# THE ORIGIN OF THE UNIVERSE

Sept 12, 2001

Jozef Rulof

1937

JOZEF RULOF

# THE ORIGIN OF THE UNIVERSE

first edition

WAYTI PUBLISHING HOUSE FOUNDATION
Apeldoorn – the Netherlands

Picture on the cover is a painting received by Jozef Rulof from the Side Beyond: 'Creation'

From the original in Dutch: 'Het Ontstaan van het Heelal'.
In the Netherlands the first edition of this book was published in 1939. The sixth edition in 1998.

Translated by: Mr. C. Dammann, the Netherlands.

Editor: Mr. R.Pilolli, U.S.A

## Authorized by the Society for Spiritual Science Foundation
## 'The Age of Christ'

Jozef Rulof (1898-1952) who was born at 's-Heerenberg, a small village in the east of the Netherlands, was an outstanding medium. He wrote a number of books, he painted countless spiritual, symbolic paintings and gave well over eight hundred lectures. All these activities were performed while he was in psychic trance, guided by his spiritual master Alcar, who lives on the Side Beyond. Jozef Rulof was also an exceptional healer. He healed seemingly hopeless cases, relieved people of their fears of pain and death and restored their faith in God and believe in eternal life.
The above-mentioned society was founded in 1946 by Jozef Rulof as instructed by his spiritual master.
In this book his master calls him André. For further information about the author and his work we refer to the publisher's note on page 563 of this book.
Finally, the publisher has elected to use the actual Dutch names of the characters in the book.

THE ORIGIN OF THE
UNIVERSE
first edition 2000
ISBN 90-70554-40-2

Printed by: Nauta Zutphen, the Netherlands

# CONTENTS

|  | page |
|---|---|
| Explanation | 6 |
| Preface | 7 |

### PART ONE

| | |
|---|---|
| Disembodiment | 13 |
| Alcar's friend | 19 |
| 'The Past' | 30 |
| The temple of the soul | 39 |
| The Origin of Creation | 62 |
| To the first cosmic degree | 75 |
| The animal world | 88 |
| Alcar anwers André's questions | 96 |
| The second cosmic degree | 116 |
| The third cosmic degree | 167 |

### PART TWO

| | |
|---|---|
| Disembodiment | 185 |
| The Divine Spark | 197 |
| The inspiring life | 203 |
| Instinct and pre-animal-like consciousness | 217 |
| Development of the earth | 234 |
| Development of the hell | 245 |
| Man, creator of light | 259 |
| Pre-animal-like human consiousness | 268 |
| Animal-like consciousness | 282 |
| The fifth material degree | 306 |
| The depth of inner life | 309 |

### PART THREE

| | |
|---|---|
| Disembodiment | 377 |
| André's mediumship | 381 |
| Alcar's past | 398 |
| The pyramid of Gizeh | 420 |
| Golgotha | 430 |
| The fourth cosmic mentality | 461 |
| Reincarnation on earth | 504 |

# EXPLANATION

Like many other books by Jozef Rulof, this book was written by his master Alcar, a spirit of light of the fifth sphere on the side beyond. Master Alcar expresses himself in accordance with the consciousness of earthly man, using the spoken language. In this book the term 'races' is used to make things clear to us; for the Side Beyond races are material degrees of feeling.

The human being on the side beyond has learned the true life and knows that all human beings have to cover the long, cosmic road, ultimately to be able to return to God.

Focal point is the reincarnation of every living being. This path of life leads him from one material and spiritual grade of life to the next. The material body of the human being represents a certain material grade of life during any of his many lives, while his inner life constitutes the spiritual grade of life he has reached. There is no standstill and every human being keeps on evolving. This process of evolution of man on earth compares with attending the forms of a school. Mother Earth confers on man the material 'forms' for his material and inner development. The form a pupil attends defines his stage of development, but not his value as a human being. For this value is contained in his soul which is of Divine origin. Just like a pupil in the first form has the possibility to reach the highest form, every human being will ultimately acquire the highest on earth.

A number of footnotes in this book refers to this explanation, stressing that the relevant passage should be regarded in connection with the entire portrayal of man and plan of evolution, as revealed by the Side Beyond.

The Publisher

# PREFACE

*Dear reader,*

This book I also received from the Side Beyond. What you have read so far in my previous books is amazing, but this is well-nigh incredible. Nevertheless, I was allowed to experience this at the side beyond, and it was subsequently committed to paper.

In this book my leader Alcar deals with the origin of creation.

This first part relates to 'The material organism'. The second part deals with 'The inner life', and the third part with 'Reincarnation on earth'. Alcar relates how he was convinced on the side beyond, and I was allowed to experience it with him by departing from the body.

What more should I say? I only wish to point out the following. In the third volume of 'A View into the Hereafter' Alcar discussed my mediumship, and in fact I did not even have that in my own hands. In this book he relates why this was essential, so that you feel that everything I received must be the pure and absolute truth, or I would not have received it. How could I, who have never heard about it, never read a book on such spiritual wonders, ever tell about this? Where would I have acquired all this wisdom, all those amazing problems, the hundreds of questions which are answered in these books, and of which we people of the earth cannot know anything?

Whether you want to accept this is up to you. Alcar says that the answer is deep within us and that you must feel it, nobody can impose that on you.

I can only say that I received this book after I had experienced everything on the side beyond. I answer for it with my life, for I know that this is sacred and that it is for us, worldly people, a mercy to be allowed to receive this. It provides answers to all our questions: Where did we come from, and where do we go to? – Whether there is an other life after this terrible worldly and material life? – Whether there are inhabited planets? – Whether we return many times to the earth? – And many more questions.

Dear reader, all your questions will be answered by the spirit Alcar, who in his final life on earth was a great artist. In the third part Alcar mentions his worldly name that he was called when he spent his last life on earth, and he explains why I was allowed to serve as a medium for him.

I am most grateful that I was allowed to receive this for those who can feel this, and dare descend in themselves to seek the answer.

I could not describe this myself, for it is also too amazing for me. Only they can who know, who lived on earth and are now there where there will be happiness once for us all.

May Gods blessings rest on this work.

The Hague, September 1939                                     Jozef Rulof

TO MY WIFE

TO MANKIND

# PART ONE

## The material organism

# CHAPTER I

## *Disembodiment*

ANDRÉ had again received a message from his leader Alcar that he would depart from his body. Alcar had already laid down through him what he had experienced during his last journey and that book has already been published*). Now he was ready to receive fresh nourishment for the mind and he waited for things to happen.

He knew that he would now experience the complete reincarnation. The spirit Lantos**) reported about it through him, though that was evidently not enough. Alcar wanted to give him an overall picture so that man on earth would understand his own life and could accept cause and effect, illness, misery, and everything related to adversity on earth. Also what the soul experienced which resides in the human organism and how this had come about. This was a deep and mighty wonder. The owner of the material organism accepted this as a quite normal event. For that was what everybody had!

Alcar had explained to him that possessing a worldly organism, the material body, meant a mighty grace for those living on earth.

But man rose in revolt and did not understand his life on earth. Man cursed his God, hated everything and everybody, for he experienced often the misery on earth, whereas there were people who had everything. Many received profound grief, others died of starvation or were killed. All this misery made them wonder whether there was a God of love and how He could approve of all this.

However, on the side beyond, André had experienced the meaning of being on earth. Alcar had explained that people were to blame for their misfortune. Yet they could not accept this, for they invariably referred to God. Didn't God love all His children? Why then this misery? Couldn't God interfere? Does He allow that thousands were killed? It had been explained to him on his last journey on the side beyond. Lantos and Gerhard had described it, and he had experienced it himself in the spheres, it was nevertheless not clear enough for mankind.

*)See the book 'A View into the Hereafter'.

**)See the book: 'The Cycle of the Soul'.

They did not respond, for it could not be accepted; it was impossible, they said. They were entitled to love and happiness and they were all children of God. However, they sought and wanted to provide evidence to the contrary, their situation did not change, could not change. A change was not possible until they had experienced their karma.

But what was karma? He would experience all this and now he had obviously advanced that far. Alcar had told him that he would learn the profoundest depth of the soul and the material organism.

The people who knew something about spiritual things, and who were interested in them, had some idea of karma, but could not get to the bottom of this awe-inspiring problem. The theosophists also spoke of reincarnation and karma. Karma was the result of something one had done in a previous life, and which should be made up in the next life on earth. However, they did not know exactly how that came about. For those who did not know anything about karma, it was just a word, they took no notice; did not ask why and what for, they were living dead. They did not revolt, they accepted. However, it was not the way one should accept, for they had not advanced that far yet. These beings still had to learn, should awaken first to which end they would return. That is what life on earth was for, which Alcar would explain to him. There was no other planet where they could learn this but the planet earth.

Man lived on the third cosmic degree; they did not know a fourth degree. On earth, nothing was known about this. Science had not yet advanced that far. Nevertheless, all life on earth would once pass on to the fourth cosmic degree. However, how much did they have to discard! How far that life was away from theirs! They did not even accept eternal life and did not understand the meaning of death. There were only a few people on earth who were convinced of eternal life and even attuned their personality to it. They belonged to the happy ones on earth. For those who could accept this mightiness lived a different life than those who were unaware of it. They accepted and bore their sorrow and misery because they knew there was a Father in heaven Who guarded them, however incomprehensible it was for them, too. Though they could not grasp it, they bore their sorrow and passed on into that power. They knew that there would be an end to everything, however long life on earth may last. They would subsequently enter an other life, and in that life there was happiness and they felt freed from all this misery. There they were themselves and were understood. They all knew that life on earth was the school for eternity.

Illness and misery were accepted. Love was understood, and they were grateful for the love they received. Those who met them felt that they bore something, which meant light and happiness, and passed them to an advanced level. These people lived and were awake. He had met them, these craving souls. How grateful all these people were and how confident. Their faith was childlike and pure, their prayers exalted and ardent. They did not pray for property but asked God to give them that by which they would learn. These souls did not evade their misery because they knew that they would develop through it.

It required struggle, but they accepted that struggle. However, this was only possible because they knew what awaited them after death. How mighty the possession of this knowledge was! Those who did not possess it, perished, were torn between hope and fear. He heard them shout: why, and wherefore, oh God, why all this? These people were nevertheless the spiritually sensitive ones. Others lived to the fullest to try and find their groove. They had lost their head and feeling, for they did not want the misery that overtook them. They wanted to oppose it. There should be something to dominate this misery so that they could forget it.

They were wrong, though, for they had not understood what God gave them. Man did not accept and could not bend his head, because man was surely entitled to happiness! What did they care about the problem of death? Yet, unexpectedly, there was something calling them to a halt. Sometimes by a gentle hint, though for many by an awe-inspiring emotional event. One being lost his beloved one, another his mother, father or child. Others again were thrown out of balance and destroyed by illnesses.

They asked why and what for. They did not understand the meaning of being on earth; hence their many questions, which were not answered. However, those who wanted to hear and could listen, those who could accept what Alcar had taught him, and what was given in many countries as nourishment for the mind, were different. They had become completely different and were open for everything which came to them from God. They were happy because they knew that there is no death and that they would see their father and mother again. They bent their head for all this mightiness brought by man who once lived on earth. They should accept as a child and submit as a child. Only children in the spirit could be convinced.

Many sensible grown-up people could not believe for they had their powers of judgement. They had studied, which took years of effort. They could not simply discard that, for what was then left of them? Nothing after all! They would then be entirely at the mercy of those fanatics, of people who dreamt; and that could not be the intention, could it?

What did people know about the hereafter? Millions of people sought the mystery of death, but for them that was the end of everything. They had not advanced any further. This was a deadlock, and death called them to a halt. They could not overcome death. It could not be approached. Up to there and then it was all over, everything came to an end.

That is what many educated people said, people who were famous on earth, and they knew the human organism and did not wonder what was behind death, for them that was the end.

However, one day they would see and experience that there is no death, and that they live somewhere and are not dead. That there are also trees, flowers and birds and all the life God created. There was everything known on earth, because it was created on earth from there. The people in the spheres are like the people on earth, except they are spiritual beings.

He heard Alcar say: 'Look and hear, André, I'm going to connect you.'

He began to observe in a visionary condition. He saw the spheres and a man in front of him and he heard this man say: 'I was ill, but I feel much better now, so I have recovered. Say, there is someone coming. Is it the nurse? Yes, it is the nurse. Oh, nurse, I feel quite well, I think I'll go home.'

'Do you know that you are dead? That you died on earth?'

'I beg your pardon, I'm dead? Don't talk such rubbish and don't scoff at my illness.'

The nurse looked at him and said: 'Truly, you died.'

The man looked around like a madman and fainted. André then saw that he woke up. He wondered where he had been taken.

Again the nurse came up to him and he heard her say: 'Do you know that you died on earth?'

'Go away', André heard him shout. 'Beat it, and call the doctor. I don't need you any more; I won't have this any longer.'

The nurse kept looking at him with a compassionate expression. She said: 'You have to prepare yourself anyway.'

'My God, you mad woman, get out of my room!' He jumped up from his bed and showed her the door. 'Go away, you shameless witch!'

André saw that the nurse went away. However, she returned with another nurse. Again he heard them say: 'Do you know that you are dead?'

Indignantly and deeply shaken the man said: 'Are you both crazy?'

The sister of the spheres looked at him and said: 'No, my brother from the earth. Your scholarship destroyed your inner life. You are dead. You died on earth and were born in this life. You live in the hereafter; this is your eternal life. We looked after you and you are now awake and conscious. If your heart did not possess this love, believe me, you would be in the darkness. You sacrificed your last property and that brought you to this sphere where you are now. Once again: 'You died on earth.'

A mild quietude overcame him. His head sank on his chest and he fainted a second time.

Strange, André thought, who gives me this vision? Is it Alcar? Why do I see and hear this event? Quietude rose in André as well, and he felt tiredness. He began to feel the familiar phenomena, so that he would soon be in that place where his leader was, and from where he had received this image. He felt himself sink away deeper and was not aware any more. He raised his eyes and he saw his leader Alcar.

'Oh, my dear Alcar, I'm with you again. Did you give me this vision?'

'Yes, André. I wanted you to feel and experience this. I showed you a true image of a man who left the earth and entered here. He was a scholar but spiritually poor. He lived on earth and was one of my friends. However, he could not accept eternal life, neither when he entered here. But he became convinced, however hard it was for him and how-ever terrible he felt. The sisters of the spheres returned to him again and again, since he just couldn't accept it. This was his transition to and his entrance on this side. He now feels and thinks completely different and he is on his way to do something for mankind. Here, convinced of his eternal condition, he asked his Holy Father for forgiveness. This problem, though simple, is immensely deep, for it connects us with reincarnation. You will get to know him later. That is why I let you experience this condition on earth. Well, my boy, we are together again. Are you happy, André?'

'Yes, Alcar, I am very glad to be with you again.'

'Now listen, I have a lot to tell you.'

# CHAPTER II

## *Alcar's friend*

OTHER journeys will follow this one, as I cannot explain everything in relation with reincarnation in one journey. To this end we will observe various conditions on earth first and will then proceed to the spheres. In the spheres, specifically the fourth sphere, the cosmic masters are awaiting us, and they will connect us with the universe and with man on earth.

This scholar was my friend on earth. I made his acquaintance in the life when I was an artist. I passed away before he did but on this side we were brought together. It was me who convinced him of his death on earth. When the sisters and brothers did not succeed, they asked him whether he had any friends or acquaintances who had already died on earth.

'Yes', he said, 'I have', and then he mentioned my name.

They asked him: 'Could you accept the fact that you are dead, when we bring him here?'

'But he is dead', he said, 'and I am alive, am I not?'

'You will feel, André, how difficult it was to convince him of his death; yet, it had to be done. Soon I was brought to him. I knew he had died and I waited to be summoned. He lay down sobbing and crying. I pointed out to him this was the truth. 'You know', I said to him, 'I died on earth, don't you? You are alive, like I am and millions of others. There is no death, my friend; we are alive. Stand up; you are better now.'

We then took long walks and I convinced him of his own condition. A brother was appointed to him and thus he, too, like Gerhard, was completely convinced of life after death. Then I went on my way, to return to him later.

I went back to my own sphere where I was further than he, and lived between the second and the third sphere, and would soon enter the third sphere.

He had not changed a bit. He was slow on earth and was no different in this life. I had to think about him continuously, and I felt I had a connection with him. I was deeply attached to the sisters and brothers of my own sphere, but with him this attachment was quite different. I could, comparing this in an earthly manner, have accepted him as my own child; yet he was not my child. As I told you: he had been my friend on earth and I had no other feelings for him. But here in my own sphere the sense of feeling is much more intensive than it is on earth. This feeling remained; indeed it became stronger and more intense. I could not free myself from it.

I consulted the spiritual brother, who also was my adviser, but he could not yet give an explanation. He only said: 'When such a feeling exists on this side, it has a profound meaning. No spirit, however high he may be, can help you; it has to awaken and become conscious. Proceed quietly and it will reveal itself. Once it has become conscious in you, you will act accordingly; then it will be possible to tell you what it means.'

I felt that I had to help him and I would return to him whenever he desired. Soon I sensed he wished to see me and I went back to him.

'Ah', he said, 'how nice of you to come back, I have been longing so much to see you. Let us go for a walk; I have so many questions to ask.

The first question he put was: 'What is your work and what are you doing?'

'I am busy finding out about my own self.'

'That is not so easy; that is what I am trying to do myself, as I have been advised to, but I can't find out how. If only I had been allowed to know this while still on earth, how different my life would then have been. I could have achieved a lot; see now, what good did I do? What have I achieved? You have given something to the earth; your products of art will remain there right through the centuries. You have accomplished something, and that must give you great satisfaction. Are you happy? Why, really, do I ask this? On earth you were the happiest man I knew. You always remained your own self. How I have learned from you, and yet I lived my own life and came no further. In your life was the calm as quiet one feels here, just as in your art. I know how you suffered and longed to be dead. Now you are here, and you are alive. And so am I. Where are all our friends? Have you met them already?'

'Yes, I have met many.'

'Where are they?'

'Here below.'

'Where, did you say?'

20

'In the darkness, we call it the hell here.'

'My God, can't we help them?'

'They cannot be helped yet. Later, perhaps some centuries from now.'

'Have they sunk so deeply?'

'Unfortunately, yes.'

'Did they recognize you?'

'Yes.'

'And yet they cannot be helped?'

'No, it is not yet possible.'

'Have you been down there for experience?'

'Yes, and to help others. There is an endless lot of work to be done there and many are waiting for help.'

He looked at me and said nothing. Then he asked: 'Where were you when you were called to see me?'

'In my own sphere.'

'Is that far away?'

'Yes, and yet so near. To be able to enter there, you have to put yourself entirely aside.'

'Did you know that already while on earth?'

'Yes, I felt it deep within myself.'

'Do you know why you were on earth?'

'I know that, too.'

'Who has given you that knowledge? Can that be learned on this side?'

'Yes, that is possible.'

'How strange it is. What is man? What purpose does the earth serve when there are so many planets? Why did I forget myself? I know I have made it up, yet I was weak. How much have you worked! I could be envious of you. If only I were like you!'

'You can learn that.'

'Is that possible?'

'Yes. Here, everything is possible.'

'What do you think I should do now?'

'I cannot tell you yet. It depends upon your own self. You have to live and see it; you have to feel and wish it; otherwise it is not possible.'

'Have you advanced that far, that you know that, too?'

'Yes, I feel it within me. I am convinced of it.'

'Ah, you are so far away from me, and yet you have returned.'

He clasped both my hands and pressed them warmly.

21

'Tell me, what should I do. I want to go on; I can't stay here. I want to go where you already are. What do you advise me to do?'

'Try to learn your own self; your own self before anything else. Only then will it be possible on this side to do something for others. Retrace deeply within you how your life on earth has been and how you are now. Time and again retrace everything; in doing so you will come to know your own self. Then you lay aside your own self; you lay aside what you must forget in order to acquiesce in the life in which you are presently. Feel clearly what has been wrong, and banish that from your life. Lay aside everything standing in the way of your advance. Put yourself under control and call yourself to a halt. No spirit, however, can help you in this process. However much you pray, however much you ask why and wherefore, nobody can make that clear to you. This must awaken inside of you; you must wake up and learn this life entirely. If you wish me to stay with you, we will make a journey together and I will show you what I possess and tell you what I know. Whenever we encounter higher conditions and depths, which I do not know myself, we will ask those who know and who are higher than we are to help us. They are only too glad to be of help. I have lived to see that already. It did not take me long to learn that, and you will see why at a later stage.'

Then we took leave of each other and I would return to him when he would call me. You know how that is done.

I continued my studies which I had started, and learned to know and understand the human organism on earth. After that, I began to prepare for the study of the universe, the cosmology. Then the psychical laws, wonders and problems known on our side. I could, however, not complete that study; it was not until a later stage that I continued.

Several years, according to time on earth, went by. Then I felt he was calling me and I returned to him. On the same spot where we had taken leave, like you have experienced with Gerhard*) we met. No need to tell you how glad he was. A similar event, André, to the one you have experienced, I, too, lived to see. Deeply we descended into each other's mind. I sensed his spiritual condition and I could be satisfied. How he had already worked on himself.

'My dear friend', he said, 'I longed so much to see you again; so much I have to tell you. I have been in so many places since we last saw

*) See the book 'Mental Diseases as seen from the Side Beyond'.

22

each other. I have to tell you everything; but you know already, don't you?'

'Yes', I said, 'I lived to see it myself.'

Yet, he told me all of his experiences; experiences I knew myself and through which everybody has to go.

'Come, let us go for a walk. Oh, I have still so much to learn. I, who thought I knew everything and put myself on a pedestal. Oh, my friend, my brother, do you know what I have been thinking about during all those years?'

I knew, but I asked: 'Well, about what, then?'

'About a new birth; reincarnation on earth. Do you know if this is possible?'

I said: 'Yes, I know.'

Then he fell silent and we continued on our way, absorbed in thought and meditation. Meanwhile, we entered a building. There, I saw my life on earth pass my mind's eye. Here, too, people were painting and I again saw my art. I learned thereby what my mastership on earth meant. I was very sensitive and yet I had not attained spiritual height.

'No', he said, absorbed in thought, 'to be a master on earth is no spiritual possession.' He felt I already knew that.

'All this is magnificent', he said, 'but once one has entered here, one can see what life on earth means. Man on earth doesn't understand himself. They don't know there that we are alive; and yet, look around you! How much I have thought about myself. Oh, if only I could return there, if only I would be allowed that possibility, how I would do my utmost. Night and day I would work and give myself entirely. I did not love, and I spoilt the love given me. Others I have not understood; I even consciously did not want to. How much I have thought about it and when I see all this around me, how they work and advance, I could cry. Yet I don't do that, because I know I have no sound reason for it. Then I would again descend into my weakness and give in to it. Come, let's go.'

Again we walked in nature.

'I would like to serve', he said. 'Serve, always. I know now that it is the only possibility for advancement.'

'And after that?'

'Oh, if that were given to me, how much I would thank that inconceivable God. Back to the earth', he said in thought, gazing far in the distance. 'Yes, back to the earth, there to make up for my wrongs.

And at the same time I would like to serve. Do you know what I feel; what I have learned to feel, and what keeps my mind occupied now? Do you know what is growing inside me, what is awaking? Oh, if only I knew for certain! Do you know what I mean?'

'I know', I said, since I followed all of his emotions.

'Is that possible?'

'I don't know. It is a law; God's sacred law, a grace, I can't give you an answer to that.'

'Where would she be? Still on earth, or already on this side? This keeps my mind occupied; I have to think all the time. I destroyed her life and her youth and I would like to make up for it. I feel it is possible on this side, but I can't find her. How I did look for her! Where could she be; can you help me? I have already made good on earth, and yet I feel it has not been enough. Here, everything is so different. You can't dissolve spiritual laws with earthly possessions. What the soul experiences and has gone through and suffers, cannot be made good with earthly possessions. One has to experience it. You have already advanced that far; you can feel and understand it. Please tell me: are the feelings I now experience known on this side? Do feel what I mean, and try to think yourself in my position. What should I do? It becomes increasingly intense.'

'Is she, to whom I did wrong, on earth? I feel remorse and I want to make it up. I feel I have to wait; but waiting for her could take ages, and I can't wait that long. I could not possibly; I can't think of anything else. I always see her before me and she asks and calls and begs for help because I stole her happiness on earth.

And yet I am here, here in this light, which is not my light. It will only become my own, I feel this, when I have lived to see and have made it up. Then I will make progress; much and much further, to there where you are now. I have made up a great deal but it was impossible to make up everything. For that, my life on earth was too short. But do not thousands of others do what I did? Is that wrong? Ah, I contradict myself and want to soothe my conscience. I know now: what I did shall remain.'

'Do I have to make up for what I did to others myself? Can't others do that for me? Do human beings on earth not pass into other hands, and do they not receive what I denied them? Can you give me an an-

24

swer to that? Yes, you can; and I know already that it is impossible, that I have to make it up myself. I feel that; I feel the answer in myself.'

'Where is she? I feel a tie between her life and mine; I can go no further and no higher; this is calling me to a halt. My God, the grace you had; you have not lived to see this. You were a silent worker and knew and understood. But, all those others and I? I wish and shall learn my own self.'

That is the way he spoke, André; we then entered an other building. Many brothers of the spheres were gathered here. They were absorbed in silent meditation.

My friend asked him, who watched over them here: 'What are they doing?'

'They ask God for strength and personality.'

'In this way?'

'Yes,' said the brother. 'In this way they have been praying for many years.'

My friend watched speechless.

He looked at them and said: 'All these people wish for personality? Is this a building for prayer?'

'Yes, here they seek their God.'

'Are you their priest?'

'No. I am not, I am only guarding.'

'Ah, you are guarding these people here? Is that your task?'

'No, that is not my task, but I took it upon myself.'

'May I ask, for what purpose?'

'I am waiting.'

'You are waiting? What are you waiting for? May I ask this question?'

The brother then gave him a long and attentive look and said: 'Are you so sure of yourself, that you ask me this question?'

'Whether I am so sure of myself? No. I am not, but I would like to know it very much. Perhaps it will help me.'

Again the brother looked at him and said: 'Although to you I am speaking in riddles, yet your thoughts and feelings are like mine. I recognize my longing in you. Yet you don't know whether you are in earnest. You are searching and asking and would like to know, so I ask again: Are you so sure of yourself, that you ask me this question?'

Then my friend said: 'I feel like you do. Do you know that?'

'I see and feel it', I answered.

'Can you read my soul?'

'Yes.'

'You know what keeps me occupied?'

'I know it.'

'Well, then tell me, what do you know about reincarnation on earth?'

The spiritual brother looked at him and said: 'Do you know your own self'?

'Not yet', he said.

'Did you profess a religion on earth?'

'Yes, but not earnestly.'

'Do you believe in God, our Holy Father?'

'Yes, I do believe in an All-Power, but I do not know much about it.'

'Can you pray?'

He could not give an answer to that question, and he cast his eyes down.

The brother of the spheres put his hand on his shoulder and said: 'Look at me, brother. They who are here learn to pray. While on earth, they prayed to their God. But there, in that life, they felt and thought differently. Here, one has to feel through everything deeply; only then is one absorbed in prayer. But some of them ask for personality, others for gifts; and yet, this is not the way.

Because I can read from your soul and I know you, I tell you: Try to learn and understand your own self. Descend into the darkness, and help others.

Praying in this manner, they will never reach their goal. Years, nay, centuries shall pass. They are praying and meditating continuously, but nothing is changing. They remain as they are. In life one has to gather real value and that means serving and being something for others, which is possible on this side. But when there is something within yourself that burns, that calls you to a halt, then there is only one way open to free yourself from that. It is a grace, which can only be given by God.

If you wish earnestly, praying continuously and find out in yourself what has to be done, it is possible. Then it could be that God grants you that grace. I can't tell you any more about it; nor can I explain more, except that it is possible to return to earth. But you have not yet advanced far enough to absorb and digest all this. However, that road is open to you, God willing.'

'Why am I not yet far enough?'

'Do you know what lives under your own sphere? Do you know life on earth, and do you know anything about your own life on earth? Do you know all the misery on earth and on this side? Is not your problem the problem of thousands of persons? Don't they all ask why and wherefore? Do you feel their misery? Do you know why you have been on earth, and have you understood your life on earth? Have you properly used the gifts granted to you? Did you know anything about this life?

Learn to know, and understand all of this, first. Descend, I tell you, come to yourself. Only then can you ask me such questions, but then it will no longer be necessary, and you will know yourself how it is, and how it has to be done. Then that wonder will descend in you, and God will overhear your prayer, because you are prepared to serve. But a serious task cannot yet be given you, because you would succumb. Centuries will pass before you awake, and then you will have to start from the beginning, like those here. They cannot be convinced however much I would like to open their eyes. Hear how they pray! Yet, they are not awake. All are sleeping their deep spiritual sleep, but one day they will awaken and then, what I told you, happens.

Life requires our entire personality. He who knows the misery on earth, and is conscious of his own life, knows what may happen, what God can grant to all of His children. When you earnestly wish and are convinced of yourself, this wonder will descend into you. Then something is conscious within yourself, which you can receive only from God. No one, but you, knows. This wonder is in you, because your prayer was overheard. But let us go outside; there is something more I have to tell you.'

They went outside together and the brother said: 'Look up, see to the left and to the right, and there, below. Here, where you are, is the first sphere; above is the universe; and below is the darkness. Learn to know all of this, first. Then know life on earth, and see how man seeks, and listen how he asks why and wherefore. Then compare your life with theirs and think; meditate night and day. You will wake up. Advance is possible, and you will learn to pray. Only then can God give you what you desire, and which is a mighty grace when you receive it. Therefore, try to acquire life on this side and on earth. Ask to become conscious. See through everything and attain this degree of seeing and feeling. That is wisdom in spirit. It may be a long time before that wonder occurs, but I will help you. I can help you by praying for you, because those feelings are also within myself. I am longing like you and therefore will pray for you.'

The brother then looked at him and asked: 'Would you like to serve?'

'Yes, with all my heart and soul.'

'Well then, I'll wait for you. Once you have advanced that far, your eyes will be opened and you will learn to know me. We will all pray and ask God for this grace. Look at me.'

Their hands clasped, and the brother of the spheres dissolved before us. Yet we heard him say: 'He, your friend and brother, knows who I am, but don't ask anything; he cannot answer you, either. One day you will be allowed to ask questions and your eyes will then be opened. Then you will get to know me and him, who is your friend and brother; and many others. Then you will understand the meaning of this meeting and everything will be clear to you. That, which is far away from you, and where no spirit on this side can enter, you will enter. Listen well to what I now say; I have accepted you and have included you in my work. From now on, you are under my guidance and protection; and so is he, who is your brother and master, as are others who do this work with me. We all belong to one order and will remain in connection with each other through all ages.

I will enlighten your paths; I have advanced that far that I may tell you this. I will connect you, in order to enable you to make up for what you once did wrong. In this way you will make great progress. Where others will need centuries, you will succeed in a short time, if you earnestly want to. You will learn to know the depth of the soul and you will learn to love. You will make journeys and the highest spheres on this side will be opened for you. You will also receive spiritual food, which will become your personality. You will live to absorb all this consciously.

I am going now, but in time you will get to know me. Know that I'll be waiting for you. The sooner you are ready, the sooner I, along with many others, will be able to start our work. I thank you, my brother.'

We stood there in amazement. My friend was speechless.

'Did you know about this?' he asked me.

'I knew it', I said, 'but not all.'

Then, André, we both descended into the darkness, and for many years we remained together. During this difficult work he learned himself. Hundreds of unhappy beings we brought up together. That is splendid work and very instructive. We learned to know and understand all those problems on earth. Deeply we descended into life, on this side and on earth. In this way we learned to know the astral world. Then we returned to the spheres for a long time to become acquainted with other conditions. In doing so, the years went by.

Suddenly he told me: 'I know it, my friend, I know it; I can go back, but only God can give that to me. Now I am awake and conscious; God can help me.'

Again we descended into the darkness and visited the deepest spheres, and after some time he felt the great wonder come to life within himself. As night gives way to day, this feeling, this tremendous wonder, developed in him. He now proceeded to deep meditation and I left him by himself.

Shortly before the great wonder occurred, I returned to him. What then happened, I can only tell you later, at the end of our third spiritual journey. Have patience until then, André; only then will I be able to tell you more about it.

You will make three journeys with me. And on all these journeys you will live to see wonders, wonders which were also shown and explained to me, which I experienced as did millions of other human beings, for which we are sincerely thankful to our Father in Heaven. I travelled over the earth and what I did I have told you already and we have laid that down in all your books. No need to say any more about that.

For what you will now experience, we will be connected by the cosmic masters, because they are watching me and they want me to explain all this to you. They are connecting us with the past and they can do it in various ways; they will explain to us the first and the last moment of creation. I will show you flashes of several lives and the depth of the soul, the profoundest problems of mankind you will learn to know on these journeys. You will see and feel that in all those millions of years the soul returned to the earth and that there is a Father of Love guarding over all of his children. You will see the origin of creation, André, this great and sacred wonder; and I am allowed to explain to you the development of the material and human organism from the first stage. Moreover the life of the soul and reincarnation on earth.'

# CHAPTER III

## *'The Past'*

NOW we will first go to one of my dwellings on earth, where I spent my last life as an artist. Then we will go to the spheres of light, where we will be connected by the masters. There, André, you will experience wonders, the reality of which you will see in other places of the universe. Bear in mind that you will receive on these journeys the most sacred, the greatest wonder created by God.

Come, we will make a start, André. While on our way, I will continue telling you what you still have to know. I am going to connect you with the past and with my own life on earth. What I want to explain to you bears relation to what I told you just now. We shall go to my studio.'

'Do you know where your friend is at this moment?'

'Yes, my boy, I know and later on I'll connect you with him.'

André looked at his leader and asked: 'Was he a scholar, Alcar?'

'Yes, but he neglected his studies. He tried his hand at art on earth, but he lacked the feeling. He lived between two worlds – the material and the spiritual world – but he was conscious of nothing. He remained a searching soul until his end on earth. There were many feelings in him. He sought and wanted to possess, but he went on seeking, as I said before; and in that condition, he unconsciously entered this life. His attunement was that of thousands of others. They are willing, but achieve nothing. Whatever they absorb does not come to perfection. They are trying to create a condition on earth, but whatever they do and establish it gives them no satisfaction. That is the very last transitory stage towards spiritual consciousness. Do you feel, André, what I mean?'

'Yes, Alcar.'

'Well then, once it has attained this heightened condition, the soul establishes something, however small this achievement may be. Man knows then what he wants and cannot be stopped at anything. He is aware of his doings and goes on, always further, not minding anything.

These beings live on earth. Those others, who are as he was, are neither good nor bad, as there is no consciousness in them. They are living dead. All this I must explain to you now.

'On our previous journey I spoke about pre-animal-like, animal-like, coarse-material, and material consciousness. In every situation the soul is conscious and can acquire this consciousness. The soul lives to see and shall relive. Whatever it establishes, even though it may be animal-like and terrible, the being lives and is conscious of what it does. One will give himself for the destruction of others, another will go for material possessions, but all will perish. But one day the human being will reach a condition of consciousness and will not know how to act. That is the condition of half-awakened consciousness.

That is searching for a great many things, for love and happiness; but they do not descend in anything, because they do not know what they really would like. And so life on earth passes by and they enter here. This was his condition. That is why he lived at the boundary between two spheres. He did wrong things in his life on earth. He caused a young life, about which he spoke, to suffer the greatest misery. By his actions, she perished. He knew this happened through his actions and that is how she entered this life.

I knew where she was, but I could not tell him because that was only possible at a later stage. So I let him talk and remained silent.

Others had done what he did, he said, but it was he who left her by herself. He did not know, however, that the child was his. While still on earth I discussed these things with him, but he turned a deaf ear; it could not be possible, he said. And yet, I knew quite definitely that the child born was his.

This was the sorrow he caused her. By his doing she landed in this awful condition and her life on earth became a hell. Then I heard about her death. Later, much later, he began to feel remorse and tried to make it up. He gave away the money he possessed. In that condition he awoke and gave himself entirely. Then he, too, passed away. All this belongs to his life.

I told you already, we met again at this side and he had not changed in anything. That feeling of remorse was consciously present in him. Also, in this life he could not free himself of it. How could he possibly have freed himself of it?

Do you understand what I mean, André? That this was blocking his spiritual progress and that what happened on earth must dissolve and be made up? One time he will be able to live and see that, but only God can help him. No spirit, however high, commands those forces. At this side it is known how it is possible, and this law is understood. While on earth, one is not aware of this, but at this side one is faced with all those earthly problems. One cause brought him in this condition.

Others cannot make it up for him. He himself will have to alleviate that sorrow. There should be nothing of this kind in us or it will call us to a halt at this side. It stops us, because it has to be made up first. I know how he will accomplish that, but will refer to that later; then I will explain everything to you.

Look, André, here I am on the spot where I lived while on earth. Once, hundreds of years ago, this was one of my studios. I brought you to this place, where I met my friend. In this house I lived and made my greatest works of art. Sit down, André, and concentrate on me.'

André did as Alcar wanted and he felt himself sink away. He saw several human beings in front of him. He knew how this was brought about. To the left and right he saw several paintings and recognized Alcar's art. He saw his leader working on a big canvas; it was the figure of a man and he immediately understood the meaning of this image. Alcar painted his friend and the portrait was nearly finished. He also felt the great gifts of his leader. Alcar descended deeply into this being and André felt the severe concentration it required. How thankful he was that his leader let him experience this. This belonged to the past, and yet, he saw it happen again; for nothing could be destroyed. Whatever man had created, remained. Amazing, he thought, is everything Alcar shows me. How great was this sight. He had experienced this several times, but he always felt the wonderful essence of this connection. This was the past, yet brought to life once more.

André felt an affectionate bond. His leader felt great affection for his friend, which he expressed in his painting. And also from the human being posing for him radiated a similar affection. But his leader possessed more light; he could see that. There was a deep bond between them. Here he felt the quiet of the spirit. He observed in silent admiration. Alcar had achieved this heightened condition by intense concentration. Alcar had been young and fair while on earth and how conscious he was of his ability! This was creation.

He painted his friend life-size. The vision then faded away and he returned to himself.

Alcar looked at him and said: 'This happened once, André. This painting is kept in a museum. But what I only wanted to let you feel is that I was deeply attached to him. Something forced us together, of which neither of us was conscious. I loved him, as I would have loved my own child. This strength was within me and although I resisted, I could not free myself from it. A power, stronger than my own, time and again connected me with him. His sorrow was my sorrow; his feelings were mine. I found myself mentally ill; I could not detach myself from him. Then came my end on earth and you know at what age.

At this side, too, I had these feelings and I impatiently awaited his arrival. Finally the time came and he, too, entered this side. You know already how we met. I want to make clear to you now that these ties were already in us on earth. They were feelings of affection from which I wanted to free myself, but could not; they were deeply rooted and dominated my inner being. How I suffered. This problem held me in its grip night and day. I thought much about it, but could not solve it, because on earth I knew nothing about occult problems.

I consulted one of my acquaintances, a scholar, too, but he could not give me an explanation. I suffered severely, because my feelings were profoundly deep. I fought against my own self; I wanted to remove this unnatural feeling, but proved unable to do it, and as I said before, it was stronger than myself. This was not and could not be an earthly friendship; it was more, it was deeper and greater.

I scrupulously kept it to myself, and none of my other friends has ever known this. I kept this a secret, because I did not want to show my unnatural emotions to anyone. They would not have understood.

Did he feel like as I did? No, these emotions were not present in him. He was not conscious of anything. I helped him in everything and I asked him to allow me to make his portrait. I wanted to have it for myself, only because of the love I felt for him, although this love was pure.

Sometimes I flung everything away from me, but these feelings invariably returned. Then our ways parted for a long time, and yet we met again. I attained what I wanted to achieve; he, however, did not achieve anything. He was torn about this failure, and everything he did remained without inspiration. He lacked the inspiration required to penetrate deeply into inner life. He lacked what I had too much of: feeling. His feelings were not deep. He lived his life and was open to nothing. In everything lay his discontent and he was good for nothing, yet he was prepared to give himself entirely. In him, too, were feelings and emotions he did not know nor understand.

I possessed love; but there was something in him, which made him fail, so that he felt incapable. An inner force halted him, and the matter he dealt with did not penetrate his mind, because his emotions failed. At the beginning he brimmed with enthusiasm but after a while it slackened. Then he began to search and he roamed about the world and it was in those days that he destroyed a young woman's life, but also awoke and yet achieved nothing.

He wanted to learn to know the soul, because these feelings were in him. This earthly life carried me to the greatest height. He, however, wanted to learn to know death and life, but he did not prove to possess the necessary strength. It was not preordained for him, because he was a scholar who did not understand his own self. Yet he felt attracted towards this study. He had been an extraordinary child, but in the years when he should achieve so much, he was poor in spirit. As I already have said, there was something calling him to stop. That something suffocated his inner life and it could not develop. He did not come to full consciousness; he remained subconscious. He lived in one specific condition, a law, which I only learned to understand at this side and which I know now. Do you feel already, André, what all this means?'

'No, Alcar.'

'Then I will tell you. It was the law of cause and effect. It was his karma and therefore belonged to his past. You will understand, André, that the first thing that should be explained to me at this side, were these affectionate feelings. This, however, was not so easy, because it was not possible at the beginning of my transition. It was not until later, when I was connected with higher entities and I accepted my own life, and I had learned to understand all those spiritual conditions at this side, that I was shown my own life. How great was my joy, and how thankful I was, when I knew and understood its meaning. I had felt correctly during my life on earth. There was a deep love within me and these feelings were pure and natural, and not unnatural at all. This was part of me, André, and belonged to my past.

In the third sphere, years after my death on earth, I learned to know my own past. There, in my past, resided those feelings, and they were related to it. Do you feel how deep this is, and that we are unable on earth to understand this? Every human being will live to see this on earth and at this side. However, only on this side are we shown the many lives we have lived. It is here that we can descend into the past. Nothing has been lost, everything is fixed – to the smallest details.

What I felt on earth was revealed here. I would not have felt those emotions had they not been mine; because what man has not experienced, he will not feel. It either is in him, or he still has to experience it. When feelings predominate, like I have experienced, this has a meaning and these forces are also conscious in us. As I said before, at this side, I was shown my past. I could accept and be happy. An other world opened for me and that very moment I understood the depth of the soul, and accepted. The higher entities summoned me and bestowed on me that tremendous grace of understanding myself to greater depth. How grateful I was! How I did pray! Weeks, nay months I remained absorbed in meditation. Deep in myself I retraced everything and came to understand the creation. I felt my life on earth and was thankful for what I had been allowed to leave there. I also understood that there were higher gifts, which could help suffering mankind, and these gifts I wanted to acquire at this side. I descended and learned to know life in hell in all its frightfulness. You know how I suffered and continued my way. At this side I also learned to know his life, and I understood what he did not know nor feel. I spent the last few years of his earthly life on earth. I could not reach him from this side, but I watched what he was doing. I saw that he had mentally fallen asleep and had succumbed a long time ago. He had resigned himself to what was in him and he felt empty and a failure. In nothing, I heard him say, am I my own self.

And yet, André, I saw he was his own self, but he did not understand this depth nor these feelings, because one cannot understand them while on earth. I saw from this side that he evolved from one condition to another. When I was still on earth, he changed every moment and now he did not feel different either. Time and again he took up another study, and time and again he failed. He could not bring anything to a successful end.

But one thing, one problem, kept his mind occupied and predominated him entirely; that was life; that was man. Slowly, he descended into life until he had no more strength left to acquire anything.

You see, he had many gifts, but no willpower; he lacked inspiration. Weren't there feelings in him to create? To do something for mankind?

Yes, surely; he had them. He would have wanted to give himself entirely, but he could not, because he felt himself unable to do it. Then he did other things.

He gave everything he possessed to the poor and accepted the life of a beggar. But his friends came to his help and brought him back to his senses; because that was not necessary. He was very popular with many people for his broad-minded views on the deepest problems. He was always sharp, to the point, and yet achieved nothing.

Do you understand, André, what kind of problem this is? What kept him going and what was already calling him a halt on earth? Was it an unknown power preventing his advancement and calling him to stop? Why were these feelings in him; and did his soul, his inner self, refuse? Why did he clash with everything concerning the universe, the soul, and man? Because this was a problem for him; it was his life and misery. His inability tormented him and, as I said, he gave his possessions to those who were in need. Why did he do these things and how did he attain these powers? There was something sad in his condition; he was forced by a power stronger than himself.

On this journey, André, and on the two to come, I will explain to you his emotions and mine. All this has a profound meaning. I will revert to this subject; then you will understand his emotions and mine, and all those psychic problems and wonders. At the end of your third journey, everything will be revealed to you; it is not until then that I can connect you. Have patience until then. Now I will show you another event.'

At this moment André felt himself sink away, and he saw his leader and his friend on earth.

He heard him say: 'I am nothing. But you? You will leave something behind. No, I cannot understand. Why do you reach that height? You are yourself in everything; but I? I am good for nothing. I'll never achieve anything. There is something of the devil in me, and I would accept it if I only knew there was truth in it. Seek and you shall find! I have been searching all my life and I can't grasp it. I am perfectly in earnest, you know that. I am grateful to you for everything; but God leaves me alone and will crush me. Do you know who stops me? Why can't I achieve anything? Oh, how will my end be?'

Then André heard him laugh and he saw him go away. Yet he heard him say: 'I shall live, my friend; believe me, I shall live.'

36

Then he saw his leader deeply absorbed in thought. Night had come a long time ago and still his leader remained in thought. André now felt something miraculous; he perceived that Alcar was being helped from the side beyond. His leader was a great artist and he was open for the other side.

He saw the astral spirit and when he observed this, Alcar said: 'Yes, my boy, I, too, was helped. An artist on earth, who can attain a degree in art, will be helped from this side. I saw visions, given me by invisible entities. Moreover, my art ripened, through my desire to understand my friend and all those gloomy moods. I have shown you this scene because I also want to explain it to you later. There was nothing of the devil in him; it was cause and effect.

You see, André, that I can connect you with my life and his. Everything under my own sphere is conscious for me, which means that I know that life, however deep it may be. At this side we learn to know everything, down to the deepest past, because it will be shown to us. Every human being, every soul has its own film of life on which he can see and know himself. I ask you: was this his fate? Had God this in store for him? Is it God's will? But why should God want this? Why was I gifted and why do thousands of others achieve nothing? Why, André, why? I showed you similar terrible conditions on our last journey. However, he was his own self and not insane. Yet, it was enough to make anybody insane. Truly, all this is strange and deep, and yet on this side we know what all this means.

In this life I also learned to understand and accept this human puzzle. On this side one knows what these strange emotions mean. Here, one knows all those laws and is his true self and one transcends into these laws. It is the masters who know and we will be connected with them, because I am allowed to explain this to you later. Only then will you understand everything, André, like I understood and accepted.

There was an enigma in him, a force compelling him to accept that. No God could help him. No spirit, however high, could solve this. It was his possession, as I possessed my feeling for art. This was his personality, his inner life.

Now isn't this inexplicable and, for man, improbable and unnatural? Doesn't it resemble being doomed? It is that deep, that man cannot accept it, because he will be confronted with a mountain of sorrow and incapacity. In this life lay the seeking of light and his God. He gave himself entirely in every respect; yet this enigma, this power, burdened his entire life. It was this silent force that broke him.

And so his life went past. Thousands of people on earth feel as he did; but why is all this? Why are they on earth and not capable of achieving anything? Wherever you go, you will see these beings. Everything goes against them. Don't you think that they yearned for a human existence? He wanted to be a scholar, but that feeling was not in him. He was prepared and studied a lot; but at the crucial moment, when his life was about to begin, he felt himself sink back into an inexplicable depth. Notwithstanding this, there was something in him urging him to begin, as he brimmed with enthusiasm in his youth. But that inner fire consumed him and he felt empty, depleted by that unnatural inner process.

Do you understand, André, how much this life possessed and yet could achieve nothing? Isn't this something belonging to the earth, and aren't there millions of people living in the same condition? Nevertheless, they try to create a proper existence, but to many it proves impossible. Is it God's will that this happens? I have already pointed this out to you in various ways. But this problem is different and relates to what I want to follow, and to man on earth. I will answer all these questions; everything I told you ever since we have been together has a bearing on his and my life on earth, and it is the problem you will experience.

This belongs to the past, and behind that, behind all this, is another past; therefore, we will descend ever deeper into the soul, and in doing so we will also learn to understand the wonders of the universe. Man is a great wonder and it is the soul, which experiences this wonder. God knows every depth, as there is a beginning and an end. God knew what He wanted and created. There is a divine end, because we advance ever higher, until the soul enters the Divine Spheres. The human organism will decay, but the soul continues and experiences life. But there must have been a beginning, and this beginning you will learn to know. And you will know reincarnation on earth, which I will explain to you in various ways and in various circumstances.

And now, André, we will leave the earth and visit the fourth sphere. There you will be connected with the universe. The masters, as I said before, are awaiting us presently. Be grateful for it, because it means wisdom in spirit.'

# CHAPTER IV

## *The temple of the soul*

FLOATING through the air, they left the earth. Alcar had shown him amazing events. How is it possible, André thought. He had experienced a lot already, but now, he felt this clearly, he would penetrate to the nucleus of life. How grateful he felt. How very mighty it was that the spirit could descend into the past. He had distinctly heard his leader speak with his friend. He had understood every word. More amazing still was that he could also feel the emotions of man. Whenever Alcar connected him with something he entirely passed to that event where he could feel and observe.

Oh, if only man on earth could experience this. They would surely change, and how beautiful life on earth would then be. He could understand the feelings of Alcar's friend. He, too, had experienced similar things. Then one felt incapable and could not understand that others did succeed. At such moments he sensed an emptiness within him and felt like an nonentity.

'Look, André, we are going towards the spheres of light. In the temple of the soul I will connect you again with the past, and there you will see several scenes concerning my and your own life on earth.'

'For what purpose, Alcar?'

'In doing so, I will show you that we are able to descend into the past of every human being, not only on earth, but also in the spheres. You will see that again on your next and final journey; however, we will then follow other lives.'

'Does that also serve a purpose?'

'Yes, because this concerns reincarnation on earth.'

'And what is the object of this journey, Alcar, if I may ask?'

'During this journey you will learn to know the universe. In the temple of the soul we will be connected with the universe by the masters.'

'As on my last journey, Alcar, when we were in the third sphere and Alouisius[*] connected me with the universe?'

'No, not that. You will now see the origin of the universe and how God has created everything.'

[*] See the book: 'A View into the Hereafter', volume 3.

'That is tremendous, Alcar. Shall I be able to understand it?'

'I will explain it to you, but the masters will show you the origin of creation.'

'Cesarino*), Alcar?'

'Yes, André.'

'How does it happen?'

'The masters know this phenomenon and how it took place. The higher masters of the fourth cosmic degree of mentality have shown it to them. They will show it to you in a visionary condition.'

The origin of creation? My God, André thought, that is tremendous.

'Do you mean how everything was born, how everything came into being, Alcar?'

'Yes, André.'

'Where do we human beings originate from? You know that, too?'

'You'll also experience that on this journey, André.'

André trembled when he heard this. The origin of everything? How is it possible, he thought, that I am allowed to see that.

'Is that why we visit the masters, Alcar?'

'Yes, only they can connect us with that event.'

'How wonderful that will be, Alcar.'

'It is awe-inspiring, André.'

'Have you seen it before?'

'Yes, a long time ago.'

'And do you know about it; I mean how it all happened?'

'Yes, André, I have experienced it at this side.'

'Oh, Alcar, if only people on earth were allowed to know this; how God has created the universe, man and animals and everything. I can't frame it in my mind. Shall I be allowed to see the beginning and the origin of everything?'

'I will now be allowed to explain to you the origin and birth of everything.'

'What do I owe this to, Alcar?'

'You are doing my work, and both of us are instruments for the higher masters, which I can only explain to you later.'

André felt happy. Remarkable, he thought; I'll see the origin of creation. Little was known on earth about it; people only guessed at it and several tales were abroad about it. One could not make heads nor tails

*) Mentor of the seventh sphere of light. See the book: 'A View into the Hereafter'.

of it. It is amazing this should be given to me, he thought.

'Have you never been able to imagine this, André?'

'No, Alcar, I have thought a lot about it, but I could not. Shall I now see the real truth?'

'The very truth, André. The entire reality, you will surely feel, is no longer possible; but the masters will give you a picture of how it happened. So you will see flashes, scenes of how it was at the beginning of creation.'

'I am so happy, Alcar. Have you known this for a long time? I mean that you may explain it to me?'

'Yes, I knew this already several centuries ago, and now that moment has come.'

'Several centuries ago, did you say?'

'Yes, André. I will explain that, too, on your final journey.'

'Shall I be able to absorb and digest everything, Alcar?'

'You will, or I would not have entered upon it. You have advanced far enough now to be able to absorb it.'

André could not stop thinking it over. My God, he thought, what do I owe this to? How grateful he felt toward his leader and the masters, who were able to show this to him. He would actually see the reality of this mighty event! How could it be possible? Time and again he returned to the subject and asked Alcar questions.

'Has it also something to do with your friend, Alcar?'

Alcar looked at his instrument and said: 'Yes, my son, his life, too, has something to do with this event. Didn't I tell you that I could not explain everything about him until on our next journeys? And in order to be able to explain it, it is necessary that you know the creation, the origin of the universe, the human organism, the life of the soul and reincarnation on earth, so that you understand all these profound depths. But not only you, also man on earth, I want to give a clear picture of what reincarnation actually is and that it is available to all human beings and animals. That is what the masters have consigned me to do. The life of my friend is therefore not the main object, yet it is involved in this and our next journeys. I will try to show you how it has been since the beginning of creation, I cannot otherwise explain everything concerning his life. I am therefore following a fixed plan.

But I, too, am only showing you flashes of how it has been at the beginning of creation. It is not possible to give you a detailed explanation. There are thousands of things which would fill volumes of books. It is my sole purpose to give you a picture showing how it happened; and you will receive this picture so that man on earth will be able to form a mental picture of how everything came into being.'

'It is mighty, Alcar; I had not expected this. You say that I have advanced far enough now?'

'Yes, now I can explain to you the first and last moment of creation. The veil which enveloped you has now dissolved; you have now become conscious in this life.'

'Even now, while still living on earth?'

'That is exactly what I mean.'

'Has this a special meaning, Alcar?'

'Yes, André; everything has a meaning. Whatever and in what way man experiences on earth, everything is preordained and has a deep significance. You will learn to know this significance later.'

'You have many surprises, Alcar.'

'Yes, André; but what you will see now is a mighty grace for you. Always remember that, because there are very few people on earth who are allowed to experience this and who are sensitive enough. You possess this sensitivity and, because you are my instrument, we both serve the masters. Surely you do feel there are several things for which you should be grateful.'

'I will never forget this, Alcar.'

'I know that, André. That is why you will see this wonder.'

'Are you going to connect me again with the earth when we are there, Alcar?'

'Yes. From the temple of the soul, I must connect you with the earth and show you in different ways that we, wherever we may be, can be connected with our past. We can descend in every human being and animal, and you will experience that, too.

From our life we can recall earthly scenes, so that we see them again before us as if they occurred that very moment. When this is possible for me, it is also possible for the masters to connect us with the past, which they know. This phenomenon is one situation, but they can see deeper than we can, because they have attained that height.'

'How mighty everything is that you are telling me, Alcar. How they try to solve this problem on earth, but they can't grasp it. Everybody asks why is this and why is that, they all seek and ask; but not a single soul knows. All the time you hear people ask: what would that be like, how was all this created, but nobody is able to give a satisfactory answer. Shall I see all that now, Alcar?'

'Yes, you will, André.'

'My God, Alcar, I still can't understand it. How is it possible? Shall I also see how the animals were created, Alcar? And nature: the trees and flowers?'

'Yes, André. That too.'

André looked at his leader and did not know what to say. Great was his leader, knowing everything. The deepest problems would now be explained to him; problems of which nothing was known on earth.

He looked at his leader and asked: 'Will you also be able to tell me, Alcar, why all these beings living in the fourth sphere and in your sphere and in all those higher cosmic degrees, have got that far already? And why I and others still live on earth and many have to starve?'

'Yes, André. I will be allowed to explain all this to you and I may now answer all your questions. When you have seen everything, you won't have any more questions.'

André trembled out of emotion and happiness.

'Look', he heard his leader say, 'the fourth sphere. Over there you see the temple of the soul, which we will enter in a minute.'

High and lofty, overlooking everything else, stood the temple of the soul. The building was made of snow-white marble and it radiated light which he could perceive already from a distance. There he was about to be shown a great wonder. How happy he felt now that he knew this.

Here, in the fourth sphere, everybody was happy. Everything had its own radiation, and people here possessed that great and pure love warming everyone. The people he saw radiated a light unknown on earth. Here the inner being enveloped the external being in radiation which could be seen. The birds sang their song for the sisters and brothers living here and who had once lived on earth. Now they were happy, very happy. He had better not think of all this happiness, because he was still on earth. Many times he had wondered why some people had advanced that far while others still lived in misery. In thousands of things people had failed. All this would now be revealed to him and he would understand why all these beings were that far.

See this beauty and how pure all these people are. See their robes!

They were loosely draped from their shoulders and this was their mental possession. It was impossible to take it away from them, because their spirit had acquired it. He saw wonderful indescribable colours.

He had been with Alcar in the fifth sphere and he had been allowed to see the sixth and seventh sphere. There, colours were still far more beautiful; it was there beyond all belief. Yet, how modest spiritual beings were; one could not imagine this on earth. They called themselves only children. He wanted to attain this modesty, although it would not be easy.

They continued on their way. How majestic the temple of the soul was. This was true art. The building had been erected in an inexplicable style. A quiet tranquility now came over him and he understood from whom it came. Now that he had entered the fourth sphere, it was only possible by Alcar's power. He could enter everywhere here by his leader's power. They met thousands of beings.

'How beautiful their robes are, Alcar.'

'That is their own mental possession, my boy, as you know.'

Yes, he knew. How far they had all advanced from earth.

'Are you going to tell me about the stars and planets, Alcar?'

'Yes, I must explain to you the various degrees present in the cosmos. You know already that there are seven degrees of cosmic attunements. All planets which can be seen from the earth, have their own attunement and belong to the first, second or third cosmic degree.'

'Does one know about it on earth, Alcar?'

'Do you mean about all those degrees?'

'Yes, Alcar.'

'No, they don't know anything about that on earth. I will explain that to you later.'

'Did your friend on earth study this subject?'

'He tried to master this subject, but, as I told you, there was an inner power which he did not understand and prevented him from achieving anything.'

'That is strange, Alcar.'

'It is, André; yet, it has a meaning.'

'And you know now this meaning?'

'Yes, that was also given me in the spheres and it was explained.'

'And you also know where he is now?'

'Yes, André.'

44

'Can't you visit him?'

'I could do that; but he is not conscious of it.'

'How is that possible, Alcar?'

'There are so many things of which one is not conscious. This belongs to the past, André.'

'Isn't he himself conscious of it?'

'No, he does not know anything about it.'

'Isn't that a great puzzle, too?'

'No, not for me; and when I can explain that puzzle to him, it will no longer be a puzzle for him either.'

'And isn't that possible yet?'

'Not yet; but the moment is drawing nearer.'

'I think that is wonderful for you, Alcar.'

'Thank you, my boy.'

'How deep is the human soul, Alcar?'

'It cannot be fathomed, André. All those problems will dissolve; but they can dissolve only in due time, when everything is in harmony.'

'Do you see him often, Alcar?

'Yes, very often.'

'How amazing; and he does not know about it?'

'No, to him I am a brother, a father now, and yet he is not aware of me.'

'That surely must be a great problem, Alcar.'

'It is, André. A problem, and at the same time a great wonder.'

Remarkable, André thought, that Alcar's friend did not know him. They had parted and Alcar knew whence he went and yet his friend did not know anything about it. It was inconceivable, and he wouldn't ask his leader more about it, because he felt that Alcar could not say any more, and he probably had nothing to do with it.

'Do they know in the temple of the soul that you are coming, Alcar?'

'Yes, André, they know that we are coming. But I still have to explain other things, and I have told you about them already. I have made my arrangements.'

The closer they approached the temple of the soul, the more the building revealed of its beauty. It stood there majestically, high above its surroundings, like a rock in the surf. There he would be allowed to enter. What architecture! The highest towers, hundreds of them, could not be seen entirely. The top of these towers seemed to dissolve and he knew what it meant. This, Alcar had explained to him on his previous journeys. The highest towers were connected with the fifth sphere. This could not be apprehended on earth, yet, that was its meaning. All these high towers dissolved in the universe, and this meant it was possible for people to evolve further. Here in the spheres everything had symbolic meaning, but after real life. A symbol was like nature; it represented life and one could assimilate that.

How this building radiated. In the spheres everything was alive and man felt God's sacred life, which was impossible on earth. There it was not possible to see the radiation of man and animal, of buildings and nature. Yet, there too, every object radiated its own strength, though invisible to man. Here, however, the radiation was visible and reflected the inner level of man and animal. Everything was amazingly beautiful. Here he felt the tranquillity of the spirit. Oh, what beauty! If only the people on earth could see this.

'The temple of the soul', he read, and above this text were some signs which he did not understand. The entire building was open. That, too, was an amazing phenomenon. How could a building be erected in that way? One could see in all directions. Alcar led the way and they entered the temple of the soul. Wherever he looked, he saw spiritual beings. Each wore his own robe and he saw they radiated light. The spiritual robe meant a wonderful possession for those allowed to wear it. He had seen this many times, but every time it amazed him and he understood how far he was still away from this happiness.

Alcar looked at him and said: 'Look at yourself, André.'

How is it possible, he thought, that I did not feel it. He, too, wore a spiritual robe. His earthly state he had dropped; he had now entirely passed into Alcar's life. His robe draped from his shoulders like the former Roman robe. He felt very happy about it; but what would people on earth think of it? Yet, it was very simple, because he would not be able to enter here, if he did not entirely accept the sphere in which he now found himself. These thoughts descended in him, and he knew from whom they came. Alcar conversed mentally, when entirely transitioned into spiritual life, it was no longer possible to speak. Instead, one person then passed into the other, establishing telepathic contact.

Amazing this robe was. Gerhard[*], too, already wore his spiritual

[*] See the book: 'Mental Diseases as seen from the Side Beyond', final chapter.

46

robe, and he had only been in the spheres for a few years. But he had worked hard and had concentrated his entire inner being on his work. Those who earnestly wanted to, could make speedy progress.

Yet, he thought, it was remarkable that he should not have noticed. Such was life in the spirit. When one thing occupied your mind, you could not think of anything else. You became completely absorbed in it and accepted that condition. This thought was also inspired by his leader and he understood him entirely.

He was now completely free from the earth; his own life and everything related to it was far away from him. Something, however, kept him tied to the earth: the fluid cord, the connection between his spiritual life and his material organism, which would remain until his death. Then that cord would snap and he would go to his place in the spheres, which would correspond with his inner level and the love he possessed. Though he had known this for a long time, it was a mighty feeling to reflect upon it at any time.

Alcar wore different robes. When his leader appeared on earth, he usually assumed a condition representing his last life on earth. He then saw his leader as a painter, the master of centuries gone by. On this side, however, André saw his earthly garment slowly dissolve, and as they went higher, Alcar's robe became increasingly beautiful until he had entered his own sphere. Once in this sphere, his robe remained like those worn by the entities living there and no further change was possible. That was also amazing. The spiritual garment slowly began to change into thousands of soft shades. That is the possession of the spirit, of the human being feeling love, and who is open to every life.

He followed his leader closely. Everybody was happy here. Look at all those people, André thought; see how they radiate! And all these beings had lived on earth; they had suffered and struggled; they had known much sorrow, illness, and other troubles; but now they were happy. How mighty it was to be allowed to see this, because all this happiness, all this greatness, was meant for all people. Each face reflected pure and unselfish love.

Fathers and mothers, sisters and brothers lived together here; they shared their happiness, and they could no longer be sad; they had gone through that and had conquered.

Look into yourself; try to understand yourself; do away with all misery and bend your head.

Yes, all of them had done that and had learned. Now, this mighty happiness was theirs and radiated from them.

Slowly they ascended and he felt what it meant. Surely Alcar went to the higher halls, if halls is the proper word. But what other word was there for a spiritual space? This defied all description.

Everywhere in this building were flowers, and he noticed birds of the spheres circling around man. Many sat down upon the hands that were held out to them and caressed them. Divine happiness engulfed him when he noticed this.

In every hall he saw the well-known spiritual fountain he had seen in every sphere. It was a symbol of wisdom, of strength and love. It is an object of art urging the human being to acquire all those gifts. Here the earthly creature lived, surrounded by flowers and birds; all this was like paradise.

Yet, this was only the fourth sphere! It could not be compared with the higher spheres he had been allowed to see on his many journeys. He had been in all spheres and had received much wisdom. But what he would see now, would outdo everything else.

Here, he would be connected with the universe where the beginning of creation would be shown and explained to him. He trembled out of happiness in anticipation of the moment when he would see how everything had happened.

Alcar still led the way. He led him towards a plateau where he saw a small building, an exact reproduction of the larger building. A smaller temple; and here, too, everything was open. That everything was open was most peculiar; he himself could not find an explanation. Was it, because all this belonged to God's own life? An inner voice told him this was what it meant. It was a miracle how everything remained intact.

How was it possible to build like that? Was this known on earth? Did it bear relation to all the spheres? And were they the architects of the seventh sphere who, so to speak, innerly bore this building, and maintained it? It was a miracle to look at. This building was like man, nature and everything living at the side beyond. Everything was open, like everyone was open here; one could see into the depth of the soul.

From where he stood he could see a deep valley. His leader stood beside him, but said nothing. Now another feeling came into him and he knew what it meant. Alcar could not explain this building in its entirety, because it was attuned to the seventh sphere; it was further and higher than his own sphere. Every inner building, if he correctly felt the meaning of these smaller temples, had its own structure. Hundreds of smaller temples were accommodated in this mighty structure. And all those buildings had one meaning which was the temple of the soul. He thought it over, but could not make it out.

He asked his leader: 'Can it not be explained in its entirety, Alcar?'

'No, André; I made you feel that already; however, I can tell you yet a lot about this building.

All these smaller temples you see belong to the whole structure and are therefore a part of it. Every building has the same architecture as the entire building, but only outwardly. Innerly, every building has its own attunement, a condition, as you will see presently. In this building, which is the temple of the soul, all spheres are present, from the first to the seventh and down to the profoundest depths of hell*) onward. All spheres known on this side are represented by separate temples and are accommodated in the entire building. Thus, every temple of the inner building, that you now observe outwardly, represents a sphere, no matter whether it is a higher or a lower one, and all spheres have been incorporated in this mighty building. On descending, or entering into a smaller temple, one is transitioned into that sphere; and observes it and is connected with that sphere, whatever it is like. Do you understand what I mean, André?'

'If I have understood you correctly and clearly, all these temples are like man and like a sphere.'

'Exactly. So, when I enter one of these temples, for instance the temple of the first sphere, and I wish to be connected with it, it will happen. How this happens, you will see presently.'

'That is marvellous, Alcar.'

'Not only can we be connected with the spheres, but also with man on earth, with planets, stars, and a thousand other things. We are then transitioned into that condition and will see what we wish to see. But there is more. All degrees of cosmic love are present here. That is, one can feel that pure love which a spirit living in the seventh sphere possesses. Do you feel how mighty this is? Thus, everything is present here. Man can be connected with the universe, with planets, stars, and other objects. One can also take up a study here and is given a course in all those laws. Only the masters living in the seventh sphere know how the

*) Meant is the deepest dark sphere on the side beyond.

entire structure was erected. Only the masters can connect us with every degree of spiritual strength and attunement. The masters live, so to speak, in the temple of the soul, and in one temple, therefore one can be connected with a master and be accommodated in the entirety. Presently, it will be explained to you what happens here and how that connection is made possible. In this temple we can be connected with the universe and with the beginning of creation. It is here where the entire universe can be shown; that all those millions of laws and problems can be solved for us here. The masters can connect us and we see it happen before us.

I will have to show you several scenes first, in order to prepare you for the great event you will experience later. I must explain to you what everything means and the significance of the temple of the soul. However, I cannot explain the overall structure; in order to do that, I have to achieve the level of the seventh sphere first. You know, I cannot go further than my own sphere, while here the strength of the highest spiritual being at this side is present. They thus manifest themselves in this building; they support their brothers and sisters, and they allow them to enter their spiritual domain and to accept it as their own possession for a short while.'

'How mighty this building is, Alcar.'

'This building, the temple of the soul, is a sacred and pure image of the spheres. Here, André, one can come to oneself. Here, one learns how to pray and to know oneself. Here, one can see his father and mother, sister or brother. Wherever they may be. We can see them again in this building. Here, one can be connected with the universe when the masters deem it necessary; and the one being fathoms the other. Then man bends his head and accepts; the mother bends for her child and the child for its mother. There is quietude and peace, because God lives here so that we can be connected with the Divine. Here, André, one sees into an other being and one knows that this being, even though one knew this human being on earth, is a wonder of spiritual wisdom. But how is it on earth?

On earth this means power and personality, social standing and property. He who has reached a high social position makes himself felt, and rules, nay, dominates everything and everybody within his reach. He is both master and ruler, and people obey and do what he wants.

But here everything is different. Here we bend our head for those who possess a higher level than we do. For those living in our own sphere, we feel great respect because they are our sisters and brothers in spirit. Here, love is might and a law.

They have been on their way for thousands of years and in that time they have attained this attunement. This is achievement; this is attainment; and all of us can achieve this.

Cesarino is a prince of love and this spirit is my master. We will meet him together with mentors Miradis, Urabis and Mondius.[*] The temple of the soul is the dwelling for the soul; it is a home given by God to mankind. It is the spark of God, which every life possesses in its human condition, and it is God's sacred purpose to bring it in that condition. It is a mighty creation, and every human being will learn to understand this temple, so that the soul – the human being – will be like this mighty building in which he lives and meets his sisters and brothers. During a previous journey, I showed you my own spiritual home. How tiny it is in comparison with this building, will now be clear to you; but I shall learn to understand it so that one day my spiritual home will be like that. All those who are here know that they can achieve it. The way to achieve this is open, because they are serving. They will continue to serve, or their development comes to a standstill. We are continuously evolving, and are prepared to make the greatest sacrifices. Nothing is too much for us. There is not a single soul in this sphere who does not know that ascending further is possible, nor how it has to be done. They all know already what will be shown to you presently. They, too, have lived to see that, since they have attained this height. It is not possible before this level is reached. Now they accept and understand their own sphere and condition. Father-love and mother-love of the earth dissolve in this sphere, and they feel universal love. You will see that, as it belongs to the temple of the soul and is the image of our own life. We will go on now, André; follow me.'

André felt that Alcar made the connection between them still closer. Humbly, he followed his leader. He saw symbols made up of flowers of the spheres wherever he looked. These symbols were in every sphere and this, too, was art. One symbol represented love; others faith, simplicity and humility. Alcar had explained all these symbols on previous journeys and he now understood these products of art. Alcar halted

[*] Mentors of the spheres of light on the side beyond. See the book: 'A View into the Hereafter'.

and waited for him.

'We will enter here', he heard him say in mental language.

'You will observe now, André.'

Immediately, André felt himself sink away and pass into a higher condition. He started observing straightaway. Alcar had entered a space. Apart from a bluish light, nothing could be seen. But in that light, something moved. It looked like the sky; here, however, it was enveloped in a dense haze. He felt accommodated in this space and there was only air. He could not describe it more clearly. He felt himself in a strange and remarkable condition.

Now he saw other colours merging in the blue, and he only saw these other colours when he thought about them, which he found very strange. When he thought of a colour, regardless which one, he immediately observed these shades. When he concentrated on something else, this would immediately manifest itself. It was most fantastic; he felt a mighty strength entering himself and he understood its meaning. Through the gifts and powers of others, he saw into the life interpreted here and it dominates the bluish haze, which remained the original colour. A strange power was present here, and he felt a great awe.

He felt a need to pray. He remained absorbed in prayer for a long time to finally observe again, for there was something extraordinary in this hall.

He felt completely empty now, and could not think of anything. He asked his leader: 'Where are we, Alcar?'

A soft voice spoke to him and he heard inside himself: 'I will connect you, André. Remember, we can only speak mentally here. Here we feel and go over in what we see and feel.'

'What is the significance of that bluish haze, Alcar?'

'It is like the firmament. The scenes you observed manifested themselves, because you thought of them. You were connected with yourself; this is the tremendous strength the masters command and which we shall have to attain ourselves. Here, man can be connected with himself through the intermediary of higher entities. I will explain that to you; be attentive.'

André waited for things to happen.

He perceived something in this blue haze. What was that? Could that be possible? He saw himself and his leader while on their way to the temple of the soul. They were approaching the building and, when they were near it, he read the inscription at the front of the temple, which he had not understood. Now he suddenly knew what those figures meant: 'Man, know thyself.'

Then they entered the temple. My God, he thought, this is also fixed. He lived here in reality. Here one attracted reality and again passed to that reality. How strange all this was.

Then he heard Alcar say: 'You see, André, everything is fixed. We can draw everything to us and pass to it again, even if it happened thousands of years ago. The smallest things will manifest themselves, however weak your concentration may be. Here, in the temple of the soul, one can see one's own film of life. It is here that I saw my own past and came to know my friend; I have told you about it. Attention now, here is another scene. All this serves to explain to you what is possible in the spheres of light. I concentrate on a certain event, on something that happened, and that event will manifest itself before us.'

André felt that Alcar concentrated himself. In child-like simplicity, he focused his mind on Alcar. He was now completely united with his leader, and he heard Alcar say: 'Don't think of anything else now, André. Concentrate on me, and try to maintain this connection.'

André now felt the pure love of his leader coming into him, and waited for further events.

He saw something appearing in the blue haze. Ah, he thought, how is that possible! He saw a scene of the earth, where he had been with Alcar. In that very place, his leader had connected him with the past and he had observed Alcar and his friend. He now saw the moment when his leader was working at the portrait of his friend. This scene disappeared and he saw another event manifest itself.

What he saw was amazing. He saw himself with his leader. Alcar was absorbed in thought and he began to see the past. He now saw two different scenes; one had happened three hundred years ago and the other he had experienced himself, although it also belonged to the past.

How miraculous the forces at this side are, he thought. One concentrated on the past and it became visible. Now he saw another event.

It was the moment when they took leave of the earth and went towards the spheres of light. He was amazed at everything he observed. Now he felt becoming detached and connected again.

He heard Alcar say: 'I will now connect you with your own life on earth. You will see that this is also possible.'

He observed and saw the house of his parents. He saw his father and mother and recognized the surroundings where he was born. How tremendous this strength is, he thought. This scene also dissolved and another one appeared. Again he saw his parents. When he saw this scene, he suddenly heard church music. What would he see now? Oh, my God, how is it possible; I can't believe it. He saw his father and mother being united in matrimony. This scene moved him very deeply. Tears of emotion and gratefulness came into his eyes. Oh, how mighty this scene was. He heard a soft voice in him say: 'Will you be quiet now, André? I will show you another scene for which I need your full concentration.'

André concentrated his mind on quietness; he did not want to disturb his leader; how grateful he felt for all this. Again he saw his mother, and at the very instant he felt a great wonder. He was entirely one with his mother and felt the great significance of this scene. His beloved mother was expecting a baby and the young life she carried was him. He was now moved by an inexplicable happiness. There was a great wonder in his mother and he conceived her pure thoughts. How deep was everything he observed; and he had to accept it. Now he saw another scene.

He saw himself in his youth. He played as a child, and all these events returned in his memory. Yes, he thought, that has happened, I know. He heard Alcar say: 'See and observe, André.'

What he now saw was surely the most remarkable event of all. He saw a dense haze beside him, and in that dense haze he saw something appear. Something took shape and he trembled when he understood what it meant. How is it possible that, of all things, he recognized his leader Alcar. Alcar had known him already in his youth. Alcar had always been his guardian angel. Again he saw another wonder. He saw spiritual children in front of him and those children were brought to him in his youth. He now saw that Alcar brought these small ones to him and that he, as an earthly child, played with these spiritual children for hours on end. Beside him, he saw his leader. Then he saw Alcar going away with the spiritual children.

My God, he thought, how great are your wonders. When still a child, he already had spiritual gifts and could see into the invisible world. That event was fixed, too, as everything belonging to the past was fixed. He was born with all those gifts; these spiritual treasures were in him.

What music, or another kind of art was for an infant prodigy, were spiritual gifts for him. Now he understood and felt his inner self. These spiritual gifts were in him as a great treasure and nobody knew anything about it. He felt he had deeply rooted ties with his mother; she had been an enlightment in his life and he felt as she did. Great were these scenes. He saw his whole youth pass along. How miraculous that is, he thought. Then everything faded away and he heard his leader say: 'Is it clear to you now, André, what the temple of the soul is? Here, you will come to yourself; this is connection. However, it is only possible through the cosmic masters. All this belongs to the third cosmic degree. Everything below the fifth sphere I can recall. I can also connect myself with other events, which lie deeper and deeper in the past and were experienced there. I can even recall my own birth on earth. I can see into everything that has been, but I need help, although all this is in me and is mine. I can be connected with my first life on earth and the hundreds of other lives which I, that is my soul, have lived and followed. The temple of the soul is the for transition into our own life of the soul. We are connected by the masters and this connection is effected by concentration. As the mother receives her child and is one with her child, begotten by the creative power, she shall and must experience this in material life. This, here, is re-living but by higher powers and forces.

We are here in one of the halls of the spirit possessing the highest attunement; it is the hall of love and it belongs to master Miradis. This mentor puts his strength and personality at the disposal of man at this side and helps him to learn to know himself. We have now descended into his own life. All this lies deep in his life. It is the heart of man living on earth; like the child, yet unborn, lives in the mother and feels what is thought and absorbed by the mother-brain. Mother-love radiates through the young life in her, and this still unconscious life does absorb all these forces and is sustained. Mother and child are one. The child unconsciously, as I said, and the mother in happy expectation. If the child would now be able to speak, it would tell its mother what it felt.

And this wonder, however incomprehensible it may be, occurs on earth; but the mother is not aware of it. And yet, this feeling, these thousands of emotions, penetrate her day-consciousness. This makes her very sensitive, all these emotions give her own life an elevated attunement. I pointed this out to you on earth. This, however, is the sole picture, André, that I can evoke in your imagination and as a true picture, in order to be able to explain this temple condition of mentor Miradis. It is mentor Miradis who connects us with our deep inner life, by allowing us to descend into his spiritual home. Consequently, we are here in this master's most sacred possession; in that what he is and owns in pure love.

I once showed you my spiritual home, which you entered. When you had entered, you were absorbed in thought and stamped on the floor to feel what the softness, on which you walked, meant. Truly, André, I am not trying to depict a symbol of a spiritual or other condition. This means experience; this is truth, for a spiritual home is as we are ourselves and the love we possess. I invited you in my spiritual home, and I knew you would not know nor understand it. And yet, you entered.

In the hall of love stood my fountain. In this temple you have seen and recognized this fountain. You know it means wisdom, strength, and love. Master Miradis possesses all this. He is a spirit from the seventh sphere, and the mentor of this one, the fourth sphere. He knows everything living below this sphere and this knowledge is his possession, up to the seventh sphere. Therefore, I can only connect you, because I am connected with his deepest inner life. I can always find and meet this master in the place where we are now. As truly as there is a God in heaven watching; as truly as the perfect child of God is Christ, Who will guard all God's children until the last one enters the Divine Spheres; as truly I am now connected with one of His children, and this being is guarding me and all who wish to approach him in love. Do you feel what it means to us to enter the home of a spiritual prince? That it is only possible when he or she, wishing to know her own self, is prepared to accept everything, and truly everything? That the past, which resides in ourselves, is brought to consciousness by him and that we then see into our lives as if it happened that very moment? That is why this was established. That is why the masters created this amazing building, which is alive throughout, and hides our inner being, our past, and all of our conditions. Is it no wonder then when I tell you that I cannot explain its overall significance? Do you feel the profound depth of this mighty building, and that it is the love of these sublime beings? That they allow us to enter and that it is an immense grace for us? So do realize, André, that you are standing on sacred and pure soil. This is the preparation for still further advancement in order to understand the sacredness of what will be shown to you presently. We are not yet in the place where the masters are, but we will go there in a minute. All this is necessary to give you an idea of what awaits you. You should feel this, my son; and if you can't, we may as well return to the earth. The masters will open themselves for us entirely. However, they demand that we are ready and have prepared ourselves.

This is meant for every spirit living here. Our presence here has a special significance. We have come here for another purpose which relates to the masters. It is they, you know that already, who sent me to the earth to make this known to mankind. And now the moment has arrived when we can be connected with them and you will learn to know the profound depth of the human soul. We will now go to another hall, André.'

André returned to himself. He did not know what to say. He knelt, and thanked his leader for everything.

'How can I thank you', he mentally said to Alcar. 'How sacred everything is; how mighty! I now understand it was a grace that you allowed me to enter your spiritual home.*) Oh, Alcar, here on this spot, I swear, I will do everything I can to be a worthy instrument; I will do my utmost for everything you are giving me.'

'Stand up, André. I am very grateful to you. Only later will you be able to fully understand my gratitude, when we have experienced everything belonging to the past. But now we will go on.'

They went again through other halls. Wherever André came, he saw spiritual beings. How beautiful all these people were.

'What are they doing, Alcar?'

'They are waiting for the great moment and are preparing themselves for that wonderful event. They are meditating, André; after that, they will see and experience. Many of them will see their father or mother still living on earth, or at this side. When beings lose sight of each other, they can be re-connected here. Wherever these beings may be, they can be seen here. Even if their ways have been separated for hundreds of years, they will be found again and from that moment on they are connected. They follow this film of life and are thus shown where they are and in what condition the being is living. When man

*) See the book: 'A View into the Hereafter', second volume.

has attained this level and can enter here, and his own soul – the twin soul which belongs to him – would be born again and thus live on earth, where he will find his twin soul. Even if this twin soul, this life, is not born yet, it is possible to be connected with this young life. Lantos told about his life, but it was master Emschor who let him experience it.*) I can connect you with the past, but others will help me. Thus, it will be clear to you that a father will find his child, and a mother hers, or vice versa but only with the aid of those possessing this power. It sometimes happens that parents or beloved ones enter this side and cannot find their beloved ones who preceded them. It is the temple of the soul which makes it possible. It is known here where these souls are, and one knows and sees for what purpose the soul re-turned to the earth. Do you feel now, André, what the temple of the soul means?'

'Yes, Alcar, perfectly.'

'What you have seen just now, is re-living. I transitioned into that past and at the same time concentrated on you, so that you saw what I felt and experienced. All these people here ask for connection. Some wish to know their own selves; others wish to see their mothers again. Thousands of people are present here, but if you ask them what they are doing here, they will not be able to give you an answer. They know they have to concentrate and do not hear, nor see you, because they are meditating; they pass into the master. Deep is everything, and also sacred. This building is sacred in the strength of love it radiates.

This can be seen already from outside and you have observed that. Everything is open and yet we are inside. This is a great wonder, too. How was it erected? I could give you an idea of its construction up to the fifth sphere; but beyond that, I can only feel and understand and would not be able to express it in words. All these people, therefore, André, are waiting for a sacred connection with their beloved ones or themselves. Some for a study, like us; others to find their beloved ones again, who are on earth or who have descended into the world of the unconscious.

Now we will go to the hall of master Urabis and you will experience other events.'

André could not say a word. All this was great. How many wonders had he seen. My God, he thought, would people on earth believe him?

*) See the book: 'The Cycle of the Soul'.

This went so far; this was so profoundly deep and could hardly be comprehended. One had to bend one's head for this. If one couldn't, connection was impossible. This was sacred and, for man on earth, a great grace. One day they would live to see it and they would be happy. Here, however, one felt this grace; one deeply bent one's head and thanked God.

He followed Alcar, who now entered another hall. André looked around him. Here, nothing could be seen either. This hall was empty. But he sensed something which made him feel happy. He felt an awe-inspiring silence absorbing him. Here he felt the tranquillity of a spirit, who stood far, very far above him. He felt himself lifted into something sacred, so that he thought he was floating. He felt that all this differed from what he had experienced a few moments ago, but he could not explain it. The bluish haze had changed into a silvery light. He knew this silvery light, as he had observed it in Alcar's own sphere. Now he felt that Alcar connected him. His leader opened himself for him. Alcar allowed him to see into his life.

How can I ever thank you for that, he thought. He bent his head and prayed from the bottom of his heart. Why did Alcar wish him to see into him? Alcar influenced him in silence and he now felt he had to concentrate on his leader.

Alcar's inner life would presently be open to him. The strength and love he felt descend in him, told him that this would happen. He humbly opened himself and he saw the first indications appearing. What sort of scene would this be?

A strong force went through him while he heard soft organ music. Through that music which vibrated within him, another scene passed and he understood its meaning. How is it possible, he thought. Alcar's marriage! The most glorious day of his leader's life on earth, for he became married. Beside him stood his soul; the woman who loved him on earth. This picture faded away and another scene manifested itself. This, too, was a great wonder.

He saw a cradle and in the cradle was a small child. He saw it trampling and stirring. The child grew, and scene came after scene. Now he saw the child again and, look... it was his leader, Alcar. This picture faded also and another appeared. He saw several people together and he understood the meaning of this picture.

He was in a hall where his earthly master taught his pupils, and he saw that Alcar was one of the pupils. This was a true scene and it had happened on earth. How great this scene was. The teacher was absorbed in deep thought. An inner voice told him who it was. How is it possible, he thought; what wonders of spiritual power. The silence which came in him, was what his leader owned during his life on earth. This scene faded also and another one appeared. Flashes from the past were shown to him. He consciously saw the past; he need not doubt anything. He also felt that, if his leader wished to show his life from his birth onward, that would also be possible. These were scenes which the soul had experienced and were momentous events. Now he saw another wonder. The end of his leader's life on earth was manifested for him. Alcar passed away and he saw his friends beside him. All were very sad, for he left life on earth too early. Nothing was lost of this event. He felt his leader's terrible struggle and also the cause of his death. This illness had been in him for years. He descended deeply into this problem of his death. God called his child and death came. A master of art had left the earth. Now he felt Alcar returning to himself and that this connection was disrupted. He looked up at his leader, but could not speak a word.

Alcar said: 'You see, my boy, I can connect you with my own past. Everything is fixed, down to the smallest events. I could connect you from my birth onward, but that is not necessary, because we will revert to that later. I can show you all my mistakes and sins, but I only showed you some events. Now we will go and meet the masters. Be prepared, André.

I can also connect you with the sixth and seventh degree of love, which are both present in this temple, and pass into mentor Mondius' inner life. Anything that cannot be shown in this hall, I can observe in a higher attunement; but this is sufficient. Come, we will go on.

You see, André, that it is possible for us to descend into our past in different ways. While on earth, before you were to leave your material organism, I connected you with life on this side and you saw that my friend woke up. You observed all this in a visionary condition and you heard him speak. Consequently, that was also fixed. In my house on earth, I showed you my own life and you passed into it. Then your experiences in this temple and, in a while, what you will experience again. But that what you have observed and experienced so far, shows you that it is possible.

60

The purpose of all this is, that you will be able to accept the mighty wonder you are about to experience. And so I have done this for a fixed purpose; because we know that what will be shown to you by the masters, is too incomprehensible for the human mind. That is why I prepared you for the mighty event awaiting you.'

# CHAPTER V

## *The Origin of Creation*

LOOK, André, we shall enter that temple in front of you.'
André saw a small temple; it looked like the temple of the soul. A golden light radiated from this magnificent building. Alcar went inside.

Did the masters live here? Here nothing could be seen either; but the inner light present here was dominated by that golden light. He recognized that light, for he had observed that at the border of the seventh sphere, which was the sphere of mentor Cesarino.*) Would he see a wonder here? Here, too, he felt himself as in space. Now he clearly felt that his leader had connected him with the highest at this side.

'Come close beside me, André.'

Alcar took his hand, and André felt that the great moment had come. He felt Alcar's hand and understood he had thus been lifted into his sphere. He would not be able to enter here by his own strength. A sacred feeling of quietness came in him.

Now he saw something move in that golden light and manifest itself. At the same time, that 'something' condensed; it was like the rising sun sending her beams over the earth. A tremendous light radiated over him; he saw several beings in front of him, and he immediately recognized Alcar's master.

Cesarino, he thought, I am so grateful to you. He saw four entities, wearing the most magnificent robes. They were the mentors of the spheres, and they all belonged to the seventh sphere. Cesarino wore a robe he could not describe. All shades of colours, from the first sphere onward, were present, but the golden light dominated. He saw the soft shade of purple enveloped in a bluish haze, assuming this golden light again. A spiritual robe was alive and radiated its light, like everything at this side. He had never seen anything so beautiful. A spirit, who had been at this side for thousands of years, manifested himself in this way. And yet, Alcar's master looked like a young 30 year old man. The other masters, too, were no older and wore magnificent spiritual robes. The golden light was predominant in these robes; this reflected the attune-

*) See the book: 'A View into the Hereafter', third volume.

ment and sphere in which they lived. My God, he thought, are they human beings? Present were the mentors Cesarino, Mondius, Miradis and Urabis, the masters of the seventh, sixth, fifth and fourth sphere.

These thoughts came in him and he knew how. The masters had come to him in a sea of light of a brilliance which he could not absorb. He could not digest it that very moment, for he felt that the masters would leave. He noticed, however, their youthful faces and their aureole of purity. The masters looked at him and smiled. An indescribable feeling of happiness overwhelmed him and he could no longer think of himself. He felt and experienced this through the powers of others. This was a tremendous grace for him and he bent his head and waited.

But immediately he heard a voice say: 'Look at us, André. We have come to you, to show you our presence here.'

André looked at the masters again. They were princes of love; and they spoke to him and addressed him by his name, which Alcar had given him. Cesarino looked at him as only a child can look, and a feeling of great happiness engulfed him.

Then he heard the voice say: 'Now the moment has arrived that you may experience the highest at our side. Master Alcar has developed you that far, with my help; for your leader carries out our wish; it is a task we all have to fulfil. So I know about your life on earth, and how far master Alcar has advanced at this moment.'

Then Cesarino looked at his leader. Not a word was spoken, however. André saw what happened and observed that the higher beings scanned his leader. Souls were connected here; a higher master descended into another being, and this being was his leader. My God, he thought, give me the strength to absorb all this. Alcar bent his head and the golden light radiated on his leader. André understood that this was a sacred moment. His beloved Alcar received the benediction of the masters for whom he performed his task. He, too, deeply bent his head for this event. A sun radiated on Alcar, yet he remained in connection with Alcar.

Then his leader looked up; his face reflected great happiness; and André heard a voice say: 'Master Alcar, how can we thank you. We have followed you in everything. The most beautiful moment has come for you. God is Love. We shall now lift the veil; your instrument has come this far. Your happiness is ours. How grateful we all are, only God knows. Your task was difficult; but you see that everything is possible.

Much has happened in the centuries that went by; but much has been achieved, and together we can achieve still more. We thank you, master Alcar. May God bless our work.

And now, André, I will show you an event, so that you will understand that I followed your leader in his difficult work and that I know his task on earth. Look up, to my right; you will observe.'

André looked in that direction and he was immediately connected with a scene. What he saw was amazing, because his leader had told him about it. It was a scene of Alcar's own life on this side. It was the moment when Alcar and his friend entered a building in the first sphere, and a spiritual brother spoke to them. He saw the brother who had spoken to them dissolve, and he heard Alcar's friend say: 'Did you know about that?'

'Yes', said Alcar, 'but not everything.'

It is amazing, André thought, but what is the meaning of this scene?

Cesarino told him: 'You see that everything is fixed. The moment has not arrived yet to explain this scene to you, but you will receive this, and your leader will explain it to you. Have a little more patience. I knew that your leader would meet his friend and the spiritual brother and I knew what his wishes were. I was there for a fixed purpose and you will also see that later. Everything, however strange it may seem to you, will become clear. You will be shown the past and you will be connected with it. You, too, are involved in this scene, and you have to do with it, which will be clear to you later. Follow your leader Alcar; give yourself entirely, and know that you are doing our work. We shall follow master Alcar in everything and support him. God willing, we will complete our work. God willing.

Now the moment has come to connect you with the universe and the origin of creation. Your leader has told you about our life, and you were allowed to see that life at our side. You descended with him into the dark spheres and you were also allowed to see the highest spheres at this side and to feel the happiness of the spirit. All this serves to give man on earth a picture of what awaits him. You have learned to know the higher spheres, degrees of spiritual love, life on earth, and the astral world. You have received that already and passed it on to mankind; but now we will connect you with the universe. This is for man on earth, so that he will receive a complete picture of his life there and at this side. You will not only be connected with this life, but also descend with master Alcar into the deepest past, and be connected with various planets. The purpose of this voyage is to show you the origin of everything.

What we will reveal to you presently has also been shown to us; and you will experience what we received at this side. It is the reality of everything created by God. However, we shall show you flashes of the true events, and all this serves to convince our sisters and brothers on earth of their Divine connection and attunement.

This serves to explain to them that they can be like God. Everything you will experience, therefore, has happened. Millions of years ago, God revealed himself in the universe. All of us, at our side, who have been allowed to see this mighty event, bent our heads for Him, who is our Father.

God created heaven and earth, man and animal but how all this happened will be shown to you. Everything you received from the side beyond, belongs to our message; also what you are about to see.

We will now retire into our own life but will return to you later. I beg Him, who gave us our life, for strength for you, so that you will understand everything. Know, that what you will observe, is meant for those on earth who do not possess these gifts. I connect you in the name of the Father, of the Son and the Holy Ghost, Amen.'

The masters then dissolved in front of his eyes. Immediately deep darkness set in. What would this mean, André thought. He could not see a thing. He held Alcar's hand in his, but he could not see him. Yet he thought he could recognize the deep blue colour in this darkness. An awesome silence set in. Never before had he felt this. What did this silence mean? Yet he felt there was life around him. In this profound darkness he heard a voice say: 'Cesarino is speaking to you; listen. Before God revealed himself, there was profound darkness.'

The voice which had spoken vibrated deeply into his soul. Now he would see the highest of events.

The voice continued: 'Only God lived in the universe. Nothing of all life living in the universe, on all those millions of planets and in the seas, existed. Nothing, my son, but God. What you observe now, is as it was before creation: darkness, only darkness. This mighty darkness is God, and out of this darkness we, and all other life, were born. I will connect you now with the first phenomena. No man, however, has ever observed this. Yet – you have seen this, because that was why your leader connected you in various ways with the past – we can connect ourselves with the beginning of creation, because we, too, received this connection, which happened as follows.

You know there are seven cosmic degrees of love. In those degrees, people are living who have lived on all those millions of planets and have already reached the fourth, fifth and sixth, yes, even the seventh degree. When the first beings had reached the seventh cosmic degree, they established communication with the sixth degree, and gave those living there this picture of the beginning of creation, so that they understood how everything had happened. This, however, was not possible until the first human beings had reached the Divine Spheres. You will realize that this event happened billions of years ago.

And it serves to show us, mankind, that we originate from God. Then, the sixth cosmic degree established communication with the fifth, and the fifth with the fourth cosmic degree. Subsequently, the masters living at that time in the seventh sphere received this message, and so we know how, billions of years ago, God revealed Himself in everything. What you experience went from sense to sense, from man to man, and from sphere to sphere, and all this is God's Will. What happened at the beginning of creation has, therefore, come to us from the highest of degrees. When this is clear to you, you will feel that we are, at this instant, connected with the origin of creation; and also that we are now passing on to mankind on earth what we have received ourselves.

These, however, are only flashes, for any spirit who has not yet reached the seventh degree, cannot comprehend it in its entirety. Consequently, you will see scenes, images of this tremendous event, nothing else. But what you will see is the holy truth, which you and also man on earth can accept. Now I am going to connect you with the first phenomena which preceded the event.'

In this darkness, André saw a very faint light appear. This light remained for a considerable length of time and disappeared. It then returned and became somewhat stronger. Again the darkness returned.

Now he heard the voice say: 'What you have observed just now were the first phenomena of Divine revelation. God manifested himself and just now creation has already begun. God revealed himself by this light, but again and again the darkness returned, and this process continued in that way for millions of years. But the process of revelation went on: Behold!'

André now saw that this faint light became stronger and more visible. Wherever he looked, this light was present. It radiated over the universe; it pierced, so to speak, the darkness, so that the darkness dissolved. The light became stronger. Still, he felt that the darkness would return, which indeed happened. But then the light returned, and it became more visible still. Again and again the light changed; gradually it became more powerful, only to weaken again. But now, the darkness seemed to have dissolved for good. It was an amazing spectacle!

Now he heard the voice speak again, and Cesarino said to him: 'It took centuries and centuries before the light had reached its present strength. What I mean to say is, that before this could happen, the entire universe, that is that darkness, dissolved in the light, and this event accepted an existence. Night gave way to day; and when God's creation has taken place, we see this phenomenon again, reflected in night and day on earth, in the spheres of light and darkness, in death and birth on earth; but this will be clear to you later. Master Alcar will explain all this to you. Your leader will therefore revert to this and he will explain several events to you. We will continue now and follow the plan of creation.'

André saw this twilight change. It became gradually stronger until it also dissolved. This happened several times, as he had seen in the previous processes. Again and again the twilight returned and changed into a stronger light, so that it became continuously lighter. In this morning-light, to compare it with that event on earth, he now saw another light appear. He experienced this mighty process like the approach of noon on earth. This event was repeated several times; it went and came back to change into another and brighter light. Now he already observed a golden radiation.

That light, too, which resembled a spiritual radiation, faded to return more powerful. The entire universe now became like the sun as observed from the earth. The universe had now changed into a tremendous fiery ball.

This lasted for a considerable time to weaken again, and a shadow now lay over the universe. Yet that golden light returned, stronger now than before. The universe had now changed into a golden ball.

Now he heard the voice say: 'Again millions of years have passed and you will now observe the universe becoming denser; the contraction process.'

That golden light weakened again and André saw other colours appear in the golden light. He saw a light blue, soft green, and many other shades, and all those colours merged into one another; but the golden light dominated everything. A contraction process had now set in; and he felt what this process meant and how it was possible. In this process, too, he saw several transitions. One moment the soft green dominated, then again the blue, then they merged. But behind it was the golden light penetrating the other colours and absorbing them. Every second, the light became stronger. Now the golden light dominated again, and the other colours had dissolved in it.

He now felt that an other stage was about to set in. Something would happen, but what? He had the feeling that heaven and earth would collapse; and yet nothing happened; but he felt that power. The firmament at this instant looked like a tightly drawn cloth. A dense haze now lay over it and the golden light penetrated it. The haze dissolved and seemed to be absorbed by all those shades.

He felt what this meant; it was the contraction process. All those shades of light again merged and he saw other shades appear. These colours again dissolved in the universe; but light was everywhere, and what he observed emanated from the darkness.

Again the golden light returned and now pierced everything. The universe was a golden ball again and there was movement in it. That tightly drawn cloth assumed shapes and an other twilight set in. The universe changed repeatedly.

Then André heard the voice say: 'You see how this contraction process happened. It lasted for millions of years. The firmament slowly densified. The entire universe, as you have seen, is a luminous glow of fire. This light, which belongs to the Divine energy from which everything came into being, preceded the creation. It was not until this was complete, that creation proper could occur. That, too, has happened, as you will see presently. You also see that the golden light continues to dominate; it will do so eternally, for it is the Divine radiation.

We shall now proceed to the next stage, and you will see what happened.'

André had understood every word. He waited for what would be shown next. He felt his leader beside him. They were one in thought. Alcar pressed his hand and he understood what his leader meant by it. He was very grateful; he did not tremble, but accepted everything. He felt great happiness. Now he was going to observe the next stage.

The universe now changed into a violet-like light and through it the golden light. Now lighter shades appeared and all these colours merged, but it was the golden light again that dominated. All these colours had merged into one colour of light, which he could no longer comprehend. The universe had now become a golden mass. He could no longer describe what he saw; the light he observed became ever more powerful. He felt a tremendous tension absorbing him which he understood and he sensed what would happen next.

A while ago he thought that the moment was imminent, but that feeling weakened and he understood that an other process had begun.

Everything he observed was marvellous. Now he saw another wonder. From that golden light, he saw thousands of other shades radiate. Never before had he observed such an indescribable spectacle. What he saw belonged to God. This was God, in thousands of luminous forms and colours, and behind this universe something lived which created all this.

Now he again heard the voice say: 'The final moment has not arrived yet, but it is approaching. This process, too, lasted for millions of years, for the golden light had to dominate; it is the golden light which brings everything to life. One day we will all be absorbed by that light; all of us will acquire what you have observed just now. The radiation of the human being, too, will become denser; for this is the transition towards perfection. In all phases of life, man and animal will experience this. This will be explained to you, too. Look what happens now.'

André felt that the moment had come. The golden light became so powerful that the universe changed into a ball of fire. This had happened several times before, but now the utmost degree had been reached. Life now appeared in this light and that life vibrated through the universe; he felt what would happen.

Suddenly, a tremendous current surged through him. He saw the universe tearing apart; that was what he had been expecting to happen for a considerable time. The universe split into millions of light balls and he saw larger and smaller balls floating on. A tremendous event had taken place. The universe had split into countless particles. God had revealed himself. This tremendous creation had burst into billions of particles, among which André observed tiny sparks.

Now André heard the voice say: 'The process of creation has begun:

the origin of stars, planets and solar systems. What you see, are luminous balls of fire; but, in reality, this is God's own light and life; God's sacred radiance. The wonder of revelation has happened.

God has divided Himself into billions of particles, and these represent His sacred life. All this life is inspiration, for it emerged from that source. God, therefore, revealed Himself in the universe. A luminous ball, therefore, is part of the Divine energy out of which it was born. He who looks at the universe, observes God's life. God lives in it; that is God; and God lives in everything which will yet be born. We emerged from this energy; your leader will show that to you. It was God's intention to reveal Himself in all this. That this happened, had to happen, you will experience. You will see much of what you observe now; many of the millions of objects which are still balls of fire, change and condense. Everything you observe at this moment, belongs to God's sacred life, and is in itself a revelation.

God's sacred life revealed itself, and this is the wonder of creation. But we will go on and follow this process of revelation. This is the first stage of revelation and the second stage follows. Thus, one event revealed itself by the other; until everything returns to His sacred life.'

All these sparks and luminous balls were suns. He saw smaller and larger suns; but all were luminous balls of fire. A wonder had occurred. God had divided Himself into countless particles and parts. God had accomplished all this.

After this event, he heard the voice say: 'What you see now already belongs to the material world. Billions of years have again passed. Those luminous balls of fire have contracted; others adopted an other condition and belong to the many solar systems we know. That light, therefore, is power and that power is energy; but it emanated from the Divine source. Surely you feel that it is impossible for total black darkness to set in.

But out of all this, and that will also be clear to you, stars and planets developed; and we will show you how this happened.'

André now saw a new spectacle. He saw that those suns contracted. Many floated on and drifted in circles. He felt they were attracted by others; yet, an other power developed which prevented this attraction. It was a tremendous, unnameable power. This movement produced vapour; and the way those suns had been created, that vapour became gradually denser. Now, the vapour had become so dense that it enveloped the ball of fire as a dense haze.

He now heard the voice say: 'An atmosphere has formed. The second process of revelation has taken place. Now again millions of years pass. Thus, in that atmosphere lives a glowing ball which remains floating in it. From this, a planet will presently appear. And now I will show you another stage.'

Far away from him, André saw millions of these objects, which had all occupied a place in space. They were enveloped in a dense haze. The golden light, which he had observed all that time, now weakened.

Again he heard the cosmic master, who said: 'The stage you now see lies millions of years later. This process has advanced in all those years; yet the end has not been reached. But when this contraction process is complete, it is at the same time the end of the process of origin, and thousands, nay, millions of planets have assumed their existence. Then this cosmic wonder has happened and the universe has been created. You know that every object is energy; as a result it contracts and this happens from the interior. By contracting, one object attracts another, but at the same time repels it; which will be explained to you presently.

This is the wonder of creation of the universe and how it happened. All objects have their own atmosphere; that power emanated from them, and it is also the protection for this awe-inspiring wonder, which also encompasses the way planets, stars and other objects have assumed their own orbit. Order rules in this vastness and that order is contained in every object. God oversaw all this.

It will therefore be clear to you that no planet can leave its own sphere; for if this were to happen or would be possible, the universe would collapse. This, however, is not possible because this, too, is fixed.

All these objects have to perform their own specific task. In accordance with the size and power they possess, they occupy a place in the universe and describe a fixed orbit. You see, it is now gradually getting darker. This is related to the contraction process and when this is complete, you will recognize in it day and night on earth.

What once was a ball of fire, is now a planet. The smaller objects are stars, and that will also be explained by your leader.

And now the next wonder.

Again millions of years have passed. The planets have contracted, and by this process life has come. Every object is life, is energy and, because there is energy, life awakes within these objects. This young life shall and must awaken and reveal itself and this is the umptheenth wonder of revelation. This life occurs in excess of millions and we see it happen on those organs. I will therefore connect you with the inner life of a planet; in doing so you will feel and see this young life.'

André felt he was connected with a planet. In this planet he saw that something was born and came to life. They were very small cells; and he saw that these tiny cells contacted others. This young life followed the same course as those enormous objects had to follow. He could see through these cells; and however tiny they were, there was life.

Now he heard the voice say: 'What you see now is the first stage of man. Millions of stages follow; yet we emanate from these small cells, and this is part of the entire creation. This stage, as will be clear to you, also took millions of years. These are small lives, but they form part of the universe; they are God's Sacred Life. This process proceeds very slowly. According as the planet contracts, this young life grows, which is the awakening of the first embryo from which we were born. Master Alcar will explain all this to you. In this way the universe was created. You now see everything is slowly contracting. All life will awaken now and the young life passes from one stage to the next. This awakening means taking possession of the planet, the process of growing, and the acceptance of the human organism. Solid portions develop which will be habitable later. The denser and more solid the entire globe becomes, the more this young life contracts until it has reached the first stage of existence. All this life has been inspired by God, because you know that it is His Sacred and Own Life. It was created by this inspiration and propelled towards perfection. The archepower which controls all this is God. You see that the process of revelation has made rapid progress, although billions of years passed, years you and I cannot pronounce. Yet it took place in a short period of time; the process proceeds further and further and all these tiny cells contract to form one whole and this assumes shapes. These shapes change again and this young life accepts a form of existence. This new form is dropped and life transforms into other and higher forms of existence, which is the perfection of the human organism. This young life only follows one course which leads it towards perfection, because an animal-like being appears from the interior of this planet, which has the Divine attunement. Organ after organ develops.

This animal-like being is not conscious of anything yet; for the instinct was not yet born. But as it grows up and is subjected to change after change, the instinct awakens and this animal-like being passes into the stage of the animal-like consciousness. But your leader will explain this and the following stages to you, for together with him you will visit the first world of existence of human embryonal life. This will suffice: Only flashes of what has been shown to us. It is roughly in this way that the universe has been created, for the actual event cannot be retold.

No spirit, however high he may be, can comprehend and explain how all this exactly happened, unless he has entered the All.

There are, therefore, beings who have already returned to God, and we, too, will reach the All and will return to God. God's sacred life lies in us. This revelation is in us and it is our connection with God. What we showed you is the experience of higher beings, who passed these scenes on to us. As it has been shown to you and happened in all those years, it is still happening, for there are still people living on the second cosmic degree who will pass on to the planet earth. That will also be explained to you. The first cosmic degree, which you observed, has at present already partially dissolved. Life of that degree has passed on to the second and third degree which is the earth. There are seven cosmic degrees, that is cosmic life, on which human beings live who have advanced less far or already further than we have. You will learn to know all these cosmic wonders and problems; we will help your leader Alcar to explain everything to you, so that you can make it known on earth. This means a mighty grace for us and for you.

We shall now return to our own life, but we shall follow you in everything. I conclude by asking God's blessing for our work and wish to add my deepest gratitude. May God's Divine blessing be with you and rest on your work. I bless you in the name of the Father, the Son and the Holy Ghost; Amen.

I, Cesarino and the other masters greet you.'

André once more looked at the masters, who then departed. The universe dissolved for him, and the temple of the soul resumed the condition when he entered here.

André looked up at his leader and knelt down. He remained absorbed in prayer for a long time to thank all for this mighty grace he had been allowed to experience. He sincerely thanked the Creator of all this for the sacred event he had been allowed to witness. The origin of the universe had been revealed to him.

'Come, my boy, great work awaits us now. I must explain this tremendous event to you, but you know that I am being helped, too. Cesarino and the other masters will follow us in our work.

I remain connected with them, until you have experienced all this.

We shall now go to the first state of human existence, which, as Cesarino said, has already partially dissolved. Yet, I can connect you there again and you will see the process of fertilization, the awakening of all life and the plan of evolution.'

André now understood what the temple of the soul meant. Soon they had left this mighty building.

# CHAPTER VI

## *To the first cosmic degree*

FLOATING through space, they went on their way and the fourth sphere now dissolved before his eyes. He knew what this meant. Alcar passed to the universe and he would experience reality. He felt the strong concentration of his leader. This was passing into an other condition. Now he would see how man was born. God created man after His own image, but how deep this wonder of creation was! He had seen it and had been able to follow it, because all those events had been recalled to the present. In the temple of the soul, he had been entirely absorbed in the process of revelation and the origin of the universe. Tremendous was everything he had been allowed to see. He had not thought it would be like that and neither could he imagine that condition. Majestic was everything, and yet, how simple did this awe-inspiring universe work. God's sacred power lay in everything. God lived in all those planets; they were God's own life. He now understood what God meant. He dared not think of all that he would experience. He could not form an idea of that either.

'Where are we now, Alcar?'

'In the universe, André. We go on, ever further, to visit the first planet, which you followed in the temple of the soul and which is the mother planet*). We shall be there soon.'

André saw various planets and other objects.

'Where is the earth, Alcar?'

'Do you see that small globe down there?'

'Yes, Alcar.'

'Well, that is the earth. The first planet is to the right and above the earth, and receives its light from the sun, as does the earth. The first, second, and third planet; these three degrees, therefore, belong to this solar system.'

'Aren't there any more objects, besides these planets, which belong to this solar system?'

'Oh, certainly. Do you mean whether there are only three planets, three objects, on which people live?'

*) The Moon

'Yes, Alcar; that is what I mean.'

'Listen, my boy; I will explain that to you. You have seen that innumerable objects have occupied a place in the universe. All these objects are planets and are energy obtained from the same Divine source and brought to life by that source. There are thousands of them of similar strength and size. All those thousands of planets have a certain degree, their own attunement and belong to the first, second, and third degree. Is that clear to you, André?'

'Yes, Alcar.'

'Well then, man lives on all those planets and proceeds from one planet to another. Therefore, hundreds of planets belong to one degree and are related to each other, which I will explain to you presently. Do you understand what I mean, André?'

'Yes, I have understood that, too.'

'When the human being living on the first degree has reached the highest and final stage, it passes on to the next planet, where it lives in a higher attunement, I mean for the material organism. In this way, the individual reaches its highest level. This attunement, the highest we know and have, to which we all belong, is for us the planet earth, and man living there. All of us, André, as I explained to you before, therefore belong to the third degree of cosmic life.

To us, the earth is the final planet and transition; because from the earth one can go on in life beyond to reach the fourth cosmic degree. Is this also clear to you?'

'Yes, Alcar.'

'We are now approaching the first degree, André.'

What André saw was amazing. There in front of him he saw the earth, and yet, it was not the earth. This planet looked like the earth; he saw a nature similar to that on earth, but here everything was withered and dead.

Alcar descended onto this planet. André felt as on earth, but walked on an other planet. Wherever he looked, there was no life. This is the domain of death, he thought. This is decaying and in a process of dissolution.

'Do I feel this correctly, Alcar?'

'Yes, André; I made you feel that.'

'And in this lifeless mass lived the first human being, Alcar?'

'Here originated, what once would become man, which you observed in the temple of the soul; the first human embryo. This planet has completed its task. Do you understand what I mean?'

'Yes, Alcar; I understand.'

'Still, I will connect you with this first stage; only then will you understand how everything is and how it came into being. We therefore descend deeply into the past; you know now that it is possible for me.'

'And this past is billions of years ago, Alcar?'

'Indeed, so it is. Pay attention now, André.'

André felt himself sink away deeply and began to observe. Life came into this lifeless mass. The inner planet teemed with life.

'What is that, Alcar?'

'These things are germs, or cells. Out of these germs, man was born.'

André saw they were globular.

He heard Alcar say: 'This is the embryo in its first stage; they are still transparent.'

André looked at that young life. And that would become man? How incredible it was for him. They looked like drops of water; he could not make a better comparison. They were transparent and this process was like the mighty event he had witnessed in the temple of the soul. When the planet contracted, it was also transparent during the first stage; and this life followed a similar development.

'Is that right, Alcar?'

'Yes, my boy, man follows the same course. As the universe has been created, it applies to all life, animal and human. There is no other course. This is the power of nature and, therefore, God. This process is infallible; for God oversaw everything, His entire creation. Nothing can halt this process. The plan of creation has come into being and now there is already life. The planet has contracted and life begins. I will connect you with the embryo. Listen to what I have to say.

In this embryo lives already that, which once will become a human being. In essence, therefore, everything is preordained and what you see is the first stage of man. Now I will show you the next stage. Centuries have meanwhile passed. You see now that the planet has become more solid, and according as this happened, the embryo developed and evolved into other shapes. The embryo, too, contracted and grew in all these centuries into a small powerful globular being.'

André noticed that great change.

'It is amazing, Alcar.'

'We shall go on, André. Again centuries have passed. The planet has contracted and has become a firm substance. The young life, too, continued its course and you see how far that life has already advanced.'

André saw that some of these beings, which looked like animals, had already grown up.

He heard Alcar say: 'Now that you observe this spectacle, thousands of centuries have passed. The planet is nearly ready to receive this young life on its surface. A firm crust now envelopes this mighty object. In the meantime, as you have observed just now, the embryo passed through many stages. Organ after organ evolved; but you see that it still lives in the interior of this planet. It has not yet reached the highest stage. Again centuries passed.'

André felt that he was again transitioned into an other condition.

'What is that?' he asked his leader.

'Water, my boy. The being, which you observe now, is already half fish, half man. Yet it has nothing human; but during the next stage, the fishy part has nearly disappeared and this being has passed to a higher level. The crust of the planet can now be walked upon, which was not yet possible in the preceding ages. The animal-like being, too, has now developed that far, as you see in front of you, André. I will connect you with the next stage.'

André observed again. What he saw was amazing. Thousands of animal-like beings lay at the shores of this ocean. Many of them had died; but all these beings had reached the waterfront.

'What does this mean, Alcar?'

'This means that the being is about to abandon its fish stage. It is now fully grown and continues its course of development. This is man at a fish-like stage. But it does not possess an organism to continue. At the next stage we see this animal-like being in possession of a powerful organism. Centuries have meanwhile passed. Those having reached the shore will soon die. But evolution continued; it had to continue, and out of this fish-like being evolved an animal-like being. At the next stage, it already lives on the dry land of the planet and has multiplied.

I will explain presently how this happened. We now return to the first stage and will continue from here later on.'

Again André felt that he was connected with the first stage of life. He saw that this life mated with other life and he heard Alcar say: 'You see that this life mates with an other life, but when this happens, it is doomed to die. This being, therefore, gave its own life, but out of it, a new life was born. Now an other wonder happened. At the same instant, the astral being was born and inhabited the world of the unconscious, presently to animate a new life. Do you feel what I mean, André?'

'Yes, Alcar.'

'Reincarnation, therefore, was preordained already at this first stage; because out of this life evolved a young life, and this young life was animated by the former. It was already stronger than during the first stage and also had an other material condition. Do you feel this too, André?'

'You mean that the inner life of the first stage was attracted by the second stage?'

'Very good, André. Thus, not only was fertilization possible, but from this second process emanated also the other, higher, material organism. This is an amazing part of God's creation; for, by continuous changes, this organism should and had to become man. This small animal-like being, as I have shown you, was therefore already essentially perfect. After each contact it died, and its animation, which is the astral being, passed to the world of the unconscious to be attracted again.

How was all this effected?

When the material organism lost its animation, it ceded to the other being, and reached its maximum age. That was the moment it passed away. In this being, therefore, an intelligent power was already present, which is the Divine attunement we also have. This Divine attunement, however, was already active during the first stage, and this small animal-like being performed the task imposed upon it by nature, which is reincarnation. Is this also clear, André?'

'Yes, Alcar.'

'Well then, I will continue. In essence, therefore, it was compelled to do so. Nature possessed this creating and driving power and compelled the material organism to give itself in order to continue the process of generation. This is fertilization.

If this had not been possible, the animal-like being would be doomed to continue this life; advancement and evolvement would have been out of the question. Then a standstill would have been reached; transition would indeed have taken place, but all this young life would be bound to die. But I told you already, this small organism lived on and evolved in all those ages until it reached the stage which I showed you a while ago.

Do you understand what I mean, André? That this animal-like being had to die as a result of contact, but was attracted again by an other being during a further stage of development? Is that clear to you?'

'Yes, Alcar.'

'Well then, that happened during the first stage. During the second stage, this small animal-like being lived on for some time and then died. You will understand that this process went on, and that its organism gradually became stronger. Whereas, during the first stage, death occurred instantaneously, the this being lived on during the second, third, and later stages for months and years, only to die then and to enter into the astral world. You have understood that, too, haven't you?'

'Yes, Alcar.'

'But also that being, that astral life, was again attracted by that animal-like and material being, which I will show you now.'

André saw how this wonder happened. There were two fully grown animal-like beings. They curled together and at that moment fertilization took place.

Now he heard Alcar say: 'Pay attention, my boy, to what I am going to tell you. This animal-like being has been fertilized, but in the same instant, it attracts the animating life, which is therefore a being which has lived already in a similar condition. It is this animating power, which brings the embryo to life, which, by birth, will accept this organism. Thus, in this embryo is already the nucleus of the human being. The organs it possesses are up to their task. During the many centuries which passed by, a strong being has grown. The mother animal-like being bears this young life, and this is an event, though at this level, which man experiences at his highest level of development. In whatever way this event happens, the cosmic problem and the wonder of creation are already experienced. Is that also clear to you, André?'

'Yes, Alcar.'

'So you see the problem of reincarnation. It is the wonder of God's creation and of being born again. What you experience now, André, is my work; it belongs to my task and I have to follow it. It is our sole purpose to convince man on earth that reincarnation is a law. It is a condition and an event, and if God had not created it, we would not be here, for we would then already have been destroyed during the first stage. But God created this tremendous wonder, and His entire creation is animated by this wonder. Animation, therefore, would not have been possible if this had not been created, if this wonder and this evolution had not been there. But it is the course which the human being had to follow during the first stage, like all life, in whatever degree, condition, and attunement it may be, has to follow man and animal, and will experience. So here we see the reincarnation. This small animal-like being already possessed that wonder at the first stage. Here, instinct was also born; and this instinct, as I said before, is the Divine attunement of creative life. This means our ultimate return to our Almighty Father. It means living life, for which purpose all those planets were created, and accepting Divine life one day.

God revealed Himself, which is for this life, passing on into thousands of lives to reach the highest, the Divine degree of life. However, we then have millions of centuries behind us and have completed this long road.

When God had not yet revealed himself, in essence everything was perfect; and this perfection is already present in this small wonder of animal life. When mankind on earth, in its perfect condition, wonders what God is and why we are on earth, this is the revelation, the truth, and reality, for it was God's wish that mankind would live through this revelation. Thus, God created the universe for mankind; He created stars and planets; but he made mankind after his own image. God wanted mankind to become conscious; and this Divine consciousness, which we will possess one day, was given by God to a being in human form. Is that clear to you, André?'

'Yes, Alcar, quite. I have understood everything you said.'

'There are already people who have lived on earth, and many other planets, who have returned to the Divine All-Power. They, therefore, have consciously taken possession of the universe; otherwise, and that will be clear to you, we would not have received this message.'

Man follows a long road; for billions of years are required to reach Divine life. But what man then possesses, cannot be imagined. What you have experienced, André, will one day be our possession. This has been the purpose of the entire creation. God gave His own self. God gave man, the highest being, these Divine gifts. God created something in which He Himself lives. It is now up to man to see to it that he is in harmony. Man, therefore, who was born out of this small animal-like being, in first instance, already possessed this Divine grace; for he created, he gave his own self; he sacrifices himself to create new life. In first instance, therefore, André, God's plan of creation is preordained; this is reincarnation, transition into an other life; it is death, and being born again; this is attraction and repulsion; this is animation, the return to God.

Similar beings attract each other; this is known on earth; and here you see that it happened; it was no different. This attraction happened in material, as well as, in spiritual respect. The animal-like being which had got that far, sought and found a similar animal-like being. That being was available; they united, and a young life was born again. What is known on earth as 'death' and that inner life is the inspiring life, was already known here, too. For life entered the astral world to be attracted again.

There, in front of you, are two beings, but at a further and higher stage. You see, they attract each other and seek connection. At this moment, when fertilization is about to happen, the astral being is already on its way. This mighty wonder, my son, is like birth on earth. This condition, this action, this possibility, is still there; it is in man on earth and is the same event. Like a child on earth is born, like the inner life, which is the soul and spirit, is attracted there, it is here also the result of this connection. In all those billions of centuries, André, this event has not changed in the slightest.

What man on earth experiences in this respect, has been present in man from the first stage of human life in a being. That urge, that power and action to unite with an other life, is the wish of God, and it has existed from the beginning of creation; from the very first stage of human life, nothing has changed in that respect. Inspiration, animation, therefore, came into being at the very moment of the wonder of creation manifested already by the very first flashes of light, which you observed in the temple of the soul.

'You see now, André, that these two beings unite, and that the astral being is attracted. The astral being passes into the embryo and is the driving power, the inner life, of this animal-like being. According as this being grows up, the instinct awakes. Man on earth in its perfect and fully grown condition experiences the same activity; but man on earth has already reached consciousness. Here, therefore, we can only speak of instinct; but we shall follow this awakening, when we visit animal life on the second cosmic degree.

What I should like to add is this: Where does the astral being live? See and observe, André. You will see the presence of the astral being in the direct surroundings of the material being. This also applies to the earth and is, as it is here, the astral world. In that world, therefore, lives the human being who died on earth. Do you understand what I mean, André?'

'Yes, Alcar.'

'But the human spirit can go where it likes and is not confined to any surroundings. That is because man lives in a higher degree. Have you understood that, too?'

'You mean, that this world is limited?'

'Very good. Indeed, André. Here, the astral animal-like being lives in a very confined space around the material life, into which it can descend instantly. But if you have understood me, you will clearly feel that, the further life advances, the wider becomes the world in which it lives. Herein we see an other and new wonder of God.

Like man on the side beyond experiences that the sphere in which he lives, although that sphere is unlimited, keeps him captive, this also applies in this case.

Inner life, that is man as spirit, lives already in the infinite. But here, during the first stage, the astral animal-like being envelops the material being and waits for connection, and remains in the direct surroundings of this material form of life. These astral surroundings, however, in which the astral animal-like being lives, are still as large as the volume of this planet.

The size of this planet, therefore, is the space in which the astral being lives. However, man as a spirit, like you are a material and spiritual being, has the universe as astral world, and every sphere, wherever it may be, is unlimited; because his spirit has lived through all those stages, from the first, second, and third degree, which, as you know, is the earth. You will also feel that we human beings will receive, ever more; we will feel deeper, nay will possess happiness, and our earthly and spiritual life will expand more and more, so that we shall ultimately enter the All. The material organism experiences the process of growing and development; but inner life expands and widens ever more, according to the sphere in which the being lives. Is that clear, André?'

'Yes, Alcar, I have understood. Everything is so amazing and natural. I have to accept it.'

'Then we will go on. This animal-like human being, here in front of you, can pass on to the second stage to continue in the tenth and hundredth stage, until it has completed its material cycle of life belonging to this planet. Then inner life proceeds and is attracted by the second cosmic degree. But I shall refer to that later, for now we have advanced far enough to answer your questions which you put forth at the beginning of this voyage. Your question of why one being has advanced further than the other, and how this is possible, I will answer now.

For, André, haven't you noticed it; haven't you clearly seen that some beings have advanced further than others?'

'Yes, Alcar.'

'Well, then, I return to the beginning and the final stage of material animal-like life.'

Again André observed. He saw young and old, large and small beings; the first and last stage. The last stage was the one during which those animal-like beings had reached the shore. Yet, he did not understand his leader, and asked: 'But did those first cells not dissolve, Alcar?'

'Yes, that happened; but here there are millions of transitions, in other words, degrees of development. The first, tenth, hundredth, and thousandth stage had already dissolved and evolved into embryonic life. These beings, therefore, were the first ones to develop. Do you think that this is an injustice? Then I will explain that to you and show that it is impossible. Because old and young is of no importance here; but a first and last degree of the first embryo is.

This is caused by external influence, to which the planet was subjected, which is the process of contraction, and is related to the solar system. Life, which was born and lived in the deepest interior of this planet, awoke during a later stage, many centuries later, to be precise. Between the first and the last life is a period of millions of years. When the first life had reached its final and last stage, down in the depths of the planet, a similar life awakened to evolve into embryonal life. You can readily accept that, for God, time does not exist. One time this would happen, and it did happen and nothing was left behind. Thus, there are beings which have already reached the highest spheres at our side. This is the reason why there are people on earth who seek the good, and others who belong to the devils of hell. By now, you also know that there are human beings, who have already reached the Divine Spheres, and have entered the All. When the last embryo dissolved, which meant the end of this planet, they had been on their way for billions of years. And still it took thousands of years for the last being

84

on this planet to reach the highest degree of material organism, to pass to the second cosmic degree; but all will come that far; they are on their way and are not restricted by time. We are all one for God our Holy Father; there is progress for all His children and everything belonging to this life, and all are on their way to the Divine Spheres. Is that clear to you, too?'

'Yes, Alcar.'

'Then do you also understand that there has to be reincarnation? Can you frankly give an affirmative answer? For, André, if it had not been there, if this wonder had not been given to mankind, God's creation would have come to nothing and it would have failed already in the first degree. But God oversaw everything; it is the mightiest that God created; it is the link connecting the entire universe. It is the link interconnecting planets and other objects.

These are the cosmic degrees and all these degrees are now inhabited. What I am after is this: What had already been present here is also for mankind on earth. For it is surely impossible that God would deprive man of this mighty principle of creation and giving birth, when he has reached a further and higher condition. If that were to happen, the plan of evolution would come to a standstill and mankind would already be doomed to become extinct here. And now, we get to know another wonder, and however strange and improbable it would appear to you, all this life here came to an end. I mean life in the first, second, and thousandth degree, which is the perfect organism on this planet; all this life was doomed to become extinct. But here, too, God helped mankind; for the inner life went on, and was attracted by a higher degree. I will explain this mighty wonder presently.

What we have experienced here also happens on the second degree, and it likewise applies to the planet earth. Both degrees André, all those planets on which man lives, as does the animal-like organism, are doomed to become lifeless; but all that life will accept a higher degree and pass on to it. The time will come when mankind and animals will leave the planet earth, but all those who have reached the highest degree of life we shall see again in our life, the life of the spirit. All these beings will leave the earth and will pass on to the fourth cosmic degree. But before this happens, millions of centuries have passed; but it is preordained, it is a law; for all life shall return to God. Then, the second and third cosmic degrees will dissolve, and we'll see them, as you are about to see when you return to your own life, as a lifeless mass. This dissolution will also take millions of years, and it will happen in reverse to its creation, which you have seen in the temple of the soul and in the interior of this planet. Again, millions of centuries will pass before this and other planets have dissolved; but also, this law is infallible and it will happen.

'Is everything clear to you now, André?'

'Yes, Alcar, but where then does the story of Adam and Eve come in? Is that a figment?'

Alcar smiled, and said: 'You are amusing, André, and wonderfully simple. Thousands of people hold on to that story; but I will tell you what it means and why it was made up.

First of all, it is a symbol. As a symbol, however, it has a value; for the people who preached it to mankind, those who created and accomplished the bible, had to show that they knew something of the beginning of creation. Whether they knew this, or not, does not matter; they achieved something. Mankind had to have something to hold on to and that was given. Because, what would have become of mankind and of God, if creation got stuck and would be doomed? In those days, not much was known on earth about stars and planets. Neither did they know God, and even today not much progress has been made. And yet, there had to be something by which mankind could be inspired with awe, and which he could accept. Therefore, it was man who created Adam and Eve, and not God; man invented that story, and it was accepted on earth. Now that you have seen all this, I ask you, can that story be true? Is it possible, now that we know this wonder? Couldn't you have answered that question yourself?'

'Yes, Alcar, I understand you perfectly. But what, then, is the last judgement? Is that also a story?'

'You have known that, too, for a long time, as I have explained that to you. But listen, that is quite an other condition; a completely different event. It is true, and yet, not true. It will come and yet, it will not come the way people think it will come, that everything will collapse and that all will be over. There will be no collapse for, as I told you already, the earth will dissolve. And that process has been proceeding on this planet for ages, and it will still take millions of centuries before the earth has dissolved entirely. Yet, there will be an end, but an entirely different end.

Man, however, can be confronted with his last judgement any second of his life on earth. He, who commits sins, must stop; for, the very moment he does, something judges, and that judgement is cause and effect. There are, however, mistakes and sins, deeds, therefore, which can only dissolve many centuries later, and which mankind will have to make good.

No, André, a last judgement, like people imagine, does not exist. God still is a Father of Love. I have also answered this question. Is it clear to you now?'

'Yes, Alcar.'

'Do you have any more questions?'

'No, Alcar.'

'Well, then I will explain another wonder.'

# CHAPTER VII

## *The animal world*

I AM going to connect you again, and with what, do you think, André? Can you feel it? No? Well, a second wonder has happened here, my boy, an amazing event; for where did our animals on earth come from? Surely this life was born somewhere and must, like mankind, have had a beginning stage? Don't you know?'

'No, Alcar, I don't know and I can't see it.'

'Well then, listen: here, André, at this spot, on the first planet, which is the mother planet, the first animal life was born; the first animal cell awakened. That was also God's work; God knew that man would need this help.

There are people on earth who think that man had to follow plant and animal life; but I contradict that. There are also people on earth who say that man, during a further stage, will be able to fertilize and, consequently, connect himself; and experience this entire process himself, but that I also contradict. That is not true and not possible; it is against the plan of creation. God oversaw everything. Would that, which was already present during the first stage and was at the same time perfect, have to be abandoned again during a later stage? No. A thousand times no! That is not possible. Listen, André, it may sound unlikely, but the animal on earth was born out of man. I will explain this wonder to you.

The animal is, so to speak, the shadow of the real being, which is man. They are, therefore, our sisters and brothers, and we must love them. But man has not got that far yet, because he kills many of our animals. But not only our animals, which are one degree lower than our mentality and Divine power, he also destroys his sisters and brothers, who also possess the Divine nucleus. When the first human embryo died, the first animal being was born out of that process of decay. From this process originated the germ, which grew to become the animal being living on earth.

Isn't it amazing? And yet, my boy, it is the holy truth. I will connect you with it. Listen well to what I am going to say: when the first human embryo died, a process of decay set in. Out of that process of decay the animal was born, as I said, and it multiplied endlessly, from degree to degree, and kept in pace with the being, which is a degree higher and further: man. Consequently, man is always ahead of the animal, and this will remain so until we have returned to the All. There, too, this form of life will surround us, but it remains in that attunement. At this side, the animal is our greatest friend and brother. You have seen that it obeys us and can sense our thoughts. It acts in accordance with what the higher being wants and thinks, and with the concentration established. Invariably, in all those millions of centuries, this animal being followed man, but it proceeded below the strength and mental degree of man. Thus it is out of us, André, that the animal being was born. When studying this process on earth, now that science has advanced that far, and man begins to understand more and more of cosmic life and the purpose of God's creation, he can follow it. If scientists on earth would not think so much of themselves, concentrated more on spiritual life and could accept emotional life, they would have advanced much further and would have understood this mighty problem.

One day they will get that far, but that will take thousands of years. Science is making rapid progress, but not yet to the extent that it can already accept all this. They search on earth, but in the wrong direction. They talk and discover, but talking is pointless; they should feel and descend into themselves deeply; for there, in that depth, is the secret of it all, this mighty event, which is God's creation.

When I speak of intuition, I can say the animal has that to a high degree. The animal surrenders unconditionally and follows its intuition, its senses, and lives. Man, however, was given a will of his own, he is like God; he is a Divine being. And as man is a Divine being, he has to follow one course, whereas the animal proceeds through thousands of material organisms. The animal being, therefore, follows thousands and thousands of material stages; what is intended for the animal being, is not meant for man. Before this mighty event took place, man was the animating and inspiring power, because it emanated from God. When God had completed the plan of creation – if I may put it this way – that which was born, man, was the first phenomenon, and there was no animal life. The first flashes of light before the Divine process would begin, which you have observed in the temple of the soul, heralded this birth. Man was already confined to those flashes of light and was, therefore, the first phenomenon of this awe-inspiring revelation.

God created man by revealing Himself and this revelation took place the moment creation started. God knew that man would develop by death and that out of the dead organism new activity and new life would appear. But God gave to His own life at the first stage, His own amazing power, because God Himself descended into this being.

I am speaking now of the first stage, because man received the very, very highest. But 'received' is not the right word, for man did not receive; man is like God, and man yielded part of his own energy: Out of that dead body, animal life was born.

Isn't it simple? In essence, man and the animal being are one, but man is the conscious Divine being, the inspiring and driving power. Man is that which is the Divine power, for we emanated from the Divine. Through all those millions of centuries, the animal being will follow us. This has happened from the first human embryo. When the first human embryo entered the process of decay, the first animal cell emanated from this process and this life was animated, because God's life is in everything. The moment this animation set in, a process started, which, in reality, equalled our first stage and had to follow the human being. Out of the first cell thus appeared a tiny animal being, it was born and could not be seen with the naked eye. Man, too, lived during this stage, and resembled a tiny drop of water, as I showed and explained to you.

Before it had obtained that size, the process had run for thousands of years. During the first stage they were only cells, and these cells, which even then could not be seen with the naked eye contracted in a natural way, in accordance with the plan of evolution and the laws of nature. But I will return to the animal being.

Now when the human being passed into embryonic life during the first stage, animal life had also advanced that far and passed to the same stage. Animal life invariably followed man, but it always stayed below us. Yet both lived in one world, but continued in their own attunement and their own astral world. These two forms of life are not connected with each other, because that is not possible. For, at the beginning of the plan of creation, as I said before, the first phenomena were directed at the human being, and only when the first embryo had died, could animal life commence.

Man on earth has now reached his perfect material degree, and the animal has assumed its highest degree, also. You see that there have been animal beings from the very beginning of creation. There has been no era during which they did not exist. This can be explained, because this process can be followed on our side by connecting ourselves with the past so that we see it again before us. On this journey, it was shown to you clearly enough that we can return into the past, wasn't it? I spoke of many, nay even thousands of transitions, which the animal being has to follow. All those species of animals which once existed and lived on this planet, have died here. What happened for the animal being, was also for man, because man also advanced further and higher, and the animal being was to follow man.

I shall explain this amazing phenomenon on the third degree, on earth; it was there that these material, but animal beings, which had already died, dissolved into the All, because they represented a lower degree of life in this cosmic plan. All this is very deep, André, but I will make it clear to you by connecting you with this invisible life.

If this had not happened, I mean the dissolution of this animal being, one could accept, as is done on earth, that man evolved through the plant and animal life before life accepted the human condition. But this is not possible, for that animal dissolved and returned to the All. But out of this material being new life evolved, and out of that stage other species of animals were born. Do you feel what I mean, André?'

'Yes, Alcar. Out of one species of animal, evolved the other species.'

'Yes, very good. Every animal being produced another animal being according to its species, degree, and power, because this animal being was maintained by the process of decay and emerged from it.

But man, as I said before, followed only one way, leading towards perfection of the material organism. The animal being, however, evolved through thousands of animal species. It accepted one life, in order to enter a higher stage in the other, but remained through all those millions of years, one degree below the thinking and sensing being, which will ultimately return to God. In everything, in whatever stage man and the animal being lived, you see the process of reincarnation. Otherwise, the animal being, too, would in first instance have been doomed to become extinct, and God's creation and the process of revelation would have been destroyed. Time and again, there was reincarnation on earth and on other planets. It means acceptance of a higher degree, until animal and man have received the perfect organism.

Man possesses the highest degree, which is Divine consciousness, but the animal also has a cosmic attunement, yet it does not reach our height. Animal and man, as I said before, are one; they know and have one inspiration and are God's life. Since man is the Divine being, he only has to follow one road.

The amazing thing about this process of evolution, however, is that when man had reached the second cosmic degree, which we will visit presently, and was neither man nor animal, the animal being had also reached a pre-animal condition. But the animal being closely followed the human being and when man had reached the third cosmic degree, the planet earth, the animal had also dropped its prehistoric organism. Yet, this animal being invaded the third cosmic degree; in former times pre-animal monsters inhabited the earth, but man had not yet reached his perfect organic condition either. You will see all that and I shall explain it to you.

You see, André, how closely both creatures are connected and how the animal being followed the Divine being. This process continued for millions of years, nay, for millions of centuries. Consequently, in your time on earth, you see both the animal being and human being in their highest material form.

It will be clear to you now why there are no more prehistoric animal species on earth: because they and man have reached a higher material degree. During the many centuries which passed, one species of animal life after another returned to the All and that prehistoric creature vanished. But we are all out of God and live in God, animal as well as man, the animal being as well as the Divine being – one energy – will return again to that source of life, but man remains cosmically conscious.

The material animal being on earth is perfect, and yet, as you see, new species of animal life are born, because the deepest energy sources of the animal being have not yet been spent. But these species are very few.

In the oceans there are species of animals which are not yet known. These animals, too, will one day pass on to a higher degree, a higher condition, and will adopt an other organism. I am referring here to degrees: in the animal world we know seven degrees of animal attunement. Do you understand what I mean, André? Then you will understand that the animal being also has seven cosmic dgrees, which are spiritual and material degrees. Isn't it amazing and yet simple?

When an animal is attracted again to the earth and is born there, its spiritual life descends into the material life and the animal acts and feels according to its present condition, which is the material organism. This organism has a cosmic attunement, but in one degree there are hundreds of transitions for the animal life, and all these transitions comprise seven degrees. The highest and lowest transition could for example be compared with the predator 'panther', and the domestic animal 'cat'. These are transitions, André, material degrees; the animal being acts in accordance with its material degree. These are transitions but in one species. Do you understand what I mean?'

'Yes, Alcar.'

'Fine, then I will proceed. Other animal species have thousands of transitions in their condition, and yet, you feel what I mean, all those beings belong to one degree, that is, the material and cosmic attunement. When you understand this amazing phenomenon, the presence of all those species of animals on earth is clear. But all those species, large and small, therefore, have one attunement. The material organism and the species to which these animals belong give the animal its terrible power; but it is the instinct, the sensitivity, which makes it act and adapt itself in a natural, and yet amazing, way to that material organism. The domestic animal cat is vicious; no less vicious is a panther. The sensitivity of the domestic animal and the panther represents one strength, one life; it is the material organism which compels the animal to act the way it was born. Now, when this animal instinct has awakened and been spent, you see very sensitive and tame animals, even though they are, in essence, like the young predator. For the animal, including the most dangerous animal, is in actual fact related to man. It was born out of man and can be raised to this elevated human condition. This explains why man can always tame the wildest animal, for in essence we are one, but we, who are Divine, possess an intellect which the animal can never approach nor acquire.

Animal and man are one in life, but we are from the first degree and the animal has to adapt itself to us. There are, however, animals which are now further and higher than man on earth. When the animal has reached the highest, the seventh degree, it has properties which man on earth does not yet have. At this side, the animal being follows us and obeys our will. He who acquired this concentration already on earth, can connect himself with the animal being.

We, spiritual beings, who have reached that spiritual degree, own that gift of power which is our personality and the love we possess. The animal being, the pigeon for instance, which finds its way home from far countries, possesses that highest degree of cosmic sensitivity in material and spiritual attunement, and is far ahead of man.

Man on earth has not yet reached his highest attunement of sensitivity, and will not possess that attunement until he has entered spiritual life and has reached the fourth sphere. The sensitivity the pigeon has is also found in other animal species. The dog, for instance, has that sensitivity and nearly attains that consciously spiritual degree, but cannot surpass it, and will not pass on to this conscious, human degree.

Also the horse and many other species possess this feeling; they are in their species in this condition and have reached their highest degree. These species of animals are very sensitive; they are closest to the human being, and approach this consciousness. Yet, all those animal species do not attain it, because it is not possible. It will, therefore, be clear to you that many animals are more advanced in sensitivity than many people on earth. The animal in its highest degree follows its intuition and this is, therefore, the sensitivity acquired by man who has reached the fourth sphere. Below it, in his immediate vicinity, lives the animal, though still on earth in a material condition. It is this sensitivity the animal possesses, whereas man lives a pre-animal life, and is below that degree.

Therefore, André, many animals on earth are further advanced than man, and it is often said: 'an animal would not do that.' By this, I mean the animal which has reached this height and has advanced that far. Still, one day man will advance that far and will reach that high stage. We are now on the third cosmic degree and go on to the fourth, but to that end we need thousands of years. Why this has to take such a long time and why this is necessary, you have been able to follow in all this, because also in that nothing has changed either. The higher we get, the more difficult our way will be. I have explained to you already that man on the fourth degree can live for hundreds of years in one material condition. During the first stage of the human embryo, it died immediately when its inspiration passed on into the other life. But gradually, this process lengthened, the seconds became minutes, minutes became hours, hours became days, days became weeks, and months... up to ten and twenty years. Then, on the second degree, thirty years and older, and on earth, still older. On the fourth cosmic degree, however, the length of life varies, and there people can reach ages of hundreds of years. On the fifth cosmic degree, however, it lengthens still further, and life there will last thousands of years. Further still, man will reach ten and twenty thousand years, to stay one day on the seventh degree. Then, the years can no longer be counted, for then man lives in the infinite.

In all those transitions, you'll feel this, André, one law applies; it is the plan of evolution, a law to return to our Father. When one follows life in this way, one begins to feel its depth, and life on earth can then be understood.

On this planet, therefore, man and animal were born and that is why it is the mother planet. But now that we have advanced billions of years, and after all those centuries, there are still beings on earth who do not understand themselves and take the lives of others.

When we notice on earth that the number of people and animals is increasing, it is caused by the transition of beings from the second degree which are born on earth. I will explain that to you on this journey. But the number of souls, of men and animals, cannot be determined; this is infinite. And yet, you will see that presently all those beings dissolved, since this planet is now lifeless. Now, my boy, you will return to yourself.'

# CHAPTER VIII

## *Alcar answers André's questions*

ANDRÉ woke up. 'How far you have advanced, Alcar, to be able to explain all that! It is all so deep, and yet, so natural.'

'Have you understood my explanation, André?'

'Yes, Alcar, entirely. It is a great wonder.'

André looked at the first planet.

'How is it possible, Alcar? Once teeming with life – life everywhere – and now everything is dead, extinct. How long will it be before this planet has dissolved?'

'Millions of years will pass.'

'Is this planet known on earth?'

'Yes, it can be seen from the earth.'

'Does this planet remain in this position?'

'No, it moves in a rotating orbit around the sun.'

'Has it still got an atmosphere?'

'No, millions of years ago the atmosphere dissolved, and this can no longer be ascertained by man on earth. That is why life is extinct here; no living organism can exist.'

'And is that the earth, there, above us?'

'Yes, that is the earth. Every planet follows a fixed orbit, which was established from the very beginning of creation. Whenever there are deviations, they concern cosmic disturbances, often caused by meteors. Yet, this planet will remain in its orbit as long as man is still on earth.'

'What are meteors, Alcar?'

'They are starlets; small objects, which, like the bigger ones, occupy a place in the universe.'

'Sometimes a phenomenon is seen on earth, which is called falling stars. What is that?'

'These smaller objects or meteors pass through the atmosphere and leave a luminous trail. They pass through the atmosphere and, so to speak, out of it again, but sometimes these meteors or pieces thereof strike the earth and have occasionally been found. When their orbit is distant from the earth, and the gravity of an other planet is greater than that of the earth, this small object is torn apart and disappears into space.'

'Have those stars their own atmosphere, Alcar?'

'Yes, but it also dissolves and then we see the phenomenon of falling stars.'

'Does that also apply to this planet? I mean, can this planet be torn apart?'

'No, that is not possible. It dissolves, but not until millions of years have passed. But before that time has come, the number of people on earth will decrease, and the earth will assume a similar condition; then the first, second, and third cosmic degree will dissolve.'

'Were these smaller objects also inhabited, like this one, Alcar?'

'Yes, but not all of them. On those which had their own atmosphere, life could awaken; on other planets, without an atmosphere, it was impossible. You see what it is like, now that the atmosphere has dissolved; it is no longer possible to live here. That applies to every other globe, be it small or large.'

'What is known on earth about this planet?'

'Nothing. At any rate, very little. The distance from this planet to the earth is measured and man on earth is already that far that he can approximate it. The people who lived here in those days, knew nothing about advancement and intellectual life. In those days, the earth had not yet condensed. At present, now that the earth is inhabited and people have reached this level, they focus on the universe and they will make progress. But they will not be able to fathom the past of this planet.'

'On earth attempts are made to reach the moon. Will that be possible in the future, Alcar?'

'No, they will never reach it.*) Nevertheless, if they want to accomplish it, those who volunteer will lose their lives. There are forces in the universe unknown to man. Now, when there are forces in the universe which hurl a small planet through space, what does man want to achieve? Those who venture too far out of the atmosphere of the earth will perish. They can cover a considerable distance from the earth; yet, at a certain moment, something in that space will halt them. There are even forces in the universe which man on earth will never know, because he himself has not yet reached that level, and will not receive it until on the fourth cosmic degree.'

'Technology goes a long way, Alcar. See how much has already been

*) See footnote page 115.

achieved on earth!'

'They will advance further yet, penetrate life deeper; they will fathom and sense the past, and change their lives. Listen, André, I will explain that to you. Mankind is now in a condition which is one degree in this cosmic plan. Whatever is present on that degree, and lives between heaven and earth, can be fathomed by them, and for that purpose they will invent instruments. But all that lives outside their own atmosphere remains inscrutable to them. Those venturing out of their own sphere at this side, immediately face death and have to undergo this.'

'Yet, they are working on it, Alcar. One often hears about it.'

'I know that, my boy. I follow everything, and with me are all my brothers and sisters on this side, who also wanted to achieve that while living on earth. Those who want to reach the moon while living on earth, do not realize that it is not possible until they are here. Yet, there are scientists on earth who try to achieve that, but they will not succeed.

Why, I ask you, do they wish to accomplish that? The moon, too, will dissolve, as will many other planets which have performed their task. But no thought is given to that. There are even scientists who know that they will perish, and that, too, is suicide. They will suffer at this side, and have to undergo the process of decay as a result of their vain feelings, only because they concerned themselves with things far beyond their own feeling and ability.

Should they nevertheless attempt it, then their technical wonder will melt away, and nothing will be left of themselves. They will be destroyed because they do not understand themselves nor the universe. For that is outside the atmosphere of the earth. The human organism which man first had, like the being you saw just now, was built differently, and had other organs than the present man on earth. The human organism must adapt itself to the sphere; for man on earth, this is the third degree of cosmic attunement. Those venturing outside this protective atmosphere, will irrevocably destroy themselves. The human organs are not intended for it. The material organism is only designed for the place where it spends its life. Thus, mankind of the first cosmic degree could not live on the second cosmic degree, and the second not on the third, and the third not on the fourth cosmic degree. God oversaw this. God provided the human soul with a dwelling, which is the human body. But God also provided the planet earth with a wall of power and energy, so that man could not penetrate it with his own power.

Those who do wish to penetrate it will perish and will have to pay with their own lives. Only God knows why that is necessary and we on this side are in the process of understanding all these tremendous powers. At this side, André, and that should be clear to you, we come to understand something of God's creation. We know that God revealed Himself and that each life is a particle of that revelation. Because we as human beings are included in this great plan and are part of it, we feel what has been given to us. God's sacred life is in everything. Every human being and animal, every material organism, however small, received its own abode, in which the soul lives. Those who wish to free themselves from it will perish.

The animal which does not know its strength loses its balance, and will perish. When this balance, which is the protection for the material organism, is disturbed, death of the material organism will follow. The soul then returns to the infinite and waits there to be attracted again. When this happens, the inner life will have to correct its mistake. If it does not do so in the life it was born again, a second, third, and more transitions will follow, which is reincarnation. Life will return to a material organism as many times as is needed to acquire the degree in which it lives. Once this life gets that far, it will proceed further and higher, and we know whence it goes. For still greater spiritual happiness awaits it in all those cosmic degrees. He who ventures outside his own degree will have to accept what is present there, for the human organism is only designed for the degree in which it lives. A dog, a cat, a bird, a predator and the thousands of other animal species which are on earth, would not be able to live on the planet where we are now, and where I showed everthing to you, because their organism is different.

Here, and on other planets, lived brute force in unconscious condition. What lived here, André, now lives on earth, but all organs have acquired a higher condition. What once lived here has proceeded further and further. They, who were here, are now one or two degrees higher, and that is man on earth in his perfect organism.'

'If I have understood you correctly, Alcar, every planet produced its own material organism, but that organism was inspired by the inner life which was born here.'

'Very well, André, you have understood me. I will tell you more about that presently.'

'Is the material organism of man on earth, perfect?'

'Man there is perfect, André, and yet, if people on earth were allowed to see their sisters and brothers who have already reached the fourth, fifth, sixth, and seventh cosmic degree they would think they saw God Himself. There, too, man is a being living in a material organism, for God did not create a second perfect condition, and this human degree is the image of the perfect child of God. They are people in a material organism, but at a higher level and more perfect; their radiation can be seen from afar. The material organism of the fourth cosmic degree is already a body of unknown beauty, but these beings cannot venture outside their own atmosphere either, or they will perish. Their bodies are transparent, like the finest material one could imagine on earth. The face of a higher being reflects the image of the universe which is seen in all of God's life. When we have come that far that I can explain that to you, you will be connected with the fourth cosmic degree and you will be allowed to admire the human being living there. We shall all go there; it is our future happiness that awaits all of us.'

'You will connect me with them, Alcar?'

'When the time has come, André, you will also experience that wonder.'

'Can the number of planets be estimated, Alcar?'

'No, that is not possible; no more than the number of souls, the living beings living in the invisible, can be determined.'

'The stars are visible from the earth; are they those luminous globes of fire, which I was allowed to observe in the temple of the soul?'

'Yes, a star is a luminous celestial body and also receives energy from other bodies, which is manifestated in light. At the beginning of creation, as you have seen in the temple of the soul, the universe tore apart into millions of particles which floated on in space. A spot of light is therefore a globular mass. There are large and small ones, but the small ones are still that large that they span thousands of miles. Each body, therefore, emanates from that golden light and radiates light in accordance with its power and size.

Just like all living things radiate their inner light down to the smallest insect, the inner light envelops the body.'

'Is that the explanation for what is observed from earth, Alcar?'

'Yes, that is the explanation, André. On earth, luminous balls of fire are seen in the sky, which are observed from afar as a star. That is why they are called stars on earth, and yet they are globes like the larger planets. Each one has its own light, for it emanates from that mighty light. We know this is energy and that everything is maintained by that power. What is observed on earth is the light which these stars radiate. A star – to adhere to this word, because that is what it is called on earth – in essence, is a powerful ball of light, and nothing else. Yet, those small objects also condensed during those millions of centuries. All those stars have become firm, and very solid masses. Yet, the inner light dominates and radiates from the entire object. Can you follow me, André? Do you understand then, what I mean? You could best compare it with the small, but fine, animal living on earth which is called glow-worm. This small animal radiates light, and yet it is a material organism.

The light of a small star, and this also applies to the larger ones, radiates around the entire body, and this light has such tremendous power that it can be observed at a distance of millions of miles. And when the origin of the universe could be accepted on earth, as we have learned to know and understand that it has been created out of God's own light, they would fathom this problem and feel and understand how simple all this is. But the scientists on earth cannot accept this, for 'death' is already calling them to a halt. They stand powerless at the grave and cry out of ignorance, because they do not understand them-selves. If they knew, they would be happy, for they would know where death would bring them and that they would be accommodated in the mighty universe. But science on earth has not yet advanced far enough. One day, however, they will solve this problem and then they will say: 'My God, oh my God; is it that simple?'

Yes, it is simple. Just like death which does not exist means life. If they do not wish to accept this, André, how could they understand the universe, God's creation?

There are scientists who exclaim: 'Oh, how mighty everything is' but if they would experience this tremendous phenomenon, it is simple, almost childishly simple. However deep everything is, everything, all those wonders are simplicity, for God is simplicity and love. When man feels that, it will move him deeply and 'this' is love. Because every-thing vibrates for love, radiates like the sun, and this is the power of love, nothing but power of love, a power which all of us will once possess.

Then, our radiance will touch thousands of people and everything living in our surroundings. Then we are suns ourselves, luminous beings like the universe, and we shall be like God.'

'Can the distance to the stars, and their ages, be determined on earth, Alcar?'

'That is not possible either, André. One counts in millions of years, and yet that figure is an estimate; to calculate it is not possible.'

'Have all those stars their own power?'

'Yes. As I told you a moment ago, in accordance with their luminosity, and that is the energy they have.'

'Will this continue, Alcar?'

'Do you mean whether these planets continue to occupy their places?'

'Yes, Alcar.'

'Millions of bodies will occupy their places eternally; others, however, dissolve because they have performed their task in this mighty whole. Such is the case with this planet. Thousands, nay millions of planets will continue to occupy a place, for one day the spiritual life will have advanced that far and will inhabit these planets. In actual fact, some are already inhabited, for there are beings in this mighty whole who have reached the Divine Spheres. Do you feel what I mean, André?'

'If I have understood you correctly, you mean to say that the highest cosmic degree will exist eternally and the other degrees will dissolve?'

'Indeed, André, so it is. Do you understand the simplicity of it all? How simple God and His creation are? The highest cosmic degrees are waiting for us and our Divine happiness is assured there. It will therefore be clear to you that, when man and animal have gone on to a higher cosmic degree, the planets, man, and animal will dissolve, because these planets have completed their task. Thus, this planet is dissolving now, because the animal and human life have reached a higher cosmic degree. This means and is the acceptance of a higher condition at the planet which receives this life. You see that it happens here and after millions of centuries many other planets will be that far and will dissolve in the All. This enormous body dissolves, like the human body on earth. The material and human organism will be destroyed by the process of decay; this planet, however, evaporates slowly but surely the way it came; the material and spiritual life returns to God, for nothing gets lost; everything remains; everything is God's own life. Is this also clear to you, André? When you have understood me, it will be clear to you that this body, this, and other planets, will also return to the invisible energy to which they once belonged.'

102

'How mighty that is, Alcar, and yet so natural.'

'So it is, André, natural, mighty, and yet so simple. I speak, André, of invisible energy, for only man and all life belonging to his condition, continue visibly. This life includes animal life, flower- and plant life and the various planets which receive us and are of the highest cosmic degrees. There is more invisible, than visible energy, which we know from phenomena in the universe.

God lives behind the visible energy; the invisible energy is that awe-inspiring power which rules everything, and which is also God and means 'life'. The invisible energy lives as spirit and is the soul of the human and animal organism. We all are energy, André, for we have emanated from the invisible. Every animal, every organism discarded, everything man possesses on earth in material condition, everything living in the universe, stars, planets, and all those millions of objects, will once return to the Almighty and Arch-Power. That is the invisible energy, in which we recognize and accept God. Nothing, nothing of all this mightiness, is lost. Everything and everybody will return to this Arch-Power, for everything that lives will once have completed its task.

Whether visible or invisible, it has to perform a task. There is nothing without a purpose, and nothing can exist unless it comes from God, and has emanated from the invisible. We, and all those living on these planets, all that exists, André, is God, is energy, and has to perform a task. The invisible energy is awe-inspiring in magnitude. That is God, our Holy Father, who guards over all of His life. Our material organism returns to God, and will have performed its task already for that tiny bit of invisible energy, which is the soul.

How beautiful is the human organism, and how deep the spiritual being. What does one know about it and all this on earth? There, one cannot even understand life and even less that we are eternal beings.

My friend on earth sought and felt already what lived behind the universe; that was what destroyed him on earth. It called him to a halt; he felt there was something deep and mighty, but he cut himself off from it as well as from what he had to learn on earth. I will show that on our next journeys; he did not understand it, could not understand it, for it belonged to the past. But how infallible all these acts, I mean the feelings of the soul, will only become clear to you later. There are people on earth who feel their death in advance, and perform actions which indicate this, and which are not understood until later when they have passed away. And there are also people who feel capable enough to take up a study, yet fail to reach their aim and don't understand it. An other law is then in force causing this failure, and that belongs to the past. For in that deep past there must be something which they have experienced, and it is only in an other life that they make it up, and then it happens, that which they have been intending to do and have been meditating for centuries.

Therefore, everything is fixed and the spent energy returns to the All. This can be determined, since we can follow that at our side.'

'How many questions could you answer about that subject, Alcar?'

'Thousands, André. I could write dozens of volumes about this planet. We do not even need to go further, as I can connect you here with the beginning of creation, and explain all those activities which life has to follow. But that is not our intention; we will go further and higher until we have reached the third cosmic degree, the earth.

I must connect you with the visible and the invisible life. To this end I follow one course, André; I'll pass into the material life and then return to the invisible life, which is the soul. Here is everything which belongs to the universe, the visible wonder and the invisible element, both of which are Divine. I follow one course, André, and I must follow it as I was so instructed. I'll answer all your questions, which is still possible yet, for presently I will proceed according to plan. Do you feel what I mean?'

'Yes, Alcar.'

'You can still ask questions about this planet; presently that will no longer be possible, for I will have to connect myself with other conditions.'

'So you will convince me of the visible and invisible cosmos, Alcar?'

'Yes, André, that is my intention.'

'May I ask some more questions, Alcar?'

'Certainly, my son.'

'Will the melting of this planet, and many others, be observed from the earth?'

'That will be seen from the earth; the scientists living on earth millions of years from now will see wonders. If they knew a bit more about this planet and could see all these changes, they would still not know what it meant. This planet melts away and dissolves as many others have already, but nothing is known about that, as they are too far from earth and man still has no instruments to establish this. But even if they could observe it, one planet covers the other; some object would bar their vision. What they observe at present, is within their reach; they won't be able to observe much deeper. But what they will experience is this: This planet dissolves eventually, to the extent, that people on earth will see that in their time. But thousands of years after dissolving, when this planet has returned to the invisible energy, they will still be able to observe this object from the earth. What they will observe is an image of that, which once was only a faint image. Still, in front of their eyes is the same planet, covered with a veil of dense haze, which in reality is the first and the last stage, that you have seen in the process of revelation. Do you understand what I mean?'

'That they will observe a flash of reality. Yes, Alcar, I understand you.'

'That phenomenon will also slowly dissolve, but it will last millions of years. Then, at the very last moment, one can see through that dense veil which will also dissolve. Subsequently, this planet will disappear before their eyes; slowly but surely it will sink back into nothing, which is the invisible energy.

Thousands of smaller and larger objects have already returned into the All. This process goes on; it shall and must happen. The picture of the universe visible from the earth, the stars and planets known on earth, all those objects will dissolve, because they belong to the third cosmic degree. Only those objects, stars and planets, belonging to the highest cosmic degree, will continue to occupy their place, but everything living below that degree will dissolve.'

'How clever you are, Alcar. I had not expected that.'

'Do you think I am clever, and did you not expect that? Listen, I am nothing yet, but I am thankful that I belong to all this. I am only a child, a tiny being of the all-embracing whole, which is God. I am not clever, my boy, all who are on earth and will enter here, will learn to know this mighty whole. Never say it again; for, knowing how everything is, I could not accept it.'

'How do you keep things apart, Alcar?'

'That is simple, André. Everything I tell you is what I possess. In the spheres, I studied this subject. I have acquired all this, nay, I possess what I made clear to you. When man enters this side, he will take possession of his sphere. I have told you about it. It is not only limited to the sphere in which they live, but they will also learn everything below their own sphere, including the stars and planets below the third cosmic degree of life. We will observe all that and it will become our property.

Therefore, what I tell you belongs to my own life, but life at a higher level and above my own, as you have also seen, must be explained by a higher being, because I know nothing about it, and it is not my own. However, when you ask me questions relative to my own condition, I can tell you enough to fill volumes, as every question concerns the All and my own life. I need not think nor remember anything, for it is in me. We are constantly laying ourselves aside, and if we succeed, we receive wisdom instead and also a higher level, because we have deserved it. We try to serve, André.

We serve by transition into other lives; this transition passes back to our own lives, because we initiated it. Therefore, everything I do for others, I do for myself, for it gives me possession, and I am telling you of it. You can ask me whatever you wish; to every question, whichever it may be, I can give you an answer, provided it concerns my property. I can tell you right from the beginning of creation up to the third cosmic degree, because I have experienced my own cycle of life, the third cosmic degree. Do you understand, André, that we really own this and how great and mighty God is? How tremendous is that which we must acquire. But isn't it worthwhile and do you feel that it is a mighty grace to be allowed to receive all this? That it has been and still is God's intention that we will pass into His life consciously? I had better say: to accept and acquire it consciously? We shall then pass into the All fully consciously, and once that far, we shall be like God. Now we are already part of that Divinity, but we must go on ever further and shall need billions of centuries to achieve this. Only then will man be the owner of this tremendous universe. I have only acquired some spheres and planets, and I have yet to acquire all those millions of transitions. To that end I must continuously lay aside myself; by serving, I will get that far.

All is love, pure love, cosmic energy, which connects man and animal. Is it now clear to you, why I can answer all your questions? Wherever man may be, I know the depth of the soul, the life of the soul on earth; that depth is within me. I have experienced all those degrees of consciousness and have acquired them. Nothing below my own sphere is strange to me, for it is my property. Also, André, what once lived here and belonged to the plant and animal world.'

'This planet used to be like the earth is now, Alcar?'

'No, what is present on earth belongs to the third cosmic degree and is materially perfect. During this stage, the plant and animal life was far ahead of the human body, so it seemed, but in actual fact this was far behind the human material being. This is what you meant, isn't it?'

'Yes, Alcar.'

'Trees and plants grew on this planet, but they did not come to full bloom; the lustrous green known on earth did not develop. Everything was different, grey and misty. The many colours seen in nature on earth, all those magnificent shades, were not present here. It was not possible, because this planet had in everything the first grade of life. Everything, whatever it was, lived far below the level known on earth. Nothing can be compared with what is present on earth. The animals were monsters and not perfect; they were unwieldy and clumsy; everything had yet to awaken and develop. What was present here was intended for progress and was at an initial stage of development.

Out of this, André, a being appeared which would become man. During the initial stage of this planet, a large process of decay took place. Everything condensed and decayed as it had come. Nothing lived on. Everything was doomed to decay, for by that process new life was born. Wherever one looked, everything was in a state of decay. This planet had no other task. This was the work of the first planet, and here the germ was born of what would once become the perfect being. Here, one condition of dying and being born ruled.

The earth is, however, to develop and prepare life for the fourth cosmic degree, to enable it to pass on to a higher planet. That was impossible from the first planet. That would have gone too quickly and the being which lived here would not have been able to digest it, no more than man on earth would be able to accept the higher level at which we live. God oversaw all this and God knew how all this should proceed, what was necessary in the beginning. What man possesses on earth germinated here. The nucleus of what man has there emerges from the first stage, because the first planet, this one, dominated the second and the third cosmic degree. Do you feel what I mean, André?

Then it will be clear to you that the shape of what God wished to create, was set here and this product was finished to the highest level on the second and third cosmic degree.

At the beginning there was nothing but water. A dense quagmire, and millions of beings, man and animal, lived together in that dense mass. Out of this process, man appeared first, then animal life.

I could tell you still more about this, but it would lead too far. On this journey, I follow the development of the human organism; afterwards, we pass on to the inner life, the life of the soul.'

'It is all so amazing, Alcar. How old is this planet now?'

'I would not be able to pronounce the number of years. Do you understand what that means? What God's creation and the universe is, and the past of man and animal means? This cannot be named, pronounced, or calculated.'

'And you cannot say how long this planet has been in the process of extinction either?'

'That is not possible either.'

'Thus, this planet does no longer radiates and has no light of its own, because it has to die and dissolve?'

'Yes, André, so it is, but it now receives light from the sun.

'Or else it could not be seen, Alcar?'

'Indeed, André, but there is still life; it is still a dense mass, or else it would already have returned to the invisible. Do you feel that, also?'

'Yes, Alcar, it is all clear. It is amazing, Alcar, if only people on earth knew.'

'They know, André. There have been scientists who knew, but they are thought to be insane. Many scientists receive inspiration from our side, but they founder and do not advance any further. They even don't know death and if death is not understood on earth, how then could they accept this death, which rules here, too. They founder on this problem and we know why they do not accept it.'

'But suppose there was a scientist who knew of eternal life; wouldn't he be able to accept this and reach the highest in his studies?'

'No, my boy. If he were to accept eternal life, this knowledge is not sufficient. Because even then they would still not understand our life, and they will have to learn that also, if they want to connect themselves with the deeper laws.'

'And when they get that far, Alcar?'

'Then there is peace on earth and only then shall we return to the earth to seek connection with them and will they accept what we have to say. Do you feel what I mean?'

108

'They want to own it themselves?'

'Indeed, that's correct, but that is not possible. If that were possible, the scientists would be our instruments for this world. They cannot achieve more; that is the highest one can gain on earth. Then a scientist is an instrument, a gifted being, and that is the object of those who bring a spiritual message on earth. But then man no longer feels himself a scientist, for he then is a child of God. They will follow their sisters and brothers who have advanced that far, and they surrender everything, because they know they are inspired instruments for whom the spiritual world sees and observes.

One day this will come and then, as I said before, there will be happiness on earth, and they will understand what happens to this planet and all others; why we die and are born; why we are on earth; what God is and what life means.'

'So you still think it is possible, Alcar?'

'That they will observe this phenomenon?'

'Yes, Alcar.'

'My dear boy, for God everything is possible.'

'Is this planet known on earth, Alcar?'

'Yes. This planet was given a name, and on earth it is known as such.'

'Can it also be observed with their instruments?'

'Yes, they can.'

'It is remarkdable that they should not advance any further. Do they also know that this planet is becoming extinct and will dissolve?'

'They know it has no atmosphere, but they cannot know nor determine that this planet dissolves, unless they can accept everything I explained to you.'

'It really is a pity, Alcar; it is nearly within their reach.'

'That is a plain truth, André. All this is very near their reach. I could lift you on earth to my condition, and speak through you to tell them about this life and help them. But what do you think they would do?'

'I don't know, Alcar.'

'They would declare you insane, a medium possessed, and a feeble-minded person. That is what you are in their eyes. But what I have to say is not meant for them. It is only for those who are craving; it is for them that I am doing this work and have returned to the earth. Yes, André, that's how it is.'

'You accept that as an established fact. Wouldn't it be possible for you to bring me in contact with a scientist?'

'It would, André, but the result would be as I told you. They cannot accept this, because they themselves have not yet advanced that far.

Just imagine their situation. They, those scientists, would be prepared to surrender to us, to you, because it is you who are my representative on earth.'

'But that is not necessary, is it?'

'In a way it is, or else we won't achieve anything. When they think about it, year after year – for they have been thinking for millions of years, since there have been scientists as long as the earth is old – we won't gain anything. They must act and proceed accordingly. However, he who accomplishes it is a prophet, but those who bring the holy truth are killed, nailed to the cross, or declared insane. No need to explain to you their degree of insanity; I have done that on our previous journey.'

'What a pity all that is, Alcar.'

'In this world, on this side of life, we do not know that word, André. We do know what it contains, and that is weakness. Those who pity are living dead; they do not know they are alive, and are not conscious. We only know laws, and those laws tell us what is possible and impossible. The scientific world baulks at mediumship. It has the fullest right to do that; but there are people on earth who possess gifts they can learn from. These gifts can be used, and we connect ourselves through our instruments. You are a useful instrument. Why you are, André, and why you possess those gifts, I shall also point out and prove to you on this side, when the time has come. Scientists, however, are too learned to realize that. If they could, their golden ornaments would drop from their chests and they would learn to know God. Those who know their Holy Father do not put themselves on a pedestal; they bend their heads and leave what belongs to the earth, and open their minds. Because they know that there is only one who knows and that is God, our Father of love. But we are not yet that far, André, though everything is possible. Now I will connect you again with the past. Attention, André. Look in front of you.'

André again saw the same scene. On the shore were thousands of beings which had already died, but others were still alive, and he felt a power entering him by which he understood what this meant.

'Do I feel correctly, Alcar? At this moment I feel a tremendous power

110

entering me. This being wants to go on, but progress is not possible.'

'Very good. I made you feel that. This animal-like being, which once will become man, wants to go on. Its instinct has awakened in the first degree, for in this are also transitions and degrees, and from this moment on life is directed at advancement. This is the deep feeling present in every life. The animal-like being feels it, and so does man on earth. There, too, that tremendous life is in the inner life of man, which nobody understands, but which means the return to God.

This power has become active from the very first moment of life. This is the mighty and inexplicable phenomemon man on earth experiences. They all want to go on, always go on, and they don't know why that urge is in them. They are all in a hurry to experience all that can be experienced on earth, but they forget that they are living in eternity, and have to experience all that is related to God. But that driving power to which I referred, and which I let you feel, is a Divine Spark within us, by which we are connected with God. That power which you feel, André, is the deepest possession of man, as well as of all other life which belongs to the animal kingdom, but the animal follows its own way and is not conscious of it. For man, however, this means the Arch-Power and the connection with the very highest.

As I said, this has been present in man from the first moment. It is all-inclusive; it is animation, inspiration, the urge for progress; it is power and personality; it is the Divine spirit within us, and it is the return to the All. If we did not have that in us, creation would be at a standstill and no new life would be born out of the first stage. This applies to man and animal, to stars and planets: all life must return to God. I said just now: if this was not in us, creation would be at a standstill, but something made us awaken again, urged us, and all other life, which evolved through thousands of stages of the material organism, until we had reached that which you see in front of you. Do you feel that, André?'

'Yes, Alcar, it is amazing and natural.'

'This is also part of the plan of evolution, and is the return to God. But you will also feel that all life has to follow one course, one action, preordained in life.

Here in front of you are thousands of beings, and they cannot go further. Here something calls them to halt, and this halt and power permit them to pass on to the second cosmic degree. The being has reached its fish-like stage, and is about to lay this form of life aside. If God had not come to our aid, existence would also have ended here and creation would have failed. For this animal-like being is not perfect; you can see that clearly, can't you, André?'

'Yes, Alcar.'

'But God, my son, oversaw everything, because there is a second cosmic degree to which man will go, and which is destined for the inner life of the animal-like being. For life also awakened on that degree, and gained the same level, but the organism is different. Now you must listen carefully.

This planet dominates the other two planets which you see in the distance and which belong to the second and third cosmic degree. That is clear to you, isn't it?'

'Yes, Alcar.'

'Well then, this planet fed, so to speak, the first transitory planets, those nearest to it which have already reached a state of existence. When those planets began to condense, the inner life born on this planet was ready and awaited attraction. Is that clear to you, too, André?'

'Yes, Alcar, entirely.'

'Thank you, my boy; I will proceed. You will feel then, that one life was fed by the other, and that is why we call this planet the mother planet, because it fed all others. Both, inner life and spiritual life, is what animates the material organism on those planets. It was not possible – and we have to accept that – to raise the human organism on this planet to a level enabling it to reach the third cosmic degree. This planet did not possess the required power, and neither do other planets. For man and animal went from one stage to the other, and that is the purpose of all those millions of planets. God surveyed it and knew it was necessary, and that is why this planet is the dominating power which the other absorbed and, so to speak, brought to life. You must fully realize that all these planets are one, that they possess one action: to raise the material organism to the perfect body you possess on earth. Is that also clear, André?'

'Yes, Alcar.'

'Well then, all those planets, therefore, had one and the same purpose, the perfection of the material organism. The stage of life here is also present on the first transitory planets, but in an elevated condition.

However, the stage in which you see the animal-like being before

112

you, is its highest level. This is a law for the entire universe, for hundreds of planets are in connection with each other and achieve something, the last of which is the earth, bringing it to completion. As I said before, God came to the aid of the being. The animal-like being had to die. When all life has reached its final stage and attained that degree, this planet has completed its million-work and returns to the All.

It will therefore be clear to you, André, that there is life on all those planets, but that from here the nucleus of all life has been laid.

Now this animal-like being as an astral being, is attracted by those other planets, which is possible because it has connection with them. I also told you that those smaller planets serve that purpose and, when those transitions have also been experienced, life goes on to the second cosmic degree to experience a similar condition and to prepare for the third cosmic degree.

I said that this applies to the entire universe, by which I mean that the fourth cosmic degree also has its transitory planets, or life intended to come there would not be able to cope with the tremendous transition, and the inner life would be hurled into the invisible, destroying the material organism. But God feeds and develops nature in such a way that birth is a law and is not limited to time. You feel, thereby, that inner life has to adapt itself to material life and reverse, or a disharmonious action starts, meaning death of the material organism and return of inner life to the astral world. Have you understood this, too, André?'

'You mean that a being cannot pass directly from the first to the second cosmic degree, as this progress is too much?'

'Very good, André, so it is. On this planet, inner life dominated, but on the second cosmic degree, the material organism dominates. This is an amazing situation, and you see that one excites the other, and yet everything is connected and logical, if it is to be accomplished in a perfect way. The transitory planets serve this purpose.

If you don't understand me, you had better ask again. All this is very difficult, but you have to know it, or you will not understand creation.

So this planet achieved this, and at the same time it had connection with all those other succeeding planets, and radiated and dominated over them. What happened here in all those centuries, what was achieved in that period, was the experience at full power. This means that all those other planets, so to speak, were fed from the mother planet, and this process, which means the condensation of all those planets, kept pace with this planet.

The large mother planet attracted those smaller planets, and then another and a mighty wonder happened. A second atmosphere, André, developed around all those planets to shroud this process, which would continue for billions of years. This second atmosphere closed off all those planets, and if this had not happened, one body would collide with an other and the universe would collapse. When the condensation process was complete, this atmosphere dissolved again and the plan of evolution could proceed. This phenomenon was guarded against thousands of dangers and God knew all this; it was preordained in His revelation. It will be clear to you now, how accurately everything has been calculated, but God controls and rules over all this. You feel there is order in this universe and that everything is bound by laws.

It will also be clear to you that it is possible for these beings to proceed to other planets, where a body was ready when life had reached this stage.

I already told you that inner life dominated the material organism here, as on the other degree. There the material body will be beautified and reach a level at which the human organism can already be recognized. I will explain all this to you when we pass on to it. See and observe, André.

In this animal-like being, you can already see a skeleton and, as can be observed, it already has the shape which the perfect material body on earth possesses. Of course it has to evolve, but a resemblance can already be observed. Here it has reached the stage at which inner life will excel material life; inner life now passes on to the other planet and raises the material organism.

Millions of years had passed before this life dropped its fish-like stage, and only then could the last being begin its transition to that higher degree. Soon we will follow these last beings, and you will then see how these animal-like beings were attracted. To this end I will descend into the world of the uncounscious, which is possible because I'll now connect myself with the higher masters. You will then see a miracle, André. But before descending, I have to explain some other things first.

This animal-like being in front of you, André, has the human condition which it had from the very beginning. It was already present during the first stage, yet this being has no head, and it also lacks the other human organs. It will receive them on an other planet, where the human organism appears. I will connect you again, and you will see that the perfect human being is nevertheless present in this unnatural being which has to become man.'

André observed. In this animal-like monster, he saw an other being, and yet it was not the inner life, the astral spirit, this was different. He saw the human shape which this being did not yet have, but which was present deep inside.

Now he heard his leader say: 'You see, André. Here, too, man already lives, as I made clear to you from the beginning; we saw that already in the first embryo. This goes on and on, and wherever the inner life will pass to, deep inside, it will follow that which God intended, and it will become man. This is the deepest condition I can show you on this planet, until these powers will manifest themselves in the material organism, which will occur on other planets. This is the driving power, the primordial force for the construction of the material organism. Presently, the lower part of the body of this animal-like being will split, and a head will detach, so that an other organism comes into being. Nature is the expressive artist achieving all this.

It takes millions of years, though slowly but surely, it will happen. To this end other planets are needed. It could not happen here because the climate differs. The only purpose of this planet was to substantiate and awaken this human animal.'

---

Footnote page 97

Ever since the successful touchdown on the moon in 1967, the relative text on pages 97 and 98 has raised many questions. In spite of many deep discussions we must admit that nobody on earth can save the situation by explaining this matter.

The above now strongly demands us to think for ourselves! In order to enlighten you as best as possible we refer to other statements by Jozef Rulof or the masters, which are related to this subject, even though made in an other context.

First of all, the masters expressly stated never to concern themselves with technical matters. Then we cite from the book: 'A View into in the Hereafter', 1st edition: 'Inventions will be made which serve the well-being of man. One day they will visit other planets, but only for the better.'

Finally, we note that we possess a tape recording of a 'question and answer' evening, held at The Hague on 17th April, 1952. That evening, Jozef Rulof speaks of the laws of hardening of precious stones on earth. He says: 'The moon was a quagmire and has not experienced the laws of the hardening of mother earth. Later, when we go to the moon with a rocket ...' People in the hall immediately react: 'But is that possible?' Then Jozef Rulof imperturbably continues: 'One day they will get there after they have mastered thousands of centrifugal forces. When, one day, your scientist gets that far ... But he won't get there, he will get there as a spirit!' (Evidently, he referred to the scientist who, at the time, was engaged in rocket construction.) Ed.

# CHAPTER IX

## *The second cosmic degree*

ON the second cosmic degree, the human organism is already perfect. Transfer directly from the first to the second cosmic degree is not possible, that is why we first have to follow the transitory planets, and why this is necessary I explained to you a minute ago. This phenomenon, André, I mean these transitions, is also a mighty wonder, for God came to the aid of the human organism, and that happened on other planets. These are the transitions to prepare man for the second cosmic degree.

You always see and feel those transitions and connecting stages which we have in our own spiritual life, and which are also for the material world. You know the first, second, and third sphere as well as the seventh sphere. In material life on earth, man proceeds from the first material degree to the second. This can be observed in the racial problem on earth, which I will explain to you later. They are the material transitions which man has to follow. Those who belong to the first transition, I mean man on earth, live in the jungle and have not yet reached the higher transitions. It will therefore be clear to you, André, that all transitions follow each other and are related to each other, that there is nothing without a purpose, and that all that lives is subjected to a specific action, but is part of the whole. What we observe and establish in creation, we find again in the material and human organism. These are the material transitions, as I said just now, and they apply to animal, man, and all planets and objects.'

'Is all that known on earth, Alcar?'

'No, that cannot be determined by scientists on earth. We shall now leave this planet, André, and I am going to connect you with the invisible life, which is the astral world.'

André felt himself sink away. He felt that he passed into the life of his leader and saw what Alcar observed. The planet where Alcar had shown him all this wisdom sank away, and he was lifted into the astral world. What he now saw was amazing. There was life wherever he looked. He saw large and small beings, all whirling along, passing into each other, and being attracted by the more powerful and larger beings, yet to follow a course of their own. He felt Alcar moving on, but wherever his leader went, this scene, all this life, followed him.

Now he heard Alcar say: 'You see, wherever we go there is life. The astral life you see will animate the organism and will presently be attracted by the first transitory stage. You will presently feel this power of attraction within you.

But listen now, to what I have to say: A while ago, I mentioned spiritual and material transitions. But there is more, and that is still deeper than all those transitions of which I already told you on earth and also on this side and which I explained to you. Now look at the astral world, André. As I said, all these transitions I have explained to you on earth and on this side, and that also applies to the astral world. Everything lives here in one world, and yet one condition is invisible for the other. In it lives the spiritual being which is the soul and the animation for the material being. It is my intention to let you feel this attraction. Now pay attention, André. In the meantime, I will descend on this planet and you will experience it.'

Something began to condense around André. Oh, he thought, now I am beginning to understand it. Yet all this life was still around him. He saw millions of astral beings, but Alcar followed one course, one purpose, and he understood what this meant. He felt entirely absorbed in this condensation. Amazing, he thought, now I understand what this is and how birth takes place. Close by, he saw shadows, and Alcar made him now feel the meaning of these shadows.

André saw they were on a small planet and those shadows were material beings living here. He now felt himself pass into an astral being, and he heard Alcar say: 'Feel clearly what happens now.'

André felt a terrible vibration entering him. He sank into a sleeping condition, but still remained conscious of what he did. As in a dream, he experienced this event. When this attraction had happened, he felt himself gain consciousness. This apparently was the small planet onto which he was attracted. When he woke up, he found himself on an inhabitable planet, but when he looked around, he saw that death had also made its entry here.

'Where are we, Alcar?'

'On the first transition to the second cosmic degree. Have you felt how this attraction happened?'

'Yes, Alcar.'

'This first transitory planet is also dissolving, but there is still life on hundreds of others. You know now how attraction takes place; it is brought about by two beings, the creative and the driving power, the male and the female organism. The genital organs have now developed that far that fertilization happens in a different way. Yet this animal-like being has not reached the human condition as we know fertilization on earth. I am going to connect you with the past again and you will observe.'

André saw that nature differed from the first planet. Here, everything had more colour, and had changed; there was also much water in which he saw animal-like beings. The animal-like being he had seen on the first planet had also reached the shore here, but the organism of this animal-like being was smaller than on the first planet, and the amazing thing he saw was the change this organism had experienced.

The lower part of the body had split, and thereby he recognized in this being, material man, like the human body on earth. Out of that former animal-like being, an other had appeared. The head was now visible and had, so to speak, emerged from that coarse body, although it did not yet resemble the human head at all. The skull was spherical, what once would be arms and legs were still only membranes, but he saw that these organs would also come to full development.

'You see, my boy, that this planet does its work, like her larger sister did. This small planet transforms the skeleton, it has this power, to make it strong.'

Alcar showed him the skeleton, which he could observe clearly.

'The material organism here, is only a shadow of its former life on the first planet where the organism was subjected to its full effect; here, this process serves the refinement of the material organism. You see that this planet has a different substance, and is very similar to the earth. But again millions of years will pass before the material organism is perfect and the being has to go that long way. It is here that the animal-like being takes its first steps to complete its way through the universe, from organ to organ. The road man has to follow – I don't need to explain that again to you – winds through the universe and finally ends in the Divine All. Inner life will return many times to this planet, which is reincarnation, and serve to bring the material body and inner organs to perfection.

Here, too, a great process of decay takes place, but this small planet is

118

firmer and more compact than the large planet which dominates this smaller one. God, therefore, oversaw everything; for what was not possible on the large planet, because its nature did not have this power and lacked the substance for the growth of the material organism, was possible on this small planet. The material organism present in a rougher condition there, received here that particular power necessary for the material development. As I said before, the first planet served the origin of the first life, the life of the soul.

It will then be clear to you, André, that when that happened, the interior of that large planet, where we were just now, could be nothing but a process of decay, because by that very process the new life had to be born.

This small planet, however, has a different task and as such it occupies a place in this enormous whole. What germinated on that larger planet and the millions of lives born there, is reduced here to one-seventh. That is simple, because this planet is subjected to an other activity and has to perform an other task than the large planet out of which it was born. The inner life waited for connection, and this life which was to be born there was also attracted and lived in an other world, the astral world, as you observed just now. During the first stage, being born and coming into being were calculated at full power. The soul which entered this life had gone through that activity, and would settle here.

That which the soul had experienced sank back in the astral world and the inner life which is the soul and, on this side, the spiritual body, passed to the unconscious. We now get to know the world of the unconscious. You know, however, that no consciousness is yet present, I mean the consciousness which the spirit or soul of man has in its material body on earth. Yet – and this is my point – this sinking back was envisaged for the later and higher attunements, which is the world of the unconscious, as described by the spirit Lantos.[*] If that had not happened, if God had not taken that into account, inner life would already, during the first stage, have suffered a certain degree of insanity, because it could not digest these experiences. Do you feel how deep this is, André?

Life of the soul, however, came to rest, and all that life and its experiences sank back into the inner self, only to be attracted later. That is

[*] See the book: 'The Cycle of the Soul'.

the explanation for the long period of waiting for a new birth.

For hundreds of years may pass before man experiences his next incarnation. Also there where consciousness has developed, I mean man on earth, inner life needs that long sleep to dissolve its experiences, but the inner enrichment remains and that is the emotional life. This explains at the same time why man cannot remember anything of his previous lives; this is given only to very few people on earth. They are the sensitive people on earth. You do feel, André, how tremendous God's creation is, and how He comes to the aid of man and animal kingdom in thousands of situations. I could explain to you many of these laws which all prove how natural and simple everything is. But I will tell you about all this later.

Now we follow material life, the development of the human organism. On our next journey we shall follow the life of the soul. Then I shall explain to you the first feelings which the inner life experienced, down to the last degree man possesses, which is the material consciousness we know on earth. I must proceed that way in order to give you a clear picture of the human organism, and of the route man has to follow from the beginning of creation. So, I follow the development of the human organism until we have reached the earth where you are still living yourself. Then you will return into your own body in order to digest all this in your material body, that is in your day-consciousness. Several weeks later I will pick you up again when I will explain the life of the soul. But now I shall continue.

So, on the first planet a gigantic process has been effected, which is the creation of the inner life for the beings living here. The great driving power which I have mentioned, that dominant urge inner life received there, the advancement to higher spheres you have observed on the shore, all that awakens when young life is born. What has fallen asleep in the world of the unconsciouss, will awake when this life is born again. This is the inspiration for the development of the material organism. Do you understand what I mean, André?

You must think well and try to follow me. What I explained to you on this journey, as I said already, is very difficult; but it certainly is worth your while to focus on me, if you want to absorb and acquire what I tell you.

I spoke of advancement and you have observed this. The animal-like beings, which had reached the shore, wished to go on, as that driving power was present in that being, which is the Divine Spark, our connection with God. That awakens, and only that, for it is the power urging the material organism on in an ascending line, the inspiring element. It is this arch-power which gives that fine organism in a short time a strong impetus on its road of development, because it is initially gifted with that.

Do you understand now that the first planet has the dominating capacity in everything? That the process of development proceeded there, but that this being could not be born there? This small planet cannot experience that process of decay on a million scale, because a transition is needed: an other climate and an other power. This small object is firmer and more compact than the first planet, and this would facilitate the development of the material organism. Do you understand then, André, that transitions are needed and that God oversaw all that?

Nature commanded that mastership and achieved it. The first planet, therefore, had no other task than the one it possessed and could accomplish, but according as we proceed, all those bodies will have to accomplish an other activity in order to develop the material organism. It will, therefore, be clear to you that this is not possible in one single state. Because, why and for what purpose do we on our side have six spheres in order to be able to enter the highest, the seventh sphere? When you understand that man was born out of that small embryo and has to follow that long way of development before reaching maturity, this here will also be clear to you, and you can accept all this. In everything we see those transitions, also in sleep and the deepest, apparent death, all of which I explained to you at the beginning of your development. In the darkness there are degrees of attunement, or transitions, likewise in the spheres of light, and we, too, know seven degrees in the cosmic picture: these are transitions to gain the highest, the Divine spheres. The child which has to be born and lives in the womb of the mother, has to experience several transitions before passing to the final stage.

In everything, there are transitions, and these transitions serve the ultimate perfection of the material organism. What we have known and possessed as man on earth, all those material transitions and, on this side, spiritual transitions, we find again in the universe. But that which is the universe and are the spheres on this side, in short all the planets, the entire universe, we see reflected in the small organism, man in his perfect condition on earth, and we can also observe that in the animal kingdom. If this were not so, God's creation as we have come to learn and understand it, would be different. But since it is so, we must accept that we go from one place to another and return time and again. This is reincarnation on all those planets, but this cannot be accepted on earth, as they do not know anything about creation. Man on earth is blocked by the puzzle 'death'. What you have observed up to now is dying and being born, transfer to an other and higher planet, and as we, mankind, are subjected to those changes, we are able to reach the All. I can prove in various ways and by numerous conditions that we have to follow a cosmic course. That course was already present during the first human stage, for it progressed from that stage as I explained before. Time and again I refer to that to make clear to you that it happens all the time, nay, that it is the awe-inspiring event which is contained in God's revelation-process, to offer us the possibility to return to God.

As I said, André, man on earth cannot accept reincarnation because of their way of thinking and feeling. They have not yet advanced far enough to feel that problem in their own lives, but those who do feel it, belong to a higher degree of mental development.

You understand, therefore, André, that the transition to this small planet which performs its task in the great Divine plan and belongs to the whole, is necessary, and that it also means reincarnation.

If, during the first stage, death had not occurred after fertilization, the end would have come already there and life would have been deprived of birth.

Is it now clear to you, André, that death is a necessity and that it means birth?'

'Yes, Alcar, that reality makes me tremble.'

'We also shivered and trembled, my boy, when we learned all this. But I will continue, André.

So, here, too, death and birth, and that is repeated until the last being has experienced this. Then this small planet which is already dissolving, will follow the large mother planet back to the source of all life. This process will not be observed from the earth either. Millions of years will pass and they will still not be able to observe these small planets from the earth.'

'Does this planet belong to the first, where we were, Alcar?'

'Yes and no. It receives its power from that large dominating planet, and yet this planet is in the neighbourhood of the second cosmic degree, to which it belongs. Every large planet has smaller planets surrounding it belt-wise. When life has experienced these, it passes on to a higher condition, a larger planet, to accept life there. The following planet is already larger than this one and these are transitions towards the second cosmic degree.'

'Is that planet known on earth, Alcar?'

'Do you mean, whether the second cosmic degree can be seen from the earth?'

'Yes, that is what I mean.'

'Yes, it can be seen and its power is felt on earth. But we will discuss that later, as the material organism has already reached the human condition, though the being is still a prehistoric creature. As I said several times, this planet is firmer than the first one, which is also for its material life. This wonder occurs in all transitions and that also applies to the animal kingdom, for that life also passes on to this planet and will awaken here and receive an other organism.

The animal keeps pace with man. In all these transitions the animal creature which belongs to the animal kingdom follows the rational being, which is gifted with the Divine Spark, and is related to God.

In all those transitions the animal has passed to other stages, meaning that it left one organism to return in another. I said that there are seven degrees in the animal kingdom. Now against one condition for man, there are seven conditions for the animal being, which are seven degrees of material life, consequently organisms. Hence all those different species of animals. In every transition we find those seven degrees and strength, and that is, as I explained to you, in accordance with the level of the material organism and the strength it possesses.

You will understand now, that the animal organism is far more complicated than the human organism; but man follows one course, whereas there are thousands of transitions for the animal, which it has to follow. The depth of the animal kingdom cannot be assessed by scientists on earth, but the depth of man can as he lives in the same condition. The human being, therefore, is not so deep as the animal being, because man has followed one course through all those millions of centuries. I could not explain all those material transitions of the animal kingdom to you, because to that end we would have to make dozens of journeys and even then you would not be able to tell all those transitions apart.

But, however deep all this is, it can be followed from the beginning of creation of man.

The animal kingdom had also passed on to this planet and we see all these species of animals on earth, but in a completely different organism.

The earth has seen the prehistoric animals, and many are kept in museums. But the animal that lived here had not yet reached that tremendous size, as this planet was also for the animal in its initial stage of development. Yet the animal follows us, because it emerged from us, and it will continue to follow until we have reached the Divine Spheres. Now I will show you an amazing event, and you will pass into that wonder.

You know, André, that we are on a small planet and also that we are in the universe. You have seen that we experience all this from our own sphere, and that it is possible for us living on this side to connect ourselves with other spheres and to pass on to another body. We are now in the universe. Where do you think the spiritual spheres are now?'

André reflected, but could not adjust himself.

'I can't connect myself; I don't know, Alcar.'

'That you cannot connect yourself is because you see and observe through me, or you should have known it. How many times have I explained that. And yet, I know, it is not possible now, for on this side we can only do one thing at a time and pass into it, if we have these strengths. Therefore you can't connect yourself, but you will experience this wonder so that you will see that everything lives in one condition and that the Divine is present in the deepest hells as well as in the highest spheres.

I will only retract you and myself and pass into our own life. But we remain on this spot. Note what happens now.'

André felt that he was lifted. Everything faded slowly and he saw that the universe dissolved. When this had happened, he experienced another wonder; a powerful light dominated the previous scene and he saw where he was.

'My God', he exclaimed, 'how is that possible, Alcar? Is this the third sphere?'

'Yes, André, the third sphere. You see that wherever man or spirit may be, he will only feel what is his own. I passed from the material cosmos to the spiritual. I withdrew into the third sphere and everything living under my own sphere faded because my own sphere now dominates. You also see that everything is present everywhere, the deepest darkness in the Divine Spheres, and that the universe dissolves, because all this belongs to the invisible energy. We returned, and that will be clear to you now, to the inner world, the hereafter, and accepted our own attunement. If I had wanted to return to my own sphere, I would dissolve, too, and assume my own possession.

So everything is in one condition, in one world, one space, and so it will remain until we have reached our last transition, the Divine Spheres. Therefore, we can be in the sphere of the earth and yet have returned to the Divine source. Yet, every sphere is separated from the others, and I showed that to you when you observed the first and second stage. You see how deep everything is, but we can follow all that on our side, because we have acquired those spheres and transitions, and possess them. Had this not been possible, God would not have overseen everything in His creation, for nothing stops life when its destiny is perfection. One sphere keeps us imprisoned from the other; we are confined to it and yet we can go on, but not until we have acquired it, to be able to enter a higher sphere.

You also know how that happens. Time after time we are going on, we can go on, and this is granted to man and animal. Between us, the third sphere where we are now, and that small planet, there are millions of transitions, conditions in which astral life awaits birth. There is life, there is invisible energy wherever we are.

You will feel, André, that I could continue endlessly, for I know those transitions; it is my possession and it will become the possession of every man.

It will be clear to you, André, that when one looks at the universe from the earth, stars and planets are observed, but there is more in that tremendous expanse. What we observe from the earth belongs to the material cosmos and is the visible energy, but what we do not observe is the invisible cosmos and what lives in it cannot be seen, nor estimated, because it can only be observed from our side. Feel that magnitude, feel that depth, feel what it means; only then will man on earth get a vague idea of his Holy Father Who rules everything.

I can still hear my friend on earth say: 'It is not what we see, but that which is behind it; that is what I wish to know, and that interests me most of all. That is what I must know and want to know, if God allows me that grace.'

Yes, André, that blue light, the sky one sees at daytime, cannot be compared with what is behind that, with the invisible God, Who lives in everything. No wonder scientists say that there is more between heaven and earth than we think. We can answer them from this side, that they are right and will live to see it. Now we shall return to that small planet.'

André felt himself sinking back. When he woke up he found himself again in the universe. He saw all those stars and planets again; wherever he looked, they occupied a place in the universe. How mighty everything was and how much did he admire his leader. He had certainly not expected this.

Have a look at this animal-like being; presently we will go on. From here, as you know, it will proceed to another stage. There is not so much life here as on that larger planet, as I explained to you. However, this being has freed itself from its former condition. It already tries to move on in a human way, but that is not yet possible, it will not be achieved until the next stage, because the organs will then also have reached a higher stage. This development enables the being to move on in a different way. Again a higher level of development, but in an other sphere, a planet, performing refinement of the material organism. The maximum age of the animal-like being here varies from ten to twenty years. There are also transitions in age. The more perfect the animal-like being becomes, the older it will grow. This is different for the animal kingdom, however, and is related to the degree of life in which it lives.

On the second cosmic degree, human life reaches thirty to forty years of age. On earth it is not much higher, but you must not calculate it by earthly standards, as they have no cosmic meaning. I do not calculate because I know, and this knowledge is fixed in the universe. I follow degrees of strength from the initial stage of man.

You can clearly see, André, that astral life is waiting here, which may take millions of years. It cannot be determined how many souls there are; we discussed that already. But life of the soul was born in the first cosmic degree, like the material organism was born.

Before following life which lived here, I must say this: I cannot explain to you the total composition of the universe, for the simple reason that I do not know the highest cosmic degrees, and that would also lead too far. But I'll try to give you a picture, so that you can feel what degrees of cosmic attunement are, to which all those transitions are connected.

126

There are seven degrees of cosmic attunement in the universe. You also know that there are transitions in those degrees, serving the perfection of the material organism. There are thousands of planets around the first cosmic degree which are all related to it and are influenced by it. All those objects have one solar system serving their development. Therefore, in the first attunement, I can pass on to hundreds of planets, while remaining in one and the same condition, since this life has not changed in any respect. It has to follow that long course, however, and all this serves the development of the material organism. I cannot follow all those transitions now, because it would lead too far. But you will now be able to sense the tremendous expanse of the universe. Thousands of smaller and larger planets belong to one cosmic degree. And there are seven cosmic degrees; therefore, in all those seven degrees, there are millions of planets. Every cosmic degree has its own solar system.'

'Can those planets be observed, Alcar.'

'No, all these planets are invisible for the earth, because they belong to the fourth, fifth, sixth, and seventh cosmic degree. On our final journey, I shall connect you with the fourth cosmic degree.

Every planet has it own place in this large whole and its own task, for God created nothing for nothing; everything was necessary and participated in this tremendous work. All these planets describe their own orbit and have to perform their own task. You do understand, André, that I could not possibly explain every detail. But by visiting some of these planets you will get a clear idea of the whole. This I'll try to give to you, so that people on earth can form an idea of what the universe is like and how all this came into being.

It is my chief object to prove to them that reincarnation on earth is a fact, for, had this been impossible, we all would have suffocated in the first stage, and creation would have been a failure, as I often explained before.

We see, therefore, from the beginning of creation that one stage follows another, and only when this was complete could inner life pass on. Have you been able to follow me in everything, André?'

'Yes, Alcar, I am very grateful to you.'

'Then I will go on; you will descend onto this planet and observe, after which we will leave.

You see, André, that life, mountains and valleys, water, greenery and air are also present here. Over there, to your right, you see the earth and, there, on the other side, that first large planet.'

Amazing, André thought. Through Alcar, he looked into the past, a past of millions of centuries ago. But he had to accept all this because it was all alive in front of him. My God, he thought, who will ever be able to understand You.

Then he heard Alcar say: 'We shall now go to the next stage, but won't stay there long, as I want to go on to the second cosmic degree. We shall move on, floating through space.'

André felt himself return to his own life.

Alcar said: 'You will continue to observe in your own life and I shall only connect you when necessary.'

'What are these small planets called on earth, Alcar?'

'Many smaller planets are seen from the earth and they are called satellites.'

'Is this planet one of them?'

'No, this one has a completely different activity.'

'Is the activity of the small planets known?'

'No, it is not known on earth; even if something were known, the real truth cannot be learned until on this side. On earth one does not penetrate to this depth. All these planets are observed there, but only when they have advanced will they come to understand the activity of all these planets and know that there must have been life on them.'

'So there are planets or stars without life, where man cannot be born?'

'Yes. Millions of smaller and larger objects have never known any form of life, and it cannot be born there. Only on those planets which were subjected to the process of condensation, and had to perform a task for the living organism, was life born. The solar systems have an other task essential for the germination and awakening. The own power and energy of a celestial body is not sufficient to awaken life. Yet its own energy radiates its system and this can be observed on earth when the sun has set. One can then see the universe, but during daytime the sunlight dominates and outshines all those bodies belonging to this solar system. But all bodies which have performed their task, dissolve, lose their power and disappear, as I told you.

See, we are already on an other transition and shall stay there for a while.

This planet is larger than the one we were on. Here, life no longer exists either. I'll connect you, though, because you will see that this was once an inhabitable planet.'

André felt that Alcar was going to connect him. What he saw was curious. He immediately saw the being which had once lived here. This being was nearly like man on earth. The material body had become slimmer; its stocky build had become more delicate.

'It is amazing, Alcar! How rapidly this being developed. How long did it take to reach this stage?'

'I'll give you a clear picture of what was needed, but when I say that millions of years went by, will you be able to accept that?'

'Were so many years needed?'

'Do not forget, André, that this process serves the perfection of the material organism. You see that this planet is directed at the embellishment of the material organism, necessitating all these transitions. The material organism has changed, but inner life has also advanced to a further stage. The animal-like being, however, still lives on in its unconscious condition. As you see, the skeleton has already changed. The lower part of the body has appeared, which you have seen on the previous planet, but here it approaches perfection. The human organism has, however, not yet reached its size; this will happen during the next stage. It has to experience some more transitions before this animal-like creature is attracted by the second cosmic degree. Here, too, in the astral world, inner life waits to be born again.

The organs have, at the same time, reached a higher stage, and this being already undergoes the reproduction process in the human way. Man here - if we can call him man already - lives in caves and entrenches himself in the ground against the changes in nature, for it finds warmth there. You see it has nothing human; and yet it has reached this stage, though it has to experience some more transitions. Its build is plump and clumsy and yet elastic. The upper part of its body is stocky, but its head can be clearly seen, and one feels that this part will attain the desired development.

The highest degree of development this being can achieve is the one it follows, and where it will be born. But now other laws come into relief, which we missed on the first cosmic degree, and have come into being during this development. Now listen carefully, André.

The lowest degree of development of the next stage is the highest on this planet. What is necessary for all those transitions, we will find on the last one, and that means that all those properties the material organism has are combined there. Thus, all those transitions are found during that last stage, and there we see a variety of human bodies, large and small, plump and slim, stocky ones, and many other imperfections. This can still be seen on earth, for these beings live there, too. There, the small organism is known which is essentially perfect, because it has experienced all these transitions and consequently has a cosmic meaning. They are the various degrees of the human organism.

Life was also on this planet, here man lived and returned many thousands of times to reach the highest stage. The being does not remember anything of its experiences there, but the soul has gained all this wisdom, which is revealed in this life. It is revealed in its search for food, and this is found, because this planet was ready to receive this life. You see how God oversaw everything. When this being was about to pass on to this planet, food was available, as on the preceding planets. Nature is again different, more perfect, I should say, more like nature on earth. Yet there was something urging this animal-like being on, and this progress and this searching are the depth of its inner life to reach the real attunement in the material life.

The animal kingdom was also represented here. The animal has, like man, passed on to higher degrees. Wherever you look, the animal being is following in our footsteps. Here, too, we see the many species of animals which were known on earth and are still present there, although the prehistoric animal species have become extinct. Extinction, as you see, goes on in the entire universe, but it means accepting an other organism. Whatever we observe from the beginning of creation, and whatever we connect ourselves with, we see death and birth while everything changes. This process has been going on for billions of centuries and we are still not yet on earth.

Do you feel now, André, what it means to be a human being on earth? In a while, when you stand in front of your own body, you will fully realize this. What the material organism has experienced – not to speak of the inner life – is unmentionable. Man on earth should accept that, but he is not yet aware of it. I hope, however, they will now realize that they will return to God, and change their way of life. If, with all this, I can convince one human being, my work and effort are rewarded. We do not ask for more, as we know it isn't possible. My masters will be satisfied and happy when they experience this, and we can be thankful that God has granted us this grace. Man on earth should learn to un-

130

derstand this grace; I do not desire more as I could not ask for more. I am happy, André, that I am allowed to do this work, and in the spheres it is known that this is a grace. Let's hope this happens and will irradiate mankind.'

'What did these people live on, Alcar?'

'On meat, André, which they found in abundance. The organs are designed for nothing else, and you surely feel that these beings still belong to the animal-like being. This phenomenon is still found on earth; man has not changed in that respect; this will only change on the fourth cosmic degree. The few people who proceeded to vegetarianism on earth are the forerunners of the fourth cosmic degree.

The people who lived here, as you will feel, were still unconscious and knew no God. They were still animal-like beings and only on earth did they change in this respect. I have not mentioned that subject yet, because it was not necessary. I shall explain all this to you on our next journey, from the instinct, up to the consciously-waking being.

You see, André, mankind has made progress and has already occupied a place on the inhabitable planets. But this being is not perfect, it still has to go on. Out of this animal-like being, as you will see presently, man will emerge. Now I'll pass on to the next planet. There is life still and it is the last transition I want to follow before passing on to the second cosmic degree. Only then will you have received a clear picture of the plan of evolution of the material organism. So, you will now see the last transition before the second cosmic degree is reached and life passes on to it.

Come, we will go on. You have seen how far man has already advanced, but we have to go ever further before reaching the earth. One transition served the strengthening of the skeleton; the next planet was for the inner organs and the process of growing of the entire organism; an other gave the being what it needed most, and all these planets had their own power and activity, which was influenced by the dominating power of the first cosmic degree.

When all these planets had performed their task, the first energy was spent, and the process of dissolving of this mighty planet and the others where we were just now, as well as those which we could not visit, could start. That happened not a second too early, nor too late, so that there was no question of domination in a heightened condition.

Everything here follows a fixed law, and that law is the material power known on earth, which is the birth of a child from the first moment after fertilization. During the first stage, every planet had its own radiation, and this radiation has been visible from the earth and is still visible of those planets which occupy a place in this mighty whole.

Even though they have performed their task, the powerful influence of these bodies is felt on earth. They will exercise their influence on other organs until the deepest inner part is consumed and dissolved and the final stage has set in. This final stage is the first moment of the process of revelation. You have seen that in the temple of the soul. It is as on earth, and this returning to the Divine source is birth and death on earth. 'Dust thou art, and unto dust shalt thou return'; this is a Divine law, and it applies to the entire universe.

It is all one and the same action; in everything we find degrees of power and attunement. The first embryo was already material energy and the grown-up being; man in his material organism returns to the invisible energy and helps maintain the universe, however invalid he may be.

Thus, André, death and birth, passing over and returning to the Divine source applies to all these enormous planets, but also to the smallest insect known on earth. When this is so, and is fixed in the universe, do you feel then that there is one power ruling all this? That we must bend deeply for God, who has given us all this? That it is a tremendous grace that we shall return to God? What more can I say to make clear to man on earth that there has to be reincarnation, or else we had not been born and would not be on earth? Can't they accept this great wonder? Would evolution be possible, if there were no reincarnation? Fundamentally, we are one with God and with nature, for it is nature that feeds and supports us.

We belong to the visible and invisible energy as material and spiritual life, of which the inner life is the Divine Spark forming our entire being. Yet man seeks, but does not know of a beginning nor end, does not know what he belongs to, and does not understand himself. He who has come to understand himself, feels that he belongs to all this. Man has to follow a long road, but once man understands where it is leading to and what purpose everything serves, he can accept it, for it takes billions of years to enter consciously into the universe.

It is certainly no earthly possession God, our Father, has given us and which we have to acquire, but it includes the entire universe. We who have reached the spheres of light, know and understand all those powers, and prepare ourselves to enter a higher stage. We know that the first human beings have already come that far, and that they watch us from their Divine Sphere and help us from afar. The perfect being of God, who once returned to the earth to teach man to know their God, was nailed to the cross. But God foresaw even that, and so did God's Holy Child; it was known in the highest spheres what would happen. And yet, this perfect human being descended to the third cosmic degree and preached the gospel. This is no longer necessary for the fourth cosmic degree; the people living there, who once inhabited the earth, have acquired that spiritual sphere and love everything that lives.

The gospel was meant for the earth, as the earth is the third degree of cosmic life. The earth occupies this place in the universe, because the material organism has advanced that far, that the life of the soul could commence.

I shall return to that subject on our next journey, when I'll explain all those transitions of the soul to you. You see, André, there are transitions in everything; these transitions are essential, because the inner life as well as the material organism would not otherwise have been able to digest this higher condition, power and energy. Wherever you look, where the human being and animal live, you feel those transitions. Slowly but surely man follows his road and will reach the All.

Look there, André, a further transition. No need to connect you with the past. This is still a state of existence.'

'Amazing, Alcar! These beings already have the build of man on earth, but how wild is their appearance.'

'Do not forget, they still have to pass on to the third cosmic degree. This body is still prehistoric. It looks like the body of the most powerful ape. It is very similar to this kind of animal, but in actual fact it has nothing to do with it. Yet, you would be inclined to think that we human beings descend from these animals and for a while one has embraced that theory. Yet, it has not been accepted. Slowly but surely, scientists are beginning to fathom the depth of the human being, but they still don't yet know how everything has come about. Nor will they accept what I told you, because science must prove it before accepting it as an established fact for further development.

As long as the earth has existed, there have been scientists who search and formulate some theory or other, only to drop it later on. But one day they will follow an other course, and beings will be born who will give science a strong impulse towards the initial stage. They are now looking for that which lives above them and is the universe, but they had better fathom the depth of the past. All that lives on earth can tell them, as it is part of creation.

These beings, André, this animal-like species with the Divine nucleus, will be born on earth.

As I said before, they live on meat and find it in abundance. These people spend their lives eating and stimulating the plan of evolution. They also live in caves, and when a young life is born and grows up to live its own life, nobody bothers about it any longer. They already have a powerful personality, and yet this personality is no more than the animal instinct. A life span as on earth is not yet attained here. This keeps pace with the perfection of the material organism. The animal-like being unites with the other life present here, and subsequently goes its way, never giving a thought to what was achieved.

In everything it is unconscious; there is no consciousness. They will only receive that consciousness or awakening until on the second cosmic degree; the instinct has then changed into conciousness. I will explain all that on our next journey.

You see that the entire body is covered with hair, as are its crude head and claws. In this animal-like being resides the primal strength of all spent and received energy. This organism was built up during all those billions of centuries. Nature has gifted it with animal instinct; it senses where it should go and slays whatever comes within its reach. This mentality is still present on earth. Yet, those beings live at a higher stage, in the third degree of the human body. When we have returned to the earth, I shall also explain that problem to you. For why are people still living in the jungle, whereas others dwell in palaces and buildings, and have a different mentality and feel themselves at a higher stage? I will prove to you that it belongs to the plan of evolution, and that those ignorant of civilization on earth still have to reach that stage.

Look there, André! In front of you you see a mother with her child. The child rests against her breast and she nurses it until that young life has sufficient strength to move about, when the mother will leave this young life and it is independent.

Its feeling is the instinct and it has no human qualities yet; those qualities forming the character still have to be born. Reproduction occurs in the way I just told you. This is in accordance with nature, for this animal-like being essentially belongs to the animals and cannot act differently, as it lacks the feelings we people on earth have. Deep human love still has to be born and awaken. But do not try to take this young life away from it; it would attack and kill you if you wanted to deprive it of its happiness, which it feels as animal. During the first few years, the young life is nursed directly by its mother, just like on earth; this has remained unchanged, although on earth the physique has developed to its highest degree. Here, too, the young life receives that mother-strength, but later it feeds like the fully grown beings and satisfies itself like the predator in free nature. But you feel and see its care; it anxiously carries its young along, but there is no trace of the father.'

'They live like wild animals, don't they, Alcar?'

'Yes, André. The father, who has accomplished this, is not aware of it, and is ready to mate again with the first female being coming its way. It is like the animal kingdom on earth, and how could it be different? The animal-like being, which is man here, does not feel different from the animal; it does not possess this consciousness and still has to achieve that inner strength and feeling.

There, André; in front of you, you see another mother. She is more robust and stronger than the other being you just saw; these are the seven material transitions, which we know on earth and are also present here. Here we find all those transitions in one condition, and that is because all those planets make their power felt, and this is present in the material organism. It is clear that the material organism has reached this stage by combined forces. We shall presently see this on earth, and they are the seven degrees for the material organism, which we know, and for the universe the planets which have jointly achieved that.

And yet, this animal-like being in its material condition is like man on earth. The material organism has reached this stage through all those centuries, and will presently pass on to the second cosmic degree, which we shall also visit.

The planet where we are now has a different substance than the previous planets, and this is to the benefit of the material organism. The robustness you see in this body, this unconscious strength this being radiates, has entirely passed on to the second cosmic degree, and there we see a different build. This thick-set animal-like being has changed there into an upright being. This bulky but elastic being which you see here has completely vanished on the second cosmic degree, and the creature has attained the normal and natural physique. Here you can meet monsters and also differently built beings, but most of them possess that stocky material condition.'

'How is their inner life, Alcar?'

'Oh, that is amazingly natural, André. This phenomenon, which may serve as an example for man on earth, is the awe-inspiring wonder of nature. This animal-like being mates in a natural way, which means, when the time occurs. It is therefore remarkable how accurately this animal-like being follows and experiences its feelings. If man on earth in the third stage could control himself equally well, he would follow the way of nature, and this event, which is sacred, would take place in a natural way. Therefore, man is in this respect below the animal instinct, for man experiences this event by his own will, by his intellectual capacity. Because man has these intellectual capacities in every respect, he has also laid aside his pre-animal feelings, his instinct, and acts in accordance with what he now possesses.

This animal-like being and all animals of the animal kingdom act as they should act, nature asks when the being is ready for fertilization. Man, however, acts for pleasure, and this pleasure is passion and animalization, an abuse of natural powers and feelings. The churches have incited that. What they did was rouse passion, but we shall discuss that on our next journey.

This animal-like being acts in a natural way, and you will understand that this is not multiplication as it happens on earth. But on the second cosmic degree a change has already set in, for instinct has attained consciousness there, and a conscious sense of good and bad exists. From the second cosmic degree onward, man is aware of what he does and is responsible for his deeds. If God had not given us all these mighty things, if we were not attuned to Him, we would have remained in that animal-like life. This animal-like being, my boy, lives as it should live; it cannot live otherwise. We, too, observe that in the animal kingdom and to whichever degree the animal may belong, it acts and lives as it should live. This animal-like being mates only once per year and then the young life is born. The next year, it mates again, but during the period in between it does not feel that it is male or female, and that is intended by nature. The animal-like being has its organs and lives; it will create or conceive.

136

You also see, André, how perfect nature already is, and that we see its resemblance to the earth. Yet the substance of this planet differs from that of the earth. There is cold and heat, but these climatic changes are below those on earth, which is caused by the orbit of the planet in the universe and by the influence of the sun. Everything is based on this influence; life lives in accordance with it and knows it in advance. The animal has, through the centuries, slowly acquired this power, which is the instinct. Here, nature resembles that on earth, but if you could feel the soil, you would immediately notice the difference. The material organism has therefore been built up by an other substance, but the second cosmic degree is different again, as is the earth.

This transition, André, also serves the perfection of the material organism which was subjected to this action and force of nature. Later you will see man as he is on earth, but also on the second cosmic degree we see various organisms; you know those degrees now. There, the head stands out far above the material body, the claws have changed into arms, and the legs have assumed human forms. This body needed billions of years to reach that stage of development. Still, it is not yet on the third cosmic degree.'

'Do these beings also dwell in caves, Alcar?'

'Yes, André. On the second cosmic degree too, and at the beginning of the third cosmic degree, on earth, man did not know houses; these buildings did not appear until later. They live in caves here, in a natural way. Sometimes they are in groups together, and yet, everybody is left to his own devices and follows his own way. You see in these caves here mother and child and all those who carry, or have, young ones. Millions of these beings lead a solitarily and lonely life which changes on the second cosmic degree and also on earth.'

'You mean they live in groups on the second cosmic degree and on earth, Alcar?'

'Yes, André. On this planet they have not yet advanced that far. Here, too, we see those seven material degrees of the human organism and the inner, but astral, being descends into the female body. Wherever we are, we see those seven cosmic degrees, which are found on earth and are the various races. All that is preordained in the plan of evolution; it is the cosmic picture or God's revelation, the transition towards the perfect human organism. The first stage we know was that first mother, but the other mother, even though present in these surroundings, lives

137

already in that second degree which we meet in the same condition.

The animal kingdom is also present here. I'll concentrate on an animal and we shall meet it. You know that we can follow only one road on our side of life; by concentration I arrive at the place I have in mind and wherever the being may be, I shall find it. That is also possible here.

Come, André, we shall go for a walk. You would think you were on earth, but we are on an other planet. I wish people on earth would not find this so unbelievable. We on our side can connect ourselves with everything living under our own sphere, and then pass on into that condition. We can travel to all those planets, the entire universe, and if we can return to the earth, it is also possible to visit the planet where we once lived. That is a great wonder for man on earth, but how simple everything really is. Those on earth who possess that gift, who can be with us by departure from their body, can stay in the spheres and observe all this beauty. He returns to the earth with this wisdom and knows what he has experienced, if he owns that gift consciously. You have that gift and the many journeys we have made together have given you all this wisdom. That is, for man on earth, the highest he can experience there. But many people will shrug their shoulders when they read that you have been with me on other planets, but here every spirit is conscious of his condition, and can, therefore, experience this sphere. Those who own inner light know what they observe and where they live; they are those who have reached the spheres of light. They who entered the spheres of light from the earth – you have heard that from Gerhard and Jeanne and the spirit Lantos[*]– all of them, every spirit, every man, have made journeys to the earth, to the darkness, the dark spheres of hell, and the many planets below their own sphere. They have learned life there and that there are planets in the universe on which they have lived.

Small wonder, when we say that we make journeys which may last centuries. They return to where they have lived and both experience all those degrees of cosmic powers; they experience their mistakes and sins; they live through accepting one material organism and passing away from the other. They experience all this coarser love and follow the instincts they have known. They go from planet to planet and then descend concsiously into the world of the unconscious and pass on to

[*] See the books: 'The Bridge to Eternal Life' and 'The Cycle of the Soul'.

those many lives. They follow everything, and one day arrive at the earth. There they have consciously destroyed themselves and each other many times and yet have met again and again through all those centuries.

Everything they have experienced on earth they experience again, and thus they travel through the universe, sustained by that tremendous love they possess and learn to know themselves. And when they finally return to the spheres, they know they have lived on all those planets and they prepare themselves to attain that further and higher condition. And they will reach this condition or sphere, for they have to go higher and are one with Him, our Father.

In this way, I have experienced all those wonders together with my twin soul and we thanked our great and almighty Father for everything we have achieved, and although we suffered a lot of agony, we had to achieve all this ourselves. With her, I followed all my thousands of lives and the many we lived together on earth. There we have known each other in dozens of lives, and in all those lives we did not know it, because, on earth, we cannot see into the past. Yet, all those lives were within us and we have experienced that process. Thus I travelled with my eternal twin soul to all those planets as everyone on earth will live to see. The reason why so little is heard about that on earth is that they have not got that far yet and do not even accept that they live eternally, and that it is possible to go further. Yet, everybody will receive that grace, and when you experience this together with your twin soul, my holy Father in heaven knows how tremendously happy one feels on all those planets. Not a soul will disturb you, for all those you meet are busy re-living their own past. My eternal happiness and I thanked God for everything from the bottom of our hearts. We kneeled down and prayed, and continued our journey which lasted centuries.

People on earth laugh at what they do not understand. They have no idea of what lives on our side, nor do they perceive what lives in the universe, but when they enter here they will get to know. Then they thank their God for that mighty power, that eternal possession, which every soul may call its own once they have advanced that far.

However, we shall reach many people on earth, and I am doing all this work for those who feel this love, and also because the time has come that they can digest it. I already said that it was not possible to bring these treasures on earth, because the mentality was still at the level of the pre-animal being. Now that people are freeing themselves from that pre-animal level, and they begin to feel there is more than they know, that death has dropped its mask for thousands of people and they are learning to understand themselves, we can come from our side. This has been going on for many years, because the need for nourishment for the mind makes itself felt. The century in which man on earth now lives is the century of spiritual enlightenment, and thousands are with me on earth to provide man in all countries with nourishment for the mind.

Now the time has come that they can be told of planets, and although all those degrees and powers make them feel dizzy, and even though they do not feel that billion-process in its entirety, it will give them an idea of what it is like. There is nothing strange in all this, nothing unnatural or improbable; it is nature, all of us have experienced it and emerged from it. Those on earth who open their minds, those who yearn for nourishment of the mind, can enlighten themselves by what is given to the earth. Travelling through the universe, André, is reserved for everybody. When it is possible for us to return to the earth, why then, should this be impossible?

What more can I say? Those who are still in doubt, who need to see this first before they can accept it, have not advanced that far. But I tell you: man on earth, prepare yourself so that you can receive it on this side. Look there, André, a being of the animal kingdom.'

André was scared stiff.

'What kind of an animal is that?'

'A prehistoric animal.'

André saw a greenish monster. Its size was tremendous and it lived in these surroundings.

'This animal, André, is found on earth in the third era. It is really very harmless and yet it has destructive feelings. Though it has attained a tremendous size, it is even bigger on the second cosmic degree. But see how perfect this animal already is, and yet it was born out of that invalid first human embryo. Several species of animals are living here, but most of them are living in the seas and are, therefore, in a different stage. The terrestrial animal had to make a long detour and is now passing on to this plan of evolution. The animal kingdom has gone through thousands of stages and this is only established on the second cosmic degree. Consequently, thousands of animal species live on the

140

second cosmic degree. This planet has a deep tranquillity equal to the place the human being, who is in the second sphere of our side and gets ready for the third sphere, feels. I have already explained all that to you and now you can compare this tranquillity you feel here. The human being lives in that tranquillity and feels it, but is not conscious of it. That is a distinct phenomenon, and we know these phenomena, as we find them on earth and on our side. It is the preparation for an other life, which is lived in an unconscious condition. There is peace here, and the tranquillity you feel dominates on the second cosmic degree.

This animal in front of you is twelve to fifteen feet large, but there are smaller species, too. The animals you know on earth, however, are not yet present here, nor are they on the second cosmic degree. You see that, as man progressed in his evolution, the animal keeps a close track. All those transitory planets also serve the animal kingdom and, although these animals are perfect, they still belong to the imperfect animal species. It is not until on earth that they reach this level and that is the third degree of cosmic attunement.

We find this greenish monster again during the initial stage of the earth, but, during its further stage, the animal differs from this prehistoric monster. The inner body of this animal nearly disintegrates but remains intact. Its skeleton has not sufficiently developed. It lives on land and in the water. But the animal passes on to an other stage, which it receives on the second and third cosmic degree.

Many species of animals have reached the negotiable planet, which hardened in all those centuries. Others, millions of them, live in the deep waters and still have to go through that stage. But when they have followed that process, that animal awakes in an other organism and is attracted on that other planet, and it has then reached a further stage than these monsters. The animals which become extinct, and that process has already set in, pass on to the All and then belong to the invisible energy. Wherever there is life, André, everything, the material organs as well as the spiritual, returns to the All. Nothing is or can get lost.

When we are going to the waters, which we shall do on the second cosmic degree, you will see how abundant life is, for the animal kingdom has branched off a thousand-fold. Wherever we are, we see life and death. In the universe, the large objects, the planets, condense; in the interior of the earth we find the same process, and on the inhabitable planets we see the development of man and animal. All that is

God and will remain God; that is energy, visible power, animated and brought to life by God. Man leaves the earth, the celestial bodies dissolve and disappear, and animals become extinct, or pass on to an other stage. In this way, this process has been going on for billions of years, and billions of years will yet pass before the earth has reached that stage and will also dissolve.

The animal you see in front of you will soon die. It already feels that influence. This is again for the next process, which we got to know on the first cosmic degree, when I connected you with it. For the animal kingdom, this is a similar condition. This animal has dropped its fish-like condition and already lives on the negotiable planet, but you can tell from that slothy body, that it moves on with difficulty. It has not yet assumed its natural condition. This is a transition and this transition lasts a great many centuries, when a different and more powerful species is born out of this animal. Other species still live in the seas, but they are also engaged in freeing themselves from that stage, and will reach the negotiable planet to accept an other organism. That is how the animal evolves. I could connect you with many beings here, but later on we shall see this process many times, and I shall be able to explain more. They are living there near man, and here we see them in the deep jungle, where they hide only to appear when hunger impels them. This animal lives on land and in the water, but there are other species living on the negotiable planet.'

'Are there already winged species of animals, Alcar?'

'No, that degree cannot be born here, nor on the other planets. That degree of development, which is the highest the animal can attain, is not found until on earth; they were born on the third cosmic degree. If you have been able to follow me, you will feel that all these animal species have to pass on into others, and that is a law for man and the animal being.'

'It is amazing how natural everything is, Alcar.'

'You see, André, again and again those material and spiritual transitions of the human and animal life, pass on from one material organism to another.'

'Will all these animal species, and those still on earth, dissolve in our era?'

'Indeed, André, all those animal species will pass on into a higher species.'

142

'Then it is all clear to me, Alcar.'

'The animal species we meet here are those monsters living at the banks of rivers and in the seas. There are not so many living on the land yet, but those which do live there are so unnaturally sized that they would frighten you, if you met such a monster. That is because the animal has to experience all those transitions, which bring it from one unnatural condition to the other, until the animal kingdom has reached its perfect organism. When it has finally assumed its definite state of existence, and has freed itself from its preliminary stages, the animal has reached the seventh material degree and continues on our side and can no longer return to the earth.'

'It has then, like the human being, reached its highest degree, Alcar?'

'Exactly, very good, so it is, André. You feel that human beings and animals are attracted by other planets, but only when they have completed their cycle on those planets and have reached that degree.'

'Will all those monsters, which are now still found in the seas, dissolve, Alcar?'

'Yes, André, but that will also take thousands of centuries, although it must happen. All those animal species will and must become extinct, or the plan of evolution would come to a standstill, and man and animal would not reach the All. Do you understand what I mean, André?'

'Yes, Alcar. Do they know about it on earth?'

'No, my son, science has not advanced that far; they can't know anything about it.'

'It is all so unbelievable and yet so natural, Alcar.'

'So it is, André; on this side we learn to understand and accept those laws of nature. Look, there, another being out of which an animal evolves, which you know on earth and has been found there for many centuries. This animal, André, looks like a toad, a tremendous monster, but its body will harden to grow a shell covering its entire body. You surely understand what I mean?'

'Is it, or will it become, a tortoise, Alcar?'

'Yes, André. Enormous animals are living here, and we find them by the thousands on the second cosmic degree. One does not know what to do with them there, and their existence is an awful torment.'

'You mean for the people living there, Alcar?'

'Yes, my boy.'

'Is this animal also present?'

143

'Yes, and we also see this animal being in its perfect condition on earth. You do feel what a tremendously long way this animal has to go before reaching that level. When this animal appears on earth during the initial stage, it is five, nay ten times larger than this animal which essentially carries its plan of evolution. Its body is still loose and flabby, but it will condense during all those centuries. We shall closely approach that animal, because it can't see us anyway.'

André looked at the animal. It had a greenish-grey colour, and its legs were already powerful. He saw that this animal belonged to the species already present on the planet earth.

'Have a good look, André, you see that the animal's skin already shows those scaly spots.'

'What a monster, Alcar. It looks like it only consists of water.'

'That is obvious, because it is an aquatic animal. Its broad head will change; its entire body will harden and its inner organs will develop. We shall see this animal again in a following incarnation. These animals have attained this tremendous size on the second cosmic degree and also on earth. Then again new lives follow, out of which, like man experiences, the true animal evolves, subsequently to pass on into another organism.

The previous planet and this one, therefore, serve the formation of its material organism, which attains full development on the second cosmic degree. You will tremble when you presently see the many animal species known there. The human being there also has an unusual size. Only on earth does man and animal assume their normal form. You will observe that wonder later.'

'Are the various seasons known here, Alcar?'

'Yes, André, but not the perfect change of seasons as we know on earth. The location of this planet, its place in the solar system, and its task in the plan of creation are such, that the living organism experiences this, which is the cosmic attunement for man and animal, implied in the condensation process. We see that in everything here. The trees differ from those on earth; what we know there as the normal wood-substance, and which is achieved by nature on earth, is not condensed here. The soil is of the same substance and the water is still muddy, a greasy mixture, in which animal life exists. There is nothing here which is already known on earth; everything on the planet earth is essentially perfect, like the material organism of man and animal. Neither do we see the lustrous green of plants and trees here, nothing of what nature has produced on earth.

Man and animal live in a transition to the real and natural state of the third cosmic degree. All this will be clear to you when we have returned to the earth.'

'How marvellous this nature already is, Alcar.'

'Yes, but everything here is in an unnatural condition, and yet - that will be quite clear to you now - perfect in its own condition. We know, however, that advancement to a higher condition is possible. Look at that plant leaf, large enough for man to hide underneath, it is about eight feet long. I shall connect myself with it, then you can pass into its inner structure.'

André passed into the tissue.

'It is peculiar what I feel, Alcar.'

'You feel that the plant lives in a preliminary stage. It feels like a downy cloth, and it is elastic as well. It would not be possible to keep these plants alive on earth. The power nature has, and which the earth receives by cosmic radiation, which is the sunlight, would make plant life here melt to form a pulpy mass. The power of nature here is such that everything lives at half-power. The energy this planet receives from the solar system is one-third of that of the earth. That is caused – and that will be clear to you – by the location of this planet in the universe and the task it has to perform. What we have seen and experienced on the other planets and was necessary for the inner organs, is here for the general constitution, which is the growth process. Hence all those huge animals. Presently we shall see this growth process in the human being, for neither does the material organism of man escape these laws of nature, as it is preordained in creation.

Everything you see, André, expands, awakens and passes through this growth process. Man and animal, therefore, experience one condition, one influence. Nature, of course, is like the organism living here, because nature produces those changes, and, as nature is, we see this reflected in man and animal. Both man and animal are subjected to it and change according as the final stage sets in. We shall go on now and pass on to the second cosmic degree.'

'How mighty and spectacular everything is, Alcar. If only people could accept it, but how could they believe it?'

'We shall convince many people, André, and the others who cannot accept it will have to wait until they learn to know our eternal life on this side.'

'Have you also been here with your twin-soul, Alcar?'

'Yes, André. Man cannot leave out a single transition after entering this side. They will learn to understand all that; nothing is lost, not even a single thought emitted will be forgotten or left out. For eternal life demands of the life that has captured a place, that everything has been made up, so that there are no more irregularities in the life of the soul, as everything must fit and every transition be experienced. We would not be able to move an inch on this side, if we knew nothing about that. We have to know everything living below our own attunement, are not conscious, don't know ourselves, because it has to do with our inner life. We shall learn to know all the lives we have lived. If there is just one thought not in harmony with our real life, it cuts us off from advancing further and from eternal life. That mistake will have to be amended and made up, or we keep feeling this disturbance and can't go on. For there are many things in ourselves which stop that process. Consequently, you can't enter higher spheres, if you don't know the lower ones. Everything living below the third cosmic degree is our own, and it is not only the depth of the human soul we have to learn, and therefore everything belonging to inner life, but also the material organs of all those planets where we once were.

Everybody, as I said before, will experience that. Then we go on and feel relaxed. We could not feel relaxed and could not concentrate on other matters, if we did not know creation. There must be no disturbance in ourselves here; we are always open and entirely free of all disharmonic thoughts. Those who wish to descend into the darkness must learn to know that darkness, even though they are higher spirits, or it is not their own. What I mean is, that he or she living in the higher spheres, has to know that, unless they are unconscious beings. Here no being can make progress unless he knows all those conditions, then he has advanced that far to prepare for higher life. He who harms others on earth will have to make it up, for it calls him to a halt. There are people who have already reached the spheres of light and yet cannot go on, because things have happened which the spirit has to make up first. On our next journeys you will experience all this. Here we feel what impedes and stops us. That is not possible on earth, because man is geared to material life. But when they enter our life, the life of the soul, which is a higher stage, you feel that they have to start thinking differently, and that our life differs from the life they had on earth.

Every soul, every spiritual being living on our side, has experienced all those transitions I showed you. That does not happen until they have reached the fourth sphere, though it is also possible in the third sphere. Yet very few do, as nearly all of us wish to reach the fourth sphere, which is the first happy sphere. Only then do we feel relaxed and capable of experiencing this; then we feel very happy to have reached the first sphere of existence, which is the spiritual attunement. The fourth sphere is – as I explained to you many times – the spiritual attunement on this side, but we go on to reach the fourth cosmic degree, where we shall arrive a few thousand years from now. Transitions and transitions again, to be able to enter this elevated condition. Above the fourth sphere are the fifth, sixth, and seventh sphere, you know all that, André; they are heavens of the spirit; after that, we pass on to the mental regions where we are attracted by the fourth cosmic degree; there we receive a new material organism of incredible beauty and an inexplicable happiness which no person on earth can imagine. Consequently, in those higher regions, people live like gods, but all once lived here.'

'It is all so amazing, Alcar.'

'If it were not true, it would be pointless to exert oneself on earth. You will gladly suffer all sorrow and human misery, when you know what awaits you there and what you will receive. God is love. We are all like God, but we must try and achieve this Divine attunement; it is not until then that we pass on into the All.'

'If I have understood you correctly, the first planet is the all-dominating one in the entire universe?'

'Very good, André. If the first planet had not had these powers, everything would have been different. The first cosmic degree had this significance. Its powers were fixed by these laws. The planet possessed no other function than what had occurred there, or the plan of creation would have been messed up. But one stage followed the other, one organ was born out of the other, and that applies to the entire universe; up to the highest cosmic degrees we see that activity. It will, therefore, be clear to you that, if the second planet had been ready and the first one had not yet completed its task, life of the soul would not be present and ready for further life; this would mean a cosmic disturbance. But

147

God oversaw everything. The first planet, therefore, dominated all those other planets and, as I said already, they were fed by this planet, the mother planet.

Consequently, all those planets follow one activity, but the first could only pass on to the second when the first stage was ready. That happened in the entire universe. The fourth cosmic degree could, therefore, not be born, and has not gone through the process of condensation, until man as a spiritual being passed on from the earth to a higher life, which is the hereafter on this side.

But even then we see transitions which are the seven spheres on our side, to pass on to the mental regions and to be attracted by the fourth cosmic degree.

That arch-power was present in the first stage, that all-dominating effect that the planet had to have, because it was this planet which had to perform that task, in which all the other planets were to participate. What happened then, I have explained to you the beginning of creation, the plan of revelation and evolution. What happened in the first stage, had to happen, could not pass on to the seventh stage, for there were no people yet, nor animals nor plants. There was nothing but the germ, that first wonder which was the human embryo, out of which the animal was presently born. Why should God create and prepare a seventh cosmic degree, whereas man and the animal being had yet to be born? Isn't that being far ahead of what one wants to achieve? All energy was spent during the first stage and was concentrated on it, and the first planet possessed that energy. That tremendous event was the first achievement and, in accordance with that action, all the other planets followed and were born out of that first cosmic degree. When the mother planet – to make it even clearer to you – still had performed its task and the young life was born, which is the condensation of all those other planets, this organ came to rest. But later, when we are on the third cosmic degree, the earth, I will give you a clearer outline of how it happened. I'll connect you then with the first stage of the planet earth and will show you to what extent the earth had condensed, when the mother planet, the first cosmic degree, had performed its task, so that you will get an overall view of this process.'

'Is it difficult for you, Alcar, to look back into the past?

'Yes, certainly, for everything is now at full power and has developed. The earth reached its highest degree already millions of years ago, and people have reached the stage for inner enrichment. We therefore live in the century of spiritual development. And yet - as you have experienced many times - I can connect myself with the past; I can pass into my own life, but at the same time descend into the initial stage of creation to experience everything again.

Look, André, we are approaching the second cosmic degree. Here, too, you would think you were on earth.'

'What is it, what I feel now, Alcar?'

'I am glad you feel that. Man who lives here, nature and all that has this cosmic attunement, differ from where we were just now. It lifts you; it is a light feeling that absorbs you. These emotional forces are also the many transitions you have experienced, in other words: Every planet has its own sphere. I let you feel this, so that you can also feel the sphere of the earth later, now that you are living outside your material organism. It is not the material body which requires this, but the spiritual body, or inner life, which is ourselves. You could have felt it in all those other conditions, but your powers are not adequate. That, again, is because you are still on earth and cannot completely pass into this life. If you were not assisted from this side, if a higher power could not connect you, it would not be possible to explain all this to you. But now that you approach your own attunement again, you begin to feel this. We shall now descend on this planet.'

Alcar descended and soon they were on negotiable ground. André was overcome by an infernal influence.

'What is that, Alcar?'

'You feel the sphere in which you are now. It is devilish.'

'Devilish, you say?'

'Yes, my boy. Pre-animal beings are living here, beings geared to the animal-like level. Evil is gathered here, evil in human form. The animal kingdom lives in a similar attunement. Look there; later I'll explain everything.'

André saw human beings. My God, he thought, is that man? They were worse than predators. They were wild and savage, large powerful beings, and they radiated a primal strength which made him shiver. He saw hundreds of these beings together. He heard them speak, but it was not speech, it was terrible shouting. He looked at this scene in amazement; he could find no words for it. He knew he could not be seen by them, for some of these beings passed close by him.

How muscular these beings were! Their bodies were hairy and they were entirely naked.

'It is unbelievable, Alcar!'

'These are not human beings; they are predators!'

Several of them were like normal people, but he also saw giants, as well as those beings he had seen on the previous planets. Several species of human beings lived together here, and now he understood what all those material degrees meant. Nature was nearly as it is on earth, yet he felt there was still a great difference, although it had nearly reached that degree.

'Are they cannibals, Alcar?'

'All of them, André, without exception. During the initial stage of this planet, they lived separately, too, as we have just seen on the previous transition. But during the many centuries which have passed, the situation changed. The human being living here has become conscious, but that consciousness is pre-animal-like. Anyone who cannot offer resistance, who cannot protect himself, is killed. What counts here is the right of the strongest, because the weaker beings are destroyed. They live close together and feel superior. They are obeyed, and thus we see thousands of them together, who have split into various groups. They go to war and wipe out whoever they meet. From the beginning of their youth they have adjusted to that, and when they have come of age, the younger ones are admitted in their midst. You meet these beings everywhere, as this planet is densely populated and is larger than the earth.

You see, André, their bodies are robust and powerful, and yet, all those degrees you saw a while ago are among them. This being feels this, and those belonging to the weaker beings, are killed. A mother who gives birth to a child and sees that this young life will not attain the required build, will kill that young life. The younger ones you have seen feel that they will die sooner or later. Yet, they remain in their midst, and tempt fate. Some separate from the group and go their own way; dozens of them are seen roaming about in the jungle. They try to find an existence, which is possible, as there is food everywhere. Yet all of them perish through the animals living here in large numbers. In addition to being killed by father or mother, they run the risk of being killed by those prehistoric animal species. Such is the life of this planet, and this mentality is still found on earth, for there are people on earth

150

who can act as they do.'

'How terrible, Alcar.'

'In essence, yes, but this is a natural condition, because the inner life has not yet developed that far. But they awaken already; because this is the first degree of consciousness, which they own. By acting in this way, they already follow a purpose, which is to be strong and remain so, and to guard themselves from destruction. On our next journey I will explain all that to you, because this belongs to the psychic world and the process of development of the inner life. Those beings, who have reached the first degrees of material development are killed here. I already said, that they live in groups. The strongest are their leaders, and when it comes to a clash, this encounter is gruesome. Fighting lasts until the others have been conquered. Then they go on, but remain within their own surroundings, of which they consider themselves the proper rulers. He who ventures into their domain is irrevocably lost and killed. They drag them to their camps; they skin and eat them like the animal on earth. This happens in accordance with nature, because frying and grilling are unknown here. Only in the third era on earth did mankind invent this, and passed on to a higher stage of development. These beings are pre-animal-like, and knew nothing about grilling, but the material organism could digest raw meat, as their inner organs were adjusted to it. They all are cannibals; it is part of their lives and attunement; it is the second cosmic degree.'

'My God, how terrible, Alcar. Have we, who now live on earth, been like that?'

'Not only you and all of us, but also those who have already reached the Divine Spheres. All have been here and had to follow this route. If this still happens on the third cosmic degree, what will the beings, which will pass on to the earth thousands of years from now, be like? You see, André, what this planet, the second cosmic degree, has achieved.'

'Have they reached the human degree, Alcar?'

'Yes, André, but only for the second cosmic degree.'

'Have such humans also been on earth?'

'Yes, these beings lived there at the beginning of the earth, but the planet earth was to complete the material organism, which happened in all those centuries.'

'Everything is so different here from those previous planets, Alcar.'

'That is very natural, André. Nature, and everything living in nature, has hardened. The trees you see are firm and vigorous and already attain the level we know on earth. The skeleton of man and animal is tremendously strong, which is also known from the first human stage on earth. We always see these material transitions. All those transitions of the material organism bring us to the highest degree, which is the material organism man on earth now has.

We shall now go for a walk and follow these humans. Nature is rugged and wild, like the humans are inwardly and outwardly. Look, André, mothers nursing their small ones the way the animal would nurse them. At the beginning, they care for their small ones and woe to him who interferes. Like a tigress she would pounce upon him or her, and fight until one of them is killed. At a later stage – as I said before – they themselves kill the young life if it is not strong enough and this happens as though it is the proper thing to do. Conscientious objections are not felt; that will come later, thousands of years later, when they live on earth.

See how their bodies are. Now isn't this organism a wonder of development and strength? If one saw such a being, which rather resembles a monkey than a human being on earth, one would be inclined to think that we descended from them. There were scientists on earth who studied this subject and even accepted it. This here is man in his pre-animal attunement and he resembles that animal creature. For this planet, their organism has developed to the highest degree. Look at this body, André, and the cruel head of these pre-animal-like monsters. See how the upper part of the body and the muscular system have developed! Follow the way they move; everything reflects the highest degree of organic power. The colour of their skin is brown-black, but their entire body is covered with hair.

This human being looks like an animal, which it is in essence. What you observe now, André, belongs to the later stage, which is the highest degree for this planet, because in the first degree these humans were not present here, and neither was life which belongs to the animal kingdom. Consequently, if I want to show you the first stage, I have to go back millions of years. But I'll do that on the third cosmic degree and give you a general outline there, so that you can see how that process took place. We, therefore, follow these humans from this moment on, and that is the highest stage they can reach on this planet. When these adult material beings have reached that highest stage, an other transi-

152

tion follows which already connects them with the third cosmic degree, the earth.

There is a lot of water here. Thousands of animal species are living in those seas, but man freed himself from that condition thousands of centuries ago. The being living here has passed on to the next negotiable planet. It has, therefore, reached its form of existence, it is already mature and is ready for a higher stage. They are all giants. These giants also lived on earth during the earliest of times. But, slowly, the material organism passed on to an other condition, the spiritual attunement, which means the perfect organism on earth as a cosmic being. The human organism on the fourth cosmic degree is, therefore, like that of man on earth, but of a different substance and it is more perfect and beautiful than the organism of man on earth. But here in a lower stage – as you see–- the living being has a material organism in accordance with nature and matching with his surroundings.

The interior is coupled with the exterior, and the animal instinct is seen to pass on into the material organism. How all this adapted itself will be clear to you. It was the task of this planet to promote the material organism and to complete it for this planet. The genital organs are like those of man on earth. The head is free from the upper part of the body and the skull resembles that of man on earth, but it is more robust and the jawbone protrudes. The eyes are deeply set and can hardly be seen through the dense growth of hair. Therefore their nudity is not conspicuous, and they resemble animal beings.

It will be clear to you, André, that every planet has its own activity, a task they have to perform for the human organism. In all those billions of years man has come that far, and yet these beings are still here, below the third cosmic degree and wait, unconscious of it, to go further, to be attracted by a higher being, a next planet. We see and find God's wisdom in everything, we see how one stage is established by the other and how out of one being, an other but higher being appears. There, André, you see a being of the animal kingdom.'

'What kind of an animal is that, Alcar?'

An enormously large animal approached him.

'Oh, stay calmly where you are, André; do not forget that we are invisible.'*)

'What a monster, Alcar.'

*) André is now in the present of the past.

'This animal lived during the initial stage of the earth. In your time, however, that animal is no longer present, it passed on into other lives and has received an other material organism. You see that the animal has to follow thousands of different conditions, while man has to follow one condition, one route, leading to the perfect material organism man has on earth. There is such a lot I could tell you about it, but if I did, we would end up in a complex situation and could not tell one thing from another. Perhaps, given time, I may explain the general condition of the animal kingdom to you, so that you can clearly see how many degrees the animal kingdom has passed before it reached the third degree on earth, and attained that material organism. Yet, the animal, like man, passes into its primal attunement and this can already be observed. The animal in front of you will one day be born on earth to stay there for a long period of time. It is now of incredible size and can grow to reach thirty to sixty feet. It is the image of what was known on earth, but the animal which lived on earth has, like man here, passed on into an other stage. This animal, therefore, lives below the other animal, which is man.

It attacks man in everything, but only when it is forced to do so: when its organism compels it. That is the eternal struggle on this planet: the struggle for life.

That struggle is part of this life and of life on earth; it does not end until on the fourth cosmic degree. Then man and animal live together, and man knows that the animal originates from him, from that which came from the Divine source. Here, however, and on earth, no pure love is known, and all who concentrate on it belong to this attunement.'

'How amazing, Alcar.'

'Look over there, André, another wonder. We have met that animal in its previous stage. It now passes on to that other attunement and is already connected with it.'

André recognized this animal. It was like the tortoise on earth. Here, it had reached a tremendous size. The head was already visible, but its shell had not yet hardened and was still composed of a fleshy substance.

'Will this animal become the giant tortoise which lived on earth at the beginning, Alcar?'

'Yes, André, we shall see that animal again on earth, but then nature has completed its task, which is the condensation process. You will see that animal there again, and also that other animal, but they will be smaller than they were on this planet. On earth, the animal kingdom has more resistance and strength, acquired in all those centuries.

Look, there are dozens of them together. Man keeps away from these animals, but these beings seek out the human being, and a struggle for life and death develops. However large these animals are, they are very vulnerable. Man is aware of this vulnerability, and knows how to surprise and hit them. It belongs to their lives; it is the instinct of man and animal. But the animal, too, knows how to attack the human being, and smells where it is.

The inner organs, therefore, are highly developed, but it is not until on earth that this instinct, that pre-animal feeling, passes on to consciousness, and they act accordingly. All of them, man and animal, adapt themselves amazingly to one another, and what the one does not possess, is not present in the other animal life, but both of them have strength in accordance with their material organism and have to follow transitions.

Nature, too, as I just said, differs from nature on earth; although at first sight, you think you are already on earth. I could call this the era of the giants, which is actually true. Everything belonging to the material organism awakens here and this planet has a capability which those other planets lack. This planet builds the material organism: is it strange that the human and animal organism should have reached this size? Trees and plants are also immensely large, although plant life dominates here.

The leaf of a plant, as you see, is as large as a roof of a house on earth, and is very thick. It has that primal strength here, but it dissolves in a few days during the coming change of climate, according to time on earth. The enormous shrubs you see here everywhere, produce a kind of fruit on which the animals, that have reached the shore, feed. There is similar food for man here, which is only present periodically, depending on the climate. They do eat this kind of food, although they are adjusted to animal food.

In the water and on land, food is abundant. In addition, there is the human being itself, which they eat.

The poisonous reptile lives here, too, but the material organism of man is immune and they can digest quantities, which would cause instant death to man on earth.

155

It will be clear to you that the first degree of material organism still living on earth is composed of a different substance than man living in the highest material organism. The pre-animal-like beings of that first degree digest raw meat without the slightest discomfort.

Look, André, another few dozen of these animal species. The animals stay together, and they also destroy the weaker organism. This is a natural law which is still in force in various ways on earth. Yet they have already reached a certain consciousness there, but it still belongs to the instinct of the second degree of cosmic attunement; although they have passed on to the third cosmic degree. Come, André, we shall move on and visit the seas.'

This land lay below him which André could still see.

'Look, over there is a vast expanse of water.'

Several thousands of animals lay on the shore. It was an awe-inspiring sight. He saw small and large animal species.

'Has all this life passed on to the earth, Alcar?'

'Yes, André. This animal life must pass on, because it has not yet reached the highest stage for the animal kingdom. The animal of the third cosmic degree, however, has appeared out of all this life. This also applies to the human organism. What you have seen so far has been living on this planet for millions of years and is therefore an existence. All this life goes on and on and we'll see it on earth later.

Life has already advanced that far that these beings are attracted by the third cosmic degree through reincarnation. Everything living here has to follow that billion-process, as the first planet and the subsequent transitions had to follow it. However, I will now connect you with the past and you can observe how everything has happened, and that every planet, and therefore every organism, however small, had to follow the first stage. Further, you will see that everything has its own sphere and has to perform a task, but that only one route must be followed, which we experienced on the first cosmic degree, and is the condensation process. Attention now, André.'

André saw the planet disappear. The entire planet dissolved in front of him, only light remained. How is it possible, he thought. Where is all this life? Where is man and all life that belongs to the animal kingdom?

'Now look there, André.'

'Over there, high above you, is the first cosmic degree, the planet which fed all these organs. Out of that condition, inner life came into being. It is this planet which completed that task. That large body fed this planet, but this did not begin until that process of development had reached its highest level and the next stage had started. This planet is now enveloped in a dense haze. It has not yet condensed; but over there, all those thousands of organs are condensing; they are all those transitions adjusted to the first organism and can receive this life, which is the inner life, the soul. You see that a further stage has already set in. Here, too, that activity is present, but life has yet to awaken. Only then does this planet proceed to the condensation process. The first planet as seen from here has reached that stage; the smaller organs are ready, and yet there, too, – as I have explained to you – a similar process took place, but these organs have to perform an other task than the mother planet.

This planet has not yet advanced that far, all energy passes on to those smaller organs, and they have started their activity with the first cosmic degree, and have been incorporated by that body in this condensation process. Here, too, we feel this awe-inspiring power which is the influencing effect. You no doubt feel that I have connected you from this place with the condensation process and I'll now proceed to a following stage.

This planet has condensed more and more. Millions of years have passed. Life has come, and this life is, as on the first planet, the first human embryo. This first life passed away when it mated with another life. But here this life was in an other condition than there. This life was more powerful and - never forget this - it received that power from that first planet. As a result of this power, and the animating life which had been living for millions of years, the condensation process took place, and accelerated on this planet.

Now that the planet had advanced that far, that it could assist in that awe-inspiring activity and development, and begin her own task in this million-process, this condensation occurred in accordance with cosmic action, which is God's sacred influence.

Life came to this planet; this life was born and had a strength which differed from that on the first cosmic degree. Now that the previous planets had got that far, all that power passed on to the second cosmic degree, and the first embryo came into being. Millions of years later, this planet had developed to the extent that the human organism reached the shore, and this life took possession of this planet. The first life

157

which reached the shore was like the being we have seen there but, and that will be clear to you now, it was composed of a different and more powerful substance. Yet it followed this route as life on all those transitions had to follow it; this is preordained in the cosmic plan.

In those thousands of centuries which followed – and it also applies to the planet earth which I'll show you there – this organism rapidly developed. When the animal-like being, which was man, had reached the shore and had dropped its fish-like stage, all these powers passed on to the first transitions and the second planet, where, in that era, this powerful creature you saw just now developed. You see, André, one route, one activity, one purpose, which is what man on earth has, the material organism which hides the spiritual body, which we are ourselves. The planet earth, as you know, has experienced a similar process, which I will show you later on. But there is still life on this planet, the animal-like life is present, and thousands, nay millions of years will pass, before this life has dissolved and has passed on to the highest stage, which is for the inner life, the planet earth.

You see, André, and that is my point, that every planet is fed by the first cosmic degree, even though the first cosmic degree has already performed its task. That planet can still be seen as a dense mass, and as long as it remains in this condition, it feeds all the other material bodies; man, animal, and also the planet on which this life exists, are spiritually and materially subjected to the influence of the mother planet. And this influence is felt on earth and will continue to be felt, because the earth is in harmony with this planet, which serves the material and spiritual life.

Now look at the earth, André. Over there, to your right, you see the earth and you can still see the condensation process, as it were. I show you an image from the past, when the condensation process of this planet had been going on for millions of years. The earth, too, is going to condense and is fed by this planet. The planet earth now receives its task; it can now commence and prepare to receive the inner life. Once the planet earth was that far ready, the human and animal beings, which had reached their highest stage here, passed on to the earth and were born there. Now I'll pass on to this life.'

André felt himself return.

'Oh, Alcar, how is it possible, how tremendously spectacular everything is.'

'We are now on the shore of an ocean. Thousands of animal species are living in this water. Again this water has a different substance than the water on the previous transitions, and all this we see again on this negotiable planet. Have you understood all this, André?'

'If I understood you correctly, everything here and where we were has to become extinct?'

'Indeed, so it is. But this is not possible until the first material stage has passed on to the highest stage.'

'Then everything is clear to me, Alcar. I am very grateful to you. Are there also transitions between the second and the third cosmic degree?'

'Yes, André. Smaller and larger planets, preliminary stages, in order to pass on to the third cosmic degree.'

'Is this planet known on earth and can it be seen from the earth, Alcar?'

'I can answer both questions in the affirmative. This planet is known on earth and can be seen from the earth.'

'Does one know there, that this planet is inhabited?'

'They don't know, but they suppose so. They cannot determine that with certainty.'

'Will they come that far one day, Alcar?'

'Possibly. When they have these instruments on earth, which will be invented, it will be possible to observe life on this planet, and on many others, from the earth. But it is not possible to try and establish contact with these planets, because man cannot venture outside the atmosphere.'*)

'Does the influence of this planet, as you say, pass on to the earth?'

'Yes, those who have not yet reached the highest material and spiritual degree on earth, and commit deeds on an animal level, are under the direct influence of this planet. That is the connection with the universe, with that degree still present in that life which spent many centuries here. It will therefore be clear to you, André, that all life we have met so far is born on earth, and there, too, man and animal pass on to other conditions to prepare for the fourth cosmic degree. That is passing on to a higher attunement for man and the animal kingdom, to acquire our own life. A ruler on earth, who destroys others, is in connection with this world and, consequently, the material organism is in a further and more perfect stage than the spiritual body. Is that clear?'

*) See footnote page 115.

'Yes, Alcar.'

'Man on earth should now improve his spiritual level; it has, therefore, not been possible to tell them about all this life before, because they had not yet reached that stage, and had to first attain that material and mental development. All those seeking evil are still under the influence of these planets and still have to drop their pre-animal feelings.'

'It is believed on earth that life on various planets has further advanced than life on earth, Alcar. So that is not possible, is it?'

'Yes, it is possible, because those are the planets which are the transitions for the fourth cosmic degree.'

'Can't they establish a connection with them?'

'No, that is impossible for the reason that all those planets are far away from the earth and cannot be observed from there. What they observe from the earth belongs to the first three cosmic degrees, of which the earth is the third cosmic degree. They should not expect anything from the fourth, fifth, sixth, and seventh cosmic degree. When the scientists know that the earth is the third cosmic degree, and that it is not possible to establish a connection with the fourth cosmic degree, they will change their attitude, reconsider their ideas, and, as a result, learn to understand the cosmic All. It is possible for a higher degree to seek connection with a lower one, but they can't go any deeper, as all those cosmic laws are not understood on earth. Man on the fourth cosmic degree is engaged in establishing a connection. But thousands of years will pass before they can achieve it.

But then, eternal life is accepted on earth and you will, no doubt, feel that they will change their attitude, so that they will receive connection. Scientists will then be born with the gifts of vision, and will spiritually depart from their material organism to the spiritual life. However, as long as they cannot accept our life and want to explain everything scientifically, they will not advance any further. Spiritual life has to be accepted if it is desired to be connected with the visible and invisible cosmos, because our life is connected with the cosmic universe. By accepting our life, André, by passing on to it, we, on our side, bring about that cosmic connection and tell them what they should do to get an overall view of creation. We can help them to develop those instruments already known on the fourth cosmic degree. The fourth cosmic degree already has a connection with the fifth cosmic degree. They know there that they, man and animal, have lived on the fourth cosmic degree. Do you feel this mighty grace, André?'

'It is wonderful, Alcar.'

'On our third journey, I'll connect you with the fourth cosmic degree and explain a lot about that planet.'

'Has everything there acquired a much higher condition than on earth, Alcar?'

'Yes, because what man possesses on the fourth cosmic degree is amazing; it is incomprehensible; man on earth cannot imagine that. Life there cannot be compared with life on earth and man is of a wonderful substance, an angel in a material attire. Love rules there; nothing but love, a condition of perfect happiness, man is spiritually geared. It cannot be described; one should see and feel that life, observe man there, in order to understand it. Man there has mental happiness, but in a material condition. Try to imagine that, André, to have spiritual happiness on a planet where illness is unknown, and everything is in harmony with the infinite. You cannot form an idea of that; you have to experience it first.'

'Is it known there that they have been on earth?'

'Yes, they know that, for it is known there what the universe is and how many cosmic degrees there are. They know all the planets within their reach and are in contact with them. In our life, on this side, they have come that far. They have experienced all those spiritual spheres, discarded and acquired them, and have, like the soul for the earth, been attracted by two beings, which is the connection known on earth and which has been established from the beginning of creation. They know that we are their sisters and brothers and still have to go that long way, but that we shall, after thousands of years, be that far to be attracted and that incarnation will occur on the fourth cosmic degree.'

'You said before that people reach a very high age there?'

'Yes, André, and that is obvious. Man there reaches an age of approximately two hundred and fifty years by earthly standards. Do not forget, there is no illness; the material organism is of an entirely different substance, because those living there are spiritual beings. You will be amazed when I say that people on the fifth cosmic degree reach ages of hundreds of years, in one material life. The sixth cosmic degree cannot be compared with the fifth; people reach ages of thousands of years and life seems to be endless. But that end comes, for one has to go higher and further to reach the seventh cosmic degree and subsequently to pass into the All. But those who have reached the seventh cosmic degree, stay there for millions of years and are also born there before entering the All.

Man on earth cannot comprehend that. But what the universe has experienced, what all those planets had to experience, which lasted billions of years, also applies to all organism living and having lived there. Do not forget that we originate from the All and all those planets, and that we are part of it and remain being part of it. Nor forget that we shall return to God consciously and then understand the entire universe. That is our life then and we have mastered all those planets.

All this will be fantastic to the earth, yet they will experience it. Not a single life, man, nor animal, can escape it. We go on and on, higher and higher, and finally live on in the infinite.

On the first planet, the first human embryo passed away when it came into contact with the other life, the driving power or the female body. The very moment that this fertilization took place, this life shed its material organism and the new life was born. This little being lived on; it went through thousands of stages, during which it died and was born time and again, but every time its life lasted a little longer. Now if that is a law, the law of the Divine plan, and applies to all plant and animal life, as well as to planets and other bodies, it will also apply as we progress and enter a higher stage. That which lasted millions of years during the initial stage, the living organism, in its supreme stage, also receives. This plan of evolution is seen to develop in everything, and this is to return to Divinity. What God created, and how creation occurred, man and animal experience, and are both part of this mighty event. Therefore, what happened during the very first moments, and what you have observed in the temple of the soul and I explained to you on the first cosmic degree, man will receive when he approaches the final stage. Do you feel what I mean, André?'

'Yes, Alcar.'

'You feel then, that there is no 'time' in the All, but that we are bound by laws and have to experience these laws.'

'How many times does man return here, Alcar?'

'That cannot be determined. We have lived in a material organism thousands of times and that is necessary, for what does man learn in one material life? When we start our next journey, it will become clear to you, because I'll connect you.'

162

'People on earth generally say: I do not wish to come back here.'

'They are in no position to make demands, André; they have to. It is a law which we must experience, which is reincarnation. It cannot be changed. People don't know what they say, because they don't understand all these powers and laws. They will return on earth thousands of times. In one life on earth, they cannot acquire that spiritual wealth, which they must possess, in order not to return there. They go on from here, but not until they inwardly own the earth as a planet, and have spiritually experienced and acquired all those transitions. They don't know that, however, and say things they don't know anything about.

They do not want all that sorrow and illness, but I'll explain to you that God did not give them that sorrow. Man, however, has not yet advanced that far that he can dominate and accept illness and suffering. When man gets to understand himself, he will ask for more, because he feels what it brings him. God foresaw everything and knew that man would forget himself. And because they would forget themselves, sorrow, misery, and illness occurred. Yet, all this sorrow, however terrible, is essential to pass into the All. But man who can surrender experiences this in a way that is pre-destined in the cosmic plan, but people who do are few. They are those who feel this tremendous process and are grateful for what they receive. God did not bring illness to the earth, nor sorrow: He brought nothing but happiness. Why is death on earth and passing on into an other world, not accepted? Why do people feel grief when their beloved ones depart? I could put thousands of questions, but people on earth don't want to listen; they wish to possess, to possess eternally, and close their beloved ones off from a higher world.

No, André, all that shall dissolve. Those who cannot surrender will have to learn it, for their beloved ones die anyway; they cannot keep them; they must go and continue their way. All that ignorance will dissolve one day. One day the earth will dissolve, will be uninhabited, like all those planets are dissolving. One day that will happen, André, but then they have overcome something; they reconcile themselves with everything and surrender completely. They know then that this sorrow is only a temporary condition. However, people on earth have not got that far, but for those who can accept all this, and adjust their lives to pass on into our life, the sun is shining, and they are grateful for everything, whatever it may be. They themselves have imposed all those illnesses. I'll show all this to you when we visit the inner life, the psychic world.'

'If only people on earth could accept this, Alcar.'

'It is not so simple to accept this, my boy. They have to determine that for themselves; we do not force them. But those who start thinking about this do not build castles in the air. They build at something living in and near them; they pass on into it and learn to know an other life. Let them do what they like who laugh at this. They are the very people who will return to the earth hundreds of times, to acquire that which those others already have. They will pass on from one condition to another. In this life, they will be rich and have many material possessions, but in dozens of other lives they have nothing to eat and have sorrow, grief, and misery. Then they roam about the streets like many other people and will be stabbed to the heart, and feel what that means. No condition will be spared to them; they will experience all sorts of earthly conditions; not a single human being can evade that, for it is all this that makes them shed themselves. All that sorrow, however, is not necessary, but in previous lives they provoked that themselves. They do not know they go on; they do not realize that one day everything has to be made up, down to the smallest things.

That is the sorrow they experience; it is cause and effect, it is karma. Man keeps returning to the earth until he leaves something behind for the benefit of mankind. Not a single being who has lived there can, and will, part from the earth without having done something for the happiness of mankind. Then they go on, and that is the gratitude for what they experienced and received. In hundreds of lives on earth, man degrades, and then he will build up, what he has destroyed in all those lives. When building up is ready, man gives himself entirely and only then is he a spiritual being.

Believe me, André, when I say that not hundreds, but thousands of lives are necessary to fully experience the third cosmic degree, the planet earth, at cosmic attunement, as the spirit Lantos told you in 'The Cycle of the Soul'. Tens of thousands of lives are required for the fourth cosmic degree, and higher, we cannot even pronounce that figure. That is the purpose of God; it is the road to return to the Divine. All of us have to follow that road.'

'When do you think, Alcar, that your work will be properly understood?'

164

'Far in the future, André. There are already people on earth who accept me, but those few must become millions. A few hundred years from now we will be accepted. At that time, a bit more will be known on earth about our lives than at present, and they will accept everything. This work, assigned to me, is coming to earth a few centuries too soon. But we do meet people who follow us. So you won't be understood there, either; but that is no problem when you know what I expect. If I can reach one person, I am already satisfied, but this very moment, we have been allowed to reach thousands of people, and all of them will help us carry our work to those sensitive to it and grateful to receive this. And in this way our work will spread, and in the centuries to come people will feel and understand us.

That is coming, André; I see it, for it is the road they have to follow and which is contained in our work. Your books, your journeys in the hereafter, the love you told about; they want to possess all this, and that makes them sensitive. And now we will go on. I have to tell you a thing or two more, yet we shall go on and return to the earth.'

'Is this planet denser and harder than the earth, Alcar?'

'No, the earth has a different substance than this body, and is harder and more compact. But there are planets with a consistency unknown on earth. Nothing on earth can be compared with this consistency. Those are the small planets which have to perform an other task. If this planet and the earth had such a consistency, life could never have come there or be born. Yet, life was born there, but no human or animal life ever lived there. Do not forget that everything lives, that everything is energy. Those are usually bodies which have to perform an other task in the universe and have occupied a place in it. They are those planets, which are observed as stars, luminous globes of fire, but not destined for the human body.

I will now fully connect you with this body; you will then feel the tremendous intensity of life here. Do you feel what I mean, André? This is a different way of connection. You completely pass on to this planet and feel its inner condition as a whole within you.'

André felt himself sink away. It was remarkable. He immediately understood what his leader meant. This planet absorbed him and he began to feel, and see, life living on it. This planet was densely populated. He saw life everywhere; man and animal had accepted this possession. How strange was this connection. He had not experienced this

165

before. This planet was within him, and he read this enormous body like an open book. Yet, he could not explain it entirely; therefore, he asked Alcar: 'Do I feel this correctly, Alcar?'

'Quite right', he heard his leader say. 'You now feel how densely populated this planet is. I am doing this, because I want to give you a similar picture on earth so that you will feel the mighty difference of life between these two planets. You will also feel the earth within you and be able to assess the difference. Now you will return to yourself.'

André felt himself return, and found it very curious.

'It is remarkable, Alcar.'

'Yes, it is possible for us, because I know all this life and can give you a clear idea of the abundance of life here. Look, there in front of you, a lot of human beings. They are making raids, and do so because they don't know any better. They plunder and murder, and think it is the proper thing to do. They use the human body the way they use animal life for food.'

'They are very powerful, aren't they, Alcar?'

'Their strength cannot be fathomed. Look, they are fighting. They are attacked by an animal being.'

André saw a tremendous monster. A greenish animal rushed at them. He heard their awful screaming and saw that several of them were attacked. After a short while, the animal had killed some of them with its horrible tail. The others ran off, leaving their dead behind. The animal made a frightening noise and trampled the human bodies until nothing was left.

'How horrible, Alcar.'

'A thing you can see on earth, but this belongs to this planet. This animal has also lived on earth, and man has felt its strength there. Now, however, it has dissolved into the eternal plan; it is still present here, but will also die out. For the earth, this is the past, but for this planet, the animal is still alive. I can connect you with the past, with the present, and with future images. What you have observed, however, belongs to the present and will dissolve, because all this life will go on. But now we'll go to the earth. While on our way I'll tell you about these transitions present between the second and third cosmic degree.'

Floating through space, they left the second cosmic degree and went towards the earth.

166

# CHAPTER X

## *The third cosmic degree*

How wonderful everything is, Alcar. How much we people on earth still have to experience. All those planets awaiting us. It is not until then that misery on earth will be over?'
'Yes, it is not possible sooner. First, all those transitory planets must dissolve, the second cosmic degree must pass on to the transitory planets and subsequently to the earth, and when all people are spiritual, peace and quietude will come. Spiritual happiness in a material organism is an inner enjoyment one finds on the fourth cosmic degree. To your left and right are the many transitory planets which are geared to the earth's level. Over there, in the centre of all these planets, is the earth. I explained all those conditions to you and I said that many organs are required to reach that degree, which is an existential planet. This also applies to the earth. If there were no transitions, as I also explained, the material organism would collapse, and inner life, the life of the soul, would succumb. But God, the Creator of this might, oversaw all this, which is for the organism of man and animal. All these transitions, which are in connection with the earth, complete the material organism, although the lowest degree is still found on earth. That material organism is already perfect, yet it is still far away from the seventh degree. On earth we know the material organisms which belong to the highest degrees, which are the fifth, sixth, and seventh degree.'
'How remarkable, Alcar.'
'It is not different from what we have experienced in previous conditions.'
'Is that known on earth?'
'No, not at all. But they do know there are various human races, although they do not understand the meaning of those races. For why has one human being reached the highest degree on earth, and why do others live in the jungle and violate others?*)
'That, too, is a natural problem which I explained to you. There are seven degrees of material organism; they who live in the first degree are

*) See the 'Explanation' at the beginning of this book.

called head-hunters. That is the material degree on earth. These degrees are present on all these planets, as I showed you. Now if this is so, why should it not be accepted on earth? Is it so strange? Haven't I shown that all of us have been like that? These humans live on earth; if they hadn't, there would have been injustice in the universe, and God would have made a mistake. The human being on earth experiences seven degrees of material organism, in order to reach the highest stage. What we have experienced on all those planets, we also experience on your own planet where you still live and which I discarded. Primitive races are still living on earth and they are the first transitions to the perfect human species. Those having reached the highest degree can no longer descend to the first degrees. Man who has reached the highest attunement passes on to an other. Yet, man returns hundreds of times in this body, which is for the inner life. The spirit will have to acquire these treasures, which is tuning in to spiritual love. Man will therefore return to the earth until he has acquired these powers, and will then go on, which is on our side. Afterwards, when man has reached the seventh sphere, he will, as you know, pass on to the mental regions and is attracted by the fourth cosmic degree. You do feel that everything links up, that one connection follows the other to which man and animal submit.'

'How marvellous all this is, Alcar, and how fair.'

'It is a wonder of justice, and man will experience thousands of wonders when they enter our life and learn to know it.'

'If people on earth only knew its meaning, Alcar.'

'They shall know, André; we are telling them already. We shall lay down all your questions and my answers and everything you have observed. Nothing will be lost; our effort will not be in vain.'

'Wouldn't they understand the earthly problem better?'

'When scientists on earth can accept all those material transitions, a completely different world opens up and they will learn to understand creation and its simplicity, because it is simple; if it were not, I would not be able to explain the universe to you. But now that we go over into it and feel all these planets within us, which I made you feel, man will feel that he possesses it.

Haven't you noticed something remarkable on this journey, André?'

'Everything is remarkable, Alcar.'

'Yes, I know, but that is not what I mean.'

168

André reflected on everything he had experienced but he did not feel what his leader meant.

'I will tell you, my boy. There are different human races on earth and they all have their own material organism. On all the planets you have observed, only the dark, brown-black race lives. These beings have been there from the initial stage up to the last transition. The white race, however, was only created by the third cosmic degree, and only lives on earth.'

'No, Alcar, I had not thought of that. It is remarkable and yet so obvious. For that type of people would not be born until on earth.'

'Indeed. Everything living below the third cosmic degree does not possess this organism, because it was only on the planet earth that man was to receive it. The earth created that organism and it developed there. The substance of the earth cannot be compared with that of all other planets. The first degree on earth received its splendid organism, but the skin colour is as we got to know it on the second cosmic degree. Only on earth is the human organism perfect. The highest degree is, as you know, like your own organism. Look there, in front of you, is the earth; we shall soon be there. Do you feel, André, now that you are approaching the earth, that a different power enters you?'

'Yes, Alcar, I clearly feel it.'

'That is the attunement of the earth. The power it radiates is present between the earth and the atmosphere; the place it occupies in the solar system is the effect you feel and it is different for all these planets. Now we are back on earth. I'll first connect you with the earth and you will feel the overall situation entering you. What you see and feel is life on earth, a condition, therefore, similar to the one on the second cosmic degree. Pay attention now.'

André felt himself sink away and a remarkable power entered him. He had not felt the earth in this way yet and now he had a general view of this planet. It was a remarkable connection. He felt life on earth. The other planet was larger. He clearly felt this mighty difference.

Now he heard Alcar say: 'You will return to yourself, André. Did you feel that those other planets, anyway some of them, are very much larger than the earth? And that the first planet dominates them all?'

'Yes, Alcar. Perfectly.'

'I will now connect you with an other image, the initial stage of the earth. You return to the past and will be able to follow the entire process, but this time of the planet you are living on.'

169

Again André descended into the unknown and the past became visible. What he now observed was amazing. In the universe lay a violet light and in that light he saw a golden glow. It was like an evening at sunset. It was of such an awe-inspiring beauty that he thought he was in the seventh sphere.

'What does this wonderful scene mean, Alcar?'

'It is a beautiful view, André, and it means the moment has come when the earth begins to condense. It receives that glow from the other planets. During the initial stage of creation, life on all those first planets has, time and again, experienced this amazing and mighty event with intervals of centuries. You see various shades of colours in the universe. The planet earth now receives that wonderful and inexplicable power, and this phenomenon preceded every condensation process. In fact the earth is, as you will see shortly because this belongs to the next event, a luminous ball of fire, though enveloped in a dense haze. When I am going to connect you with that moment, the earth will dissolve before us. The light of the sun darkens; the first planet has completed its task. The other planets, which receive life from the first cosmic degree, are ready, as you see. Thousands of planets have hardened and condensed. Up to your right you see the second cosmic degree. You see, André, it is in a further stage of condensation than the earth. All those smaller planets belonging to the second cosmic degree are now going to condense. The first transitions between the first and second cosmic degree are ready. Now I pass on to the initial stage of the earth.'

André felt himself sink away still deeper. The earth dissolved before him and now became a luminous disc, in which he could see. What I observe is as in the temple of the soul, he thought.

'A wonderful sight; how is that possible, Alcar?'

'I will go on, André, and will show you transition after transition. Attention now, this is a mighty phenomenon.'

André saw that the earth started to condense. He saw dark parts appearing in this light. The dark parts spread over the entire body. He now felt he was in the centre of the earth, and to the right and left, below and above him, he saw the earth condense. Slowly this amazing light condensed. The light took other colours, like he had observed in the temple of the soul. One colour slowly changed into another, and he understood this phenomenon.

This lasted for a considerable time; then he heard Alcar say: 'As you know, millions of years have already passed. These transitions, which form the first stage of the condensation, lasted millions of years, before that process could go on. I now go on to the next stage.'

Again André saw that he was connected with an other process. A dark shadow now lay over the entire earth. Above him in the universe he saw something condense, completely closing off this planet. This mighty organ was now secured from outside. André felt what it meant: the atmosphere was forming. This atmosphere changed into an other light, and now he could no longer observe it. Yet he felt that it would stay and was nearly ready.

He looked at the universe and could observe the other planets, and saw that the earth passed from one condition to another. The dark haze which covered the entire earth became ever denser. In that darkness he saw shapes which changed into others, subsequently to compact as a dense mass.

That will become the earth, he thought; mountains and valleys formed. My God, how mighty is everything I see.

Again he heard Alcar who said: 'You will now see the next stage.'

André saw movement below him. He could perceive something in that dark mass. It was as if a dense mass of clouds contracted. This mass became denser and denser; it was as if the earth had changed into a ball of fire. It resembled a huge fire but he could not comprehend it. This went on and the earth now equalled the darkness of hell. He understood the meaning of this majestic event. During the initial stage, the earth had been like a blazing fire. That mass had condensed to such an extent that he compared it with a fire of tremendous magnitude. He could not think of an other explanation.

This remained for a considerable time. The power that brought all this about was indescribable. It looked like it had been lit from the inside. When something is on fire, dark clouds of smoke billow up, but here they stayed together, which he found amazing. This phenomenon was like a fierce hurricane sweeping over the earth and spreading death and destruction. The earth was like an erupting volcano, but the entire mass remained close together; something kept it that way.

He now felt the meaning enter his mind. How marvellous, he thought, it was brought about by what was above him, the atmosphere. The earth continued its process and he saw a following stage. Alcar now held a mental conversation with him.

That rolling mass condensed and he saw what it was to become. My God, how wonderful is Your power, he thought. That mass of clouds changed, and he saw that it became water, nothing but water, and in it he saw life. How is it possible, he thought; he had observed a similar process on the first planet. In this water, the first life was born. Yonder he saw the mother planet and all those other organs.

Tears ran down his cheeks now that he was allowed to see all this. It moved him deeply. Oh, how great is God in heaven; such might and power! He, who saw this, knew he was a tiny part of it all.

The earth followed that process, and now he saw that the condensation process had attained the next stage, because something separated and condensed in the water. Again he felt what that meant. That will become the negotiable planet, called earth. When this is complete and entirely condensed we will see the firm soil. He understood his leader, because he saw that it happened.

'I am now going to connect you with the next stage', he heard Alcar say. 'Millions of years have passed again, and you will see what happened in that time.'

The earth had come to rest. He saw land, trees and flowers, although as on the second cosmic degree. It was not the earth as he knew it.

'This is the first era experienced on earth, of which nothing is known today', he heard Alcar say. 'Thousands of centuries have passed. In the many waters on earth, a being has appeared like you have seen on the first planet. Here, man also followed a similar process and had passed on from his fish-like stage. Here, too, the lower part of the body split, the animal-like being reached the shore and man gained the negotiable planet. But once again billions of years have passed and in all those years the earth has reached this stage and has advanced that far. Now I'll pass on to the next stage and again millions of years have passed. Look in front of you, André.'

André was scared stiff. What he now saw he had seen before. He saw man and animal, as on the second cosmic degree. Man and animal had accepted their material condition. They were large and powerful. Were they the first human beings who had lived on earth, and were those animals the prehistoric species now extinct on earth?

He saw a wonderful vision passing by. Out of that luminous ball of fire, the earth had developed and out of that water, man, and animal, and yet everything was one condition, one event; one stage developed out of the other. The image he saw was wild and rugged. The animals which lived here were enormously large, although not quite as large as on the second cosmic degree, and man was hairy and strong, though his body differed from there. This material organism was more refined and more perfect, but the skin colour was dark. The white race was not yet known in this period.

'Everything is amazingly beautiful, Alcar.'

'This is the wonder the earth has experienced and where we were born. You will return to yourself, André, and I'll explain several events to you.'

André looked up at his leader, but could not say a word.

'Has all this moved you, my boy? It has deeply moved me and all beings who have seen this process. Now that we know what God's creation is, we work out how we have to live to thank our Holy Father for everything, no matter how our lives have been. We now see the first stage of the earth, the first era, about which, as I said before, nothing is known. You have seen that everything follows one course. All this did not come into being at once, but one stage developed out of the other. In this tremendous space, lay the All-encompassing and the simplicity, which we see in the entire universe. Had the third cosmic degree been ready before the mother planet had completed its task – I told you about it, but it will be much clearer to you now – chaos would have been the result. If man on the second cosmic degree had already been able to reach his highest material condition, one planet would, as it were, have crushed the other. But here is this Divine order, which we also find in our own material organism. Everything is present but one organ depends on the other, and acts through the other; it receives power and energy from the vital organs, and all this is also present in the material organism of man. What we observe, know and feel in ourselves also happened in the universe. The smallest insect - I told you about it - has the same activity as the planets have experienced. Feel how mighty it all is, and how simple the way it happened. This is amazing for man on earth and yet, if they could observe all this they would be silent at all this simplicity.

The planet earth is ready, but over there the mother planet is dying, as are the many other planets which have completed a similar task. Billions of years from now the earth will also die. When the last being

173

of the second cosmic degree has come here, and all those beings have reached the spiritual condition, the earth will accept what all those bodies had to accept and will dissolve to return to the invisible energy. At present the earth is building the material organism. Man must go to his highest attunement and will receive that here. You see that man lives here and the animal is also present, but all that life will die. Now look over there, André.'

André saw an enormous monster.

'Do you recognize that animal, André?'

'Yes, Alcar.'

This animal arrived on earth from the second cosmic degree, just as all life you observe has lived there. This is the mightiest and most sacred wonder of God we know; because every planet produced its own life, although all these planets were connected with each other. You see, André, the animal has now hardened.'

'Is that a tortoise, Alcar?'

'Indeed. But the animal is in the first stage of development. It is enormously large, but it will discard that size on earth. Man, too, has a different body than man in your time. Material life on earth begins, and the earth will beautify this material organism. Many thousands of years will pass and, during all those centuries, beautification proceeds. It is nature that changes this organism inwardly and outwardly. The skin colour will also change, and the enormous size is dropped. Man has a fixed cosmic degree and that attunement is approaching.'

'Is that the reason why people were so large, Alcar?'

'Indeed, you saw that on the second cosmic degree. Here on earth, size serves to reach perfection. At the same time, inner life, the life of the soul, develops on earth. However, man is still a prehistoric animal; in all those centuries, this animal being will change and attain that human degree. Everything reflects the plan of evolution. All those organs are present to pass on to this beautiful human organism we now possess, but it requires thousands of centuries.

Man and animal passed from one era to the next. In one era, thousands of animals species were born and died again to pass on to an other organism. The prehistoric animal species dissolved, and out of this process the many other animals emanated. Then a time came when the winged animal was born; man, too, had already gone through various changes. The dark skin colour became lighter, and the earth beau-

174

tified the fine organism, so that man could pass on to his final stage. Still, for all of us, in your own time, the highest condition and material degree have not yet come. Dark races are still living in the jungle, which have to pass on into that condition and attain the highest degree. These races should not be confused with the oriental type, because that type belongs to the perfect material being. The being in reduced and yet beautified shape, as seen in the first cosmic degree, is found again on the second cosmic degree. Man now living on earth has the perfect human condition, which comprises seven transitions before the highest degree is attained.

What happened on all those planets, we find again on earth. However, a different process occurs on earth, which is for the embellishment of the material organism.

It is therefore not surprising, André, that there are still dark races on earth. In the billions of years, which have passed, these beings have not yet advanced that far, and millions of years are still required. But however long it may last, it must happen. A time will come when there are no more dark people on earth, then all those species of people have passed on into one species, which is the highest material degree we know. Then man can no longer be born in the jungle for the simple reason that man has passed into an other race, the second material stage. But as long as there are planets inhabited with a second cosmic attunement, beings will live in the jungle and the first stage cannot dissolve, because they emanate from an other planet and pass on to the third cosmic degree. It will take billions of years before the last human and animal beings will arrive on earth.

You surely understand that the earth must exist and that there is no question yet of destruction or perishing, for God would then destroy His own life, which is of no use for the creation. In time, the earth will dissolve, but then life has lived on all planets, and discarded them, and has passed on to those regions which are ready for the fourth cosmic degree. It will now be clear to you why we find all those conditions on earth. Why there is sorrow and misery, and why all those different material organisms exist, you can now accept and understand. If scientists would know all this, they would feel how far they have advanced, how much they have learned and discarded, before they entered that material degree. But as long as they cannot understand their own lives and continue to see death as a process of total destruction, they will not advance any further, and remain blind to God's creation. All of us, who once lived on earth and have entered the spheres of light, have experienced all this. It is our origin, out of that which happened, we emanate.

A magnificent image has been shown and explained to you, André. I can't follow the various eras now, it would be too much; what I told and showed you, André, will suffice. On our next journey I will tell you more about it. But you now understand the meaning of being on earth.

The way the earth completed its task is wonderful. The other planets, too, had to perform a tremendous function, but the task of the earth is awe-inspiring.

When man lived in his first and prehistoric era, food was available for him and also for the animal kingdom. Also, in later times, when the human being of the first material condition had reached the second, third, fourth, fifth, sixth, and seventh stage and the human organism as well as the inner organs had reached a much higher and more beautiful level, the earth also provided food for all this life. In whatever stage man and animal lived, there was food for them.

But man, who was still in a pre-animal condition, awakened, and with it good and evil came into being on earth; which certainly, already existed on all those other planets, but there man had not yet been conscious of it. You do feel that the inner life followed the material life, and could not attain that high degree. Even at this moment, now that millions of years have passed, inner life has not changed in the least. There are still pre-animal-like beings on earth in that material and spiritual attunement. And it will again take millions of years before every being has accepted the human condition.

We are again on earth, André. We have made a long journey. Are there things you have not understood?'

'There are small beings on earth, yet they are people like we are. What kind of degree is that, Alcar?'

'From the first cosmic degree onward, you have followed various stages of the human organism. These small beings lived on those first transitions, and what happened there also applies to the earth. You have been able to follow this process from the first stage on. What was born there is born here, but on earth this life receives a perfect material organism. What happened on the first transitions, is also found on earth because here a similar process came into being. Is that clear, André?'

'Yes, Alcar.'

'On the second cosmic degree you saw that those small beings, which were born out of the first stage, were destroyed. But here these beings united, which resulted in the various races populating the earth. That happened on earth, but it already occurred on the first transition, and on the second cosmic degree it was no different, but there, as also happens here, one group attacks the other. The groups which formed there have here grown into large tribes and races. Every degree unites, and this has been since the beginning of creation. No other creature can experience the life they possess. Nowadays, now that all those human races are being understood and investigated on earth, this study is taken up, but the real essence, the depth of all that life and of the material organism, will not be understood on earth, because they cannot follow the wonder of creation from the very beginning. That would still be possible - and I return to that again and again - if scientists could accept eternal advancement and reincarnation. That reincarnation - and that is my point, and is why you have been allowed to experience all this, and why I have shown you that on this journey - is for the material and spiritual organism. Both organisms are one; both intermingle. What is possible for the material organism, is also possible for the spiritual organism. If, during the first stage, the human embryo had not been animated, if that life could not have passed on into an other organism, we would not, as I have shown to you, have come onto earth and we would not have known that mighty wonder: creation. But God oversaw this, for God gave man a material organism and, although this organism was like a prehistoric animal species, it had to change, and that was the purpose of all those planets. The power those enormous objects possess, however strange it may sound, are also present in the material and spiritual organism. Everything is in harmony, and we find this compilation in everything.

In various ways I have shown to you, that this has to be so, or else we would not be beings with a Divine Spark, and would never be able to enter the universe and accept it as our own. In everything, from the very first moment, there is reincarnation. I can show you this in hundreds, nay thousands of conditions. Anyone on earth is an incarnation. Trees, flowers, and the entire animal kingdom have been on other conditions, other planets. If they had to stay there, they would not have advanced that far. If the first human being was pre-animal-like, and it took millions of years before it had advanced materially, it must be the soul, the spiritual body, which has experienced that. I will explain and show all that on our next journey. Now man has advanced that far, and the spiritual being owns this magnificent material organism. But inner life, the soul or spirit, will return in it thousands of times to acquire spiritual love, for this mightiness is God's pure love. Man not only needed millions of years for his material development, but also for his inner life. Both follow one course up to the very highest, which are the Divine Spheres. What inner life could not receive on the first cosmic degree, it acquired on the second. Thereafter, inner life received this magnificent organism which the earth would produce. But inner life, the life of the soul, which owns this organism as its dwelling, will return to acquire the spiritual love in this organism.

I showed you this mighty phenomenon on all our journeys. Later on, when we shall visit the first cosmic degree again and follow all those planets – most of them at any rate – and we see inner life grow and awaken, it will only then be clear to you that there must be reincarnation, or else all that God had created would have been in vain. And could that be possible? Would God, our Father, not have overseen that? I need not repeat that time and again, my boy, but I would like to repeat it on earth many times, so that their eyes finally open and they accept that this must be so, or we would not return to the Divine, and heaven would remain closed for us. But you will do it for us; together we shall lay down all this. Those who are honest, and do not place themselves on pedestals, will be able to accept it. Those who realize what nature is like, and that the earth has this cosmic image, and that this sacred event is also present in the mother, feel the sacredness and the simplicity of all this, how unbelievably deep it may be. Now what was possible for the male and female creature was also present during the first stage. What God accomplished billions of years ago, has remained in all those billions of years. But we go on, further and higher, once to enter Divine life.

And now, André, we shall return to your own organism. This journey is nearly over. I have been allowed to show you the creation of the universe. The masters had assigned me to do this and I have completed my task, at any rate for the material organism. On our next journey we shall follow the inner life of man and animal, in so far as my task concerns animal life. Then, as I said already, we shall again visit various planets and follow the life of the soul, pass from one world on to another, the astral world where the being lives that will be attracted. I'll explain and show you wonders of spiritual powers. All those wonders you experienced up to now were born and created through Divine inspiration.

What you have seen up to now, belongs to the visible energy, the invisible energy you will experience on our next journey. From the first moment of activity, when inspiration became instinct, I'll explain all this to you. You do feel what that means. Then we shall pass on to all those lives on earth and I'll explain why man returns there hundreds of times, and why it is always the earth, which attracts that being. That, my son, belongs to reincarnation, as did my friend whom we shall follow on a subsequent journey. Only then can I explain your own life and mine to you, and tell you why you have these spiritual gifts, which really belong to the life of the spirit, and why we are together and have to experience all this, necessary for the earth and humanity.'

André felt a sacred quietude enter him. This journey had been amazing for him. How great Alcar was. How tremendous was what he had been allowed to see, and yet, it was not sufficient; he was to receive still more.

He took his leader's hand and said: 'Alcar, how can I ever thank you.'

'Don't thank me for everything, thank God. But listen, I still have more to tell you. Meanwhile we shall go back to your material body, but we shall do it slowly so that I can explain one or two things to you, because I want to know whether you have understood everything.

When we were on the first cosmic degree, I spoke about the prehistoric animal species. The animal that was born there passed into an enormous organism in later times. As you have seen, this animal also lived on earth. I have also explained that this animal has to experience thousands of transitions and organisms before reaching the highest degree in its condition. I said that there were hundreds of animal species in one degree and I compared that with the cat and the panther you know on earth. But what I want to say is this: these pre-animal species we have seen on those planets, have dissolved in the All. Not only materially, but also spiritually. Do you feel that, André?'

'Yes, Alcar.'

'Splendid, then I'll go on. What applies to all those planets, also applies to the animal kingdom; it had to dissolve, because the animal living on earth was born out of those animals. I also said that the animal kingdom is deeper than the attunement of man, although that attunement is Divine. That is also clear to you, isn't it?'

'I perfectly understand you, Alcar.'

'The animal, therefore, has in its condition a degree, its material organism, but passes in that degree on to hundreds of transitions. The thousands of bird species - and how many are there on earth - have seven material and spiritual degrees. The seventh degree, and that is my point, goes, as we do, higher and higher, like for instance, the pigeon and other species. We find those animal species again on our side and they are our spiritual friends in this life. Also the dog and the horse we can call back on our side and they stay near us, although they live in their own world. That is marvellous. So you see that the noble animal species has the highest material degree, or it would not be able to advance on our side. If it has not yet acquired that degree, we find the species as predators, and for predators there is no room on our side. Do you feel all that, André?'

'If I have understood you correctly, Alcar, a pre-animal monster cannot live in the spheres of light?'

'Indeed; very good; that is what I wanted to explain. On this side, in our life, there is only room for the higher animal species, to which the various winged species belong. A pre-animal monster, therefore, has gone that long material and spiritual route and passed on into a higher species to return, just as we do, to God.'

'And that applies to man and animal, Alcar?'

'Yes, André.'

'So the time will come that brown-black people are no longer on earth?'

'Indeed, André', those human degrees, as I said, must also dissolve. I am glad you have understood everything. Races will indeed be present, but the first six degrees dissolve into the seventh degree, because the soul must experience that.'

'If I have understood you correctly, there will only be higher animal species and spiritual people on earth when the end of the earth is near.'

'That is obvious, André. Only then, as I said, will there be quietude and peace on earth and man will live in a paradise, which is God's intention. But millions of years will pass before that stage is reached. That is the final picture I can show you of the earth. The planet earth will then undergo what the other planets already experience; the earth has completed its task.'

'How mighty is everything, and yet so natural, Alcar.'

'So it is, André, mighty and natural. We can solve the most difficult problems, because we know the material and the spiritual organism. If man can accept this, I assure you, quietude and peace will come on earth.'

'May I ask another question, Alcar?'

'Yes, André, you still can.'

'Can you explain to me, Alcar, why a pigeon has that wonderful instinct?'

'Listen, André. A pigeon has the highest material and spiritual degree any animal species of the animal kingdom can acquire on earth. Fundamentally, that animal and all other animal species belonging thereto, as I explained to you, have a more advanced and higher feeling than many human beings on earth. The animal acts in accordance with its inner possession and those feelings of the man who has attained the spiritual spheres of light on our side. The intuition of this little animal, according to which it acts, is the telepathic degree we also have.

This little animal, released far away from its home, concentrates on its own possession, in this case its home, and it is infallibly attracted to that place. Do you feel what I mean, André?'

'Yes, Alcar, everything is now clear to me.'

'So everything is feeling, which we had to acquire. The animal has also advanced that far in those millions of years. Whenever I wish to connect myself with anyone on earth, I will find that life, wherever it may be. The pigeon acts as I do and arrives at its destination. In other animal species, other organs have developed to the highest degree, and their attunement is between the first and seventh material degree. The many species of birds of migration which travel to warmer regions in winter are not essentially different. That is why the animal kingdom is more complicated than the human being. Have you understood everything now?'

'Yes, Alcar.'

'You have seen a lot, for which you should be thankful to our Holy Father.'

'Shall I know all this consciously, Alcar?'

'Yes, André. To acquire all this in day-consciousness will be more difficult than in the past, but I'll help you and you will get through it.'

Soon they arrived and André entered his home.

'Everything is so amazing, Alcar.'

'We'll take leave now, my boy. I'll pick you up soon, when we shall return to all those planets and follow the life of the soul from the beginning of creation. Farewell, André, God bless you.'

André knelt before his leader and thanked him for everything. He descended in his material organism and the journey was over.

THE END OF PART ONE

# PART TWO

## The Life of the Soul

# CHAPTER I

## *Disembodiment*

SEVERAL weeks had passed since the last spiritual journey André had made with his leader Alcar. He had assimilated everything he had experienced on this journey and was prepared to receive nourishment for the mind. Alcar had told him that he would spiritually leave his body today. He would be shown inner life from the beginning of creation. He had gone to his room early and waited for Alcar to release him from his material body.

It had been difficult for him lately. His mind had had to absorbe all this. Night and day he had meditated and pondered on everything he had experienced during his last journey. During the first days, Alcar had said, he should not think of anything but his material life. He had done so, but time and again all those spiritual experiences came back in his mind and he did not know how to cope with them. Yet, he had to go through it, as it was within him, his spirit had experienced it.

His inner and spiritual life dominated and his nerves could not bear that. There were moments he could not tell one thing from an other which made it very difficult for him. He felt he lived between two worlds, of which spiritual life dominated, and yet he had to remain himself, which was not easy.

The first days after he had made his spiritual journey went by as usual. He felt free from all these spiritual laws and experiences. Yet, all these feelings returned consciously and he lived in an inconceivable condition. He felt very far away from the earth and yet he was on earth like everybody else.

Deep within him resided all that power, nevertheless he had to acquire all this, in order to possess his experiences.

Alcar had told him to meditate. On the side beyond everybody meditated. When people had died on earth and entered spiritual life and were convinced of this life, they secluded themselves to contemplate all this in order to acquire it, when they were ready for fresh nourishment for the mind.

He, too, now had to do likewise, and he understood why Alcar had said that it would now be more difficult than after all those other spir-

185

itual journeys he had experienced. The tremendous power of everything he had experienced weighed heavily on him.

In the spirit, when he was on the side beyond, everything was straightforward. But now he had to digest this in his material life on earth. However difficult it was for him, it was a marvellous period, because he went through everything again. Once he had started, he left no time unused and the days passed in a flash. In this condition he was no longer aware of time; in thought he was constantly on the side beyond. He followed everything where he had been with his leader Alcar, and in doing so he progressed step by step. Whenever it became too much for him, he stopped and waited for new energy.

He had been doing this for several days when he felt he could not go on any longer; his nerves could not digest this awe-inspiring experience.

From the start of his connection with Alcar, his leader had always seen to it that he could sleep. A good night's sleep was vital, he could not miss an hour. His life on earth was too intense, because he lived a double life: the life of a spirit and that of man on earth. Inner rest was essential and it was always given him in his sleep.

But now he could no longer sleep and it frightened him. He had gone to bed early, but could not fall asleep. He concentrated on it, but he could not control his material body, though he had succeeded before. He was aware of this danger. A mighty problem faced him. He pondered what powers he could use, but he failed, because his inner life dominated. My God, he thought, will this work out well, how do I get through this. These problems had never thrown him out of balance, he was always in control of himself, as his material body should be free from disturbances. He often wondered how his nerves could digest all that spiritual wisdom, but he knew, that he was being watched by his leader Alcar.

But this time he was in a disharmonic condition. All these spiritual degrees, attunements, stars and planets, all these animal conditions and all that he had seen in the temple of the soul, were swimming before his eyes, so that he could not tell one thing from another and all this prevented him from sleeping. His head and nerves could no longer cope and he was afraid to lose himself. Would Alcar come to his aid?

Without perfect health in his material life he would be of no use to Alcar, because material and spiritual body must be in harmony. Nothing should be the matter with his material organism lest he would perish by what he experienced on the side beyond and had to pass on to mankind.

It was not the object to build up something and then run it down; it was not the way and would be terrible.

It is a mighty grace to be a medium for higher spirits, but people should realize what his life was like and what it required.

He had been awake for several hours and could not sleep. He turned from one side to the other, concentrated on sleep, but this time it did not work. He prayed fervently but in vain. Now what?, he thought.

He concentrated on his leader Alcar and after a while he began to observe. There was Alcar; he would soon be asleep now and be fit in the morning to start to meditate, and acquire everything. How happy he was when he heard his leader say: 'Can't you sleep, André?'

'No', he said, 'I cannot get asleep, my mind keeps me awake.'

He heard his leader say: 'You cannot and may not sleep now, my boy, I am keeping you awake.'

'I beg your pardon?' André asked full of surprise.

'I don't want you to sleep, André, you will stay awake until morning, but then you will sleep. I'll tell you a few things about this condition.'

'Is it because of my experience at your side, Alcar?'

'Yes, André. Your inner life strongly dominates your material body, the nervous system, but you know that I am watching and that nothing will happen to you.'

'Do I have to stay awake all night, Alcar?'

'No, that is not necessary.'

'Why then do you keep me awake?'

'Because your spiritual life dominates and you can't sleep anyway. Better meditate now and ponder on everything until sleep overtakes you. Day time is now too short for your inner life; together we shall try to harmonize again. Do you see what I mean, André?'

'Yes, Alcar, it is quite clear to me.'

'Now listen to what I have to say. If people on earth knew this, there would not be so many neurotics. Spiritual life now dominates the material organism. When this happens, people think they have to sleep; if, instead, they went through all their problems and troubles, in short everything that occupies their mind, by meditation until they had fully considered their problems, an other condition would set in, and they would return to normal life. That is the balance between spiritual and material body, and the nervous system will relax. Then, a stroll in nature, especially along the beach yields wonderful strength. But man is not attuned to nature and would rather take medicine, paralyzing the vital organs and constituting the nervous system.

Your nervous system is now overstrained and your spiritual body, which is emotional life, dominates; but a few hours' sleep will be sufficient. It demands your full attention and concentration. However, you want to sleep, the time of night compels you to rest, but this is wrong. If we would go for a walk and return in the morning, you would receive more rest than by staying in bed for days on end. However, that is not possible, as your family would get anxious; we shall do it our way. If I don't succeed you will leave your material body, although you would have to assimilate that.

You clearly feel that your mind dominates, because of all those problems I made you experience and the nourishment for the mind you received on this side. I have given and shown you, André, the very last you can receive as our instrument, and which we reveal to mankind. A few years ago it would not have been possible, you would have succumbed; but I proceeded cautiously and guided you from one spiritual condition to the other. As a result you awakened. We passed from one sphere to another. On our first journey to the darkness, as you remember, our life overwhelmed you, and we had to return to earth. Yet you had to go through it, so that I could explain everything concerning our life to give mankind a picture of life on this side. Ten, nay twenty times you fainted, because the powers of darkness dominated your inner self. Those who do not know the darkness, which is hell on this side, cannot form an idea of it. But everybody dying on earth and entering here, will experience it and they will wonder how you could have endured and assimilated that on earth without disturbing your life on earth and particularly without sapping your material body.

You got through that as well, you earnestly want to serve us. Your faith in our work and your love for it gave you that strength and opened you to our help. And another thing: if you had not kept your gifts pure and clean, you would irrevocably have perished and have landed in some asylum, because you would have fallen into the hands of evil. However, I could always reach you and I am grateful to you, so that I could explain our life.

I progressed further and deeper and knew many years beforehand that the time would come when I would be allowed to show you the very last of our life. You know, André, nothing for nothing: this too, all this spiritual wisdom, you will have to pay for with your inner energy. But I am with you and I'll help you with everything and we shall get through this as well.

If you have understood me correctly, you feel that daytime is too short to have spiritual and material harmony and to fall asleep. The seven degrees of sleep I explained to you before. You cannot attain the fourth degree now, your spiritual body will not allow it, as the preponderance present in your spiritual life is too great. This strain dissolves by meditating, staying awake, and natural harmony between spiritual and material life returns.

But man who does not know this, leans over backward and wants to sleep. Yet he will not fall asleep, and when he takes to medicine he tries to attain the desired condition by force and will not achieve his aim.

For isn't it true, that the spirit will free itself and man will wake up and sedatives have no effect on the material organism? The tremendous power of emotional life which is the spiritual body, man or scholar cannot fathom, as he does not know the spiritual body and does not accept its action. They will wake up anyway and no material means nor concentration will be of any use. They consult various doctors, or turn to natural cure, but they forget they have to go back to their youth, to the first moment they could not sleep, because that is the cause of the disturbance. The disturbance occurred in that period and the spirit cannot omit anything. You do feel how deep this is and I could tell a lot about it, as it concerns life on our side and is the eternal action of inner life.

Inner life compels them to meditate, but they do not think of that.

You know our life, André, you know how we meditate before we can settle down. Even if you were not able to sleep for days on end, it would not be as bad as forcing yourself to sleep.

On the side beyond we cannot move an inch when our mind is not at peace and problems keep us occupied. All these cares, struggle and sorrow and the many diseases people suffer on earth, deprive them of their sleep. But I assure you that we cannot sleep either when something keeps us occupied, because we live and are conscious; our life is like earthly and material life; nothing has changed. We have to be in harmony with everything and this also applies to people on earth. When something keeps our mind occupied we stay before falling asleep, as Gerhard*) explained to you.

Having woken up, our inner life is ready again to receive fresh nourishment for the mind, but we cannot fall asleep before our mind is idle and another action can set in. This action manifests itself in natural tiredness, and that is for our life, our inner life and the material organism for man on earth. When it is not completely in harmony and the material organism or the spiritual body dominates, a disease is caused. It usually concerns the nervous system, but people suffering from some disease will experience an aggravation of their complaint. This has an enormous action, because when someone suffers from a complaint; when vital organs are affected, for instance the kidneys, these organs dominate the mind, because the illness is more intensive than spiritual life and the latter responds to the action of the material organism.

Everything is interrelated and connected and it is not possible for those people to sleep. Although not normal, that sleep is better than the other condition when inner life directly concentrated on the nervous system and overburdens the material organism.

Your case, André, is different; your material body is in perfect health. Only your spirit is awake and conscious, even over conscious, and now we check this so that you will fall asleep in a few hours. You should try to stay fully conscious and not fall asleep. Slowly the dominating force will flow back into your inner life; this will restore the balance and the inner strain is reduced. Do you feel what I mean, André?'

'Yes, Alcar; thank you for everything.'

'Think of our life and follow me. Do not concentrate, in other words, do not try to acquire what I explain, but listen to what I say. This way you will restore the balance between your material body and inner life. You allow your inner life to do its work. When ready, your consciousness descends into your inner life and your material body experiences sleep.

The human body and its inner life are profound; both are powerful, one is dependent on the other; although inner life dominates the material organism on earth in everything. It directs, guides and keeps it intact, as the material organism lives through our inner life.

It is now four o'clock in the morning, André. Wait a moment and you will hear.'

*) See the book: 'The Bridge to Eternal Life'.

190

'It is amazing, Alcar, that you know that too and think of it.'

'Do not forget, my boy, that I also live on earth, and follow you and know everything that happens on earth. Listen, the clock strikes four and now you will soon sleep. Inner life has performed its task and the material body can now sleep. You feel that sleep slowly returns, and you yourself control it.'

André felt that he got tired and blissfully relaxed. He knew where this relaxation came from and who brought it about.

Though very far away, he heard Alcar say: 'Sleep, my boy, know that I am watching and will continue to watch until our work is finished.' He then was fast asleep.

When he woke up in the morning, he felt fit and cheerful. He did not feel tired any more and remembered what Alcar had told him. He immediately began to meditate, and continued until that day was past and he was going to sleep again. Yet, there was something, he had not yet experienced in all those years. He felt a terrible stress at the back of his head. He felt like he had to carry all these planets and was in the middle of those enormous objects and that all this was in and around his head. It was an awful sensation; yet he felt composed. His entire body was tense and strained, and he felt he could not cope with it himself. If only this will not be too much for me, he thought, I am not myself now, my nerves cannot stand this.

He concentrated on his leader Alcar; soon he saw Alcar near him and heard him say: 'I am going to help you again, André. You will leave your body, and you will see from this side what I am going to do and what the condition of your nervous system is like.'

'Are we going to make an other journey, Alcar?'

'No, not yet, first you must be fully prepared and have assimilated everything in day-consciousness, before you can receive fresh nourishment for the mind.'

André felt himself sink away and knew what would happen. When he opened his eyes he was in the life of the spirit. Alcar stood in front of him and received him.

'Alcar, my good Alcar.'

'You are hard put now, André, but all those difficulties are outweighed by what you have experienced. You will get through and your nervous system will again obey the will you impose.'

'Does being here give any rest, Alcar? My body is now fast asleep, and I am on this side. Isn't that rest, or is it not the same?'

'I can answer all your questions. No, this is not the rest you receive in your material body. First of all it would not be possible to leave your body if I did not bring that about; and if we would now visit the spheres, you would find in the morning that you could no longer think. The nervous system of your material body is overstrained by the tremendous power you impose on it; which is, when you are in your material body, the inner life or the spiritual body. Do not forget when you leave your material body, that your body is free from spiritual life, because this life which moves and directs that body, then lives on this side outside the material organism. To those living on earth, your material body is apparently dead. Your material body is one percent active. You are the ninety-nine percent living here. Obviously, your material body cannot function at full strength; it cannot act and recovery of your nervous system is not possible. Is that clear, André?'

'Yes, Alcar.'

'Well then, my will-power dominates all this; also your leaving your body, and, as I said, I control your material body. Your material body is experiencing something, because inner life, you yourself, has left its organism. When something is paralyzed it cannot function.

When the nervous system is strained and sedatives are administered in order to sleep, the natural functioning is paralyzed and recovery is excluded. Sedatives only give temporary relief, but later we are confronted with the same process; the organs are affected and forced out of action. Therefore, André, it is wrong to take too many sedatives for this disorder. You will understand that leaving your material organism does not provide the same rest as a good night sleep. The present condition of your material organism is deeper than normal sleep and the organism is deprived of its normal functioning. Leaving the body cannot help either, unless both bodies are in harmony. To leave the body, the spirit must be sensitive and not be strained or overburdened and there should be no sorrow or misery. You will also understand what these gifts require before we can use them. Thousands of people could leave their body and all of them would become mentally ill. One body would dominate and completely destroy the material organism. This, and this only, is the reason why the mystic warns against occultism, it is the domain of the spirit, and those not acquainted with all these effects are irrevocably lost. But I guide you in everything, and watch over your

192

spiritual and material bodies.

I'll do the following: I'll descend into your material body and relax your nervous system, I will live on earth again and you will live in my world. My concentration restores rest and peace in your organism, after which that nervous stress has disappeared. Farewell, André, I take possession of your body.'

André saw this miracle happen and Alcar descend into his material body. How miraculous life on this side is, he thought. How well he was protected; his leader saw to everything. Now he was alone on the side beyond. He observed an amazing scene. How great Alcar was and how mighty everything he experienced. How well Alcar took care of him. Whoever could accept this and all his recent experiences? Nothing was known on earth of what happened now. Miracles in the spirit.

He saw Alcar completely pass into his material body and then awaken. His material organism now resumed its activity and his organs continued their task. If anything could convince people of eternal life, it was the miracle he now experienced. And they would believe it if only they could see and calculate it. But how could scientists on earth calculate it? Those who could not accept it would never find out. To him it was a great miracle, and the amazing thing was, that a spirit, a man who had lived on earth and now lived in eternity, could descend into a material organism and take possession of it. He witnessed yet another miracle. He fully understood what his leader meant. Alcar commanded great mental and tremendous will-power. Because Alcar was further advanced than he was, and could bring this about. He himself had no complete command of his material body, which was quite natural.

He heard Alcar say: 'Think of yourself, André, and reflect on everything given to you recently.'

He did as Alcar wished and found it quite amazing; everything was straightforward, he penetrated the deepest problems without the least trouble. He did not want nor dare to move away from his body although it was possible. He also felt that he remained in communication with Alcar and that he could even speak. Spiritual life was awe-inspiring. He watched Alcar and saw a powerful blue light radiating from the back of his head. Yes, he thought, that is where the strain is. How amazing this is, he thought. Alcar radiated his head, because the nerves in his head were overstrained. That powerful light was his leader's. He could now see through his own material body. Nothing was concealed from him. He saw and felt the severe strain and understood what Alcar did. Meanwhile, he followed everything he had experienced, which was easy now.

He saw himself in the temple of the soul, he descended to all those planets and slowly returned to his material body. Yet he remained near his organism, but he experienced and contemplated what he had received on that journey. He felt that several hours had passed. Within him was the quiet and stillness of spiritual life. A dense haze now enveloped his material body and he felt that his leader had arranged it. It was the light-blue radiance he had observed a minute ago and he understood why his leader had done this. It secluded him from other influences. He also felt what his material body had received and that his nervous system was relaxed.

Several hours had passed and Alcar was still in his material body. He walked around in the vicinity and he could see everything clearly. He passed through everything and he could touch material objects but not move them. It was night on earth, but in the world he now lived in, it was light. He knew what this meant, Alcar had explained this too. It was his own inner possession; without it he would now wander in darkness. His mental possession told him that he would have light on the side beyond when his time had come. And although his light was not as powerful as Alcar's radiance, he felt reassured and happy.

For the spirit there is no night and day. The radiance and love one inwardly possessed provided light on this side. A little bit of light was his possession and he could be content. It was already strong enough to make him see. He would do his best to make it a strong light. He concentrated on it, he wanted to serve; for this power could only be obtained by serving. He felt that he was getting tired and understood that this feeling came from his body. When he had sensed this, Alcar had left his body and rejoined him.

'Well, my boy, that is done.'

'Did you achieve what you wanted, Alcar?'

'Yes, André, completely. Aren't you tired?'

'Yes, I felt tired a moment ago.'

'You see how intensely the solar plexus reacts and conveys material strength. This plexus enables you to feel your material condition. I have relaxed your nervous system. When you return into your material body, you will soon fall asleep. You have experienced everything again, but you have to start anew tomorrow because it happened outside your body and your material organism must also experience it. Here, on our side, everything is different; you are free from all those disturbances and you are yourself. That body still belongs to you, and you are its working power and operate it. I have rendered you a service; you relaxed through my power. When you wake up in the morning, that strain in your head will be over. In a few days we can continue and resume our work. You have understood what I did, haven't you?'

'Yes, Alcar, I think so.'

'I merely concentrated on the nervous system, that was all. I relaxed it by concentration and tomorrow you do the same and meditate calmly. Farewell, my boy, I will watch.'

André descended into his material body and woke up. How tired I am, he thought. His body felt very tired, he could hardly lift his legs. He looked at his leader, who was near him, and fell asleep.

In the morning, when he woke up, he felt very fit and knew what he had experienced that night. He began to think again and thought all day. He saw the moment he entered his organism, when leaving his body and the journey had ended.

In the evening he heard Alcar say: 'Wash yourself with cold water tonight, André, before you go to bed; go for a walk and concentrate on nature.'

André went for a walk and felt very fit when he entered his house. Then, before going to sleep, he washed himself with cold water and after a short while enjoyed a sound and natural sleep.

When he woke up, he had slept for nine hours and felt he could move mountains. The first thing he now did, was fall to his knees to thank God for everything. Then he prayed for strength for Alcar; that he might always receive that strength. He was ready, yet he retraced everything again from beginning to end and this time he progressed more rapidly. Very quickly he went the long road he had followed with his leader. When he was ready – he clearly felt this – he could, if Alcar would connect him, speak for ten hours on end and tell people of the universe and all those planets. It had now become his own knowledge, his own inner possession; his material body had absorbed it and he was happy with the experience. He also felt different, as if he had grown older and had lived for hundreds of years. Yet only eight days had passed since he had made this disembodiment.

He had been Alcar's instrument for nine years, but to him they seemed nine hundred years. That was how he felt, for he had had to digest so very much in those nine years.

He could now fathom the deepest problems at a glance. In a flash he felt the depth of every problem, spiritual or material. Most simple for him were the spiritual problems people on earth presented to him. He had achieved this because he wanted to, and he faced everything in order to be a worthy instrument for his high leader. It took all his energy, his deepest inner strength and personality, but when he had gone through he would not like to do without. How well he now knew people; he could see into everybody. Now he knew how God's creation had come into being; how everything was created. It was awe-inspiring, and yet so simple. How difficult all those days had been, but he was ready again to leave his body.

Several weeks had passed. He would now learn about the life of the soul, which was even deeper than what he had experienced. He would get through and acquire it and then he would understand creation.

# CHAPTER II

## *The Divine Spark*

HE waited for things to happen and he soon began to feel the first signs. Slowly his spiritual body was lifted and entered the spiritual world. Alcar stood in front of him. He approached his leader and took both his hands.

'We are together again, André. You have acquired everything you have experienced during our previous journey. You will now experience new miracles. We shall soon be on our way and you know where we shall go; back to the first planet. While on our way, I shall explain a thing or two.'

They floated away from the earth.

André felt very happy.

'How shall I thank you, Alcar, for what you have done for me and are still doing.'

'It is to my own advantage, my boy, if your material body is not in good health, I cannot work. I have to watch your health and you help me, because you follow me in everything.'

'If people had sufficient concentration, Alcar, surely there would not be so many neurotics?'

'Exactly, André, those who control their condition are master over their material organism, at any rate when no other ailments undermine their bodies. One is often powerless to do anything about them, and many die from those ailments.'

'What do you think of my patient, who has not eaten for three years now?'

'She is a miracle, André; I mean her material organism.'

'I don't understand, Alcar, why doctors are not interested.'

'There are so many things they are not interested in. This patient is a miracle to them, but if they would examine her, it would still remain a mystery that she stays alive without eating. If they knew the powers of man on the fourth comic degree, they would exclaim: My God, how is it possible that there are people who can keep alive on light, air and warmth.'

'Is food not required there, Alcar?'

'No, André, and that is very simple. Isn't it remarkable that, according as man concentrates on spiritual life, the material organism reacts immediately and does not require what it used to consume to preserve the body. Again we see that the spiritual body dominates, even must dominate; because it is obvious that higher beings do not require food and only consume what is necessary to maintain the material organism.

On the first planets, man ate raw meat, and on earth, too, people eat meat; but on the fourth cosmic degree all are vegetarians. The main nourishment is what nature provides and there are thousands of sorts of fruits. All this will also change on earth. Your patient is in an amazing condition.

You know the way her material organism feeds; I explained that to you. She only needs small quantities of juice, that's all.'

'Will she die from this ailment, Alcar?'

'She will pass away like everybody else. It is not true that this advances her passing away, or she would have been on this side long ago. She is alive and remains alive. She does feel weak and tired, but still does her work; she is busy from early morning till late at night and lives like anyone else of normal health. And yet, her condition is a great miracle.'

'But what is it, Alcar, that keeps her alive?'

'There is food for her in the atmosphere, André, and I am speaking the truth when I say that man will no longer eat in the highest attunement, and only take what is present in and around him in the atmosphere. Do not forget that everything that grows and blooms from the earth is present in the universe as invisible energy, which can also be used as food when our inner life attracts and receives it through concentration.

Well then, that patient does not have that strength and does not know anything about it; but she obtains food unconsciously from that invisible reservoir. That energy is present; she inhales it and her spirit, which is very strong for earthly standards, now dominates her material organism. In essence it is very simple, but for people on earth she is a great mystery. This, however, is her condition.'

'It is also surprising, Alcar, that she still does her work.'

'She has a strong will and a pure faith. By means of her faith she absorbs that invisible energy; it is the love she possesses and we know that love is everything; it is the strength by which we adjust ourselves to the visible and invisible and pass on. In addition, she receives your radiance.

Once again, for people on earth she is a great mystery, but I see through that mystery and know how it works, know her life, materially as well as spiritually.'

'Do all people on the fourth cosmic degree already live as she does?'

'No, not yet, they live there on what nature provides. But the higher man advances towards his attunement, the purer becomes his inner life. Once there, they live again in a material body, and are spiritual beings living in a material condition. When we can no longer eat meat because we discarded our earthly organism many years ago, and when you know that we love everything and all life, that we pass from one condition into a higher one to acquire ever more love, you do feel that we shall experience a life quite distinct from that we had on the planet earth. On the fourth cosmic degree they adjust themselves to advancing further and live on in pure love. As I said before, there is serenity and peace and people are sisters and brothers in spirit.'

'Do they know there what the Divine Spark is, Alcar?'

'They all know they are children of one Father, and that they themselves are that spark which is related to God. The more love they acquire, the greater that spark of God becomes; it strengthens their inner life and they pass to the higher spheres. Their inner light shows us how far they have advanced. The spark of God which is within them and constitutes their whole being, which they are themselves, radiates according to the love they acquired.'

'On earth they cannot find out, Alcar, what exactly the spark of God is.'

'That is obvious, my boy. Do you know yourself what that spark of God is like and how it has come into us, now that you have experienced the plan of creation, André?'

'No, Alcar, I must frankly admit it is still a great problem for me. I know what it is, you explained it; but how it all happened and has come into us, is not quite clear to me.'

'So your question was rather meant for yourself, than for man on earth?'

'Yes, Alcar, also for myself, as I would like to know it.'

'Listen. I have explained how God's creation was accomplished. You have observed how everything happened and that everything which lives in the universe is God's own life. A planet is a spark, a mighty source of energy, and that applies to all planets and stars which have taken their place in the universe, and to everything belonging to the invisible energy. I told you that. In everything, in trees and plants, is God's life that is why it lives or it would not exist. It lives because it has to live, because it is God's life; but there is something different in animal and human life. It has been in us from the beginning of creation, because we and the animal kingdom emanated from that tremendous event. God split, divided Himself in billions of particles and from that moment on it was preordained that man was to have a will of his own, and that will, that is that being, is a particle of God. During the first stage man, this particle of God, possessed no consciousness. This particle should first of all receive a splendid organism; that was the object of the entire creation and that was to become man. The spark of God, as will be clear to you now, is fundamentally energy, and this energy originated from God, what is called God. Our entire existence, André, as a human being, is that spark of God, as are all those planets, everything living in the universe. But man, and this will be clear to you now, not only received God's own life, he also passed into His sacred life. God wanted us through His attunement to become like God, to pass consciously into the universe and to acquire that.

A spark of God is the animal on earth, a piece of stone, a fragment of iron, but we are the conscious, inspiring beings who have received this gift from God.

Therefore, André, we people represent our Holy Father; God gave us His own self; He is in and around us and remains so eternally. Like we concentrate to pass on into something, to achieve something; like we have to think with our entire inner being in order to attain and accomplish the object of our attention, God created us and all existing life which serves us and which we need to consciously enter that Divine condition. That Divine power is present within us; we are that power and it is up to us to go for it; to become the conscious Divine being. Is it clear now what the Divine Spark is?'

'Yes, Alcar, quite. It is me.'

'Quite so, my boy. You are that spark of God, you are a particle of God, you emanate from that which is God, your life represents God's own life. Everything belonging to creation is God, or a particle thereof. His holy life is within us, but it is up to us to acquire it.'

'That inspiration, if I put it correctly, Alcar, has been there from the first moment, hasn't it?'

'When you observed the first flashes of light in the temple of the soul, it happened for a fixed purpose. We were already represented in those flashes. By that action, or concentration, if I may put it that way, we were to receive ourselves. We received our personality by that inspiration or concentration as we emerged from it. It is clear that the human will, the personality, is implied therein; and that will is the relation to God, is His sacred life, which we have received. If this had not happened, we would belong to what is the universe. We would be invisible and belong to the invisible energy, like everything belonging to that form of life.'

'Are you now thinking of the darkness?'

'Yes, André, when nothing, nothing existed yet.'

'Is this inspiration present in everything, Alcar, in all life created by God?'

'Yes, André, but we know conscious and unconscious inspiration. Is that clear?'

'No, not quite. Does a stone, a tree and all other life comprising nature belong to the unconscious energy, Alcar?'

'Excellent, André, that is correct. When God created the universe, there was only inspiration. The first to appear were the stars and planets, the solar systems and thousands of other objects. Subsequently man, and this being was to have the ability to create. This also points to our Divine attunement. The next process, or the life that appeared, emanated from the first; because the first already possessed that miracle and created an other form of life. Then the animal kingdom came into being which emerged from the process of decay. But behind this, as a further stage and development to which the entire universe was subjected, was the condensation process of the universe, and all that life belongs to the unconscious energy. Is that also clear, André?'

'Yes, Alcar.'

'It served as unconscious energy; it served the first and second being, man and animal, as a condensed mass; it became the negotiable planet. Do you feel what I mean, André?'

'Yes, Alcar. A question strikes me, but I think I should not pose it.'

'I know what you want to ask me; so speak up.'

André looked at his leader and asked once more: 'May I ask that question; am I not ungrateful?'

'Everybody will ask that question; so speak up, André.'

'Well, what I thought is, Alcar, what was present when there was only darkness, before God revealed Himself? Can you explain that?'

André looked at his leader and waited for Alcar to speak. He felt the quietude of his leader enter him and he saw that Alcar concentrated on something. A tremendous power passed through him.

His leader was still silent and it occurred to him that he should not have asked this question, when Alcar said: 'No, my boy, I cannot answer that; only the cosmic masters, those who are cosmically orientated, can give you an answer; I can't. I feel this all-embracing conception; the answer is deep within me, but I am not yet aware of it. I am unable to express this inconceivable, mighty and impenetrable miracle in words. Still, the higher masters can give you an explanation, but you and I and man on earth will not be able to comprehend that process. At this side we have great respect for God's own life, and above all for that, which nobody knows yet. They received it the way we received the image of creation from the highest heavens. The masters cherish that wisdom as the most sacred possession, and bow their heads for what was present before creation.

Yes, André, God was present. God was and is eternal and will always be. When there was darkness, we were there too, because there was life and that life was God, were we, the animal and all those planets and stars. And now it would be revealed. That has happened and man and animal have advanced that far; they have returned to God. I cannot explain the essence of this problem; we have only learned the action and revelation, because it is what we are. I, too, bow my head for the most sacred, the moment when darkness still prevailed. This darkness contains what is also present in us, and which is not known on earth and will never be seen, because it is that invisible energy; it is God's own life and that cannot be seen, it can only be felt, but not until we have entered the Divine Spheres.'

'I am grateful, Alcar, that you have told me this. That question was put to me; however, it is too deep, too mighty and too sacred, but I kept thinking of it. When everything was ready, Alcar, and the planets condensed, how did the Divine Spark awaken?'

'The Divine Spark would awaken in us, André, and you will experience that on this journey.'

# CHAPTER III

## *The inspiring life*

WE would awaken, André, because we are Divine. We have to go on, ever further and higher, and as we advance and seek the good, we shall awaken. Everything is love; we therefore have to acquire the Divine love. That is our way, and it is only for man, because we have to return to God.

Look, the first planet. In order to explain everything, I have to connect you again with the past, with embryonic life.'

Alcar descended on the first planet. Again André was on this tremendous object where every human being had once been. They sat down on a high mountain.

Here everything would die. André thought of this process.

'This here in front of us, Alcar, is the visible energy; and what is around us and in which we live belongs to the invisible energy? If I understand you correctly, the ores and minerals a planet may contain, are present in the invisible?'

'Yes, indeed, everything emanates from the invisible.'

'Also gold and silver and other metals?'

'Yes, everything.'

'How amazing, Alcar.'

'If it had not been present in the invisible, it could not have come into existence. Although science has advanced quite far, it will advance further in the future. As true as gold is found in the earth, it is also present in the invisible. Everything the earth contains is present in the invisible; because everything is energy.'

'Do you think progress will be made in that respect?'

'Many inventions will be made, I discussed that already. It is now the technical age.'

'Do you know many inventions which will be discovered presently?'

'Yes, I see many, even very many.'

'Could you, Alcar, if you want to, mention such an invention?'

'Yes, I could, but it does not interest me. I only concentrate on the life of the soul; that is my task.'

'Yet it is remarkable that you could, Alcar.'

'Yes, André, I could, because I know many inventions.'

'Is that also your possession?'

'Yes, mine, and those who live in my own sphere. We see all those possibilities and we could bring them about, but man lacks nourishment for the mind, and that is most urgently required. Man should now learn his own attunement and when they know on earth that progress is possible, they will live as they should and as God wants them to, they will then receive wonders, and we know all those wonders. This very moment we know already what people will possess in five hundred years. There is more that they do not know, than they have already accomplished. But what good does it do, when all those wonders are used for the destruction of the highest being God created? That is their downfall, because there are already too many technical wonders on earth.'

'Can't you stop it?'

'Haven't I explained to you in the dark spheres, that the demons of hell bring this about? Haven't we visited the geniuses and masters of evil? God gave us, people, a will of our own; the Divine Spheres are open to us; we received everything; we have our happiness in our own hands. Haven't you known that for a long time?'

'Yes, Alcar, indeed.'

'What we can do is pass this on to mankind. We bring them happiness and through it they will learn to know themselves. The masters sent me and thousands of others to the earth to tell them of our eternal progress and to open them inwardly. We shall proceed in this way and once we shall have finished. When people on earth seek higher life, all those inventions will be used for the well-being of mankind. It is not until then that we shall come to the earth from this side to bring them all those technical wonders. Everything is established, André, but we on our side wait until they have advanced that far, until they understand their life on earth; this cannot commence until then. I am going to connect you with embryonic life. We will stay on this spot; from here I can explain everything. Pay attention, André. You can ask questions; that will be possible.'

André felt himself sink away. The condensed planet dissolved in front of him, he saw the past and the first stage appear. He recognized this stage from his previous journey and knew which moment he witnessed and what Alcar wanted to show him.

'Again you see, André, that the planet is condensing. We shall now descend into the astral world and reality; but first I will connect you with the first stage of the human embryo, because it is there that life, that driving force, that power, that action: the instinct began.'

André watched. He saw millions of cells.

'You see, my boy, we have again descended into the past and there in front of you lives the first embryo. When, as I explained, it came to life, when that spark, that life, passed into embryonic life, it was to become man, not only materially, but also spiritually. The power that brought this about is the Divine inspiration. This emanated from God; it was God's will and if this had not happened, one life would not have touched the other and the embryo would not have come to life. But the Divine inspiration passed into the embryo; nay, this young life was inspiration and the plan of evolution began in material and spiritual form. But what happened before this, André? Do you feel this miracle? Have you understood me on our previous journey? What wonder are we about to witness? Do you feel the depth of the process of revelation? I can go on asking you questions, but you must answer me first.'

André calmly thought for a long time, and said: 'I think I have understood what you mean. Out of this one body millions of lives were born. Is that what you mean, Alcar?'

'Indeed, André, that is what I mean, but how did it happen?'

Again André reflected upon this Divine wonder.

'How deep this is, Alcar, I do feel its entirety, but I cannot express myself.'

'Then I will help you, listen. I want you to feel and understand this. Haven't you noticed that we experience on this planet what happened in the entire universe? That out of this body millions of lives must appear, because this body also divides itself, like God divided Himself? That this applies to man and animal and all other life? Thus, out of this body emanated inspiring life, sparks of God, because a planet represents God's life. Every particle, however tiny, is God's life and will represent God as material and spiritual life. We have followed material life; inspiring life commences here. Each particle is inspiration, and is part of this planet and is the spark of God, because we were born out of God. It was accomplished by the condensation process; the process of revelation commenced when this planet divided itself. Everything we witness here points to this wonder; it could only happen here. Consequently, it was here that the soul was born; but it only knows action; there is definitely no consciousness; that must be born yet. Is that clear, André?'

'Yes, Alcar, now I feel this mighty event. How deep it is, and yet, how natural.'

'So it is, and we encounter this wonder in the entire creation in a perfect and mature condition. Thus, what happened was brought about by the driving power of the All-power, of which it forms a part.

'My point is to explain to you what inspiring life means and how everything happened. That first action, the touching and repulsion of embryonic life, was essentially nothing but the inspiring life, which we, human beings, had received as part of and attunement to God. Here, on this location, the first human stage, we feel and see already the direct attunement to God, because we, as inspiring and sensitive life, are a part of Him. Do you feel what I mean, André?'

'Yes, Alcar, perfectly.'

'Well then, during the second stage of human embryonic life, this action was no longer receiving, but it happened on its own power and this was the first ability man had acquired. During the first human stage man received it from his holy Father; during the second and further stages this was no longer necessary. Consequently, inspiring life was born during the first stage.

It will also be clear to you, that I could not and should not have told you anything about it on our previous journey, because you would not have understood it and you would not have been able to distinguish between one life and the other, nor between all those actions.

What happened for the material organism and what man received, was also meant for inner life, the life of the soul, which was to become the inspiration and the spiritual body. Therefore, life of the soul is the nucleus of all life, as it is the depth, the first and most sacred action; yes, it is the spark of God and the Divine inspiration, which every being and every animal can acquire and which belongs to the highest being. I speak of animal and I actually mean the animal being that we shall also follow for a while.

When the first human embryo contacted the other, one was the creative and the other the driving power; both merged, and these, as I explained to you on our previous journey, were the male and the female being. Although those organs were not yet perfect, fundamentally they

206

were ready, and the power to bring about reincarnation was present. After this contact, as you know, the first life died, the young life would be born, which actually happened. I'll connect you now with the astral world and we shall follow this process of attraction and birth. I'll connect you deeper, that is, with the preceding phenomena.'

André clearly felt this and he heard Alcar say: 'What do you see, André?'

'Nothing, Alcar, I don't see anything.'

'Indeed, my boy, because there isn't anything yet. There can't be anything, any life, in this world, because that which will be present later has to be born yet, or, in other words, the first human embryo still has to die before inspiring life will enter this world.'

'What kind of a wonder is this, Alcar?'

'This is the wonder which precedes embryonic life, and therefore birth of the first human embryo.'

It is amazing, André thought. He did not see anything and there was no life either. Where was the astral world? It was empty, entirely empty.

'Is that correct, Alcar?'

'Quite, André. Better ask me a dozen times if you think something is not clear to you, André.'

'Yes, Alcar, but this I feel and is clear to me.'

'Then I'll continue. You will experience wonders, André, psychical or spiritual wonders.

There is nothing here, absolutely nothing. You see an empty space, which is quite natural, since there were no astral worlds yet; they were still to be born. When the first human embryo was born and had matured and connection was established, that first cell died and it was not until then the astral world came into being, and that world which was to become the invisible world, was born.

It became the hereafter. When you leave your body, you enter this world and when man dies he will enter it. Do you feel, André, where the spheres emanate from? And that our life is the same condition as that empty world in front of you, but that we and all other life live in the billion-stage? That we have advanced this far? That embryonic life of man and animal has evolved and reached the human and animal stage? But here, on this location, everything was born; this is the origin of creation; the visible and invisible world.

I'll continue and you will soon see that the astral world is filled with billions of little sparks or living beings. After the first embryo died and passed on, the inspiring life accepted the astral sphere and waited to be attracted again. I'll connect you now with that first stage and you will see the astral world of the first human embryo as an inspiring and living being.'

André observed, he saw billions of luminous little sparks passing by.

'I show you this world in a luminous atmosphere, André, or you would not be able to see anything at all, because there was no light yet, there could be no light because radiating man had to be born yet.'

My God, André thought, how much you know; how is it possible. How marvellous and natural all this is!

'You see, André', he heard his leader say, 'all are moving. In actual fact it is inspiring man and has to become the Divine being. At this stage and long after it is unconscious, you can see that it is alive, because it is moving. This little being or life must be attracted, or birth would not be possible. This life is indeed attracted because this process goes on and on. From the first stage we pass on to the next and I'll show you a second stage. I wonder if something will strike you.'

Again André was connected with the astral world. What he saw was amazing. There was more movement and he could see all those little objects better, they were clearly visible.

Wherever he looked, there was life. To the left and right, above and below him were these little beings of light.

'Did you feel me, André?'

'I see them clearly, but I don't know what it means.'

'I will explain that. This is the second stage, and it is, as a result, further advanced than the first. There is more power during this stage than during the first condition. So the spiritual energy is stronger and denser than in the first condition, because it can be observed more clearly. During the following stages it is of course still stronger and more visible. The reason is that the first embryo in material condition has passed to the second stage, and therefore also that enhanced attunement has set in here. Did you notice, André?'

'No, Alcar.'

'I'll connect you again with the material world now, and subsequently return to the astral world. Do you see the second embryonic stage, André?'

'Yes, Alcar.'

'You clearly see that this little being has become larger and has condensed. Therefore, inner life follows the material world and is an integral part of that body. Both bodies must merge into one another, and this merging process is a law. It is like we are in our lives and material man is on earth. We are the energy for the material being on earth; we are the will man possesses. It is therefore the inspiring power for what lives in front of you in the second stage of embryonic life. What we are as spirit and as man is on earth, is already the material and spiritual consciousness – and all that, as I said before – this young life has yet to acquire. That, André, we shall now follow.

Look, André, how attraction occurs. I connected you with it on our last journey, but now we follow this process in its general development.'

Again André saw the second stage. He saw that two cells connected. The moment this happened, a similar being descended from the astral world and entered both material cells. He then saw that the connection was interrupted.

'Could you clearly follow this, my boy?'

'Yes, Alcar, very clearly.'

'Then we will follow this little being. It will live for some time; then you will see an other process, as it has to die. I'll keep you connected.'

André kept looking. Among these billions of lives he followed this one cell. Amazing how Alcar could achieve this.

He heard him say: 'Purely concentration, André. I am one with that little being and recall the past. You see what I see and what I want you to see. I can do that, because it is part of reality. If it were not possible you would feel and notice it. When a spirit in our world wants to connect himself he can establish this connection when the object belongs to God's creation, and he possesses the required strength. He must have this strength at his disposal, otherwise it is not possible. I can only show you what is present in my own life and what I possess. You know that too. You can still see that creature, but I am about to connect you with the next stage.

That little being in front of you has lived for several hours after connection. So, after several hours this little material being passes over and the inspiring life enters the astral world.'

André saw this wonder happen. The little being still moved, but he felt its movements weaken. It went on slowly, still moving. It was an amazing sight. It was exactly as if man on earth gasped his life away.

'Now watch it', he heard Alcar say.

André felt that the moment had come.

'What is that; do my eyes deceive me, Alcar?'

'No, you see it clearly, André, the astral spirit, the inspiring life is entering the astral world. It is the second time you have watched the process of connection, attraction and death during the second stage of embryonic life. That is birth, death and descent of the inspiring life. This still happens on earth. This is reincarnation as it has been in all those billions of years. If this young life had not been able to attract inspiration, this young life would have suffocated and continuation and reproduction would be out of the question. No, God knew and oversaw all this; that is why God created His own being; why God gave this being that inspiring power; that is why we possess that spark, that awe-inspiring will, by which we control our own fate, happiness and rest, peace and harmony. I'll have to explain all that to you on earth. Here, however, everything was preordained in the first instance. Isn't it a wonder, André?'

'Yes, Alcar, and yet so natural.'

'Now I will pass on to the animal world for a while, that also belongs to our work and I have to disillusion anyone who thinks that we, Divine beings, emanated from the plant world and animal kingdom, and that we had to follow that way and life. Once more: I irrevocably contradict this.

I return to the first stage, because animal life was to be born during that stage. We follow an identical condition, in the first degree, though now for the animal world. Look there, in front of you, André, a similar connection takes place. During the second stage, as you have seen just now, this being was to live for several hours. I explained this to you a minute ago and on our previous journey. Now look what happens. That little being dies, and we follow it. The astral life has already entered here, but the material being is submitted to a process of decay, out of which the other life was born. Do feel that it is already in a state of decomposition.'

André saw this amazing process develop. He saw that this tiny body dissolved into a slimy condition. Out of this process, however, something came to life, although it could hardly be seen. Yet, however tiny it was, this little decaying cell produced little animals.

210

He heard Alcar say: 'I showed you the result, but a long period of time passed before it was born. Now watch the process again, André. What do you see now?'

'I see hundreds of these little animals, Alcar.'

'Very good, that is correct. Out of the first human peel, to put it that way, hundreds of animal lives emerged.'

'How amazing, Alcar.'

'That is the mightiest wonder we know and at the same time the most natural. I showed you this already on our previous journey.'

'Is this known on earth? Do they know this wonder, Alcar?'

'No, scientists on earth are searching for the initial stage of man and animal, but they do not know yet which organism was born first.'

'Can't that be established?'

'No, that is no longer possible. I made it clear to you, however, that the process of revelation was concentrated on one being, and that was the human being. The next wonder emanated from this event and was the creation of the animal kingdom. Scientists should to able to feel this process; it is not possible to calculate it. This planet created inspiring life for the entire universe and it is the all-embracing event of creation. This body had no other task.'

'But then, scientists cannot penetrate this depth, because they live on an other planet? Do I feel that correctly, Alcar?'

'No, that is not clear, because every planet created its own organism; but here the nucleus came into being for the entire universe, in other words: what happened here, we find again on earth. But there is more. Scientists attempt to explain the origin of the universe materially and that is not possible. When they do not gear up to the spiritual or invisible cosmos, they will never understand nor be able to explain its origin.'

'You mean to say that they can only establish the origin of man, planets and stars and everything present in the universe when they follow inner life?'

'Indeed, André; otherwise they cannot penetrate the initial stage, because death is calling them to a halt. We have seen, and it was explained to you in the temple of the soul, that we, man and animal and everything present in the universe, were born out of nothingness. This nothingness manifested itself in a twilight, it became denser and denser until the process of development started. When scientists on earth accept an All-might or All-power, they will penetrate the initial stage, which accommodates the Divine mystery. They investigate the existing world, but it is behind it, billions of years ago, in the distant past of animal and man, that reality resides.'

'Can't they accept that, Alcar?'

'No, because they do not know nor accept eternal life, they do not understand themselves; they do not feel the profoundness within themselves and 'death' calls them to a halt. Time and again I refer to this, have to refer to this, as it bars their way, it deprives them of their connection with the invisible cosmos. Reality is behind it, behind that veil, the mystery of 'death'.'

'Do they know how the condensation process happened, Alcar?'

'Yes, André, they know this process; they have understood and followed it in thousands of conditions.'

'Do they also know that the earth has been a transparent ball of fire?'

'They know that too; they have been able to establish that.'

'Why then do scientists not get any further, because they have certainly made a lot of progress.'

'As I said before, they search in the existing world, they follow the activities and eras of the earth but they do not progress, and feel that they are powerless. Something is calling them to a halt. Once a certain point is reached they cannot advance any more, because they see the planet earth as a ball of fire, a glowing mass, and life, including that of animal and man, can no longer exist. It tells them that no life could have been possible previously, and that a second creation has taken place.'

'But that can't be possible, Alcar?'

'I am glad you feel that, André. No, it is not possible; there has always been life and a second creation conflicts with everything related to the Divine. The planet earth went through various eras, transitional periods, such as the ice age, the glowing and condensation process. We, on our side, see through this and know all these conditions. Not an inch of the earth remained untouched; the entire earth experienced this process, nevertheless there was and has always been life.'

'And is that the deadlock, Alcar?'

'Yes, André, that's the end, they feel completely bound up. Even now the planet earth goes through all these transitions; we still see this process take place in the interior of the earth, although it is hardly perceptible on the surface. If all this would stop, if there were no more erupting volcanoes by which this glowing process can be observed, believe me, we would experience on earth what happened here millions of years ago, which is the dying-process of this planet.'

'You mean to say that the inner planet lives precisely because of those phenomena?'

'Yes, André, that's correct. That is how we recognize the inner life of every planet. Here, all this ceased long ago; besides those phenomena did not occur here, at any rate not with that primal force and violence.'

'Did this planet go through other activities, Alcar?'

'Yes, André, because every planet has its own activity and occupies its own location in the cosmic entirety.'

'You did not tell me anything about it, Alcar?'

'No, my son, that is not necessary, you would not be able to tell one thing from another. I only follow the natural phenomena as we came to know them on our side and by which I try to explain the process of revelation to you. That will give you an idea how everything has happened. I hold on to a fixed plan and will not go further and deeper than necessary.'

'So you do not intend, Alcar, to follow the entire creation and the development of the earth?'

'No, André, I have not been told to do that, I only follow my assignment.'

'But you could, couldn't you, Alcar?'

'Yes, certainly, I could follow the entire process of the earth; we could write dozens of books about it, but that is not the intention.'

'Are there scientists on earth, who are beginning to think differently, Alcar?'

'Yes, certainly; some feel a different creation, but they, too, do not advance any further. There are scientists on earth who know and accept that one thing was born out of the other and they also feel, which is most important, that everything they observe is only temporal and must dissolve like many other material things.'

'You know that these scientists exist, Alcar?'

'Yes, we know that these scientists were born on earth, and they will give science, their study of geology, a powerful impulse; but they, too, will fail, because this theory will not be accepted. These scientists know and feel that life on earth is only a transition to something higher. They have started on the spiritual way and when they continue they will make progress; but one theory after another will be dropped. The learned of today, will be a great nought in the universe tomorrow and especially an earthly being.'

'If I understood you correctly, Alcar, inner life is fixed to the material cosmos?'

'Yes, André, and they have to follow that way, in order to advance any further.'

'This planet has condensed like all others, has it not?'

'Yes, but the activity and condensation, the many transitions the earth experienced, are not present here. Every planet created its own organism, condensed for the inspiring life to accept an existence, but the planet earth was to complete the organism of man and animal. To this end the earth received all energy when all these planets had fulfilled their task, as I explained to you. This planet is dying, there is death wherever you look.'

'How mighty this is, Alcar; I can't find words for it.'

'It is mighty, André; and yet we can see through all these laws, because we have experienced them.

We'll continue and return to that wonder. This cosmic mystery lives right in front of you, and in this way we see all miracles created by God, as we can connect ourselves with them. You see, André, that animal life was born out of the first human peel. All these lives will connect again with other beings, which is the way this awe-inspiring process occurred. The animal kingdom, as you know, emerged out of us, out of the first process of decay. Out of all this; and that is my point and the reason why I had to explain this again so that you can understand the origin of what I'll presently show you, how the 'astral animal world' also emanated. I'll connect you with that world, because that young life also passed over and entered the invisible world. Do you feel this mighty wonder, André?'

'Yes, Alcar, but it never crossed my mind.'

'Look there, in front of you, another sight: the astral animal world.'

André saw that life.

'I have only connected you with the animal world, but now I'll pass on to our own astral world. Now watch it, André. You can clearly distinguish the astral animal being from the astral human being.'

'All this is so amazing, Alcar. I have no words for it. How wonderful; both live in the same world and yet one world is separated from the other.'

'Very well observed, because I wanted to explain it to you. Now, when man on earth attracts inspiring life, the astral being - I am now referring to our own world - the inner life descends into the embryo and accepts that life. The inner life therefore returns to the first stage and enters material life, which is the mother; it is the inspiration for that young life. I want to make clear to you, André, that this process, this event, has been proceeding in this way all those billions of years and it still happens that way in the perfect material body of man on earth. Do you feel what I mean, André?'

'Yes, Alcar.'

'The inspiring life therefore accepts the first stage to inspire the human embryo on earth after fertilization. The inspiring life is still unconscious, but we shall follow it and presently the inspiring life will acquire instinct.

I have shown you the astral world of our own life and of the animal kingdom. Also the inspiring power and the prospective mental body; how the animal kingdom was born out of the first peel; and the entrance into the astral world.

Now we'll continue and pass on to an other stage. I'll show you what happened several centuries later.'

Again André saw the astral world. My God, he thought, what is all this?

'You see nothing but life, André. What you observe are the thousands of transitions. Centuries have passed and you now see the first and last degrees of development together. We see a similar scene in the material world. There, too, the young life has multiplied. We find all those transitions together in the astral world and also in the material world. Attraction and birth, death and connection have increased to a billion-process, and yet only centuries have passed. Do you know now the number of souls, how many people live on earth? And what the first planet had to achieve, and what its task was in this mighty event? That cannot be fathomed nor calculated; it has to be accepted. It is not only awe-inspiring, it is Divine, only an All-power could oversee and establish it.

During the first stage you saw an empty space; now there is life and all that life we see again on earth. All that life will become the inner human being: the inspiring power for the material being; man. That life is the driving power, the spark of God and at the same time a part of God and it will return to God. I cannot give you a clearer picture of inner life. In all happened here, in front of you, André, inner life was born for the entire universe. Do you feel what this means? Here on this planet, which as you know is the mother planet, this process took place. Reincarnation was preordained to it, and those who cannot accept this will have to wait until they die on earth and enter our world where they will be assisted by their sisters and brothers and must acquire this wisdom. There are many people on earth who will shrug their shoulders at reincarnation, but others will feel it, because deep within them this truth and reality is present. I explained this to you again to prove that reincarnation had to exist in the first instance, or God's creation would have failed and we would have been destroyed during this stage.'

# CHAPTER IV

## *Instinct and pre-animal-like consciousness*

ILLIONS of years passed. Life awakened and accepted various
stages. I cannot follow all those stages, it would be going
too far. One stage followed another; before the instinct awakened and the animal-like being had acquired this, it had to experience
many transitions.

Feeling has now developed, brought about by the material organism.
Is that clear to you, André?'

'You mean that according as the material being matured, inner life
developed, Alcar?'

'Splendid, André, you grasped it. Fundamentally, there is feeling or
action but that feeling, the instinct, is still far away. To that end man
and animal must have attained their mature material degree. I showed
and explained that attunement and mature condition on our previous
journey. You have seen these beings on the shore when many had already died. That is, as you know, the highest degree for man in the fish-
like stage; but there is no instinct yet. The animal-like being had to
pass on to an other planet before it was to acquire that attunement of
feeling. Here, there was only action, it cannot be termed instinct or
consciousness. It will therefore be clear to you, that inner life could not
attain the degree of consciousness one has on earth, because this is the
initial stage of material and spiritual life. Inner life is not ahead of
material life, and this process or development is reflected on earth, as I
will explain to you there. If there was no reincarnation, there would be
no development for animal and man either and we would have suffocated during this stage. There was bound to be reincarnation; in this
short life man and animal could not attain the Divine attunement. Is
what I explained to you on this planet so unbelievable, so improbable
or unnatural? Did God create a perfect and mature being? Is that possible now that we have come to understand creation? God created the
universe. God created stars and planets; every planet has its own task,
and the mother planet dominated all other planets. Here, inner life was
born for the entire universe. If that is true, we have to accept the cycle
of the soul, which is reincarnation for animal and man.

217

There is life here, André; but there is no question yet of instinct or animal consciousness, because we would not receive and acquire that degree until on the first transition.

Here, a condition was created in an unconscious degree, which is and has always been for those planets, which had to perform a task in the plan of creation. There was action and life, but that life had not yet accepted an existence, neither materially nor spiritually. All this was accomplished because it was implied in the great plan.

I hope you understand me, André. I want you to understand all this, as it proves that we, man and animal, received everything from God during the first stage and that we have to acquire all other qualities, and to follow that long cosmic way through the universe from this place, this planet. That mighty wonder started here, on this planet. You will now understand this marvellous event. It was our Holy Father, God, Who oversaw everything. It was this object, this planet, which had to fulfil this task and it did so infallibly. This planet, the mother of all those other planets belonging to the third cosmic degree, gave birth to the first life and first material organism. This planet was to accomplish animating life, not only for man, but also for the animal kingdom. This tremendous event happened, because all this was controlled by one power, brought to life by the All-Soul, and therefore created by God. God is the fountain of wisdom, the source of all love, of which we all are particles, which are the Divine Spark within us. God, my son, is the natural law of life in billions of forms. God, André, is perfection, as you have been able to see. We were to experience an unchanging law, laws of life and energy, which is reincarnation. All that, André, took millions of years; but God knows no time. In all those years one law was revealed and that is 'Life', Gods own life, revealed in millions of forms.

Here, André multiplication took place; that law became effective. I ask you: Why should all that no longer happen on earth? Has anything changed in all those millions of years? Are man, the activity, the Divine Spark and animation different than during the first instance? Could God, Who is the source of all life, deprive us of that activity? Nothing has changed, André, there was only development: a perfect human and animal organism emanated.

Here, my son, death and birth originated, there is not the slightest change on the planet earth. Is all that so incomprehensible? So unnatural? We all are children of God and it is up to us to acquire that Divine attunement. God lives and works in creation. God revealed Himself in millions of forms and all those revelations represent His own life. It is the spark of animation, which is attuned to His Divine life.

What more can I say? Can you accept all this? Is everything clear to you, André?'

'Yes, Alcar; I understand.'

'Then we'll go on. All those children of God who had reached the shores on this planet, were ready to accept subsequent life. From that time onward the instinct and a will of their own awakened. This will that man possesses is contained in this process. Man received a body and independence, but inner life, the animation for that organism, awakened on the first transition. The Divine Spark, therefore, is the personal will, the animation; it is activity, feeling and thinking; it is the driving power for material life and the return to God. Whatever form animating life has, it owns that will and that Divine Spark; it is independent and can do as it pleases. That is why inner life will be born again, pass on into thousands of lives and awaken in those lives, in order to reach the Divine Spheres. Thousands of transitions are required and, André, that is the purpose of the material and spiritual life; two worlds for material and spiritual man, as the visible and invisible wonder of creation. Invisible man drives the material being, passes from one body on to the next, causing life of the soul to awaken.

When man had reached his final and highest stage on this planet he could not advance any more. Yet, the urge to go on was present; the Divine energy of this being drove it onward. However, no other body was available and life was doomed to die. Inner life, free from those material ties which kept it imprisoned, floated on in the astral world. That inner life was attracted by the organism on the first transition.

When the first planet had performed its task, as I explained to you, the first transitional planet was ready and could receive that life. I connected you with that event because you were attracted and there is no need to do that again. We'll go to that planet and follow the inner life of man. Any more questions, André, you can still ask them.'

'No, Alcar, everything is clear.'

'Then we shall go on and won't return here.'

André returned to his own life. All that time he had observed through Alcar's power. Everything he had experienced this time was amazing.

'How simple is the way all this was established, Alcar'.

'Life had to follow but one way, to undergo but one activity, which was initially infallible.'

'Wasn't it in following stages?'

'No; for man who became aware of his powers, destroyed this process. What happened in an infallible way, in which man had no part, life also received on the planets that followed, but there it became conscious. When we have advanced a few more degrees I will show you how man forgot himself and did not understand his own creation. Then, André, man already controlled and destroyed all this mightiness he had received from his God.'

'I understand what you mean, Alcar.'

'If you understand me, you know that when instinct awakened and man had passed on to the creative and driving life, his downfall was irrevocable. Born out of pure love, this first planet had performed its task and placed that great wonder in the hands of this being. The first planet created all that, brought it about, for God wanted man to become his own creator, and to this end he received a will of his own and all these powers; you will see how man acted. One life was killed after the other, and though not yet aware of this terrible event, man in his highest material degree was to do this consciously.

You will understand, that when the first planet, the mother planet in the universe, had passed this on to all children of God, it was ready to return, which process has been going on for millions of years. All this was brought about in and around this planet. That activity, André, we see again in life on earth, in the mother organism, the soul this organism has, and is the same activity which took place in the first instance. That does not only apply to the mother body on earth; it can be seen in the entire creation, because it is no different in the animal kingdom. When the mother animal has performed its task there and the young life goes its way, this is a law, an event which we have learned to understand during the first stage.

But on earth it is full consciousness of animal and man. We see this again in all those thousands of conditions of the animal kingdom, and man, as happened here, cannot act differently, because this mighty power was given to the smallest organism; that is a law, as created by God. This happens every second on earth and in the water which also contains life and on thousands of planets accommodating life. The event you have just learned to understand happens everywhere.

This is the serving power or the mother-organ, like the first planet has been; every organism has received this task. All that is life, André; God's own life; why then should all other life in other and higher conditions experience this in a way different from the way envisaged in the plan of creation? That is not possible; it cannot be possible, because it is the law of reincarnation and it is the mother organism that owns this wonder.

Look, there is the first transition we visited on our journey and that I connected you with. There is no life here either; but I showed it to you and I'll do so again. In front of you, you see the human beings which lived here.'

André began to observe.

'When man passed on, I mean inner man, animating life, a material organism was ready for animating life to descend into. Though it was not possible on the first cosmic degree, it could happen here. The urge the being had on the first cosmic degree, it received on this planet; instinct was born here because a different material organism was available. Now that the lower part of the body had split and inner life had advanced that far, and as always this perfect balance in everything, in every transition, the being became aware of its ability and crept on and that was the first progress of the human being on the negotiable planet. During this process instinct awakened. During the first steps it took, the being experienced such events and, after a short while, it meant the end of its material existence. During the next stages the material organism became more perfect, it advanced to its proper attunement and accepted its existence for this planet. It looked for food and in doing so it passed into a degree of feeling: the instinct.

We have now come to the phenomenon instinct. Thus awakened what is called instinct. The human but pre-animal-like being felt hungry, caused and evoked by its material organism. It was to become self-supporting and with it, instinct developed. Now man lived on the planet, which was not possible on the first cosmic degree and it will no doubt be clear to you that man had to awake here. Now that man had accepted an existence and had advanced that far, it gave inner life experience, and this experience was an activity evoked from within, which revealed itself as feeling hungry. You see this unity in everything, that one activity evokes the other, because this activity passed from the ma-

221

terial organism on to inner life. Thus, the material organism gave birth to the instinct, and it was on this planet that man advanced to a will of his own, which he used. On this same planet all those experiences graded up the growth process for both organisms, the process of evolution commenced and pre-animal-like consciousness was born, which meant good and evil for man, though he was unaware of it.

Here, André, man killed for the first time and good and evil were born; man broke a law, as I told you. Here, man forgot himself; he became ruler and destroyer of everything, of all this pure love he received from God. Man lived here in a pre-animal-like condition and this animal-like being was to become the Divine being. It was the beginning of that eternal road towards perfection and it would take billions of years.

Life here had only one feeling, which was hunger, activated by the material organism.

I explained what age these beings could reach and I do not need to go into that again. What you should know is the following, then we'll go on to see how the instinct awakens; which was already present here, though in the first degree, because it also has transitions. Before the being attains the highest degree of instinct it passes, like we do, through seven transitions and degrees. The instinct also has degrees, belonging to this and the next transitional planets which we got to know on our last journey. Material life has seven degrees, as I explained to you, and this also applies to spiritual life. For material life they serve to attain the highest organism and for inner life to enter an other and higher consciousness. Do you understand what I mean, André?'

'Yes, Alcar.'

'You will feel then that all those transitions of the material organism we saw and man received and experienced, are also for inner life because it is related to the seven cosmic degrees. These seven cosmic degrees are, as you know, conditions of existence in the universe, of which the seventh is the highest and belongs to the Divine Spheres.

It will be clear to you now that inner and animating life is passing on to a higher stage in accordance with material growth, and that which is the pre-animal-like consciousness does not awaken until on the second cosmic degree. Is that also clear?'

'Yes, Alcar.'

'Then I'll go on. Look at the astral world; I'll connect you with it; see

222

how much life is present here. Nothing is known here about our astral world and the darkness or hell, although it must become our astral world, that is to say like our hell is. Man does not have intellect yet, it must still awaken. Again we see how all is one, how one thing emanates from the other, how the hell in our life emerged from this condition. I will explain that on this journey.

This is the astral world, André. You only see life, but the astral world we know, which is darkness, you know the hell on this side, is different. Man in the darkness has built a world of his own and how that happened you will experience when we have returned to the earth. In this way I will show you that both worlds I discussed, change. We see that again on the inhabitable planet. The material being has changed and inner life has advanced to a further and higher stage which is emotional life. This happened for the multiplication process, reincarnation on the inhabitable planet. All this life is waiting in the invisible world for a new birth.

You see, André, how everything condensed. The development of both worlds continues, necessitating all these transitional conditions, degrees of material development, which are also present in the psychic world.

Here in this astral world lives the human being, which will be attracted by the material being on the inhabitable planet. The astral being will have to experience all those transitions, subsequently to pass on to a higher planet. We shall now go on to the next transitions.'

André returned to his own life.

'I'll now go to the condition where life was still present. You know the ensuing planets and you can imagine how far material and inner life have advanced since we see all that life again on the second last planet to the second cosmic degree.

We'll float on through space, André.'

'It is wonderful, Alcar; but I understand everything.'

'You should when you can experience all these degrees and activities. On the planet we are now going to visit, man still lacks the pre-animal-like consciousness; he will not receive that until on the second cosmic degree.'

'If I have understood you correctly, Alcar, birth of man also gave life to good and evil. Are they to blame?'

'They were when they had acquired all those qualities. Whether they were to blame does not apply to this planet here; for man was unaware

223

of good and evil, that feeling was not awaken until on the earth, the third cosmic degree. However, what they did become aware of, was what they felt after their deeds, and this feeling was the Divine attunement. Man on earth began to feel remorse, and this feeling was the transition to intellect and spiritual life. All that caused the Divine Spark and inner life to awaken. I'll explain that presently on the second cosmic degree.

Look, the last transition to the second cosmic degree. As you know, material life is present here, and we see this life again on earth.'

'We have been here before, haven't we, Alcar?'

'Yes, André, we have. You see that people live here and you know them from our previous journey. Life on this planet is fairly quiet; on the second cosmic degree, however, pre-animal consciousness has awakened. Man here lives in his normal human but animal-like condition and I explained how natural their lives are and that they live accordingly. Good and evil are not yet known here either and man lives as he feels inwardly and in accordance with his powers. His feeling is still unconscious. His material organism has attained a higher condition, but inner life will reach this perfect degree on the second cosmic degree, where it is in control of itself. Manslaughter and violence dominate, whereas here there is quiet and peace. All this indicates that this inner human being is not yet conscious. This animal-like life only lives for the perfection of both organisms. Here, material and inner life are one, on the second cosmic degree inner life is already lagging behind material life. This stage we see again on earth. There the material organism is perfect, too; but inner life stays behind all those material degrees we know.

What I am concerned with is that which you observe here.

You see that inner life follows the development of the material organism, which means the awakening of both organisms. The animal-like being already has a powerful and strong organism, of which the inner life makes full use. It adapts itself and the strength the material organism now has serves the awakening of inner life. Man is able to move, but inner life learns and acquires this. It is really simple; we see this in the child on earth: as the child matures, inner life develops accordingly and, as you see, this also happens here, it is a law, the law of natural development for inner and material life. Man here is in balance but he will lose that balance, and as a result Divinity in man is lost.

This phenomenon is the transition to all other conditions of consciousness, from which emanate all those passions and character traits we possess on earth. If man could have lived on in this pre-animal-like stage, good and evil would not have emerged and we would not have known all that misery. Man, however, had to go on; man is Divine. He proceeded ever further and higher and after he had experienced those various transitions feeling awakened. This feeling developed and passed on into pre-animal-like consciousness. You will come to know that degree and we'll see how good and evil have come to life in all those centuries. The only good thing we observe here is the care for the young life present in the mother life. This is love and this pre-animal-like love must awaken. This feeling will become stronger as man has a higher material attunement. Consequently, everything is in the process of formation.

When young life has reached mature age, it will go its own way. The mother no longer bothers about it, although it is part of her own life, but she is not aware of it. You feel that there is no spiritual consciousness here, not any more than in the animal world. Even on earth, but then consciously, mothers act like this pre-animal-like being. What happens here as a natural phenomenon, the mother on earth does fully consciously, although she has the perfect material organism, and has had to follow that long road of development; she attunes to a pre-animal-like event. That is awful, it happens more than once and man will be severely punished. You also see how many animal-like beings are living on earth, and all of them have reached the highest material condition. I mean the white race*), as I explained to you.

Here, André, man acts in accordance with his natural attunement, however, man and the animal kingdom cannot stay here, but must return to God. God gave man everything, but this Divine being perished because of all this. We will now go on to the second cosmic degree, for it was there that pre-animal-like consciousness emanated.

We'll soon be there, André. If you have followed me in everything, you will understand that, for the material organism, I had to dwell at length on the first cosmic degree, where I had to explain most, and that for the inner life I had to be on earth. Because on the planet earth inner life has attained full consciousness and man will pass on to the spiritual stage. It will also be clear that man did not yet know God nor religion,

*) See the 'Explanation' at the beginning of this book.

pure love or faith; things man on earth has acquired. All that had not yet come into being.

We'll pass on to the second cosmic degree. Look, André.'

Alcar descended on the second cosmic degree. They had been here where those enormous pre-animal-like beings lived.

'There, in front of you, you see man who lives here. He has the pre-animal-like consciousness. In all those millions of years material organism and inner life have advanced that far. No need to explain the material organism; you know that. Here, André, as I said before, manslaughter and violence dominate, for pre-animal-like consciousness has awakened. A still higher consciousness cannot develop here; that is impossible as you will understand. It is not until on earth that man will acquire it. It is amazing to see, André, how inner life follows material development and the inner human being acts in accordance with the strength of his material organism. Man indulges here and still doesn't know anything about a God of Love.

During the first stages of this planet, this life evolved from the embryonic life. Inner life, however, was born during the first stage on the mother planet, where we have been.

When this planet was ready and life could commence, the planet earth condensed to receive inner man. You know that too and I need not go into that. We won't stay here long either; we'll return to the earth presently; for that is where human consciousness came into being. Yet, I'll connect you with the astral world. Look and observe, André.'

André saw that he passed on into the invisible world. How mighty the picture was that he now saw. Astral life had condensed tremendously. Wherever he looked, there was life.

'You see, André, this is not yet the astral world we know as our hell. Nothing has yet been built up in this world, for good and evil built a world of their own. The higher spheres of light are for us what the dark spheres of hell are for the demons in life after material death. You know that man who enters the side beyond from the earth, will receive his spiritual dwelling when it is present in his inner life. The demons of hell descend into this darkness, they are those who seek evil on earth.

There are no spiritual dwellings here because man has not advanced that far, he lacks this ability, as he is unaware of God and pure love. Inner life has to experience a law, the law of development of the material organism. It is not until then that life accepts its final condition,

226

that inner life has completed its cycle on the earth and prepares to enter the spheres of light. I'll refer to it presently.

You may already have noticed one event. If you have followed eveything properly, André, it will be clear to you that God does not and cannot punish, that man has made himself impossible in this cosmic order. We'll learn more about this on earth. Do you feel what I mean?'

'Yes, Alcar; I felt it.'

'Millions of years from now, all this will have dissolved, by which time man has passed on to the planet earth. All those planets below the third cosmic degree must dissolve; only inner life will proceed until man has reached the highest spheres. The material and inner world pass on to the All, dissolve and are part of the invisible energy. You also know that only the Divine Spheres will remain and occupy a place in the universe.

You will now return to your own life.'

'How mighty everything is that you are showing me, Alcar.'

'Look, André, hundreds of people live together. When an animal on earth looks for connection and it takes place, people find it a natural occurrence. But if they would see people connecting here, although they are pre-animal-like beings, they would close their eyes and leave. Here, however, man is like the animal on earth. Connection can be observed with animals, though not with others because the animal feels it and does not allow man to observe. This, too, is part of animal instinct; but the more familiar animal, which has adapted to the human being, connects because it follows the natural course.

But these are men and they experience fertilization like the pre-historic animal. That is quite normal, André, for they do not know any better. We can follow this. Look, at this moment the astral being is attracted and I will connect you with the invisible world, so that you can follow this process.'

André saw that the inspiring life was present. How is that possible, he thought; if that world did not exist, no life, no development would be possible.

'At this moment, my boy, connection between two material beings has been established and, as you see, the inspiring life which already has lived thousands of times, descends into the material organism of the mother. The very moment that connection takes place, inner life is attracted, which is a new birth on the inhabitable planet. Look, André, an other condition, a life-and-death struggle. That happens frequently and many will die.'

These beings fought like wild animals. André saw that they were tearing each other apart. Soon, some were left laying about to die. Nothing but murder and violence, passion and animalization.

'You see, André, how they are attacking each other. That has been going on for millions of years and for the time being it will not end. I'll connect you with this being and will let you experience a material transition and also the way the inspiring life detaches itself, just like it happens on earth.'

André saw this wonder happen as on earth. He had been allowed to follow the dying process of several people.

'Will this spiritual body also be collected, as is done on the side beyond when somebody dies on earth, Alcar?'

'I am glad you ask this question, André. It is not possible and not necessary here, as man has not yet reached that level. Do you feel what I mean?'

'Have these people not yet reached that stage because they still have to receive the perfect human body and their inner life has not yet advanced that far?'

'That is correct.'

'How natural this phenomenon is, Alcar.'

'It shows us that the inner life has yet to awaken. I will explain this on the planet earth. It is only possible when inner life has attained a sphere of existence, for us the hereafter, which means a spiritual condition. None of these beings has a spiritual attunement; this is still pre-animal-like consciousness. One more thing. This is an astral world, but a world of unconsciousness. The spirit Lantos[*] told you about that. Inner life is attracted by the material being, but when man on earth dies, the inner life returns to this world, which is the world of the unconscious. In our life, the life of spiritual man, the hereafter is a conscious world in which people live who have achieved a spiritual world of existence. Do you feel this too?'

'Yes, Alcar. You live in that world, don't you?'

'Indeed; so I and millions of others have advanced that far, but here in this condition this world did not exist, as inner life still had to awaken.

[*] See the book: 'The Cycle of the Soul'.

228

You will learn this great wonder on earth too; you will see and observe how man has developed.

These people have no spiritual attunement, it does not exist, it is not until thousands of years later that inner life has acquired these powers. Nothing we possess and have acquired in life after material death is present here. All those questions, for instance, where will inner life be born; will it become a king or an emperor, a scientist or a beggar, rich or poor, will illness or misery be its share on earth, we do not know on this planet. That belongs to the earth; inner life can only experience those laws on the planet earth.

Those laws did not come about on earth until in the third era, they emanate from man. What is attained here is that the highest material being attracts the inner life attuned to it. When two perfect material beings connect, these two persons will attract the highest inner being. As you know seven degrees of material and inner life are present here. This is a law; a natural law, which we all have to follow.'

'Does this not apply to the earth, Alcar?'

'You mean, whether those laws do not belong to the planet earth?'

'Yes, Alcar.'

'Yes and no; man has disturbed these laws of nature. Here, equal beings attract each other and that also applies to the earth, but on earth we experience cause and effect. Here, things have not advanced that far and nothing is known of cause and effect; man experiences and will experience, connections are made and interrupted. It will be obvious that everything man has on earth could only originate on earth. Inner life awakened and all those spiritual laws we know on our side took effect when people had advanced that far. Here we are still in a process of development for the inner and material man.

An other wonder. You know I can connect myself with the past; you experienced that in various conditions. We descended into the distant past, and I can do this because I am connected with the higher masters. We'll follow that being in front of you, André, and to this end we'll return to his deepest inner life and past.'

André looked at this human being; he lay down to sleep. He was entirely naked and hairy like an animal. His body was large and strong. A giant on earth was a dwarf as compared with him.

You see, André, this man has the male organism, but I see more and I'll let you see that. I'll connect you with his inner life. You will see the

229

past because I remain connected with him.'

André observed. He saw a scene and he understood what it meant. It was the first material degree of man on this planet. He knew those material degrees; there were seven of them.

'Do you see this condition, André?'

'Yes, Alcar; is this the first material degree?'

'Splendid, André. Now look at this man. Inside him resides the animating life, which has been in the first degree; he has discarded that life and organism. The inner life returned into a material organism hundreds of times before it attained the highest material degree for this planet. That being passed away and we see inner life again, but in a different organism. But there is more and I'll show you an other life.'

André observed again. In front of him he saw a mother and child. The mother carried this young life and nursed it.

'What does this mean, Alcar?'

'This means that the soul has descended into the female organism. Look well and feel that this is correct. On this planet we can only feel it; on earth we can observe it because inspiring life has passed into an essential being, which means that we recognize inner man. That is not possible here, because inner life has not yet acquired the spiritual attunement. The outward appearance of man is recognized by his inner life; but it is not until on our side that we see that animating life is the image of the material organism. If the inner life has lived in an other organism, we can see this, because the material face is related to inner life. We therefore recognize that other personality and know it has to do with an other life.

That, as I said, cannot be seen here, it can only be felt, but what we can observe is that this being in front of you possessed the female body in its previous life. This mother, André, has the same inner and inspiring life as the creative organism. Do you feel this wonder?'

'Yes, Alcar; I see it'.

'That is the wonder of reincarnation. If this were not possible, creation would come to a stand-still. This Divine wonder is given to every life that is inner man.

This mother with her child was the second last reincarnation of this life, this human being. I won't follow all those previous incarnations; but you'll realize that it also applied to them, or inner as well as organic life would have become extinct.

This animal-like being, André, has attained the perfect material degree and will presently be attracted by the planet earth to be born again. Inspiration was born since the first planet, and we already see this inner life again in the pre-animal-like consciousness; it has covered that long road. The reason why inner life receives the female organism is to permit the soul to experience the serving feeling or creation. I have explained that on our previous journey, but you will experience that on our next journey; this belongs to reincarnation on earth.

This mother is a pre-animal-like being and experiences this mighty event in accordance with nature. Man on earth is not generally different. There, too, man experiences this event and does not feel the mightiness of this ability, which is the creative and driving power.

We see and know how people on earth live and do not understand nor see or feel anything of God's creation because they do not realize that they emanated from this mightiness. One man curses the other, and that in a perfect material organism!

Here, André, man, at any rate inner man, is as on earth. And yet, there are people on earth, who attune to higher life and acquire these qualities, who feel love and know that they will advance. However, the earth is over-populated by animal-like beings, and those beings live in a perfect organism. Here people satisfy themselves on the life of others, but they are not aware of it. People on earth, however, are aware of good and evil and of a Father of Love, a God Who loves all His children; they have advanced on their cosmic road but they still indulge themselves.

If it was not possible to advance, André; if there were no other planets to admit higher spiritual as well as physical life, man would continue living in this stage. That, however, is not God's intention, for all this life has to return to God. They have Divinity and they form part of it. Thus, we have become acquainted with pre-animal-like consciousness. This planet created this powerful and mature organism in a pre-animal-like attunement. The earth embellishes this organism and inner man experiences this progress and adapts himself amazingly well to that material organism. We have been able to follow from the very beginning how amazing this adaptation is. It happened in all those degrees, and why should this be different on earth? If the Creator of all this had not overseen it, there would not have been any progress; however, one stage was born out of the other. That progressing life created its own organism, because it possessed this grace from its initial condition and will retain it eternally, until we have reached the All. The urge to create is present in every being or life; it is at the same time the most sacred gift we received from God; God has laid this mightiness in our hands.

Do you feel the meaning of all this, this grace, this power and might, André? That is why we are Divine; God gave us everything; it is up to us to understand this mightiness and to learn to feel why these powers have been given us. God as the Creator of the universe, of man and animal, granted us that Divine power. I ask you: Is this understood by man? Do they feel on earth why they are there; why they are 'man'? What it means to be 'man'? What it means to have received this? That we will become like God and that we have to acquire those powers? That all those thousands, nay, millions of planets serve that purpose, or we could not return to God? What more can I say? This should be clear and man can follow it. Here, André, human beings live and they cannot stay here. All those who live here will be born on the planet earth. If this is so, it is also possible to advance further and higher still, and we know this is our hereafter. But even then we proceed to acquire the highest cosmic degree, where God's perfect Child lives who returned to the earth to announce the existence of our Almighty Father in Heaven. Christ, the perfect and Divine Being, returned to the earth, and I'll tell you on earth why He descended to the third cosmic degree. That was a law, too, and it was a grace for the perfect Child of God to be allowed to represent His Holy Father, the All-Power, the All-Inspiration. Because that is what happened, and it is a grace of God, which so many people on earth do not understand and feel yet, because they do not even understand their own life and can't solve the problem of death which calls them to a halt. It was not possible for Christ to bring them nourishment for the mind on this planet, because they are unconscious and have not advanced that far; they are pre-animal-like people. It was only possible on earth.

This is the psychic attunement of this planet and all, none excluded, will come to the earth. Man on earth will attract them. Millions of beings are still living here, and the process of birth and death is experienced; as on earth. You will understand, André, how many centuries will pass before the last being has passed away and has received a new body on earth. This is fixed, it will and must happen. Everybody, none excluded, has been here; all of us were pre-animal-like beings. These are wonders and spiritual laws of the second cosmic degree; on earth we see and experience other wonders. I'll tell you about them, André, and explain everything.

We'll now go to the earth and won't return here either. Have you understood everything?'

'Yes, Alcar; it is tremendous.'

'It is, André, but most natural. We'll move fast now.

Look, in front of you, André; that is the planet earth. I have a lot to explain to you on earth, first of all the development of the planet earth, in order to give you a clear picture of inner life. I'll have to show you the initial stage of the earth and to this end I'll return to the first stage of the earth. Subsequently, I connect you with inner life, and I'll also explain how the astral world condensed for man and the animal kingdom.'

# CHAPTER V

## *Development of the earth*

ALCAR descended to the earth and André felt entirely free of the other planet. 'We'll sit down here, André. From this spot I can explain everything and we'll pass on to the planet earth.'
They sat down in a lovely vicinity. André looked around. How beautiful the earth was, here he lived. Yonder, far from this place, lay his material body. How mighty all those wonders were. If only people could accept this, how happy they would be on earth. He was very grateful that he had been allowed to experience all this.

'Where are we, Alcar?'

'In your own country. Wherever we are, I can always connect you with the earth. Now listen carefully. On our previous journey I explained material life to you and the way all those planets were created. When we arrived on earth I told you how the plan of evolution of man happened, but now we'll follow psychic life. It is essential, however, to follow man along his way on earth from the beginning. I explained at the time that the first planet is the mother planet, which dominates all those thousands of planets. The earth, too, received its power; it was directly influenced and nursed by the mother planet. You know all that and it is clear to you, isn't it?'

'Yes, Alcar, perfectly.'

'Then we'll go on and descend to the first stage; I'll connect you with the embryonic life.'

André felt himself sink away. The earth faded before his eyes, he began to observe and saw that the earth began to condense. There was no life yet; but it would soon come.

He heard his leader say: 'I explained this on our previous journey. Yet it will take thousands of centuries before the earth has condensed to the extent that life can commence. I do not want to stay in this condition, I'll show you the next stage. Before I go on, I'll first show you a mighty wonder.

Although you see that the earth condenses, it is by no means fully condensed. The earth is nevertheless already in connection with the astral world and inspiring life is waiting to be attracted. Consequently, from its initial stage the planet earth attracted inspiring life, and I'll show you that life. I explain this to you, so that you feel how closely both lives are connected with each other, and that this attractive force is already present in and around the earth. Do you understand what I mean?'

'Yes, Alcar.'

'Very well; I will connect you and you'll see the astral world in which inspiring life lives, which inspires material man on earth. Attention now.'

André clearly saw what happened and he understood the meaning of this scene. The earth began to condense, but around this tremendous object he perceived another force in the form of a dense haze, a cloud. The planet earth lived, as it were, in it. He saw this haze below and above him, to the right and left, it was present wherever he looked. The earth floated as in a spiritual shell. He felt how deep all this was, and he understood what his leader meant.

Now he heard Alcar say: 'This is the inspiring life for the earth; but that haze, too, will condense and it happens according as the earth becomes available. The planet earth was a transparent mass during the first stage, as you have seen in the temple of the soul, but that transparent ball of light condenses, and that also applies to the inspiring life. Both are one in every respect. That cloud you observe is the inspiring life returned to the first stage, as I explained to you before. This is for inspiring life, André, now you will experience another wonder which I'll connect you with. Remember, you can only feel it.'

When his leader said this, he felt a tremendous power surge through him. What is that? he thought. I am being radiated by an invisible power and that power absorbs me; it warms and feeds me.

'What wonder is that, Alcar?'

'That wonder originates from the first planet, the mother planet. Do you feel now that the mother planet accomplishes everything, that the earth is nursed from there? This is power from the first planet and the earth condenses through this power. The earth, therefore, did not possess this power and would have remained a transparent ball of fire if no other powers had assisted it in its task, but God oversaw everything.

Shouldn't we bend our heads deeply for this event? We know that this is God's sacred life and light which is condensed through an other power, the atmosphere. But there was another dominating power which controlled all this, and that is the mother planet.

This, André, is to feel sacred respect for that which is creation. See and feel, my son, that this is the power of the first planet and of all those thousands of other planets. All those planets feed the planet earth, for it is the earth, which has to perform a sublime task in the Divine plan.

This is a great wonder, André; but don't we see that wonder in nature, too? Doesn't a branch of a tree receive its power from the entire tree? Doesn't a mother on earth feed her child during the first moments of life; and isn't the earth the child of this dominating planet, which, like the mother organism on earth, performs its task? This, André, is God's work, and it is mighty and natural. It is a wonder of life, of power and of pure love. This is God's work; we emanated from it, we were born on earth. It has been established by this all-embracing power. The earth, therefore, received its activity through this influence; and in this awe-inspiring event was the order of the All-Soul.

God oversaw everything; nothing disturbed this great process, because that mighty guidance, that infallible activity is in everything.

The earth therefore receives its power and experiences this activity; it will also attract inspiring life. That activity is at work now, but later, I mean thousands of centuries later, we see how far the earth has advanced. Is that also clear, André?'

'Yes, everything; and I thank you, Alcar.'

'You see, my son; inspiring life is ready and is waiting.

The earth continues to condense and presently the first connection will be made and the first life will be born. I'll connect you and you will now pass on to an other stage.

If you do not understand me, you must tell me and I'll explain.'

André observed again. He saw that further stage in front of him and he understood what it meant. He had observed this life on the first planet. This was embryonic life out of which man would be born. He saw these unnameable cells which floated on and moved. It was an amazing sight to see this again.

He heard Alcar say: 'You see that this is a further stage. Many centuries have passed. I can tell you that thousands of centuries passed before the earth had condensed to the extent that embryonic life was ready. All those cells have already been animated by the inspiring life. When this material life commenced, the inspiring life immediately descended into this little cell, as happened on the first planet. My point is, and that is why I must explain these first stages again, that the inspiring life, which we have got to know as mature beings on those other planets, fundamentally returns to the first stage, so that it can be born in this life, on earth. Inner life descends in the embryo as the Divine Spark and as inspiring life, and drives material life onward. This, my son, is the great wonder, and this mighty wonder happens in the mother organism, it has the perfect organism on earth, and we have experienced it on all those other planets.

Thus, that cell in front of you will become man. Inner life, which we have followed on our long way, lives in it.

Inspiring life of that pre-animal-like human being, the spiritual energy, the soul, which has discarded its material life that far, has to accept the first degree again in order to be able to enter this material shell. If this were not possible, there would be a disturbance and one life would dominate the other and destroy it. However, inner life adapts itself to that material organism, which, during this stage, is embryonic life. I speak of embryo, my son; here in front of you lives the embryo and that is also present in the perfect human body. The being as man would have to cover that long road, and when it has advanced that far, this being owns creation, because that wonder is implied in the mother organism. These organs are present in the mother organism; in this wonderful product of creation the entire creation is reflected. What happened here, happens in the mother organism, it is the wonder of creation, that great and mighty gift we people received from God, which God has laid in our own hands. I want to prove herewith that man is his own creator and that he received this from God. What all those planets have experienced the 'mother' on earth experiences now. What happened in a billion-process, now happens in the mother organism; it is man's own property. Now try to feel this, André, try to imagine this wonder. God gave us everything; I told you this many times; now, however, it is getting through to us, now we see and feel, what it all means. When people on earth connect, then, André, they experience the 'plan of creation'; it has not changed. And this event is defiled by man. We know life on earth, we on our side know how man lives. One-thousandth of the male semen is sufficient to establish this awe-inspiring wonder. Man does not realize nor feel this; it happens in an unconscious condition, because man does not understand his own life, death and birth, nor the universe.

This wonder, André, happens every second on earth when two people connect and birth is engendered. Now I will explain another wonder.

You know now that inspiring life of the second cosmic degree descends into this small cell. The inner life returns to embryonic life. We also know that this inner life has lived before and has acquired several qualities in that life. Yet, and this is the wonder I want to explain, inner life retains all these qualities it has acquired in all those centuries. All those qualities of inner life will awaken as the material organism matures. They are part of that pre-animal-like human being, they are his acquired property. That astral being which affects embryonic life, is in actual fact the pre-animal-like but inner human being we have come to know there. Do you feel this wonder, André?

That inner life returns to nothingness and yet, it has, when we see mature man, the qualities it had already on the second cosmic degree. When we presently follow the first material but mature human beings, when the earth has performed its task, we know that inspiring life is present therein, which life we have come to know on the second cosmic degree. But even now, in this condition, it is also present and it inspires embryonic life. In nature and in all those millions of years, nothing, absolutely nothing has changed; we still see it happen in your own time, the children are born on earth in this way; the embryo is inspired in the mother body; this event is as at the beginning and origin of the earth. Is this not awe-inspiring, André?'

'I have no words for it, Alcar.'

'I'll go on now, André; follow me and keep concentrated on me.

Inspiring life is present in this bluish haze; but when material life condenses and we advance many centuries, we see that both conditions have changed considerably. A further stage now follows and, first of all, you'll see the astral world.'

André saw what happened; it was a wonderful sight. The astral world had condensed. He saw millions of beings in this spiritual world. He now felt the wonder of both lives. The planet earth had gradually condensed and a similar process took place in the spiritual world. Oh, how wonderful, he thought, how natural everything is.

Then he heard Alcar say: 'Do you see in what an amazingly natural way everything happens? Do you see that both lives follow one condition and that the material organism cannot be ahead of inner life? All that changes when we have reached the perfect material condition; but

238

when man fertilizes and connects, then happens what I explained just now when I told you of the mother body in its perfect material condition. The astral world will also condense more and more according as the earth advances ever further and we pass from one stage to the other. I am not going to follow all those stages; you know them already and it would lead too far; I'll connect you now with the thousandth and tenth-thousandth stage and we'll see what happened in those thousands of centuries. Observe André.'

'What is that, Alcar?'

'I told you I was going to connect you with other and subsequent stages. You see millions of lives. All that life, which will become man, lives in the deep waters and has now attained the fish stage. I'll go a little further, and we'll see that some of these beings have reached the shore. Pay attention, André.'

The same instant André observed. What wonder was he going to experience this time? It teemed with beings. They were on the shore, in the water, wherever he looked, everywhere was life. And this was to become man, man on earth. He witnessed an unbelievable problem.

He heard Alcar say: 'Some more centuries further and we'll see beings, man, already living on the negotiable planet. Look, there, André.'

André trembled because of all these wonders. Indeed, there were beings; man lived there and had emanated from them. The earth had advanced that far; now he saw happen on earth what he had experienced on the first planet. Oh, what wonder! How unbelievable this was for man on earth, and how natural, how clearly had he been able to follow everything from the beginning of creation. A tremendous problem had now been solved for him. He saw the first terrestrial people! The first man, my God, how is it possible. He was inwardly moved to tears watching all this on earth. Deep within him he felt profound respect and gratitude for God and his own leader for being allowed to observe this wonderful event on the planet earth.

'I have no words for it', he said to Alcar, 'I can hardly speak for it has moved me deeply.'

'I can well imagine, André. It is wonderful. This was accomplished by the good earth; all these people appeared from its interior. I was as you are now; I felt trivial and insignificant when I was shown this wonder of creation on earth. You feel all this very deeply, because you still live on earth. All, none excluded, feel that way when they die on earth and enter this life, and if they do not want to understand their own lives, a spiritual brother or sister on this side descends with those disbelieving brothers and sisters to the origin of everything and of themselves, and then happens what you now feel and experience. Then they are silent and do not speak; but those who are allowed to see this, are inwardly broken and bend their heads. If anything can convince man of his insignificance on earth it is the origin of the universe. We on our side can connect ourselves with the initial stage of the earth, because we, living on this side, have experienced all that.

Here, we were born, but millions of years were to pass before the perfect material organism had developed. It still took that long before the planet and all those material degrees of the human organism were ready, like your own material organism is now perfect.'

'How deep, but how natural everything you show me is, Alcar. I am so grateful that I can't say much, but do feel my gratitude.'

'I feel you, my boy. I, too, and all beings allowed to see this, were grateful. I tell you, André, look at this wonder and feel what it means that God is the Father of all of us. Do not forget that God gave us all this and that we, human beings, were born out of this process. I understand that you can't speak, for it is so mighty that it cannot be expressed in words. You only feel the insignificance of our personality, even though man has his perfect organism, when you follow him and see how he lives and destroys God's life.

We emanate from the earth, from nothingness, from the invisible, which is God.

We will go on now and follow the first human beings on earth. You see, André, that human beings already live on this negotiable planet. The earth is not yet ready though, because there are still human beings living in those waters. Those beings must first leave the water before life commences on this negotiable and condensed earth. But even in this era there were seven degrees of material organism. We see the first and thousandth stage, which comprise all those degrees we'll presently see on this negotiable planet.

I'll skip a few centuries. What happened in this period? Those, which had reached the shore, also developed and multiplied. In those centuries those first material beings attained the human condition and they were the prehistoric beings which lived on earth. I'll show you that process of evolution, you will see how far they have advanced, which

240

you will find most amazing. Look, centuries have passed again.'

André experienced one wonder after another. He saw these people: how coarse and crude they all were. He observed the male and female being and all were hairy, like animals. They were still animals, but he recognized man by their bodies. See, how powerful those bodies are, though this first man had a monstrous physique.

This was accomplished by the planet earth and was to become man. This wonder had reached that stage.

'These beings, André, could proceed and occupy the earth. However, human beings were still living in those deep waters, who had to discard their fish stage. I'll go on and we'll see what happened.

Many of the first human beings who had reached this negotiable planet died when their cosmic time had come, which is normal death; others, however, were attacked by prehistoric animals, dragged into the water and served as food for these enormous animal species, which, like man, lived here. The animal was in essence good-natured, but man awakened this animal being, which happened already on the second cosmic degree. We saw there how the human being destroyed the animal kingdom; and the soul, of man as well as of animal, was attracted by the planet earth and would be born here. When the animal kingdom awakened on earth and had received this awe-inspiring material organism, a struggle developed between man and animal, which continued for thousands of centuries.

Before I go on, I'll return to the animal kingdom, for the animal followed man and attained this material organism. To this end I must connect you with the first stage.'

André felt himself sink away deeper and he began to observe. He heard Alcar say: 'This is the world of human embryonic life. What I explained to you on the first planet about the animal kingdom, happened here too, for here on the planet earth it was one and the same condition and event. I showed you the spiritual world, how inspiring life condensed and subsequently how embryonic life was inspired. However, you will now see another wonder.

There, in front of you, André, you see this world which also comprises the astral world for the animal kingdom. This world is therefore in the human astral world, as on the first planet, and it is also invisible for human inspiring life. When the first human 'peel' died and decayed, the inspiring being descended from the astral animal world and, after a long time, the first animal being was born. Not merely one, but dozens of beings; they were so tiny and small, that they could not be seen with the naked eye. And yet, after many years, when this process proceeded, we see thousands of these beings in the waters, because all those beings rapidly multiplied. I won't follow all that, you see that wonder also materialized here on earth and that it was already in advance. That enormous animal being on the second cosmic degree animates the material animal on the third cosmic degree, the earth. This was one event; for man and animal had to go on. Every planet created its own organism, though brought about by the mother body. The earth, as I explained to you, condensed and enlarged many animal species, which sometime pass on into the true cosmic organism.

I now go to the final stage where we were just now, and we see both man and the animal kingdom again.'

André felt himself return.

'This is also wonderful and natural, Alcar.'

'Indeed, André, a natural law has manifested itself.

Now I'll pass on centuries and in those centuries we see that man has multiplied and so has the animal kingdom. I said that a terrible struggle developed between man and animal and many people were destroyed. The earth condensed, the last beings living in the waters appeared and life on earth commenced. During all those centuries millions of human beings had died and returned to pass on to the highest material degree. Now we see an entirely different condition.

At this time seven different species of material beings lived on earth, and these material transitions were also present in the animal kingdom, but in the animal kingdom these material degrees had become very extensive, because out of one species many other animal species had developed. The highest material degree of man was the black being, but it had a prehistoric material organism. And there was more.

At that time, André, there was no white race yet; that still had to be born. During the centuries that passed, this material organism got ready and, again, we see an earth, which differs from the one in those other conditions.

Human beings now lived in all corners of the world, divided in groups. After centuries had passed again, these beings awakened as did the animal kingdom so that both attained consciousness. Man had pre-animal consciousness and when he passed on to it, that violent struggle of

242

which I spoke, sparked off. Man attacked the animal and the animal attacked man. Human passions awakened and constituted their personality. Centuries passed.

In those centuries man joined together, because the animal forced him to. Man in those days was no match for the animal, even though there were animal species, which were not malicious and would not attack human beings, not even when they were killed. But there were species, which would attack the human being; this hatred developed on the second cosmic degree and was inherent in the animal on earth, like man had brought his pre-animal consciousness with them.

The groups became larger as the number of human beings increased, the struggle on earth in particular became more violent, though no longer against the animal but against those human beings born in a different place. Every second human being was killed. The more advanced human being slew the others who had not yet attained that highest material degree. It was no longer a struggle of man against man, but they went into battle in groups of hundreds and those they met were killed; the strongest therefore conquered. In this era the more advanced people joined together, as did the lower degrees of material organism, and we still see this in your time on earth. This has not changed either.

One group attacked the other; but something proceeded and that was the planet earth, which went on completing the perfect material organism. Some centuries later these material organisms have appeared on earth, and the picture of the earth has changed again. The higher and further man advanced, the stronger became hatred for the other man and also for the animal kingdom. That hatred became more conscious and fiercer, so that the prehistoric aspect had vanished forever.

Those groups of people became tribes, and after a long time these tribes became nations which produced rulers. These people lived in groups of thousands, scattered all over the earth. It will be clear to you that they developed into all those various races and nations, white people already being among them. This race began to dominate and the earth also proceeded. What used to be a quagmire in centuries gone by, condensed and those regions, too, became populated. This occurred all over the earth. The earth continued its difficult task and brought this about, to which end it had occupied its place in the universe. People joined together still closer and killed everything coming their way and proceeded to large scale fighting. Thousands were killed. The higher degrees passed on to a higher stage of feeling, but the lower degrees were all cannibals.

In this era, the earth had completed one third of its task, and this was a great wonder. For those living in a lower degree of material organism, meeting and seeing the white race*) was a great wonder. They did not understand it; but the whites knew what to do with them and attacked them. Materially more advanced man, therefore, dominated the planet earth, but he did this by manslaughter and violence. In this respect nothing has changed either in all those millions of years.

We see nothing but animal violence, killing, all the time these beings were not capable of other things, although that time would come.

Centuries passed again, in the meantime the perfect human organism was ready, and we see that the seven material degrees are present in the highest degree. Finally the earth had advanced that far with its task and we observe the following situation.

The lowest degree of material organism was the prehistoric animal-like being while the highest being lived in a material organism which became perfect in those thousands of centuries which followed. Then the planet earth had completed its task and we learn to know other laws. One law steadily remained effective, the process of dying. In those thousands of centuries billions of people had died. What happened with all those beings? We'll follow that now, André; after that I'll return to the development of the earth.'

*) See the 'Explanation' at the beginning of this book.

# CHAPTER VI

## Development of the hell

I AM going to explain other wonders to you. I'll return to those first human beings who have reached this negotiable planet, for these beings were to die. We'll follow them as spiritual beings, in other words: I pass on to the psychic world. The planet earth was ready, but what happened in the astral world? There was a world for inner life, too, and that world became the image of the earth, but in a spiritual condition. I am going to connect you with it.'

André felt himself sink away and he began to observe.

'You see, André, there is darkness. The spheres of light, in which we are now living, did not yet exist, for man had no inner light yet; inner spiritual man still had to be born. Now listen carefully. When the first human beings died on earth, they returned to the astral world and waited there to be attracted again. In that era there was nothing but birth and death, return to the earth to pass into an other material organism. All those beings, inspiring life, had to follow that course to attain the perfect material condition, and they were to return until that attunement had been acquired. These beings, as will no doubt be clear to you, could not progress any more because they had not acquired a world of existence, and would not advance that far until during that further and higher stage of the earth. They were to return to the earth to receive the highest material organism; only then would they have completed their cycle on earth.

There is still darkness which is the astral world we saw on the second cosmic degree and which I connected you with. So nothing has changed, at any rate not in the astral world, in all those thousands of centuries the spiritual world has not changed, because inner man had not advanced that far. Is that clear, André?'

'Yes, Alcar.'

'Then I'll skip centuries. Yet there was activity, something happened in the astral world, unknown to anybody. In the astral world an other world came into being. Man created that world. I'll explain that process to you and we get to know the hell.

I explained that man proceeded in his material condition on earth

245

and awakened and this awakening meant hatred, passion and animal-ization. Every sin they committed, every mistake man made by taking the life of others, all those horrors made the astral world condense and that became hell. In that world a second world developed through hatred, passion and violence, and this world became the world of existence for those who had completed their cycle on earth. I'll pass several thousands of centuries and show you what happened during that period. Look and observe, André.'

'My God, what is that, Alcar?'

'The hell, André; hell in life after death. Man is creating hell and the astral world has condensed during those centuries.'

André saw another world in this darkness. How is it possible, he thought.

'Could this not be avoided, Alcar?'

'No, my boy.'

'Do people already live here?'

'No, not yet, they will arrive presently when man has reached the highest material degree.'

My God, how terrible, André thought.

'You say that the astral world, the hell, is waiting for man?'

'Yes, André; it could not be avoided. Alas, darkness is waiting. This would become hell in life after death and man built it himself, for man has passed to a condition of consciousness, inner life has acquired it. Man created hell, God did not want it. God gave man everything, His own life, but it is man who created it. As I said, conscious evil developed on earth and man created it. Do you feel all this, André?'

'If I understand you correctly, Alcar, I feel both worlds. The first astral world is the natural world, if I may put it that way, but an unconscious one; the other world is a conscious one.'

'Indeed; that's right. For man has to go on; and although this is hell, this world is at a higher stage than the world of the unconscious. One day the end on earth will come. Inner life became conscious; it acquired an animal-like consciousness and attunes to something, which would be the spiritual world of existence after death on earth. We have come to know this dark sphere as the hell, a conscious world. Both astral worlds were one but invisible for the other. I'll skip some centuries again, and you will see how the hell condensed.'

André observed that next stage. How is it possible, he thought, he saw a mountainous landscape. This was hell, the shadow of reality. This was the conscious spiritual world, but hell in life after death; darkness on the side beyond.

'No people live here yet, Alcar?'

'No, not yet; not until thousands of years later.'

'How terrible, Alcar! Did man have to go through evil first in order to reach higher life? Was it preordained in the plan of creation? Was it God's intention?'

'You ask me many questions, my son, but all people will ask those questions if they do not know the material and spiritual creation. Yes, my boy; was all this necessary? Why all that evil when man is a Divine being? Listen carefully; I will explain that.

In the first place God gave man His own life, as I told you many times. All this is evidence of God's pure love. It has been like this from the first moment, as God's sacred love was present in the first stage and man received that love, he received everything and got a will of his own. All this was still unconscious on all those planets, but here on earth man was to become conscious. When this happened, as we have seen, man forgot himself and slaughtered God's own life present in man and animal. Man, therefore, did not understand his Divine attunement. But he should learn to understand himself. Man passed from one condition on to the next, but in all those lives he forgot himself and killed. The astral world condensed through passion and animalization, and the condensation process increased alarmingly. Man was to live in that world when he had acquired the highest material degree and died on earth. Inner man entered this life, but not until he had completed his material cycle on earth. Do you feel what it means, André?'

'If I understand you correctly, I feel that this world had to be, or the development of man would come to a standstill and further advance would be out of the question.'

'Very good, André; that's correct. Inner man had to go on, he could no longer descend into the world of the unconscious, he was conscious, although it was an animal-like attunement. Consequently, his inner life attuned to an other world, which is hell in life after material death.'

'Now I understand, Alcar.'

'Splendid; I'll go on. You asked, could man avoid this? Was this God's intention? Did man have to go through evil to acquire the Divine Spheres? I ask you: can man acquire Divinity in a few centuries? All this is the Divine love he has to acquire. Is that possible in one short life on earth? Is that possible in ten, twenty, say hundreds of lives?

Look around you, André. Look up and down, to the right and left; look at the stars and planets and look at everything living in the universe, then try to imagine the invisible worlds man will get to know. All that is God. We people must learn all that and acquire it. Is it really not worthwhile to live for that and give it everything you have? Man will have to earn this and accept it in full love, for that is God's will; that is why we are Divine. God revealed Himself in man and in all life, but man destroys this life. As a result he created another condition, which meant darkness, cold, misery and sorrow to him and that is not what God wanted. He knew that His children would forget themselves. Man was to become conscious and millions of lives are required to attain the supreme degree.

Therefore, did man have to go through evil to attain the Divine Spheres? I hope this will be clear to you.

I also asked those questions as did all my sisters and brothers on this side; we know now that it was ourselves who created hell. Through that very misery, darkness and cold, André, we would awaken and understand and appreciate our future happiness. We would get to know ourselves through all the misery and I'll presently explain how this happened. Again, God knew all this and let us have our way, God had nothing more to give; we received everything in the first stage. Doesn't it speak for itself: 'God has nothing more to give.' All this sorrow, all this great human misery exists on one planet. All these horrors are only known on earth, thereafter comes Divine happiness, which man has then earned, he is busy returning to God and he has already covered a long way.

Again I ask you: Is it not worthwhile to live for that? Having to be on earth and to experience those thousands of lives for all that tremendous happiness? People have everything in their own hands, André, and they will begin to understand life on earth when they become spiritually conscious, and acquire this consciousness. God does not punish, He cannot punish, but man punishes himself. God created heaven and earth, but man created darkness. Man became the creator of light and darkness and would live in these two worlds after death on earth. Thence, further and higher towards perfection, back to the source we came from. Is this also clear to you, André?'

'I have understood everything, Alcar; and I bend my head for these truths.'

'Thank you; then we'll go on, as there is more I have to show and explain to you.

Thus, the animal-like being returned to the earth and so did the astral human being. On earth, man did nothing but fight and yet, according as man progressed, intellect awakened and one thing emanated from the other. I'll return to the material world. People on earth lived in caves, but this is going to change. When we follow life on earth, we see that people have progressed. They had made weapons of stone and wood for their collective struggle and after those weapons other useful discoveries followed. Some races, however, were more advanced than others. As you know, there were already white people, and this race was beautified by the planet earth until this material organism had reached the highest degree.*)

They invent something to protect themselves against the animal kingdom. When fire was discovered, they proceeded to other things, they made huts, which the highest material degree had known for quite some time. This proves that inner man developed and became interested in other things. They also became interested in the soil, and they started farming. All that pointed to progress, which continued steadily. Only then did man become aware of his abilities and powers and his feelings changed, although he retained his pre-animal-like state of consciousness. Many centuries later we see a different world again.

As I said, one thing emanated from the other, and this went on. All these people did not know a God; consequently, religions were unknown. However, feeling developed, and with this feeling faith, although for them it was only fear, fear of the elements. When nature revolted, these beings became restless, especially when many perished and were destroyed by the elements. Not only the elements developed faith, the motherly feeling also awakened in a higher condition and consciousness, and this feeling led to faith, also for fear of losing what was dear to them. You feel, André, how far the inner human being had advanced.

For fear of being killed, they knelt down and when that drove the enemy away, it was a power superior to theirs. This created faith and all races, I mean the higher species, felt it was a higher power than their own.

In later times, there were other things to which these people clung. Thus, the foundation of their primitive faith stemmed from their fears

*) See the 'Explanation' at the beginning of this book.

and anxieties. When I show you the picture of the earth many centuries later, a lot has changed again.

The earth experienced various eras. Everything living on earth changed; everything living on the land and in the waters experienced this material and also inner evolution. The various races joined more and more together and all those degrees of material life spread over the earth. Millions of beings of every species were present on earth and other laws had become effective.

When people on earth had advanced that far, hell in life after death was still empty. Now that degree was attained, millions of human beings had completed their cycle on earth and were about to die. But their inner life was in a pre-animal-like condition. Man had not acquired anything in all those centuries but had indulged themselves and lived their lives to the full. They had received one life after the other. In one life they had killed their fellow-men and in thousands of other lives they had done no differently and yet, time and again they received a new material organism until they had acquired the beautiful, perfect material body. Their ego, an animal-like being, lived in it, but that being also had the Divine attunement. There was no inner possession yet and that very last life on earth passed in passion and animalization. Wherever one looked, man and animal lived together. Their struggle to the bitter end went on; the lower brothers and sisters were killed so that the highest degree was lord and master on earth, to which these beings belonged.

Then their end on earth came and they entered an other world.

You do feel, André, that these were the first people of the hell, people who could no longer return to the earth, because they had completed their material cycle and were attracted by that other world. In this case the dark spheres, the astral world, or hell in life after death. These people were free from the world of the unconscious and entered a world of existence. We discussed this on the second cosmic degree. Now you will be able to understand all this.

In a short period this number grew alarmingly, for every second beings came to the side beyond. Those who had not yet completed their material cycle, returned to the earth and entered the world of the unconscious upon death. From this moment on we see various spiritual worlds in life after death; in the first place we know the darkness, or hell, then the world of the unconscious and the astral world for the animal kingdom. The animal kingdom also has its astral world, and that world, in which inspiration for the animal being lives existed from the very beginning of creation. The astral world has always existed for man as well, I explained that on the first cosmic degree. Now, however, inner life has become conscious and man entered a higher stage, in this case hell in life after death. The astral animal world has also condensed, that world has also changed, because those prehistoric animal species passed on into other animal species. It is fundamentally as for man in both worlds, the material as well as the spiritual world.

The next point, André; ask me if you do not understand me, only then can we follow the human beings living in the darkness.

At the beginning of creation there was darkness. That darkness was in essence energy, and that energy God. Invisible energy, therefore, which condensed into suns, stars and planets and revealed itself in man and animal. But all that life is God.

In the darkness, the hell, there are spheres, different worlds for man and yet, and that is my point, the All is present here. God lives in that darkness, although man is not yet aware of it. God is invisible energy, God is light and darkness. God, therefore, lives behind and in all this, because if God didn't, man and animal could not go further and higher. We have seen that one thing awakened the other and revealed itself, and once man became conscious he could see in other worlds, because this Divine life has not as yet attained the source of all life, to which it belongs. Therefore, André, progress is possible, there must be progress or we human beings would not develop any more and were excluded from progress. Do you feel what I mean, André?

We are now confronted by a great event, for how did the situation change? Man has acquired a condition of consciousness, lives in the darkness and is not aware of progress. But in this darkness is the Divine light, lives God, is the All, are the Divine spheres. Now isn't this in-comprehensible? Can you feel this, André?

Man therefore must awaken, must go ever higher and that happened. This also awakened in man, he began to see and feel and understand himself. But this process of understanding himself took centuries, because man continued to concentrate on evil, but there is an end to everything; also to the darkness which they, the first human beings, entered. In all those centuries we see that many material, and also spir-itual wonders have happened. But what did the beings do who entered here? We shall follow them. Have you understood everything so far, André?'

'Yes, Alcar; I am moved by reality.'

'I can well imagine. Those who learn to understand God's creation in the natural way, who feel and experience the laws of nature, bend their heads deeply for all this simplicity, all these infallible laws, and recognize the Divine aim. They see and feel that it must be like this, that this is the real truth. Now I'll tell you of other wonders.

These people, who, as I said, awakened, for they all fell asleep and this spiritual sleep was deep, so that years by earthly standards passed, saw and experienced that they were alive. I explained all those conditions to you in hell and you know that when man dies on earth, he will arrive here in an unconscious condition.

When the first beings woke up from their deep sleep, they jumped up and ran around in the darkness like mad men; they did not know or understand that they were dead and had died on earth. They touched and felt themselves and wondered why this deep darkness prevailed.

Where is the starry sky, where is the light, that sunlight and everything we see on earth? Where are we ourselves? Thus wondered those first human beings who inhabited the darkness. Are we alive, are we dead, and where are all those people, our father and mother, sisters and brothers, in short, all the things we had on earth? But there came light in their dark lives, and this light meant that they were not alone. Thousands, nay, millions entered that darkness and all of them wondered about the same things, which man in your time still does when he dies on earth and enters this life. All, non excluded, I mean those who had attained the highest material condition on earth, entered hell in life after death. Aren't you surprised, André?'

'No, Alcar, because they had no inner light.'

'Very good, my son, you follow me in everything, thank you. No, there was no light yet, but man was to become creator of that light; for, as I also explained just now, man has the Divine attunement. God's own life and light are in man, but they had not advanced that far. Now what happened on this side, in the astral world? Once awakened and conscious in their animal-like life here, all these people roamed about and passed on into each other. They began a terrible life, because they felt passion and violence, they were only open for evil.

There were only men and women here, there were no children, only mature people could live here, because they had attained that attunement. What they could do in material life, they did here too, they had no inner spiritual possession, they experienced all those passions again, they attacked each other and struck down whoever came their way. Here in the darkness, André, they indulged themselves again and their life was as it had been on earth.

That continued for a considerable time, though for many it came to an end. These beings, who deeply thought of what they had once known and yearned for it, suddenly felt drawn away from their condition, their darkness and hell. It was an other force, stronger than their own; a force which attracted them and brought them again on earth, but this time as astral beings. But darkness remained, as there was no light in them. They were attracted by material man on earth who had the same attunement and the astral man passed on into this inner life, whether he wanted or not, and experienced a new life. These beings were attracted by the inner but material man on earth. Do you feel now, André, what would happen and what would result from it?'

'Did they pass on into man on earth?'

'Yes, that happened; but there is more.'

André thought for a long time and said: 'They experienced what man experienced, Alcar.'

'Very good, André; but there is something else still.'

André thought again, but he could not get on to it and he said to his leader: 'I don't know, Alcar.'

'You are honest, my son; but you should have known.*) What have I explained to you on our last journey but one?'

'Oh, yes; I should have thought of that. I know now, Alcar.'

'You see that you must think and feel, or we don't get any further. I am doing this because I want you to know and understand all those spiritual laws, also in your life on earth, presently when you are again in your material organism. It will be of great value to you, because you will then see and feel all these laws, which is spiritual wisdom. So listen carefully and ask me if something is not clear.

Now, obsession arose on earth and insanity developed. One thing developed out of the other, out of the preceding being an other emanated which was obsession and insanity for man on earth. The astral spirit was attracted by those earthly beings, and the more sensitive of

*) See the book: 'Mental Diseases as seen from the Side Beyond'.

them passed on into these spiritual beings and were obsessed.

An illness, a mental illness had come into being and these mental illnesses will remain, they will continue to ruin the human being until there are no more bad people on earth and on this side. Then these illnesses and symptoms cease and can no longer exist, man no longer finds man to take possession of from this world and every soul will then feel what is good and work for it. Is this clear to you?'

'It is horrible, but again natural, Alcar.'

'You see that the astral man again passed into his animal-like life and brought hell and horror on earth. You know how they can connect with man on earth, I explained that. In those days life on earth was terrible, but even now, in your time, it is no different. This awful illness is still on earth, and many go to ruin because they are open to evil. Now imagine that hell in life after death and on earth. All were influenced, non excluded. Life on earth went on, people joined together and the astral being lived in and around them. It was a spiritual and material chaos. Man on earth was stirred up, because these demons lived in and around them and now hatred, passion and animalization really did burst out, which was beyond description.

Man on earth was in fire. Urged on by the demonic being, man forgot himself as never before. The human beings were destroyed by the thousand and many women were defiled and besmirched. This can no longer be retraced, but this era when man felt like that and had sunk so deeply, cannot return, even though man in your time thinks that evil dominates. This was horrible.

What is man like in your time? They think there is no end to it. Those who seek the good, feel the terror of those few who hold power over thousands of lives, dazzling others with their ideas as if they were the true prophets. But that is worldly, it is material; it is temporary, it will and must happen because man on earth lives in his own wilderness and has no feeling to start a higher life. We have followed that from this side. I showed you on this side through all those journeys we made together, that man is to blame for this downfall, and that he has acted in that way, even if he now feels differently than those demons. In thousands of lives, I assure you this is hidden in the distant past, but we can show them on this side, they massacred thousands and thousands of lives, they animalized, like those who made themselves rulers of the earth. These beings now think that they are different, but they know

254

hatred, passion and violence, they slaughter their fellow-men. But I know and thousands on this side know, as well as those in the spheres of light and those who have returned to the All, that all those times will pass, that all that misery will dissolve when the individual awakend and tries to create an atmosphere in his surroundings the way God so dearly wants us to. But they are not different, although their hatred and life are not as bad as of those of all others. In these times people were not savages, but devils. Those spiritual monsters lived a life on earth similar to the life they had lived in the material organism.

That is what the poor earth was like in that era, it was terrible. When would this end? The end is not yet in sight; but it will come, though not until thousands of centuries later.

The earth continued and ignored all those beings living on its surface. It developed the material organism and beautified it, but according as this human organism became finer, inner life became increasingly horrible. We see, André, how far that material organism has advanced and how far inner life is behind. But how far indeed was the material organism ahead of inner life? It could not be drawn up; that gap cannot be tided over thousands of years. All this happened, had to happen, because inner man had to awaken.

Those millions of beings, who had returned to the earth would awaken. They saw and experienced many possibilities to live on earth again, to give full rein to their passions, and exactly in this way they got to know other laws. What happened?

Something awakened in them because of all the things they experienced, so that they began to understand those adventures. Children were born by them, which, as a matter of fact, still happens on earth in your time. They experienced whatever they wished, because millions of people lived on earth who wanted a similar life. All these human beings on earth were open for murder, passion, violence and animalization, and they attracted them because they had the same attunement. In this way they gave full rein to their various passions. When, afterwards, they calmed down, when the fire of passion was extinguished and they were satisfied, they were open for other things and they helped man on earth with something or other.

And how amazed they were that man acted in accordance with what they had urged them to do. This was no longer evil, but something of value in their lives. When they had lived to the full, they began to

255

protect these beings, for fear that they might pass on into other hands. You surely feel that out of all this, out of all this misery and animalization, all that hatred and passion, good was born. Slowly but surely something developed in them and they saw and experienced that, when they began to provide for happiness of man on earth, to protect him against many other things, as this was also possible, there was more light. Then there was something that made them feel less cold and sad. Something that warmed them encouraged and lightened them.

From this moment on inner man awakened in these beings, not only because of what I told you, not only by all those good things they did and by inspiring the beings they could reach; there was something else deep down in them which would make them awaken. That was the Divine Spark, the Divine attunement, for life would go on; they did live in the All, as I explained to you; life would advance ever more, and man began to feel and experience this.

Now there was something in these beings which urged them on; something they had awakened in themselves; because deep down in man is a nucleus, a power which is the connection and attunement to our Father in heaven. They awakened this and it urged them on, and as a result inner man awakened. This process started in all those millions of beings, each in his own condition. Slowly but surely they began to feel it; because, as I said, when they did good things for people on earth their world was not so cold and dark any more, and it was as if something was present in that terrible hell which warmed them. And that is what they wanted to have, it made them go on.

Yet, these feelings weakened time and again and they assumed that animal-like life; they drained people again and killed them; their inner life was again in fire and they felt as before. However, they went on and had to go on and they started that other life, but each time they returned to their former lives.

This process of trial and error continued for thousands of years. These beings nevertheless awakened and the struggle between good and evil had begun. Something already sought nothing but good and inspired man on earth to seek good, even though these material beings were not aware of it. A great many centuries passed. These souls lived in the dark spheres and were in life after death for thousands of years. The astral world condensed, as I said, in an alarming way.

Life on earth passed from one era to the other. Wherever one looked and human beings lived, there was horror; hell and the devil had set in. Everyone wanted to possess and every human being lived to the full. Compare this world with the one in which you live and tell me if anything has changed. We still see this on earth, people still kill each other and steal each other's happiness. This came to life in the distant past and now that we as well as the earth are billions of years old, man has not changed a bit and pre-animal-like beings in human shape are living on this planet. There is no love yet; they do not feel and understand themselves yet and do not know they have been on their way for billions of years and will return to the Divine Spheres. We are still laughed at when we speak of eternal progress; man does not understand death. Man shrugs his shoulders at spiritual laws, depths and truths, yes, at all these things, this entire truth which is all the same deep down in him.

My God, when will they begin to feel that You are nothing but Love? Hear my prayer, feel my love, you man of the earth, I would not be able to lie, to talk nonsense; this, what lives on this side, is your own past, your life and your Divine attunement. Where will it all end if they continue to follow this way? But once there will be an end to all that misery, all that madness, because there will be no more bad humans.

These human beings, André, not only struggled against all those unknown illnesses, which are still not understood on earth, they also had to contend with thousands of other things and misery, which made life on earth a hell. One being poisoned the other and they were in need of everything. Nobody had anything he could leave on earth, there was no property, because they were not in any way gifted. That would come, though thousands of centuries later. Is it clear to you, what sort of chaos prevailed on earth? And that these times find no comparison?

There is still grief, sorrow and misery on earth, but everything is different, quite different from that time. That is how man acted; and that is what we were like, André, I and you and the angels on our side. Those were our first lives on the planet earth. This changed, however, but it took a long time before those who had already felt that inner warmth awakened again. And there were many who had felt and experienced it; because millions of beings emerged out of every degree. Do you feel what this means?'

'Yes, Alcar.'

'Well then, all these beings lived all over the world and they began a higher life and their world started to change. This is the moment when the spheres of light were born and man became the creator of light.

Man as creator of light, do you feel what that means? This being possessed this power, this awe-inspiring truth. Man searched for the good and sought what would give him inner warmth. Centuries later this process came true, because what do we see then!

Light came around them. The good things they did and established on earth for mankind built an other world in the spirit, which became the spheres of light.

# CHAPTER VII

## *Man, creator of light*

EVERY good deed man did on earth and in the spheres changed his inner life, his surroundings and his own level. He got light, inner man awakened. They developed it, so that this light became stronger, which they observed in and around them. Inner man began to radiate light, to awaken and to feel love for all life. The more good deeds they did, the stronger this light became and it irradiated their surroundings. The delightful feeling to be able to do something for others, made them happy. Now, they were worthy of the name man. Now, they were children of God and all felt how much they had to make up. But they gave themselves entirely and sacrificed themselves for suffering humanity.

Man returned to the golden light and acquired it, as we have seen in the temple of the soul. You see and feel, André, that we emanated from that golden light and would return to it. We were to acquire that light. Man began to earn God's own loving radiance. The revelation of God now commenced in man, because these people understood they could go further and higher. They would make every effort; they understood how they had to live, and serving man was born.

When the first flashes of light pierced the darkness, God revealed Himself and the plan of creation, of which I told you, commenced. For all these people it meant that they had freed themselves from the darkness and had covered that long road. When the first flashes of light appeared, the aspect of the earth changed. These beings, who had lived in the darkness, now saw by their own light how far the earth had advanced. In all those millions of years they had been spiritually blind; now they understood the process of death and birth on earth and thousands of laws of the life of the spirit. Those who had advanced that far, taught others who had not attained that level. They already were the spiritual brothers and sisters of the spheres.

More advanced man in life on earth could be picked up upon death and brought to the place of his destination. Surely you feel, André, that only those people could be picked up who had completed their cycle of life on earth. Thus, every human being was brought to his spiritual attunement. The greater the number of people on earth who had reached the highest material degree and had inwardly acquired something, the more the image of the spheres changed. For also on earth, in material life, there were people who were beginning to seek higher things. An ever increasing number of people arrived on the side beyond who had completed their cycle of life on earth. These beings built at the spheres, at their spiritual dwellings and yet, the first, second, third, fourth, fifth, sixth and seventh sphere had still to come into being, because they had not advanced that far. The light they possessed, was like that in the Land of Twilight on this side, the sphere of which Gerhard*) told you. The spiritual world, however, came into being. Vegetation appeared, the spiritual spheres began to condense, because the spheres had to follow the same course, like everything else had experienced natural development.

Again we clearly see, André, that one thing emanated from the other and that everything in the entire creation had to follow one course which remained unchanged, also now that man is conscious. Some centuries later we see that the first sphere has been established. You know that the first sphere is an image of the earth. This world was created on our side by inner man and this became, as you know, the hereafter.

I'll pass on several centuries again.

We now see a wonderful thing. The first sphere came into being and proceeded to pass on into an other condition, which was to become the second sphere. In life after death everybody who had attained this level, owned a spiritual dwelling and, in accordance with their progress, they saw its exterior become more beautiful. Thus, not only their own spiritual organism, but also everything around them became more beautiful and pure. Everything came to life in this way and they learned to understand the spiritual laws. They followed the development of nature and learned thereby. Now, a feeling for art awakened and temples and buildings were built. These highly attuned beings, who had become conscious in the spirit, became also aware of the higher powers in man, and one art after the other came into being.

In the spheres, in the various temples and buildings which still exist, we can follow the initial stage of man, his entrance into the spiritual world and how it all happened. Nothing has been lost; here, too, everything is fixed.

*) See the book: 'The Bridge to Eternal Life.

260

Earthly and spiritual life went on and as time went by we see every-thing on earth and in the life of the spirit change. Millions of beings, all from the earth, who had laid aside their material organism there, helped and built their own dwelling and sphere by doing something for others.

I will now, before going on, tell you another wonder. Those who were in the spheres of light and prepared to receive their brothers and sisters who were about to come, experienced an amazing development. There was something in the spheres, they felt it clearly, which was not perfect. Fully concentrated as they were, they had not given it much attention, but when the picture of the spheres changed, when people there also had to perform a task, though most of them worked in the sphere of the earth, they perceived a very beautiful scene, a wonder of God.

From the beginning of creation, the animals continued to follow the gifted cosmic and Divine being; both beings were always together. Those who experienced it fell on their knees and wept for emotion. Birds were around them, my boy, and they sang their song of joy and happiness. The animal had passed through its thousands of stages and had, like man, reached the spiritual spheres. What a marvellous scene! What mighty grace for man and animal, for both had got that far. The ani-mal knew no hatred any more, it had experienced all those organisms and the highest animal species had reached the spiritual attunement. They descended and perched on the hands of their higher sisters and brothers. My God, such happiness, such a wonder and grace! Now they really felt what had happened on earth. A Divine problem had been solved. The animal also progressed and would join them on the Divine road.

What was it like on earth? Not much had changed on earth. Fighting continued and man indulged himself. I will go on in the spiritual do-main and we see how man reached the Divine Spheres.

Once advanced that far, man continued to serve and in doing so the spheres changed, as did his own spiritual level. After the first, the sec-ond sphere came into being and in these spheres trees and flowers grew and bloomed; and according as man advanced, the spheres and every-thing living in and around him became more beautiful. The inner light man had acquired radiated on others, the spiritual dwellings radiated the inner light of man and temples and buildings arose. Many brought their knowledge and happiness on earth, and one invention after the other was made. Life on earth had started and the intellectual world awakened. We'll follow spiritual man and we see that sphere after sphere came into being and was acquired. Millions, as I said before, helped building; all contributed to their own possession which became the conditions of existence, the spheres, which belonged to all of them.

Gradually, one sphere after the other came into being. Man progressed ever more and the spheres became higher and more beautiful. One sphere developed from the other and in the life of the spirit, too, one thing emanated from the other.

The universe also changed, that is to say the universe of the spirit. Whereas the spiritual sky in the first sphere was as on earth, the second sphere was far ahead of the first and the third sphere was more beautiful still; but the fourth could not be compared with the first three spheres, it was that beautiful and superior.

Those who had reached the fourth sphere, very clearly felt that they were entirely free from the earth and that nothing material remained. They also felt that they lived in the All and that those Divine powers were in and around them and that they had to acquire them. These beings no longer returned to the earth, as they could make themselves useful in the spheres. There, too, a lot of work had to be done. Meanwhile teachers arrived, who had studied earthly and spiritual life. They instructed the others who were to return to the earth on a mission, because they knew what mankind on earth needed most of all. Thus, one thing resulted from the other. Millions of astral beings were now on earth urging mankind to seek the good.

Man also progressed in the spheres, we see the fifth, sixth and seventh sphere come into being. In the seventh sphere the light of man has changed into a golden light. In this sphere we see the image of the golden Divine light which man had to acquire. This spiritual and Divine light was to become as we were allowed to see at the beginning of creation, in the process of revelation. Man was to acquire it and that happened too.

We now see a different picture in the spheres. All spheres from the dark spheres onward were inhabited; and billions of beings lived on this side.

How tremendous the light of the seventh heaven was; for after the fourth sphere the spheres are spiritual heavens. How great happiness was of man living there, and yet man had to acquire four more cosmic degrees, in order to enter the Divine Spheres. The people who had arrived in the seventh sphere and had completed their task, prepared to take leave of their brothers and sisters. Those who had performed a task there assigned this task to others. The mentors passed on, and with them millions of others. An other planet, an other solar system awaited them. Coming into being of these spiritual spheres also took millions of years.

You surely feel that there was no longer darkness for them; darkness was only for the planet earth. They had freed themselves of darkness and had acquired the highest spiritual attunement. This meant for them the end of the third cosmic degree, and they would be attracted by the fourth cosmic degree. Great happiness awaited them and they were to have it in a material condition. They also had to experience transitions, planets in connection with the fourth cosmic degree. The astral world was a world of light and these spiritual beings were attracted into this invisible world; they were the inspiring beings for the material organism they were to receive there. We call this invisible world the mental regions. In that life, as I said before, they received pure happiness, a condition man on earth cannot imagine. However, you will see them when we begin our next journey.

When they had arrived there, these people experienced inner life, the same event they had experienced from the beginning of creation. On the fourth cosmic degree, a planet, material embryo was ready; the development of those planets, the activity and the experiencing inspiring life, are as we have seen in creation. I cannot tell you how long condensation of the fourth cosmic degree took, I cannot feel all those powers. What we know we received from the cosmic masters as was shown to you in the temple of the soul. The process of attraction and passing on to those planets, André, you surely feel, has not changed, it could not change, because it applies to the entire universe. Yet, everything must have been different there, as inspiring and inner life had been down that road a billion times and therefore reached the mental condition of consciousness. But everything belonging to the material and spiritual condition and representing a particle of creation, had to follow but one course, which we have been able to follow in the first three cosmic degrees.

Now I will explain the 'ulitmate' in a few flashes, that is, when man entered 'Divinity'.

As I explained, every cosmic degree, at any rate from the third cosmic degree onward, has its own solar system. These solar systems are invisible from the earth, and we discussed this on our previous journey.

When people had reached the fourth cosmic degree and life had commenced there, the fifth cosmic degree condensed, and the sixth cosmic degree was also in a seminal stage. We have been able to follow this process in the first three cosmic degrees. And since we know that creation is as we have seen, we must accept that all those higher planets had to follow a similar development in order to receive approaching inspiring life. It was therefore not possible, André, that the sixth cosmic degree would be ready before the fourth or third cosmic degree, as it would cause a disturbance. How could life commence, when we know that the wonder of creation resides in the condensation process. It had to happen in those very first hours of condensation, when inspiring life passes on into the embryo. I explained all that on the first cosmic degree, and this is, as I said, the wonder of creation.

God's infinite wisdom is in everything; it is the Divine wonder you have learned on this journey. It happened this way with all following cosmic degrees, man entered the seventh cosmic degree, subsequently to enter the All.

As you know, we have received this knowledge from the cosmic masters of the seventh sphere. My master Cesarino told you about it in the temple of the soul. You see, André, man has to follow one course and everything, in the entire universe, has to adapt itself to one purpose, everything is subjected to one activity and this activity is the plan of evolution of man. This is, as you see, the same for material and spiritual life. We have been able to follow that on this side, for when the first spiritual sphere was ready, the second followed and we see this process in the entire creation. One thing originated from the other, out of a previous one developed an other world, an other human being, in a still higher attunement. The human being advanced ever further and entered the All.

Man, as Divine being, had now reached his ultimate end; man had returned to Divinity; had consciously acquired the universe and was like God. From this moment on, God's creation was accomplished, and this holy life had returned in Divinity.

Look at that long road, André. How many billions of years have passed? I cannot pronounce that figure. Now the universe was inhabited; no sphere, no place without life. The lowest condition was in connection with the higher one; and in this way we subsequently see all conditions interconnect. When this happened, man in those higher spheres or heavens knew that human beings lived in material and Divine happiness of such intensity, that they could not comprehend it. They also knew that people were living on the first three cosmic degrees, who had to cover that long road and lived in sorrow and misery, darkness and cold. One connection was established after the other, one message came through after the other; for the masters of the highest spheres had mental contact with them, that is from feeling to feeling, like I am guiding you. Is it so strange, that we should know all this, and that we also know that sorrow and misery are only on earth and that man has brought that about himself. Do you feel now, André, that man is creator of darkness and light? God gave us everything, we inspire and experience all those heavens and subsequently return to the source of all life.

Can't you be thankful, now that you know all this and is life on earth that terrible? We had to experience sorrow and misery only because we had brought it about ourselves, and had to make up for it. God did not want that misery; but God wanted us to make up for what we did to others, for burdened with all those debts and sins we would not be able to enter spheres of light, because we would collapse. What more can I say? Only this: they, who have reached the Divine Spheres, will remain there and all those millions of planets will eternally continue to occupy a place in the universe.

The animal, too, came to us and now Divine beings are living there in a Divine happiness, which I am unable to tell or describe. One day we will come there, too; Divinity awaits us.

It was known in the Divine Spheres where sorrow and misery was suffered, and that the earth was the planet of good and evil. They knew that something had to be done for the earth, to convince man of a God of love. And this happened, too.

Our highest Master, Jesus Christ, was born on earth, and we know His life and how God's perfect Child was received there.

I'll return to the earth and we shall see what happened there. The earth provides an amazing picture; in those millions of years quite a lot has changed. But since we know how long it takes for man to free himself of his condition and desires, you will also feel that mankind

265

could not have advanced much further, although there were beings in those days who had attained Divinity. It was no longer possible to founder in the higher spheres, they progressed step by step having a set purpose in mind. This was quite different on earth. There were beings, who had reached the spheres of light, but there were also people who lived on the second cosmic degree and were to be born on earth. Even now, in your time, as you know, people are still living on the last transitions of the second cosmic degree who have to pass on to the third cosmic degree, to be subsequently attracted by the earth. It is not until then that they will begin to follow that long road.

We see a changed earth in that million-process. Cities have been built; thousands of inventions have been made and all this they received on earth from astral man. There is nothing on earth, unless we brought it, because inspiring life sees and thinks through all matter and wants to help suffering mankind. We have given thousands of things to the earth. On our next journey you will see and experience that all art, music, painting and sculpture, has come from this side, and that beings returned to the earth with a task, were consequently born there, to leave behind what they came to accomplish. I will tell you about it on our next journey; for I and millions of others belonged to those chosen and blessed beings, who were allowed to bring something of beauty to the earth.

In those days 'religion' developed and the prophets, referred to in the bible, came on earth. I will not follow those times; it would lead too far.

Fighting on earth still continues, though intellectual beings were also born. Now, the earth and people had advanced far enough to receive the religion of God. You surely know what would happen? Christ would be born on earth. Christ descended from Divine heaven and was born on earth. His sacred life is known to us, God's perfect Child was crucified.

My God, my Father, forgive them; they do not know what they do.' That is what God's Child could say! And God forgave them. Jesus Christ knew he would be killed, yet, God's pure and perfect Child accepted His task.

Do you understand yourself, man of the earth? Know that Jesus Christ came to you, that His death is your salvation. Look up to all this and accept; I come to you in His name, in His name! Cherish love, and feel that everything is as I said. One good deed everyday; one good thought will already help Him, our Master Jesus Christ, and us who returned to the earth to convince you as sisters and brothers of your spiritual and cosmic life. Discard all your mistakes and cherish love; eternity awaits you; you and your beloved ones.

Christ, my son, returned to His own sphere. Man, however, has come to know his Father of Love; but we know how life is lived on earth and how His sacred life is defiled. Man wanted to forget and again plunged into a pool of mud and misery and forgot himself.

This is the picture of the earth and all this belonged to the past. Now, I'll continue in your own time. Do you want to ask any questions, André.'

'No, Alcar, I have understood everything. How thankful we should be on earth, that we were allowed to learn all this.'

'Indeed, my boy. Those who feel it, will be grateful for everything given from this Side.

We'll now go to the first material attunement and see how everything on earth is at present, we'll pass on into these seven degrees of material and inner life.

# CHAPTER VIII

## *Pre-animal-like human consciousness*

WE shall move on floating, André. We'll go to the jungle where human beings live in the first material degree, their inner life has the same attunement. We'll pass on and proceed in your own time.

All those human material and inner degrees have not changed yet. Good and evil dominate on earth and those first degrees are despised. No white man will compare himself with those who are in these dark bodies. The whites are the rulers of the earth but they don't realize that all are God's own children and that these dark beings, too, will ultimately reach that material stage. Thousands of years will pass, though, but it shall happen. No child of God is put behind the other and none is given preference over the other. One day, the beggar will be rich on earth, one day we'll see emperors and kings in beggar's garb. But they are not aware of that; it is all deep down in them, hidden in that incomprehensible inner life.

Look, that's where I want to be. We are in the jungle, André. Children of God are living here.'

André saw these people. They looked wild and savage. How well did he understand this attunement, how well did he understand their inner life and the deep meaning of it all. How wonderfully perfect creation is.

These human beings are like those living on the second cosmic degree; but their material organism is different. They come from there to the earth and the inner life descends into this organism. The earth is billions of years old and, as you have seen, these human beings still live on earth. There are even human beings unknown to man, who have not yet seen the highest material degree, the white race.\*) Now review all those degrees, all those planets and all those billions of years; consider what I explained to you on our first journey, what you have observed from the beginning of creation, then you see, André, that these people are still on earth, that they don't know a God in heaven, a Father of Love, and that they will learn all that when they have acquired a higher degree. This pre-animal-like but human being is a child of

\*)See the 'Explanation' at the beginning of this book.

268

God and we have followed that process. They live like man on the second cosmic degree feels. There , however, they have a pre-animal-like monstrous body, and that is why I can speak here of a pre-animal-like but human attunement. This body has developed in all those thousands of centuries to what they now have. You have been able to follow that. They, too, live in groups. Now isn't this remarkable? Why do these beings live like that; why do they separate from all those other tribes? These beings belong to the dark-coloured race, and that is the first cosmic stage for the third cosmic degree. We have learned that, André ; it is still as in the initial stage of the planet earth. We see this again in your own time, and it will go on because that first material degree has not become extinct yet. That will not happen until there are no more people living on the second cosmic degree.'

'Where do they arrive, Alcar; or where do they go to when they die on earth?'

'You should not have asked that question, André, you could have answered that yourself. They go to the world of the unconscious, André, that's where they go.'

'Don't they have to go on? Can they already enter the hereafter?'

'These beings only live in the first material degree and there are seven degrees. You'll feel and understand what this means. These human beings return to the world of the unconscious and will be born again. Is that clear?'

'Yes, Alcar, I should have known. So all those degrees are together in the world of the unconscious?'

'Yes, André, they are bound to, because there is only one world of unconscious life, where inner life lives to animate the material organism. We know only one world on this side where this life lives to be attracted by the material being. All those various attunements are in that world, from the lowest up to the highest degree, which is the spiritual attunement.'

'Do you know how many times these beings have to return in the material condition, Alcar?'

'No, I cannot assess that. As I said, man has to return to the earth thousands of times and it cannot be fathomed for inner life either. Man cannot in any way change his return to earth, André. When the cycle of life on earth is not completed, either material life will attract us, or we have to return until the spiritual world attracts us, and we have inwardly advanced that far.'

'How amazing everything is, Alcar.'

'It is all enormous and natural, André. Man, however, cannot imagine this; but all of us have experienced it, and everybody will. This cannot be changed. The earth attracts inner animation for its own material organism and this inner life cannot go higher, because it is connected with the earth. That is an infallible law and we have been able to follow that from the very beginning of creation. No human being or animal can evade that. They will and shall all go back, because they have not advanced that far yet, neither materially nor spiritually.'

'What would happen, Alcar, if these people were killed as occurs so frequently on earth?'

'Why do you ask, André?'

'I thought: what would happen, if these people were no longer there and inspiring life yet waited to be attracted; or if man has killed these human beings; or if they were killed by a natural disaster; surely that is possible?'

'Let me tell you first of all, that this is not possible. However, I want to answer this question and say this: If that were to happen, inspiring life would pass on to the next degree.'

'Is that possible, Alcar? I thought it was not possible, that both lives had to be one?'

'The way you feel and think is very good, but you forget one thing which you are not aware of, as I have not discussed it yet.

You forget, André, now that the earth is ready, the organism is perfect and the earth has completed its task. Do you already feel what I mean? Do you feel that this was necessary for embryonic life and that it would happen there. That at this moment one transition is no longer of importance? That there are people on earth living in the seventh degree who connect with the fifth degree and that children are born? I will explain that to you later. It is, therefore, possible for material life, because the planet earth is ready; but as a cosmic transition it is not possible; in other words: passing from the earth to the fifth cosmic degree where spiritual and divine angels live, is not possible. One transition is of no significance; though, as I said, extermination of all this life is not possible; that is not why God has created all this life; all this belongs to creation.'

'Then, surely, it is not possible for entire humanity to perish?'

270

'No, André; that is not possible either; because no matter how far everything has advanced, creation would be a failure and God would not be a God of Justice and there would be disturbances in the plan of creation. Every life returns to God, that is a law; and to this end planets are required to acquire that development. Nature and what God has created cannot be destroyed. All of us share this. What belongs to the first degree and has to perform its task there, does not have to do it in the third degree. No natural disasters destroying all life of the earth will therefore occur, André. That is impossible, such a disturbance does not exist and cannot occur, or it would have happened during the first stage.'

'So man on earth does not have to worry about it, Alcar?'

'No, André; it cannot happen, or God had not overseen His own creation. Nothing has gone wrong in all those billions of years. Everything happened as was preordained. These laws are infallible; we have been able to follow and experience that on all those planets. And such a disaster would occur on earth, where this awe-inspiring process is established? The earth, which has to perform a great task, where man becomes 'man' and has to prepare himself for the fourth cosmic degree? The earth, with all those wonders and cosmic laws? If this were to happen, we and God would dissolve and nothing would be left. God cannot destroy His own life.'

'If I understand you correctly, Alcar, nobody can destroy himself?'

'No, André, that is not possible either. Temporary material life can be destroyed, spiritually it is not possible. Thousands and thousands of people try, they put an end to their material life and yet enter into an other world and are alive. Didn't Lantos give a description in 'The Cycle of the Soul?' Those who commit suicide will either wait to be born again, or continue life on this side; total destruction is not possible.'

'Do these people know their condition, Alcar?'

'Yes, of course they know their own lives; but I feel what you mean. Your question should be: do they know themselves? Do these people understand why they are here?'

'Yes, Alcar, that is what I mean.'

'The answer is no, André. They know they are alive, and that's all. They feel like man on the second cosmic degree, they hunt and kill and eat human flesh and are like wild animals.'

'But if these people are still on earth, why then can this connection with the second cosmic degree not be accepted? Where do these beings come from? Why do these beings live on earth?'

'We have been able to follow all that and I can tell you that no human being can say: I know myself; I understand my life; I know who I am.

Now that you know and have experienced all this, you will think and feel differently; you know that all these human beings are children of God. They live their own lives, they separate from the mass; they live in caves and holes and are prepared to slaughter other races and eat their flesh. I ask you, is this being so strange, so incomprehensible now that we know where he came from and how it happened. Can't you see deep in his soul and don't you fully recognize this being, materially as well as spiritually? Now ask those questions to a learned man on earth, who has made a study of it. What will he reply? He does not know; for how should he know this black woman and man, these two beings? Doesn't he look down upon them like a deity? And yet, one day, he had this black skin; for God knows and makes no difference. Once all white people lived in the jungle; all of us have been here.'

'How interesting, Alcar.'

'Not only interesting, André; but natural. If this had no meaning, the entire creation would disintegrate. If this had only been for these people and not for those millions of whites, God would not be a God of love and creation would not be right. One thing would be in contrast with the other; there would be a wide gap, which could not be narrowed. Have you seen any unbridgeable gaps on all our journeys? Have you been able to detect one unfair deed in the entire creation? Have you seen anything unnatural? Have you experienced that on this side and on earth? Can you indicate an untruth to me? If so, you have not understood me, and you should have asked me, André; I could have pointed out God's justice to you. I can't contradict myself; I followed nature, and God's life and laws cannot lie and cheat, only people can. Man betrays his sister and brother, and his God, and renounces his own attunement.'

'How will they take this, Alcar?'

'They will condemn this, and all your other books, because they cannot accept it. But that does not matter, we'll show them on our side, and I and thousands of brothers and sisters in the spirit, their material brother and sister, their father and mother, who are here and have accepted everything.

272

Here, my son, in this deep and dark jungle; here in this black material organism and in all that misery, your life and mine on earth started. I call to my sisters and brothers on earth: 'Man, you man of the white race, look at your brothers and sisters on earth. Look at those who live here, who are on earth like you are; fathom their material and spiritual condition and you will recognize yourself. God's own life lives here. Here lives the first and second cosmic degree; we recognize in this material organism God's sacred laws; you lived in it as the inner human being. This life goes on and has to go on; because the spark of God is also in them.'

'How simple everything is, Alcar, since we know this. Wouldn't scientists accept this either?'

'No, André, they will not accept this either; they will, as I said before, deny all this, like they condemn your other books. They concentrate too much on what they know and do not advance any further. 'Death' still calls them to a halt. They'll not advance until they can bridge that gap; then they'll feel that there is no death and witness the distant past. One man kills the other, they dare to criticize, but they don't understand themselves and deny everything coming their way from this side.

Once more, André; it does not matter to me. I and many others have patience; for one day they will enter here; we'll convince them on this side; they will die there, one after the other.'

'Why are these beings so anxious, Alcar?'

'There is fear in them, and also the hatred of millions of years ago. One race slaughtered the other; we have been able to follow all that. This commenced during the initial stage of the earth. In those days other dark races attacked them, but later the whites came, and they really knew how to deal with them. The white race, ignorant of this grace of God and not understanding its own material attunement, massacred the dark beings. They wanted to possess and that was their downfall. Those who were ahead of these beings wanted more, it was not enough yet, although they had received that magnificent body.

No, they returned and those poor in spirit were killed off. Does it not clash with everything God is, with everything bearing God's own life? Do you feel now why they are so anxious? That fear, André, is already millions of years old; but not only man, the animals also attacks them; you have learned that hatred which is still there. The white race has cursed its Divine attunement and they also curse God when they look down upon these beings and think that they have to bring their own civilization to these people and impose it upon them.

As sure as there is a Father of love in heaven, as surely all people of the earth once lived in these dark jungles and were despised and ridiculed, but all that is not understood; they don't want to understand it; but it is the holy truth.

This, however, only happens on earth; because there are no dark material organisms on the fourth cosmic degree. Everything and everybody there is white and pure, like the most delicate material known on earth. But here these people still exist.

You see, André, that they are no longer like those hairy people on the second cosmic degree; that is not possible. The earth has developed this magnificent material organism and completed it. Look how powerful they are. They do not comprehend science and everything the white race has. They only 'feel'; they can't do anything but feel and that in a pre-animal-like way. This is man living in a pre-animal-like, but material condition.

What do these beings have to acquire? Just imagine this and you will wonder when they will pass on to the highest degree. How long will that take? Where do they stay in life after death and do they proceed there? We'll follow that; though I first have to explain some other conditions to you. Then we will go on and follow all these attunements until we have reached the highest material and inner human being. Now look at the astral world.'

André observed.

'What kind of a world is that, Alcar?'

'Their world, André; that's where inspiration lives which has come here from the second cosmic degree and is attracted by these material human beings. This inspiration or inspiring life, is in and closely around them as a result of their lower attunement. But you see that they are human beings who have lived on all those planets.'

This astral life surrounded the material being as a dense cloud. André saw this clearly and observed that this life was attracted. It happened the way he had observed on the second cosmic degree; nothing had changed. The human organs had changed somewhat, they had become more beautiful, but the functioning was as it had been from the first moment.

274

Has anything changed in this mighty process, André?'

'No, Alcar, nothing; it is all as it was.'

'Yes, as on the mother planet, in the first stage. But now it is established by this magnificent organism. And in this perfect material organism are those seven degrees. Isn't it a mighty wonder that it proceeded during all those billions of years? Isn't it amazing that nothing has changed? Yet, man on earth is ignorant, does not feel this tremendous wonder. Man just lives as he likes; he is not aware, not of a God, nor of creation or of the beings who live here.

Inspiring life descends into the female and male material organism. The soul, therefore, experiences both material conditions and that, too, is a mighty grace. Why does this have to happen? This existed from the beginning and happened there as a natural event, but it is not until now that it proceeds at full power and action. It was also present on the first cosmic degree, I showed you on all those planets and you experienced it. It was present on the first cosmic degree, the mother planet, and also on the second cosmic degree. I connected you there; you have seen that wonder and been able to follow the attraction. I ask you: Why does inspiration descend in both organisms? Why should it be that it has the mother organism and gives birth to children in one life and receives the creative organism in the other life? That is a wonder, André, a sacred wonder, which God oversaw. I have described this already in your book: 'Mental disorders as seen from the Side Beyond', and we have been able to follow it again in all those stages.

Man on earth still owns this wonder; man has to own it, or he would not be able to develop any more and could only create, not being aware of spiritual inspiration.

This is, André, to be able to awaken spiritually, to evolve. This is, to enable every soul to learn and understand pure mother love and to fathom the wonder of God in all its depth; it is the origin of creation, though as individual life.

The mother experiences this wonder. That first activity and the origin of creation are present in the mother organism. The mother organism owns that power and capacity; because the first stage of embryonic life takes place in that body. The embryo awakens and lives in the mother, as happened on every planet, and that life is also closed off by a dense mass, the human and material organism.

Do you feel what it is, what it means that inspiration has to descend in both organisms? Isn't this a sacred wonder? Man on earth will laugh at it, although he knows this wonder of birth, but its meaning, no, he cannot accept that. Thousands of years will pass before they will accept and understand this and be able to follow me in everything. I do not return for those who laugh at this, it is not meant for them, only for those who crave and yearn, who are longing to learn more about this mighty event; who want to understand the miracle and wonder of creation and especially their own lives and attunement. Everybody will and shall become a mother; that inspiring life is a man and a woman on earth; it is creative and driving, the serving life. God gave man everything and man also received this from his Father in heaven. These beings will enter the male and female body thousands of times. It is, as I said, to awaken, to experience the plan of creation.

These human beings, however, are unaware of it; they do not feel this awe-inspiring event and pass from one condition on to the other. Also those who have acquired the highest material degree, all those scientists are unaware. And yet, this is the essential event, which awakens the human soul. If that was not a fact – we have been able to follow that – we and all that life would never have been. If the mother body had not existed, the earth and all those other planets would not have come into being. This is a similar condition; the human body experiences the plan of creation, and is the plan of creation, because the creative capacity resides in the human body which holds the serving power.

God knew all this, and with all this, God gave Himself, God created a being representing His creation in miniature. Creation is therefore embodied in man and animal and we see this awe-inspiring wonder reflected in them and in nature; which connected the universe and is the cycle of all life. God gave Himself entirely; God created wonders and man possesses these wonders but does not understand them.

Is the connection between a man and a woman a different condition, a different event, than we have seen during the first stage? Is it all different?

I ask you, André, has anything changed in creation in all those millions of years? Hasn't it happened there, and on the second cosmic degree; and wasn't this for all those other planets? Don't we see it reflected in material and inspiring life and in the entire universe? Haven't all of them passed on to this activity? Look at the earth, the animal kingdom, nature; wherever you look there is reincarnation. But man

276

does not understand himself. Man who is the thinking being sees nature in a different way than we do who know nature. We pass on into all these wonders; we have experienced these wonders in ourselves. Yes, we are different, so very different from man on earth; but we have acquired all that, we have laid ourselves aside and have come to understand our Father in heaven; because we know now how it all is and what it means to be on earth. We have bridged that gap, that wide gap; we have learned to know God and understand the depth of life here present. We passed on into all those laws and acquired them.

We know creation now and that what was born at the beginning of creation is still present on earth and in man. But they are deaf and blind and do not listen to those soft inner voices. They do not see that these wonders happen every second and do not understand that tremendous love tied therein. God knows his children, God gave one the creative power because he did not know nor possess serving love. One day man will and must create. He will awaken, because he creates and by what he creates; then he receives and experiences this sacred wonder.

Look, how everything is alive, how everything returns and it happens by an infallible power, a law, and that law is God. God returns to man every instant, but man does not see or hear anything of this return. Man calls why and what for and asks for gifts, for happiness and for that which cannot be given him until thousands of years later, because it is not until then that he will understand the tenor of what he asks. Then it comes; but if it comes and it is not like he had imagined, he rejects this wonder and exclaims: No, not that; that is not what I mean; that is too difficult and costs too much strength. He rejects all these gifts and curses himself and his Father in heaven. I could go on like that, André, but one more thing I would like to say. Those who want to feel it, can understand the depth of creation, because it is within them. Those who want to see open their eyes; but not their material eyes, for they are spiritually blind and will remain so as long as they do not witness inwardly, and discard themselves. In doing so they will learn to understand themselves, when an immense power radiates from them and they experience creation; they will experience what happened billions of years ago and still lives within them because they still live on earth.

Reincarnation is inherent to all that; we see the first moment again and we recognize it as the beginning of revelation. Human beings are living here who are unaware of all this, who are despised by the white race and who cannot be compared with them. Human beings are living here who are unaware of God's perfect Child; who have the first material degree and will return to the earth thousands of times. These beings also live on earth, in the cities, although they wear silk dresses, and decorate themselves with marks of honour. We see through it, however, and recognize them immediately and we notice their spiritual poverty. Their deeds point them out; we have listened to their discussions, we saw who they were the way they behaved. The pre-animal being still lives in that beautiful body. These beings live in the highest circles of society. We'll see them there again, André; and I'll prove that when we get to it. It is not only here that they have no feeling for all those things, there they haven't either. Scientists don't know anything about these material degrees and when they are discussed it is fantasy. Living dead are also on earth, in the highest material degree and I'll show you who belongs to them.

These beings here are spiritually dead and perish through their own ailments and animal-like life. But even in the highest degree they have to contend with illness and perish in misery and sorrow. Here, they do not know of a God; there they do but they do not act accordingly, they only experience and they are heading for disaster with all their possessions. In many respects these beings are ahead of them, because they are children of nature and give themselves as they are. But there in the large cities, we see people in disguise, as no pre-animal-like being could, and they look down upon these beings.

And yet, the wonder of God also lives in these dark bodies; they, too, are God's children and have to cover that long road. Thousands of years from now they will have advanced as far as the people in cities and villages and will have attained a condition of existence on earth. One day, all these beings will occupy an important position in material life and they will be doctors and scientists on earth. One day, they will be the blessed ones and we'll see them again, but then they will be like most people on earth and still belong to the living dead. One day they'll pass on to the highest material stage on earth and live their lives to the full like they still do there and as happens every day.

Later, after thousands of years, their eyes will open and they awaken on this material world, when they possess that perfect and beautiful body but have changed beyond recognition. Yet, they have received

278

everything from their God, but neither do they know then where they came from.

I ask you my boy, why did I take you along to this jungle, to these dark brown-black peoples, whereas there are so many beautiful things on earth? Why do I pass on into these beings? Didn't you wonder? Do you understand why I have to be here? Why don't I take you along to the spheres of light, where I could explain such a lot to you? Why don't I speak of those pure spheres and don't we go to those regions where man is happy in his life and why don't we take long walks in our spheres? Why do I stay here, whereas there is so much of beauty on earth that people are still unaware of? Do you feel, André, why I am here and do you understand that everybody living on earth must have been here to attain the place where he is now? This is where our life on earth began, this is the first degree of material and spiritual attunement. This is where we came on earth and our long way on earth begins in the jungle. This organism is the first material degree and they will and shall acquire the seventh. This is where the cycle of life on earth begins and the foundation is laid to start securing ourselves a place in material and spiritual life. Here we begin our existence on earth and it is magnificent to look back on it now that we have acquired the highest degree. We, human beings, will experience God's creation in this organism, and awaken. Here our long road on earth starts and this is reincarnation on earth. Should this not happen, it would again be an injustice and no love. But God does not want that. God is justice; our holy Father is a God of Love.

These beings go about naked; they do not know all those earthly pleasures man now has, which make life more comfortable. They go about like wild animals, they have no light, no warmth and are poor, so very poor. As compared with life of those who have everything on earth, their lives are miserable and terrible.

But, André, we know better. Man has to go through this. In the future they will live in an other organism; if they wouldn't, if that would not happen, God would be an unfair God; God would be a God of revenge. But God is love and has been in the entire creation, as we have experienced on all those planets. Man goes on, must go on; it is a law; it is experience and quite natural. Man should know that law and try to understand creation.

Man on earth who possesses the white body does not know all these laws because he does not inquire after them and does not feel them. What has he got to do with these people? What could he learn from them? Why do all these types of people live on earth? Man seeks and tries to solve this enigma, and yet, he will not find the truth. 'Death' is a deadlock and exactly behind it is the solution. The answer is here, in our lives on this side; they will see and understand all this after their lives on earth, but they cannot accept it. Dead is dead; when they die it is all over forever. These people think they are learned, they want to solve the mighty word 'creation'; these people try to analyze these dark souls.

Seek, you learned men of the earth, but first seek your own spiritual and cosmic attunement; seek and feel what death is and means.

But they don't; they put themselves on a pedestal and continue to solve it in their own way and they will never succeed.

Look within me, André, and feel why my soul is crying now, and my heart breaks when I think of all these things. Because, one day, these beings here will also have everything and put themselves on pedestals, and death also will be a deadlock and they will not wonder where they came from. They will go there and have to pass on to it. We, living on this side, see and know it; all this was revealed to us, we have experienced it, and so have all those higher spirits, and man on earth and these black souls will experience it later.

Is this so strange? This is and belongs to reincarnation on earth, as a result we must accept that we will pass on into many lives. This is the great wonder these beings will experience and which keeps the entire universe connected. This is majestic and a grace; it is mighty in its simplicity and infallible for every being who experiences it.

The human being will deeply bend his head when he feels creation and when he experiences the depth of inner life and material life; for that makes us awake. Black people are living here; but God's wonder is in them just as it is in the white organism. When people on earth are prepared to follow this course, they will comprehend this deep mystery; an other course is not possible.

Is it clear to you now, why I wanted to be here, André? We'll go on from this place and pass on to these seven material degrees. This is the first degree and at the same time the poorest, the most miserable one found on earth.

You see, my son, they live as they did on the second cosmic degree, they are divided into groups and feel as they did there, but have a different organism. These are already human beings; on the second cosmic degree they were animals. This is a human condition, this is a pre-animal-like but human stage.'

# CHAPTER IX

## *Animal-like consciousness*

W E'LL go on and leave them and visit an other group. They are slightly ahead of these beings and therefore belong to the animal-like condition in regard to their inner life. Do you have any questions about these human beings?'

'Yes, Alcar, if I may put this question: Can they attract a higher being?'

'No, not yet. I say not yet, because later on it is possible. Once they have experienced all degrees. They here attract that being, the inner being, living on the second cosmic degree, as this life is attuned to their material condition, because we have seen that material balance is necessary for animation, which is inner life. But there comes an end to it, and I will tell you about that when we have reached the highest degree.'

'What happens, Alcar, when these people connect with a higher degree?'

'The material organism will split. Children born out of this connection have lost their natural attunement. Do you feel this, André?'

'Yes, Alcar, it did not enter my mind. Is this known on earth?'

'Yes and no. Scientists know of it, but they cannot fathom this depth because they don't know and don't accept these material degrees. They are unaware of all these truths; they do not know that the spiritual and material creation are one and that it has been so from the beginning of creation. One has to accept all this in order to learn and understand the material degrees of the human organism and that these material divisions have come about in that one attunement passed on into the other.'

'Does the material organism really have this power of attraction and can the material organism bring about a change?'

'Yes, that is possible. The action is as follows: Those two different degrees of material life have their own activity and attunement. These two degrees connect, let's say the fifth degree and this one, the white race and this body in the first degree. What will happen? In the first place the natural attunement is lost and I can tell you that the primitive life dominates. The higher the material organism advances, the further it moves away from its arch attunement. The arch attunement at full power and activity, and therefore in perfect health, cannot be surpassed by anything; in it resides the tremendous power of all those planets, dominated by the first stage which is the mother body known to us as the first planet. This means that it is material and possesses that arch power in that material degree. This is obvious, because inner life, the life of the soul, belongs to a higher attunement. That soul or life has that dominating power in its own material level; but in this case, the lower level dominates. Is that clear, André?'

'Yes, Alcar, but what is the action or attunement of inner life like?'

'When a child is born out of this connection, that inner life has the same attunement as the mother, though it is possible that the child is different; in which case it has a different meaning, of which I will tell you later. The child may then have more intellect than a child of parents of the same attunement. This is a remarkable phenomenon brought about by the higher organism.

We see, for instance, this child awaken, and this event differs from all those other children born out of one attunement. It has more intellect and this activity is brought about by the higher material organism. In this dark, black child, in this organism lives something of that higher organism and that activity can be seen. It is only temporary; when that organism has reached maturity the first stage will dominate and inner life will obey that organic supremacy. Do you feel what I mean, André?'

'Yes, Alcar. Is that why the human race is unnatural?'

'Yes, in so far as you mean that different degrees have connected.'

'Yes, Alcar, that's what I mean.'

'The human race, all those seven degrees, have passed into thousands of degrees. I want to tell you about that when we have reached the highest degree. There are no pure races on earth any more. The seventh degree is contaminated, it has passed into other degrees; in other words: In that highest degree flows the blood of the second, third, fourth, fifth, sixth and even of the first degree. Is that clear?'

'Yes, Alcar; perfectly. It is amazing how much there is to it. Is it of great moment for all those material degrees?'

'Yes, it has a deep meaning and not one, but thousands.'

'Can you keep track of them?'

'Yes, we know all those events; not only those events and possibilities, but the history of all seven material degrees as well. As a result, André, that magnificent material organism has weakened in all degrees; that's why these inner disturbances, illnesses and other torments exist

283

on earth. Believe me when I say that man is to blame for his own sorrow and misery and for all his illnesses as well. Man has defiled his own attunement. That is not possible in the animal kingdom; an animal would not do that; that life acts, as I explained to you, in accordance with his natural attunement and cannot act differently. But man has passions through which he has destroyed his own attunement; this attunement therefore passed on into a different degree. As a result the natural attunement weakened and an unnatural condition set in. This happened millions of years ago and cannot be restored.'

'So there are no people on earth having the pure natural material condition?'

'No; as natural attunement, not one.'

'Is that where all those illnesses come from?'

'That's why this natural material organism weakens and declines. All the organs are there, have always been there, but the tissues, that million-process, have weakened. The material organism in the attunement of the highest degree is a magnificent organism, and if this attunement had remained pure, all those illnesses we know now would not exist; that same organism would have more strength, and be more resistant, also against summer and winter because that organism has the same strength and activity as nature in which it lives and out of which it emanated. In that period it was perfectly natural, but the white race has multiplied this process too, has returned to those lower degrees and defiled its own material attunement.*) The children born did not act differently on reaching maturity; that is why the process has multiplied and the natural attunement is lost.

Now, this organism is weak, the scientists examine all these illnesses; they go back to the third and fourth generation to try and find out what caused them. Though this is possible for various illnesses, the real source is millions of years old. Yet, man on earth wonders where all those illnesses have come from, and because of them they curse their God, or beseech Him to be delivered from them.'

'What chaos has become of the earth, Alcar.'

'The earth is a planet of quiet and peace; it has completed its task, but man has disturbed that peace and quiet. They have defiled everything and everybody. They have not only forgotten their God, not only the animal kingdom which still shows its teeth when this high being

*)See the 'Explanation' at the beginning of this book.

284

approaches, but they have forgotten themselves in everything and through everything and made a hell out of this planet, where life holds God's own life and forms part of it. They have not only forgotten themselves, they also defiled God's sacred love; they tred on mother love and descended in the deepest misery to experience and to give full reign to their passions; they forgot they are children of God, and are Divine. They defiled everything and laid down a curse upon mankind and cursed the arch power within them. This was bound to have consequences, and nature punished them; for their own body could not stand it. It went from bad to worse and now that they have come to their senses, they call out: Oh God, help us, help us and deliver us from all that misery.

But God in heaven cannot alter this; they wanted their illnesses and misery themselves. Whoever it is, wherever he lives, however far he has advanced and feels now, all took part, not one excluded, all of us have forgotten ourselves.

But we come back to make it up; all on this side come back, not one person from the earth who enters here and sees and experiences that process, can advance; they will return to the earth and do deeds, nothing but good and do constructive work. They serve; which is giving their inner life; they make up what they once destroyed. They are still asleep and plead: Oh God, deliver us from all that misery! God, however, looks on and waits and cannot change anything. Now they seek and ask, now they come to their senses, now that everything is defiled and they experience the misery caused.'

'You said, Alcar, that this happened millions of years ago; are the people of this era to blame?'

'That is a question everybody will ask. What concern is that of ours, what have we got to do with it? We lived a pure and clean life; we love God and pray and go to church every day, don't we? Isn't that what you mean?'

'Yes, Alcar.'

'I can imagine, André, that people who are unaware of this would ask me such a question; but you should not have asked.

I ask you, André; has man got to do with that what happened millions of years ago? Haven't I explained to you just now, that these people lived in the jungle and that all of us have lived there? Haven't I explained to you, that we are billions of years old, that we have lived on earth thousands and thousands of times and lived in those times? Don't you feel, that there are still people who connect with a lower degree? That they will again defile their own attunement? They do not know anything about these laws and are therefore unaware of what they are doing. This is still possible on earth because there are still seven material degrees. Those black people will also reach that stage, they will curse their God and defile their attunement, not a single person can evade this. They do not have that property, that personality, they do not have that control, that love, but live to the full, because passion and violence are in them.'

'If, from this moment on, man owned that mental power, and continued to follow the natural way through all those centuries, would all this misery dissolve, Alcar? Is that possible?'

'No, André, that is not possible. I told you that this is millions of years old. It cannot be changed. These people have not advanced that far either to be able to control themselves in everything in future. That's why they will also forget themselves and pass on into what they want to possess. Is that clear now?'

'Yes, Alcar; how natural everything is.'

'It is bound to be.'

'Can that no longer be done on the fourth cosmic degree, Alcar?'

'No, that is impossible; only on earth. People there are awake and conscious; here, they are spiritually blind and have poor feeling, they have passion and violence. There, everything is different; no illness, no misery, no passion, nothing of all that earthly misery; there is spiritual happiness in an earthly body. There, inner and material life are one in everything, in a natural condition and pure.

Can you imagine something of such purity, sublimity and perfection on earth?'

'No, Alcar; I can't; and nobody could. Will doctors never be able to feel or assess that depth, Alcar?'

'You mean the weakening of the material organism?'

'Yes, Alcar, that's what I mean.'

'No, that is impossible; it is too far in the past.'

'But if children are born out of perfectly healthy parents, is that weakness still present?'

'Even then, even if they have never been ill and have died a natural death, that weakness is still there.'

286

'You would not think it was.'

'But it is, because the natural core has been lost for millions of years.'

'Amazing how much you know about that. How is that possible?'

'Is it now clear to you what the cycle of life on earth is and means? What it means, that one of your books is titled 'The Cycle of the Soul?' That is one and the same condition and event for material as well as spiritual life. It means all those material transitions, all those thousands of lives together, which we have experienced. When we have experienced that inwardly, by inner life, we ourselves, an other world will attract us and we go on in the hereafter to prepare ourselves for the fourth cosmic degree. Then, all those questions, all those illnesses dissolve, and our life will be natural, in an unstained and pure organism, so that nothing will disturb us there. But before we pass on to that, we return to the earth and do something, give something; bring something of ourselves, because God gave us His own Life and we therefore bring our inner knowledge and tell them how to live, and we are ready to serve all the time. Those who do not want to go back, do not understand themselves, do not know our lives, nor God and neither the earth and life. Those who say they do not want to return to the earth do not understand anything of creation. And those who have not advanced this far and laugh at all this or shrug their shoulders, belong to the living dead. They are convinced here and then they yearn, like we all do, to be allowed to do something for mankind, for ourselves and especially in gratitude for everything we received from our Father.'

'There are so many people who do not want to return, Alcar; and they recoil when they hear of it. I know and hear it all the time. Who wants to come back to this hell? Is life on earth not dreadful? Not one of all these people wants to return.'

'Do you find that strange?'

'Yes, they do not understand what they say, Alcar.'

'I will tell you something, my boy. Those who speak like that and do not want to return, do not understand themselves. People who speak like that, do not feel all this; they are living dead. There are also people who cannot imagine that a mother could cry herself to death because her child was taken away from her. They would not be able to. Are those people more advanced in life on earth than she is? No, we know those living dead, people who speak like that. Haven't I shown you, when we visited those poor mothers and all those mentally ill people on earth living in a deranged condition, that those who speak like that and are amazed at their condition, do not yet have that feeling? Haven't I explained that they still belong to the living dead and do not own that sacred feeling? And if they do not have that feeling, could they yearn for it? Is that possible? Those people, André, will not acquire that attunement of feeling until hundreds of years later and will then cry like all those mothers and speak no longer about not wanting to return. They will and shall experience that. That is a law and means justice. We shall return and are in no position to make demands, as we have not attained that material and highest spiritual degree yet. Oh, those poor of spirit, who have done nothing but cursing the life of God!

When we live in the world of the unconscious waiting for an incarnation, we receive exactly that what we do not want, because it is the very thing we do not own yet. Those who say: I do not want to return and only say so for fear of all that material misery, are mentally dead, they are not awake and conscious and they will return and experience exactly that what they do not want to receive. Those who do not want, will receive and those who want to receive, won't, that is as far as earthly things and conditions are concerned and if it is only to possess, to be rich. Christ knew before He descended to the earth, what awaited him, and what was for Him, is also for us. One day, we'll experience what He did; one day, we'll also possess our entire personality.

Then we don't ask to give us this or that; or we won't descend. No, André, however it may be, we descend and desire to give everything we have. It is not until then that we are awake and conscious. Those living dead, however, do not want that; they annihilate what others built up and think they have a right to destroy all this, but they are fast asleep and won't wake up for the time being. They have nothing to give either and belong to the living dead. All these beings only love one person and sometimes they don't love anybody, or only when they get something in return. Those living dead will stare their eyes out, because they will have to return since they feel that way. The earth would be beautiful if people could want God's creation. But if they were able to determine their birth and death, if these powers were in their own hands, it would be real chaos. Man received everything, God's own life. Man only wants to experience beautiful and desirable things; only that life on earth in which he has everything. Thank God that we understand nature, that we know the laws of nature and that people cannot alter

288

them and have to obey them. It is not God Who sends them back, they are attracted by their own attunement, their mistakes and sins and by all the wrong things, which lie in their past. This has to be made up, when they will be able to take leave of the planet earth and enter life hereafter.

Wherever they are and whoever they are now; after a while others will take their places and they will fall back and pass on into an other condition, back to the earth to make up for everything. It is all straight-forward; these are material and spiritual laws. There is an end to every-thing and the lowest degree passes on into the highest and the highest descends to the lowest to help. Those who curse some race will perish. Those who violate the love of others will also go to ruin, as they make mistakes and will have to make that up in an other life. Those who do not know God, will understand Him one day. Those who do not seek me, Christ says, will neither see nor find the Father. Those who do not accept us, do not accept God, for we have come in the name of God; thousands descended to the earth with me. Thousands with me speak of love and faith; thousands with me know that all who speak like they do will return.

They all think they can return to God in one single life on earth. Is that possible, André? Can we acquire all that in one short life on earth? Now that we know that we go further and higher and other planets await us? What then is the use of all this? Has it been God's intention to create heavens with which man on earth has no connection and will never receive that connection? Review all this and imagine if that is possible. Feel all these possibilities deeply and ask for mental inspira-tion. There are millions of beings on this side, who will come to testify of their mental happiness and bliss. But death is a deadlock for man and will remain so. They will awaken, though, all those people must go further and higher; one day they will be grateful to have received all this about our lives, about creation and the laws and powers. We'll proceed and finish our work; we, on our side, as I told you, shall wait until they all enter here.

Look, André, we are on the spot where I wanted to be; is our conver-sation clear to you?'

'Yes, Alcar.'

'Well, then we'll go on.'

André again saw people and they were like the ones he had just ob-served, though they were slightly different. Among them were those he had seen there but he also saw smaller human beings, they were dwarfs.

'Another degree, André, one degree higher than where we were just now. Those dwarfs live here too and have come to them. Do you recognize this attunement?'

'You mean those dwarfs?'

'Yes.'

'Weren't they on all those planets, those transitions, Alcar, between the first and the second cosmic degree? '

'Indeed; that's where we met them and here we find them again. I told you about them on our previous journey. Isn't it amazing to see these beings again after all those millions of years? What happened there would also happen here. They pass on into an other material condition, but before all have died thousands of years will pass. That degree then dissolves and they accept a natural condition. Do you feel what I mean?'

'Yes, Alcar, I know. Do those others already belong to the second degree?'

'Yes, you see that their bodies are different and although the change is not conspicuous, it is a different degree, the second material degree we know. These people, too, are inwardly different, they feel and understand more and are not that shy any more. Many inner changes can already be seen, they are different in- and outwardly.

But why do these people not live together? Wouldn't it be simpler? Why do we see that again in all these transitions on earth and do those groups of black people*) not join together? Isn't that strange?

Listen, André, they cannot join together even if they wanted to. These degrees cannot be connected, they live separated. It is a law that keeps them apart. This is nature and is the first and second degree. This wonder is deep down within them and they react to it as to something natural. The two degrees cannot stand each other. And why? Is that so inconceivable now that we know all these degrees and have been able to follow them from the beginning of creation? These human beings cannot be connected because nature calls them to a halt like in our life if we want to go beyond our proper sphere or attunement.'

'It is amazing Alcar.'

'But natural, André. It is very normal and yet deep, very deep, because it is part of God's creation.

*) See the 'Explanation' at the beginning of this book.

290

These people feel differently. They are no longer pre-animal-like, but animal-like. They too cannot refrain from killing and eating their fellow men, although they are generally ahead of those we just visited. They proceed to do other things because they have feeling, although animal-like. They do not know a God either and are unaware of all those higher degrees. Yet they have something which raises them above those others and that is the second material degree which gives them this feeling. They still receive; they did not acquire anything, they receive until they make something of themselves. They will not get in harmony with their life until they are no longer able to kill. They learn in each life on earth. What they have acquired in one life on earth will remain their own. That's how they go on. But how much longer? Until the highest degree in which they will also live and forget themselves. That is what the entire creation is like, they pass from one life on to the other.

People want to possess and when they have it they want something else and that is no good either. One material organism, as will be clear to you, gives them more than the previous one. God gives inner life ever more. In all those material degrees lies earthly happiness acquired on earth. They received this from our side and it is present in all these degrees. You will feel that every material degree has its own power, and that happiness and those things which make life on earth more pleasant form part of it. Do you feel what awaits them? That they will receive this, but that they will also forget themselves? That, according as they advance, they want to possess all those material things, all riches of the earth; but that it will also ruin them? This goes on, André, until they have reached the highest degree in the material world, and this will happen; they have to complete their cycle on earth. We shall see that and I will show it to you. They do not know any better and do not know the riches of the earth; just watch them collect all that earthly trash. These passions already awaken here. In the jungle, far away from the intellectual world, they collect earthly things; that is their human happiness and their inner self. That is the being, the soul that is their personality.

And that personality grows, awakens, must awaken, after they have attained a higher stage, which, for them, is the higher material organism. As a result they themselves, the inspiring life, will develop. Their present development attunes them to animal-like consciousness. Here, we see the initial stage of human passions, which we will see again in a refined condition in the highest degree.

See, how they do their faces and already adorn their dark bodies. See where that leads up to and you will find yourself in the inhabited, intellectual world, in the large cities, where everything is different. That's where we also find those qualities; where people collect all sorts of things and have developed a passion for them.

These people are still living in nature, in the jungle; but the more they advance, the more they will lose their natural behaviour and they will pass on to a higher consciousness. They may become kings and emperors and the intellectuals on earth, or be poor. One day they will have advanced that far and have acquired that stage; but then thousands of centuries have passed. Slowly but surely they will pass on into those other material degrees. Nature or creation will bring them that worldly happiness. God gave man everything and as a result man would learn to understand himself. Do you understand, André, that this will happen and that these people are already ahead of those others?'

'Yes, Alcar, I see and I understand you in everything. Do these people, when they die, also go to the world of the unconscious?'

'Yes, they are bound to. They cannot yet enter the spiritual hereafter. They have to return thousands of times. First of all to acquire their highest material degree and subsequently for their inner life.'

'If I understand you correctly, they are already building their hell?'

'That is also correct, because they cannot think and feel differently. They are still unaware. They pass on to the world of the unconscious time and again. That is a sacred law, which I explained to you in various ways. They will return there, until a higher world, the spiritual world, attracts them. Then they cannot return any more, even if they wanted to.'

'How amazing, Alcar.'

'We see and find that natural law in everything. It is reincarnation, it is creation, it is the return to God. There are thousands of beings on our side who would like to go back, but it is not even possible; only God can give them this wonder and grace . I will explain that to you on our next journey when you will see how this happens; we'll follow one of these beings. You will also see how infallible inner life is and that the soul will experience what it destroyed in its previous life. These people proceed, materially as well as spiritually. They return to the earth and wait on this side to be attracted again.'

'Are they not aware of it, Alcar?'

'No, André, that is not possible. The soul has this higher feeling, it is within them. When they receive a new organism, it must therefore be of a higher degree or they would come to a standstill in the plan of evolution. However, the material organism attracts what belongs to it as inner life. Neither man nor spirit can change that, because it belongs to God's sacred creation and is, therefore, a law.'

'How long do they have to wait for a reincarnation; do you know that?'

'That may take hundreds of years or less. The higher man advances, the longer it takes to reincarnate. Materially perfect man, he who has acquired the perfect human body, often has to wait five hundred or a thousand years before receiving a new body. These beings, however, return sooner and for the first degree it varies from fifty to one hundred years. This is simple and natural and when we have to advance ever more, it will take longer on those other planets, because man in his material body will live to be hundreds of years of age. There they know and experience other laws, which I'll explain to you on our next journey. There they understand what it means to receive a new material organism; they have learned to understand these laws and they live there in great happiness, a happiness they will always retain. The higher we come, the greater the distance between inner life and the material world.

I explained that on the first cosmic degree. Thus, inner life waits to be attracted again between the first and second degree, these transitions. It is born again, as it has to go further and higher and has to cover a cosmic road. Everything is ruled by natural laws. Nature either calls us to a halt or attracts us, which serves material life and man as inner and spiritual life.

So, when you live in hell, I explained that to you, but it will be more comprehensible now, you have reached a world of existence, however terrible it is. However deep the misery in which these people live, they are conscious and have acquired a world of existence. Those who have not yet acquired a world of existence live in the world of the unconscious and will have to acquire that world.

When the first people arrived in hell and had to accept that there was something that stopped them, that they could not return to the earth any more for incarnation in a material organism, they shaped their own condition and became the rulers of the hell.

Something called them to a halt when they had completed their material cycle, but had not acquired anything inwardly in all those centuries. How these people would like to return to earth and receive a new material organism! And how these people, who are the demons of hell, would live their lives to the full again and take possession of the earth! Don't you think they would rather have life on earth than having to stay in that darkness? They have experienced that and gone beyond their natural limit; an other world attracted them and prevented their return.'

'That is an amazing law, Alcar.'

'This law is like all the other laws, André. We'll see again in life after death what we have experienced on earth. The hell is a condition reflecting our inner selves. The material world serves inner man. When inner life has completed its cycle on earth, it is quite simple that we human beings should enter an other world, because we have to acquire Divinity. A spiritual law detains us and we have to accept that, whether we want to or not. These people will also experience these natural laws, as they have to go on, ever further, until they have completed their cycle and continue in spiritual life. That world will be as they feel inwardly. The first beings who passed on in evil, so that hell began to take shape and darkness set in, could not return any more and had to accept that. We who now live on this side, also had to accept that, just like these people will experience that later on, for every human being will experience that, because man forgets himself in all those lives on earth. One day there will be an end to it, though millions of years will meanwhile have passed. As long as one single human being lives on earth, he will have to follow all those laws, he will also seek evil and find a world on this side reflecting his inner self.

There has to be an other world when man on earth departs from his material organism. Those who inwardly bear a higher world, which means doing the proper things and loving God's life, will pass on into an other world, the spheres of light, which you have seen on this side, but not until they have experienced all those degrees of life of the material world. God gave man everything. How many times have I repeated these words; I must repeat them; it does not penetrate the minds of people that all this serves to return to God. It is worthwhile repeating them, as we feel in those words the All-Power, the All-Love we have to acquire. In various ways, I refer to it time and again, I try to convince you.

Thousands have come with me to the earth to bring what they know about our life and have acquired. Each of us selects his own attunement to convince man. And this has been going on for millions of years. When the first human beings who populated the earth had attained their highest material degree, they could not return to the earth any more. But they returned to the earth in the spirit, as spiritual beings, to live their lives to the full through man in his material condition. That also came to an end. They began to realize that is was possible to advance. Thousands of years passed before they had acquired this feeling. The people who had experienced the first rays of light of the spiritual spheres within and around them and felt that it was possible to advance, dragged the others along and tried to convince them. What they achieved on earth added something to their own lives. The good things man did, became the heightened condition in which they would proceed, because an All-Condition, Divinity, awaits them. We have been able to follow all that. It became clear to us on all those planets and it also applies to the earth, to all these people, as they have to experience it as well. This happened during the initial stage of the earth and this process is still going on. The age of the earth, my son, cannot be assessed, nor how long it will last; but one day all this unnaturalness will dissolve.'

'So everything man has on earth, good and evil, emanated from man, Alcar?'

'Yes, André, that's correct. Everything on earth and on this side has been accomplished by man. No sphere could exist if man did not sustain it. The darkness will and must dissolve when there is no more evil, the earth and all this material life belong to that, but life goes on and higher to pass on to the fourth cosmic degree. Everything is fed and maintained by man. The material and inner world of these human beings is one condition. Every deed has its own attunement; man creates darkness, hell by his passions which force him to do wrong, and those who helped create it, will once have to pull it down, because man has a higher attunement. Every sin punishes itself; those sins are within us; we did wrong and by doing so we created darkness and the hell could condense. There is not one human being on earth who did not

295

create hell; we have to go through that and will forget ourselves, because we must learn to understand ourselves. As a result, Divinity will awaken within us; we hold that power, that Divine strength, in our own hands, it is up to us to make the most of it. Every grain of sand of the hell, a spiritual substance, but after reality, must dissolve in order to destroy what we did wrong. As man begins to feel and understand his own life and seeks the good, he deprives the dark spheres of power, but others are adding to the dark spheres, and this is the struggle between good and evil we have to experience on earth and on our side. One day man will advance that far, just like the first human beings of the earth did, and the spiritual light will penetrate them.

When the first human beings experienced it and felt what God's life on earth and on this side meant, they went on their knees and bent their head. When that Divine Spark burned in them and inspiration became more and more intense and seethed in them; when they were ablaze with inspiration, they hurried back to the earth to help those who could be reached. We, too, have experienced that and those who follow us, like those who will awaken later, will experience it. One day these people will also awaken, they will create the dark spheres, and continue to do that until something else awakens in them when the higher spheres are open for them. Then the inspiring fire is within them. It lives and sets them ablaze; they will always feel that fire; that is feeling and means spiritual possession; it is related to God's own life. Then they are ready to give everything, their entire inner being.

Who, then, would not want to go back to the earth? Millions would, but then it is not necessary any more and not possible.

They will proceed on this side; there is work for them and they will give themselves completely. We all started in this condition on earth. Once, André, I lived on the second cosmic degree and passed on to the earth. Here, I became acquainted with life on earth; but I was not aware of it in this condition. One time, in this condition, in this dark body, I killed my fellow men and I ate human flesh. How was my life and that of all my sisters and brothers; how much have we suffered and destroyed? But we had to be here; we had to pass on into this in order to attain the highest cosmic degrees.

Everybody will experience it. I have seen all my lives and I returned to the earth in hundreds of lives. I was shown all those lives on this side. I also know why I was on earth and became a master of art and why that happened, as I have learned to know that wonder on this side. I know all those laws. I have experienced those and other laws and I'll explain them to you on our next journey, when you will get to know me and many others entirely.

I showed all this and I know all these wonders and planets, I experienced them and I am now in the spiritual spheres. I have been, André, like these human beings; but I am not ashamed of that any more, because I have made all that up, all that misery and all my mistakes and sins. I helped create the darkness, because I caused misery and sorrow and should have brought happiness. I have experienced all that, and so have billions of beings, and now we return to the earth because many people have advanced far enough to listen to us. Now we are convincing them.

How much have I suffered and how much have I had to work on myself to make it all up. Learn through me, André, and my sisters and brothers in the spheres. All of us have suffered and we want to preserve you and all people on earth from it. Seek the good and continue doing so.

I cannot yet reach people on earth, as they are deaf and blind and do not believe this truth, they will have to see and experience that for themselves. Man lives his own life and ignores this subject; he does not feel the sacredness of all this, nor the great grace, though, one time he will experience it all.

I lived here, André, and started my cycle on earth. You will get to know it, my life and that of others and why we must pass all this on to the earth.

How are these human beings now? Could we curse them; haven't we done the same? There is nobody on earth, who has not been here, all of us, none excluded, were here in this jungle. Here, we were born and would die to be born again. Try to imagine that long road and how long it will be before they have acquired that highest material condition. Millions of years will pass before they have advanced that far. By then we'll be on an other planet and don't know misery and sorrow. We and all those who go with us, have deserved that and received that from God. That applies to the entire universe; to receive, deserve and acquire. This goes on and will continue infinitely, and we'll experience all those laws. People will experience all these wonders they don't know yet, but which are within them and they will finally awaken and become conscious. Then they will fall on their knees and cry their eyes out for gratitude and they understand their Father in heaven. Once, all will feel what it means to be 'man'.

Life on earth begins here. They desire to possess and they'll own what is so beautiful in their opinion. Pieces of stone, pieces of wood, and a fragment of iron which the higher human being has lost or forgotten; they collect these things. This is a particular character trait and we received that feeling on the second cosmic degree. That's where we got these feelings because that's where pre-animal-like instinct awakened, and this feeling is quite distinct from animal-like consciousness. You know that distance of feeling; you experienced it.

That feeling came in us when we attacked those other groups on the second cosmic degree and robbed them of all they had. It was there that these feelings came into being and with them we came to the earth. From the first moment that we opened our eyes we felt desires. When we had advanced to the extent that we could move about, we wanted to possess all those things. When we got older these feelings became stronger and we knocked others down by our physical strength, merely because we wanted to posses what they had. That is an arch-feeling that passed into the instinct, which many people, even in the highest material condition on earth, still have, and which you will see and experience.

People are killed for this trash which is now gold and silver, diamonds and pearls, all those precious things on earth which are only valuable for them. That is what everyone wants to possess, but they should be able to discard them. That is not possible, because they have not advanced that far so that they have to return many times. Returning is a torment for them, because they begin to sense what awaits them. People do not want struggle and sorrow; they want to keep all these material things, to enjoy all this trash which we started to collect in prehistoric times.

One day all this end. Then, we only collect mental treasures and acquire all those qualities forming our mental character which cannot be taken away from us. They will cheer us from the side beyond, for the more mental treasures we collect the more our inner being changes and develops and we adorn our spiritual dwelling. That is thousands of centuries away from those who live here, and also from them who have already attained that material level. One day they will die and enter life after death. They also collect these things, that earthly trash, in hell;

you have seen that, André. They also adorn themselves in hell with pearls and diamonds but this trash is as false as their spiritual lives.

Look at these magnificent material bodies! See how this body lives and radiates how strong it is. It sparkles with vitality. See how ardent they are and how childlike and natural! But you know after all that I told you just now, that they are animal-like. However vital and powerful this body is, the core, the natural attunement is lost; because they also suffer from many dreadful illnesses they carry within them or from other illnesses they contract during life. We will leave these people now and visit others. I have to tell you more, but we'll leave here.

In this condition, André, which is the animal-like attunement, there are seven more degrees. In that first degree, where we started, there are seven transitions, to which belong those small dwarfs and many other tribes. I'll not follow all those transitions, as you will understand all this now. You see that those transitions are present, we have seen those transitions on all planets. Everything we have seen and been able to follow in the universe is reflected in human life. These small beings we find here among those races, are the many transitions present between two material degrees in order to pass on to that higher degree. We even see these human beings again in the perfect body. All that must have a meaning. On earth it is attributed – at any rate by the scientists who made a special study of it – to improper functioning of some glands, which retard the perfect growth process. This may be true for some of these beings that entire tribes suffer from one and the same condition is possible in the case of other illnesses but not for this process. This is no illness, but a material, even cosmic, condition; because their organs are normal, although their build and size are not as should be for the human organism in its perfect condition.

At a later stage, these people will pass on into another organism, which is the normal size and one degree of the seven material attunements we know.

Now that we have advanced that far, the material organism is well ahead of inner life. These material bodies are fundamentally perfect but their inner life has only reached the pre-animal-like and animal-like attunement. I explained that already on the second cosmic degree, and you will now experience it. Now that they have reached the third cosmic degree, they still live in their animal-like attunement and they have to follow two more degrees before passing on into the white race.

Pre-animal-like man still lives in these two dark races and they have this attunement.

This is their inner possession and the love they have. The pre-animal-like, animal-like, coarse material, material and spiritual attunement or consciousness live in these seven conditions. People are living in all those conditions of consciousness; we are acquainted with the first two. Presently you will see and experience that all these conditions of consciousness are represented in one human being whom we find again in the highest material condition.

We'll now go to the third degree or transition and these beings are animal-like beings; they also kill and murder as much as they want. These people are living together in various groups. We have been able to follow all those groups from the second cosmic degree on, and we find that natural process again on earth. Three degrees are therefore living in these dark woods. The fourth degree is already in contact with the other, the white race.'

Alcar floated over the earth and André observed and experienced all these wonderful things. How deep life is, what does man on earth know about it? Who could ever fathom this? Everything his leader explained was wonderful. He had experienced a lot, and more was to come still, it was not yet sufficient. How thankful he felt for everything!

'Look, André, a next degree.'

André saw other people. They looked wild and ferocious and yet, their material bodies were different. They were not that coarse and did not have that pre-animal-like appearance. How far were these people still from the perfect white body!*) There was a lot of difference as compared with his own body. Blood also circulated in these bodies; they had the same nervous system and were similar to the perfect body, but they could not be compared with his own material organism. How mighty all this was. These people could not be fathomed, he knew all these people now; he understood the degrees and knew where they came from, how the earth had worked and developed this material organism before it had attained that perfect condition. They had adorned themselves with all sorts of things. How beautifully they had made themselves up with lots of beads! He got to know a different kind of man, a different attunement of feeling. Hundreds of these people were together.

*) See the 'Explanation' at the beginning of this book.

300

'Are they dangerous, or can they be trusted, Alcar?'

'No, not yet; they are still dangerous, André. They also forgot themselves and had to, because they lacked that inner strength. This is a higher degree, but inwardly they still have the animal-like attunement.

There is more life in them, more feeling and intuition. They have already some feeling, which is religion for us. They have, however, no religion yet, they are still unaware of it. It will be thousands of years before they have advanced that far. But you feel and see that there is more feeling and they are livelier than the others we have met. They don't fear other people any more, they have to control themselves. The others were timid and anxious, these are bold and ready to attack anybody coming within their reach. This degree lives like the previous one in separated groups, but the core of this attunement lives together in a main group, although they are unaware of it and cannot comprehend it. This applies to all those transitions, which include the highest degree. The present race is also widespread, but is one; they all have attained one material degree of organism, although they speak other languages, which has nothing to do with all this. God did not create languages, not any of all these earthly things which man established. God created the universe and man is ruler over all planets. They live in different organisms, each in his own attunement.

It is remarkable that these beings should have more feeling than the others. We can accept that, as we know the activity of all those material bodies. The closer they approach an other race, the more they learn from them, which adds to their knowledge. That knowledge is nothing but earthly wisdom, events occurring in their daily life, which cannot change their inner life; to the contrary, it will urge them to seek evil, because they want to have all the things the higher condition has.

It will be clear to you how much these beings have to suffer. They are peaceful in their natural condition, but completely upset when in contact with higher material degrees, because all those human qualities confuse them.

When the first human beings lived on earth and came in contact with others, trade commenced. The property of one group was desired by the other and it is still the case at present. But the higher beings cheated the others who did not know anything about it. You can follow all that in human history; these unfair things still happen, the higher being degrades himself for the sake of property.'

301

'Can't they attract a higher feeling yet, Alcar?'

'No, that is not yet possible, that will happen in the fourth degree. That's when cause and effect begins. Then we get to an other domain when man begins to make up for what he has done wrong in former lives. By that time they have experienced all material degrees. Do you feel what I mean, André?'

'Do they first have to experience all material degrees before cause and effect begins?'

'Quite so; that is what I mean. This animal-like attunement attracts that inner life which belongs to their material attunement. No other inspiring life can be attracted. We will follow these beings. This condition also has transitions and all these transitions bring us in contact with the fourth degree. When we have passed through them we go to the fifth degree, where the black race changes into the white race. Consequently, the first degrees only live separately in the jungle. In the fifth degree people live spread over the earth, as do the human beings of the sixth and seventh degree. Once race differs from the other, which is quite clear, because this has to do with the climate. Yet they are and remain one, which is the material attunement; but as inner being they pass from one body on to the other.

We will now go to the fourth degree, André; where I'll continue.'

Floating through the air, Alcar left this place. André felt that he got somewhat nearer to civilization. He no longer saw the jungle, where people lived in hiding. Here they lived in nature and he observed that this was a higher condition. People lived everywhere, but his leader went on.

Now Alcar said: 'We'll stay here. We have reached an other, the fourth degree, of material organism. Look at those people in front of you.'

Remarkable, André thought; these are different again; who on earth is aware of that.

'Is that known on earth, Alcar?'

'Yes; why not? They do not understand it, though. These people are different from those we have met. Their material organism has acquired a finer condition. Look at this organism, André; see how remarkable it is and how different their shape and build are. It is known in the scientific world, but they do not know why. Whoever would be able to assess that? They do not know all those laws, they do not know how everything was predestined from the beginning, how it all happened and how creation has come about. This is the fourth degree. These people are different, outwardly and inwardly. They discarded centuries ago what the other three degrees still do. They do not want the food of the jungle any more, their material organism requires other things which grow around them. Every constitution asks for the kind of food it needs. They eat meat, like those others, but no human flesh.

You see that they have advanced inwardly and outwardly; for it is the inner being that wants it and the material organism will take what it can digest. Everything is in harmony; not only spiritually, but also materially. These are material and spiritual laws. This is natural in so far as they attune to nature, because everybody has a will of his own and does things not in compliance with nature. They get in conflict with these laws and have to digest that.

There is already something within them representing their religion. They possess a feeling, which surpasses the faith of the perfect material being. In essence these beings do less harm than perfect material man. Nature calls them to a halt. They live naturally, in accordance with their inner being and they have respect for the stronger being. They feel the presence of a supreme power, which they recognize in nature; the elements make them anxious. That is beyond their comprehension. When they progress they seek support and worship those forces of nature. Pre-animal- and animal-like consciousness have then attained a higher attunement of feeling. The inner being has the animal-like attunement, although they passed into the fourth material degree. You see that the material organism is now far ahead of inner man. In these four degrees we have passed to the animal-like consciousness. Transitions now follow and all these transitions of the material organism pass on to the white race. That is the fifth material degree.

These people represent the fourth degree and that is their proper attunement. Around it are all those transitions and it is remarkable when you follow it. It is as we have seen in the universe. In the centre lies the mother planet surrounded by all those planets, which are related with the proper attunement and are the transitory planets. Now this is remarkable and we see that all over the earth, in all the material degrees we know. Gradually, all those beings pass on to those transitions and receive an other body until they have completely acquired the proper attunement, which is a higher material degree for the human being.

They gather knowledge in all those transitions and all this knowledge is what the earth possesses, what the other degree knows and acquired. You feel, André, they do not yet possess what they should in order to enter our life and hell in life after death.

You also feel that all these beings have not yet reached a world of existence, and not only materially; they have to experience another three material degrees before they pass on into spiritual life, as I will presently explain to you. One law detains them and takes precedence over all other laws, which serves to acquire the highest material degree. I will continue and pass on to the fifth degree, though I'll return here where we are now in the spirit to follow inner life, because those other laws will take effect, which is karma and cause and effect. I said just now that one law takes precedence and works infallibly, and that is, as will be clear to you now, that man proceeds, always has to proceed, to acquire that highest material degree. Do you feel what that means, André? Do you feel then that all these people commit nothing but sins and mistakes, but that they are unaware of it, and do not feel it? That they commit murder and destroy and that they have to make up for all this? I'll refer to it later.

'The earth therefore compels inner man to go on, which is a natural wonder, too. Do you feel these laws, André?'

'Yes, Alcar; though it's getting complicated.'

'I said already that we shall get to know other laws and that a material and spiritual chaos develops on earth. This development continues infallibly; man nor spirit, however high, can alter that. In this apparent chaos lies the quiet and harmony of the supreme being; nothing whatsoever can disturb that, though it is incomprehensible for people who are unaware of it. Nature goes ahead, ignoring everything including man; the planet earth rules over all these laws, life living on earth has to experience those laws, and I am explaining these Divine laws to you. Do you feel, André, how mighty everything is? The planet earth detains inner life; it is a Divine law every soul must experience to reach the perfect material degree. Thus, inspiring life follows only one course, but we have to experience the seven material degrees. We know why all this is and what purpose is served.

There is encompassing justice in all these degrees of development, André, as it has been from the beginning of creation. As I said before, everybody will experience it; all must cover that road and will receive that body and all those earthly pleasures. That goes with it and they will also have it because it is tied up in the other incarnation. All this is strange for man on earth, and yet it is true. People living in the large cities feel different from those living in the jungle. You feel what I mean, André, and so every degree of the human organism has its own condition which they created themselves. It is the holy truth, and I'll show it to you; I am already showing that everything serves a purpose and that we have got to learn God's laws. Nothing is coincidental, nothing is wrong and nothing in creation will come to a standstill. Everything goes on and proceeds, ever higher, until we have approached our Father and pass on into His sacred life.'

'There are dark people on earth, Alcar, a remarkable race which is intelligent, don't they belong to this degree?'

'I see what you mean, André. No, that is a different condition and has nothing to do with the cosmic material attunement. Those races are coloured people of which they have the deepest degree. There are many racial species, coloured people, who have nevertheless reached the highest material attunement. Is that clear?'

'Yes, Alcar; but have those people acquired their colour by nature?'

'Yes, the coloured people you mean have nothing to do with these beings. Look at these beings and then at those you see as coloured. How great the difference is! These people have not advanced that far; they are primitive, clumsy and shy. They live apart from the crowd and cannot yet adapt themselves. Those coloured people have more feeling and live among the whites. They, as will be clear to you, are in a completely different condition and have contact with our inner lives. Their material organism is also perfect and cannot be compared with these degrees we have followed so far.

I'll now go on to the fifth degree, at any rate to a region where thousands of people of this degree are living, because this degree is spread all over the earth. We will find them in all corners of the earth, and they live separated from the sixth and seventh degree.

We will soon be there, André.'

# CHAPTER X

## *The fifth material degree*

I'LL show you some beings of the fifth degree. Then we will return to the fourth degree where I have to explain a lot about inner life. We do not need to visit the sixth degree and in the seventh you live yourself. We go to the North; that's where people live belonging to the fifth degree, although the majority of the fifth degree is widespread. They live by hunting and are not ungifted spiritually. You'll feel that development has reached the stage where inner life commences which is displayed in intelligence. Look, André, the fifth degree.'

André looked at these people.

'Are they known on earth, Alcar?'

'Yes, they are called Eskimos. Formerly, many thousands of centuries ago, they had a different name. All other people belonging to the fifth degree live in the South, West and in the East. In those millions of centuries, the fifth degree has, like the sixth and the seventh, spread all over the earth, because many of them were in search of property. Yet, the core of the fifth degree is present here. Their bodies are hardened and can stand this climate. Their organism has a powerful skeleton. Many have a religion, brought by an other degree. Yet, they are children of nature, and it is not by chance that they live here.

The seventh degree will not be able to pass on into this kind of life; nor will the sixth degree. This life cannot experience an other attunement, I mean pass on into everything. That is not possible, as the material condition adapts itself to their inner life. Both belong together, although the material organism is far ahead of inner life.

As I said, they are not ungifted. But, they find it difficult to live among the seventh degree, as they cannot very well adapt themselves. Although we see transitions among them which means, that some of them can adapt themselves to the sixth and seventh degree, but their material attunement remains as it is.

Millions of years ago millions of people lived here, but they spread during all those centuries and now live all over the earth. Their inner life is in amazing balance with their material life. The reason is that they are living alone here and do not tolerate the influence of other races. That is why I visit them, because the pure fifth degree is present here.

'The sixth degree we find in India, and also in China and Japan and other parts of the earth. The core of the sixth degree lies in the Far East, as does the core of the seventh degree which has spread all over the earth. This, André, is the material condition of the human organism and the seven material degrees of the earth. All those millions of beings live their own lives, but, and this is remarkable, they adapt themselves to the organism they have, although they are not aware of that. These people live here and are happy, and that is one condition for all degrees. But what does this happiness mean for the seventh degree? What does the happiness of the first degree mean for the sixth? Everybody feels and has his own material life and that is not because they are a race, but the degrees which determine the material degree and condition of man on earth. Man is tied to that and cannot free himself. As I said, nature and the earth bring this about and it means reincarnation on earth.'

'It is amazing, Alcar.'

'Yes, a mighty wonder of nature, André. And this wonder has existed from the first stage of the earth; it occurred from that time on, and this law is still in force, because inspiration lives and waits for a new organism. Those degrees can therefore not dissolve, because inner life has not advanced that far; it has to experience that school of life materially as well as spiritually. Is all that clear to you, André?'

'Yes, Alcar.'

'These are the material degrees of the human organism. All of us have had to follow that long road including those who have already reached the Divine Spheres. Feel this million process and you will understand your own condition on earth. You'll also feel that all this must have a meaning, that God is fair and that there will have to be an end to that jungle stage. All these races are known on earth, but not the spiritual meaning. There are even people on earth whom they do not know, who retreated far away from the inhabitable world. All that will and shall dissolve, because they are God's children, too. Any questions, André?'

'No, Alcar. I now understand life on earth.'

'Fine, we'll go on then, as I must now give you a general survey of inspiring life which lives in every degree and inspires material life.

Wherever we go there is life, man and animal live together. Each follows his own course, his earthly, spiritual and cosmic road, and knows and has his love, but also his sorrow and misery. We'll now return to the fourth material degree.

# CHAPTER XI

## *The depth of inner life*

A LL this belonged to material life and you have some idea of the material and inner condition of all those human beings. I'll now follow the life of the soul about which there is a lot to tell. What happens when inner man has experienced the seven material degrees? I am going to explain that now.

You have clearly felt and fathomed their inner and spiritual life in the first material degree on earth. The depth of their inner life can, however, not be fathomed, if one does not know all those degrees of material organism. Where did that inspiration come from? We know now that inspiring life for the first material degree has come from an other planet where it reached that particular condition and has a pre-animal-like attunement. That inspiring life arrives on earth, which is similar, but slightly different from the planet from which it came, and receives an other body. Do you feel what I am getting at, André?'

'No, Alcar, I have no idea. I can't feel it.'

'You are honest, André. Now listen. That difference I told you about is caused in that the material organism has attained a higher degree. This organism differed from the one we have learned to know and which they have received on the second cosmic degree. The body on earth is more delicate than that of that other planet. And this materially increased strength, which the earthly body possesses, raises the inner life. I told you about that on our last journey, when we followed the animal kingdom. The animal acted in accordance with that material strength and, as you know, it was dangerous. A cat, we have made this comparison, lives in the same degree as the tiger, since this degree also has seven degrees of material strength.

'It will be clear now that inspiring life born on earth will, nay, has to act in accordance with that material strength during the first stage, which is the driving power for inner life. You see, André, that this activity is also present in the human and material organism, as we have experienced in the animal world. Inspiring life, however, is now on earth and proceeds to extricate itself from that animal-like attunement. Then follow the transitions and those people live spread around the first degree. During that time inner life gradually adapts itself and adopts qualities of those other transitions and inner life awakens. I have explained that to you. When the soul has attained the fourth material degree, inner life has lived hundreds of lives on earth but is still living in that condition. Again inner life is attracted, time and again to reach the seventh material degree. When this has been achieved, as we have been able to follow, spiritual chaos sets in, of which I told you.

The planet earth has accomplished its task and inner life now commences. Man who lives and dies in the seventh material degree returns to the earth again and begins his inner life, which means making up for what he did wrong in all those lives. This is that awe-inspiring law which is innate in every man. It is the Divine attunement within us, which calls us to a halt and compels us to settle and make up for what we have done wrong in all those degrees. That experience and return to the earth is karma, cause and effect, of all those thousands of lives in which we killed one life after the other. Inner man has to experience a tremendous mountain of sins and mistakes. Only God, Who knows all His children, knows how awful it all is. Not any man, just follow him in all those material degrees, has made the most of his life because he does not know himself, and has therefore not acquired anything of value in life after death. He has nothing in the way of spiritual property, does not know the pure love that we have, necessary to enter the spheres of light.

It will be clear to you, André, how mighty everything is, but man cannot fathom the profundity of this process. The planet earth has completed its task, inner life can begin, and the law of cause and effect now comes into force. The law of cause and effect now calls a halt and its power is tremendous. We see all these conditions of consciousness in one organism. Inner life, which has attained the seventh degree, now descends in the fourth degree in order to make up in that material degree. Do you feel what this means, André?'

'No, Alcar, I don't.'

'Then I'll explain, listen. Inner life, which already belonged to the white race, now descends into a dark black body to experience the law of cause and effect. This happens from the fourth degree on because inspiring life cannot enter the first three degrees. Man who killed his sister and brother in the fourth degree is now attracted by that inspiring life, because he is connected by hatred, that terrible power. You see:

souls attract souls, one life will now meet the other and make up. That hatred or passion, however deeply subsided in inner life, has developed and attracts that life and we see cause and effect and get to know that Divine law. Though the cause lies thousands of centuries back, the soul returns to that state and meets that life on earth to make up. That applies to every human being and herein resides the depth of inner life.

If this did not exist, man would not be able to reach our spheres and it would not be possible for inner life to make up and start its karma. But it happens, just like everything happened; it is a law, it is God, it is our attunement to the All and our connection with it.

I have experienced all that, André. As I said, I have seen all my own lives and everybody who has reached the fourth sphere on this side will experience it. When I, as inner life, had discarded all those material degrees because I had to acquire that condition of existence on earth, I returned, had to return, to the fourth degree in a dark body to start working at my past and make up for everything. I saw myself there in that brown-black organism and these are the transitions - the coloured people you meant - to make up for something. That is the sole reason why we find intellectual people among them, gifted people like the higher race on earth and we see that again in all those degrees. Man who experiences this law is, of course, unaware of it; he does not even accept eternal life. And all this lies behind death; and it is not until we accept life after death that we learn to understand all those spiritual laws.

In that life, when I began to make up for my hatred and my ruin, something of the higher race attracted me, and I could not bear life among those black people any more. I had accomplished my task, though, because I had that strength which detained me at the place where I lived. Later on, however, something urged me on; I sought and was never satisfied. I did not belong there and wanted to have what those other people on earth had. I wondered why that great and mighty difference in the earthly and material organism I lived in existed. I looked at the white people but was at a loss to understand it. But deep down within me there was something that urged me on, that I did not know nor understand and would never become clear to me. In that life, I was the slave of someone else and that encompassed my entire struggle to make up. It will be clear to you how amazing that is, now that we know all this.

'An other law came into force which I did not become acquainted with on this side until in the fourth sphere. I passed away in that dark body when I was sixty-five years of age. In that life I had made up and my life on earth came to an end. I was, and that's my point, to reach that age. My birth and death on earth were therefore preordained. I was not to die earlier or later. I learned to know those laws in the temple of the soul, André.

Try to feel this depth and if you do, you understand that birth and death on earth are preordained, that it is nothing but karma, which dominates this law. My death on earth meant the end of cause and effect for that life. My death on earth was a great loss for those who loved me, they felt grief and sorrow; but for me death was a grace, as I was to pass on into an other condition. I had made up in that life, my own karma called a halt to further life on earth. I passed on and waited for the next reincarnation in which I had to make up as in that previous condition. I will now follow my own life so that you'll get a clear picture of some lives. You'll see that God does not call the human being, does not say: now it is enough, but it is our own condition that does so, which is our past. It is a natural law, the law of cause and effect, which brings this about.

In the spheres of light I saw several of my lives and I saw that I was attracted in the North after the life I told you about. In that life, I received the female organism. However, five hundred years had lapsed. During those five hundred years I lived in the world of the unconscious and when I was attracted by my parents and was born there, I experienced the fifth material degree.

I shivered and trembled and felt deep respect because of the great wonder I was allowed to experience through the cosmic masters, who connected me with many lives, which served a purpose, as I will explain to you later. I wanted to have children in that life and they were given to me. But the human being living at my side cursed me and my life became a hell. I passed on when I was fifty years of age, inwardly broken and torn. And why all this? Once I had destroyed that man's life. I had tortured him to the extent that he could not cope with his life any more and crushed himself. I was the cause of his death and had to meet him again which happened, as it was preordained. Again I entered the world of the unconscious. The next life I observed and into which I had passed was in Egypt. All this is so amazing, André, and mysterious for people on earth; but believe me, I'm telling the holy truth.

I assisted with a cosmic plan, an event related to deep human history. I assisted with the building of the pyramid of Gizeh. I saw myself, and the one I destroyed. We were employed bringing up blocks of stone one by one. The man I destroyed stole my love. I had been waiting for a long time for the right moment and that moment came. During a struggle I pushed him over the side and he died a few days later. In doing so I created sorrow and grief again. That life was chaos and I entered the world of the unconscious. I was born again and I saw that I lived in Egypt once more. In that life I was his slave. One day my master was out hunting when we were suddenly attacked. I jumped in front of my master and the animal killed me. A very simple event, but it had to happen. I died at a young age.

I have lived thousands of lives in those millions of years. In one life I had the male organism, in an other the female. Every human being has to experience that, to make up and return, to be born on earth and to die again. Then, the entrance into the spiritual world; constantly into the world of the unconscious to wait for a new body in which to descend, and make up for what happened many centuries ago. In every condition I passed away at the right time. In every life I did something to settle my sins and mistakes. In one life I had to give myself, in another I was destroyed. As a result, I evolved, if this had not been possible there would be no end to my life on earth and I would never have attained the spheres of light. One law detained me, connected me with those beings, and sent me back to earth to make up.

Just imagine that condition on earth, André. There is not one human being on earth unless he is there for a fixed purpose. In the first place, to acquire the highest material degree, and when that is accomplished, to make up for all those mistakes and sins and to discard the past. Not a single soul can evade this. How could people ever attain the spheres of light if this was not possible? In the spheres of light there should be nothing within us, which belongs to the earth: it will stop us and block our entrance to those pure spheres.

No human being can enter the spheres of light until everything has been made up, there should be nothing that could defile our spheres. We have experienced all those transitions for material life; would it be different in the spirit? I explained to you that I and everyone else has helped build the hell, but when I had experienced the material organism of the seventh degree, mother earth set me free and that million

313

process could commence. I'll explain some other lives on our next journey, now I will stay at this life and follow inner life of man.

If anything was ever just it is this law. If any law calls us to a halt, it is this very law. How deep everything is!

Human hatred brings us back to where we awakened that hatred. A murder will connect us later again with the being we killed. This happens from the fourth material degree on. In one life we are in this part of the world, in another somewhere else, one day in the West, then again in the East, the North and the South, to experience dozens of lives. All are spiritual laws, André, and that is what inspiring life has to experience. God is just; God oversaw all this, all those depths and possibilities for inner life. Not only I, but all those living in the highest spheres on this side experienced these laws. When everything had been made up, I passed on and entered an other organism and experienced my last life on earth, when I was an artist.

Now I live in the fifth sphere and you know what my life is like.

You will experience many wonders on our next journey, André. As I told you, I'm going to connect you with the life of my friend and we will follow some of his lives on earth, which gives you an other picture of reincarnation on earth. Look, André, we have returned to the fourth degree and we see these black people again. I'll now follow their life.

What is their inner possession? They don't have anything at all. They desire to possess but they live their own life and will presently pass on. Now fathom these people. Feel how their lives are and why they are on earth, you know all those material degrees now. You can recognize these people, André, because they only follow one road, which we also followed. It is here, where those who lived in the highest material organism, descended to make up.

Intellect descends into the fourth degree, and arch-instinct into the fifth, sixth and seventh degree. There are people on earth living in the seventh degree who are animal-like beings. How do they live? They kill thousands of people. We also see that in the sixth degree and it is no different in the fifth degree. All those material and spiritual degrees are spread all over the earth and live to the full. You can't tell them apart. Try to follow and feel it and tell me whether you understand the depth of inner life.

Who understands himself? Who knows why he is on earth? Who recognizes his slave or his former master in the beggar he meets? That

314

cannot be fathomed, as it lies hidden in the depth of the soul and that constitutes the human character. That's why it is here that man begins to build at his character and personality and to enrich his spirit. Could you follow me in everything, André?'

'Yes, Alcar, everything is clear to me, it is tremendous. Is this known on earth? Do the scientists know this depth of the soul?'

'No, they don't know anything about it, they don't understand themselves and won't accept it. Where will it lead them? What is the purpose of all this? It brings them on that other road, a road winding through the universe from the beginning of creation, which has now reached the earth and even entered the Divine Spheres. Look at all those millions of beings, all those children of God. One drags himself along and has nothing to eat, another tries to understand himself, they all do something, they are all making up and live. One law urges them on and passes them from one life on to another, ever further towards Divinity. This has been going on for millions of years and there is no end to it yet, all of those will return who have not experienced their karma and made up for it. Black or dark in one life, so that they are despised by the white race, master of some art, king or emperor in the next.'

'My God, how can you tell things apart', André said when he followed all this in his mind.

'How God tells things apart? Is it not clear to you yet and don't you feel, André, that this was preordained from the beginning of creation? When the first flashes of light appeared, which you had seen in the temple of the soul, everything was already preordained. God knew what man would experience, and has to learn in order to enter the Divine Spheres. But isn't it as I asked you before ample compensation for what awaits us? Is it possible to skip all those sins, to go on and simply forget them whereas all those laws are in force which have to be experienced? Didn't we live unconsciously in all those lives? Had we advanced that far that we understood that life and knew ourselves? No, a thousand times no, we had nothing and could not acquire anything, because our inner condition had not reached that stage. I'll explain that to you and show it, because we go on, ever further, and we'll see what man does in all those material lives.

Come, André, we'll leave and follow inner man to the seventh material degree.'

André was deeply lost in thought. They did not speak for a long time. How is it possible, he thought, who can accept this? All this is unknown on earth, and yet, how mighty and natural everything his leader told him was. Who was his real self and who understood creation? How misinformed people were. What is scholarship on earth? he thought. What did scientists really know about creation, about all those dark souls living in the jungle? Why did they live there? Now he had learned all those incomprehensible things. This was a revelation for him, he could never have imagined that it would be that magnificent. He reeled at all those wonders he had experienced and yet his leader still continued to show him more wonders.

'Have you ever met that man from your time in Egypt again, Alcar?'

'Yes, though centuries later.'

'How amazing that is, too, and how mighty, Alcar. And all of us will experience that?'

'Without exception, André.'

'Do you know my lives, Alcar?'

'Yours too, my son.' Alcar looked at his instrument and said: 'Are you not eager to know where you have lived and how your lives have been?'

'Oh, if that were possible, Alcar.'

'It is possible for us, André, and consequently for you; but we have other plans for this journey and that forms no part of it.'

'So you could connect me with my own life on this side?'

'You mean with your past lives?'

'Yes, Alcar.'

'Yes, I could. At the beginning of our previous journey I connected you with your life, and mine, on earth. I showed you my life in various ways and told you about them. I also connected you with your parents, with your youth and I showed you many other scenes. If that is possible, I can also connect you with those other lives.'

'I'm prepared to accept everything, Alcar.'

'It will happen, my boy, just have patience.'

'Shall I experience it on our next journey, Alcar?'

'Yes, I promise.'

'I'm grateful to you, Alcar! I'll see my lives! How amazing, how wonderful! I'm thankful to God for that! Why is so little known about that, Alcar?'

'I said and explained that to you. This is quite simple. Only sensitive people can feel something of their past, but one should be able to look into the past, be clairvoyant and have these gifts in order to observe something. But above all there has to be someone on this side who brings that connection about. Do you feel what I mean?'

'You mean that I cannot see by myself?'

'Indeed, that is what I mean, it is not possible. The past is deeply hidden in the soul. People on earth do not even understand 'death', not to speak of this depth. Look at all these human beings. See what they do and how they live. All of them go to ruin, they go on and on, and live their lives to the fullest. Something raises them; in every being resides a power which is the connection with our holy Father. But they do not know the depth of their own lives; they cannot fathom it because they are animal-like human beings. Do you feel this, André?'

'Yes, Alcar. So it is only possible to look into the past, when one has inwardly advanced that far?'

'Yes, it is not otherwise possible.'

'Then this is clear to me, Alcar. It also explains what people had told me they had experienced.'

'Which is, André?'

'I spoke to somebody, Alcar, who visited an other country he had never seen before, yet he recognized many things and could orient himself. He knew exactly where he was and found it very strange. I got the feeling, he said, that I lived here before. Does this belong to his own past?'

'That is possible. Some people can feel the past, but in order to look consciously into the past a connection from this side is necessary. Life on earth occupies man completely and he cannot orient himself. However, when he feels something, the past usually dominates and it suddenly penetrates his consciousness, though he can't find an explanation for it.'

'Is it also possible, Alcar, that qualities manifest themselves in this life, which we have acquired in an other life?'

'Yes, certainly, but all those qualities passed on into our feeling, a condition of consciousness. Do you feel what I mean?'

'Yes, Alcar, I understand. Can these feelings be recognized?'

'That is also possible, for instance, feeling for some kind of art. I told you about that. This is most clearly seen in children. Sometimes such feelings manifest themselves at an early age, whereas these phenomena

317

cannot be observed in other children. On earth, these feelings are referred to as talent, intellect, but that is not the truth. The soul has acquired these qualities in the previous life, or perhaps many lives ago. It is at any rate a fact, when such feelings arise, that they emanate from the depth of the soul.'

'If I understand you correctly, Alcar, I feel that those people who live in the fourth degree in their present life, will not feel anything of the past because they have not experienced anything?'

'Very good, André, that is obvious. Their one life is like the other, but when they advance, you surely feel that, intellect awakens and these feelings mean talent or intuition for something they try to accomplish. Is that clear?'

'Yes, Alcar, perfectly. How simple it is. You now follow inner man from the fourth degree on, Alcar, is that the reason why you do not visit the first three degrees?'

'That is obvious, too, André. All those earlier lives are alike; in other words: they have not the slightest depth. The first three material degrees only serve to pass from the pre-animal-like on to the animal-like condition. These are conditions of consciousness in an animal-like degree, the human character is not formed until in the higher conditions of consciousness.'

'Is the experience of these human beings of no importance?'

'Yes, certainly, but do not forget that everything the soul experiences in life on earth will be reflected in the character, and that, if these qualities belong to the earth, they are of no value in the spirit. Do you feel this too, André?'

'Do you mean to say that, when I have learned something of the earth, an earthly matter, it has no meaning on this side?'

'Yes, that is what I mean. For this side, only feeling is of importance, and this feeling must be the pure love we have on this side, which means light in the life of the spirit. Do you feel that too, André?'

'Yes, Alcar, you made this clear to me before, I now understand what you mean.'

'I'll presently pass to an other condition and I'll follow a human being who continued his way from the fourth degree and we see this soul several times again in material life on earth. I want to give you a clear picture of what inner life has to experience before reaching the highest material degree. I have known the soul I'll tell you about and I

318

have met him several times in life on earth. Follow me, André, and listen to what I'm going to tell you. We will move on floating. The soul we are about to follow lived in the fifth degree and you know how far those people have advanced and what inner feelings they have. Before the spirit I want to follow had reached that level, he had been on earth hundreds of times. The human being was unaware of all those lives and he waited in the world of the unconscious to be born again. He has already experienced the jungle, the first degrees, and also the fourth degree and passed on to the fifth degree. Every birth, as will be clear to you, gives more property to the soul as man, as inner life. That property is the earthly property the parents may call their own. Do you feel what I mean, André?'

'Yes, Alcar, it is quite clear.'

'If you understand me, it will be clear to you that inner life can receive more riches as it approaches the highest material degree. People in the jungle have no earthly possessions as compared with the property of man in the large cities. This is, as you feel, a mighty difference, which awakens inner life. You'll also feel that as inner life proceeds, this progress is reflected in material life, which is a remarkable phenomenon, though it has a natural effect. It also shows us the human development, development towards a higher consciousness and this higher consciousness requires, and even demands, an other and individual condition. This condition is life on earth, so for the child the parents where it was born. When this soul or inner life receives rich parents and will and can experience this life, it adapts itself and we can now feel how that life will be, whereas inner life born to poor parents cannot experience that because these people lack the earthly means. Surely you feel what I'm hinting at and what purpose I have in mind with this explanation? This life, André, was born again. What was impossible in the pre-animal-like and animal-like attunement is now possible. The parents have earthly means and this inner life, their own child, is spoiled. This is earthly property. The child grows up and it adapts itself marvellously to this new life, but the inner life emanates from that animal-like life, in which it lived in its previous incarnation. All those previous lives had been experienced unconsciously. This is not seen nor felt on earth, as man on earth is unaware of spiritual consciousness. I speak of animal-like consciousness, André, but inner life must proceed ever further until it has acquired spiritual consciousness. But the soul has to acquire more. Inner life only experiences material life in the first four degrees, because this life has an organism. That is very simple and natural. What all those people do not realize and are unaware of is, that they will have to become conscious as inner life, which means awakening. They live, because they have to live, they act, because they all have to act, and all this is imposed by their material organism. Do you feel, André, how great and deep everything is? Do you feel that when inner life advances, it has to lose itself? That this life emanates from that animal-like and unconscious state and is going to lay all that aside? And that hundreds of character traits, acquired in that higher life, will take that place instead; and that all these beings are unaware of reality and conditions of existence, and can't possess anything? I'm following that soul and we see that it is now going to lose what it has known and experienced. All this is feeling, to pass from one condition of unconsciousness to the more conscious reality. That is the mother life, or the perfect and pure mother love, and this is the mightiest thing mankind has received from God. In the animal-like attunements connection and bearing children happened in an unconscious life because, and that should be quite clear, they had a material organism and had to act accordingly.

They accomplished all that. The mother organism underwent that event, both felt and experienced; yet, these beings were fully unaware of higher emotional expressions, and they were the slaves, the tools of material man. They experienced all this in an animal-like way, and we, human beings, were to experience that all-encompassing event in a human and subsequently in a spiritual way. Hardly anybody on earth possesses this spiritual way, because all this would then be part of spiritual consciousness.'

'What you told just now is amazing, Alcar.'

'I must explain this to make you feel that becoming conscious is only possible when two human beings connect, and the mother organism experiences creation. Did you feel that clearly, André, if you don't, you won't be able to follow me and the beautiful essence of what I'm going to explain will be lost. Ask me if something is not clear.'

'It is amazingly deep, Alcar, nevertheless I feel what you mean.'

'Think quietly, my son, we have got plenty of time. You must feel it or I cannot go on.'

André pondered on everything and began to feel the depth of this

320

problem. An amazing world opened itself. My God, he thought, who knows these laws? Who on earth will think of that?

'I know now, Alcar, and I'll try to put my question as clearly as possible. If I understand you correctly you mean that people are living on earth, because as a spirit they have a means which is the human and material organism?'

'Splendid, go on, André.'

'In that means, or tool, as you put it, the spiritual human being or soul lives. The soul experiences in all those degrees in accordance with the strength and activity of that organism. Inner man performs all those acts and he does so in all these degrees because he has this organism. I now feel that all these beings live like the animal, Alcar. I cannot express myself more clearly.'

'It is very good, André, all these people live like the animal. But they are human beings and because they are they have to pass on to a higher life and leave the animal-like attunement. Now what happens? They lose themselves, but will find themselves again by experiencing all these problems of life. Is that clear, André?'

'Yes, Alcar, but then there are only a few people on earth who live as man should. Have those who live as man attained the spiritual condition or attunement?'

'These human beings have reached the material condition, André, the spiritual attunement lies beyond it.'

'Then I can follow you, Alcar.'

'Thank you, André, I'll go on. This soul, of which I spoke, will have to experience it. From early youth this child is unmanageable and we wonder how it will live as it grows up. Follow that young life now and see how it lives. The only possibility to awaken is to experience creation, which the soul can only experience in the mother organism. Man who has not advanced that far, must receive, experience, in order to awaken. As a result, his love develops and the soul passes on into another and higher consciousness. In this way, the soul experiences all social conditions. He feels at ease in all those lives and this has been going on for millions of years. The soul passes from one life on to another. From the fourth degree into the fifth, then into the sixth, in which this inner life has to awaken. The soul will receive in life on earth, which is the birth of a child. This is the process of revelation given to the individual human being, in which life must awaken. Awakening time and again, André, in various conditions of consciousness, as I explained to you just now. In all those lives one evil after the other is done, because this life is unaware of a higher love. When the parents have the means to make life agreeable, it gives satisfaction to inner life and something awakens which will form part of the character. Inner life, however, cannot experience much in the fifth material degree, since there are no means in all those degrees and the character cannot develop. I will pass on and continue in the sixth degree. The last life on earth this soul had completed was the death of this human being at an advanced age.

Hundreds of years later this life was born again. The soul had the male organism and this life also passed in passion and animalization. Again this life returned to the world of the unconscious and waited to be born and we see this soul again in the male organism. That life was spent in a similar way. However, all those experiences on earth deeply wounded the human soul and left something behind which man acquired. Again, death came and this inner life entered the astral world. What will happen now? This soul is again born on earth, grows up and awakens. This life desires and this desire awakens as the material organism grows.

What kind of condition is this, André? Can you feel what is going to happen now? Is it clear to you how this life will be?'

'Too deep for me, too incomprehensible, Alcar, I don't know.'

'Well, listen and try to follow me. I'm speaking of the sixth degree of material life and we must go on to enter the seventh degree, which we will do presently. An amazing event takes place in this life. The soul now lives in the female organism. What it has acquired in all those lives is nothing but passion and animalization. It is in disharmony with everything, with nature and life itself. The consciousness it has lives at the surface, we call it day-consciousness and it is nothing but violence, murder, animalization, destruction and similar devilish passions. It has no father or mother love, it has no faith, no religion, it has nothing.

Now that life returns to earth, for God gave this soul a new organism. God wanted that, if it would not happen, this life would never reach the Divine degree. It must and shall receive, or it won't advance and its development will come to a standstill, because the plan of evolution must proceed, as this life is a particle of God, and represents His own life.

322

What will happen now? How will this inner life feel now? What will it desire? To what parents will this child be born? Questions, my son, nothing but questions, but I'll give you all the answers.

The parents are like she is. The soul has descended into the mother organism and, as I said, it can become a mother. But we know the life living in that organism; is not ready for that body. Yet, that mighty wonder happened which nobody understands. An amazing event, but a very common event on earth which can be seen every day, every second. When the creative and the serving organism connect a new life is born when this body is perfect. We see that on earth, not only for man but also in the animal kingdom. This has happened from the very beginning of creation. This occurred already, as I showed you, during the first stage. God knew and oversaw all that, for the soul would not and could not awaken if it had not experienced creation.

Now that inner life has descended. The parents have attracted and received in accordance with their own inner attunement. Now that law of attraction of the soul of our level is in force. It has one degree, one attunement, the parents and their child are one, although the parents are advanced in creative and driving capacity, because they connected, or it would not have happened.

I make this clear to you, because the strange emotional life, which is known on earth but not understood, awakens in that inner life. It is the struggle, that awful struggle to pass from the creative on into the driving life. The soul is neither man nor woman, it only has passion and animalization. It has everything, which is, however, animal-like, and now it awakens. Something in this life is now conscious and that is the previous incarnation. This was experienced very intensely and is the only thing that is alive and awake in day-consciousness. Life or the soul has the female body, but it feels male. Do you understand what happens, André? Do you feel how deep, how incomprehensible these human beings are, who are despised on earth? I told you about them when we visited mental patients and I explained a few things. Now you will experience it again, because we follow the development of man.

Now this life is neither man nor woman, and that in the sixth degree of material life. It is in the last three degrees that we see these phenomena awaken. It is a curse because this soul wants to experience, but this inner life can only experience the way it feels, which conflicts with nature. However, there are other beings on earth who feel like they do and the instinct which is in the soul knows this intuitively, but everything is abnormal and unnatural. This is no love, this is passion and however horrible it is, that passion passes on to a higher consciousness, but not until other lives have been lived. This life is hell and the soul receives in this life only what it wants to have and what is pursues. This entire life is lived in this abnormal condition. This soul passes away at its proper age after a pre-animal-like life. This had not yet happened, but its experience produced that unnaturalness, the male feeling lived in this female organism which this life could not alter.

Feel that horrible struggle this hideous condition caused, feel how terrible this life is, how it has felt all those years, how it has struggled to quench that awful fire of passion. But that fire remained, that is the way it was and could not be changed, only God could. But God knew what was necessary; God knows and feels how it has to be and what the soul will receive and experience in its next incarnation. Feel how deep this inner life is, feel the agonies it experienced, feel how its heart broke for desire. Whenever it met a similar being, it was attracted to it. That being acted on it like a magnet, and its struggle to pass on into mother life started again. Then death came and put an end to this struggle. Death was the saviour and a grace, though not for its parents. Not for those who know nothing about death and regard it as something terrible. For this being death was a grace, a saviour and a friend, but it did not feel that either, because it had wanted to live and experience, to satisfy what was deep inside. But, it passed away, had to pass away, for God said, now it is enough.

It was not until two hundred years later that it was born in the next life and came on earth, again in a female body. We see this life again, André, in the previous life poverty, in this life riches. How good is God for His own life, for now she needed riches. In this life she was spoiled and could receive everything. These parents, too, were as she felt, both gave themselves entirely, but in her mother lived a similar life and she was not entirely pure and free of those feelings either and not completely a mother. The mother lived her dual life, her child awakened and reached maturity.

However, there were no desires in her, but as she grew older, something awakened. When the material organism reached maturity her consciousness awakened, her inner life passed into day-consciousness and something awakened in her again. Both sexes had now awakened in her, though the mother organism possessed the dominating feeling and the power for motherhood and she became a mother. However, this life was not perfect, she was a mother and yet she wasn't. She had feeling, she had experienced this and yet, she did not care about that young life, which was her own child. Soon she freed herself, left the father and child and went away. She did not understand anything of her own inner life yet. She was a bad woman and had none of the qualities a mother should have, for what mother can leave her own child? Is that mother love? Has this soul that sacred feeling? She experienced this sacred connection, but she was not aware of anything. But why did she act in this way, why did she go away? She sought but did not know what, she had to go, nothing comforted her, nothing could console her. We see and know these mothers in life on earth.

Whenever she could experience this soul felt at ease and there was no struggle any more. But after a short while that struggle was there again and she sought once more, because she could get whatever she wanted, as she was rich in this life. And so she went on receiving, became gradually older until she finally passed away and entered the world of the unconscious. Death had also put an end to that struggle. Yet she had learned in that last life. In that animal-like life she had received something she had not known nor felt, because an other power, a passion within her dominated. She had experienced something in an unconscious condition.

That wonderful event had happened in her. She had experienced creation as happened in the first degree. She had experienced that wonder present in every mother, which is creation. In that first degree, too, we experienced it unconsciously and we would experience this mighty event unconsciously thousands of times. Do you feel, André, what my point is, and why all this is? Do you feel, my boy, that the soul must acquire the consciously creative feeling, and that this is only possible through the mother body? That we, human beings, consciously pass into creation? That the soul unconsciously experienced this mighty event in all those thousands of lives? That it must awaken in those lives? That this is God's intention and if it would not happen, we would never be able to attain spirituality, nor the spheres of light? Feel this mighty event and realize that it is necessary and the only way to awaken.

Nothing happened in those millions of years, which had to happen to experience this consciously. The soul must awaken on the planet earth, as will be clear to you now. This soul had experienced the plan of creation and this experience, that terrible struggle that was going on in her, this feeling, my boy, awakened her. The soul had advanced that far now, it had experienced and felt it just now, after all those millions of years. We know this life and where it has lived. Is all that so incomprehensible? Could this soul have acquired a higher consciousness on an other planet? Was that possible? Haven't we followed those people and don't we know what their inner life is like? Again, André, was this possible in those other lives. No, André, a thousand times no!

This soul would not awaken until now, now it is ready, now it becomes conscious, though many lives are necessary.

Three hundred years passed before a new material organism was ready for her. You feel that to be able to accept a new life, an ever-increasing number of years is required. Yet this life returned to earth in a transition between the sixth and seventh material degree.

I see her again as a child of farmer parents. That's where she awakened. Her parents had seven children and she was the third child. She again had the female body, and why, André? Can you feel that?'

'No, Alcar, it is too deep for me, I don't know.'

'Listen, I have explained that to you. In our life when we think of something we will and have to pass on into it, or a disharmonic condition will set in to the effect that we'll lose our balance and attain a deranged condition. Gerhard explained that to you[*], I told you about it and you have experienced it in the darkness. When we visited the darkness and you thought of something but did not consciously pay attention to what you thought, for instance, when we visited that man who had been cremated.[**] You followed me after I had told you to wait, you were immediately attacked, because you left your condition and attunement by thinking of it.

That means passing on into an other condition, it is experiencing something, and that experience emanates from our deep inner self, and is therefore present in inner life. These are spiritual laws and belong to inner life; it is the concentration and moment life experiences. You also know that nothing can be skipped in the spirit, and that what one desires and wants to experience will happen, because man has a will of his own. That will is deeply hidden in our life, and it is the soul, which

[*] See the book: 'The Bridge to Eternal Life'.
[**] See the first and second volume of the book: 'A View into the Hereafter'.

has these desires. The soul desires, experiences in accordance with its inner attunement, it is a condition of consciousness of life itself. That's why I ask you, is it so strange that this soul should receive the mother body again? Isn't it natural? Development proceeds and does not decline, because that activity is not present in creation, we don't know such activity of laws. Onward, ever further to awaken. What comes after that previous life? How is the inner condition of this soul? Could this life go back, does it not have to go on? It can only receive the mother organism and this wonder happens.

This encompasses that wonder of God and various spiritual and natural laws. It is predestined that inner life will receive this organism, the mother body, and pass on into the female body before this child awakens in the mother organism. Do you feel now, André, what kind of wonder this is? That it had to happen and nothing could change it? That it is present in inner life and that science, the scholars on earth, will never be able to assess that, because it is a law of nature? The soul therefore receives the mother organism, as this is the sole reason that this life returns to the earth now that she has inwardly advanced that far. The soul receives the mother organism to acquire mother love, and consequently attain a higher consciousness. Imagine that. This is no material event, but a spiritual one. This is not a material, but a spiritual law, André, and inspiring life dominates this law and inner life, as a human being will receive this body. It was therefore preordained that a girl would be born to these parents. The soul has this power and this is a law, because inspiring life lives in it at that moment, which is the plan of evolution, the continuous advance for this life. Isn't it a mighty wonder? Do you feel, André, that people cannot alter this and that they do not know these laws? That we only see and experience that in our life?'

'I have no words for it, Alcar.'

'I have a lot more to tell you, André. Yes, my son, this is a wonder. We find this wonder in all material degrees and spiritual lives, because it has been so from the beginning of creation. It is a wonder and a grace of God of which people are completely unaware. It is the life the inner life experiences, it is the desire to experience, but beyond that is a law and this law compels inner life to follow the road it began, or life would not proceed. What is destined to be born and to awaken in nature will be born and awaken, it has to advance and not to go back, or God's creation would come to a standstill and there would be injustice. However, we have not yet experienced injustice, nor the return to an other condition of consciousness. God's life, everything created and activated by God, will have to return to Divinity.

The inner life again descended into the mother organism and it received one life after the other and enjoyed the bliss of heaven, which is the plan of creation.

The creative power, man, lived in her environment. He was to become her husband, even if he lived at the other end of the world, if he were to meet her, it was bound to happen. Then a new law comes into force and they are connected. I said that he lived in her vicinity and seven children were born out of their marriage.

A very normal, earthly event experienced every second on earth, but beyond that, in this world, the deep mystery of the soul resides. This soul became a mother, though she did not yet have that deep and pure mother love. This happened because it had to. Millions of children are born in this way, but it is no spiritual experience, it happens through the passion of him or her and they pass on in that process.

She was therefore no spiritual mother, because she lacked feeling and inner consciousness. It was her husband who wanted this and she surrendered willingly. This sacred event was still not perfect nor conscious, and she was poor, very poor in spirit, because this was not accomplished out of pure inspiration. Can you feel that too, André?'

'Yes, Alcar.'

'Well then, she died at a mature age and hundreds of years passed again, because this life was not conscious yet. This inner life was attracted again and descended on earth. She was born on an other continent and again received the mother organism. This child grew up and awakened when it reached the age of eighteen. She felt attracted to art. Though her parents were not rich, they had the means so that she could strain herself to acquire that study.

Where did those feelings for art come from so suddenly?

You can't feel that, therefore I will tell you. This soul experienced creation and by that great and mighty event those feelings had passed into other feelings, which displayed in her life. The feeling to create was in her. Do you feel now, what awakened in her, André? This awe-inspiring feeling, that event, the experience of creation manifested itself in her and art now appealed to her. This feeling, that urge now lay in her, but she did not understand it, she did not know where these feelings came from. Man does not wonder about this, because he did not understand himself and is unaware of all these laws. She wanted to create, nothing but create, she was strongly inspired and this would happen. She married and gave birth to a child, a boy. This, too, is a spiritual miracle, yet this miracle and activity cannot be felt.

She gave birth to one boy, André, and because of this child, this soul attained an other and higher condition of feeling, because the creative power was present in that life. That relation between mother and child brought her, the mother, in a higher creative condition and she felt capable of achieving great things. Consequently, her inner life was not only upgraded by her own feelings which had awakened in her by her previous life, but also by the life she had attracted and which had come to her. The child also became an artist and even a great artist, and when this was noticed and experienced on earth the child owed it to his mother, because the mother fancied art but she would not attain that level. It was the mother, though, who had given him that feeling. She had the feeling to create the desire to accomplish something and this is creation. Her child who came on earth was to become an artist. She passed into that urge to create during pregnancy, but her inner life had already awakened in her previous life.

In the plan of creation lies activity, and that activity is feeling, and means love. She had experienced that in that other life seven times; it was not until now that this experience made a deep impression in her inner life, and had awakened her so that she began to yearn. But she would not awaken forever until in a later life, and that also happened.

She passed away at the age of sixty-five and it was six hundred years before she would return to earth.

When this moment came, her inner life was rested and prepared and this wonder happened. She was born in yet an other country, but what did she possess, in which body did this soul descend this time, André?'

'I cannot answer that, Alcar.'

'She descended in the male organism. The creative feeling she had acquired in those other lives now gave her the male organism. She had lived in hundreds of other creative bodies, but in the pre-animal-like and animal-like condition of which inner life was unaware, it only has animal-like consciousness. Yet those feelings became manifest in these people and we see the creative feeling awaken.

How remarkable all that is, André. We see that process develop in the first three material degrees. We see man possess what God as Creator of heaven and earth established, and this Divine power lies in the creative organism, the male body. Creation is fixed in this organism, but the mother organism experiences creation.

We on this side see and feel that activity and from where these feelings come. It is the urge to create, and it is that what we have received from God by which we are Divine. God, my son, created the universe, man and animal, but man passes consciously into this feeling, acquires this feeling which is reflected in art. In art, yes, what is art? Where does art come from? What is the origin of art? Out of creation, André. Out of that which is deep inside us, out of the All and God, because we represent His own life. And this Divine gift resides in the male organism, for this organism creates an other life, it received this power from God.

The higher inner man, the soul, advances, the more beautiful art becomes. Do you feel that as inner man grows and develops, the feeling for creation is becoming conscious?

Do you also feel that every race can and must have its own art and that this has to do with all these material degrees? That the feeling for art is displayed in all these degrees, and some time has to reach a level related to and inherent with the seventh material degree? That it is no coincidence, but awakening? We see all that and know all these conditions of consciousness, because we have experienced all this.

When I go a little further, and ask man on earth what is art? What could he say? He will only repeat my question, shrug his shoulders and go away when I have explained my feelings.

Art, my son, is the awakening of creative feeling, which is present in the male material organism as activity. This also explains why the male being as creative artist can reach that level. The man is creator; he has received this power from God as a cosmic being. The soul who awakens in this body creates, in it resides that might and power which the mother body lacks and cannot have because this amazing organism experiences an other activity. Only the male being creates and attains the very highest in art. Art reflects the inner life of the artist. To man on earth this is art, for us on this side it is consciousness in creation.

Do you feel that everything is fixed to it, André? That this feeling is the Divine Spark and means awakening of inner man? That this is because we belong to creation and God has put this in our hands? We see this feeling awaken. We have learned to understand this feeling in all those material degrees, every soul has this feeling to some extent, because we are all life and form part of creation. The higher the soul advances, the more beautiful art becomes inner man proceeds and inspiring life awakens. As I said, this soul had received the male organism in hundreds of lives and the female organism an equal number of times. But, in all those lives it learned nothing in respect of those properties, which constitute the character and the personality a higher level of consciousness. In the jungle we cannot speak of a personality, nor on those other planets where the inner life and the material organism are developing. All those lives are essential to develop and progress. What does man learn in one life on earth? What does man learn in those first degrees, and what does man learn, when he is ignorant. He is unaware of human love. What man acquires in one life is spoiled in the next, because he does not yet possess anything, no personality, no consciousness, no pure love, everything is animal-like.

Once again, André, what does man learn in a short life on earth? Follow all those human lives and see how they get old and spoil one life after another. See how they live and make life unbearable for others. How they want to possess, deceive and cheat other people. It is all rough and rude and no spiritual possession. I explained many times how life on earth proceeds and what people make of it. They live to be seventy and eighty, and what have they achieved? They only worked for their property, for their own life and for that of their children.

When you talk to all such people about love you will see how they shrug their shoulders; how they laugh and call you a dreamer, merely because it is too unbelievable, too unnatural for them, and because they are unaware of a God in heaven. What they need is a lot of earthly property. What they want is the happiness of the earth, which everybody can acquire and will experience because he has to. However, they forget their inner life, which goes on, ever further to return to God. Follow all those people on earth and see how they curse their God.

They pass from one life to an other and they follow their own way in all those lives, because that feeling is in them which is their inner life, their spiritual attunement. In this way they experience because it is a law, a force of nature and they will receive what they desire. That is still possible, soon it won't be because other laws will take effect of which I'll tell you and which I have connected you with. That is making up, my son, that is experiencing their sins and mistakes, that is their karma.

Man goes on and ascends on the social scale. He ascends ever further and reaches his aim. Then, André, they will fall and land in the depth of their own inner life. They have no spiritual level yet, they will forget themselves and they will perish. That is an infallible law, because they have not advanced to the extent that their own inner life calls them to a halt. They fall; they have to fall to start all over again. With no deeds to connect them with higher life, there is nothing to look back on. The soul must first have this strength, we are inwardly protected against destruction against anything we may come across or experience in life on earth. There is something within us, which says: till here and no further, because I see and feel an other life, I know I live eternally. I love God and have understood my Father. I do not live for myself but for all those people, because they are out of God and are my sisters and brothers. I feel no passion, no destruction within me, I want to live and prepare to proceed, because I am aware of eternal life and want the good.

How long will it take for people to speak and feel like that, my son?

They have nothing of all this; no spiritual property, nothing, they live and experience and have to acquire all of it. They have to acquire all this because God gives them millions of opportunities. They receive a new material organism time and again, but they defile all these organisms. They not only annihilate themselves; they also curse Him Who has granted them this awe-inspiring gift. They cannot act differently, because they have not advanced that far, they are people who still have to acquire all these powers. They have not yet learned to understand their God, nature, their father and mother. They do not yet possess the faintest feeling of love for him or her who accomplished that, who gave them life. However, all of them, including their father and mother, live an unconscious life, they don't know themselves, they fail again, because they are unaware of spiritual love, of advance, and of a God of love. That's what they have to acquire; that's why they are on earth, that's why God gave them all this love, because God knows that they can't acquire that in one life on earth.

If this would not be possible, André, as I explained to you many times, we would come to a standstill. I explained to you in thousands of conditions that this is essential or we cannot advance any more. It is the soul, which acts and asks and answers all those questions itself. The soul can and will accomplish all those wonders, because it is inspiring life. It is out of God, and will return to God. It is perfection and has a Divine attunement. We shall acquire that attunement, though thousands of lives on earth and on all those planets are required in order to attain that level. We would awaken in all those lives on earth and this awakening takes place.

We passed from one body to the next. In the first one we learned to feel and in the next we acquired that feeling. We learned how to speak and to speak a lot, which is possession. We learned something related to art, which other people did not know and we went to other countries to get acquainted with man living there. What we knew and possessed inwardly belonged to the earth. All this was given us to make something of ourselves and that happened. But what was it, nothing but earthly personality. There was no spiritual personality in us. People wander over the earth and acquire things others do not have and they live to the fullest. But why is all that? It also serves to awaken, and belongs to life on earth. In this way life on earth passed and there was no time for anything else. In that life on earth all these people had acquired the wisdom of the earth. When they passed away they entered an other life for which they had no qualities. That life was like they were themselves; which means their personality and inner life. That inner life was living dead for that other world and could not live there, because it still had to experience the perfect material organism on earth. Having returned to the earth to receive an other organism, this soul passed on into other conditions and became a ruler.

This possession had been learned and acquired in all those lives and it belonged to the creative power residing in this inner life. This also meant ruin. This downfall is deeper as wealth becomes greater. God gave man everything and man acquired this which becomes the personality; but that personality is terrestrial and of a course materiality; those living in it are the rulers of evil and they live on earth to destroy. The more wealth, the greater the personality, the deeper the downfall, because all this has no meaning in life after death.

All this is necessary to become a personality. Those powers will presently pass on to the spirit and it is not until then that man, all those souls, begin an other and higher life. Then their inner life matures and radiates, there is something within them, which guards them against animal-like life, it is the spiritual property and the love they have acquired in that life on earth. In this way the process continues ever more.

When the creative power awakens in inner life, life proper begins, all these urges like hatred, passion and violence awaken in a powerful concentration, but merely to possess. It is not until the soul passes on to it, as I said a while ago, that this inner life receives the greatest blessing on earth such as a lot of possessions. Everything belonging to and present on the earth is for this soul, because it must awaken inner life. Together with this creative feeling all those terrible qualities representing the character and personality manifest themselves. When the creative capacity approaches and becomes conscious it seethes in that inner life. It is a burning fire and inner life is awake and conscious. That life hovers. Many lives pass, the soul is restless and they have every reason to curse their Divine attunement and it is impossible to call to a halt. Evil in man has awakened and the arch-instinct again dominates and man lives the way an animal would not be able to. They perish hundreds of times, they return time and again in one condition in order to leave it and start a different life. I cannot follow all those lives. This is a picture of what will and must happen, which this inner life I told you about and has now descended into the male organism, will experience. This life now passes on into creative power and the soul receives the material organism, that beautiful human body. Now he can move, he is his own master, which was not possible in that previous condition. In the mother body the soul has to receive. This reception is the second personality; it is passing on into that creative capacity, to accept and to serve. In the spirit we have a healthy respect for serving love, but on earth this serving is experience. The soul has to give itself completely through the being living in the female organism.

The creative body demands, it compels and creates, that is the first personality and it is its own master. It can do what it wants, thereby forgetting itself. Oh, that power, that arch-being, it will awaken. It can move mountains in that organism breaking all existing laws and cannot be reached. The female being cannot do anything about it, cannot alter it and cannot achieve anything because it does not have that strength. In that body resides the first moment you have observed in the temple of the soul. That first moment is an awe-inspiring power, which cannot be assessed; and which nobody knows or feels unless he is on this side and understands all these powers, all those planets, and accepts and experiences this wonder of creation in the spirit.

334

Now what power is this in the male body, which can awaken the arch-instinct? What kind of power is contained in it? It is the all encompassing; it is what God has incorporated in all His life and which comprises His own life. It is the attunement to God and the activity of all those planets, which created everything. This is the miracle of creation and it is billions of years old. This existed from the first moment, as a result of which everything emanated, the power, which interconnected stars and planets. This is the universe, heaven and earth, it is as I said before, the all-encompassing life, it is God Himself.

Consequently, the male body is the animation, is the miracle of God, because God established that miracle, that arch-power, in a material organism.

See and feel whether this is so, whether you understand and feel those powers. That miracle resides in this body. My God, if that awakens! What will happen if this has to awaken? Where will it lead to and what will the end be like? That end is incalculable. Oh, my God, why did You give that being this power and this wealth? See how it curses You! Hear how people lament, no man on earth can stop him, because this soul does what it wants. It rules and dominates everyone. Follow that life, André, and look at its horrible life.

This must happen because this life will awaken. Life on earth has to experience this and has to pass through that stage. This life will attain the utmost on earth. That is the purpose of life on earth and it is not until then that it has reached its aim. That child will experience it, the soul we follow, and which has now descended in the male organism. This life also passes and death follows. It subsequently enters the spiritual world to descend on earth later on in an other organism.

The soul will again receive the male organism, because it has to proceed. This seething and cursing life passed but it is cursed in this life and it will receive what it did to others. Now this inner life revolts. It does not let itself be dominated and does not allow itself to be tortured. It does not want anything of the sort. It is on earth and it has no earthly property because the parents are simple people. The soul nevertheless creates a condition of its own. It is not like the previous life, it is not aware of it anyway because it cannot know that it has already lived this life.

This life, this human being is on earth and lives among millions of others. It seeks and finds and what is experiences and will experience proceeds to an awe-inspiring level. Yet it can't reach that level because it does not have that earthly property like it didn't in that previous life. But it seeks and wants to achieve, this life has a power, which urges it on and cannot be stopped.

In this life on earth this soul achieves nothing, it shapes its own life, it strikes down when its way is blocked. This soul has no spiritual quality yet, because there is nothing in this life in the way of self-control. Where did it acquire that great power? This life revolts, it is arrested, frustrated and those who try to stop this life will perish.

We see these beings in all social classes, André. You will find these people wherever you look. We'll follow this life. This life cannot be arrested nor stopped. This human soul seethes, a power has awakened, capable of moving mountains which wants to create and possess everything on earth which makes life pleasant. This life wants earthly property, honour, fame and glorification. This life wants to be something, a personality; it wants what is felt on earth as awe, it wants to rule over thousands of people. Yet this inner life is stopped.

On its way this inner life meets others who want the same. It is not merely this soul; there are millions on earth who want it and that is how struggle begins. This is the moment when this soul will destroy and it does, because it knows no God, no commandment or love. The love, which cherishes all life, is not yet present in this inner life. This life goes on and the moment when this life will perish has not yet come. Finally the moment has come; this life is attacked and destroyed. There is an other power on earth who decided, the way this being acted in its previous life, because it had the power. This life was also killed, because it once murdered, extinguished the light of others.

A bad human being perished and entered the life on this side to wait for a new birth, which will and shall happen.

Where does this end? How far can these beings go? Is nobody calling them to a halt? Is there a God in heaven and can a God consent to it? Will He not interfere? Must this life go on killing others? These souls spread sorrow and misery over the earth, they destroy everything and everybody they come across. How can God consent? We hear all this in the spheres of light, we receive this and we can't do anything either. No Father, nobody can help them on earth. God gave man a will of his own.

God does help, but in a different way, a way people on earth cannot

336

and do not want to accept, unless they understand all this. God helps, helps all the time, God helps all His children through the ages. Try to follow me, André. This life must go on, must awaken, must return to the earth to learn to love.

God is love. Would God be a Father of Love if he did not give this human being the opportunity to make up? Would God be a God of Justice if this were not possible? Must this soul continue to live in hell? This soul received an other material organism again and once more a male body. What will happen now? In early childhood this boy had a will of his own. The parents could not understand this child and wondered where this soul came from. How is this possible, the child is like the devil? That's the way parents speak. They wonder why and what for, how is it possible. The parents did not understand this because they were religious and prayed to God. This child would not bring happiness to the parents, because they soon realized that this boy meant evil and doom.

We know this being. We know that it will seek until it has found what it had when it left its last life on earth. It will and must, when this inner life grew up it looked for friends; these friends were bad and led the young life to ruin. This had to happen and could not be avoided, however much the parents prayed and bemoaned, their child would perish, for in this life a powerful hatred fired and it would live with this hatred. It would grow up with it, which hatred led to its cause of awakening. It would be connected with it, because that connection, that power resided in this inner life, it lived in it.

When it had reached maturity that life wanted to possess, wanted to love and did not control itself in any way. It sought earthly property and love and it took to drinking to stimulate love and passion. That force deep within the soul, which was its emotional life, urged him to drink and awaken that hatred, not only when he was alone but also with friends who were on earth for a similar experience.

That was not all. In the hell on this side, there were thousands, nay millions of beings who had already reached their spiritual world of existence and could not be born on earth any more because all of them had completed their cycle on this planet. Yet these beings were on earth, I explained that process to you, they wanted to escape the darkness and cold of their existence. They wanted to experience, sought human warmth and that happens through all those earthly people, because they know how to achieve that. All those monsters and devils of hell descended into inner life as a result of which all those earthly people were in the hands of evil.

Now they lived, André, they plundered and murdered for possession, to fuel that awful fire of passion deep down within them. That animal-like being within them wanted ever more and continued until it could not be satisfied any more. Now it had come to an end. A terrible life and death struggle made an untimely end to this life. It again descended into the world of the unconscious and waited to receive an other body. Yet, God did not call a halt to this soul, this earthly being. To the contrary, this soul was to return to the earth again.

When this soul came on earth again and grew up, evil became increasingly violent, the depth into which this life descended could no longer be fathomed. It went from bad to worse, but that animal-like being in that depth was not yet satisfied, this soul had not yet attained the perfect material organism of the seventh degree for which it had to return.

Centuries passed before this soul descended on earth again in a different organism. It awakened on earth in a similar condition and it sank even deeper in this life than in the previous one. The parents who had attracted this inner life lived like animal-like beings. They never wondered why and what for, they had no possession and neither had their children.

The soul we follow had left home early in youth and lived in an other part of the world. This life had intellect, but that intellect was an animal-like instinct, which awakened in this human body. This inner life now commanded others to steal and murder, so that it became a massacre. It had reached a high social position. It perished again in this life. This inner life entered life after death with thousands of sins, mistakes and crimes.

Hundreds of years passed and this life had to go back to the earth again. It now entered the seventh material degree; it had lived in the material transitions during all those previous lives. It had not known parents, nor felt sister and brother love; this soul had descended to the deepest hell and had acquired it. It had killed thousands of lives and when it had attained the cycle of the earth this inner life belonged to the masters and geniuses of evil. This life had to go back, though; it still had to experience the highest material degree on earth.

Having spent many centuries in the world of the unconscious in a sleeping condition, this soul had come to rest. All this resided in the depth of this inner life, all those sins and mistakes which cannot be fathomed nor felt. Centuries passed before a material organism was ready on earth, this soul was attracted again to experience material life, to descend in the highest organism and to die. This being had everything; it possessed art and many properties constituting the character and personality, but in an animal-like attunement. This life had slept many centuries and a great wonder had occurred during this sleep. It had passed into an other condition; nature had brought it there. This inner life had come to rest, as I said, and had returned to the first stage when the cycle of the earth started. During that pre-animal-like stage, this time as a human being in the highest organism the soul can receive on earth, this soul consciousness sank back into the deep subconscious, effected by the material organism.

It is this enhanced material strength which stops that consciousness to prevent that arch-power from destroying that fine organism. The nervous system of the highest material organism is not designed for that arch-power in full consciousness, reasoning consciousness must live in it. What happened with this soul was a natural law and the help of God.

This material body locked that arch-power and this life began on earth in a condition of waking and half-waking consciousness. Full consciousness lay in the depth of the soul; it was the subconscious of this life.

This subconscious is the balance, the boundary between material and spiritual life. Now what happened? This inner life, was again attracted by parents and these parents were neither materially nor spiritually awake. The soul, which descended in life on earth now received a different organism and received the female body.

Who understands this inner life? During her youth she was quiet and downcast. In this life this soul created a condition of its own. However, she did not enter a relationship, she lacked the feeling, she had no desires. Sometimes, however, she yearned and was overcome by an awful feeling, which emanated from her inner depth. It was the activity of her material organism and was connected with the monthly natural law. Oh, how she could cry and yearn. But when that period was over she felt relaxed and was herself again. Her life passed that way; she did no good and no evil. She passed away when she was seventy. She had not experienced anything in this life, nor acquired or destroyed. Again she entered the astral world in life after death.

She had to wait for an other organism. This time it did not take long, because she had not experienced anything in that life, nature had soon performed its task. How deep those laws of nature are. God knew and oversaw everything. God already helped this soul, though people on earth are unaware of it. If God had not interfered, if nature had not brought this about, this inner life would not have been able to cope with that horrible struggle. The Divine attunement, my son, made her sleep so that the soul kept its balance and would begin an other process.

This inner live descended in the mother organism again, though in different surroundings. This environment offered more activity and property, which incited her to experience life on earth. She married and gave birth to two children. A different life was to begin. However, this life meant her struggle against her bad inner self, she had to overcome herself. How great God's love is. God knew she would not be able to bear all those sins and crimes in day-consciousness and made her inner being sleep. Do you feel that, André?'

'Yes, Alcar, but what sort of amazing event is that?'

'That applies to any being who has exceeded the limits of nature. These souls have to relax to prevent the material organism from collapsing through that inner urge and power. I explained that to you on the first cosmic degree. We see that this has not changed either. Inner life has to adapt itself to the material organism. Nature brings this about. Do you feel this deep spiritual mystery, André?'

'If I correctly understand everything, Alcar, consciousness now descends into the depth of its own life?'

'That is correct.'

'In that case this life as a child is not natural?'

'That is quite obvious, for it isn't possible.'

'And these souls do live on earth? Who can feel that, Alcar? Who understands these souls since this depth cannot be fathomed? What a mystery.'

'I could ask many more questions, and yet this had to happen, or inner life could not be attracted.'

'So, when such a soul lives on earth as a child it will be quiet, because a spiritual law brought it in that condition?'

'Yes, André, we must accept that.'

'Will this soul awaken?'

'That will happen and we'll follow it.'

'And nobody knows anything about that, can't feel it, because he does not understand this depth?'

'No, André, man on earth does not know anything about these laws of nature, and spiritual bounds. Thousands of people living on earth have exceeded all these natural laws. Here, in the life of the spirit, we learn to know and understand all those laws. It is not possible in material life on earth.'

'Does this soul not have to make up for all those sins and mistakes?'

'Certainly, as I said, it is now going to start a different life, though many lives are required. This inner life awakens slowly but surely. The first thing that awakens in it is the feeling for its children. These were the feelings rising from that depth to become conscious. I said just now that she gave birth to two children. She was quiet and desired. This life passed in peace and happiness and yet we know who she is. Death came and she entered this life. One life now followed the other and in all those lives her balance would be restored. This process continued. Gradually, she began to feel and her inner life awakened, she became conscious. The depth of her inner life now passed on into day-consciousness. Mother in one life, in the next she descended into the male organism to acquire this consciousness. After awakening she forgot herself because she had not acquired spiritual level yet. One life was even worse than the other was. She got nothing but sorrow and misery though her misery could not be compared with what she had done to others. Thousands of years passed and we see an other wonder.

The planet earth let her free and you surely feel what will happen now. Now she had to experience her karma, after all the misery she had received she faced the law of cause and effect. A mountain of misery and sorrow blocked her way, she had to make up for all this. Her sorrow made her collapse and she died insane. But she would return. She began to make up for every life in which she had caused misery. Yet she sinned and made mistakes again because she did not yet have spiritual consciousness. She passed from one life on to the next. She was no longer open for murder and animalization. She had learned something in all those lives, which was within her. She now had to restore that balance; she was thousands of years behind her material organism. In

341

all the lives she was going to experience she wondered why and for what reason she had to suffer that much. My God, help me, I am crushed and defiled. She experienced misery after misery. This soul had lived in all countries of the earth and had caused misery everywhere.

This human being would nevertheless reach her end, but this soul had only received. She had done nothing for all she had received from God, because this had not been possible in all those thousands of centuries. How have all those lives been? What does man learn in one life on earth? Nothing, indeed. What did this soul achieve in all those lives? She did wrong again. She had the coarse-material feeling, although she also did good things, since good and evil are done in every life. As I said this life awakened, it passed into other and higher feelings. She had many qualities which all had to change now in spiritual properties. To this end lives were needed in which this soul should achieve that.

God is a Father of Love. How mighty is the grace man receives; we shall receive anything the earth possesses, we shall live in all ranks of society. All of us create a condition of our own. All try to advance on earth to secure a condition of existence and this happens according as we awaken. That is the way we proceed ever more.

This soul would also awaken inwardly and pass on to a final life on earth. This soul had experienced wonders and problems and she now faced her last problem. The soul would now pass on in full consciousness and would become aware of that terrible depth. She would now, after those many lives, awaken in the spirit. In her final incarnation she passed into the mother organism and she was to retain this organism as her cosmic attunement. Dozens of lives had meanwhile passed in sorrow and misery. I do not want to follow them; I'll now proceed to her final life. As I said, the depth of her inner life surfaced. Nature got into balance and what remained in her she would now experience, since her inner and material organism are one.

Her spirit now consciously entered the final material organism. When I speak of consciousness it does not mean that she was aware of all those lives, but her inner being was awake and conscious. This child was born and in her youth her parents already felt that she was an extraordinary child. She possessed a tremendous power, the final thing she had to make up. Now she wanted to experience. That feeling seethed in her, it was inspiration and seemed unquenchable, that feeling was the intellect of a gifted being. There was something in this soul which awakened her. The Divine Spark roused her inner fire, but she had no spiritual level yet. What she had experienced in all those thousands of centuries was making up for all her previous sins. She had only experienced her karma and had not been able to do anything for herself. She could, therefore, not acquire anything because her guilt exceeded anything she could receive and acquire which is spiritual possession in our life.

Do you understand why she was on earth? Her inner life was still hundreds of years behind. In those centuries the material organism had been very far ahead of inner life and now she had to make something of herself. And she did, she created a life of her own in art. She became famous in that life and was worshipped; though she perished again. Again, because she did not yet have pure love, although she had completed her material cycle. She lost herself in that last life, she had not been able to acquire spiritual love. She remained childless in that life and entered our side advanced in years. When she awakened she lived in an other world and this was our hell, a hell she had created herself. She had built at it in all those lives and broken down again. I explained that to you. She had not been able to free herself in that final life. There was still darkness in her and no inner light. She awakened deeply moved. People lived beside her who were like she was. Yet, there was something in her which made her awaken so that she began a different life.

Her mother who had passed away long ago drew her into an other condition and she saw and felt how much evil she had done. She returned to the earth and saw where she had lived. She did not know or understand anything of all her previous lives. That was not possible, she did not even understand herself. Her mother helped her and prayed for her.

Half a century passed before she had freed herself from the dark spheres and she entered the spheres of light. You feel, André, how much she had to do for that.

At this side she became conscious of her own life. Here she was shown how she had lived. It was not until then that she felt remorse and in that condition she could be reached.

When she entered the first sphere her spiritual and higher feelings, awakened. Now she prayed to her Father and thanked Him for everything. However, there was something, which increased her feeling of remorse, because she had done nothing at all for all that grace. She had left nothing on earth. She had only lived to the full and had received thousands of things from God. She had only freed herself from darkness and had passed on to the light. Now she prayed for many years on end, and asked God to be allowed to be born again on earth to do something for all that wealth she had received from God.

She went on praying. Would God hear her prayer? She could not otherwise free herself from that remorse. Again, God comes to the aid of this soul. Her beloved ones, who had followed her to this side, knew where she would go. She would show her gratitude by doing something on earth and performing a task. She would help develop the earth by bringing nourishment for the mind, for man needs this nourishment, man perished as a result of all these material things.

That's what she brought on earth and she gave herself completely. She laid intense joy in everything. She knew of life hereafter, she had spiritual property. She would awaken with it as a child. When her life began she was already inspired by her own feelings; the remorse within her and this life was lived spiritually. Subsequently she returned and proceeded on this side.

I showed you flashes of a soul, André, of a human being, whom, as I told you, I have known. These are no stories, I met this soul on earth time and again and she now lives in my own sphere. I lived with thousands of them during my time on earth; there we met and lost each other. She now lives in the fifth sphere and is an angel in the spirit.

God is love. God knows everything and is just. All sorrow, illness and misery is over and she'll go on and on to pass on to an other planet. We'll meet again on the fourth cosmic degree. We know there that we have to live so many lives, for life there would not be perfect if we did not know that and that feeling was not in us. We all go further. One day, God awakes us and says: 'Look, my children, heaven awaits you. I guard over all of you.'

The soul weeps for joy because God, our Father, is so good. Now that we learn to understand that great problem, we fall on our knees and don't know how grateful we'll be.

Such is life on earth, André, and every man will experience that. They have to in order to return to the All. I had to tell and explain this in order to give you an image of material and spiritual life on earth. It is only for the earth, only the planet earth knows struggle, sorrow and misery. It is to pass from pre-animal-like on to spiritual life. Is all this clear, André?'

344

'Yes, Alcar, but I would like to ask you a thing or two. Does attraction occur in all lives?'

'Yes, from the first sins and mistakes man takes up his karma. That is what you meant, isn't it?'

'Yes, Alcar, it is amazing how everything happens and is predestined. Is it fixed upon birth when the soul will die and how man will pass away?'

'Yes, that is a law and is fixed too, but the way in which a person passes away and the cause of his death have nothing to do with it. Life comes and goes when it is called.'

'How deep the human being is, Alcar, I had not expected this. Who can follow this?'

'We can follow that in the spheres. Not a single thought transmitted can escape. Every man will see his own film of life and every man who has attained the fourth sphere can observe this, as you have experienced in the temple of the soul.'

'How many fathers and mothers have we had, Alcar?'

'Thousands, my boy, but father- and motherhood is only of consequence for the earth. Father- and motherhood merge on this side into universal love. I explained that to you a long time ago and I do not have to go into that any more.'

'Isn't this a great problem for people on earth, Alcar?'

'They will remain problems and wonders for them, for others it is imagination. It belongs to our life, everything I showed and explained to you belongs to reincarnation on earth.'

'Is it possible for people to become spiritually conscious while on earth?'

'Oh, yes, many are. The soul I told you about did not awaken until on this side, but others advance that far on earth and consciously enter the spheres of light. Millions of beings live already on earth in a spiritual condition and have acquired that attunement.'

'Does this also happen in a normal condition, I mean not when they ask for it?'

'Yes, André, millions of people have advanced that far on earth.'

'If I understand you correctly, religions will dissolve one day and those religions were given to people to hold on to.'

'That's right, but haven't you known that for a long time?'

'Yes, Alcar, but now it is quite clear to me. Did everything given in all those centuries from the side beyond serve a definite purpose?'

'Yes, I will explain that to you on our next journey. Everything and all higher thoughts emanate from this side.'

'Your art too?'

'My art too, I and all masters who lived on earth at the time were part of it.'

'It is amazing, Alcar.'

'Do not forget that the earth is the only planet where great sorrow is experienced. We have been able to follow that development. People do not understand their own lives and death is still a horrible monster for them. Death spoils life on earth and disheartens them to make something of life on earth. Death breaks all energy and they succumb to it. This must cease, and as soon as they can accept, there will be peace and joy on earth and they will think of meeting again on this side. Those who accept this may be quiet and happy and adjust their view even when they have lost their beloved ones. One day they will meet again on this side. However, one soul has to depart ahead of the other, when a mother is left behind, the father can visit her from this side and support and help her on earth. All that is possible, if they seriously want to go into all these problems and wonders, a firm connection will develop and they learn to understand life of the spirit. One day this will happen but not until after several centuries.'

'Where are we at this moment, Alcar?'

'In an other country. We floated ever further and have gone from one country or continent to the next, though you did not notice. I followed one road, which brought me to the places and cities I told you about and where this soul lived. You listened to me and could therefore not observe.'

'I could have, Alcar?'

'Yes, certainly, I could have connected you with all those lives but it was not necessary and would be too much for you.'

'You mean like on our last journey, Alcar, when you connected me with your own life?'

'Yes, that's what I mean.'

'How can I digest all this, Alcar?'

'Don't be afraid that this life will overwhelm you, I'll help you and it will be easier than when you returned from your previous journey. You are now conscious of our life and you can digest everything, however deep it is.'

346

'Can people in general not digest this?'

'In order to penetrate the deepest spiritual problems without spiritual help on earth, André, you first of all need a strong nervous system, and in particular feeling for these laws. A scientist or whatever he may be on earth cannot acquire that depth without this spiritual connection. One should feel this and be able to discard one's own personality.'

'I am so happy, Alcar. If only I were allowed to tell mankind about it and that you would help me from this side. I'll pray that you may receive that grace.'

'That's very nice, André, it might happen, but first we must record all this. That is a mighty task, you will receive it. It is the intention of the masters that we present this to mankind. It is possible now because many yearn for nourishment for the mind and they will receive it, we are spread all over the earth. Many others are working with me on earth through instruments, all of them mediums who have to accomplish a task. We are all grateful to God to be allowed to do this, because we understand the meaning of all that sorrow, all those illnesses on earth. We are now awake and conscious.

I am most thankful that this task was assigned to me, how have I prepared myself! I geared up for all those questions for two hundred years. I'll tell you about this on our next journey. Now there are people on earth who belong to the sensitive persons, they want to receive, because religions do not give them what they want, what they need.'

'You said, Alcar, that all those religions will dissolve, but what did Christ bring for mankind?'

'Do not compare the life of Christ with religion, André. Our great Master taught love and belief in God. What Christ brought is for all planets up to the highest, the seventh cosmic mentality. It cannot die, it cannot be destroyed, it inspires all of us and it is God's sacred life. Christ brought Himself, brought Divine life. We can reach God only through Him, through nothing and nobody else. All those religions will disappear because they lack the true core and the clergy put themselves on pedestals. This remains, André, this is eternal because it is perfect, through Christ we learn to know and understand God.'

'If I correctly understand everything, Alcar, there are no people living on earth who are free of sorrow?'

'No, that is not possible, only those who understand themselves and have to perform a task on earth know that what they experience should not be seen as sorrow, but serves to awaken and to make up. Everything then changes; it is no longer sorrow but a grace. However, all those millions of people live in this condition for it is their attunement, they do not want sorrow and do not want to know about the past.'

'In all those degrees up to the highest degree of material organism people live in cities and villages and all over the earth, who have sorrow and misery?'

'That's right, so it is. Everybody lives in his own condition, which is their cosmic attunement, that is: they have accepted an other life and make up, it is their karma and why they are on earth. There are no people on earth who are free of sorrow; these people cannot be on earth. They would not be on earth any more, but on this side or they would have already reached the mental regions to be attracted by the fourth cosmic degree. It is not possible for people to live on earth who are free of all sorrow and you will not meet a single person who does not know sorrow. When they know all those cosmic degrees and can accept, that sorrow is a different sorrow because it is making up for what they did wrong in the past. They know that happiness and rest will follow and remain forever. God knows all His children. God will not allow any of His children to receive unnecessary grief. Yet people think and say that God has imposed all that misery, but we know better. We have learned to know our life and know that it is not God Who imposed that misery, but that it is cause and effect, making up for what we did wrong. If people on earth could accept and understand it, if they resigned to all this and experienced it in a natural way that deep sorrow would soon dissolve.

People think God punishes, we know, however, that God cannot punish but that people have violated the laws of nature and have to get in harmony again. Those forces and laws of nature shut them off from further advance because of the numerous passions and the misery done to others. Man attracts the very laws in which that mental disturbance resides because they have to be made up. Thank heaven that this happens, or we would continue to live in these depths of misery and would never advance. Now that we know that everything is love, quiet and peace, that God does now know sorrow or misery, man will have to solve all those horrible things. I explained to you how this happens, and not any man can free himself of it, can evade it, as it is man who attracts it.

348

Everything on earth seems horrible, but when we get to know life it is all different and natural. How many people are there on earth who do not know anything about eternal life? They are unaware of all these laws and laugh at those who tell about these wonders. Do you feel how spiritually poor these beings are?

Thank God that the time has come now that we may come back to mankind to tell them that we are alive. We now know what is possible and will be. We now live in that time and feel happy about it. Oh, those poor people who do not understand themselves and do not know that everything is love and that God is a Father of Justice. God looks on how people forget themselves, but God knows all His children. They ask for happiness and earthly property, but they don't know the depth of their own life. They don't want to have anything to do with the past; they want to live and be happy, for everybody has a right to happiness.

Every second people are born on earth, but they should awaken and be born spiritually. Inner man is and remains missing. The earth is a paradise, that is what God wanted, but man changed that paradise into a terrible hell. Poor people, poor earth, but there is life in it, the life of God. The earth gave people everything, a place to live. But how do people act?

It will have become clear to you, André, that there is nothing on earth or on this side, unless it is brought about by man. There is no sorrow unless man wanted it, created it.

Haven't I shown you in dozens of conditions that what we have done in other lives is our own fault? Haven't I shown that there must be reincarnation or we could not progress on the eternal road? That everything is fixed and that these activities are part of ourselves? Is there anything incompatible in what you have seen? Those who are honestly prepared to open their mind and to give themselves completely will feel and understand this and recognize cause and effect.

God's simplicity lies in everything and maintains everything. It is up to us to understand and acquire that simplicity. One thing emanates from the other. What man owns today he will lose tomorrow. All this awakens him and he will feel that a law is in force to make him bend his head. If he can, he has advanced and his life on earth was not in vain. One day all human beings will come on this side and are confronted with all these laws. They see that our life is true and that we spoke the truth. It is not until then that they will be grateful for what they received on earth from this side. Mankind now receives an image of creation; we act on them all over the earth. People on earth must know that their beloved ones are alive and that they will meet their father and mother again. They must know that they have their happiness on earth in their own hands, they must feel that life on earth is only temporary. They can't imagine greater happiness. Wherever they are and live, in whatever condition they are, paradise as God gave it to us human beings was never understood. One day there will be happiness and they will get to know their Father of love and that they are to blame for everything. This is hard; nevertheless we also had to accept it. However terrible their life on earth is, the time will come when they bend their head and thank God for everything. It is not until then that they will understand they are to blame for their own misfortunes. Could you follow me in everything, André?'

'Yes, Alcar, I thank God for all you have told me. Now that I know all this I understand paradise. I have also become more understanding of Adam and Eve, and everything written in the bible.'

'Those same two people, André, still represent mankind on earth. According to the scientists creation then began. There had to be a beginning and those two people, Adam and Eve served that purpose. Follow them, we still see these two beings together, they proceed from one century into the next and they do not learn to know and understand themselves. These two souls were to represent creation. Man would be given an example and in those days these two people served that purpose.

Then God spoke, but it was the voice of beings who lived already on this side and brought this message. That story was given, but it is not understood yet. There is truth in everything brought to earth in those days in the field of spirituality but the core is missing.

Adam and Eve represented the creative and driving capacity and that is still present in man, nothing has changed. Adam and Eve still live on earth and are dispelled from paradise, because they have not yet come to themselves. People on earth have not changed in any way and many centuries later they will speak about these two beings, not realizing that they live in the same condition as these two beings.

There are many things like this one in the bible and when one realizes the reality of them and understands the intention of those who accomplished it one feels the holy truth, but then everything is different. Those who assisted did not understand that message.'

'What a pity that they misunderstood everything, Alcar.'

'Yes, André. People on earth do not want to understand. Christ came and this had been predicted centuries ago and when He came people regarded him as an ordinary human being and they nailed the holiest Man who ever lived to a cross. But Christ's life and belief remain forever, because it is Divine, Christ was like God and brought this message on earth. I told you about it and it will be clear to you.'

'Do you know what is right and what is wrong in the bible?'

'Yes, but you should know it too, you can feel that, André. Those who love life will enter the spheres of light. Those who destroy life will descend into the darkness. Feel what love brings, what pure love is and accept it, accept everything written in the bible. But no passion, no destruction, no misery and egotism, only sacrificing love which Christ teaches. Everything else is the work of man, was produced by scientists and has no meaning. Christ brought Himself and sacrificed Himself for mankind. He knew in advance what would happen. Nevertheless, Christ came to the earth to tell us about our Father in heaven. It is only by Christ that we can reach the Divine Spheres.'

'Did the people who lived in those days already have a connection with the Side Beyond, Alcar?'

'That spiritual connection has always existed, André. From the moment on when astral man could not return to the earth any more. From that time on life on earth began and astral man tried to get into contact with those who had not yet completed their material cycle. Centuries went by, but when the spheres of light were born and it became light in and around them, when they felt and understood that it was possible to advance, they quickly returned to the earth to convince their sisters and brothers in material life. You know that this is possible and nothing has changed in this respect either. Thousands, nay millions with me are doing just that at this moment. They already brought the message of eternal life in those days.'

'I heard, Alcar, that many people were killed merely because they had told of an other life or religion. Is that true?'

'Yes, André. Those times were terrible, though it is not so long ago that all mediums were burnt alive and killed if they spoke of things which mankind did not know or understand. Yet, there were many people who, although they knew they would be killed sooner or later, opened themselves for their invisible helpers, astral beings, who spoke through them. They were not afraid of death or of destruction, they all knew they would die sooner or later. Although not one of them would escape they made themselves available. All of them were inspired, the holy fire of Christ was within them, and they had that pure sacrificing love. When their task on earth was accomplished great happiness awaited them. Thousands of people have been killed merely for what they told. It was a horrible time on earth, but what happens at present? People have now advanced to the point that they no longer destroy our mediums, although nothing has changed in some countries. There are human beings in many countries who defile our work and of thousands of others. Oh, when those people enter on our side! They forget that millions of human beings have given their blood and lives for this work. When there are people on earth who pose as prophets it is their own business, but if one human being suffers misery and sorrow and loses his belief in God as a result, darkness awaits them for they will have to make up for it. Thousands of people left life on earth because they told of a God of love and were connected with this side. At present, André, man has advanced a little or you would have been on this side for a long time.'

'Would they kill me, Alcar?'

'You and all other mediums working for us.'

'I am prepared to give my life for all this, Alcar, they may kill me.'

'That won't happen any more, but I'm most grateful for these words and to all people who dare speak like that. No, my son, those days have gone. We have advanced a little, inner and material man has changed as has the planet earth.'

'Knowing all this, Alcar, I must say that progress is slight, because thousands of years have passed.'

'That is true. We have not made a lot of progress though much has changed. Now, in your time, mediums are no longer killed, they are ridiculed and sneered at. Now it is all diabolical work and they live under one roof with the devil. Many people curse and yell, but if they had their way, I assure you, they would drag you out of your house and kill you. Mankind has advanced to the point that they don't allow it.'

'Is that, Alcar, why the Side Beyond influences man and provides all that nourishment for the mind?'

'Yes, André. It is now possible to bring nourishment for the mind on

352

earth. It is the century of technical miracles and spiritual development. We can now convince those who are open to it of eternal life. That was not possible some centuries ago, it is not so long ago that they killed our mediums. Look back and feel how recently that occurred.'

'How slowly this development proceeds, Alcar.'

'A more rapid development is not possible, my boy. You can follow that on earth. It took millions of years before the earth was an inhabitable planet. Millions of years were required for the first human beings to live on earth and it took as many centuries to make something out of that life. This is reflected in the entire creation.'

'I don't understand, Alcar, why so few people know something of eternal life, for there are so many millions of people on earth. They do not understand death. They don't know anything about eternal progress. They find reincarnation something horrible and having to return most terrible of all. The clergy speak of eternal damnation and perpetual burning in hell and they frighten people. It is so narrow and heartless.'

'Is it not clear to you, André?'

'No, Alcar, I don't understand it.'

'You forget that inner man still has to be born.'

'But the earth is millions of years old?'

'When I speak of millions of years it sounds impressive, but it is only one second in eternity. We on this side understand creation and we know how difficult it is to achieve something on earth. Every development proceeds slowly particularly in regard to the spirit. The earth is billions of years old but it is not until now, in your time, that the spiritual age begins and that it is possible to tell people of eternal progress and miracles. Follow man on earth and you see and feel that this stage has come.'

'It is incredible, but I must accept it.'

'Indeed, you must accept it, mankind has not advanced any further. How recent are the times when the masters of art lived on earth? Sculpture came first followed by the painters. There were three centuries of art. The spirits brought art on earth in those centuries.'

'Spirits, you say?'

'Yes, André, for all those masters were born for that purpose. That mighty event was controlled from this side. All those artists were instruments, it was fixed in the great plan.'

'Did these artists know that they were spiritual instruments, Alcar?'

'No, André, they did not know or understand. Yet, all of them once lived on this side and were born again for that purpose. I'll tell you more about it on our next journey. My point is to show you that this happened not long ago and that it was only possible in these three centuries to bring art on earth. All the masters of music lived on this side. I lived on this side, was born again and when I had accomplished my task I returned to the spheres, but my art was on earth. And why was all this? To raise mankind to a higher level, André. Man needed something of beauty. It was understood on this side. The art we brought was for the eye, the heart and the mind. Our art is tangible and can be seen, but the work of the composers can only be felt. As a result mankind would awaken.'

'And has mankind awakened, Alcar?'

'Not all those millions, André, but dozens.'

'And that's why all that trouble was taken?'

'We sacrifice ourselves for one single human being, my son. We know we cannot reach millions of people. One living being, André, the others are living dead and cannot yet be helped. One child and it is a child of God, this child wants to awaken and that is why we come to the earth to convince this being of eternal life. We on this side know what is possible and what is not. You can't understand that yet. Neither do you understand that they do not accept reincarnation and speak of damnation and eternal fire. We know all that, we know all these people and how far they have advanced. Do you believe, André, that they will welcome you with open arms? This is not understood, André. But a few centuries from now they will idealize our work, but then you'll have been on this side for a long time. We go on, others will continue our work. You'll not understand how mighty our work is until you are on this side. All masters of art understood this, what we are now bringing on earth serves their eternal happiness. Whether they want to accept all this is up to them, André. It is given to the earth and we shall reach many people.

This is strange for you, but not for us, because we know life on earth. Now that we live on this side we see through all these phenomena. Mankind has not advanced that far. We know, André, how difficult it is to convince people of something higher. Once again, we are only at the beginning of spiritual development. Just now, in the twentieth century, it is possible to tell them of our life. And that is comprehensible because they do not understand death yet. Just imagine this, André. The earth is billions of years old and yet death is not understood. Every second people on earth pass on and enter this life. They only see death and go on doing so, because they have not inwardly advanced any more and do not feel an other world within them. Is all this so strange when we know that thousands of centuries are necessary? Work that out for yourself and feel how difficult it is to correct one single mistake and discard it. We make mistakes and commit crimes hundreds of times again although we are trying to discard them. We fail, it is nearly impossible.

With many ups and downs we reach our aim. An entire life on earth may pass and yet we failed to discard small things. Then we pass away and it is not until on this side that we see how terrible our life has been. On this side we learn to understand ourselves and we realize that we have not taken the trouble to discard all our mistakes. Here we are also faced with the same condition. No human being or spirit can help us; we have to do it ourselves. God gave us everything, gave us His own life and His own Divine attunement. It is, as I told you several times, up to us to make something of it.

We'll advance that far by experiencing life. That's why all those thousands of lives are essential. We don't achieve anything in one life on earth; we can't achieve anything. We therefore receive all those lives from God and pass from the male organism onto the female organism. Truly, my son, all this is a mighty grace.'

'I have even spoken to scientists, Alcar, and they found reincarnation something terrible, the greatest stupidity an intellectual person could profess. They thought the idea of having to start on earth time and again as a child and to spend all those wasted years before reaching maturity narrow minded. What is the use they said, that short period left to live on earth? Many people even passed away when mature. Then what, back to the earth to start again as a child? No, they could not imagine God to be so narrow minded.'

'What did you reply, André?'

'Nothing, Alcar, I said nothing, I could not answer them. They were scientists, people who had obtained a degree. If they don't feel it, who does?'

'These people have not advanced that far, André. We find these people especially among scientists. Simple people feel and understand more of all these spiritual laws than scientists on earth. Theologians speak of damnation and eternal burning and they are also scholars, they made a study of it. All those beings, André, have yet to awaken. All that learning has no meaning on this side. Those who speak like they do show who they are and prove that they have no feeling, no belief and no respect for creation. They belong to the living dead.'

'Although these people are sometimes religious, Alcar.'

'That is quite possible, André, these people also live on earth. Some human beings enter our side who did not believe in a God and there was light in them all the same. They passed from the earth straight on to the second sphere and you know what that means. Though they did not believe in a God, in their life on earth they loved nature and all other life and nature is God. You feel how deep everything is and yet how simple. All those other beings find it terrible; they cannot accept spiritual wonders and are spiritually blind. All this indicates that we are only at the beginning of spiritual development. All this is in a seminal stage, André. Human but spiritual feeling must be born now. It is not until then that they can accept this and yearn to be allowed to learn about all this. So let them talk and don't take notice. We go on. You can convince them on this side, it is not possible beforehand. They will stare their eyes out and bend their head. We cannot convince them of all those wonders until they have reached the spheres of light and they will see and experience the purpose of all this. Man has not yet advanced that far, André. The earth is billions of years old and yet it means nothing. Did people, who lived before Christ, have any notion of all the technical wonders man on earth now possesses? How many inventions have been made, though that was not possible until now. Had scientists advanced as far as in your time?'

'How then do you explain the Egyptian period, Alcar? Hadn't they advanced very far?'

'Thank you, André, for these words and that you know about it. Yes, my son, those people had advanced very far, but that high civilization and knowledge had quite a different meaning, when we know what happened in that period. I'll also explain this to you, but on our next journey. I'll then explain and show why these people had advanced that far. You will be amazed when I say that those people cannot be born any more.'

'Did you say that they can't be born any more?'

'No, André, at any rate not in that condition, for that event. Mankind must now try to advance that far by its own effort. That is already in progress, and in several branches of study they are already ahead. This wisdom was given them in those days from our side, as was all art on earth. All this must seem strange and amazing to you, however, you'll get to know these wonders too.'

'Isn't it difficult to achieve something on earth, Alcar?'

'No, André, it is not difficult, especially not for those who steal it from others and enrich themselves at the expense of others. That is quite simple. We are concerned with the spiritual development. We followed one man on earth, we saw how this soul lived and developed spiritually. Now look at all those people. Follow them and see how they create a condition of their own. Anyone can attain that wealth when they have a feeling for it. Do you hear what I say, André? Feeling, for everything must be felt and one must possess that feeling inwardly in order to acquire that material level, be it wealth, a social position or thousands of other things. That is what man created, they acquired that during all those thousands of centuries. This, however, belongs to the material world. All those earthly people have advanced that far in the many lives that passed and they belong to the materialistic world. The spiritual world now follows. They will change all those material qualities and feelings into those of the higher consciousness. They will free themselves of the material world and will begin to enrich themselves spiritually. Thereafter, André, follows consciousness. As I said before, thousands of centuries were required and how long has spiritual development, craving for a higher life, been going on? Do all these people not live like wild animals couldn't? Haven't we been able to follow that and haven't I shown that to you? Don't you feel that thousands will awaken in the material world and only one in the spirit? All this work, all this nourishment for the mind, André, is for that one being. It is for him that we come to the earth; we try to convince this man of his eternal life, because that is now possible. The others, the materially disposed beings must awaken yet and cannot be reached. We know this, André, we know the mentality, the material, nay the pre-animal-like attunement of all those people. We see how far they have advanced on their cosmic way. Do not look at those billions of years behind us, look at the 'now', the present and feel what life on earth means. Now is the age of technical wonders, as I said before, and of spiritual development. Isn't it remarkable that this spiritual influence is now being felt all over the earth? Those open to higher things won't fail to notice. The others experience their life on earth and perish. Those who think they should defile our work must suit themselves. The masters who lived on earth centuries ago, look at them from this side and smile, for they know and understand why they were artists on earth. It was not until on this side that they understood what inner and spiritual value their art had and why they attained that height.

Here, they became aware of all those spiritual laws and wonders, and understood the deeper meaning of this miracle. It is a wonder that only we know, and that inner man experiences in material life on earth.

All this, André, was given to the earth and people must acquire it. They are at the beginning of spiritual development. Inner man gradually awakes. It was not possible until now to bring nourishment for the mind in which they recognize the depth of their own inner being, and as a result of which they discard all coarseness.

When I speak of spiritual development it means that human evolution has reached that stage. On earth one now speaks of civilization, and because there are people who speak like this, it is possible for us to get through to them. They are awake and conscious and are open to higher life. They free themselves from violence, passion and animalization. Thousands of years ago we could not achieve anything, it would not even have been possible a few hundred years ago. You were burnt alive then; nowadays you are ridiculed and laughed at. But that does not harm you. Within you lies the conviction of our life, the knowledge that you have conquered death and the heavenly peace of the spirit. You depart your material body and experience all this and they will also depart, but that means that they pass away on earth. You return to earth with a treasure of spiritual knowledge. You experience wonders and problems they are completely unaware of and which they cannot accept because they have not advanced that far. When a scientist on earth declared that the earth rotates around the sun and continued its orbit, and that the sun did not rotate around the earth he was also ridiculed by the entire scientific world. They know better now, they understand these laws of nature and bend their head for this man. Is it clear, André, why there are so few sensitive people living on earth?'

'Yes, Alcar, it is clear to me now, thank you.'

'Any more questions?'

'Yes, Alcar, some things are not quite clear to me.'

358

'Which are, André?'

'You spoke of good and evil and of maximum limits. I wanted to ask you: Is it possible for material man on earth to exceed these limits?'

'Certainly, André.'

'Is it also possible before inner life has acquired the highest material organism?'

'A very good question, André. Yes, that is also possible, I explained to you that God interferes and helps the soul, which has exceeded these limits. I explained that this soul came to rest in the world of the unconscious, in a deep sleep, because that dominating life would destroy the material strength.'

'What is this activity like on earth, Alcar?'

'The material organism cannot absorb those devilish powers. All this is very deep, but I'll try to explain it more clearly. The soul returned to the astral world and waited to be born again. That last life of this man was terrible, he exceeded the maximum limits and enters the world of the unconscious. If he would be born immediately and there was no period of rest, this inner life would disturb the embryo and fertilization would be interrupted. Do you feel what this means?'

'You mean that that inner power, the inspiring life, would destroy the embryo?'

'Yes, my son, that would happen; you felt it correctly. This was prevented because inner life came to rest. Let us assume that this was not possible, that inner life remained in the same condition and was attracted in that condition by two material beings. What would happen? What condition would the child be in upon birth? What phenomena would be seen in that child?'

'Insanity perhaps?'

'No, André, because that is spiritual consciousness and only possible in a mature material condition. It is not possible for the child. But listen. The material organs cannot digest that high tension, to put it that way, and the child would die an unnatural death. The material organism would have to accept death by suffocation and so we see the opposite of insanity. There is no harmony, there could be no spiritual harmony, because inspiring life dominated. It would first of all destroy the embryo and secondly these powers and activity are not present in creation, we have not experienced that activity on our long way. Material life would not be able to attract inspiring life and inner life would not be able to descend, so that there is no question of fertilization.'

'Is that known on earth, Alcar?'

'No, not all this, they know, however, of disturbances of the nervous system which make fertilization impossible.'

'In that case they should be able to accept this as well. It is one and the same activity, I should think?'

'Yes, André, it is one and the same activity; they do not want to have anything to do with an astral personality, they have not advanced that far yet, at any rate not the scientists. And exactly the astral personality dominates; though, as we have been able to follow, the inspiring life came to rest through a law of nature or through God's help. Should this nevertheless happen, which, as I said, is not possible, we would observe quite different phenomena and we would learn different laws. What do you think would happen?'

'When the soul would be born again in the same condition, Alcar?'

'Yes, André, that's what I mean.'

'Well, I don't know, I don't feel it, Alcar.'

'I'll tell you. If that was possible, André, every man on earth would know of his former lives; they would understand death, creation and a thousand other spiritual laws and wonders, for the soul as inner and spiritual life would consciously descend into material life, in this case into the embryo. Is that clear?'

'Yes, Alcar, I now feel this wonder and its possibility. It is remarkable.'

'Since inspiring life returns, as we have seen during the first stage, we must accept all these laws of nature. It is one condition for man and animal. Because inspiring life has to follow and accept that course, the entire personality descends into the depth of this inner life and only acquires consciousness as the years go by and the child grows up. Do you feel that too, André?'

'Yes, Alcar, it is remarkable and yet so natural. Have you told me about this before?'

'Yes and no, we did not yet descend to these depths, though I explained it to you before.'

'Do you know all these activities of inner and material life, Alcar?'

'Yes, André, though there are many I did not yet discuss.'

'Do you mean the connection with the embryo, Alcar?'

'Yes, André, that is a source of wisdom, perhaps I could explain that one day.'

360

'You don't know for certain?'

'No, my son, we could write dozens of books and that is not the intention since people on earth have not advanced that far.

I could explain to you and the scientists on earth the origin and development of the universe through the mother organism, and not only that, I could also show the way in which they will learn to know all these wonders.'

'That sounds wonderful, Alcar. So you could go on endlessly?'

'Yes, André, there is no end to this wisdom. The embryo connects me with creation, from the beginning to the end, which is the All. I could show you wonders and also explain them. For example: in the embryo, that tiny foetus which is in the mother organism and becomes a child, the entire creation is already fixed during that stage. Scientists on earth have already advanced to the point that they recognize the human fish-like stage. But we see more. We see in it all periods of the planet earth, the planetary system, the universe, and also all previous transitions the human being has lived. That billion process, André, resides in the embryo, it is inherent to it, it is creation.'

'How remarkable that is, Alcar. If they can recognize the fish-like stage, can't they accept all previous and following laws?'

'No, my son, they have not advanced that far. The moment that two human beings think of accomplishing the material connection inspiring life is attracted that very moment. This attraction is the first stage, the twilight you observed in the temple of the soul, when the process of revelation began. When God revealed Himself, a luminous condition set in, in other words: the darkness dissolved. This phenomenon showed itself the way God revealed Himself in man, when this man wants to create. When the creative being, man, thinks of that, performs accordingly, then he creates a condition and happens what God meant in the process of revelation, and what we have learned to know. That very moment we see the process of revelation occur, God put this process in the hands of one being, the creating individual. After this deed, this willpower, man created and fertilization was accomplished. The serving and driving being accepts this action and a wonder occurs. That wonder is the first stage of every planet, it is transparent but will condense. You surely feel that everything whatsoever is present in the human embryo, and that we recognize God's revelation in spiritual and material form in it and that it is not perfect until the child is born.

What happened in those nine months took billions of years in creation before the universe was ready. That, André, is why the universe is present in the mother organism and I could go on endlessly. What now happens every second I can find again in the universe, in the mother organism and in the embryo and I can explain and especially show the course of development.

When man thinks of this, and that's why all this is sacred, he does nothing but what God did in infinity and which became the universe.

Man creates, because he gives life to an other human being. Man creates in a small way what God did in the infinity. As a result I return to the very first stage of the first planet and will be connected with this wonder. On that planet one life gave its own life to that other little cell, now the perfect human being does so and remains alive because he possesses these forces of nature. There, however, material life died at that first moment. You see that when the creative individual gives of himself and the mother receives this sacred wonder, an activity is established which we have been able to follow in creation, and represents the entire creation and the universe. God, my son, has put that mighty and Divine event in the hands of man, because we human beings are Divine and have received His own life. We will become like God, but we must deserve it.'

'How awe-inspiring all this is, Alcar.'

'I could go on, my son, I could fill volumes, but that will not be understood either. On this side, André, we see through all those wonders and laws of nature, we learn to understand those laws and feel their activity'

'Did you make a study of it, Alcar?'

'Yes, André.'

'Is that possible for everyone?'

'Everyone who has reached the spheres of light can go in for some study or other on this side.'

'Those living in the darkness too?'

'No, because they do not even understand themselves, are unaware of the spheres of light and are living dead. These beings, as you have known for a long time, do not even know that they died on earth and those who do know are spiritually poor human beings, who are at an utter loss and seek animal-like life. They are unaware of all those laws of nature; they live in the darkness, feel no love and are obsessed by their own misery. They must first discard that dark life.

We cannot qualify for a spiritual study until in the fourth sphere on this side, it is there that we have discarded all abnormality belonging to the earth and have consequently entered normal life. Those living there have the feeling; they have advanced that far on the spiritual road and understand the meaning of life after death. They know that they can and shall proceed ever further, they know they can return to the earth and, above all, they understand creation. It is not possible to make a study of it previously.'

'How long does that study take, Alcar?'

'Such a study requires hundred of years. Don't forget that all these beings are connected with the universe and have to acquire all those laws of nature. It takes no less than dozens of years before they have learned and felt the true meaning of the problem of birth and death and the many laws of nature related with it. In this spiritual life we do not learn and calculate what we are being taught, we must be able to feel and experience it, it does not otherwise get through to us and it would be useless to spend time on it.'

'So man must have advanced that far, Alcar?'

'Yes, André, indeed. They must have that feeling inwardly or no master can help or teach them. Here we see who possess sufficient inner light and they can make some study.'

'How remarkable all this is, Alcar. I have no words for it!'

'God's simplicity lies in everything. Death dissolves here and we human beings pass on into those wonders, because we are those wonders. This, too, is a great problem for mankind on earth, but all of us here have experienced it. If the word 'death' would be abolished, everything would be different. Here, that word instantly disappears. And that also applies to all other wonders. When man of the earth enters here and cannot accept that he has died on earth, the sisters and brothers will convince him. I showed you such a scene when we started our first journey. If they still can't believe it, they are asked if there are any relatives on this side who passed away on earth. That is usually the case and they are brought to them. You should see them then, André, that very moment death disappears; they don't know that horror any more and bend their head. They are prepared to accept everything and understand that they do not possess anything.

Many scientists have to be convinced in this way. It is not until then that they are open to spiritual truth and yearn to know more about it. Then they get to know all these wonders, but only, as I said before, if there is light in them. For many of them hundreds of years go by before they can qualify for a study on this side. They are led to the spheres of darkness and back to the earth where they have to learn thousands of spiritual things. First, death, the process of dying on earth, then the most important and most difficult event: birth. When they know something about it their guides pass on into the universe and if they are ready to learn life on other planets they are brought there. You should see them, all those learned men. Broken, they return to the spheres of light. Many only cry. They have to cry and can't help it. Something has broken in them, earthly life and everything related is now far behind them. They subsequently follow their own life on earth and it is not until then that they feel how horrible they were to demolish what they did not understand. They attacked everybody on earth, their sharp tongues criticized everything and everybody who spoke of spiritual laws and felt the simplicity in everything. That has to be made up. They now live in the life of the spirit, form part of this mightiness and have done nothing but demolish. And yet, they entered a sphere of light. God saw and knew all that, and so did we who followed and watched their work on earth. We are usually their fathers and mothers, sisters and brothers with whom they were connected on earth. These beings will convince them and that is possible because darkness lies far behind them. Others descend into that darkness and are lost for hundreds of years. Many exceeded the limits of laws and cannot be helped for thousands of years. Such is our life, André, these are spiritual laws everybody will have to learn and especially acquire.'

'A while ago you explained those maximum limits, Alcar. Now what happens if man cannot return to the earth?'

'You mean those who live in the darkness and have completed their cycle of life?'

'Yes, Alcar, those I mean. Have those people exceeded these limits?'

'Certainly, André.'

'What kind of people are they usually, Alcar?'

'They are usually rulers of evil, people who have killed thousands of beings on earth. When we were in the darkness to learn life there I showed you the deepest spheres, the spheres of hell we have on this side. I connected myself with one of those beings and told you what I observed. All those people lay there like living dead, they had perished in their animal-like life. Do you remember, André?'

'Yes, Alcar, I can well remember.'

'Well, those people have exceeded the maximum limits in nature and now live the life of the spirit, they have completed their cycle on earth and cannot return any more.'

'Is there no end to that? How do these people get out of that condition?'

'I told you already, we'll visit them on our next journey when I'll explain all that. Again God comes to the aid of those people and how this happens is an other great wonder we human beings and spirits know nothing about.'

'Are those people born again, Alcar?'

'Well felt, André, there is no other way. Do you feel what will happen, how these beings get on earth and in what condition they will live?'

'No, I don't know, Alcar, I can't imagine.'

'As I said before this is also a mighty wonder of God given to man. If it was not possible, André, I assure you, these souls would not advance any more and would be doomed to live there eternally. They perished in their own animal-like life, they destroyed everything, and they have no material possibility of existence. Yet, they are also God's children and belong to creation, and form part of all this. There must be a way out for all those poor people, I'll explain that to you later when we see again that God is love and that no child is lost.'

'So human beings can break these laws in both conditions, Alcar?'

'Yes, André, they can forget themselves in both conditions to the extent that they no longer feel life. Is that clear?'

'Yes, Alcar, but difficult to grasp. It is all so wonderful and mighty, yet, so simple and natural. Are they the rulers of evil, Alcar?'

'Yes, all are rulers of evil, these people brought destruction and misfortune on earth.'

'That's exactly, Alcar, what people on earth don't understand, that one man has the power to kill thousands of other human beings.'

'Isn't that clear? Haven't we been able to follow all this? Haven't I shown you that God gave us everything? Haven't we got that power in our own hands? Haven't I shown that this applies to every human being? That people on earth will experience it when they yearn for it? All that is possible, André, man creates his own condition, man is his own lord and master. All these people perish and also those who follow them. When a ruler has power over thousands of people and these people do not feel that they will perish, support and help him plunder and murder, these human beings are demons and darkness will await them. Mankind does not yet understand that God does not approve of that and has not given them that power. But this has nothing to do with God. Those who have advanced ahead of all those people do not join them and follow their own way. These people are different, they see through all that violence. Those who follow these rulers will perish; those who follow their own way seek the good.

One day, all those people will awaken and see and experience their own deeds. One day, André, there will be an end to all this violence. It is still possible on earth; these people still live on earth. You see again how little progress inner man has made, how far he still is from higher ideals, how long it will be before these beings also awaken. All those rulers will perish, even though they think they are doing a lot for man-kind on earth. They who take the sword shall perish with the sword. Christ brought this message, but people act in defiance of everything and go their own way. They destroy mankind and believe they are help-ing them. Look at those lunatics, look how they act, André. I told you about them on several occasions. Mankind calls and implores to be delivered from these demons, but they live and remain alive and that, at any rate their death, is predestined. One day, however, all that dis-solves, all their ideas will be destroyed. What has been established through the blood of mankind; what has been brought about by ha-tred, passion and violence, will dissolve, believe me that is a law. Noth-ing will remain, it cannot exist, because it is as they are and the feeling they have. These people live in the darkness on this side, they lie there and are seemingly dead. Yet, something is alive in them. In the depth of all that misery lives the spark of God. Once, however, this particle of God was on earth as a human being. You will see them, André.'

'What do you think of the rulers who still live on earth in my time, Alcar?'

'They will also perish. Every wrong thought must be corrected; every deed must be made up. Now just imagine all their sins and mistakes. They created a mountain of misery. They have destroyed or ordered to kill not one but hundreds of people. Nobody will stop them or can stop them; this is what they achieved on earth. It is the highest man can attain, at any rate in material life on earth.'

'Is that also part of creation?'

'Part of creation, André? How could you ask that question, though I know what you mean, it all belongs to inner man, my son. You see again how little progress we have made in all those billions of years. This is still possible on earth; people still listen to these demons and follow them in their animal-like life. This time they wonder why and what for and implore God to help them. People do not yet pray enough, they must pray more ardently and ask God for help. Man created this himself. The soul we followed acted no differently. That is how man lives on earth and attains the highest. That is worldly possession, it is wealth and power and it is reserved for everyone. Those who yearn for it and hold out their hands for it will perish. Yet, all human beings will experience it as it makes life on earth more comfortable.

Is this part of creation, André? I repeat your question and answer: No, a thousand times no, it has nothing to do with God's creation. This belongs to inspiring life and this life is animal-like conscious. We have been able to follow this life and we know now how little progress all these people have made. It is up to them to free themselves from it and seek the higher life. Those who follow them and accept are all animal-like beings and belong to that attunement. The planet earth is ready but mankind lags behind. Material life is far, very far ahead of inner life, but all these human beings do not want to realize that. They follow those demons and disturb peace on earth. Wherever they appear passion and violence, animalization and ruin dominate. The earth is a paradise, could be a paradise if there were no people. Man is like the devil of hell and has taken possession of it all, he wants to rule and destroy. That was not God's intention. We now come to the earth to make clear to them what kind of beings they follow, who they are and what awaits them after death. Inner man is millions of years behind material man. They must try and correct this. That happens the way each of us has to make up for his sins and mistakes. All this is for mankind, the inspiring life on earth.

How grateful they should be to be allowed to receive this. Now there are human beings on earth who seek higher life and all this nourishment for the mind is meant for them. They shall and must awaken like all of us who have reached the spheres of light awakened.'

'What do you think of the present situation on earth, Alcar?'

'What we think of it? On this side we see everything differently, André. We cannot help them. Mankind has to experience this and begin a different life. It is chaos again and people are anxious because they realize this will come to a standstill. Mankind has not advanced that far yet that it wants to live in quiet and peace. Each human being must come to rest and everybody must begin his own life. One being hates the other and wants to possess what the other has acquired. This very earthly property will cause mankind to perish, André, because they don't want to do without. How is life on earth without wealth? Do all these human beings not desire this happiness; don't they yearn to possess much wealth? Everybody has lived in wealth and has known poverty, grief, sorrow and misery, but they are not aware of it any more. All this resides in the distant past, a spiritual veil keeps it concealed. Not one single being accepts it, they want to experience, to possess and yet their lives pass in poverty.'

'If they know all that, Alcar, they are fortunate to possess little of all those treasures?'

'Indeed, André, it could mean happiness if they understand it which means that they are living a higher life or live in some condition of consciousness. It is also possible that all these people will receive this wealth after some centuries. In that case they will subsequently return to material life again and who knows what they will then receive.'

'How deep everything is, Alcar. However, there are people who are rich, and lead a good life as well, which means that they seek higher life. These beings can't be bad, can they?'

'That is a different condition altogether. There are rich people on earth who also hold a high social position and have to accomplish some task or other.'

'Is that also possible, Alcar?'

'Yes, certainly, all those people know no poverty, no grief, sorrow or misery, I mean not the kind of misery they have to experience as a result of their own karma. Do you feel this difference, that this is a different condition?'

'Yes, Alcar, that is clear to me, though it is getting ever more complicated. I can hardly tell things apart. When do we know on earth that we experience our karma? Surely nobody can feel or know that?'

'That is not necessary, André. Life on earth is to awaken. We have

368

seen people living in the first degree who are animal-like and pre-animal-like conscious, but all those souls cannot remain there and in the jungle, they will consequently pass on to a higher life. They pass on into that other condition between the fourth and fifth degree. That is where their struggle really begins. If all those people could accept everything, they would not create more sorrow and misery and would not revolt. But the first human being who can control himself in these material degrees must still be born. Not any human being has that inner quality in all those material degrees. From the first to the highest degree they seek property and that's how all those thousands of lives are spent. How far have all those people advanced on the spiritual way? How is their inner life? What is their cosmic attunement? In what condition of consciousness do they live? Is it the pre-animal-like, animal-like, coarse-material or material attunement? Can you answer these questions now, André? We have experienced all those degrees. I told you about them in various ways, I explained something of my own lives, we followed the life of all those black people and I connected you with the astral world. We subsequently followed that one soul and now you must answer me.'

André reflected a long time on that and felt what his leader meant. He said: 'They have no spiritual property, Alcar, they have forgotten themselves in all those lives and they seek all that material wealth.'

'Thank you, we have not been there in vain; you understood me. No, they have no spiritual level, they seek and go on seeking and they murder, plunder and destroy if they don't get it willingly.

These people live in all those various attunements. All these people are animal-like beings, even though they have received the highest from the planet earth and God. Thousands of centuries, do you hear, went by. In all those centuries these people experienced death and birth again. In those thousands of years they seek something, and they spare no one to achieve the object in view.

Don't these people live on earth? Don't you see these beings every day? Are there no rulers in your time who think they have a right to ill-treat their fellow-man? Who terrorize thousands? Are they spiritual beings? And can these people reach Divinity in one life? We know now that it is impossible and why these people are like that, we have been able to follow their attunement.'

'Can't we help those people by praying, Alcar?'

'To pray that they will live a different life?'

'Yes, Alcar, that's what I mean.'

'No, my son, unfortunately no, that is not possible. Listen. Never before did people pray as much as in your time. In your century people pray as fervently as never before. Isn't that a mystery? Why do people pray so much nowadays? We know all that, only we, living on this side. We overhear nothing but prayers and they go higher and higher, from sphere to sphere, from heaven to heaven and finally reach the cosmic masters we met. Then on to Him, to Christ and subsequently to God, our holy Father.

Now what? Does God help all His children? Does God allow these animal-like beings to murder all those others? All those rulers, André, have attained the highest on earth, their development has advanced that far, but they also have a will of their own. Nobody, do you hear, nobody, no spirit, no human being, no angel, no cosmic master has ever supported them, it is their own acquired property. This applies to every human being, for God gave us everything.

This is no nonsense, this is reality, it is what we can achieve on earth. God gave Himself, God's life is within us. People can acquire that might and power, that all-encompassing. There is a limit, however, and this limit may not be exceeded; within this limit these mortals, André, can do something for the bliss and well being of their fellowmen. When they have advanced that far, you feel that they live for their fellowmen. Their might and power are incredible and so is the task laid in their hands. All these gifted people are able to make or break whatever they want.

What is their life like now? Do they live for their fellowmen? Do they share with others what is within their reach? Do they contribute to the bliss of all these people? Do they sacrifice themselves for mankind, like Christ once did?

Man prays, asks and implores; he calls to God for help, and yet, nothing, nothing happens.

To all those questions I can only say this. Man has a will of his own; man received everything and it is up to him to seek for the good.

As I said before, we live in the century of technical wonders and of spiritual development. People can accept the technical wonders because they can see them. But that we live in the century of spiritual development they and you too, André, cannot accept. And yet, I'm speaking the holy truth, man now prays, begs for nourishment for the mind, asks for the help of God to deliver him from these demons. Now we come to the earth to convince them of all this, of the origin of the universe, of man and animal, of spiritual attunements and thousands of spiritual laws. Only this knowledge can help them and deliver them from that chaos.

Once again, God gave us everything, but God cannot help us now, because we have a will of our own and we must use it only for the good.

Man of the earth, my sisters and brothers, seek the good and try to bring quiet and peace in your own home. Accept that you live eternally and will soon enter this world. God guards and does not allow that any of His children receives misery. Feel what this means.

No sorrow can and will be your share if the law of cause and effect does not apply to you. That means that you have made up everything whatsoever in the distant past and are now on earth for some purpose. Do not stop praying, for all of you will be helped. God guards, although your faith is in your own hands. You have received everything from your God. Be aware that those who departed watch you and help you from this side. There will be an end to this chaos too.

Pray, pray and don't lose your faith and confidence, even though mankind appears to perish. Know that you'll die on your fixed and cosmic time, that everything has been arranged in advance. So go on praying, it is your only salvation, one day the good will triumph.

Show what you want, what is within you and be prepared to die, and try to seek the good in that chaos. Begin today, it must happen now, for tomorrow you may be taken away from life on earth and live on this side. Then, pure love is your only salvation and bliss in this life of reality. May God give you the strength to bear your cross, may God protect you and yours. We are essentially one, but we have completed our cycle and all misery is over. Accept this message, it is a mighty grace to be allowed to receive all this in your material life.

A faint light wavers at your human horizon. It is the light of spiritual awakening. Feel, you man of the earth, how faint that light is, and yet, now that we see it, it gives us faith and confidence to continue our work and complete it.

Christ once lived on the planet earth and brought us Divine happiness. It was not accepted, not understood and its meaning is still not felt. Peace and quiet could have been on earth already thousands of years ago. Mankind, however, did not accept, did not believe and perished. From that time on, life on earth could have been a paradise, but there has been no change, nothing has changed after all those centuries. All those spiritual laws are still there, but death still rules, it is lord and master on earth and causes fear, as well as grief and sorrow. Look through that black mask, you don't see castles in the air, but eternal life and us who went before you.

We who live on the side beyond have learned and understood the message of Christ and we accept that the entire cosmos is inhabited. We have learned that we are like God and we will pass on into it. You must acquire this. You must accept that you live eternally, it is not until then that you will awaken in the spirit and see your sister or brother in your fellowman. Love each other like you love yourself. Look up, Divine happiness awaits you. It is up to you to earn it, to acquire all this. Is everything clear, André?'

'I have no words for it, Alcar, and I thank God for everything.'

'Any more questions?'

'No, Alcar.'

'Then we'll return to your material organism and this journey is also finished.

Come, André, we'll float on towards your material organism. I'll soon call for you. We'll again pass into the past and you get to know my own life and that of my friend. I'll help you in everything, so don't worry.'

'Shall I be able to sleep, Alcar?'

'Yes, André, you will sleep, because your mind is entirely open now and on our next journey you'll understand and accept what that means.'

André felt happy. How much he had received, it was incredible, and however deep it was, there was pure simplicity and reality in everything. He had experienced wonders; he had learned spiritual problems and especially the depth of the soul, all those thousands of lives of the human being. Life is amazing, he thought, and mighty. Now he would soon be in his body and live on earth.

He returned to his earthly body, feeling a different man.

Now he had to digest all this. Alcar looked at him and said: 'Yes, my boy, this too and all that you'll yet experience. One day your last journey will come and then you are here with me and we'll set out on a journey for many years, because there is no end. Look, André, we have returned.'

André looked at his material body. How well did he now understand his own material organism.

'Farewell, André, we'll soon be together again, though it will take a little longer than last time. Be strong, may God bless you.'

André thanked his leader for everything. He descended into his material organism and this departure from his body also belonged to the past.

THE END OF PART TWO

# PART THREE

## Reincarnation on earth

# CHAPTER I

## *Disembodiment*

ANDRÉ was again informed that he would depart from his body. Four weeks had passed and during that time he had reflected on everything and acquired what he had received on his last journey. Nothing had disturbed him and his inner wealth had increased.

How wonderful everything he had received from his leader was. The depth of inner life, birth, death and returning to the earth, all that was tremendous. He had not expected that he would experience it and now he was ready again to join Alcar and receive fresh nourishment for the mind. He had gone to his room early and waited for what would happen.

During the last few days he had experienced new developments. It was very peculiar; when he thought of everything and experienced it again, when he descended into the distant past he became aware of a peculiar sensation. It rose from his deep inner self or subconscious, but only when he meditated and thought of all these wonders he had been allowed to experience, otherwise he felt nothing and was his own self.

He clearly felt that someone else lived within him. When he descended into the past, he felt he was taller and broader, and a different personality altogether. It was very strange indeed. This was no condition of trance, because when he was in trance he departed his material body and was not aware of anything any longer. In this condition he was conscious of his own life and yet that other personality was within him. It was a remarkable feeling he had not experienced before. If he did not intensely concentrate on himself, that other personality dominated his own self, he then sank back into an other life and that other personality consciously passed into him. This was the strange event he had not experienced before.

He clearly felt that if he did not want to, he could sustain himself and was still master of his own material body. If he consented and wanted to experience these phenomena, that other personality passed into him with feelings that were not his. He acted differently and felt he had a beard. If he wanted to remove that beard, he found it was not possible because it belonged to that other personality.

He repeatedly noticed that he stroke with his hand along his chin and it made him angry. At such moments he threw everything away and he thought of his own life on earth. Imperceptibly, that other personality returned.

There were feelings and phenomena in him, which not only he was aware of but also his friends and acquaintances. Whenever that other personality dominated, a very refined feeling developed and the way he spoke differed from his usual manner. He spoke carefully and it was remarkable that he could speak an other language.

When he gave in to those feelings willingly, he clearly felt that this civilization and that foreign language belonged to that other personality.

He also felt that he was drawn to an other country, invariably in the direction where he had been with Alcar when he had shown and explained the past of his friend. These were remarkable feelings; one feeling was even stranger than the other.

In his own life he did not adhere to earthly things, he did not care about them, but in this condition he was attached to them.

When he gave in willingly and surrendered to that personality, he experienced many other phenomena and feelings related to that other being. He then felt like a very rich person and that was a heavy burden on his mind. He wanted to have an other house, the house in which he had been living for many years was not good enough any more. He also felt a strong desire to ride horseback, he dared not tell all this to his friends who asked him what was wrong with him. He was afraid they would have misgivings about him, about that which had to do with his gifts, his leader and the side beyond. For him all that was sacred, but these feelings were very strange.

Should he tell them I am not André, I am someone else? Could he, André, say that?

They would think he was insane and everything he had received from his leader Alcar would not be of value any more. No, he could not tell them anything and he kept it to himself. He wanted to know more about it himself and only his leader could explain it. He could not tell them anything at all now, for some fresh feelings had come into him. These feelings made him shiver and he now discarded everything related to that personality.

He himself, as André, was very happy in his life on earth. There was a feeling of satisfaction, surrender, patience and contentment in him

378

and he could control himself in everything. Life on earth meant nothing to him. He lived for his gifts and for his leader and he felt quite happy with what he had received and achieved during all those years.

Since that other personality had come into him, he no longer felt satisfied and he sought and wanted to have everything, which could make life on earth more comfortable. Where was his own personality? This was not André, this was somebody else and he did not want to possess these other feelings, because his inner happiness had disappeared with these feelings. When these feelings manifested themselves it had given him a fright and he thought that somebody had influenced him, that he was nearly possessed.

That was not true, however, for he immediately felt quiet again when he concentrated on something else or on himself. He nevertheless began to think and feel again. He had wanted to ask Alcar what it meant, but he had not yet done so and had not received connection.

When he tried to see the face of this remarkable person, the image dissolved and the figure disappeared. He thought it was his imagination but that wasn't true either. He did not imagine things; he was far too sensible for it.

He thought, has all this something to do with what I have experienced on the side beyond? Or was it because he had experienced too much, that all those spiritual laws were getting too much for him and that those feelings were his own? Was it really imagination, or the influence of some spirit? Was he open for that? He had never experienced anything like it in all the years he had been in connection with Alcar. This was new to him, and strange, very strange. It was not a condition of trance, because it was too conscious in him. It was a very strange phenomenon and it could therefore not be his own.

Alcar had told him that he was now conscious in everything and that the spiritual veil around him had been removed. This meant that he was entirely conscious and that he could receive anything given from the side beyond. He could now see through everything, there was nothing that stopped him in the spirit. He now understood everything, could digest everything, he had been able to sleep well and felt very relaxed. Yet, that other person lived in him and he attracted him when he contemplated everything. For days it had preyed on his mind. During the last few days, when he was ready to depart from his body again he had not felt much of this other personality and had completely been himself. He was very curious to know if it had some meaning and he would ask Alcar.

He already felt that his leader Alcar was on his way and it would not be long before he would be in life after death again. Yes, his feeling was correct, there was Alcar.

Instantly he heard his leader say: 'Here I am again, André, you will soon be with me. I'm going to release you from your material organism straightaway.'

André felt his spiritual body rise and he felt soundly asleep. He was not aware of anything any more and awakened in the spirit.

'Well, my boy, we are together again in life after death and you will again receive nourishment for the mind and I'll explain quite a few things. We'll leave shortly, on our way I'll tell you a thing or two and where we'll go first of all. Come, André, we'll go on floating.'

# CHAPTER II

## *André's mediumship*

ANDRÉ was with his leader in the spheres again and he was very happy.

'I felt such strange things, Alcar.'

'Strange things you say?'

'Yes, perhaps you could give me an explanation. During the first few days I felt quite normal. However, the more I pondered on everything the more an other personality manifested itself within me and I could not free myself. Those were remarkable phenomena and I found it all very strange. Does it mean anything? Do you know anything about it?'

Alcar looked at his instrument and said: 'Have you felt that thoroughly and clearly?'

'Yes, Alcar, and it drew me towards the place where we have been on our first journey. Were they my own thoughts?'

Alcar looked at him again and said: 'It is remarkable indeed.'

André felt that his leader let it pass. Would he have imagined something? Perhaps Alcar did not know either. Yet it was very strange because he knew exactly how it had entered him. He could not have imagined it, because it had even taken him by surprise. Why did Alcar let it pass, should he not have asked? Was it so strange? He had felt it for days on end. A very different human being had lived within him during those days and he did not know how to cope with it.

Again he said to his leader: 'Have I imagined something, Alcar?'

'I don't think so, André, and we will look into the matter on this journey. Have a little more patience, when we have advanced that far I may be able to answer. I am now engaged with other things and lost in thought. Can you accept that?'

'Of course, Alcar, thank you.'

He was not quite satisfied, though. It was not the answer he had hoped to get, for it was no explanation. Surely Alcar knew what he had felt in those days? He would wait; perhaps this problem would be solved on this side.

That's why, he thought, I did not get an answer in my material body either. I would certainly have received it, but it was perhaps not possible. He had experienced that before and the problem was solved afterwards. Perhaps that would also happen this time and he no longer thought about it.

'Where do we go, Alcar?'

'I am going to connect you with my own past and I'll show you some of the lives I have lived. Then we'll go on.'

'Shall I see something of myself too?'

'That will also happen.'

He was very happy, for what was he going to see and what would he experience? He would see his own lives, lives he had experienced. How wonderful that would be, he would be able to understand himself completely. How much he had already learned about himself, but only through his leader. He would receive everything and that was a mighty grace. He understood that everything had happened from the beginning with a fixed purpose. His mediumship differed from that of many others on earth. He saw because he should see. He received because he should receive and departed from his body because he departed through his leader. His own thoughts frightened him. Did he possess gifts? He only now felt that he actually possessed nothing at all. Lately he had felt this more clearly. There was something, which connected him with the past and he felt an unknown problem behind it.

'Is your mediumship not clear, André?'

'No, not really, Alcar. I know what I am and could do on earth and yet I feel it does not belong to me like all these other mediums possess their gifts. It frightens me, Alcar.'

'You need not be afraid, André, though you have felt it clearly, very clearly. Listen, I'll explain that to you, that was not possible before now.

When I was on this side and acquired life in the spirit and wandered over the earth, I thought of all these things. I had a fixed purpose in mind and made my plans for when I would work there to convince man on earth of our life. I told you about that. When I had completed my study on earth, I returned to the spheres. I was connected with the masters and asked them to give me an instrument on earth through which I could pass on my experiences. The higher masters, among whom Ubronis[*], gave me advice and I waited. I knew in advance that you

[*] Mentor of one of the spheres of light on the side beyond. See the book 'A View into the Hereafter'.

382

would become my instrument, but I had to wait until the time would come when I could influence you. I also told you about that.

You had these powers. There are many clairvoyants on earth, but every clairvoyance is different, and this concerns the condition of the human soul. The more spiritually minded human being feels and sees in a different way than the material individual and he consequently has a completely different connection with this side. A human being can have gifts of his own, he sees whenever he wants, and their spiritual assistants help their clairvoyants. When they see the controlling spirit passes on what he observes on this side and in this way the medium expresses on earth what the controlling spirit sees and wants to pass on. Those are usually messages from this side, from beloved ones living in our world. All these beings have a connection with this world and are instruments, but they remain as they are. They don't know our life, because their connection is different. Our spiritual life remains closed for them, although they receive messages. Is that clear, André?'

'Yes, Alcar.'

'However, there are also people who think and feel that they are medium, they are sensitive, but that sensitivity is such that they cannot serve us. Nevertheless, they open themselves for our world and our life is being defiled. Well then, I had other intentions. I wanted to keep those gifts in my own hands; which means that my medium would only see and experience what I saw on this side and wanted to pass on. But I went further. I opened your mind and brought our connection about. You know that if I do not act on you, you cannot observe, nor paint or depart from your body, because you cannot do anything on your own. And that was exactly what I wanted. If I could achieve that you would have to listen to me and be unable to do anything yourself, so that you would follow me in everything and your gifts would not be squandered. The more you exerted yourself to get to know our life, the more I could give you and the gifts you possessed as feeling would develop accordingly. You were and remained dependent on me and will remain so. In reality, therefore, you have no gifts, they belong to me. What you have is feeling, is your own life, and I eagerly made use of that life and I could connect myself. You only have gifts when I have connected myself with you. Do you feel that, André?'

'Yes, Alcar.'

'That is the strange feeling you have been experiencing lately, I mean that feeling of being nothing. What did I achieve by it? In the first place that your gifts would remain pure and in the second place that you are not only a medium but above all that you would acquire what I taught you and that it meant spiritual property for you. I wanted you to achieve something, and that when you would depart life on earth you would own something in our life, which you would have deserved by following me and giving yourself completely. It was not so simple, though. You know your own struggle on earth to lose yourself as a personality and above all to earn an other personality. To that end you had to discard yourself completely. You should have no desires any more if I wanted to develop you in a short period of time and if you were to follow me in everything. Several times it was so terrible that you did not know how to cope with our world and your life on earth, and yet remain yourself. You know how much you suffered, how terrible your struggle has been; though I also helped you in it. All those other mediums do not feel and experience that, they remain themselves and do not know this struggle. For you, however, it was your school, your occult school of hard knocks on earth, I may say, but it also served to enter this life consciously while you are still on earth and are used as instrument. What you now own and know of our life is your own spiritual property; you own inner life, but not more than that. It sounds hard, André, but I have those gifts and not you, even though you live through me and you have those powers. For what did I do?

I made you conscious. I wanted you to become man, to feel our life and to acquire it. When I gave you something on earth, passed on messages from this side and told you of our life, you would have to digest all that in your material organism, which is the most difficult life we know on earth for a material human being. I also wanted you to have no earthly desires any more, I wanted to eliminate your material life and to prepare you for our life and I tried to achieve a lot. Your fierce struggle really began when I had advanced far enough for you to depart from your body. You know how everything happened and that I first had to convince you of all these spiritual laws and I went ever further until we could go to the third sphere. Although all that happened on my powers, you gradually began to feel our life and to experience it in your life on earth, and that became your inner possession and your life on earth. You would have to find yourself in it and would not have earned it until then.

I made you experience everything. I gave you nourishment for the mind, but if I had continued to develop your physical gifts, in the period when you were dematerialized and I held spiritual seances, you would have remained a physical instrument and you would not have seen or experienced anything of our life, of the spheres and hells, of the depth of the soul and the beauty of life on our side, as these powers belong to the mental gifts.

You know, André, that I suspended those gifts and began to develop your mental gifts. It was not until later that you understood why I had done so, when I began to write through you. That does not belong to you either, if I or an other intelligence of this side would not give you anything, and not act on you, you would not be able to put anything on paper related to our life.

I achieved that, André, and also that I could one day give you everything, which is the final problem on our side, which these three departures from the body confirm. If I could continue in that way and you would listen to me and continue to follow me in everything, I could easily give you ever more, open you entirely and we could have departure after departure.

You acquired all that, you devoted yourself, because you wanted to serve and give yourself completely for our work, though you felt you were nothing, could not be anything, for you remained completely dependent on me and that was exactly what I wanted.

As a result you could not do anything on your own, you could not make things up and your gifts remained pure. You cannot pass on spiritual messages if I do not give them to you. You do not know anything about curing if I do not give you the diagnosis. You would not be able to depart from your body if I did not want you to and release you from your material body. You are nothing, you are merely what you experienced through me and what I gave you in all those years, what you received from me through all those departures and what I made you experience in your life on earth. All those conditions, such as the various problems I helped you with and the many deathbeds you were allowed to observe became your own property and developed your inner life. Only that is your own property and neither spirit nor human being can take that away from you. You therefore discarded yourself completely. It is your property in our life and you served man and me on earth.

Yet, everything will soon return within you, you consciously pass on into our life and acquire that. You consciously feel our life while you are still living on earth. That is my intention, which is what you deserve and receive, like others have gifts. They also acquire a lot, but they know little about laws and spiritual problems, because the connection is different.

At the beginning of your development you laid yourself, your entire being and personality in my hands, you lived through me and in return you received spiritual wisdom. The others who serve on earth as instrument have a different experience, but I wanted you to acquire everything of our life. That is a great difference and it happens with many mediums, but the majority has a different connection.

I want to make clear, André, that, during the first years, I took away your entire personality, that you lived through me, but that you did not remain behind. You were always prepared to follow me, and when I have finished and explained everything from this side, you know what others do not know and can't know, what God intended with creation and how everything happened. What is essential for a pupil on earth - that he has to follow his teacher in everything in order to acquire his capacity to which end he has to exert himself - also applies to you and in return you receive our life. For you it is a spiritual study and you will obtain a degree in it. I'll see to that, André.

The deeper I can descend in our life so that you can experience everything with me the sooner I will reach the end which end I will explain to you on this journey. That is possible now, it wasn't in all those years, but now we have advanced that far. What is the end of his study for a student on earth is the end of your spiritual study for you. This is a great wonder and has to do with what you felt on earth. When I have reached that stage I will explain everything you have experienced and felt during the few days preceding your departure from your body. Being an instrument on earth served to consciously pass into our life. You also have what other mediums possess, but I kept those gifts in my own hands to keep you entirely pure. When people on earth know this they should also accept our life and everything you received through me, because it was not you but I who told of this life.

Do you understand, André?'

'Yes, Alcar, yet there are people who say that I am a dreamer and that this emanates from my subconscious. They cannot accept it and they think that I fool myself. They can't believe it, though I knew that I was allowed to experience all this through you and could not do anything myself. But they don't want to accept that.'

'Leave them alone, André. Those who cannot or do not want to accept should suit themselves. We know that everything is pure and I took that into account from the beginning. Everything you told through me about life after death is pure and must be true, or I would not have been able to reach you, so that you would never have known or received anything about it. If I had not acted on you, even though you possessed feeling for these gifts like other mediums, you would never have acquired this depth, this connection. You would have been able to see and hear, perhaps you would have been able to cure, but you would have been unaware of our and my life and all those spiritual wonders and laws, because I had not given it to you and could not have established those departures from your body. Do you understand that this is a very different mediumship, that it relates to your inner life and that, as a result, you entirely pass into our life?'

'If you had not been there, could an other control have given me those messages, Alcar?'

'You mean to say, would you still have become a medium?'

'Yes, Alcar.'

'Yes, that would have been possible, but you would not have received what you now know of our life. I am supervised myself, I am a member of a spiritual order and that is why I get help from a higher level. You surely feel the great difference in connection and this also has a meaning, which I will explain to you on this journey.

As I descended deeper into your life, you not only experienced this on this side but also on earth. It is especially on earth that you would have to learn our life, so that it would pass into your inner life. I gradually went deeper and I could do so, because you were always prepared to give yourself completely for us.

We already advanced that far, that I was allowed to show you the beginning of creation, an event that only few mediums can experience. It is not only a mighty grace for you, both of us are concerned, it is our work, my work and yours, which you'll understand later on.

What I know of our life, all those gifts and wisdom I put into your hands as your development advances. That also applies to all mediums who keep their gifts pure, the spiritual help can gradually increase in accordance with the task assigned to him or her from this side. The greater the number of mediums, who can free themselves from earthly ties and life, attune to our life, the more nourishment for the mind we can give, and that is what the earth needs. There is a great shortage of good instruments and those who possess gifts should know that it is sacred and require sacrifices. Those who own these spiritual treasures must disengage themselves from all that earthly business and concentrate on us. Those who think they can experience life on earth and also be an instrument will find that their gifts will disintegrate sooner or later, as we cannot keep them free from all those earthly influences. We help them in everything, also in life on earth, we give them spiritual wisdom, solve their problems and misery, but we demand of them to follow us and give themselves completely for our work. Those who are not able to do this and wish to acquire earthly happiness are irrevocably lost. They will experience that their spiritual connection becomes weaker, their spiritual life and all messages they receive will decrease in strength and truth. This cannot be correct, for we give ourselves entirely, we are ready day and night to help them, but in return we demand their complete submission. You have always been able to do that, André, and I'm grateful to you for it. It is the most difficult mediumship there is, for those serving on earth as an instrument must not only live their own life, which is difficult enough as it is in that chaos, but above all digest what is given them from this side. This means, as I said, to sacrifice themselves.

We, on the other hand, completely give ourselves and help them in everything. There are many mediums on earth and all those mediums who have to perform a task, who are in connection with our side, who can receive clear and true messages, are in our hands. That is a heavy and great task they are charged with. They hold the joys and sorrows of thousands of human beings in their hands. God has given all this, they receive that from their Father in heaven and it is a mighty grace. All these mediums are under one guidance and live all over the world. It is remarkable that all of us describe one life, one in English, the other in French and someone else in an other language known on earth, because we are all members of one order, so that we can never contradict ourselves. However, there are millions of spirits in the sphere of the earth, those who return to the earth as astral beings, but who sometimes don't know anything about our life and are living dead as are those who attract them. Spiritual messages are then defiled, they serve themselves and that has no meaning in the spirit.

Here in our life, André, everything is preordained. I knew in advance what I would accomplish and could achieve. You might ask, was it all that difficult?

Yes, you should not forget that when the soul passes on into life on earth it does not remember anything and that only inner life is awake and that man does not know anything of former incarnations.'

'Is my mediumship connected with reincarnation, Alcar?'

'I already explained that there is no human being on earth unless he has to do with former lives, and that all this is preordained. I know this is not a direct reply to your question, but I cannot answer it yet, I will do that when the time has come and when I have advanced that far. At any rate you understand that your mediumship on earth is in my hands and that I see to it, that you receive it according as your development progresses. So you have to earn this mediumship. But there is more. I said already that I had made my calculations in advance and not only I, but also the masters on this side. If we had not been able to, we could not have acted on you, as we would have done more harm than good, which would not help mankind. I can assure you that we pondered everything before my work was to begin and had to be prepared in every respect to properly perform my task. One single mistake from your side would have been enough to destroy my work and that of the masters, that would be no progress for mankind on earth, but would add to the misery already present and we did not fancy that.

You will realize what was expected of me and of you and that all has a deep spiritual meaning, which I cannot explain until I have reached that stage. I want you to know, André, that not everybody will receive this, it only happens with a definite purpose like everything given to the earth from this side. At present, I cannot go any further into this matter but you will be amazed. I tell you already now that these will be wonders for you as well, although quite different wonders than those you have received and experienced in all those years.'

'You're making me very curious, Alcar.'

'I can imagine, but you'll have to suppress your curiosity. Your life on earth had to develop the way we wanted to. In the first place your full submission, then all your love for our work and mankind.'

'Did you know for certain, Alcar, that those powers were within me?'

'Yes, I knew, but there are thousands of dangers in material life and those dangers could be your own desires to possess, like other people. Do not forget that I could not change your own will and that I had to watch how you would do your work and live your life on earth, that it would be in harmony with our world and that I could reach you. In life on earth I could do absolutely nothing at all and had to leave you there, entirely to your own devices. How many mediums have perished? How many have understood their task?

They forgot themselves for the sake of wealth, and attracted that which cut the other guides and me off, so that those mediums passed into other hands and their work was destroyed. I had to try and avoid that and you assisted me in the process.'

'How awfully difficult your life now appears to me, to have known this in advance and having had to watch how I would live my life.'

'That was a deep and great problem, André. It is that deep that I'll tell you about it on this journey and explain all those conditions. This was so deep because, as I said, we weighed it up in advance, just like Gerhard experienced it when he would descend into the hell in our life and thought he would succumb. For this work one must be able to sacrifice and that has happened. One must be able to give oneself completely or the essence of our nourishment for the mind has no meaning. I would not have reached the depth I wanted to reach for the nourishment for the mind you received from me and which is your development on earth.'

'It is getting ever more complicated, Alcar.'

'Yes indeed, and you have clearly felt that. It is the most difficult problem there is and ever will be. Man on earth may be an artist or qualify for some study, but living as a medium and human being on earth between two worlds is the most difficult thing there is. I brought you reality and exactly because everything is true it is difficult and you had to overcome that. Many people on earth qualify for a study and give out, although they have their feet firmly on the ground. You had to take leave of the earth emotionally, during all those years you hovered between heaven and earth but you remained yourself. Your nervous system was in no way disturbed, and it also gave you spiritual wisdom. If I had not been the one I pretended to be, you would irrevocably have perished and would have landed in the hands of evil. Man can feel from your own condition, your own life on earth, that this must be real and pure and the absolute truth.

However, all those laws and powers are not known there, they are unaware of them and do not feel the depth of what I want to give and have brought so far. That was why your life was so difficult, but now you passed through all that and you are entirely open. Being open has a specific meaning, which I can also explain later when I have got that far. That is why we made arrangements on this side. You should not possess anything you could learn on earth. I did not want you to qualify for a material study, that is why you were born in that small town. Your parents were not to have material wealth, nothing, so that they could not let you study. Your mind had to be completely vacant for me to use you as an instrument, otherwise your own acquired knowledge would have destroyed mine. I'll also tell you about that.'

'So writing, Alcar, that's what I should do and is most essential?'

'Indeed, André, only that, just our message. The other gifts you now have are of secondary importance. Man needs nourishment for the mind more than treatment for his material and physical illnesses. We have been able to help many people and alleviate suffering, but what I have to tell is most important. If I can convince just one human being, as I told you several times, our work is rewarded, but we have already reached thousands of people. Your books will find their way and cannot be stopped. In them I tell the holy truth, the truth only, I could not act differently. Your gift of painting is also of second importance, however splendid it is. We are not understood yet and that is indeed not possible, but we quietly continue our work, as do all those who work with us on earth. This work has been going on for thousands of years and yet so little has been achieved, but you know why.

Thus, I had made my calculations in advance. When you were still a young child, you were already under my guidance. That's when I started. During the first years of your childhood I brought spiritual children and you played with them. I showed you in the temple of the soul. One day you were nearly drowned and I came to your rescue as I helped you with many other things.'

'Did you know that I would be born in that small town?'

'Yes, André, I knew. The masters had shown me and I waited.'

'It is remarkable, Alcar, and that I'm unaware of it, I mean of an other life.'

'That is not possible either, I'll explain that to you on this journey. It was our intention, as I said just now, that you would not acquire any earthly knowledge. You would, therefore, be born to parents who did not have the means to let you study, as earthly knowledge would have an adverse effect and obstruct your mediumship. The less you knew the better for me. You did not have to ponder anything and to wonder whether it was you yourself or I who gave you everything. All this was to your advantage, you received it from me and you could submit yourself completely. A learned man cannot be an instrument for this mediumship, he knows too much and that knowledge is an obstruction.'

'Did you know that in advance too, could you assess that? Did you have that in your hands?'

'No, I could not assess that and I did not have it in my hands either, but God helps the soul in everything.'

'If I understand you correctly, you can't do anything about it?'

'No, André, nothing. Those are Gods sacred laws and we have to wait.'

'So it was a grace for me to be born to poor parents, Alcar?'

'Certainly, André, it was a mighty grace indeed.'

'How is it possible, Alcar, and how deep this event is.'

'The soul, my son, at any rate man returning to life on earth attracts this. In other words: he will receive what this being desires, though that is only possible if that being has to perform a task on earth. If the soul has to return to the earth to make up for something, it will take care of itself and those are God's laws.'

'Did I yearn for this and did you know me before I was born in this life on earth, Alcar?'

Alcar looked at his instrument and said: 'I'll explain later, have a little more patience and I'll be able to answer those questions too.'

This is also remarkable, André thought.

He asked: 'So your powers and those of the masters cease to exist between the world of the unconscious and the earth and then you can't do anything?'

'Very good, André, no, nothing; Lantos told you about that. Master Emschor explained that to him and that also applies to me and everybody living on this side. When man descends into this world and it is preordained that this soul has to bring something on earth, these incomprehensible laws, which we don't know nor feel, will take effect. What we do know is that everything on earth is in harmony, nothing is wrong and the soul will receive what we or others need for our work.

What could I have done if you were born to parents who wanted you to qualify for some study? What could I have done if your parents had wanted you to become a scientist, if your father and mother had been bad people and you had grown up a good-for-nothing? I could have prevented that, but that environment would have defiled your inner life. All those events would have made my work impossible.

So I knew beforehand, and this is a grace of God, that you would be born in that small town and we are grateful that this happened. I'll tell you more, which will be miracles to you. Already when your mother carried you I knew that you would become my instrument and would be born there.'

'I beg your pardon? As early as that?'

'Yes, the masters told me beforehand to whom and where you would be born and that I should prepare myself.'

'You are ever going deeper, Alcar.'

'Yes, I am and I have my reasons for it.'

What a problem, André thought. Where does it all end?

'Where it all ends, André?'

'Yes, Alcar, that's what I thought.'

'At the plain truth, my son. You have experienced it, haven't you? Hasn't everything happened the way I wanted it? Isn't God love in everything?'

'It is amazing, Alcar. If I understood you correctly you knew you would achieve all this and that I would acquire that level as a medium?'

'Yes, however difficult your struggle has been, how often you may have thought that you could not go on any more, I knew we would succeed and get through all this struggle to reach our aim and accomplish my work and that of the masters.'

'Has my dear mother something to do with that?'

'Yes, André, you are like she is, both feelings are one.'

'Is that a sacred law? I mean did she attract me?'

'Yes, that's right, just because of that.'

My God, André thought, how amazing. All my questions are answered and yet it is a big problem for me. How deep everything is again.

'Was I closely connected with her, Alcar?'

'Very closely, my son. That connection and unity of soul was very deep.'

'Was that why we understood each other so well?'

'Yes, André.'

'Mother is a wonderful woman, Alcar. Oh, she is so good, so pure and generous. All the things that dear soul has done for hundreds of people and me. Oh, if she would know all this. She has read my books; she senses me and says I receive this from our Lord. She prayed day and night and was not afraid and yet she sometimes looked at me as if she wanted to say, what is going to happen with that boy? I asked her about all those things in my youth, Alcar. There were people who wanted to buy me. They said there is something extraordinary with that boy. In my youth I saw the universe in a cabbage and whenever I asked if that was possible she shook her head and walked away. Do you know about that?'

'I know everything, because I put those thoughts in your mind.'

'As early as that?'

'Yes, André, I was always near you.'

'Oh, you must have had a hard time with me. Were all those inspirations yours?'

'Everything that connected you with our world.'

'Then you could not have thought of a better mother for me, she has really everything.'

'I know that too.'

'How well everything fits, Alcar, there is no flaw in it, everything is right, it is almost beyond belief and yet I have to accept it. If people could there would be happiness on this side. How many people want nourishment for the mind? They think I am able to do all this and make it up, Alcar, that it all comes from within me! I, who was unaware, and never knew what you have given me. Oh, if that would happen one day, if people would consider this and want to acquire it, they would no doubt change. What a pity that they do not know anything about their other lives. They cannot remember anything and keep asking me: Why don't we know anything of our former lives? But there is nothing in them, nobody who knows anything about it. Everything is gone, there is nothing left of those hundreds of lives.'

Alcar listened while André was speaking ardently and said: 'Do you think that everything is gone?'

'Yes, Alcar, because they can't remember anything.'

'Let me tell you that nothing at all is gone. You should have known

André. The soul descends into life on earth and passes into an other life. When the soul has the male organism in one life and descends into the female organism in the other, how could they accept that while they do not even understand death? How could they understand the depth of inner life on earth when they don't feel their own life? Everything is present deep down within them. You will experience that on this journey when it will become clear to you.'

'Is it on earth as it is on those higher planets, Alcar?'

'No, people living there know where they have lived and can experience and digest that, they know the depth of their life. All those people are cosmically conscious, clairvoyant and have various gifts, everything is different there. You just wait, André, it cannot be accepted yet on the planet earth, but one day they will. They won't understand that there were mediums in those days who had advanced that far and received this on earth.'

'Will that time come, Alcar?'

'Certainly, that time will and must come.'

'And you have come a few hundred years too early?'

'Yes, André, I told you already I am, and so are the others with me. Yet, one day they will realize and accept all this. Our work is not in vain, don't ever forget that. We have been able to convince many people and more will follow. This will gradually get through to inner life and people will acquire these treasures.'

'What do the masters say, Alcar?'

'My masters are satisfied, quite satisfied. Everything proceeds as desired, there is no disturbance, you are doing your best.'

'So I have only come to earth to serve you?'

'No, to make up as well.'

'So I have made many mistakes and have to make up for them? Do you know my mistakes, Alcar?'

'Yes, at any rate one big mistake.'

André bent his head. He thought as much, nothing for nothing. Work and pray, make up and serve. It cannot be otherwise.

'May I ask a question, Alcar?'

'Of course, André, do.'

'I would like to ask you whether I am making up for that big mistake, and if not, whether you would help me so that I can make up for it, while I am still on earth?'

'A good question, André. You have started already.'

'Thank God, and will I accomplish it?'

'Not only accomplish, but also overcome everything. Everybody, whoever it is, is on earth for a purpose or he would not be there any more. All make up, do something for others and are there for us or for themselves. If they are there for us, that life is taken advantage of in that man serves. At the same time something is made up and you too are making up. You receive something and serve me and not only me but also yourself and others.'

'It is wonderful that I may know this. Do you know that big mistake, Alcar?'

'Yes, I know that too.'

'It is amazing that you should know me entirely. I suppose you can't tell me what it is?'

'Yes, but I can't explain until later, when the time has come.'

'Then I'll wait, Alcar, and I am very grateful to you. How remarkable everything is, how can people ever accept this? You are going ever further. Will there be an end?'

'Yes, that end will come, when I have given you everything from this side. Then my task will be completed and what the masters wanted and intended to bring to earth will have been accomplished.'

'Is your work then finished?'

'Not quite, for there are some other things I have to do and for which I need your help.'

'Oh, you mean writing the books?'

'Yes, that is what I mean. What I would give; and you would receive, and belongs to my task, will then be accomplished.'

'Do you refer to the nine books?'

'All this work, André, is part of it. That is what the masters intended and what I was to pass on, that is why you are my instrument and it will then be accomplished.'

'So there remain no deeper problems on this side any more than those you are talking about?'

'I could fill dozens of books, for there is so much to be seen and experienced here to tell about it, but this is sufficient. In all these books man finds a clear picture of his death on earth, the return to and birth on earth and the amazing problem how God created everything, which you'll receive in three volumes. That is sufficient and if I'll tell you a bit more and record it through you, it will come, but I don't know yet, because I, too, am only an instrument. This, however, would and had to happen, the masters were certain about it.'

'It is remarkable, Alcar, that you have already advanced that far and that it is invariably known on this side what must and can happen, as against the questions 'why and what for' on earth. Here they know what they want and what can be done, whereas on earth they do not advance.'

'No, but they do not want to as I explained to you. People must accept and they will one day, we can only wait. So do not ask anything, even our highest Master did not ask anything and He was crucified. What then should we want? As I said, it is sufficient to convince one human being, but we have already convinced thousands of people; aren't you happy about that? When you are here forever you will really feel your happiness and later we will be understood. Then you are here with me and we'll make long journeys again for many years to come. Go on as you do, André, and we will both be happy. You know now why you are on earth. Later, as I promised, I'll show you some of your lives, as you would not be able to digest all of them and I can't follow them all. You will also get to know me and many other wonders.'

# CHAPTER III

## *Alcar's past*

M ANY wonders await you on this journey. I connected you each time with the past and I can always do that.'
'Where do we go now, Alcar?'
'To Egypt. I have lived there and I want to show you my life and that of my friend. I said on our previous journey that I met him there. A quarrel separated us and he lost his life through it. However, I'll pass on to that time later; first I have to explain some other conditions. I'm going back thousands of years and during those thousands of years I lived on earth several times. During the first life that I'm going to follow I had the female organism. That is an amazing and incredible problem, but every human being who enters here will experience it.

I also pass on in other lives and that is the most incredible of all, though it is the truth. It is merely for the soul, the soul must experience that or we would not advance. I explained that to you. Inner life must develop and that is only possible when we can experience the plan of creation which requires human organisms.'

'So, after all, that material body is only of secondary importance, Alcar?'

'Yes, André, but haven't you known that for a long time? However marvellous and mighty that earthly body, is it is not important any more and will die. New people, new material bodies are constantly coming on earth, invariably occupied by the same souls, never by others. We know that inner life was born on the first cosmic degree and had to follow that million process. The earthly material organism is subjected to the process of decay, the soul returns to the spheres and will wait. That process goes on, has been going on for millions of years, and is still in progress. However, people on earth cannot accept it. In nature I could draw their attention to thousands of examples of reincarnations, in a germ, that minute seed, lives the multicoloured perfect flower. People know all that, but they do not reflect and do not feel that this wonder means reincarnation for the vegetable kingdom. It is no different for mankind and the animal kingdom.

This is where I wanted to be. This is where I lived, André. Here I gave birth to two children.'

'I beg your pardon? You gave birth to two children?'

'Do you find that incredible?'

'No, I don't, Alcar, but it is so remarkable.'

'Here, André, I cursed myself and others. This was my life and here I began to make up.

Look, André, I lived in that quiet environment on the edge of this forest.'

André felt himself sink away deeply, the present-day earth disappeared before his eyes and a different world, the past, revealed itself. Then he began to see. My God, he thought, how is it possible. In a simple hut he saw a human being, to the left and right animal skins were suspended. He understood what it meant.

'Now I connected you with the past, André, look at this mother.'

She was an old woman and she sat there quietly. A mountain of misery surrounded her; she was poor and embittered. There was hatred in her; he clearly felt that. It was quiet and he looked up at his leader. He dared not speak a word and he waited for what would happen.

Alcar said: 'I'm going to connect you with her. Try to feel her and ask me if you want to know something.'

André felt himself descend into this being. What am I going to experience now? he thought. There was terrible hatred in her. She thought of putting an end to her life, because she was alone and deserted. Where were her children? Now that he thought of it he immediately saw another image.

He heard Alcar say: 'I'm going back forty years and you will see what I was shown by the masters in the spheres.'

André now saw that she was much younger and he saw two children, a boy and a girl. This picture faded. He subsequently saw that some years had passed. The girl was ill and her mother sat beside her sickbed. She was preparing some herbs over a fire.

'An other image', he heard his leader say, 'that child will pass away.'

André saw it happen. How terrible it was for her. Somebody entered. It was a robust man who looked around and approached her. André was going to witness a remarkable event. The man spoke to the woman and André could understand those words. He could, because he felt what this being wanted to say. Before he had pronounced his words, André knew already what he was going to say. He asked Alcar how this was possible.

'We know no languages in the spirit, André. On this side one must feel and experience, merely feel and we are connected by those feelings and pass on into the human being. It makes no difference whether the event happened in the past and neither in the case of foreign languages, it is no impediment in our life, we connect by feeling and know what they think and want to say. You can follow him now in all his feelings.

Once I destroyed his life. Now he will destroy her, she will perish through sorrow and misery. She cannot endure all that misery. It breaks her heart. He is a hunter and he was famous for it in his time. This life was thousands of years ago, André, and yet we can see and experience it again. This child is going to die, André, and that event is also fixed and on time, this young life will pass away not a second too early or too late. Her husband, who was invariably away from home, stayed away when this child passed away. That was hard, very hard and he, too, will have to make up for that.

How can people forget themselves in that way? He loved someone else and he left her in all her misery. However, she received what she had once done to him, but he did wrong things again and that is what we are like as human beings when we do not understand ourselves. He should have stayed and waited for his end. Only God could have given him what he so dearly wanted, but he took it, lived his own life and thought of nothing else.

Some years went by. Her boy grew up and this child was also taken away from her. A wild animal killed it. Now she had nothing left, she was entirely on her own and deserted. Will she be able to cope? Will she be able to hold out? Has this soul already advanced that far and does she have those powers, which are spiritual property? Isn't this life terrible? We do not know the depth of inner life and we do not want to see the pit brimming with sins, and yet, we have to make up for those sins. However, she could not endure this, André, and she put an end to her life on earth. Look and observe, my boy.'

André saw this horrible scene. She had strung herself up. My God, what misery and he looked at his leader. Alcar was lost in thought.

It was long before he could speak and André said to Alcar: 'You have had to experience that, Alcar? You once put an end to your life? And now you are in the fifth sphere?'

'I am not ashamed of it, André, because I have made it up and have covered that long road. This happened once. I saw all this in the temple of the soul together with a lot of misery, when my own film of life was shown to me.'

André's eyes filled with tears. This moved him deeply. His leader was an angel of light and yet he had done it centuries ago. Alcar looked back at his past life and that required courage.

'I lived in this material body as an astral human being, André. I, a particle of God, lived in it, because I am spirit and man, I am soul and life. As a human being I did not feel love and my soul had to experience that. I lived, but I did not understand that life. I had to acquire it and to that end many other lives were needed. I had returned here to make up, but all that misery broke me and that's why I put an end to that life. As a result – and that will now be clear to you, I told you of the soul we followed, she also perished time and again – I did more bad than good and I had to experience this terrible mistake. My soul, I myself, was eaten up with hatred towards the one who did this to me. God could not possess love, for this was unbearable and I cursed Him and all those who spoke of Him. There was faith in me, though Christ had not yet come to earth. There were other prophets, however, and we had learned to know a God.

Can you sense my feelings, André? I will return to that time, you can feel that I am the one who lived in that material mother organism. What do you feel, André?'

'My feelings lead me from her to you, Alcar, I feel that very clearly.'

'That's correct, André. I descended in that time and accepted that life, my inner life of that time, for a while. We can pass on into it and we are as we then felt. I'll go on now and show and explain a bit more.

In this life I forgot myself, and what happened now, what happened to me and to my body? What happened to me will happen to every human being who puts an end to his life. I was attached to this material organism and had to experience the process of decay that Lantos described. This was my end on earth and my entrance into the spiritual world. Look at that corpse, André. Beside that material organism you see that other being, that astral one and that is the spiritual or inner life, which is I. I experienced being separated from my material organism and had to wait until it had decomposed.

That corpse was not found until months later and was buried. Here below is my material body, when it was buried this hut was pulled down and I was forgotten. This was the end of a human life on earth.

When my material body had decomposed after many years – Lantos*) described it and he did so for me, otherwise I would have had to give you a complete explanation - I wandered about in the astral world, an empty space, to which there seems to be no end. However, that end came and that world also dissolved for me and I entered the world of the unconscious. There I waited for a new body, because I had to proceed and be born again to make up. In this life, however, I had destroyed more than I had made good, although this life had not been in vain, which I could hardly understand or feel. I would have reached a very high age in that life, but I put an end to it when I was sixty-four years old and wandered about in silence for fifteen long years, the years I should have lived on earth. Lantos told you about that too, and I do not need to explain that to you.

Do you understand, André, to continue this subject for a while, why Lantos was allowed to tell about his life? He did so for me, because I had too much other work to do. In addition he could tell about his own experiences, for there was depth in his life and a mighty wonder which is reincarnation on earth, represented in Marianne.*) He told of his life on earth, his entrance into the astral world and what he experienced in the life of the spirit.

I said that after that long walk I dissolved in the world of the unconscious and waited for a new birth. If reincarnation would not be a fact and had not been created for the soul, if God had not given us that mighty grace, believe me, I would have had to live on in that empty space by myself, deserted. There would have been no change for me and those who put an end to their life on earth. How could I have left that world? Who could free me from it? No man and no soul, only God. But I was to receive a new body, because I still had to make up and to that end I came on earth again.

After having atoned, after having experienced that misery, because that deed had to do with that life, I returned to the earth and was born again. I'll refer to it later. Now we'll first follow this astral image so that you can see what I experienced. I'll pass on into a different condition.

You now see that I am free of my material body, we shall follow it.'

André observed. He saw the astral being beside the corpse and also that new life entered this lifeless mass. He subsequently saw this being moving away and Alcar followed his own shade.

*) See the book: 'The Cycle of the Soul'.

'A remarkable event, André, but horrible for those who have to experience it in reality.'

The astral human being wandered and so did his leader in his present spiritual attunement. It was an incredible scene. Alcar continued to follow his own shadow. If he was ever shown a miracle it was at this moment. If he was ever inspired with awe for God's holiness, it was by this event. My God, how deep everything is, how true Your life is. A human being as spirit, as life, followed the true and honest reality, the past walked in front of him. It was unbelievable and yet so natural. He felt both beings, from the being in front of him he got to that other human being, his leader Alcar. His leader was a spirit of light because he lived in the spheres of light, in a condition of pure happiness, but in front of him wandered nothing but sorrow and misery, that being had to perish out of ignorance and need. Oh, how horrible, André thought, though he felt the deep truth of this event.

André saw that she sat down and fell asleep immediately. That is how Lantos had experienced it and so had Alcar and perhaps he, too. He saw that she woke up and went on again, towards the unknown. André saw her go and followed her. He dared not look up any more, was that Alcar? It was nearly too much for him, he could hardly believe it, but he had to accept it. He looked at her again and saw her fall down. She then fell asleep again from exhaustion. Oh, he thought, such misery. Had this been shown to his leader in the spheres and did he have to experience that there? It was horrible. This being lay there, but he dared not ask questions now. Yet he felt an urge in him and he sensed that Alcar wanted him to ask.

André asked, looking in front of him: 'How long did this sleep last, Alcar?'

'It lasted for months, André.'

It is unbelievable, awful and horrible, he thought. Now he saw another scene. He saw she got up again and started her mad journey.

Alcar said: 'This journey lasted fifteen long years, André. I have experienced that, my son, and that is why I know what grief and sorrow and all other misery on earth means. There is no sorrow on earth, which I have not experienced. However, this was not enough for me. I had to suffer in many other lives, because evil had accumulated so alarmingly in all those hundreds of lives that I would have to return several times to restore my own spiritual balance. I had destroyed lives, made others unhappy and I had to make up for it. To this end I returned to the earth and would do so many times. All this misery, and this is the most awful thing we can experience, was not enough yet, because I had done this myself and did, therefore, not belong to my karma. There was more to come, because I had to make it all up, even the last wrong thought.

God oversaw everything, only God knows what His children have done in all those lives. In one life I was rich, here I was poor and later I had many worldly possessions again which made me perish, as I'll show to you presently.

When those fifteen years had passed, André, I dissolved, and an other world attracted me. Another wonder happened, my son, and you will also see and experience that wonder. She, André, in front of you, this human being dissolved and you know which world attracted her. She will live there and wait. She had to wait for hundreds of years to be attracted again. Yet, she had to go back to the earth, for all those people to whom she had to make up lived on the planet earth. And that wonder happened.

Now realize how natural everything is. You have seen how the universe condensed. I subsequently showed you how embryonic life condensed and dissolved, when one life passed on into the next. We have been able to follow that in everything from the initial stage. Condensation and dissolution, connection and attraction, birth and death, that is God's creation. This soul dissolved again and was attracted by an other world. Asleep and unaware of anything she would prepare to be born again. She is still a shadow of reality. Look, André, how she dissolves, how she gradually disappears, presently you will not see her any more.'

André watched it. He had got to know another wonder. It was awe-inspiring, like everything was awe-inspiring and wonderful.

'Now she is gone, my son, down into this deep darkness. I explained all this to you before, and now you have been allowed to experience this great wonder. She, this soul, returned to the first stage, although she was on earth as a human being. I myself descended into that world and was unaware of everything. An other world admitted me; I lived in it and came to rest. You will feel that now, André, take care and concentrate on me. Sit down, André.'

André did, as Alcar wanted. He sat down and felt sleep overwhelmed him. He looked at his leader and Alcar said: 'Do you feel sleep over-whelming you, André?'

'Yes, Alcar, very clearly.'

'I have connected you with this world and I can do so, because I experienced that. Is this clear?'

'Yes, quite.'

'Very well, I'll connect you completely and you will feel what this world actually is and means.'

André felt himself sink away still deeper, so that he became fully unaware. He subsequently felt himself regain consciousness, though that mysterious power detained him.

He heard a voice as from far away say: 'Do you hear me, André?'

What was that? He heard someone whisper his name, but he did not understand what it meant.

Again he heard: 'André, do you hear me? It is me, your leader and...' then he did not hear any more.

He did not know how much time had passed, when he woke up and opened his eyes, he saw Alcar.

'Where are we, Alcar? How did I sleep!'

'We are still in the same place and have not been away. What did you feel, André?'

'Sleep, and yet it wasn't. It was as if losing consciousness, something like that, Alcar.'

'Did you hear me speak?'

'Yes, but not clearly, it was very faint. As if from a great distance.'

'Do you know now what this world means? You did not even know any more where we were and you did not clearly hear me speak and yet I spoke very loudly.'

'I wanted to listen and it seemed as if your voice stopped and I sank away. Is that possible, Alcar?'

'Yes, that is correct, and you have only been in that world in an unconscious condition for a few seconds as compared with several cen-turies or even longer for others. The soul is finally attracted and will be born on earth. A blissful quiet resides in this inner life, it is not aware of anything any longer. Nothing but quiet and rest and yet this inner life is ablaze, it accommodates hatred, passion and violence. That rest is necessary, for if this inner life would be conscious, as I told you, it would suffocate the embryo into which it descends. Now you can comprehend this wonder, it is also open to us. The soul descends into the embryo as the spark of God and this, too, I explained to you on our last journey. Do you understand that this is necessary and that a new birth is a grace? And do you also feel that this has been so from the beginning of creation and that people can therefore not know anything about all those former lives any more? That inner life will awaken in the mother body and can only awaken therein as the child grows within the mother? Now isn't this a great wonder? You felt it yourself and could follow it.

Thus, in this world there are millions of lives, sparks of God. All are human beings, they once lived on earth and all will experience this, but are unaware of it in their next life on earth. You experienced a mighty wonder; a process of nature and this is the astral world and the world of the unconscious. Could you follow me in everything, André, and are there any questions about this subject, for I'll presently pass on into an other condition.'

'I have been able to follow this, Alcar, though I would like to ask you: What makes one fall asleep?'

'A very good question, André. I'll explain that as well. First of all you know that this world is unconscious, which means that we can't feel any more, in other words: we lose our life and consciousness. It is therefore a world in which no existence is possible. You still don't know what caused this condition, do you?'

'No, Alcar, I don't know yet.'

'It is quite obvious. This world, André, is the one – you should have known because I explained it to you – when we visited the first cosmic degree. When there was no life yet and the planet was not ready and embryonic life was yet to be born. Do you feel now what this world means?'

André thought for quite some time, but could not find the answer.

'I don't know, Alcar, you may find it terrible but I can't find out.'

'Thank you, my son, for your honest admission. You could have known, because I told you about it. You have seen and experienced it.'

'I have seen and experienced that world?'

'Yes, even in various ways.'

'On the first planet, Alcar?'

'Yes, there and nowhere else.'

André thought again and considered everything, but he could not find out. He looked at his leader and said: 'No, however much I try I don't know, it seems a mystery to me, a new problem.'

Alcar smiled and said: 'I'll help you, André, stop thinking. You could have known, though I can imagine your ignorance.'

'So you understand that I cannot feel or know it any more?'

'Yes, André, you are still living on earth, if you had been here, if you had discarded your material organism everything would be different. But listen. When we were in the temple of the soul and the masters connected us with the beginning of creation, what was the first phenomenon you saw?'

'I know the answer now, Alcar. You mean that darkness, the invisible cosmos?'

'Indeed, you see that you know, but you did not realize that we had to return that far and deep for this condition, that is the meaning of this world. So you return to nothingness. Is everything clear now?'

'It is a mighty wonder, Alcar, and I have no words for it. How is it possible, who would ever think of that? Having to return that far, to the very first stage of everything, no, I did not think of that.'

'You see that in many conditions we have to return to the initial stage in order to be able to answer many questions, for that's where the answer is found, the holy truth of everything. The soul has to return to the first stage to enable inner life to pass into the embryo. I have explained that to you, so I need not refer to it. That first stage is part of the darkness, before God revealed Himself. So there was no consciousness yet – I do not speak of God but of the human stage – and because there was no consciousness the soul is subjected to this activity when we enter here as human being, as spirit. You have been able to feel it, unconsciousness seized you. Is that so strange?'

'No, Alcar, I understand you perfectly. It is a revelation to me, a mighty and sacred wonder.'

'You will agree with me more than ever before that we human beings will return to the spark of God as inner and inspiring life, in order to pass on into the embryo.'

'What is the activity of my own material organism? Why didn't I think of this, what is the disturbance, Alcar?'

'You had better speak of an impediment than disturbance. The material organism still has that power to prevent you as a thinking and feeling being from complete transition, even though you have departed from your body. Do you feel that too?'

'Yes, Alcar, it is clear to me now. I feel that is the reason why I cannot penetrate to this depth, because my own organism prevents it and I experience feelings and actions.'

'Indeed, so it is. I am entirely free from earthly and material vibrations. I can connect myself, descend deeply into the past and I do not feel the slightest disturbance, because I belong to this life. The entire creation is open to me; I can through one condition follow the beginning and the end of human life. That will now be clear to you and we will go on. I'll just connect you with an other problem and that is also a wonder. I experienced that in my last life on earth when I was an artist. I am going to connect you with the one we just saw and who went away. That is possible from here. Look, André, at the man who left me and did not return any more, he was a terrible man in this life, but in the life preceding this one it was I who destroyed him. He also had to experience dozens of lives before he passed to his final life on earth.

In my last life on earth when I was an artist, and consequently many centuries later, this soul was my teacher of art. Who could ever have thought that, who could know this and who will accept it?'

'How is it possible, Alcar.'

'I have been able to follow all that in the spheres of light. He became famous and he will always be remembered on earth. Now just imagine that and stay in this condition. Who could ever have thought of that? If this had been his and my last life, if there was no reincarnation, neither of us would have become artists. Keep this picture of the future in mind and feel how mighty and deep it is. If God had not given us the grace of reincarnation, there would have been no change for him and for me.

Look at him. He already has an impulsive nature and he has every quality to become an artist. There he goes, this soul people cannot fathom. He hunts and goes on hunting till his dying day, though one day he will be a famous artist.

It was not until in the seventeenth century that we were on earth together and he was my master. We had already met in the spheres and there, too, he was my master. We were subsequently born and both accomplished a mission. Now imagine this, André, we would not accomplish that mission until thousands of years later. Wouldn't we be grateful to God? Observe my life and his. The earth will not forget us;

our art is here and will remain so.

Each of us, however, went his own way and I had not seen him in all those centuries. When this life was over, his soul, he himself, was attracted by other lives and he would make up. To that end he had to pass from one life on to another, from the male body to the female body. He would return to make up for everything, for all his mistakes and sins, and to leave something behind on earth during his final life. That is the wonder of reincarnation on earth, it is because our mighty Father in heaven gave us that grace.'

'What a wonder, Alcar. Did you know on earth that you had met him before?'

'No, it was not until I had reached the third sphere that all my lives were shown and also this one. On earth I did not know anything about it, nor did he, because we had not advanced that far.'

'What happens, Alcar, when everything has been made up?'

'Then auras will tear apart and hatred, jealousy and all evil dissolve and we can go wherever we like. We try to earn something, to make something of ourselves and that is when we receive grief and sorrow, we have to endure and experience, for that is the final making up.'

'Is it possible when we are confronted with fresh misery that we put an end to our life again?'

'No, we have experienced that. Lantos described that very clearly. He felt in the inner life of that unfortunate mother that she contemplated suicide, but Lantos saw that it was impossible. Master Emschor made him feel that. She could not put an end to her life a second time, she had done that before and as a result of which one learns. That same knowledge was in me, for many times I was on the verge of suicide again, because I had to make up in those other lives and was faced with a lot of misery, but I could not resolve to do it and I experienced all that misery. Such a deed and experience leaves a deep wound in the human soul. That struggle and sorrow reside in us, but we are not aware of it and our deep inner-self refuses, it causes a halt because we have experienced that terror. However miserable life on earth may be, we'll never be overcome by suicide when we have experienced that process of decay, which seriously wounds our inner life.

That very power protects us in other lives and we see that grief and misery strengthen us, that we mentally grow through them and that we acquire spiritual property through the life we experience.

We make many mistakes, André, but once a mistake or deed has deeply penetrated our inner life, I assure you, we won't let it happen a second time, because we have had to suffer so much from it.

When I committed suicide, which I did not understand at all, it protected me several centuries later when I was confronted by the same problem and if I had not experienced it before, I would have forgotten myself again. For we learn, even though we think that it is not possible, because we do not know the depth of our inner selves. One day we shrink from making the same mistakes, André. Nevertheless, we often make the same mistake, but in time this comes to an end. When a human being puts an end to his material life, it is the very, very last thing we can do. The deep sorrow within us, the horrible event we had to experience can never be forgotten and inner life will warn us even in unconsciousness. When we receive misery and sorrow again, that experience will manifest itself and we feel a contradictory force develop within us, which are the experienced misery and all that sorrow of former lives.

If we could not return, it would be impossible, for it is exactly in the material organism that inner life awakens and man will experience that for which he has received an other new body. Is that clear, André?'

'Yes, Alcar, everything.'

'Then we'll go on, come and follow me.'

New wonders had been explained to André, one wonder was even mightier than the other. What misery! And yet, Alcar was happy now. How great God was to tell all this apart. How mighty everything was. Not one human being could oversee all that on earth, this should be experienced on this side.

Floating through space, Alcar went on and André felt curious what he was going to experience. How his leader had suffered. Now he really understood why Alcar knew about all that misery on earth. Through misery the soul awakened and man passed on to other conditions. Thousands of lives had been experienced before man could take leave of the earth forever. How could people on earth ever accept this? Yet it was all so simple and natural, or life would come to a standstill and man was after all a Divine being. When would we ever get there? He had seen enough of this life and he understood that this could not be attained in one life. Some people faced a high mountain of sins and mistakes. For instance, all those people who tortured and killed others. Not one human being, but thousands. Wouldn't they have to make up for that? Could they do that in one single life on earth? In that life in which they had destroyed those people? He accepted everything and fully understood Alcar.

'Do you only follow your last lives, Alcar?'

'Yes, André, I'll explain some of my lives on earth to pass on to my final life, in order to give you a clear picture of what I want to show you. I cannot follow all my lives, because we have lived in thousands of conditions. That would be too much and is not necessary either. I'll explain some lives in which I was connected with my friend. The many other lives have an entirely different meaning, they were important but without depth. I'll follow one course and I'll presently explain other wonders to you. I therefore follow what will be sufficient for you to get a clear picture of reincarnation. Naturally, I will not follow the lives in which I was a living dead, for thousands of lives passed in that way. So you see that I was a living dead too and I have nevertheless reached the spheres of light.

You will also realize that life on earth serves to acquire feeling, merely feeling which becomes the alleviating and healing love which supports others and it is not until then that we live the way God wants us to. We must acquire pure and absolute love, which requires thousands of lives on earth. Man on earth is unaware of all those lives which is a mighty grace, for human strength, our nervous system, is not designed to bear all that sorrow consciously.

Look, André, we are now in an other part of the world, in the Far East.

My parents lived here and I'll show that to you. I must explain some other conditions to you. Ask me if anything is not clear enough. I'm going to connect you with the past, at present our house no longer exists. You will observe, though, for that is fixed.'

André felt himself sink away and pass on into an other world. He saw a large building. An ancient building decorated with towers and figures appeared in front of him. A remarkable scene now developed. His leader entered that building and he followed. His leader halted in a large hall, after having passed through various smaller rooms.

'Look, André, a mother and her child.'

André saw both beings and he looked at this image in amazement. How remarkable, he thought, what a mighty wonder!

He heard Alcar say: 'This mother was my mother, André, and this life precedes the one I just showed you. In this life, however, I experienced hatred and violence and I destroyed him who enters there.'

At the same moment André saw a human being enter.

'My father, André, and I destroyed him. In a vicious way I put an end to his life on earth. I pass into this condition just now because I wanted you to know him and to understand why I had to make up. I also defiled my mother's life, though she was ahead of us on the spiritual way. I have made up to my father and will make up to my mother although in an other life. I now come to the most remarkable thing of all these lives. Do you feel what I'm about to say?'

'No, Alcar, I don't know.'

'Look and think, my son. There, in that other life I was a mother, his wife, here I was his child and had the male organism.'

'My God, why didn't I think of that, Alcar?'

In astonishment André looked at his leader and did not know what to say.

'It is a wonder, André, a sacred wonder. What more should I say? I could fill volumes on this subject, tell about cause and effect, the attraction and repulsion of both souls, but above all about the wisdom of God our Father, Who brought all this about; I could not otherwise have served and made up for my mistakes. Everything dissolves; I don't have to explain any more. I was tortured; I put an end to my life because he left me. I suffered terribly and so did he. But this is not God's will, André, this is cause and effect, wonders of laws of nature which we only know on this side, but experience as human beings on earth. I deceived and robbed my mother. We were rich in that life and possessed everything man can think of in life on earth. After my father's death I left and did not return. I perished in that life and my mother died of grief. Thus I had killed both. I was not punished on earth; I could not be punished, because I killed him in solitude. Yet, one Power knew and watched my deed. God knew, though God did not punish me. Oh, how I did pray when I understood that deep problem, but it was not until in the spheres of light; there I bent my head and thanked God for everything.

God did not punish me; to the contrary, I received a new body and was born again. How was my life? He could do with me whatever he wanted and the punishment I received at his hands was, as compared with what I had done to him, a blessing. If I had not committed suicide, deep human sorrow would have been my lot, but that should not have been necessary. Herein resides an other problem. Hundreds of laws are associated with it, André, but I cannot explain all those laws, as it would lead too far. Why did he not kill me? I had killed him before, hadn't I? That force is not present in nature, it is a law of God and God does not know hatred. Something quite different happened, because I served, I had to serve for I became a mother. By this motherhood, giving birth, by carrying his life which I endured, I made up. I owed that to him and I made up. I gave myself completely and no human being on earth knows this depth, for it is part of God's wisdom and All-love. Should I want to explain this big problem to you, I would be connected with the universe, with infinity, cause and effect and thousands of laws. I could explain it, though, for we have experienced these wonders and laws ourselves. He left me because he did not need me; he, too, would have to make that up all the same. Listen, my son, and realize how deep all this is. He also had to make that up, for a spirit of the light acts differently, cannot act the way he did. Thus, God gave me all this and I cursed Him, Who is nothing but love. That is how we all are: all His children and still God loves us, God gave us His own life. Have you understood this, André?'

'Yes, Alcar, I am ever more bending my head for everything.'

'I am very grateful to you, André, we will go on and you'll see an other wonder. Come, follow me.'

André was deeply lost in thought. Who knows himself: who dare say, I'm good, I know, I feel it, it is true? For him all this was a lesson, a lesson of life that he would never forget. He could not ask any more questions on that subject, he did not know how to think. People on earth were like that and they were unaware of all these wonders and laws. God, yes, who knows God? Not one human being on earth knew God, for they would also know all these laws and wonders and that was not possible.

'Look, my son, we are in an other country, this time in the West. My parents lived in the country and worked hard to make a living. Why would I be born here? Who attracted me? I'll show you.'

André began to see.

'How is it possible, Alcar. Is she your mother again?'

'Yes, André. It was she who attracted me; I had to make up to her.

413

Who connects us? Is it God? Is it a law? If so, that law and also God are infallible, because hundreds of years have passed. Now isn't that in itself a great wonder, that two souls find each other on that large planet? Can we human beings ever assess these laws and wonders? I ask you, did God want me to return to her? Problems again that we cannot solve, for we do not know these laws although we experience them.

Isn't it amazing, André, because I destroyed the life of these two beings on earth. I did not think of any laws or a God, I only thought of my own life. Yet I was born here, but we did not have all that wealth. This time my father was a different soul, he was a stranger to me, but my mother had to do with him. Now what happened in this life? I'll tell you about it, listen.

When my mother carried me, so she had the female body again, she fell into a pit. This happened between the fourth and fifth month. Apparently nothing was wrong, but a few months after I was born she got into trouble and could not walk any more. She received help and I grew up. My father passed away when I was fourteen and my mother and I were left behind. I had no connection with my father, André, in other words I did not have to make up to him, only to my mother and that's why she would meet him. So you see that we have to experience many problems.

I said just now that my father passed away when I was fourteen years old. We both remained behind and I cared for this soul, I worked for her and did my best day and night until I was thirty. When I was thirty years of age she also passed away. She had suffered much though it was not her final life; she had to return to the earth and to other lives. I would meet her once more, which was in Jerusalem, though many centuries later. I will refer to that later when I have got that far, I'll now proceed with my own life.

So I met both beings and did for them what I should do. Our souls attracted one another and it is not God, but the law of cause and effect that brings all this about. Something invisible connects the human being; sorrow caused to others calls us to a halt.

I also had the female body. I connected with a being and a child was born. It was a girl and the soul living in that material organism once became my friend. From that time on I see this life again several times and I therefore has to do with this inner life. I had met this soul before, thousands of years ago, when I stole her love. I had lived many lives again, and met and ruined other beings and experienced that karma but now this karma would have to dissolve, though not until many centuries later. These laws had not yet taken effect, because my own lives dominated this karma and we get to know other powers and laws. Do you feel, André, how amazing this is? Do you feel that a different power dominates this karma, for what happened?

An illness taking a heavy toll on life on earth, broke this family and I was once more left behind. Had I not suffered enough yet? Had I not fully made up to my father and mother? I was confronted by a new problem, for I faced my own life, suicide. I thought of suicide, I wanted to put an end to my life, because I was entirely alone on this big earth. Just imagine that life, my son, feel what it means having to live it. I found God terrible and destructive and I won't repeat the words with which I cursed God. And yet, André, you do feel how God guards all His children and that we human beings cannot understand that, although this awakening is to show what I wanted. I remained alive; I did not put an end to it and died an elderly woman. I had not put an end to my life but wandered about lonely and deserted, for something made me stay and that is what I explained to you. I would awaken in my own life. Something within me resisted all that misery. Do you feel how we awaken, André? Finally the end of my life on earth came; I passed on and entered the world of the unconscious again. However, I was to return many times. I returned to the earth; now we'll leave here and I'll explain an other life to you.'

'It is all so remarkable, Alcar.'

'Indeed, André, you see that we have to prove what we want.

This law dominated my own life and that other karma and yet I was again connected with my friend, though this tie was broken again and we both passed away. I, however, had to show what I wanted, I had already experienced that activity, that earlier life, but I was not entirely free of it and was still connected with that life. I was left behind which is also amazing, for why I should be left behind and not the others? For me, however, this karma should be dissolved. I had to prove what I wanted to bear my sorrow or perish again. I did provide that evidence; I felt that invisible power and that power dominated my own life. That is the All-Father. He guards and forces His own life upwards, and although this life receives misery, it has to go through it, or its development would come to a standstill and would not advance any more.

Consequently, that life was only for myself, but I had not earned any-thing yet.

We now see, André, that one life may be faced with many problems and that we do not know these problems. Nevertheless, everything has its meaning. If we are prepared to bear, there will be an end to all that misery sooner or later, for there must be an end to it, because we have to pass on into other lives and make up in them as well.

We are now going to the North, where I also received the female organism. I had to make up to the one who attracted me there. I had destroyed him as well, but in quite a different way. I had broken him inwardly.

You see, André, one problem follows the other and it often has to do with the previous one. Try to feel all this deeply. In that previous life I met my mother and made up what I had to make up. My friend, my own child died at an early age, yet I was again connected with that soul. What I want to point out is this: in one life I met three beings, I had to make up to all of them and I also experienced my own karma. It will now be clear to you that I can't follow all my lives as we could not tell one life apart from the other. But there is more, for why did this child pass away so soon? Why did that other being who was my husband pass away? Why was I left behind? Problems again, but we know now that my feelings to commit suicide dominated. Who provides for all this? Who wants us to experience that and who looks after this cosmic order? I don't have to explain all that to you, we could follow that in everything. We must accept it and have to experience all these prob-lems.'

'It is very complicated, Alcar.'

'Nevertheless, God's order resides in it, we just have to follow it. When I began to explain my lives to you, I told you that I would only show you those lives in which I had to make up. However, in every life we make mistakes and sin again and that must also dissolve, for I was left behind.

We made a scanty livelihood in the far North. My father was a fish-erman. I was already cursed upon my birth, for he wanted to have a boy and he was not given a son. Look, André, there you see me in this environment. How could you ever feel that other life in the Far East and yet, that urge, power and desire reside in the inner life. My father was sturdy and wild and embittered both our lives. He attracted me for

I had destroyed him in an other life. My life and my mother's were messed up and when he was at home we were nagged from early morning till late at night. He was worse than an animal. That lasted for several years. My mother perished and I remained behind with him. I had to go through that until I was thirty-five. That life was awful. Again we get to know new wonders, because in this life I made up as a child. My mother's karma dominated mine and she passed away a broken-hearted woman and nothing could be seen or felt of my inner life. Then God interfered and I got off. I married when he did not return. I got happy. Three children were born, but I had no connection with any of them. These ties belong to him who was my husband. All these beings experienced their material degrees and you know what that means. We experience other problems of life, connections for inner man. This life passed in peace and quiet and I entered the world of the unconscious. Once again I would return to the earth. In all those conditions I had acquired mother love and I proceeded to the creative power. In one life I received wealth, in another I had to create my own condition. In one life it took hundred of years before I was born again, in an other less time passed before I received a new body. This also has a cosmic meaning, but I won't follow that now.

I subsequently experienced an other life, which was in Egypt again when the pyramid was built; we'll go there soon. All these souls with whom I had to do, André, followed various other lives and experienced various problems, their own karma and they also had to make something of themselves. There is not one human being, listen what I say, who will meet lives, souls, he has nothing to do with. Do you feel what that means?'

'You mean to say that we only meet those people with whom we have to do?'

'Indeed, only those to whom we have to make up. All those other people, all those millions on earth, experience their own karma and meet people whom they have to do with; they are their fathers, mothers, brothers or sisters, for one law brings them together and that is the law of cause and effect.'

'How remarkable that is, Alcar, and also how natural.'

'It is, my son, every human being has to make up for his own sins and mistakes and can only do so to those to whom they brought grief and misery. God does not permit them to meet one single human be-

417

ing with whom they have nothing to do. This also shows God's Justice. On the other hand they cannot miss out any human being, for all sorrow or misery must dissolve and we know how that happens. These laws are infallible and no human being can evade them.'

'There is hardly any home without sorrow, Alcar, have all those people to do with one another?'

'Yes, André, they met in the past, that sorrow will dissolve now even though they may think that God curses them. Follow life on earth, you now see through all that misery and you understand that all are making up.'

'It is amazing, Alcar, how natural everything is.'

'It is not until all those people have made up that they start working on themselves and that is to acquire nourishment for the mind. We'll first of all meet those souls to whom we have brought the deepest misery, as that karma dominates. We'll subsequently follow other conditions and everything will dissolve as a matter of course.

There are conditions into which man has brought himself and has to wait for thousands of years before he awakens. I'll explain that to you in the dark spheres, in the hell, as I promised to visit the rulers of evil, those who violated all laws.

Come, André, we'll leave, I can answer your questions on our way.'

'Where are we going now, Alcar?'

'To Egypt, to the pyramid, for it is in that country that I received a new material organism. In that life, as I said, I got to know my friend. We were both on earth, but a quarrel separated us during which he lost his life.'

'Why are Orientals open for reincarnation and why do we in the West know so little about it?'

'The feeling of all these people is closer to nature than that of the Westerners. That is an arch-instinct into which they pass on. I told you about that. The Westerners cling to a dogma and need that because they have discarded those first stages of feeling, they have advanced further and higher in a material condition, but lost their natural attunement. As man advances an other condition gradually awakens, though he moves further away from his first stages, the arch-instinct. These beings live in those first stages and also in the very highest, and they feel mysticism in everything and they have their own God. People living in the jungle have often advanced far more and are closer to nature

418

than those who have attained the highest organism on earth. Their natural feelings bring them closer to God than the intellectual people on earth. They are children of nature and have remained so in everything. The intellectuals, the more civilized peoples have acquired different powers, but they have discarded the powers of nature and with those powers and qualities their inner feeling. Man in the East lives with the soul of the deceased and consequently accepts the inner personality.'

'Is it known for certain on this side where the soul will be born, Alcar?'

'Yes, André, but only the masters can connect themselves with it. I told you about it. However, it is not in our hands and neither in theirs. It is subject to the most remarkable laws we know.'

'How has God arranged everything, Alcar.'

'There isn't the slightest disharmony in anything, my son. There is order in all those laws, the order of the All-spirit. Only we violate these laws, for when we have to make up, we don't accept but ask why and what for and put an end to that life, because we think that dead is dead.'

'If I understand you correctly, Alcar, there is not one human being on earth who did not put an end to his life on earth?'

'Yes, André, that's right, all of us murdered and destroyed and when our own karma calls us to a halt, we put an end to our life. Then, however, we experience other laws, laws that have to do with that deed and we see that we live. I want to tell all this to mankind, I want to open their eyes and guard them from their own ruin. As I said before, if I can reach one human being I'll be satisfied. It is a mighty grace to guard one human being from all that misery. We all put an end to our life on earth, without exception. We all asked why and what for and cursed God in heaven and yet we have learned to understand ourselves, we now live in the spheres of light and others have already reached the All. Such is our life, in this way inner man awakens.'

# CHAPTER IV

## *The pyramid of Gizeh*

W HAT kind of building is that, is that the pyramid? Why was that pyramid built, Alcar?'

'I'll tell you, André. It is very remarkable, yes, and it is Divine. It is absolutely a great and sacred wonder and this wonder is not understood nor felt, although they are now trying on earth to unscramble that Divine mystery. That building, André, represents a Divine mission.'

'A Divine mission you say? Can a stone building have that power and was it built on earth for that purpose?'

'Yes, it was built there to announce the birth of Jesus Christ, but there is a lot more which is not yet known on earth. I told you about it on our last journey and now I am going to explain that to you. The high-priests and scientists of those days together with their king knew all about it, but the priests received that great truth from this side, for they were assisted from this side. I told you that in those days everything was received from this side and that mankind must now acquire these treasures which it began centuries ago. In those days the priests were already in connection with our side. It is not known on earth why and how they had advanced that far, only we living on this side know. How it all happened is not known on earth. At present, in your time, there are no such scientists on earth, although they have achieved much. Yet, many centuries ago, there were people on earth who had advanced that far. That is a wonder indeed, for these people who were capable of understanding a Divine construction do not live on earth any more and cannot be born again. I said already that it was envisaged to convince mankind and this happened as follows.

The cosmic masters descended from the seventh cosmic degree to the sixth and brought this mission. This happened in the same way we received that other mission as you were shown in the temple of the soul. This mission subsequently reached the fifth cosmic degree and these masters then communicated with the fourth cosmic degree and passed this Divine mission on to them. Finally it reached the third cosmic degree, the mentors of which set themselves the task, as they were meant to do to bring this mission to mankind on earth.

A Divine mission had thus descended from feeling to feeling, from master to master, out of the very highest and had reached the earth.

In those days mankind was ahead of our time, although only for this event.

That message was to be brought on earth, to that end people were required to serve as instruments on earth, people who possessed this sensitivity, learning, intuition and other talents and had acquired them as inner property. Only human beings could receive and accomplish this. Among the people living in those days were the greatest scientists that ever lived. Among them was the high priest who had the general management. This message, however, could not be given to one human being, many people were required. The people of Egypt fully understood that task. Now what happened? The Divine Man would be built from stone. Not only materially, but also spiritually and Divine. This building was to represent Christ as the perfect Divine Being. The building would not only encompass the life the Divine Human Being was to experience on the planet earth, but also eternal life and the Divine attunement. That was the way this building had to be erected. In the first place to announce the coming of Christ, secondly to represent His sacred life and thirdly mankind would possess something related to the existence of the earth. The priests were under the direction of capable spirits and all were up to their task. They received the inspirations and indications from this side and the scientists had to look after the construction and supervise it. The high priest received the entirety symbolically, and the scientists materially. I know that twenty-five human beings have worked on the pyramid and have accomplished this Divine event.

When they had received all their messages the actual construction started. This side guarded the overall process and their instructions were obeyed on earth. Consequently, no mistakes were made in the construction of this mighty building.

As I said, this building encompassed first of all the coming and birth of Christ. The Saviour would be born on time, not a second too early or too late, in addition, his life and suffering, his death at the cross, resurrection and the return to God. The pyramid also represents the problem of mankind, as man on earth, as spiritual being and the Divine attunement. This building not only encompasses the entire mankind but also all events man on earth would experience. Thus, the masters looked ahead thousands of years. There is no end to the pyramid, although people in your time think they can attain it. That is not possible. Thousands of years will pass and the deepest meaning of the pyramid will not have been established because it cannot be determined, except for the cosmic masters. It is a Divine mission, it is perfect.

The pyramid was erected in the centre of the earth. This had to be, because God also occupies a place in the entire and inner universe and that also applies to the perfect Child of God, though not only for that reason.

Condensation on the first planet started from the centre and this also happened on earth. The first human beings were born out of it, all power and energy was concentrated there. The Divine and perfect Child of God was to be born in the centre of the earth and from this centre people flocked to all corners of the earth and settled there.'

'How remarkable that is, Alcar.'

'Yes, it is remarkable, André, just imagine this work. Look, we are now where I wanted to be, the centre of the earth. Here are many pyramids and also the pyramid I mean.

It stands here like the Divine Human Being and it shows us the way towards perfection. I helped to build it, André, though I was no scientist, no priest, I was one of the supervisors and helped. It encompasses thousands of wonders. Stone was available, though what it took to transport those tons of stone to the site and to move them up is indescribable, for in those days there were no machines. Even if they had been available their use would not have been allowed, for man had to sacrifice his own flesh and blood. To that end one gave oneself completely. The whole of Egypt was engaged in it, everybody did something and wanted to help. It was there that I met my friend, but there was an accident and he fell down.

You may have wondered whether the people of that time had such a sensitive and pure connection with us, the spiritual world, and whether they were such great mediums, for those people could not accomplish this by their own doing. Man who had attained the highest material degree, I told you about it, had not advanced enough yet to understand a Divine mission, not to mention this wonder, this Divine structure. Isn't that strange? People on earth search and wonder, they admire these builders, scientists and priests, for among them were the geniuses of the earth, who would never be born again.

I repeat, André, what I said before, we shall never see these scientists on earth again. They cannot be born any more, and why not? Why had those mathematicians, those astronomers and priests so endlessly advanced to feel and calculate this depth? What gave them these high feelings, civilization and exceptional intuition? Had these people already advanced that far and have we declined? I could go on, André, and ask you hundreds of questions, but nobody on earth can answer them. They admire those who accomplished this and rightly so, for the pyramid of Gizeh is a Divine wonder, a Divine revelation. It was erected in stone, the coming of the perfect Child of God was fixed in stone, as were a lot of other wonders, but that was the main thing.

I ask you, has science declined, are those scientists no longer on earth? No, André, they will not return to earth again, all those artists, all those scientists in feeling had come to the earth and were born solely for this event. These beings had reincarnated and they came like Christ came and this monument would be ready for Him. Do you feel what I mean? I'll now return in the spirit.

When that Divine message had reached the third cosmic degree, that is the mentors of the third cosmic degree, but the seventh sphere on this side, it was deliberated. One of them had to return to the earth and would be born in Egypt. That being became a high priest. Many others would come with him. They all came to the earth for one purpose: to build a Divine monument, which meant a Divine task. Thus, all those spiritually perfect beings accomplished a tremendous task in stone and the perfect Human Being Jesus Christ brought Himself.

Those who do not accept this, do not feel that these beings who had to calculate such a Divine event and represent it in a cosmic symbolism, to which man is bound from his youth up to his end on earth. One could not do it if it did not imply a wonder. This encompasses the wonder of reincarnation because all of them were born.

In the spheres I saw them go to the earth, that was also shown to me. In the spheres it was deliberated, arranged and calculated how this wonder would be created. This was accomplished in the seventh sphere and the mentors of the seventh, sixth, fifth and fourth sphere descended to the earth to study. The amazing wonder happened. The pyramid represents many wonders, but the deepest wonders we know on this side are not understood.'

'How is it possible, Alcar?'

'I am telling you the holy truth, André. All those mathematicians, all those gifted people, those priests among whom the high priest, a master of the seventh sphere, the astronomers, who had continued and completed their study on this side, who as spiritual beings could visit all those planets, who had learned the activity thereof and owned all this as their property, were born on earth.

Isn't that a great wonder? The mentor of the seventh sphere supervised this mighty plan and was the connection with this side. All those spiritual beings received a new material body and the place where they would be born was determined in advance. Thus, all were born on earth, which was only possible by way of two human beings, the male as creative being and the female as the driving and serving organism. Imagine this wonder, André. They all came on earth to accomplish this. What had been decided beforehand was effected infallibly.

On this side everything was ready, everybody had his own task and was up to it. I have seen the spheres where they lived; this is also preserved on this side. They were together all the time, everybody followed his own way and they knew what awaited them. Years of preparation and meditation went by. During those years this structure took shape and was completed but still only in the mind.

Finally this awe-inspiring process could be started. They dissolved in the world of the unconscious one after the other and waited for the moment of attraction, one after the other was born on earth in Egypt, where this building would be erected. They were all born to parents who had the means to allow their child to study, and, above all, were attuned to their inner level. Every soul, mathematician or priest followed his own way, which was allocated to him beforehand on this side. They would not be able to qualify for anything else. The mathematician completed his study and so did the astronomer, the priests were trained for their priesthood and the mentor with his king were in charge.

Just imagine that! Everything happened according to plan and the work could be started. They were all there and were quite unaware, the connection with the Side Beyond had yet to be established, and eventually was. The high priest received that connection together with all other priests. He departed from his body and received his instructions from this side, it was explained to him what was to happen, like I explained everything of our life to you.

424

Slowly, they awakened and became conscious and the spiritual veil was lifted from them, so that they knew why they had come on earth. This mighty wonder, my son, you'll also experience in its entirety on this journey. That is what they were on earth for and for nothing else. The mentor of the seventh sphere supervised this Divine work, but who were his leaders? Can you imagine, can you feel that, André?'

'No, Alcar, I can't.'

'I'll tell you. The preparation they all had received in the spheres was also necessary on earth. There they also needed years of meditation before the spiritual connection was established. All cosmic degrees were subsequently connected, which means that all degrees, all those planets received one connection. From the highest heaven, the seventh cosmic degree, instructions came through to the sixth, fifth and fourth cosmic degree and the mentors of the fourth cosmic degree communicated with the earth. This, however, was the only time in the history of mankind that a higher cosmic degree established a direct connection with the earth. It was possible for this purpose and that is why this structure is Divine.

The cosmic masters of the fourth cosmic degree remained in communication with the earth until the pyramid was completed. They received their messages from the fifth, sixth and seventh cosmic degree which are the Divine Spheres. I explained all this to you so that you can understand it.

When everything was ready and meditation and the spiritual connection had been completed, actual work was started. I said already that the stone material was available, for they were also shown on earth from this side where this material could be found. Everything tallied perfectly, but the actual building was a superhuman task, though they received support. By inspiration they received the simplest means to move the stone blocks up which weighed several tons. Yet many people perished and were crushed.

As I said, many wonders are represented in the pyramid. In the first place the coming and birth of Christ, His sacred life and death. In addition I told you that all events on earth, the entire mankind up to the last human being who will live on earth, are laid down in this building. Also the development of the earth and, besides, the pyramid represents the universe, all the cosmic degrees and the orbit of the various planets. In short, the entire creation is fixed in the pyramid, also what

425

we now follow, what you have experienced, man as the creator of darkness and light, everything, everything is fixed in the pyramid.'

André had listened in admiration and looked at that stone structure which predicted the course of events.

'So thousands of years have been looked ahead, Alcar?'

'Yes, and only those who know and control material life can do that. They are the cosmic masters.'

'It is incredible and yet one has to accept it, Alcar.'

'There is more, André. Beneath the pyramid is a second building. However, nothing is known of that. There are many corridors there, which are related to the entire monument. In addition, every block of stone has its own meaning. In your time the depth of the pyramid has been discovered and time and again people will be born who will reveal it. Every century has its own meaning. Every century will see human beings penetrate a little further into this cosmic mystery. That is also fixed and all those beings will be born at the right time. According to the bible the pyramid can be unveiled, but also in the bible profound truths and realities have been falsified because nature and the cosmic meaning were not understood. Every scientist who makes a study of this will and cannot go further and deeper than he has feeling. You no doubt feel that later, when they accept eternal and cosmic life, scientists will have advanced much further, they will penetrate ever deeper to unveil this Divine mystery than those who are at present engaged in it. A scientist who does not know anything of cosmic life and cannot accept reincarnation will never get through to the deepest meaning, because death will call a halt again and he will not proceed beyond the depth of his own life.

This, however, has been accomplished for every human being, for we all have to follow Christ and it is only through him that we can attain the All, which is called the King's chamber. That is the utmost a human being can achieve, but we know how deep everything is, that we proceed ever further and that it is laid down in the pyramid. I could write volumes on this subject, but that is not the intention. You do feel, André, how wonderful and deep everything is. This is beyond description, I would not be able to do that by myself, for I would have to visit all those cosmic degrees and look ahead thousands, nay millions of years, which I can't. As I said, I could nevertheless fill volumes, merely relating what has to do with my own attunement.'

426

'Are all those terrible events, like war, also fixed in the pyramid, Alcar?'

'Yes, the last terrible massacre mankind on earth experienced was also calculated on the dot. The course and evolution of the earth and of mankind is calculated and fixed. As I said, they had a comprehensive view of everything, these gifted beings, who were to come to the earth with that task. But this does not apply to the normal earthly and material human being, for he has not advanced that far yet. From time to time, as I said just now, people will be born on earth who will reveal part of the pyramid. That will gradually proceed and the human condition can be calculated for every human being and as long as there are people living on earth, for that is fixed. However, it is not possible to calculate the end of all things. Time and again this stone structure will be there, and call a halt to man, for on earth only good and evil, light and darkness dominate. This building, André, represents the resurrection of the Divine Man. All misery is laid down in this building. This building represents good and evil, like man is in his life. One road ascends through this stone structure which is the way indicated by our highest Master Jesus Christ, the way we all have to follow in order to enter the All.

Isn't it remarkable that we find everything I explained to you on our three journeys represented in this building? It encompasses man and his Divine attunement, that man must become 'man'.'

'What kind of statue is that, Alcar?'

'That is the sphinx. Those who sense that statue feel and understand the pyramid. The sphinx demands, calls, compels us to come to ourselves and to descend into ourselves. Only then are people allowed to enter here. It says: 'Man, know yourself, become what I am, hear what I have to say.' Man, however, does not listen. This statue has a deeper meaning and has to do with the bible. Look at this face, André, and feel what it wants to say. Listen, it has to tell a lot, though few people understand it.

This is meant for man, but man passes by and enters. The sphinx calls us to a halt and says: 'Up to here and no further and bend your head. You, children of God, look at me, all of you who want to enter here.'

André saw that his leader knelt down and so did he. He listened attentively to what his leader said: 'Like the universe is and God's own life is the true love within you. You are a God of love, take my sins away and allow me to approach you. My heart belongs to you and our Father in heaven. I shall try to achieve what you demand of me. I'll bend my head for that is what you want. I see that you are smiling. You make me feel that I understand you and accept your life. Through you I receive true life and I enter reality. In your shadow I'll learn to understand my own life and to love my God. God is within you. Eternal life resides in you. May God give people on earth the grace to know you. We shall try to get the better of ourselves and to discard ourselves completely and ask you to open our eyes. May God help us. Amen.'

It is Christ's wish, my son, to understand this wonder, otherwise it would be better to stay away from this mighty building. An all-embracing love radiates on us and on all those who enter here, and we will have to acquire this all-overpowering love. Through the sphinx we learn to know God in heaven, and as a child of God, as a particle thereof, ourselves. That is laid down in this structure and it is the meaning of the pyramid.

There is an other wonder which I will explain to you. Look at this building, André, look up to the highest part of it. Don't you see anything strange at the pyramid?'

André looked up and said: 'No, Alcar, I don't see what you mean.'

'Listen, André. Isn't it strange when I tell you that the pyramid is not complete?'

'You say it is not complete? What kind of mystery is that?'

'That is a spiritual mystery, one with a Divine meaning. I'll explain that in a few words. The top of the pyramid is lacking.'

'Indeed, I did not notice, Alcar. Has it got a meaning?'

'Yes, André, as I said, this is a spiritual mystery with a Divine meaning. The top of the pyramid is the seventh cosmic degree the very last material attunement man can attain. We know that the All, God, follows and we also know that no spirit, however far he has advanced, can explain God in His entirety. Do you feel, André, what my point is and what this means? The seventh cosmic degree is the end of material man.'

'My God, how is it possible, Alcar, I understand its meaning, here human and spiritual powers cease to exist.'

'Very good, so it is. That's why the pyramid could not be completed, as one should be able to essentially understand God and God cannot be represented in stone or in writing or art.'

'How remarkable, Alcar, and yet so natural.'

'It tells us, André, that the human being who has reached the seventh cosmic degree has understood his Father in heaven. Consequently, the All cannot be described nor explained. That is why the pyramid is not complete and that is what I wanted to explain to you. I'll proceed.

As I said before, André, I helped in building this structure. Here I met my friend. I told you on our last journey that he stole my love. We quarrelled and he attacked me. A struggle followed and he fell down. A few days later my friend passed away. He was twenty-eight. I did not want to kill, it was a concurrence of circumstances. It was predestined, though, for I have seen all this in the spheres.

The moment it happened I was overcome by an awful feeling. It was as if I killed my own child. We now know it was true. At the time, however, that strange feeling and great mystery were within me. That feeling stayed with me during my life, until my death, and I suffered terribly. We had both met again without knowing it. We returned to the astral world and had to wait to be born again. I passed on to several other lives and met my twin soul. I met her again during my last life on earth and you know who she is.*⁾ As I said, I passed on to several lives and in two of them I met my friend again. In one life he was my master and I was his slave. I died at an early age, a wild animal put an end to my life, but I saved his. I told you about it, so I'll continue. My star now began to shine and his faded. His way was a different one than mine, as he still had to make up, whereas I had nearly finished. I was ahead of him on the spiritual road of which we were unaware. However, I would return to the earth many times, because I had not yet earned anything. Centuries passed. Once again he would become my child, but that time I would be his father. This is that other condition of which I spoke. That wonder also happened. She who once was my mother now became my wife and he was our child. That happened in Jerusalem, where I was a merchant. That's where we'll go now, that's where I have to show and explain other wonders to you.'

*⁾ See the book: 'A View into the Hereafter'. André meets her in the fifth sphere.

# CHAPTER V

## *Golgotha*

Y OU understand the pyramid and you know the meaning of this
amazing building. Come, André, we'll go on and on, up to our
final condition. There is still a lot I have to explain to you. The
pyramid was complete and we are now going to the place where one
waited for the birth of Christ. The perfect Child of God would come
and gave Himself.'

'How superior that is, Alcar, I have no words for it. Is it a place of
pilgrimage?'

'Yes, André, but man does not feel how deep and how sacred everything is.'

'Could we learn to understand ourselves through the pyramid, Alcar?'

'Indeed, André, that is the purpose of this structure. It was known in
the spheres that man would forget himself and that thousands of years
would pass before man would understand this stone building. If this
side had not influenced one being, a field-marshal, people would not
yet be aware that it had this meaning.'

'Did this knowledge get lost?'

'All beings who helped build it passed away. This is the great mystery
and secret, man must learn to understand it and himself, he has to exert
himself, nothing for nothing.'

'Oh, now I understand, Alcar, that is quite natural. They would not
have understood anyway.'

'Very good, André, that's right. Everything is laid down in it, even
the darkness, when there was nothing yet. Man became the creator of
light and darkness, but the light he must earn himself. Aren't all those
wonders present in nature? Haven't I explained all that to you and don't
we find it again in the pyramid? Are death and eternal life not fixed in
it? Though it can be seen every second in nature, in the universe, people look on, have no feeling, no understanding and think that others
and we are dreamers. They are living dead and have yet to awaken,
though only after thousands of years. Those living dead people nailed
the perfect Man to the cross and all of us assisted in it.

All of us who were born on earth at that time and later, also those

430

who are still living there, all of us nailed the perfect Man to the cross. It still happens every second, for we don't know ourselves. My God, You must forgive us all, for we are making up for it. That's why I prayed, my son, and asked God for strength. If there is one sacred and pure church on earth it is the pyramid. However, they enter that structure like they visit a museum worth seeing. They forget that they enter the heart of God and His perfect Child. They don't understand anything at all of the deep and sacred meaning.

For the sake of this building the masters descended to the earth and souls were born. If there had been no reincarnation, this building, this temple of God, could not have been accomplished, as there were no scientists who could have achieved it. Why are such geniuses not on earth any more? They still do not understand why people were so learned in those days. Where are those artists, where do those people live? They came from the side beyond, my son, like everything else on earth. I'll show that to you on this journey. Music, painting and sculpture, everything was arranged from this side. These souls descended to the earth from here and were allowed to transform their feelings into art. But such artists are not here any more. Now isn't that a problem? Why did those artists live on earth? I told you already, but I'll repeat it, because the earth needed art and feeling. However, all this art is not felt. They understand what they possess, but from where it came, in what way and for what purpose, no, they can't accept that. When I say 'they', André, I mean the scientists of the earth, because they have to learn and understand all those problems. However, they remain living dead, for they have not advanced far enough to feel these things.

I belonged to those who were allowed to bring this to the earth. We also had to make up for something. When my work was finished I passed away like they did when the pyramid was completed. Wonders, André, all of them, and yet it is said that there are no wonders any more, we don't know any wonders. They wait for wonders and are faced with them but they are spiritually blind. Do they need any more wonders? Are there not enough on earth? Isn't the human body a wonder, a revelation when they know all this? Do they need more wonders, which they do not understand anyway? Oh, those fools, those poor in spirit. This is why we come back to the earth, we, too, are allowed to accomplish a small mission.

Look, André, we are in the Holy Land now. In your time there is nothing sacred any more. The white and brown people continuously quarrel and hate one another. A curse rests on this Holy Land and it is caused by man. It is still the Holy Land and it will always remain so, for Christ lived here, Gods holy Child and here He was nailed to the cross. The world goes on and people live, but they live to the full.

Come, André, I know this city and you too will get to know this Holy City. Once we lived here, I as the father, my mother as my wife and he, my friend, as our child. I'll show you that image, I retain good memories. Here I awakened, my son, and became conscious.'

Alcar now turned into a very narrow street.

'Our little home has disappeared, but I'll find the spot where I once lived. Spirituality is and remains forever, it cannot be broken nor removed. Look, André, one of my many dwellings on earth.'

André began to observe. He saw the past in front of him. That home was built of stone and clay. What was he about to experience this time?

Alcar entered and he followed. His leader said to him: 'Do you see that woman there, André?'

That very moment an other image manifested itself and he saw what his leader asked him.

'Yes, Alcar, I see and it is amazing.'

'My wife, André. I'll show you a few scenes of that time and connect you with her inner life. Look at her inner radiance! Look how she radiates and what her inner level is like. She is thirty years old and she once was my mother. It is an incredible wonder and yet this is the holy truth. Her soul is prepared to give much love. She has a rich spirit. The inner property encompasses everything man has acquired in thousands of lives. From a sphere of demons we try to acquire something and to that end all those lives are needed, as I told you on many occasions.

I'll show you an other scene. Look, my son, the past is open to you.'

André saw an other human being. This man was tall and broad and in the prime of life. With him was a child, a boy of about six and they entered the home. He felt what this meant. That was bound to be Alcar. He looked at his leader and waited for Alcar's confirmation. The woman embraced them both. They subsequently sat down and he heard them speak. This, too, was amazing, for he understood every word spoken. They discussed every-day matters concerning their child.

Alcar said: 'That's me, once it was me, André. I lived here. This is my mother of centuries ago and this child is my friend I told you about.

There was quiet in this life, at any rate during the first years and I learned to know myself. In this life and in many others I came to rest and I passed on into an other level of feeling. I explained that to you on our last journey. I had to work hard for our daily bread. Here, in the Holy Land, that was not yet holy and of which nothing was known, although there were rumours of something wonderful, but there was no certainty. It was not known that Christ would come. That happened a good many years later, but we did not live to witness that.'

'Can this be shown, Alcar? Could you connect with that wonder too?'

'Certainly, André, everything is fixed and I'll also show that to you.'

'People on earth sometimes say that this is a legend.'

'Those who say so curse themselves, like those who lived in this era cursed themselves and nailed Christ to the cross. I connected you with the past in various ways, I showed you my own life and that of others, you witnessed the origin of creation, we could follow everything, why should this not be possible? I'll show you, my son, not only the most horrible event on earth, but also what happened on this side and when this holy feast is celebrated on our side. I'll get around to it in a moment, André.

As I said, the first years passed smoothly, but then misery started. I'll show you that image. Look, my boy.'

André began to observe. The image faded and an other appeared. He saw a sickbed. There lay a sick person and he understood this image also. Presently he heard them speak and he saw that the child had grown up and sat beside the sickbed of his mother. He now was a young man, big and strong. André felt attracted to him but he did not know why.

'You still need me so much', he heard the mother say, 'and now I'll pass away.'

Did she know she was going to die? Was she not afraid of death? Had she acquired that? Again he heard: 'You must look after your father, you must love him with all your heart and not be so quick-tempered. Will you look after yourself?'

She stroked his head and his dark black curls.

An intimate scene, André thought. How is it possible that such a scene can be recalled again? This happened centuries ago. The young man sat beside her and looked at her. Then he said: 'You won't pass away, you'll stay, I'll do my best.'

André felt that Alcar maintained this connection. He heard Alcar say: 'She passed away a month later and entered the spiritual world. Both of us stayed behind. My child was twenty-four.'

André still saw this scene and he got a remarkable feeling. He felt like it was himself, as if he were this young man when he concentrated on him. Yet, that turbulent nature this young man had was not his, though several qualities of character were similar. I just image things, he thought, for Alcar said nothing. This image faded and he saw an other one. A pity, he thought, this feeling was remarkable and he would have liked to keep it a little longer.

He saw this young man again, but now out in nature. He was outside the town and strolled about. Evidently he expected someone. Then he sat down. It was a remarkable image that André now witnessed. Those other feelings had come back to him. Over there, in the distance, he saw someone coming, the young man looked at the person, he jumped to his feet and hurried towards this figure. Again André got a strange feeling, for he also wanted to hurry towards that other being, but at the same moment he could not move on, something stopped him, called him to a halt. He felt himself again and André saw that it was a young woman, whom the young man ardently embraced. They stayed there for some time and when night fell he returned home. These two people loved each other. This image faded again and an other scene appeared. Several years had passed now, for André saw that the young man had become older. He also saw his father. The son had married now but had stayed with his father. This image also faded and he saw an other one. He immediately felt a great change. The quiet had disappeared now, for he felt anxiety and grief. This feeling dominated all his other feelings. He saw him enter. He saw his father in the corner of the room. When he entered his father approached him and André heard him say a few words, which made him understand the entire scene.

'You scoundrel, you liar, you are in the hands of satan.'

André looked at his leader. A shudder went through him when he heard the man speak those terrible words.

'That happened, André, he deceived her. She suffered a lot, but she, too, had to make up. This marriage, out of which two children were born, failed completely. However, I could do nothing, for he did not listen to me. How beautiful were those first years and how awful were these. We had lived through her who had passed away and only now did we become ourselves. I was left behind alone and I felt the misfortunes of my own life. My soul languished away and I suffered from all that misery. That's how I lived on and the years went by. What had happened to him? I did not see him again for we all went our own way.

The end of my child was, like mine, awful. She, however, passed on into other hands and had a lot to learn, for she was also guilty. My son and I have not met again; it was not until in the seventeenth century that I saw this soul once more when he was my friend. I told you about that, how deeply I loved him and how unnatural these feelings were. At the end of our journey I'll tell you some more about it. I lived to be seventy and the end came in poverty. Alone and deserted, filthy and infected I entered the world of the unconscious.

I had learned much in this life, he, however, had destroyed himself. Not until in the lives following this life was I to become conscious.

I'll pass on to the time when Christ would be born, André, for there is nothing more to say about that life. Could you follow me in everything, André?'

'Yes, Alcar, I could follow you, but there was something within me that I can't understand or explain. Perhaps you can help me. When you showed and explained all this to me, it was as if I were that child, your own child. The feeling I got was so strong that I can hardly be mistaken; though I don't want to imagine things. I can't express those feelings in words. In addition, I understood every word spoken and it shook me. Do I imagine this, Alcar? Every word vibrated in my soul, it was as if I spoke myself and I was overcome by a profound sadness. I can't explain it.'

Alcar looked at his instrument and said: 'So, André, you have felt that? Could you feel that vibration deep within you?'

'Is it because you connected me with him?'

'Indeed, André, you have felt that. That you understood that language is something you have experienced many a time on this side. We can understand and speak all languages of the world, because we are connected with man in feeling.'

Again Alcar looked at him, but said nothing and passed to an other subject, but André referred to it again and said: 'It is remarkable, Alcar, as if I knew him.'

'Is my answer not satisfactory?'

'Yes, Alcar, but I don't understand it yet.'

'Just wait a little and this will become clear to you when we come to that. The time has not come yet, have a little bit of patience.'

André bent his head and waited.

'We were Jews here, André. Every human being living on earth, regardless of his race, once lived here and has had to follow these laws which are laws of nature. We pass on into all the human races and there is not a single place on earth we have not lived in and experienced. All this is related to the material organism, the many degrees and the many races living all over the earth. We pass from one life into another and we'll acquire something in those lives. Come, we'll go on, I have to show you quite a few things.'

'How long was it, Alcar, before Christ would come?'

'Christ was born several centuries later. On earth he was not understood. The perfect Child of God would die on the cross. People in those days had risen in revolt. The Romans were the rulers in this country and in this chaos Christ was born. I'm going to connect you with that time and you will observe that this is no legend. May God give that mankind on earth will feel and understand this sacredness but we have not advanced that far. Come, André, follow me.'

André followed his leader. Now again he got strange feelings. He saw the old city and those narrow streets were familiar to him. It was as if he recognized every stone. My God, he thought, what is this? He wanted to banish all those feelings from his mind, for this could surely not be possible. This was self-deception. Yet, he thought of it repeatedly, as if he had to, as if an other power, stronger than him, wanted that. He knew this city, there was nothing unfamiliar, and the most remarkable thing of it all was that he knew where Alcar was going. He kept following his leader. Alcar left the city; he could follow no other way than this one. But why did he know that? Did Alcar make him feel that? Oh, he thought, why did it not cross his mind? How stupid I am, Alcar let me feel all this and when his leader did so he was in telepathic contact with him. This experience had now changed somewhat. It was more within him, he experienced it more clearly and profoundly, this was closer to reality, as if it were part of himself, as if he lived here once more.

Look, he thought, this seems familiar to me. And over there, I know that too. In front of him was Golgotha and over there Mount Olive. Everything was familiar to him. Once out of town, he felt something else. He knew all those old walls, and what was that? Could he trust his eyes? Again he felt that shudder; it vibrated deeply down in his soul. He saw boys playing. Oh, he thought, now I understand. These are Alcar's thoughts. This belonged to his own life. Alcar is thinking of all this, of his life, of those days and he sees the past and experiences it. I am connected with Alcar, that is why I begin to see and feel these remarkable things and I feel them the way Alcar does. That's what it is, André thought, it must be.

His child was playing and here were all those memories. These were images from the past and those images affected his leader, opened something which was experienced many centuries ago. This must have been something very intimate, André thought, never before had he been able to follow his leader so deeply, so intimately in everything. It all recurred now that his leader was here again and passed into that past. It was amazing and he had not experienced anything like this before.

Alcar stood still and said: 'Have you been able to follow me, André? From afar I sent to you what I once experienced and observed again.'

'Yes', André sighed, 'everything, everything like never before, I experienced it that intimately. Now I know why I felt and experienced it so intensely. It is mighty, Alcar, and a great wonder. There is your child, Alcar.'

His leader was lost in thought and André looked on.

Alcar said: 'Do you see that high mountain over there, André?'

'Yes, Alcar.'

'Golgotha, my son. Any honest human being should, on hearing this word, not be able to commit sins and to make mistakes any more. But people on earth do not want to be children of God and are unfeeling, they do not feel what it means. We'll go there presently because I have a lot to show you up there. I ask you to prepare yourself for that, André, if you do not want it to break your heart, to make you collapse of grief by the reality you will experience.'

André was frightened, but immediately recovered. That was strange too, but he understood that his leader helped him. He still saw Alcar's child.

'Look', his leader said, 'look, André, how happy my boy was. These were the most beautiful moments of this life. How many times I found him here. At the time I did not know or understand anything of what I now know and feel. Look at his youth, André. There is not any grief or misery. This is how the soul returns to the earth, that is the way we all are. There are hundreds of lives behind us of which we are completely unaware. And yet, how simple everything is. Though he is eight years old, the end of his life is already within him. This youthful life received the misery he once inflicted on someone else. We first have to meet one another to make up for it, it is not until then that all the other lives follow. I cannot be sad about it any more. We know that it is not fate, that it is fixed and that all of us will experience it. Rich in one life, poor in another, though we create our own condition, we try to create our own world in every life. Creating it is so simple, especially when we seek evil. Everything then happens as a matter of course and we achieve what we want to. We see ourselves as rulers of good and evil, of darkness and light. Nobody can stop us, for we have that in our own hands, we live the way we want to.

Follow this child and feel how deep this inner life is. Now what can we acquire in a hundred lives on earth? Hundreds of lives are lived in evil; we are demons, devils of hell and destroy the life of God. In those lives we violate the laws of God, and we want to acquire those laws to hurt others, to destroy, to dominate them and everybody else.

We are ready for every call, we give ourselves completely and we do not wonder whether that has to be made up. And so inner life descends into the material organism and life on earth begins.

My God, how mighty and natural everything is, how great is our life, how deep and sacred Your love. Time and again we receive Your life and what do we make of our life on earth?

God does not call us to a halt, André. God gave us everything. It will be clear to you more than ever before, especially after everything I'm going to show you soon. I'll pass on to the time when Christ would be born. Prepare yourself; cling to me, ask God for strength, André, the most sacred event that you can experience on this journey and will ever experience, awaits you.

There were rumours about an infant prodigy. Somewhere in this country an infant prodigy was born to very simple people. That child was a child of a carpenter, and though it was not eight years old yet, rumours spread about this infant prodigy throughout the country. In Egypt the first Divine wonder had already come true. The pyramid of Gizeh had predicted the birth of this child and the polar star lit the upper part of the pyramid. That very moment Christ was born. The first prophecy and the first Divine wonder of that mission had come true. The pyramid had now confirmed one event. A flash of light cut through the universe and God's sacred light returned and that same moment it was certain that man would forget himself. Man received a son of love, but man threw that golden light away. Man cursed himself by that deed. Anyone who could have opened his inner eyes at that moment could have observed this. The pyramid stood as a symbol of reality and how old the earth will become, when mountains and people perish, this remains, it is God's will. It cannot be destroyed, he who thinks he can demolish it destroys himself. The golden light was thrown back into God's face, man on earth did not accept.

In those days the pyramid was enveloped in a dense haze and remained that way. Hundreds of years would pass before man would open his eyes after having slept all those centuries.

The birth of Christ was fixed in the pyramid and this wonder happened precisely to the second, as did the reflection of God's sacred light, that golden light of love. Both events were one fact, one condition and a law as only a Divine wonder can be. Man, however, violated a Divine law. We were to experience that and we have.

Come, my boy, we'll go up. I'll help you in everything. Golgotha awaits you. You will be connected with reality. I'll be allowed to explain three mighty but spiritual problems to you, you'll see that with your own eyes, although two of those problems belong to the past.'

André saw a narrow road winding upwards to a high mountain. He walked beside his leader, who was lost in thought. What was he going to experience now? He was at ease and he felt a strange quietude. He felt that Alcar gave him this tranquility and he remained in mental contact with him. Inwardly André trembled, for he knew only too well what awaited him. My God, he thought, do I have to experience this too? Who will ever believe me? And yet, Alcar had lived where they had just been, this was Jerusalem. Here Christ lived, and here in this city He was nailed to the cross. Feeling the past was amazing. There was no disturbance at all, he understood everything. Everything could be recalled on this side and experienced again.

The quietude within him deepened. They ascended slowly and he trembled at every step. A cold shudder went through him. When he thought of these events he could cry. A strong power surged through him and he began to feel deeper. He understood that too, for it came directly from his leader.

Steadily, his hands folded on his back, Alcar walked on. André had to think if he wanted or not, a tremendous power surged through him and that power made him think. Something was alive here, and that something he felt within him, were the events.

When he concentrated and felt deeper he saw shades. Here were unnamable beings, visible and invisible human beings. He now saw them very clearly. The visible beings were the material people and that was the Jerusalem as it was in his time. The invisible beings were the spiritual people who had died on earth. Concentrating on them he could see them more clearly. Wherever he looked these spiritual beings were all over the place. They all had knelt down and were lost in prayer. He felt deep respect for them.

Yes, he thought, here one comes to oneself; here one can experience and pray. But he saw still more. Over there and to his right and left he saw thousands and thousands of beings together. Did Alcar make him see this? It was bound to be so, because a minute ago he had not seen this. He saw rows of them and now they dispersed. Why had those beings come to this place? Were they pilgrims? All had died on earth and lived on the side beyond. He knew they had passed away, for he could tell by their radiation. Material people were different; a material body radiated a different light. Most of them wore spiritual garments, though others did not. He understood that also. These beings had not advanced that far and had not yet acquired those garments. He kept following Alcar. Thousands of people were gathered here, but now only those who had died on earth. Many of them now lost themselves in prayer; others joined them in their walk upwards, for Alcar had not yet reached the highest part.

He saw that many of them cried. They let their tears trickle down their cheeks and were not ashamed of it. All these people were like children. Look at their faces, feel it and pass on into them, André thought. He wanted to feel it and tried to pass on into them. He had felt something similar at the pyramid. What wonders were on earth and man was unaware of them. All these beings were like children of eternity. In their arms they had spiritual flowers white as snow, they were transparent and did not grow on earth. They also radiated a powerful light. Oh, my God, what grace to be allowed to witness this.

Alcar still went upwards. To their right and left other people followed. They all had flowers. These flowers were theirs; he saw and felt that. Flowers of the spheres, from their spiritual home. Such flowers grew in their environment and had grown through their grief. They had all colours, every flower had developed to full beauty through struggle and grief. In this way the spirit nurtured his environment. As a result everything grew and bloomed, as they did themselves. These were the fruits of their work. They had worked on it while on earth and it was their possession in the spheres.

Oh, he felt and understood them all. They brought all these flowers to God's holy Child. These flowers were for Christ and these presents were accepted, because this was accomplished through grief and sorrow and the deep love they all had. They wanted to lay their inner presents at the feet of God's holy Child. This occurred to him and he understood that Alcar followed him in everything. Mental conversation, there was no other way of communication.

They all had these treasures, although there were also some who had nothing to offer. They nevertheless followed and went their way up. He felt where Alcar was going. Now he heard people sing and it was as if heaven tore apart and all angels descended. It came to him from afar and it got ever nearer so that all could hear it.

Golgotha was one sea of human beings. All around he saw nothing but spiritual beings. On they went, upward where that terrible event had happened. Soon his leader would be there, one more bend and they would be at the top. He followed Alcar and waited for what was about to happen. He dared not ask questions any more, he would wait until it would be possible. Now they had arrived and Alcar knelt down, so did he.

André could not think any more. Instinctively he began to pray and his prayer became deeper and more sincere. Words did not come to his mind, he only felt. Yet, those feelings were real and pure, like a child would think. How can I ever make up for this, he thought. My God, I'm only a puny human being, I still live on earth, I work for my leader and I follow him in everything. I'll do my best, Father, and I'll see to it that what I receive will remain pure. I'll not defile this work and I'll do everything that is good and what my leader wants. Father in heaven, I have no flowers, I have come empty-handed, because I do not yet belong to all those happy people. My place is still on earth, but once when I'm on this side forever, I hope I'll be allowed to lay my flowers at the feet of Your Child. Have mercy on me, oh, Father. I know I am nothing if your envoy does not give me anything, but I'm grateful to be his instrument. Father in heaven, give me strength for my work, forgive me my mistakes and bestow on me Your love, so that I can love all people. Oh, God, how can I thank You for having been allowed to see the universe, I know now that everything is love. Forgive me if I make mistakes but I shall see to it that I change them into good deeds. One day I'll enter this side and return with arms full of flowers, received by my own struggle and grief. I hope to able to earn that, Father, I'll do and accept everything. Thy will be done. Amen.'

André felt empty, he could not think any more. All the strength he possessed he had spent on his prayer, but he now felt a quiet happiness. He felt himself one of all those thousands of beings, for they all were lost in prayer. They subsequently raised their eyes and looked into the infinite cosmos. But what was that?

In front of him he saw the cross and that cross looked like a luminous column. It was of tremendous size and it radiated a golden light. God's sacred light, he thought. This golden cross stood on the spot where God's Son had died. This was the holy truth and the inner radiation of Christ. He understood that this belonged to the past. He saw gold, luminous gold and this light was Divine. Whoever would see this would not think of a legend any more. They would kneel down quietly in profound gratitude. Oh, how mighty this was! Once more all bent their head and prayed for strength. How great this wonder was! This was the most sacred event he had experienced on his spiritual journeys. This was the real and true light of Christ. All received the blessing in gratitude. Quiet, spiritual happiness and pure love descended in him. He bent his head still deeper and a golden sun shone on him.

He clearly felt its warmth; it penetrated him and warmed his entire being. That light had now enveloped all. The flowers piled up under the cross and their radiation mingled with the light of the radiating cross. Then he saw another wonder.

Around the cross he saw a golden sun and that sun radiated the entire scene. How great this sacred event was. The cosmos was created out of this light, the universe had once been like that, and he had been allowed to watch that in the temple of the soul. This golden light remained in and around the luminous cross and shone and radiated on all those spiritual beings. In gratitude they bent their head and kissed the earth. They were born out of the earth and they were like the earth, a particle of that golden light. He felt holy respect for all this.

Now he heard singing and all present joined in: 'God is love, God is life, God is just in everything.'

Angels were singing on earth and in heaven. Suddenly the universe tore apart and the heavens became visible. He recognized all the spheres on the side beyond. This must be something special and had a meaning, which he did not know nor understand. He would wait for Alcar said nothing. This was like a great feast at which Alcar and he were present.

The spheres were entirely open now and he could look into every sphere. The highest spheres were never visible, Alcar had not told him that and he had never experienced it before. What wonder did he see now? Was something about to happen? Why were the spheres entirely open, so that one could see from the first sphere into the highest?

There, high above, he recognized the radiance of the seventh sphere. What did all this mean? Why were the spheres open? He wondered again. He had never experienced it on the side beyond. This was a revelation of God, for who else could do this? Oh, he began to feel; Alcar extended his influence on him.

'Christmas in the spheres is about to begin. On earth it is celebrated later, in the spheres much earlier', he heard in his mind. Christmas, the holy feast of Christ! My God, how mighty everything is.

'That's why all these spiritual beings have come here, they celebrate the feast of Christ and are connected with Him. This is therefore the connection with God's perfect Child and it is experienced on this side.'

He subsequently heard Alcar say: 'I'm so happy, André, that you are allowed to see this. We see it every year. The seventh sphere connects with the first. Millions of beings are present here and will witness that terrible event. They have all come for that reason and shall, like we, observe the past.'

Thank God, André thought, I could not digest that by myself.

'Look at this light, my son, it is the universe and it is God's own light, the light you have seen in the temple of the soul. This is reality. This is the true event when Christ was nailed to the cross. Behind that material cross and invisible for people on earth was God's own light. For God watched over His Child and came to His assistance. But God was slapped in the face. God allowed this, and His Child was murdered. Yet, all this was present, we and billions of others have witnessed it, from the highest down to the lowest sphere on this side. All those who bend their head, who want to give and open themselves, can be connected. All this is sacred, never forget that, André, this preceded the crucifixion. Those who accepted Him as God's Child, observed this and they are the fortunate ones. Yet, this event can be observed here and this will remain so, every year we are connected again. Bend you head, my boy, and be grateful. I felt your love, be happy. May God bless you and our work.'

Singing of angels resounded again and the earth vibrated. A shudder went through all present. What was about to happen?

They all looked downhill. André heard a tremendous noise and screaming, the sacred silence had gone. People were coming this way. What was he about to experience? Was Alcar going to connect him again? All who were present knelt down again and prayed. This screaming came from the city. It was awful and André thought he could feel it.

A feeling of deep sorrow came over him. He cried, he could not restrain his tears any more, for he understood what he felt and what would happen. Oh, God, how terrible! The first people had now reached the foot of the mountain. Millions of souls witnessed what had once happened. This was Christmas in the spheres; the spiritual world was connected with the past.

'Crucify Him! Crucify Him!' He could hear nothing else. There they came. Not a single spirit stayed on his place, they all descended. Warriors took up their places on a plateau. André now felt that he passed to an other condition and he began to see the material world. The crucifixion was witnessed on this side as it once happened in reality.

Man, know yourself and pray, pray that you do not belong to them. Every second Christ is being crucified on earth. These words lashed his soul. He heard the words and it was as if they were meant for him.

Christ has been nailed to the cross; God's holy Child has been murdered. When God's Child was nailed to the cross darkness came over the earth. None of all those present dared look up, these spiritual beings experienced in their deep inner life, this real, this terrible process. All were praying and asked for forgiveness.

'Do not steal, do not rob, do not break hearts, do not abuse love given to you for you crucify the Christ', a voice spoke in André. That voice vibrated in his soul. Every word entered his mind and was understood.

'My children', he heard the voice again saying, 'God is within you,

God has always been within you. His own life was destroyed and you see how God's holy Child was understood. There is a curse on man on earth, on all of us. It is up to us, however, to spread this event and to open their eyes. You are all here on your pilgrimage and you accept. God bless you all.'

There was subsequent singing. People beamed with happiness. High above them they saw that horrible scene. No one dared to look on and André understood why it disappeared, it could not be witnessed any more. Who could ever bear this? Reality had been shown, they had seen and felt it, to feel any deeper and watch it any more was impossible. They did not yet have that strength and they would collapse. He saw, however, that this process went on. There were the tyrants and there were the two others who had been murdered together with Christ. Nobody spoke, but those who concentrated on this inhuman process could see and experience what once had happened.

My God, who could see and bear this in full consciousness? Many had collapsed already, but he stayed and felt and he understood from whom he received this strength. He clung to his leader and he now understood his words, before they had ascended. No, he did not want to collapse. Oh, how he cried inwardly, he would rather not watch any more. This was quite enough, but a power stronger than his forced him to watch what happened here. That power wanted him to observe. Here were spiritual beings and many had collapsed, but he had to see and experience, although emotion nearly made him collapse. My God, what sorrow, he could not bear it any more, but that power made him hold out. He could not watch it and his soul cried for help. Yet, he held out, the power within him was that strong. There were the tyrants again. Now he thought he was going crazy with grief.

Oh, my God, not that, do not allow that Your Child is murdered. Kill us, sinners, but leave Him alone. He gave Himself, His inner being, His blood and all His love. Yet, He is murdered. Hear those strokes, hear how every stroke destroys His holy flesh, and tears it apart. Oh, my God, how can You accept this. This end is fatal and will mean a curse. How horrible this is. Oh, strike me down, don't let this happen, we can't bear it, it breaks the deepest inner life. Oh, God, have mercy on them, they do not know what they do.

André still heard those hammer blows and saw those horrible beings around Christ.

He could not bear it any more. Yet, time and again that power forced him to keep watching, hearing and feeling. He had not expected this; it was beyond watching and unbearable. Oh, Alcar, help me, I can't bear this any more. I'm conscious of what is happening here, thousands have collapsed and I also feel I can't cope any more. Why do I have to experience this? My God, how could people have done that consciously, how dared they!

Oh, what misery!

Now they were pulling the cross up. Those other two people had already been crucified. André cried, he could not cope any more. Where was Alcar? Oh, how could he be left alone, this was unbearable. How could people have done this, still, there were beings here who witnessed it, but he saw tears, nothing but tears, because all who experienced this cried and were inwardly broken.

How would this end? Christ had to die. Once more he looked up, then he felt the strength that made him watch this scene weaken and he felt himself sink away, so that he was no longer conscious.

He did not know how long he had been unconscious, but when he opened his eyes, he saw his leader Alcar. 'Alcar', he cried, and he fainted again. He regained consciousness for the second time and looked around. A pair of hands radiated his head and when he looked up he saw two eyes looking at him. He could not utter a word and burst into tears.

He was, however, not the only one who cried, the spheres of light were open, billions of beings had witnessed this and all wept for grief. Yet, there was happiness in them, for the golden light radiated over all of them and that light made them happy. Christ had revealed Himself, Christ gave man everything and wanted man to listen, see and feel.

'Therefore, my son', he heard André say within him, 'I could not do anything about it. All of us, all those millions of beings trembled for grief, just like you.'

André listened and it made him feel happy. He had not wanted to follow this, out of respect and love. Yet, he had seen and followed everything, he had even heard those blows and that was too much for a human soul still living on earth.

'Alcar, how can I ever thank you.'

'Do not thank me, André, thank God.'

André looked around and saw that the spiritual beings returned to the spheres. Some still stayed behind and were lost in prayer.

'Does this happen every year, Alcar?'

'Yes, André. All meditate and experience the birth and death of Christ. All look into the past and feel the deep grief, the torturing pains of what happened here. This will go on for thousands of years, people keep coming and going, we will always see people here. Here they awaken and become conscious and learn to know themselves. This is the truth, the holy truth. Our Christmas is a feast of meditation and prayer. Everyone is connected with Christ in this place. This happens on earth and consequently all come to this holy place. Then the spheres part and the highest spheres are open. Man sees and experiences on this side and tries to acquire those spiritual treasures. We know what this means, it is up to man on earth to acquire this. We follow this road from the beginning up to his death, for which we need months of preparation.

All are open and know and feel the pure love. Oh, if only people on earth knew this. If they could feel, concentrate themselves for one second like we have to in the spheres, in order to learn and understand ourselves, to understand the deep and sacred meaning of Christ's coming on earth. But their material life and all their possessions obsess them. They celebrate for years on end and do not stop. They lack respect and do not feel anything, they only experience what the earth possesses. They don't want to hear about this, because it requires struggle, it means feeling the grief caused to God's holy Child. These beings were pilgrims, André, and all are awake and conscious.

Presently, this feast will be celebrated on earth and when you are in your body again, you'll think back to this. Then you'll feel happiness, nothing but pure happiness and you'll know that Christ died for you, and you'll also know that you must follow Him and you'll be grateful that you were allowed to experience this as an earthly being.'

'I'll never forget this, Alcar. It is deep within my soul, it was a terrible experience. People can't bear such grief, can they?'

'Why should earthly people not be able too? The deeper one descends into this the more intense and grievous one will feel that sorrow. All of us who live here try to feel that depth, but suddenly we can't feel or think any more, it tears us apart and we are not conscious any more. Sorrow has then overwhelmed our inner being and it is not until then that we feel how Christ has suffered. You thought you would lose your mind and that's what many others thought. Yet, there is one power watching over all of us, there is one feeling that makes us experience and that is Christ. Your heart bleeds and you would wish to give yourself, but that is not demanded of us. We could not give our life anyway, for it is too insignificant, but we feel the wonder come over us and that wonder warms us. It lifts us up, it opens us and leads us to unknown levels which we will attain. We submit completely and feel the depth of this horror. Then the Christ awakens in us, we are glad. That is why we all come here and want to try to acquire those powers. Awaken, man of the earth, it is not too late yet. People have forgotten themselves, André, and here people will have to make up for all that. Christ lives in this place. Here, mothers will find their children again and all are connected. A soul that is not aware of our life and cannot be reached is brought here. Then it will fall on its knees and the greatest sinner will come to himself. Many, however, will again live their life and will perish for the umpteenth time. One day they will awaken and only then will they return here and feel what it means. They feel that Christ must awaken in them and when this does not happen in vain, there will be joy in heaven.

They all brought flowers, my son, and all those flowers have been grown by their grief. That was their sorrow, their grief but they conquered themselves and by sacrifices, great sacrifices, they received the light, the light in which they live. Then their spiritual dwelling radiates and they all have possessions, many spiritual possessions and they know themselves.'

'I also heard singing, Alcar, here and somewhere else, but it was so far away and heavenly, did I hear correctly?'

'Angels were singing, André, angels were singing for Christ. Are you prepared and strong enough to experience this once more? I can connect you again and show it to you, so that you can see how all this was experienced on this side. This was the material event, but what happened on this side? Could you experience this once more, André? It is meant for mankind on earth, you see for them, because they are all longing to be allowed to know something of this past.

There was darkness all around, but in reality there was light. The heavens emptied, for all were on earth when Christ was crucified. Christ saw that and all sang for Him, surrounding Him with all their pure love. At that time not a single being remained on this side, they were all in the sphere of the earth. Yet, they could do nothing and had to watch his crucifixion. They knew that this horrible thing would happen. It had been known on this side for hundreds of years.

Even when people were reincarnated and came to the earth for the Divine monument. It was known in the spheres that with the pyramid grief and sorrow would develop, they created this deep grief and were aware of what they achieved. All this was known and it happened.

Just feel this, André, and think it over, try to understand that everything is fixed, because we on this side know all human ways. Christ came and would die. He gave us human beings everything and led us to Divinity. By His death people received a religion and began to learn true love.

Shall we go on our way, André, or shall I connect you?'

'Yes, Alcar, gladly, I want to be strong, connect me again and do not go away, Alcar, I'll pray and ask God for strength. I'm so grateful to you.'

André felt himself descend again into the past and he began to see.

From the place where they were they looked down upon Jerusalem. Again he heard that wild screaming that made him shudder. There they were, on their way to Golgotha. He could see everything and experienced this monstrous event again. There were thousands of people about. Many watched this scene out of sensation; others felt heartbroken. He could see them and he recognized them all. The misery came ever nearer and he thought he would collapse, it was that awful to watch. He felt he was connected even deeper than a while ago. He heard singing again which he had heard from afar. He clearly saw what happened. He saw Christ wrapped in a snow-white garment.

André felt himself sink away, yet he wanted to experience this and he made every effort to hold his ground. Heading the procession he saw thousands of angels carrying white flowers. They were to the left and right and high above the perfect Human Being. A holy power emanated from all this. He saw magnificent garments and the masters of the spheres were on earth in radiating beauty. Suddenly the singing ceased and he felt a deep concentration develop within him. He felt and understood why this happened. All respectfully drew back, for one feeling dominated their feeling. André also felt it and again he heard singing.

My God, how is it possible. Alcar made him feel what this meant. Christ had made all of them feel that not they, but He had to make this sacrifice. They were not allowed and could not help Him bear. Christ wanted to make this sacrifice alone and He gave Himself completely and did not want them to bear as well. On the way to Golgotha man received a lesson. Christ remained Himself under the deepest grief and humiliation. God's Child endured. Christ gave everything, He wanted to accomplish this alone.

André trembled, for he felt that man had to be alone when the deepest sorrow came. The moment when everything was demanded up to the last bit of strength, one had to do that individually or we would not have given ourselves completely. He felt this lesson, but people would not be able to. The intense concentration now dissolved into singing. All on the side beyond had felt this. They drew back and looked on when that process of murder began. The silence within them and the feelings of all these angels enveloped Christ. He knew and felt this and He looked at them and thanked all His children.

Again André saw the universe tear apart and that the spheres became visible. Then darkness closed in, also there where had always been light. What did this mean? Was He left alone? Why was there also darkness on the side beyond? Did that have to be now that this horrible event was about to begin? Darkness not only prevailed on earth but also on the side beyond. What did it mean? Now he began to feel and he understood what it meant.

When Christ was crucified there was darkness on earth and neither was there light on the side beyond and it was as if heaven and earth perished. Mountains seemed to disintegrate, thunder and lightning were heard and seen and the earth shook and trembled. He grasped Alcar's hand. Near the edge of the plateau thousands of people were together and when the earth shook and tore apart people began to shout. Now they knew he was no human being, but the Son of God. The soldiers and tyrants took to their heels. People were crushed to death and darkness still prevailed. Had God deserted His own Child? Was He left alone at the most terrible moment? André understood, because Alcar made him feel it. Now everything had to be given, this was sacrifice experienced by one's own strength and not by those of others.

He subsequently heard a soft and pure voice say: 'My God, my God, have You left Me?'

It was not until this moment that André understood this darkness, which was not understood on earth. This was the last, the very last strength a human being could give. Confronted by the very, very last moment man decided for himself: That was as God meant it to be it was God's sacred and strict will. Christ had to experience it as well, but it is also meant for man, nobody can evade it. Everything, everything, the last remainder of strength was spent. Christ surrendered. It is accomplished, he now heard within him.

He subsequently heard singing and darkness gave way to the golden light. The spheres revived and people became visible once more, but the perfect Human Being had died. In this darkness, hidden from human eyes, it had happened. He understood this too and felt the deep significance of this sacred process of dying. He had been murdered, a sun of Love had been killed. Man had cursed himself; man had laid violent hands on the most sacred being.

André felt himself returning into his own life. He had experienced, felt and understood this consciously.

'God, give me strength', he prayed, 'never, never to forget this any more.

Then he looked up at his leader and thanked him deeply. Tears trickled down his face. This was what people saw on the side beyond and they knew that this would happen.

'Christ wanted to do this alone, André, but we must also experience our struggle alone, not any human being can help us. This is the lesson people have to learn and those who do not want to will have to all the same. God left Him, His Child, in fact alone. When darkness closed in Christ understood this would require the very last of His strength. The supreme moment had come. We'll all be faced with that moment and then we must show what we want. God did this and yet, behind that darkness God looked on and watched and Christ laid His flowers at the feet of God, His Father in heaven. These flowers cultivated by His sorrow, and grown in His holy heart and awakened by His own life, these flowers God accepted and a golden light radiated the head of His Child. It is accomplished. It is the end of every soul and awaits all of us. Not one soul can avoid it. We'll have to give ourselves. We'll experience that sooner or later.

And isn't that worth it? Can't we give ourselves for what we all receive? Look at those who are on this side, they all have experienced it already, otherwise the gates of the spheres of light will remain closed for us. God demands everything, the very last of our strength, and no human being, nor spirit, can help us. People should begin during life

451

on earth. Every second can be their last moment. Time and again they fall on their knees and appeal for help. Yet, it comes back time and again, for we have to go on, ever further and higher, that's why God gave us all those lives. That is the purpose of life on earth and we pass from one life on to another and learn to understand ourselves.

Then we make up, André, and discard everything that is wrong. You have been able to feel the sacredness of it all, my son. What Christ experienced we shall experience and receive. Heaven is open to us, we still have to cover a long way, but one day we'll get there and will be met by those who are there already. Christ will say: 'Enter, My children, I thank you for all your love.'

We then have returned to God and entered the All. I have explained two sacred problems to you, you were allowed to see them with your own eyes and the third problem, my son, is our Christmas, which will remain forever, in all eternity. This also belonged to the past and you see that everything remains, that everything is fixed.

Now we'll move on, André, and continue our way. There is a lot more I have to explain and show to you. You have been allowed to witness this sacred event. That can only be witnessed here and it will remain forever, also when the earth dissolves and passes to the invisible energy. Every man will experience this if he wants to and is on this side. Here man becomes conscious and learns to understand himself.'

Alcar descended and André followed his leader, lost in thought. Everything he had been allowed to experience was deep and sacred. How grateful he was for having been allowed to receive this as an earthly being.

How horrible this was but how mighty and elevated. How pure the life of Christ was. It was deeply tragic and it had overwhelmed him, though at the beginning he had felt thoughts telling him that he had experienced this before. As soon as these thoughts had occurred to him he had shaken them off and began to see and experience. However, these thoughts now returned in him. They were like those he felt when he walked with Alcar through the streets of Jerusalem. Now that his leader went the same way back he felt those thoughts develop and he began to recognize everything again.

His leader had not given him a direct answer, perhaps that would also come. It was as if he had never been away from and still lived here, his feeling were that clear. Yet, he tried to discard these thoughts, because he wanted to wait. If an answer were required he would get it from Alcar. His leader would not let him go about with problems on his mind.

Over there, he would be able to find his way about, was the garden of Gethsemane and there the Mount of Olives. Or was he again receiving Alcar's memories now that his leader concentrated on them? That was also possible. He followed Alcar at some distance. Presently they would leave the Holy City, but he found it difficult to leave, he would rather stay here. He was still trembling because of this horrible experience. Why did this have to happen? This occurred two thousand years ago and as yet man did not stop. They persisted in their hatred and went on cursing. Oh, all those spiritual beings, how did they feel this event! All were inwardly broken. There at Golgotha, they again experienced the suffering and death of Christ. It had not gone, it remained there like every thought man had transmitted and that was simple because everything was fixed and could be seen again on this side. Alcar had shown him in several ways. He understood everything now, except why Jerusalem appeared so familiar to him. Had he only imagined it? It was a strange perception and yet so natural. Perhaps one day he would receive an answer. Alcar had left the Holy City. His leader went on and he would experience other wonders. Oh, if only people on earth would be able to imagine this. He lived in the hereafter and saw all this. When they would die and arrive here they would be faced with the same problem he had experienced just now. He had understood everything, because Alcar had first shown him the amazing event on the side beyond and he had subsequently seen the reality on earth and on this side. He heard the tyrants drive nails through Christ's hands and he thought he would die that instant. He had seen that Christ had been pulled up and that the two other murderers had been murdered together with Christ. How horrible people were in those days, though they were not different now, they were even more vicious than in the past. How could a human being forget himself that much? There were even people who looked on while Christ was murdered. Who would ever wish to see that?

On the side beyond thousands had collapsed. They meditated and would experience this, but they collapsed through all that grief. Now of all times they would learn to understand themselves better and begin an other life to acquire spiritual love. He would do that too. Later, when his life on earth would come to an end, he wanted to have spiritual property. How well did he feel the grace to be allowed to communicate this to mankind? What a great task he had to perform. He would not defile the spiritual connection with Alcar. Didn't Alcar take much pain to convince people? All this awaited them when they would die on earth and arrive here.

'Farewell Jerusalem, I don't think I'll return here before I have passed away.'

He would try to bring flowers, to lay those flowers at the feet of Christ. Oh, how very well he understood the meaning of those flowers, how they had grown. If life on earth was correctly understood and one lived the way God wanted, one had to accept all that struggle. Those flowers then grew spontaneously, they were cultivated in one's soul and they radiated through all that grief. Those who had suffered most and had fought that struggle by themselves had the most beautiful flowers. When it got dark it had given him a fright. He had understood that too. One day man is faced with the very last moment and has to show what he wants. The angels had wanted to help and support Christ, but Christ decidedly declined that help. God's holy Child had to cope with it alone. And that was only natural, bearing in mind that man had a will of his own and had received everything from God. When darkness set in and it also got dark on the side beyond it was as if God had forgotten His own Child. Christ also felt alone and deserted, though that was not true, for God watched behind it. That was the very last moment and applies to everybody, because all of us will face that moment and must show what we want. Everyone will experience that darkness. No human being or spirit can help us. No father or mother, we have to determine and experience this ourselves. We have to go through this. It is the evidence we have to lay at the feet of God. For this Christ had died and suffered. What Christ had experienced we would also experience, it cannot be avoided. That darkness was horrible and yet, behind it was God. Thus, it had been God's intention, God demanded everything, only then did those flowers of the heart grow and radiate. It was not until then that it was allowed to lay them at the feet of Christ and God's holy Child would not send us away, but accept them gratefully.

He heard, as it were, say within him: 'How did I suffer. Was this not meant for all My children? Did My Father in heaven not demand everything of Me, even the very, very last?' André was convinced that that

454

was the way. Those who lost their beloved ones on earth and accepted could cultivate flowers if they could surrender completely. Those who lost the ones dearest to them and were nevertheless grateful cultivated those light-radiating flowers which would be accepted. The angels brought all sorts of such flowers and that was so wonderful, something so Divine he had never seen before. Yet, it was also meant for people on earth, for they should try to accept everything.

How beautiful death really was. How well he now understood death. Yet, he was laughed at on earth and he was a dreamer, but one day all those laughers would have to take that laughter back, when they were faced with that final problem and were snatched from the earth. They did not laugh any more and reality made them tremble. No, then they would not be able to laugh any more, they would fall down and ask for help and be grateful when someone spoke with them. They would nevertheless also be helped, that is by the spirits of love who cultivated flowers, to present them one day to God's Child. They cultivated flowers by helping others and how were these wonders of nature? He observed their radiance. He felt very grateful that he had been allowed to witness this mighty event and he would always be thankful for it.

Jerusalem now lay behind him and he once more bade that old city farewell.

'I'll return when I have died on earth.'

Alcar looked at him and said: 'Anyway, we'll come back here once more on this journey, André. On that occasion I'll have to explain another wonder to you and I'll connect you with it too. That is related to reincarnation on earth and you'll have to experience that also. That wonder is also fixed and means a mighty grace for us. You will see it and be grateful that it has been given us. First, however, I must explain other conditions to you and after that we'll return here.'

'You mean to Golgotha, Alcar?'

'Yes, André, where we were a while ago.'

Now what would this mean? he thought. These were all spiritual problems for him and all those problems were solved and Alcar explained them. Strange, he thought, that we should return here again. Was there more to be experienced? He was reduced to silence and he waited.

He subsequently thought of Alcar's friend and asked: 'What has become of your child, Alcar?'

'From there he entered life on our side. He experienced the process of decay and when he had experienced that and the years of silence which he should have spent on earth had passed, the world of the unconscious also accommodated this soul and he waited for a new birth.'

'Haven't you seen him ever since, Alcar?'

'Not before my last life on earth, in England. Between Jerusalem and his last life on earth are many other lives. I have not met him again in all those centuries, but I could follow his lives in the spheres. He descended in the female body*), was born and died at an early age. These early transitions always have a spiritual and natural meaning. It is usually because the soul has to acquire the childlike feeling and for the mother body, because we have to become conscious in it and it is necessary for the development. He died at an early age and he subsequently entered the female organism again and reached an old age. That happened several times in succession and when he had experienced that he accepted his proper attunement, which is assigned to us from the first cosmic degree. So you see that the soul has to acquire both organisms and that is to awaken, for we could not awaken if we could not consciously experience the plan of creation.

I saw him again in Memphis and that was at the time when Lantos met his beloved one and he was the brother of Marianne. However, I cannot follow all those lives, my object is merely to give you an idea how everything is and that people on earth will and have to meet each other several times. One day they will see that on our side.

He subsequently lived in the West and returned there several times. He was born there twice and in both lives he had the male organism. I could tell you much about that, for many people of that time are now again on earth and I could connect you with them. I could connect you with his fathers and mothers, sisters and brothers, and above all explain those lives to you.'

'Is that not possible, Alcar?'

'No, my son, that would be too much and all this will not be accepted on earth.'

'What a pity. Are there people living on earth, Alcar, whom I have met in other lives?'

'Yes, André, very many of them now live on earth. I could show you wonders, but I can't pursue all those wonders in greater depth. I will

*) He was born a woman.

explain some of them to you later. I could even point out your own mother of the past who is also on earth now but with whom you have nothing to do. This is the holy truth, but incredible for those who are completely unaware of it and cannot accept it either. I see and know that she is on earth, as are many others of those days during which my friend and all the others lived, which was in France.'

'How amazing that is, Alcar.'

'Yes, it is amazing, yet, people take no notice and think it is ridiculous because they know nothing about it any more.'

'How is it possible, my own brother of those days now living in another country, a different language, other friends and acquaintances and perhaps sisters and brothers. I can hardly accept it, Alcar, though I have been able to follow you in everything. When are you going to tell me about my own lives?'

Alcar looked at his instrument and said: 'At the very last moment of this journey I'll explain many lives to you. So have some patience.'

'I'm very happy, Alcar, and I'll wait. What did your friend do, Alcar, I mean in those other lives?'

'In his first life, in the West, he tried to acquire art, but he did not get far with it. In his next life he joined the army and became an officer, but he was killed. After that he once more returned in an other life and became a scientist. His name is still known on earth and I could mention it to you.'

'How amazing everything is, Alcar. How many fathers, mothers, sisters and brothers have we had?'

'Thousands, my son. How could it be otherwise? Is that so strange when we know we have to return time and again and that this has been going on for billions of years? Can't we accept that? People flounder on death, but when they begin to see spiritually, that is when they enter life on our side, then they look into their own lives and have to accept. I asked you many times: can we become like God in that one short life on earth in which we achieved nothing but passion and destruction? Just ask yourself that question and let people on earth wonder about it. They will say that it is impossible. What then did God intend with creation and did God cause all that sorrow and human misery? We know now that we are to blame and not God. We know, and I have clearly shown that to you now and on our previous journeys, that we have forgotten ourselves in all those lives. Thus, we have landed ourselves in this condition through our own fault and God has nothing to do with that. Now feel all that earthly misery, but people do not think any further. They do not search their inner self; they don't dare, because they are afraid. Yet, they can't believe it, can't accept it, because it is so incredible and they do not know anything about creation.'

'I don't quite understand, Alcar, you said that the scientists on earth know of embryonic life, can't they conceive the life that follows and must follow? We would have died, wouldn't we? How then do they explain the perfect human being? Did that embryo suddenly mature? Was man suddenly ready? I don't understand that. Isn't that a great and profound problem?'

'A lot of questions, André, clear questions, but they have not advanced that far. Unfortunately, no, they do not think or feel that this is a deadlock. As I said before they feel and think that a second creation has occurred, but they don't know anything about that either and come to a deadlock.'

'It must be quite remarkable for a scientist when he begins to feel and understand these wonders. How happy I would be if I was allowed as a scientist to know all this. I don't understand those people, I can't imagine that they do not feel this. How natural everything is that you showed and explained to me. We do not acquire anything in one life, we killed others, or do other things and yet, they can't accept this?'

'No, my son, everything is too deep, too unbelievable for them.'

'There are even many spiritualists, Alcar, who can't believe this and do not wish to know anything about reincarnation. For them all this is nonsense, imagination and deceit. All these people say that there is no reincarnation. I know now how narrow-minded all these otherwise sensitive people are. I only know this now and also that I have to digest all these marvellous things alone. However, it is such a great pity and sad to hear these people speak like that.'

'I know that, André, but wait a little and have patience, this side now influences mankind and every spirit and leader of some importance tells them of their thousands of lives and of their own distant past. Wherever spiritualists live on earth reincarnation is discussed and later, after a few hundred years, they will know about it and accept us. I'm telling them now about spiritual wonders, I may and can speak of spiritual laws and wonders, for if I were not allowed, believe me, I could not have uttered a word. I would defile my own inner life and spiritual attunement and I would be a liar and such people live in the darkness. My sphere is the fifth on this side and you know where I live, you know me as a human being and as a spirit. What I have been allowed to explain to you now and what we bring on earth is miraculous, it is beyond their mental grasp and inner possession, but everything is the holy truth, God knows that I have experienced all this. Many people, however, will be grateful to us, André, that they may read about this already on earth, and acquire these powers. God gave us those various lives, all those possibilities, how could we otherwise get rid of all that misery? How could we ever make up for it in one life? I have shown you the darkness to convince you that reincarnation must happen, otherwise those human beings who live there in crevices and holes and who have been there for thousands of years, would never advance any more. This also applies to hundreds of other conditions and yet, how will people on earth react? I know the answer, André, for we know in advance what we can and will achieve. If priests and theologians, scientists and even spiritualists who do possess feeling do not feel this, what will people say who know nothing at all of eternal life? Yes, my son, it is sad indeed, but, as I told you, once the time will come when all those clergymen and in particular the spiritualists who cannot accept us now will understand us.'

'What will they understand, Alcar? Do these people think there has been no death before and that they only live on earth once?'

'Indeed, André, they do not get any further. They are unaware of reincarnation, though it is a mighty grace for us and everybody will experience it. All of us who live here have seen and understood that in the fourth sphere.'

'Where did you go after Jerusalem, Alcar?'

'I was subsequently born in Italy, and I returned there twice. That first life ended through a piece of stone, for I wanted to acquire the art of sculpture. Once again I returned there and attained a great age. After that I was born in the Far East, one life in the female body. I then returned to the South and when I passed away I entered the hereafter. I could not return any more. At the border of the Land of Twilight where Gerhard entered I also awoke and was convinced of my eternal life. I had experienced my karma. I'll refer to that when I have got that far. I'll explain to you how I attained the first sphere, which you know already, though I did not yet tell you about it myself. I told you that my friend lived in France and that he was a scientist in that life. He returned there again, was destroyed in that life to be born again. His final life was in England where I met him when I was an artist. In that life he was also a scientist, I told you about that.

I have explained many lives to you so that you received a picture of my friend and myself. My point is merely to give people on earth an idea how everything happened and that every soul must experience this. When they know all this they'll lead a different life. We want to convince them of their eternal progress, of their karma and cause and effect, but in particular, that we are Divine and have to attain the All.

There is nothing strange in all this, how improbable many human conditions may be. It is a long road winding through the universe. I have been allowed to explain all this to you, for the earth needs nourishment for the mind and we want to protect mankind from total ruin.

Those who follow us serve, serve themselves and will, as a result, receive spiritual happiness. Those who accept experience their own karma, will progress ever further and will one day enter the spheres of light. All this is not fiction, nor romantic, it is the holy truth and reality and I have been allowed to make that clear to you. I have experienced this, André, and all those who are on earth will experience it. I have no more to say on this subject and we'll go on.'

# CHAPTER VI

## *The fourth cosmic mentality*

'WHERE do you go to now, Alcar?'

'I'll now pass on to the fourth cosmic degree. On our way, I'll connect you with other conditions, but our destination is the fourth cosmic degree. I promised to connect you with it.'

'Do you pass on to that planet, Alcar?'

'You mean the way we did on all those other planets we visited?'

'Yes, Alcar, that's what I mean.'

'No, my son, that is not possible there and I'll explain that to you presently. You will all the same receive a clear picture of life there and what condition they live in.'

'You said that those planets belong to a different solar system?'

'Yes, André. Thousands of planets are millions of light-years from the earth, and all those planets are not visible from the earth.'

'How can those distances be calculated on earth, Alcar?'

'Many emit their radiation and inner light and the distance travelled by that light in one year is calculated on earth and we arrive at figures that can hardly be pronounced. The scientists call them light-years.'

'Can the distances be calculated on earth?'

'They approach reality, but it is not possible to do so accurately.'

'Can't they calculate the distance of all those planets, Alcar?'

'They can calculate the distance of some planets, André. Now listen. We are now in the spiritual or invisible cosmos. You see and have observed everything from our own world, our hereafter. If I want to pass on to the material world I have to connect myself with it and we then see the universe as it is seen from the earth. You clearly see that there are no stars and planets, for we belong to the invisible cosmos and have reached a condition of consciousness in it. Is that clear to you, André?'

'Yes, Alcar, I could follow all this.'

'Now I'll pass on to the material universe. You feel, and you have known for a long time that we know a material and a spiritual cosmos and that we people and the animal kingdom, in short everything that lives, belong to that. What we have observed in the universe is also present in ourselves. Our inner life is the invisible cosmos, our material

461

organism is the material cosmos, both form part of this all-encompassing, which is God. My inner life as a human being therefore belongs to the invisible cosmos, is our hereafter and forms the worlds of existence for the spiritual human being. I have reached the fifth sphere, but my sphere belongs to the third cosmic degree, as do the two spheres above mine. It is not until beyond those, I told and explained that to you, that I'll pass on into the mental regions and will be attracted by the fourth cosmic degree, that is by the first transitory planets. All that is beyond my capacity and spiritual level. And what I do not possess on this side, or the love I lack and have not acquired, I am unaware of. A master who has reached the seventh sphere is in communication with the fourth cosmic degree. Later, when his task in the seventh sphere is over and accomplished, this being will be attracted by those planets and the inner life descends into the mental regions, for us the world of the unconscious. The earth retains inner life and only releases it, as I explained to you, when we have reached the highest material degree on earth. Even then we are not free, because, as you know, our inner life will draw us back and we have to make up what we have done wrong in many lives.

Once a master has advanced that far, he can also impart some of his knowledge and wisdom to others, and present us with part of what he owns and knows. For he, this master, is already in connection with the fourth cosmic degree. The fourth cosmic degree is within him, he is ready, and he feels what is felt there, because all those beings have lived in his own sphere. Had this been impossible, the pyramid of Gizeh would never have been built on earth, as there would not have been beings capable of receiving those messages. We know, however, that the entire universe is inhabited, not only materially but above all spiritually. Astral worlds came into existence, sphere after sphere emanated and was inhabited. The origin of the universe was shown to the masters, they received a clear picture of the development of all those planets. Since this is now possible, André, and others who are open to it have advanced that far and understand it, I can now connect you with the fourth cosmic degree, because I am being connected through the masters. This is part of my work and it is my task, otherwise it would not be given to me. The masters constantly, as at this moment, guide me and they give me the powers by which I can connect you. Do you understand what I mean?'

'Yes, Alcar.'

'Then you will understand that we are going ever further, and soon we will no longer be able to observe anything belonging to the firmament and the third cosmic degree that can be seen from the earth. The farther we get, the darker it will become and even if we go to the right or left, up or down, it does not matter, for there is no distance, no higher, no left or right, there is only space and this space expands. There is no beginning and there is no end, there is only life. So you'll presently see nothing but darkness, because we go to an other solar system. That solar system, as I said before, cannot be observed from the earth and will never become known because it is the fourth cosmic degree and mentality.'

'How mighty this is, Alcar.'

'It is mighty, André. It is the expanding universe. This is known on earth and it is admitted that we can't be the sole inhabitants in this mighty expanse. They know that the universe expands and that there is no end and that there are more solar systems than the one to which the earth belongs. We cannot only see all those planets any more; we can't see the sun either, that luminous ball of fire which warms the earth. Everything will presently disappear for we enter an other part of the universe. I should not and cannot speak of an other part of the universe for, as I said, there is no centre, no left or right, no height or depth. There is only space and life and all that mightiness is God.'

'It is getting dark already, Alcar.'

'Yes, I see, André. That gives us an other picture which connects us again with creation, this time with the beginning when there was still nothing. The further we go the darker it will become. It will become as dark as you have seen in the temple of the soul. The silence we will presently feel is beyond description. It can only be felt. Material beings, however, cannot feel it, for they would collapse. Human beings could not live here. If man, as I also explained to you on our first journey, would venture outside his own atmosphere, he would suffocate or his organism would shatter. Other laws and powers are in force here and everything that does not belong here will perish. Nobody will ever come here, this is a transitional condition, which is an astral world, yet, thousands of planets are floating in this space. It is therefore possible, my son, how incredible it may be, that we already passed through other planets, but all those objects are invisible for me, even if they

463

were material. Consequently, I not only can't see the spiritual higher condition any more, the material cosmos is also beyond my reach.'

'How deep this is, Alcar.'

'Yes, André, it is and if you properly feel that might and power you'll understand that man on earth will not hear anything from the fourth cosmic degree for a long time, because that planet is too far away from the earth. Those other planets to which the earth belongs and which occupy a place in the universe have no human consciousness. People living on them are unaware of good and evil. Those people cannot send messages to the earth; they are living dead and have to awaken yet.

Don't you think that if people were living on those other planets, who had acquired a higher world of existence, they would not try to establish a connection with the earth? If they were ahead of people on earth and had more feeling, wouldn't they be anxious to tell people on earth we are alive, we are people like you? I know, believe me, they would wonder and would have tried to establish a connection with the planet earth a long time ago. But that has not happened in all those billions of years. Those who live on all those planets of our solar system are mentally dead. Their feeling is poor and they have to go to the earth in order to acquire feeling. They have to become humanly conscious. It is thought on earth that there are people living out there who are ahead of them, but the people living there are like those prehistoric beings we have come to know. They have no feeling either; they are living dead and still have to awaken. The people of the other planets of the fourth cosmic degree, however, can reach the earth, but there is a wide gap, which is 'death'. As long as man on earth cannot accept eternal progress he will not be able to understand the cosmically conscious human being, this perfect human being is considered to talk nonsense. The scientists, as I told you, will never achieve anything as long as they do not accept our world and everything we have to say, which we received from the scientists on this side, the masters of the seventh sphere who inwardly bear and possess the universe as the third cosmic degree. Man, however, lives and does not know about life and death, he does not want to know and perishes. They rise against death and they ask and cry why and what for. So you'll understand that people from earth cannot feel this silence, that they would collapse. If they could be here, they would cry for fear because they would think they would die.

Look, my son, we have advanced. That is the way it was before creation, André. However, to our right and left some glimmers of light are perceptible. That dim light still comes from the solar system to which the earth belongs. We go on and on and presently you won't see anything at all. You'll feel an incredible silence. Look, André, darkness sets in.'

André did not see anything any more. His leader was also invisible for him. In this deep silence and darkness he came to himself. My God, he thought, how mighty everything is.

Alcar said to him: 'Do you feel this silence, my son?'

'Yes, Alcar.'

'It was like this before creation, André. Everything emanates from this darkness. God revealed Himself. We don't see anything now, we can only feel. Everything is sacred, also this darkness and this silence. Presently glimmers of light will penetrate and that dim light is from the solar system to which the earth does not belong. The picture we then observe is like the first faint light you saw in the temple of the soul; here it means that we approach an other solar system. You see, André, the darkness is dissolving. Soon it will become lighter and we are gradually approaching the fourth cosmic degree. During daytime, if you could speak of daytime, there is pitch-darkness, because there is no solar system here. And then to know that there are thousands of solar systems in the universe! Yet we see emptiness, darkness. We are passing from one cosmic degree to another. One degree is hidden from the other and invisible. That is the entire universe of which we know nothing and which only God knows. Darkness, André, nothing but darkness. Isn't it as if God speaks to us? Hear my voice, how it sounds and how far it penetrates, how deep and mighty everything is. You think there is no end to it and yet, in a while, it will be light again. Light of a sun that radiates many planets, which belong to the fourth cosmic degree of which we know the main planet.

Now we are many, many light-years away from the earth. People on earth will not believe us, that is not necessary. When I succeed in teaching them to understand death, I will be satisfied, that's all I want.

Look, André, it is getting a bit lighter. Everything is different there. This planet has a different atmosphere, for the material organism differs from the organism on earth. The organism on earth is coarse as compared with that on this degree. Man on earth is a wonder of creation, but there the human body is transparent and resembles a spiritual being of the fourth sphere on our side. You know how they radiate, although that is their spiritual garment, on this planet the material organism is like the inner radiance of the fourth sphere. Just imagine that. To be allowed to live in a material organism and in a life of happiness, love, and purity and where everything smiles at you. Where people are as we know the masters of the seventh sphere.

The masters of the seventh sphere and all those living there with them arrive at the lowest material degree and they begin their first life. Although there is also a highest material degree of the body, there is no black and brown any more and the animal-like degrees have been experienced. That belongs to the earth and all those other planets visible from the earth.

Look, André, it is dawning, as if day approaches. This has a meaning. They know night and day too. I could be there in a few seconds as there is no distance for us and master Cesarino will guide me. We'll experience this through him. The light becomes more powerful and that is an indication that we enter an other solar system. That awe-inspiring silence dissolves, for light is also in motion, it is energy, although we won't feel it. Everything is motion. In that deep darkness one feels the Divine silence. Concentrate on it and you'll feel that this silence is not there any more.'

André did as Alcar said and now felt a different silence than a while ago.

'How amazing, Alcar.'

'This twilight is already in motion which is power and activity and this activity already dominates this deep silence. It contains many secrets. Once people on earth have advanced to the extent that they can utilize the sunlight thousands of possibilities will be open to them. Many discoveries can be made in respect of sunlight, for its activity is awe-inspiring. On earth people have not advanced that far that they can extract these powers from the cosmos; one day, however, inventors will be born on earth who will discover that wonder. That day has not arrived yet and it will take thousands of years. The inventions they have made up to now are nothing as compared with what is present in the cosmos. People on the fourth cosmic degree are well ahead. That level cannot be reached on earth because the material condition of the human organism is not suited to it. They cannot advance ahead of their own cosmic attunement.

However, one day they will concentrate on sunlight and try to make use of that energy. As I said before it is the age of technical wonders though they will only achieve part of what is present in the universe. Do not forget that sunlight is energy of a magnitude of power and strength that cannot be imagined. Some scientists already concentrate on it, but it is not yet possible to achieve something because these scientists must have a different inner attunement and adjust themselves spiritually, which means that they must feel deeper than they do now. Everything is linked with their inner life, which makes them assess and feel the tenor of all these secrets. I'll let you experience another wonder so that you know where we are.'

André suddenly felt overwhelmed by a deep sleep, though he remained conscious of everything and asked: 'What is it, Alcar? I nearly fell asleep.'

'It is because we are in the mental regions. I left you to your own power for a moment and because I did not concentrate any more you immediately fell asleep. Unconsciousness sets in and your mind is not aware any more. I am also influenced by that activity, but the master helps me. I constantly keep my mind concentrated on it or I would also fall asleep. So we are now passing through the mental regions of the fourth cosmic degree. There are more wonders and you'll feel and experience those too. Attention now, André.

You now experience that everything is one and integral. I connected you many times in this way, but this time it is greater and mightier still. You know that we are going to an other solar system and we'll visit an other planet. Although we cannot live on it, we can observe but nothing else. Here are also our hereafter, the hell and the astral animal kingdom as well, yet the way we feel we are far, very far away from the earth and the hereafter where I live. Do you feel what I mean?'

'Yes, Alcar, it is almost incredible.'

'I'll show you, my son. Now you'll get a clear picture of what lives in and around us, of which nothing is known on earth. Look, I'll first connect myself with the hell, the deepest darkness in our life. We have been there before, you have seen all those demons and you also know the land of hatred. I explained that to you. My point is this: I'm going to connect myself, André, now look, there is the darkness, the hell in life after death on earth.'

At the same moment André began to see.

'My God', he exclaimed, 'how is that possible!'

This world has changed. He saw the darkness, the hell he had seen on his journey with Alcar where the demons lived. He also saw those holes and pits in front of him where people lived.

How is it possible, he thought and he was amazed that he understood all this so well.

'I understand what you mean, Alcar. Is this the lowest sphere but one in the darkness?'

'Yes, indeed, we have been there before. That sphere is also present here. Everything is here and that belongs to the third cosmic degree and the astral cosmos. So you see that all spheres on this side are infinite. I connected myself with the astral cosmos and yet, just now we were in the material cosmos, which is the universe. Just imagine the infinity of everything, and also the narrow-mindedness of man on earth who believes he can achieve whatever he wants. Those who experience this will feel their own insignificance, but also what awaits them and what can be acquired. In this condition I connected myself with the demons, the animal-like beings who live here. At that time I explained to you and recorded in your second book*) that they try to attain the land of hatred, once they arrive there their spiritual and animal-like life begins again. Yet, André, we are near the fourth cosmic degree, in the mental regions and in thousands of other conditions and I can show and explain all that to you. You also feel that I now live on my own powers again and act accordingly, because this sphere is below my own attunement. Do you now understand, André, what might and power every human being has to acquire and what awaits all of us? Isn't it worthwhile experiencing life on earth? Is all that misery that terrible? See what we can achieve, try to imagine all those astral and spiritual worlds and then on to the fifth cosmic degree! It is incredible, we must nevertheless accept it, for that's what awaits us, and it even becomes our property. We know and we'll get to know all those spheres.

I can also connect you with the second cosmic degree and enter that astral world, so that you'll see those pre-animal-like beings again. That sphere, that world, is also here where we are now. You see, wherever we are I can concentrate and pass on into it. This is the infinite cosmos; it is the All, the infinity of every condition, sphere or heaven, that closes us off from the other for we have not advanced that far. Thus, André,

*) The second volume of the book 'A View into the Hereafter'.

spiritual and material transitions. It is not until we begin to feel and acquire those higher transitions, which is only possible by serving that we begin to see and advance. I can ascend now and we'll see two more dark spheres. Then follows the Land of Hatred and when I ascend further you see light appear and I could continue up to the fifth sphere, which is my sphere. Yet, we are in the cosmos and float towards an other planet, an other solar system.

Here and wherever you are, live animal-like beings and those beings have arrived here from the earth and have completed their cycle of life on earth. These beings cannot go back, but if they had that feeling and yearned for it, as I told and explained to you, God would come to their help. However, they cannot be born in their present condition, for they are 'beasta', who exceeded the limits of greatest evil, broke the laws of nature. I'll explain all that later when I return here and connect you again. You asked me those questions on our last journey, in a while I'll answer all those questions. For the present, however, I'll attune myself to a higher condition and we'll observe that. I'll subsequently pass on to the following sphere and so on, so that you will see that all those astral worlds are in one world, which is the universe.'

André felt that Alcar returned. He saw one sphere after the other dissolve. Now he saw the Land of Hatred, then the Land of Twilight and subsequently all the other and higher spheres. It became gradually lighter and he already saw the first sphere on the side beyond. Everything he experienced on this journey was remarkable. Alcar ascended further and higher still but he only did so in feeling. They remained where they were, far away from the earth and yet he experienced all those spiritual degrees of the third cosmic mentality. How complicated everything was and yet all those spheres were separated from each other. Then came the second sphere, the third and fourth sphere and now Alcar passed into his own sphere.

Slowly but surely his sphere dissolved before him and could only be seen as in a dense haze. Alcar went on and withdrew into that other world. Then the darkness they had been in returned and he felt that Alcar passed again into the material cosmos. He saw that deep darkness as it had been before creation and this also changed and that twilight condition they had just been in set in again.

'Could you follow me in everything, André?'

'Yes, Alcar, it is amazing, everything is really one world.'

'It is all one world though every condition has its own attunement, a world of its own, transitions in a material and spiritual condition. The astral worlds are together; we find all those higher and lower astral worlds in that one space. We live in the All, André, which will now be clear to you. We'll go on and soon reach the fourth cosmic degree.'

Alcar now rapidly floated towards that cosmic degree. What was he about to experience now? It became ever lighter for a golden light like that of the rising sun on earth radiated towards them. This was a different atmosphere than the one on earth, this one was brighter, he clearly felt that. His leader steadily went on and the light in the sky became stronger as they approached. The sky already had a golden glow. He now saw an other wonder. The further they got, the more that golden light faded and a deep purple-blue dominated the golden light.

'Is that the firmament, Alcar?'

'Yes, André, as on earth, but this firmament is brighter than that. This blue is deeper, brighter than on earth. It radiates everything. The further we go the brighter the firmament will become.

Look over there, André, those are the transitory planets for the fourth cosmic degree. Here, we also find these transitions as planets for it is impossible to pass straight away on to the fourth cosmic degree. We'll go on now but observe from our world. Over there the fourth cosmic degree floated in this amazing universe. As I said, it is not possible for us to descend onto the planet and to live among them and observe. We cannot connect ourselves with them because they are more advanced in feeling than we are. Only the masters can.'

'My God', André exclaimed, 'how is it possible.'

In front of him he saw a planet like the earth. The firmament had now assumed a clear light-blue shade, the colour was as in the fourth sphere. In the fourth sphere a purple glow was perceptible in the firmament and that glow was also present here. He saw a magnificent scenery, temples and buildings, which made him think he was in the fourth sphere, the Summerland on the side beyond.

'Do I feel this correctly, Alcar?'

'I made you feel it, André. The fourth cosmic degree in a material condition is like the fourth sphere in our life. You know the beauty of our Summerland. You know how pure that sphere is. You see in our sphere that the flowers radiate light and in a sense that happens here in a material condition. This means cosmic happiness, this means having

470

a fairy-tale-like happiness in a material life. We'll descend close to this planet and we'll see man of the fourth cosmic degree. I'll pass on to that and explain a lot to you from some distance. We remain floating in space.'

André experienced this wonder. How could people ever believe him? There in front of him he saw people. Oh, how amazing, and such silence! His leader had approached them very closely. How Divine these people were and what beautiful garments they wore. He saw these garments in all shades. They wore them the way a spirit on the side beyond did. It was mighty to see all this. He trembled for happiness at the sight of these people.

He heard Alcar say: 'Steady, André. Don't forget I'm also guided by other powers and that this also moves me deeply. I have experienced this several times and I always feel very happy when I see them again in all this beauty. They are people in a material organism. Look, André, how they radiate and how delicate that organism is! This is human beauty. These garments are like those of the spiritual human beings of the fourth sphere, but materially, because this material condition is similar to the one of the fourth sphere on our side. I could have explained this to you on our side, but this sight reflects their overall condition.'

'How amazingly beautiful these people are, Alcar. I could not have imagined such holiness.'

Like the fourth sphere, young and beautiful! Look at those buildings and this environment, and here women, men and children are living. Oh, such happiness. It was like paradise, André thought.

'This is already a paradise', he heard his leader say. 'Isn't the fourth sphere on our side like paradise? This is a paradise, but a material one. Fancy that. Here are birds of unprecedented beauty and flowers unknown on earth. What people have here is also found on earth in various things, but on earth everything is in a lower condition. Did you expect that, André?'

'How could I have expected this? It is a great wonder. How beautiful these people are. All this beauty has moved me deeply. These people cannot be compared with the human body on earth, they are transparent, Alcar.'

'I told you. These beings are like the spiritual beings living in the fourth sphere.'

471

'Can people on the side beyond see all this?'

'Yes, but only those who have reached the fourth sphere, it is not until then that they can be connected with it.'

'And I still live on earth, Alcar.'

'For you it is quite an other thing, because it belongs to my work. You have seen the seventh sphere, you have been to the sixth and seventh sphere with the highest master, a prince of love, and only because you serve as an instrument on earth for the masters. Otherwise it would not have been possible, André. Only those who have entered the fourth sphere will come here to see what awaits us. Isn't it a mighty grace? Can't you be grateful to be allowed to see this while you are still on earth?'

'I am very happy, Alcar, but people will not accept it at all. This is going too far, it is beyond them, too incredible for those on earth.'

'Those who cannot accept and believe this had better ignore it, André. We do not want to impose it on them. The others who can accept a life after death will begin to think and gratefully accept everything. These sensitive people can imagine this, when they hear of all this bliss, of all this spiritual and material happiness. They will feel this within them and they will be grateful to us for having been allowed to receive this image of what awaits us all.'

'It is tremendous, Alcar, I have no words for it, and to think that I am allowed to experience this.'

'Accept, my boy, that this also belongs to my work or it would not have happened. You receive everything now and all this is spiritual and cosmic consciousness. You are spiritually awake and conscious now and you can absorb all this. You will presently see and understand why you may experience all this and what your mediumship means. I'll also explain that to you and what I have told you about it is really nothing; only flashes of your inner life and mediumship on earth. You serve, André, so do the masters and I too. Don't ask why and what for, but observe; we'll go into that later. Now you must observe everything for people on earth should also be able to imagine what you saw as a human being departed from his body. Look at this nature, André, it is like the Summerland. You know the quiet and peace of the fourth sphere, but these people are still deeper and more conscious, because all these beings have been in the seventh sphere. Their appearance however is like that of the spirits of the Summerland, it radiates and it is pure like

472

nobody on earth is. The earthly organism is beautiful and strong; here their build is quite different, including the inner organs, in short this planet built an other material organism than the planet earth. The atmosphere is different, the orbit of this planet differs from that of the earth, and everything is in a different condition unknown to the earth. The flowers and trees are also different and the water is crystal-clear and human life is so clean and pure as only the perfect spiritual being can be. Just imagine such happiness, feel what it means to be a human being and feel what awaits all of us. My God, how grateful people on earth should be when they die. All sorrow is gone and great happiness awaits them.

You can observe them now, André, the masters have established this connection. When they proceed to other things and concentrate on something else, contact with this world will be broken. So see as much as you can, in a while it will no longer be possible.'

André looked at everything and took in as much as he could. How is it possible? he thought. Look at these garments and these beautiful people! He saw cosmic beings, angels in a material organism. It is almost incredible, he thought, and yet there they were.

'Do you feel, André, that Emschor could not show this to Lantos, that Lantos could not be connected? It is not possible unless one lives in the fourth sphere on this side. Lantos would nevertheless be convinced of all these laws and the possibility to proceed, for it belongs to our work. Lantos and his soul are also instruments of Cesarino as are all who work for the masters. So you see that many beings are working with us to convince mankind of our life and we all serve that purpose. Master Emschor and Lantos were one, Lantos was once his own child, and both of them along with many others help us to accomplish that. That had also been calculated in advance and master Emschor knew that this would happen.

This beautiful image that you now observe belongs to this great work and we may well be grateful for it.'

'It is all so amazing, Alcar. This is a paradise and people here are happy. Here worries and shortage are unknown. Is this planet free from them, Alcar?'

'Yes, my son, everything here is love, they know they can advance and they know their Father in heaven.'

'Is everything they have here also on earth, Alcar?'

473

'I said before that many things known on earth are also present here. People on earth have music and other art and great many other things, art, however, has reached such an incredibly high level here, that we would not be able to understand it. Art is like their own life, in accordance with the love they have. Life is not cursed here any more; they don't lie nor deceive. Everything is different here.'

'Are there kings or rulers?'

Alcar looked at André and said: 'How could such beings live here? All that belongs to the earth and they have discarded that long ago. That happened already in the first sphere on our side. Could those who have reached the first sphere act like those tyrants, I mean those who destroy others? No, my son, that is not possible, you should have known.'

'How is their life, Alcar?'

'Their life is like ours on this side. There, too, are masters just like in all spheres on our side, because leadership is essential, though they are princes of love. They are respected the way we feel for the being who has advanced beyond us and has more love. They provide for everything, they love their children and give themselves entirely for those who have reached this level. Everything reflects their wisdom, their life is pure and sacred and that in a material body.'

'That is how everyone looking for higher life conceives happiness.'

'Yes, that's the way those who feel the true fire of love think, that's how all of us imagine the world and how the earth could have been. It is difficult to imagine happiness, pure happiness that is, in a material condition, yet man here enjoys this happiness. Now imagine this happiness, André, no hatred, no jealousy, no deceit, no violence, no egotism, no passion and no war or any other violence, nothing of all those passions, all those troubles man on earth experiences. Here is only peace, holy peace and true love, though we are only on the fourth cosmic degree.'

'Have they got money like on earth?'

'No, André, that is not possible either, life here is different. There is only inner value. All these earthly things are absent and yet everything is present here and that is for everybody. There are seven degrees of inner life and those seven degrees are like the seven spheres on our side. The lowest degree of inner and spiritual attunement is the human being who lives in the seventh sphere on our side. A spirit from the seventh sphere starts in the first degree and gradually advances. Those spheres, those degrees of inner life we also find on all those other and higher planets. Only the transitions, those other planets, which form part of it, have not yet attained this attunement. However, there is only one material degree and that body is ready. Do you understand what I mean, André?'

'If I understood you correctly everything is completely different from the earth and it is only here that one passes into that perfect material organism.'

'Quite so. Those transitions, which are planets, have their own attunement and although inner life has already covered that long way, it is all the same not ready to accept this attunement, that is this life. If a being from the seventh sphere would be directly born here it would cause some disturbances, for this material organism is more advanced than inner man living in the seventh sphere is. We find this on all planets and that even applies to the highest cosmic degree, which is the seventh cosmic heaven.

It is a refined material organism and the soul who enters it must be in harmony with this material attunement.'

'It is difficult to believe that transitions are still necessary for those higher beings.'

'It is quite clear, though, André. Just think of our own life. The more we advance, the more difficult it becomes to attain these higher conditions.

I live in the fifth sphere and there are two more spheres above me that I can reach, but it will take hundreds of years to acquire the love they feel and have in those spheres. They live in and around me and yet I can't see them, I am not even aware of their life and presence. They, however, do see us and they feel and know what we are doing and the way we think.

All those spheres are present, there are buildings, temples and flowers, for I have shown that to you on these journeys and a while ago, yet, I do not see anything of all that beauty. Everything lies in and around me and I must try to acquire it.

I am already connected with the sixth sphere but I am still a stranger there, although those living there will receive me with open arms and they are glad that another soul has attained that level. That also applies to them, they must be able to prepare themselves and those transitory planets serve that purpose. Then occurs, what the beings in the third and fourth sphere on our side receive time and again, that they are going to experience what they have acquired. That very beautiful organism demands all spiritual concentration and you will no doubt feel, André, that this life is beyond description. The masters know what is required for that. If inner life is not fully prepared for it, this disturbance, as I said before, differs from the one on earth and they will lose their balance.'

'Are there illnesses here, Alcar?'

'No, André, there are no illnesses here, no nervous disturbances or all those terrors people on earth know, for the inner human being lives his natural life and adjusts himself to those laws and he tries to acquire still higher laws. This planet therefore has one organism, but the inner human being can advance to acquire seven degrees. So you see, André, it is quite distinct from that on earth, for on earth we have seven material degrees.

Nature on this planet is like it is in our fourth sphere, the birds are amazingly beautiful as are the flowers and all other life are beyond description. All those disharmonic conditions of the planet earth are unknown here. The misery and sorrow of the earth is here pure and unselfish love. These cosmic human beings are all perfectly happy and this happiness awaits us, André.'

'Are these people born as on earth, Alcar?'

'You mean whether that has changed, André?'

'Yes, Alcar.'

'No, my boy, that is the same for all life, human or animal, so also here. There is but one possibility and we receive that from the first stage. That is for the entire universe. God created two bodies for all planets, the creative or male and the driving or female body. On this planet it is a sacred event. It is the most sacred event God has created, for it is creation which the human and Divine being received from his All-Father. Here it is sacred, André. The further we advance, the deeper we penetrate what is most sacred of all, and we'll feel deeper and purer, which is completely unknown on earth. The feeling they possess is beyond my own power. However, we know how they feel, how their life is and how they think, but we cannot comprehend this pure bond which exists between two human beings, because we have not advanced that far. They live a different life than we would want and could. When a child is born they know the attunement of this young life beforehand and above all where the inner life, the soul as spirit and as human being, lived, who it is and where they have met and known this inner life. Do you feel this marvel, my son?'

'Yes, Alcar.'

'There is a lot more of which people on earth have no idea, because they don't know this paradise-like condition. They are all, without exception, clairvoyant to the highest degree. These people, André, are cosmically conscious, cosmically orientated, they know who belong to them, for all are twin-souls.'

'How superior this is, Alcar.'

'It is bound to, André. All those who have reached the fourth sphere on our side are spiritually conscious and have consequently reached the third cosmic consciousness. If I were not cosmically conscious, the consciousness belonging to the third cosmic degree, I could not have told you or explained to you anything of all this mightiness belonging to our cosmic degree. However, it is in me, I experienced it and I can connect myself again with that which is below me. I see through all those degrees and I know the laws of nature both materially and spiritually. I know what I have to do to be in harmony with this mightiness and yet I'm only a child, a small particle, a spark of this mighty entirety.

If I can say what I see and hear what others who are not in my sphere can't see or hear but which is there, those higher beings will surely be able to, for they all lived on our side and were in the seventh sphere. They know all the cosmic laws of the first three cosmic degrees, they have experienced those degrees, they understand their God of Love, they know they can advance, in short they are conscious in their condition.

When a child is born here they can clearly see from its birth how this life will be, for there are no mysteries any more for the human being and every being knows what he will achieve in that life. When I speak of being cosmically orientated this means that they understand their own life and that they experience this life as inner possession. The life in which they are born is therefore entirely open for them. All are one and know, they are conscious in their degree of life and this is cosmic consciousness.'

'What remarkable things you are telling again, Alcar. How I am yearning for it.'

'It's the holy truth, André, that's what awaits all of us. We are also longing for it and we are doing our best to get that far. We on our side, however, live relaxed and proceed consciously, like they do. We cannot sin and make mistakes any more, like all those in our life who have reached the highest spheres can't sin and make mistakes. In our life there is no disharmony any more and I'm only referring to the first sphere on our side, not to speak of the higher spheres which are spiritual heavens! All these beings who have experienced many transitions before they passed on to this planet have a tremendous love and are one in everything. When they have advanced that far both pass on and accept this mighty happiness our heart is yearning for. They have both earned that happiness.'

'You mean those who are attracted from the mental regions, Alcar?'

'Yes, André.'

'You speak of both, what does that mean?'

'That is an other wonder, my son. You know that all human beings when they have got that far will receive their twin-soul. There even are people on earth who have their eternal twin soul. But most people on earth, and only those who yearn, long, feel and can give much love, who are conscious in their feeling and love will receive their twin-soul on this side, that bond is forever.

However, that is only possible when they love and understand themselves, the life of their own soul and all other life. Souls, people, then receive the mightiest bliss man can ever receive and that is the twin-love. The happiness you'll then feel within you and own is beyond description. You think that the universe is within you, that God Himself lives in you. This feeling, this happiness, my son, is tremendous. It is so mighty and great that you float and feel like being adored. Everything smiles at you. You pass into the eternal quiet, you feel connected with God, and you feel pure love for man and animal and the life God created. There is a sacred fire deep within you, the Divine fire out of and by which created heaven and earth. All that mighty life will find a place in your heart and she or he who belongs to you feels like you do, loves like you love, carries the way you will; both will bend their head for all those pure gifts. No sigh, no incomprehension, no hard word, no false note will disturb that quiet. It is not possible, for both beings are one, one in each other's lives. They thank their Holy Father in heaven for this awe-inspiring bliss and accept, they are happy, for they have got that far.

478

When man after all that labour on earth receives this happiness on this side and assumes his spiritual dwelling here, which has been prepared by the angels of our world to give these souls a warm welcome, man kneels down and does not know whom to thank first. It is always our Holy Father in heaven Whom we must thank for that mighty bliss. Man will see his twin-soul, or will wait until she or he will come, and there will be feast on our side, spiritual happiness and they will be joined together forever. That is an awe-inspiring event, André, you know that because you were allowed to experience that in my own sphere. When I was allowed to show you that mighty event you saw that Christ manifested Himself and that they ascended. They were two pure beings who had completed a great task on earth and could finally proceed. They then live in Divine bliss for thousands of years, but they have to go on until they have experienced the seventh sphere. Now what will happen then?

No spirit can separate these twin-souls, they are and remain one life. Yet, the time will come when both live in unconsciousness, for both will pass on into the mental regions simultaneously. Do you feel this wonder, André? They are attracted and born on the first transition and they will meet there again. They already meet and recognize each other in childhood, they play and grow up and they know that they belong together. This consciousness has already fully developed when they are ten years of age so that they know they are together forever. That is present in their inner life. They advance ever more and follow each other. They finally reach this planet where they find each other again. They are born not a second too early; their parents are also aware of this. Try to imagine this and compare this consciousness with that of man on earth. However, it is not possible to make a comparison.

People here are awake and conscious and the human being retains his cosmic attunement, that is the driving or the creative organism. However, before they retain that attunement, and you'll feel that too, André, inner life will also pass into both organisms, which serves to accept and acquire the depth of this inner life and material life as a natural attunement, subsequently to accept their cosmic attunement again in the final degree. That is the organism they received at birth during the initial stage of the first planet.

Consequently, the further inner life advances the deeper it becomes. To that end inner life experiences creation here as well and that experience is a sacred wonder for those living here. Through this sacred wonder all beings living on this planet will awaken in a higher level of consciousness.

So they know, André, that they had the male body in their previous life and that, in the subsequent life, they will have the pure and sacred mother organism. And exactly by being allowed to know and feel all this, their bond and this connection are sacred. They know that they are one with God at the moment of connection, they feel one with God and they understand that the process of revelation is within them and that they experience it. They also know that they will receive a cosmic being and that this soul has been on its way for billions of years and that it is their father or mother, sister or brother they have known on the planet earth. Before these beings connect they'll kneel down and try to become an integral part of this mighty event. They'll seclude themselves and meditate. They'll experience the most sacred event God has created. What manifested itself in the universe will now be revealed in the mother organism. They are aware of what happens and they feel the deep significance of connection.

For them it is a sacred event. For them this event is the connection with God, for God laid this mighty event in the hands of man. These beings, André, prepare themselves and this preparation is necessary for they know that a great wonder is about to happen. They are all aware of this awe-inspiring wonder and those who are aware experience it in pure submission. You cannot imagine the depth of this sacred wonder, which is defiled on earth, for on earth it is often experienced in an animal-like way. Here they know that they attract the inner life, which yearns for it and is a child of God. They know they should be prepared to receive their sister or brother. And they are prepared, they are awake and conscious, for they experience creation the way God has given it to all His children.

When the mother feels that this wonder awakes and the young life grows and awakens, the mother is already connected with her child and in her deepest inner life she speaks with this new life. The mother will descend deeply into that other life, which is in her, with which she is one; they are one in feeling and in pure love.

That child, this young life, André, awaits happiness! We get to know another wonder, for the mother who receives one of the twin-souls will visit that other mother and they will stay together. They, too, are one

480

and speak of future happiness for him or her living in their body. They hear wonderful music, which is indescribably beautiful and makes them live and be happy. They pray and are completely in harmony with all and with themselves and they thank their Father in heaven for all those feelings, for all that bliss. From the connection onward they seclude themselves, they walk in the pure nature and prepare to receive this young life. They exclusively live for this young life within them. This way they feel God, feel and experience the wonder of creation, they descend deeply into this most sacred event in order to experience it consciously. When the moment of birth arrives no doctor is required nature is the healer. This knowledge is within them, all are natural, the spirit has it in its own hands. The mother secludes herself and gets ready. Heavenly music vibrates in her soul and those sounds give her an enhanced attunement. In this condition of prayer and meditation, of pure sounds of the soul, man is born. The more they advance and acquire inner value, the purer and mightier birth will become. These mothers do not need the help of others, everything is within them, they are like nature, they are conscious. The child radiates like a child of God can in that attunement. Within a few years it will be awake and conscious. It observes this world and it feels and assesses, even recognizes the inner life with which it is connected.

The mother organism is very sensitive, for the natural activity brought it into this exalted condition. As I said, the two mothers visit each other and will stay together for a long time. Their children are twin-souls. They emanate from an other planet, lived on earth, advanced through the spheres on this side and the long journey to the fourth cosmic degree has been attained. This young life is like an open flower and the love they all feel is awe-inspiring. There will be a feast for these young beings, for they have reached this degree. This child is brought up in a sphere of love and at an early age it already speaks of wonders and problems, this young life consciously passes on to the acquired level.

Consequently they experience this great wonder together. They are one in everything and are perfect for this attunement. Their deep inner life subsequently awakens and they reach maturity. They live their life together and they assume their duties appointed to them by the princes of love.

Subsequently, they experience creation. A law of earth does not bind them. This law resides in them for their yes is a sacred word and lie and deceit are unknown here.

Father and mother are unknown conceptions here, though I have to use these words in order to explain something of their sacred life to you. There are no parents here, no father or mother, they are all sisters and brothers in the spirit and love everything that lives. These are spiritual and material laws that nature imposes on them and these laws are experienced in a natural way. Nature here calls a halt to man and all obey, for all are one with nature.'

'How wonderful that is, Alcar. Who can accept this?'

'If people on earth feel this they will accept all this. The conception of being father and mother dissolves in the spheres, on our side we only know universal love. We already pass to that attunement starting in the first sphere. If we can't dissociate ourselves from being father or mother we can't advance any more, for this belongs to the planet earth. This is an earthly and material feeling and we have to discard these feelings.

Now that we know that we on this side, in the spheres, have got that far, we must accept that those living on this planet have advanced ahead of us and that all those earthly laws and conditions no longer exist. Universal love is above all earthly love, father and mother love dissolve in it and that is no different on this planet.'

'Is help during childbirth still necessary here, Alcar?'

'No, André, as I said before, they possess this strength, the material organism of this planet is like nature and is not defiled in any way.'

'When I understand you correctly you mean that everything happens on this planet in accordance with nature?'

'That's right, people here are spiritually and materially one.'

'It is marvellous Alcar. One simply must yearn for this. You have explained all those material degrees of the earth, but isn't there one degree that experiences birth in a natural way? Do all those people on earth need help, Alcar?'

'No, my son, there are human beings on earth who are like nature and who experience this amazing process by themselves, without help. They are the human beings we met in the first, second and third material degree and they, like those here, do not need all that earthly assistance. It shows you that the intellectual human beings have left the natural way, even though all those beings think that they are ahead of all those poor souls in these dark bodies.\*⁾ They have created a condi-

\*) See the 'Explanation' at the beginning of this book.

tion that is not natural any more. They drape themselves with decorations, they are well dressed, but they discarded their natural attunement. They lost themselves in their beautiful and rich lives and they do things people in the jungle would never do. That is instinct, nature and intellectual man has lost and defiled those laws of nature. Is it that terrible when I say that the natural core has been lost? That they adorn their bodies, but that the inner being spiritually starves to death?

In those jungles no doctor is needed, nature has developed to the extent that the human being, the inner life, has acquired this strength and they experience this the way their bodies and nature are. That harmony is restored on this planet, their spiritual and material life have one attunement, their life is natural.

On this side, my son, they have advanced that far and that is their inner possession. Scientists are not needed here.'

'Are there no scientists here, Alcar?'

'Yes, certainly, but not for illnesses because there are no illnesses here.'

'How incredible that is, Alcar.'

'Indeed, André, but I'm telling the holy truth, or there would be no happiness here either. The scientists of this planet are cosmically conscious and are in communication with other planets, the planets of the fifth cosmic degree.'

'Can't the scientists here follow all the sciences of the planet earth?'

'Only those sciences that belong to their proper life, in other words, they try to acquire the laws of nature.'

'That is also amazing, Alcar. So there are no lawyers, no doctors, theologians or sciences known on earth?'

'No, André, because lie or deceit are not known here, every person knows himself, they are spiritually and cosmically conscious and do not need religions any more. All that belongs to the planet earth. Lawyers are needed on earth, because there is evil. Do you feel this wonder, André?'

'Yes, Alcar, I understand you perfectly. Don't they have telephone and television, Alcar, for that is a great wonder, isn't it?'

'Those are indeed great wonders, André, but they are no longer necessary here.'

'You said that those wonderful inventions are not needed any more, Alcar? They belong to the greatest wonders the earth has, don't they?'

'Indeed, my son, but I'll explain this great problem to you, listen. This great wonder, André, is the inner possession of those who live here, they have acquired it. Do you feel what this means?'

'You mean to say that these people possess a technical wonder? How is that possible, Alcar, that can't be accepted, can it?'

'I'm telling the truth, though. Don't forget, my son, that all these people are cosmically conscious and clairvoyant to the highest degree. A material invention of the earth is the inner possession of this being. Those living here attune to that other human being and can manifest themselves far away from their own body. The material inventions of the earth are the inner possession of those living here and consequently are spiritual gifts. People here no longer need these material connections. If one of them would like to speak to some other being thousands of miles away from him, he inwardly attunes to him and a spiritual connection is established. They can manifest themselves on that spot; they depart from their material organism and experience what they want. All these people here experience spiritual wonders, but in a material life. These are wonders we know and have acquired on our side. They speak with each other over great distances and pass on into each other. This spiritual connection is infallible. Distances are no longer a barrier for them because they have spiritually advanced and developed that far. They can see into every other life and they can establish a connection wherever that life may be, then happens what they want. Their sharp and infallible intuition and concentration establish this long-distance conversation.

They don't need all those inventions of the earth, although they know and have material wonders not yet known on earth. They move in space to which end they possess technical wonders very similar to those on earth, but here everything is perfect.'

'Can accidents occur here, Alcar?'

'No, André, that is not possible any more.'

'How incredible that is, Alcar.'

'And yet so very simple, my son. For no human being can die here before his time, especially not by an accident, for it is fixed and known a long time in advance.'

'You mean to say all people living here know in advance when they will die?'

'Yes, that's what I mean, André. When they move into space, they know beforehand whether something can and will happen and they prevent this disturbance.'

484

'You are going ever deeper, how amazing this is, Alcar. It is nearly unbelievable and yet I have to accept it for the Side Beyond has already advanced that far.'

'Indeed, André. The scientists on this planet co-operate and all are working for one purpose, the connection with the higher planets, which has already been established. They communicate with those who are ahead of them, to which end they have instruments. Although technical science is well advanced here, their inner spiritual possession dominates their material abilities. Only those inventions are and can be made which are useful and only serve to help mankind, to make life more comfortable. No other inventions will come about. The inner condition of the human being is taken into account in every respect. Everything is geared to it and everyone lives and works to acquire inner possession. Their activities cannot be compared with those of the earth. All that toil is unknown here. Each being has material and spiritual happiness; there is no shortage here, all live in perfect happiness.

They designed all buildings and temples themselves, like in our spiritual world. They also have vehicles which can rise from the ground, but, as I said, accidents do not happen any more.'

'Has all that been calculated, Alcar?'

'Not only calculated, André, but intensely felt. As I said, they oversee a technical wonder, which means that they know beforehand whether a machine will operate properly, for they can feel that. That is difficult for people on earth, although it is possible. There are people on earth who feel that an accident is going to happen and they act accordingly. Is it so strange when I say that they can feel that and inwardly possess these powers? When this happens on earth, these people usually receive those messages and feelings from our side, they are warned by their beloved ones. Here, however, they have acquired those feelings, which are spiritual gifts for they have attained that higher attunement. So they know this in advance and prevent material destruction.'

'How marvellous all this is, Alcar.'

'Every human being will attain this, my son, all of us will come that far. Those who pass away are not mourned, for they know that they will return soon. Now we get to know other laws. The return happens the way we know in the world of the unconscious for the third cosmic degree. What may take many centuries there does not happen here any more. As I told you, what the world of the unconscious is for the planet earth are the mental regions for this cosmic degree, though everything is different.'

'Don't they have to wait that long for a new organism, Alcar?'

'No, André, here cosmic harmony rules. Life on the transitory planets lasts longer than on the first three cosmic degrees; as inner and material life advance a change sets in. People live on all transitory planets, but inner life is now in harmony with the material organism and that is the cosmic balance. This cosmic balance has been lost on earth, for there are people on earth who could have been in the spheres of light many centuries ago, but they still live in the spheres of darkness.'

'What kind of mystery is that, Alcar?'

'This spiritual and cosmic mystery belongs to the planet earth, my son. I'll explain that to you and it will be clear to you how natural everything is that we have learned up to now. Listen and try to follow me.

It tells us, André, that the more we advance the more our inner and material life will get in harmony and that we return to the natural attunement. When inner life is ready here it will be attracted immediately. On earth, however, this is not possible and sometimes it takes centuries. And why does it take centuries? Because evil dominates on earth, that is, that life living there is in a disharmonic condition and brought this about. Violence, animalization, destruction by others and suicide dominate on earth. All these passions cause cosmic disturbances for inner life. As a result, souls enter our life too early; they pass away before their cosmic time and wait to be attracted again. Consequently, the astral worlds for the planet earth are overpopulated because of these disturbances. The soul, who puts an end to life on earth, as I explained to you, must and will return on earth in order to experience the third cosmic degree. Thus, back to earth. However, there are millions of souls who violated these laws and it therefore takes centuries before all these people receive a new body. This overpopulation is caused in that all these beings have to experience these lives again in order to be able to reach the spheres of light. Is that clear to you, André?'

'Yes, Alcar.'

'Well then, everything is different here. There is no passion here, no violence, no suicide, and no destruction, there is cosmic harmony on all those transitory planets for this cosmic degree and it will therefore be clear to you that we get to know other laws. Here, André, man is cosmically conscious and in harmony with nature. As a result we learn to know cosmic harmony, because inner life has advanced that far and man and animal are in natural harmony.

The further we advance the more material and inner life are one in everything. In the mental regions one soul waits for one body. In the case of the planet earth, however, thousands of souls wait for one organism and this explains the disharmonic conditions of the planet earth, which we have encountered on our long road and which I have been allowed to explain to you.

Is it clear to you, André, how amazing all this is? And, most of all that we people have our happiness and sorrow in our own hands? That people on earth are completely unaware of this? That each being must get in harmony with creation and acquire these laws of nature?'

'Yes, Alcar, I understand you in everything, it is also natural.'

'This cosmic and natural harmony must be present here and that is awaking, passing away and being born in the next stage, in an other organism that is ready.'

'How old do these people get, Alcar?'

'That varies in accordance with their level. That process begins already on the first transitory planet. By earthly standards people will live to be one hundred and fifty years, and when the fourth cosmic degree has been attained even older and they'll exceed two centuries. Thus, the age of the material organism and inner life is gradually increasing, because we proceed to the All. Is that clear to you, André?'

'Yes, Alcar, and it is very natural.'

'It must be, my son, and it has a cosmic meaning as well. The highest age life will reach on this planet exceeds three centuries. On the fifth cosmic degree and this is again a spiritual mystery for earthly mortal beings, people live to be thousands of years and the inner and material life has passed on to other and higher laws, of which I don't know anything either. In the seventh material cosmic degree there is hardly a material end.'

'Does the soul not have to wait longer, Alcar?'

'No, André, because there is cosmic harmony again. Starting from this planet we get to know these laws of harmony and however unlikely it is for us as well, there is no change in that respect, even though material life lasts thousands of years. These are therefore other and higher laws than those we have encountered so far and this is one event.'

'You mean that the process of dying and attraction of inner life is one activity?'

'Yes, André, and in it resides that cosmic order.'

'Now I'm beginning to understand, Alcar. What happens when we have reached the seventh cosmic degree? Do you know something about the age of material life there?'

'I told you a while ago that figures are almost unknown on the seventh cosmic degree and there is almost no end to life there. The soul nevertheless passes into the astral cosmos and man has returned to the All. We cannot follow or understand the laws in force in the All. Creation can be followed up to the seventh cosmic degree, but what happens after that no spirit nor human being knows anything about. I explained that to you at the pyramid. We have to require all those cosmic degrees.'

'If I understand everything correctly, Alcar, the All is like the mental regions?'

'Very good, my son, but the Divine attunement. No time is wasted unnecessarily on all these planets; people don't do things which they regret later on for that is not possible any more. Here, on this planet, André, a human being will achieve in one life exactly what should be achieved. People on earth do not think of laws of nature and live to the full. All people here know what they are living for and what is expected of them. All these beings serve.

When people here die during the first stage, they pass on into a subsequent life, at an other and higher level. On earth, however, we return many times to one and the same stage, because we have forgotten ourselves during that stage.

The further people advance, the longer they live. Is that clear to you now, André?'

'Yes, Alcar. If I understand you correctly this only applies to inner life?'

'Exactly, that's what I mean. There is only one material organism, but there are seven degrees for inner life, transitions of development. On earth we see black and brown people, but the highest body in material condition is that of the white race*), here, however, man has only to do with spiritual degrees for which he will return. Again, it is the process of death and birth and receiving a new body, the male as well as

*) See the 'Explanation' at the beginning of this book.

488

the female organism. In all these degrees people live in the female and male material organism in order to experience the depth of inner life in that higher condition. Great respect is felt for the mother organism, the mother organism is most sacred, for it experiences creation and therefor goes through the soul.'

'What amazing things you tell me, it makes my head spin, Alcar.'

'Mine does not, André, and none of them who live on this side and on this planet. Those who live here know all this. I'm also grateful that I know this and I build on it, I'll concentrate on it. I said already, that I hope I'll have advanced that far in a few thousands years, though I already have spiritual happiness and quiet in me so that I can prepare myself. I'll dedicate my entire life to it. I thank God that He has given me the grace to bring all this on earth. I'm grateful, my son, that I live and am awake, that I am a particle of all this mightiness and that I have learned all that on this side. What you now experience, my son, is sacred. This is only given to a few on earth. It is a grace to be a medium for it and you can be happy.'

'I am, Alcar.'

'I know, André. We are all happy when we can do something for our brothers and sisters on earth.'

'Is all that hard work man on earth has to accomplish not necessary here any more, Alcar?'

'No, it isn't. For instance coal is not needed here, for there is a force of nature which is also known on earth. It is electricity, though its use is more advanced. Sunlight is collected and processed, which is stronger than electricity, it is not yet known on earth. This power is known on this planet. People here know the meaning of this enormous power; it can be traced back to the primary stage. Thousands of inventions stem from it, which are used here.

People here are vegetarians; not a single animal is killed. Animal food is not used any more: the refined organism could not even digest it. They live on natural food, the products which grow in nature. There is natural food everywhere, just like in our spheres. If one wants food, one goes into nature and picks the food if nothing is directly at hand. This atmosphere differs from the one of the planet earth and this also has a cosmic meaning. Consequently, every planet has its own atmosphere and its life is in accordance with it. Heat and cooling off are also known here.'

'Is all the cattle we have on earth not present here, Alcar, and not needed any more?'

'No, killing cattle is not necessary any more, though we know that noble animals like the horse and many species of animals live here. Man and animal, however, are one. The animal here gives itself entirely to the human being and the advanced human being gives himself to the animal and is most grateful for all this love. That is God's intention. Here, everything is pure like nature.

Their garments are made of a silky substance and are like the spiritual garb seen in the entire cosmos.'

'It is amazing, Alcar.'

'So it is, André, and yet so natural.'

'Are all those animal species we have on earth only for the planet earth?'

'Yes, André, every planet produced its own organism and this also applies to the animal kingdom. Only the higher species of animals, as I explained to you, go with us to the All and they'll attain that degree. You also know that all those animal species will and must dissolve into the highest species, which is the animal that has attained the highest degree in its species. All that cattle, all those thousands of animal species belong to the human condition on earth, is that clear to you, André?'

'You mean to say that when inner man has got that far the animal has also advanced to that stage?'

'Yes, that is what I mean, in essence this happens on earth. One day all that cattle will become extinct, for it will not be needed any more. We know, however, that this animal has also reached a higher stage in the course of this evolution.'

'Have they got machines which are used on earth for a lot of things, Alcar?'

'Oh yes, they do have them, André, but not like those on earth. Thousands of machines do the work for the human being here to his advantage, but not like on earth for the benefit of a few, while others are starving. That is not possible here, there is no starvation, no shortage, man is happy here. Everyone has his own task, as I said before, assigned by higher beings. Mother love is the dearest possession and bliss known here, mother love dominates and supports this planet. It is the mother who experiences this cosmic and Divine wonder and holy respect is felt for the wonder of creation. Those living in the female and

490

mother organism have to adapt themselves to this natural activity and this event is sacred. You may think that this life is very complicated, but it isn't. It is in fact very simple, for one understands oneself here and one is conscious in everything.'

'What should one learn as a child here, Alcar?'

'Children and grown-up people must learn the laws of nature. On our side, too, we do just that. Their life is like ours in the seventh sphere, though in a material condition.

The masters are constantly in communication with them. The mentors say that our life of this planet is like we have learned to know it in the seventh sphere. What we have observed and possessed in a spiritual condition we also have here and it is the possession of all. You surely feel, André, that those messages have reached us too.

'Feel how wonderful it is', they said, 'and you can imagine what our life is like. What you know there, we have extracted from the cosmos in a material condition. Here we know that we will die and be born again, that we have to learn and that learning is our spiritual development, like the masters told us when we lived there. We have temples and buildings as in the fourth sphere, but ours are material and radiate, as we all have inner radiance.'

They were also asked: 'Have you got your own language?'

We know all languages of the earth and we also have our own languages, though they are hardly used, for we use the spiritual language. Why should we needlessly complicate matters when we can pick up each others thoughts and feelings? We try to live like we have learned and acquired in the seventh sphere. Consequently, our life here is a life of pure happiness. You can imagine our life, but also realize that we are material beings and possess all that in a material condition. You all know the wonder of creation, but we experience it consciously, none excluded. Imagine what it means to be conscious with the All-Father. We are so very happy, for God lives in our midst and we feel close to Him. We are in communication with our brothers and sisters who have already reached the fifth cosmic degree, and that life, that happiness cannot be compared with ours. We receive many inventions from our sisters and brothers of the fifth cosmic degree, but we can only prepare and apply them when we have advanced that far and have acquired the highest inner degree. We only want to use those inventions that can serve us, but what we can do ourselves, we will achieve with our own efforts. You know the quiet and peace we have. We are all like you, but the sixth higher inner degrees are ahead of you.

We also experience the celebration of our Master Jesus Christ, which is no different than in your sphere, though the higher masters feel the sorrow and pain suffered by the Master more intensely. They explain to us how it should be experienced and felt. This depth means descending into His holy life. What we could experience on the planet earth after which we returned to the spheres, we also experience here when we are all one. Nothing has changed and it also applies to the fifth cosmic degree and all planets. It is experienced and that will remain so, for we feel the great injustice done to Him. We establish this connection from time to time and we receive your feelings. We know your life and we return to the past and you know the connection required. He who has established this connection with you lives in the fifth spiritual degree and the masters assigned this to me.'

That is what this mentor said to all of them, André, and once I was allowed to hear this conversation. I was also connected. I told you of a spiritual connection between this planet and our side, which happens several times. I was allowed to experience this through my master Cesarino, for he established this connection, he was the instrument to receive these messages.'

'It is remarkable, Alcar.'

'All the beauty present here, André, is the possession of the material beings who live here.'

'I have no words for it, Alcar, I don't know what to say. Is there night and day here?'

'We find that throughout the universe. This planet also describes its own orbit around its sun, though it differs from that of the planet earth and that can be seen and felt. They know seasons like on earth, but these are in no way related to the earth.'

'Surely they know time and have established a measure for it?'

'Time exists on all planets and this applies to all material bodies inhabited by life. Life brings this along and not only life but nature compels man to act in accordance with it. Not only the planet as a cosmic entity, but also the material body needs sleep, because it is essential for the organism.

Consequently, this also applies to these people, although these beings are higher than material man on earth is. As I said, this planet has an other atmosphere than the earth. That is why nature is different and that the produce of this planet is quite distinct from that of the earth. Fruit growing in this nature is deliciously juicy, like in our life. Man has concentrated himself on it, that is what they live and work for and they give themselves entirely. We know they make tremendous progress and although much has been achieved this process goes on ever more.

The search for material perfection is within reach of man and this also applies to the earth. On earth new and better types of fruit are being cultivated which is possible in nature.'

'So there are a great many things, Alcar, which are known on earth and are also used here?'

'Yes, indeed, especially what nature produces but also art and sciences, though everything is more perfect here.'

'If I understand you correctly, Alcar, all those institutions essential on earth for self-preservation are not necessary here any more?'

'No, André, as I said before lies and deceit are unknown here, people do not steel and fight, here is spiritual quiet.'

'How delightful that is, Alcar. So nothing is ever wasted here and man does not desire the property of others.'

'As I just told you all those earthly passions are not known here. There are no rulers here, such people are only known on earth where they are essential, here they aren't, for everyone can be trusted and every being possesses true love.'

'It is amazing and great happiness awaits us people of the earth. If only they could accept this. That, however, will not be possible.'

'I told you that they cannot imagine this, though we'll convince many. Others, however, think we are insane and dreamers, but that is up to them. One day they'll get that far and will also experience this. No illness, no restlessness, no death, no fear of the future, nothing of all this earthly misery is found here. Just try to imagine. My God, who would not want to live for that?

So, all that earthly misery is unknown here. Everybody knows how to live, what age he will reach and thousands of other things, for they are conscious in everything. It is not until now that man uses his inner gifts and although some also do on earth it is not in this condition and attunement.'

'How is the arrangement of such a planet, Alcar?'

'You mean how it is looked after and managed?'

'Yes, that's what I mean.'

'Oh, that is very simple. The masters live in the centre of the planet, just like on our side. The masters look after us all and we after others down to the lowest degree. In this way everybody is connected and that connection emanates from the centre and encompasses the entire planet. From this centre they issue their instructions which are punctually and faithfully executed, for everybody is doing his work in a perfect way because they cannot make conscious mistakes. This is the spiritual connection and the planet is governed like our spiritual world.

People on this planet, André, are quite distinct from inner and material man on earth. Oh, that pure love they possess here! That fire, that spiritual fire is their inner possession. To be allowed to live in such a condition, in such a splendid material organism, to play music, to paint, to sculpture, all that, André, is so superior and pure and nobody on earth can imagine that.

Here is spiritual and material happiness. My God, how could we thank You! Such is life here, André, on the fourth cosmic degree, which you have now been able to see. It is a grace only few people may experience. This is the honest truth. One day we'll also be here.'

'How long will it be before the animal-like human being will enter here, Alcar?'

'You mean the animal-like human being of the earth, don't you?'

'Yes, Alcar, I meant that degree of consciousness.'

'Possibly ten, twenty or perhaps even a hundred thousands years.'

'Before they are born here?'

'Yes, it may take that long.'

'And coarse-material people or those who are already open to spiritual things and can accept all this?'

'For coarse-material people it may take thousands and thousands of years and also for spiritually sensitive people.'

'How is it possible, Alcar, that long?'

'Yes, André, do not forget that the more we advance the slower progress will be. It may be a thousand years before I reach the seventh sphere, and thousands of years will pass before I enter the mental regions and before I'll be born on this planet.'

'It is a long way we have to cover, Alcar.'

'That way leads us to God, my son.

Once you feel spiritual ground under your feet, you feel safe and advance quietly. You can't hurry, that would be wrong, for you cannot keep that pace up. We on this side proceed consciously and we know what we can achieve. In the spirit you cannot leave anything out and yet all of us will be born here. We prepare ourselves, we serve and we sacrifice ourselves for life, we give ourselves entirely, we work and pray and advance step by step.

Gerhard staked everything, which he could because he possessed those powers. But he won't be able to in the second and third sphere. It becomes increasingly difficult and an other life is required. Those spheres cannot be reached that easily. He made a lot of progress within a few years, but the years would increase tenfold for him to enter from the first sphere into the second or into the third sphere.

People on earth who begin to feel that they'll live eternally should calmly adjust themselves and allow the Holy Ghost to act on them. They will reach our side and they can proceed. When they experience everything they will hurry back to the earth to tell their relatives that they are alive, they'll return to the spheres with renewed courage to acquire the higher feelings.'

'So insanity is not known here either?'

'You felt that correctly, André, though you have known that for a long time. No, that is indeed impossible. All are spiritually conscious and insanity is in essence the influence of a lower consciousness. That is unknown here that is past and is not possible any more. All those illnesses and spiritual phenomena belong to the earth. You know why, I explained that to you. The material organism of the planet earth is ill and society is worse. Nothing is in harmony with nature in accordance with which they should live. It is incomprehensible that the number of people killed is not greater, for when the earth is observed from this side one trembles and shivers because of all evil, all the misery but if you tell them of eternal life, they look at you and think you are insane. Here it is different. They yearn for spiritual wisdom and receive it. Here everyone adjusts himself and receives and experiences the greatest bliss.

If only it was like this on earth, if they only wanted to destroy death, they would have advanced and the aspects of the earth would change.'

'Aren't there religions here, Alcar?'

'No, André, but you have known that for a long time. Nothing of all those earthly religions and religious hatred are known here, these earthly aspects are not present. People here yearn for spiritual nourishment, which is satisfied. They only know life and they love this life in pure love. That is all they need and it is their religion, it is the perfection that man needs. They only know Christ, for their feelings for God's holy Child are deep.

How do people act on earth? We hear their prayers, but we also know that their prayers are not pure, because they ask God to destroy their enemies. The priests do the same and go on praying in this way. However, such clergymen only live on earth.'

'So, there are no clergymen here, Alcar?'

'No, my son, those people are not needed any more, for they do not even know themselves and what can these beings do for others? They do not know their God; nor Christ or life, they are also living dead. Here, however, one lives and is awake and conscious. These people do not lock themselves up, they live life as nature and God wants them to. All those religions belong to the planet earth, for it is there that we, people, begin to awaken for advance. All, none excluded, my son, love, they have true love.'

'What a mighty difference with the earth, Alcar.'

'Man on earth holds happiness in his own hands. Those who seek the good and live accordingly, the way God wants, acquire inner happiness and know that God guards them. Life on earth is difficult, but only because it is a school of hard knocks for spiritual life. It cannot be evaded, for people must go back to the All. We know what awaits us, the spheres on this side and this life on the fourth cosmic degree. Shouldn't we do everything for this? Man here lives in a material paradise and God has reserved that for all His children.

Life is lived here for the happiness of others and it is not possible for one of them to feel unhappy. They live here as in a large family governed by princes of love who guard them all and serve the life living here. We'll find this situation towards the end of the earth. The earth will change, and the good will prevail when there are no more demons in hell, when the first and second cosmic degree have passed on to the third cosmic degree and those pre-animal-like beings have reached the highest and spiritual attunement.

On earth people must be urged on to seek the good, that is not necessary here any more. One time all that misery will disappear from the earth when there are no more illnesses, no passions or violence,

496

then all people present on earth are awake and conscious and know where they are going to and what awaits them. We are not understood yet, André, and we don't blame them. One day, however, they will get that far by which time we hope to be here and live in all this beauty.

How must we thank our God. My Father in heaven feels my deep gratitude, André, I'll never forget this either. I'll always think of this and we'll do our utmost to acquire this happiness and wisdom. To that end we have to learn a lot, but we'll manage. My heart feels it and it warms my soul, this is the driving force to accept to give ourselves entirely like God wants us to. How blissful everything is and love radiates and flows towards us, in essence we are already connected.

All of them cultivated those spiritual flowers and they, too, collapsed many a time before they had advanced that far. They covered a long road and yet, they once lived like wild animals on the second and third cosmic degree and felt nothing of all this love and inner richness. Now that we know this it urges us on to make a start, for this road is open for us, we want to start, won't we, André?'

André looked at his leader and thanked him profoundly.

'I'll make your ardour my own', he said. 'I shall and want to do that at all cost. I want to destroy my pedestal and myself, for there should be nothing left in me that could obstruct my spiritual progress.

Oh, if people on earth knew this. If only they wanted to discard themselves and find fault with themselves and not with others they would be well on their way. However, they invariably look at others, they are at fault. I notice that all the time, Alcar.'

'We'll experience that for a long time to come, for they forget that they are there to learn. They forget that they could not be there any more, if they had experienced their own karma and had made up. Nothing for nothing and not a single child of God will get unnecessary sorrow. Man looks for happiness, but that happiness does not come until on this side. They will not begin to feel their happiness until they have finished with their many lives. Every being seeks and attracts what they are themselves and have achieved. An animal-like being descends into the material organism and inspires that material life. What would happen if they also had this in their own hands?

People wonder why and for what reason they receive such a child, but deep down within them they have to do with that inner life and merely because of that they attracted that life and will make up.'

'That is not possible here any more, Alcar?'

'No, thank God they have advanced that far. These people are angels and they can only attract similar beings and this inspiration lives on our side. Do you feel, André, that nothing has changed yet and that nature still acts infallibly? That we shall attract in accordance with our inner being? When we have experienced our karma an other life will descend into that material organism and that life will do something for the earth. It is remarkable how well everything has been arranged; God oversaw this and knew how it would happen.

I was allowed to explain many wonders to you and if people do not seize this with both hands they are not worth being children of God. Yet, I should not speak like this, although I know they will trample upon this nourishment for the mind, they will abuse it and not accept it. Nevertheless, we reach many people and in a few hundred years we will have advanced that far. Then there will be people on earth who understand us and are grateful to hear about this. They will continue our work, because they feel how sacred everything is, how deep, how great and pure this message is which was passed on. I'll explain that once again and you'll then feel and see how I arranged everything before-hand, so that no mistakes could be made. I guarantee your mediumship, I hold these gifts in my hands and it is my task to tell you of our life.

Those who do not feel this do have to learn it. Later these people will be on earth and read our books, André, and then they'll make every effort to reach the spheres of light.

Then we, and all who follow us, will be understood and all will be grateful that we were given the grace to tell this. They will fold their hands and bend their head and know that they can proceed. It is not until then, André, that they will seek themselves and do not ask why and what for any more and that death is spiritual happiness and reunion on this side.

Yes, one day we'll be that far, and we'll be far, very far away and prepare ourselves to accept this. We follow Christ and all who have received God's life will have to follow Him.

An animal on this planet is thousands of years ahead of the rational being on earth. There are many species here that follow the Divine being in everything. They are grateful when being spoken to and they feel what this higher being wants. On our side they are the spiritual messengers, they have a similar task here, but in a material condition.'

498

'Did this planet also bring all this about, Alcar?'

'Everything we have seen on the first two cosmic degrees and the earth brought about, is present here, but only the seventh degree of animal species, of which I told you. The higher the more beautiful all life becomes, whether human or animal and everything growing in nature. So everything is perfect here and beyond description.'

'What a wealth, Alcar. I see the entire planet in front of me and also how everything happens.'

'I make you feel this, just as I did on our side. In the centre of this planet, my son, there is a mighty building and this building is the image of the pyramid on earth. However, this building is a Divine temple and has a different meaning. In it people concentrate on the All and are connected with those higher spheres and planets. I cannot describe this profusion, for this happiness is too profound for my feeling, but we know how everything is. There are buildings we have in the seventh sphere and which are of incredible beauty and the height of which cannot be seen, the upper section dissolves in this bright blue and they know why. I showed you this on our side. Everything is as they are inwardly. The architects who live here are spiritual artists. Their feeling is highly developed and mighty and that is what man seeking higher life creates. Everything living here belongs to them.

Material property is unknown here, they live in everything and with everything, for personal property does not exist, they discarded that a long time ago. Do you realize how mighty it is to be able to feel like that and to be allowed to live and to receive in this way? Wanting to live for that is a sacred feeling which is present in all of them. Nobody will disturb; they would not be able to. Everybody knows his own task and knows what is required of him or her. Everything here is perfect, spiritually perfect. As I told you, the technical wonders here are beyond description and beyond comprehension. They are thousands of years ahead of the earth. They float in space, for them there is no distance and they know this planet. There is no being who would not know what he possesses, for they own it inwardly. They have an infallible intuition and their main possession is that they know themselves.'

'You said, Alcar, that this planet is larger than the earth?'

'Hundreds of times larger than the earth, André.'

'And then to live on it as a large family?'

'Yes, billions of beings live here and yet it is one big family. They all travel, years on end and thus take possession of their beloved planet. They are one with everything here and even a grass-stalk is sacred to them. They know every patch of soil and have been there and they are lovingly welcomed on their journeys by their sisters and brothers. Do you feel, André, how great this love is, how mighty is their happiness? Their houses are open, for these houses are also the property of others and they are happy to receive and welcome their brothers and sisters.'

'Is that for everybody, Alcar?'

'Yes, this happiness is for everyone, my son, without exception, there is no distinction here.'

'What many wonders did you explain to me on this journey. How simple this life is and yet how profound, Alcar.'

'The depth of this life is their feeling, André. The further we get, the more we advance, and the simpler it becomes, however difficult this may seem. Only people on earth make their lives difficult. They do not understand anything of creation and lose themselves in everything and they feel very unhappy when husband or wife or child passes away. They cannot be helped and think themselves very unhappy. Here, on our side, that father or mother awakes and sees that life. Then there is no misery or grief any more, only happiness.

All this is known here, for I told you that they know where they are going. To be allowed to die here is a mercy and this also applies to the earth, though they don't feel it and they cry their eyes out. So on earth everything is different.

This difference is due to a lack of inner possession, of faith and confidence. That is why it is so sad on earth, they are living dead and feel lonely and abandoned. Here one being supports the other and they understand what is given to them. No more tears of suffering and grief are shed here, for they do not know what sorrow is. It is true that they can cry, but only for happiness and bliss because of everything they received from God. It shows their love and they weep for deep emotion and gratitude. Is this not a great and mighty happiness? Look at all that, André, and proclaim it on earth. Tell them what it is like here and that they will receive all this. A planet where billions of people live in harmony, isn't that a cosmic wonder? Don't we feel that we'll become like God? Has that Divine quality not always been in us from the beginning and haven't you noticed and felt it everywhere? I explained that Divinity in many conditions and wherever we were we saw and felt that Divine suggestion. Pursue it, feel accordingly and respond to it.

Feel the depth of you own inner life and descend into that depth. What you feel is either evil or misery, but if you descend deeper and deeper into yourself you will feel the quiet of God and you touch your own Divine attunement, for the spark of God lives in that pure quietude. You fall asleep and the tranquillity of the spirit descends in you. Poets on earth feel what all this means, but people who live like wild animals curse everything I said. Yet, that quietude is God, because it touches that which is His own life. They do not know hell or damnation here, preachers who say that, André, live in darkness themselves and are living dead.

I could go on, for there is no end to everything here. It becomes ever more beautiful and purer.'

'If this planet is hundreds of times larger that the earth, it must be a great expanse. Are there planets which are still larger, Alcar?'

'The higher we get the larger everything becomes and we get the feeling that there is no end any more. On earth powers of nature and wonders are known, we on our side know spiritual laws and wonders, but these people here and those who have advanced even further know cosmic wonders and cosmic laws of which we, André, know absolutely nothing. Everything becomes ever greater and wider and the more we advance the more everything expands and its extent can no longer be felt. They know, however, that this is true and that it awaits them.'

'If I correctly understood everything you explained to me on all our journeys, Alcar, our life on earth is exactly the opposite of this life here. If we can accept everything on earth, that means losing everything, then we'll actually receive, is that correct?'

'Did I ever say something different, André? Isn't that what I always taught you? Those who can accept, my boy, have well advanced and will soon receive everything. Precisely when we are prepared to lose everything and bend our head for God, an other power acts and lives in us and then happens what God has reserved for us. How great is the human being who can say, my God leads me on the right way when I am wrong and I'll be grateful when this happens, whatever my life will be like. These people here, André, give everything and the more they can give the more their inner wealth increases. Their inner light then radiates over their environment. People here give, on earth they ask and demand, here they only serve, and they could not live differently.

This belongs to us, if we want and we can receive this, if we bend our head. This will be our property, if we open ourselves and it is spiritual wealth. That is what we are all longing for. Have an other look at everything, André, I feel that we'll have to leave soon.'

'Does Cesarino let you know that, Alcar?'

'Yes, André. The way they live and receive here, and are in connection with others, is like our life, we in the spirit, and they in their material organism. You can still observe, soon this will not be possible any more and we have to return.'

'That again is a wonder, Alcar. I have assimilated everything and I am most grateful to you, I won't forget it. Does Cesarino know what you explained to me?'

'This mentor has connected himself with me. I know of all these possibilities, but in order to pass on into this, higher powers are required and this happens the way you experienced when you were permitted to visit the sixth and seventh sphere. My powers are insufficient. I, too, am only an instrument, you see how the masters are following me. This is their work, and mine and yours and that of many others.'

André looked at this paradise, he would not return here again. I wish you all farewell for thousands of years, and he sent his gratitude to those united in happiness. He felt grateful, very grateful to the Creator of all this mighty life. He knelt down and prayed for this happiness. When he opened his eyes he saw that his leader was also absorbed in prayer. Alcar also looked up to heaven and thanked his Holy Father. André trembled for happiness.

Then he suddenly exclaimed: 'What is that, Alcar? Everything is fading away, I can't see the planet any more, a dense fog is covering it.'

'Didn't I tell you just now that our connection would be broken? That is what happens now and we must leave.'

'What wonder, how you are one, Alcar. Now I understand what was shown to me in the temple of the soul.'

'Cesarino has broken our connection, André and we must return to our side, where you will experience yet more wonders, which I am allowed to explain. Come, my son, however difficult it will be for you, this happiness has come to an end. Once, even though it will take a great many years we, too, will live here together and with us many sisters and brothers of the spheres. All will arrive here and accept this possession.'

André could not see anything any more. Alcar returned and they floated towards the side beyond.

'I could pass on into our own world here, but I want to linger for a while in this silence. You want that too, won't you, André?'

'Yes, Alcar, I'd love to. I must digest this first, presently I'll be ready.'

# CHAPTER VII

## *Reincarnation on earth*

I also need this, my boy, for this is also a mighty event for me.' They floated on and both were lost in thought. André did not know what he should think of first. He felt, however, what he should do. This should not last too long, for there was still a lot that Alcar should explain to him. Once back on earth he would have enough time to ponder on everything. How good his leader was, for he definitely needed this; Alcar had experienced thousands of wonders and could cope with them. There was a longing in him now and he realized that this meant struggle on earth. He now had to try and digest this in day-consciousness and that was not so simple. It was essential, though, and he would do his best.

Oh, what happiness and beauty! How pure those people were. Yes, he thought, they are transparent, finer still than the most delicate substance on earth. These people were material angels. He could not stop thinking of it and this was awaiting people on earth. To acquire this, one should like to live. Oh, such beauty! How amazing life on that planet was. On earth man fought and killed as much as he liked. Nobody could stop those animal-like beings. Wherever one looked there was misery. There was no peace anywhere on that large earth: hatred, envy and deceit everywhere. What wonders he had been allowed to see here!

It was getting dark, they had already left that solar system. Now he felt that deep silence. Oh, that Divine silence. He now lived in nothingness and that very nothingness was God. It was here like it was before creation. He understood everything and he felt as if he had never been away from here, as one of those on this side; creation was that clear and transparent to him. He felt and saw that it was like that and had to be so. This was amazing and yet those feelings he had had before, returned. It was as if he had been told of them before. It did not come from the left or right or from above, no, this emanated from his deep inner being and he began to feel it again.

It was strange, yet he could not free himself from that. He had never heard of that on earth, but on this journey he had felt it many times and even very clearly. He had not been aware of this feeling on those other two journeys, now, however, it was conscious within him. This was strange, very strange, it was within him and he could understand it, but he did not know from where this mystery came. It was most remarkable and he felt this had to do with himself. It was exactly as in Jerusalem, but now more profoundly than there. How was that possible? He lived on earth, didn't he? Did this also belong to the past? To his own past?

He did not yet know where he had lived, Alcar would explain that, so he would wait and not think of it. He felt the silence overwhelm him, and he passed on into it. This was like it was before creation when man had yet to be born, when there was nothing. Darkness, deep darkness and yet, everything was there though it should be felt. But who could feel that?

No scientist on earth, but learning is terrestrial and this could only be felt. One had to descend deeply into oneself, for it is there, we had experienced it.

'Did you feel', Alcar suddenly said, 'that not only our inner life is calling us to a halt there, but material life as well?'

'Yes, Alcar, I felt that.'

'On earth we can see through all substance, there, however, that is not possible any more. We also face that depth and cannot enter and you see that I can only explain what lies within my reach and what I have experienced. Everything else is invisible for me.

Here is quiet and peace. We are again in the silence, in the Divine silence. Darkness now prevails in the universe, yet there are thousands of solar systems and everything is moving. All those thousands of heavenly bodies are moving and nothing disturbs in this mighty universe. The entire universe is in harmony, but where earthly human beings are there is disharmony, for earthly human beings disturb. Here you feel the purity of nature coming into you. Now we float on in the universe and are happy beings. God created heaven and earth; God created us human beings, the animal kingdom and vegetable world. God created the entire universe of which we are part. There is already light in us, André, but we have to acquire all this mightiness. Do you notice, my son, that it is getting darker all the time?'

'Yes, Alcar, and also quieter.'

'Presently, it will become light again and that light is of the solar system to which your own material organism belongs. When that dies you will be with me forever and we'll go on, on this side.'

'Once I'm here, Alcar, then what?'

'I told you many times that we'll make a journey that will last many years. Then we'll experience everything once more and that will take years. After that, I'll return to my own sphere and my task will be finished.'

'What about me, Alcar, could you tell me that?'

'You'll proceed alone for some time to do other work. That work is already waiting for you. You'll give yourself entirely to it and after that I'll await you in my own sphere. We'll go on together and proceed to reach those highest spheres.'

'Shall I be allowed to work together with my sisters and brothers of the earth I now know, Alcar?'

'Yes, André, that is possible. You'll see all your brothers and sisters who follow us on earth again on this side. You'll be allowed to work together, to make long journeys, you'll be united in love, in pure love of the spheres.'

'Oh, what happiness, Alcar.'

'It will happen, André, you'll receive all this happiness. All will enter here, where great happiness awaits them. I'm telling you this now and you may rely on it.'

'Does your twin-soul wait for you all that time, Alcar?'

'She waits already from the moment I went to the earth, but she helps me, André, we both do this work. There is no parting in the spheres, you know that. You were once allowed to see my sphere and you have even spoken to her. We are one and I am never alone. Wherever I am she follows me, and I her and we never feel separated. Yet, I am always in the sphere of the earth and she is in her own heaven, but parting is not possible. We are forever united and we'll remain united.'

'It is all so mighty, Alcar. When we arrive on the fourth cosmic degree, do I recognize you and you me?'

'From now on we are one forever and all those with us will remain so. Isn't it marvellous to be allowed to know that already? This is the spiritual connection, André, and those who are connected in the spirit have acquired that. Ask those who have reached the fourth sphere and all will confirm that. Believe me when I say that we are prepared to give everything. This seems much and yet, it is nothing as compared with

506

what we received. God gave Himself, His own life, His attunement. Those who lose themselves receive that what God is. We try to acquire that cosmic consciousness and we give ourselves completely for it.'

'Where do you go now, Alcar?'

'To the darkness again where we were, for there are many things I must explain, related to reincarnation on earth. I'll also tell of those who broke all spiritual laws. Reincarnation occurs from all transitions, from those regions that are inwardly prepared.

Everyone who yearns to make up what he did wrong can do so and returns to the earth. I'm going to explain that every being can experience birth, reincarnation on earth, if he really wants to. When they live in the astral world and have completed their cycle on earth, their return is a mercy. That is the wonder of reincarnation on earth, it is deep and mighty and like everything else, sacred. It is amazing and it is only known here. When this soul lives on earth again that inner life is not aware of it any more and some ask why and what for again.'

'Shouldn't they have reached a certain level?'

'You mean a spiritual level, don't you?'

'Yes, Alcar.'

'No, that is not necessary, but, as I said, only God can grant it to man. When inner life receives an other organism they can achieve more in that short life on earth than in a few hundred years on this side. Do not forget that when one lives in the darkness, one does not have anything but darkness and cold. Try to imagine that condition. That same being now receives a material organism on earth. While on earth, it will irrevocably meet that inner life to which it must make up. The soul only returns to the earth for that purpose. Thus, God comes to the aid of this life. Millions of beings receive this mercy. They would not otherwise make any progress, though all these beings are children of God. Millions of beings live in the darkness who yearn to come back. Among them are people who broke all laws of nature. How do all these souls get out of that condition? Can you imagine anything more horrible? Not being able to move, to feel no space, any life any more, nothing but darkness? We know these conditions on this side, André, and I'll show and explain them to you.

There is a beginning and an end. There are also conditions in which the soul lost itself, so that there is no viability or possibility of existence any more. And that is logical, it is very natural. We can break these laws, because we belong to this mighty life and are part of it. These laws of nature are not known on earth. I learned to understand these laws when I made my journey on earth and on this side. I learned that God is love in everything. How many beings haven't I met who were yearning and went on yearning and nevertheless there came no end to their misery. All these people lived in the darkness and could not free themselves from it. That must happen in material life but, as I told you, it is a mercy of God to receive a new material organism.

A suicide who has paid the penalty on this side because he destroyed his life on earth feels here what he did and lost. When his end has come inner life will call him to a halt and only this law can help him, which is reincarnation.

That is the final moment to show what we want, or we sink back into a deep and miserable life. That is the darkness we have got to know on Golgotha and that applies to every human being.

Well then, that suicide returned to life on earth and faced that condition again. Would he again put an end to his life? He does not know that he committed suicide before, though it lies within him. If he has no spiritual property he will perish again. This is a problem for him, a tale of woe, although an opportunity, a possibility to get out of that condition. How can this be overcome on this side? Is it possible, André? Can man prove on this side that he won't commit suicide?'

'That, surely, is impossible, Alcar?'

'Yes, my son, it is only possible on earth, one has to have a material organism. Now what happens, what will these people experience?

Hundreds of years pass on this side. During those centuries they cry and ask why and what for. I mean those who are trying to acquire something, who feel that they can advance. Can and may I not prove that? In the darkness they can advance if they want, but they cannot shed those feelings and this stops their development. Consequently, when a suicide is born again and wants to commit suicide, I explained this already, something will prevent him from doing so and that is the past, his inner life, which he experienced on this side. In that life on earth he achieved that and he was only on earth for that purpose.

'By telling you this I want to make clear how great this mercy is that everyone can receive. It is incredible how mighty it is to be allowed to be on earth again out of that profound darkness. For there is light on earth, André, everything that makes life agreeable is there. Here is noth-

508

ing but cold and misery. Just imagine this life. So, God is coming to our aid in various ways.'

'And if they fail again, Alcar?'

'That is hardly possible, André. Before they pass into that condition they have brought themselves to that stage; in other words, they have acquired that much willpower that they will not fail again. Consequently, it is pre-established that they will achieve this.

I also saw others. They did not live in the darkness, but in the spheres of light. They, too, can return on earth. I told you of a mother who wanted to experience motherhood. She yearned for fifty years and finally her prayer was answered and she was born again. Those are wonders, André, God helps us in all these conditions and we must be grateful for that. Those who want to learn will receive everything from God when their experience will help them reach the spiritual spheres.

On all our journeys I spoke of spiritual and material laws of nature and now of the mercy of God. If that mercy did not exist, I would not be known on earth, there would never have been any art, nor music or sculpture of the level people possess. However, I was born on earth together with many others. The pyramid came also into existence, for these beings came from this side as well, as I told you, and there are thousands of other conditions.

Once a human being lived on earth who interpreted the life and suffering of Christ in music. On this side this soul asked his Father in heaven to grant him that. He received this mercy. I'll soon connect you with that life and you will see this human being. To this end we'll return to Jerusalem, as I told you before. This soul lived there and that was because he wanted to feel Christ and interpret all that sorrow and misery by music. Do you feel this wonder, André? This has happened and that is possible for thousands of conditions, but only when the soul wants to experience something or has something to bring on earth. Those who are connected with these laws know what great wonder happens and only those who experience that know. No human being or spirit on this side can tell anything about it, because it is a mercy which only God can give.'

'Is that why so little is known of reincarnation, Alcar?'

'Yes, nothing is known of it, André, we only know that it is possible. Ask all those who live here, nobody knows. When this happens, inner life dissolves in the world of the unconscious. You know that condition. They arrive in an unconscious state and inner life is born and awakes on earth in that condition. In that life only that will happen for which inner life came to the earth. Material life runs its normal course, but inner life will experience that and it is fixed and must happen. Those are the many problems of life they must experience on earth. Once again, André, if God's children want the good, everything is within reach of inner life and we'll receive that as human beings.'

'Would a spirit of your sphere know of his reincarnation, Alcar?'

'Yes, for one is conscious and that consciousness makes us act and feel on earth and our feeling demands nourishment for the mind. No human being on earth can take that away from us. When a soul comes to the earth for art, it will achieve that; this inner life will turn to art. Even if parents have other plans, which often happens, the child will follow its own way, and even if it causes a rift between them, it goes and must follow that way, nothing can change that. That is why the soul returned to the earth and not for anything else. This inner life naturally also experiences thousands of other things; it will forget itself in that life or make something of it. We are then connected with various conditions of our own past. I explained that to you of my own life. Inner life awakens on earth; the human being experiences that, awakens and becomes conscious. Good and wrong things are done, but it is not possible to sink lower and deeper than they already have. That inner strength makes them hold their own, it makes them carry on and they experience their art or that for which they have come to the earth. Is that clear to you, André?'

'Yes, Alcar, and it is also amazing.'

'Yes, it is, though it is more a mercy than a wonder, for this event is beyond all existing spiritual and material laws. I'll now pass on to our astral world, for you see that we have already approached our own solar system.'

André felt that Alcar was going to connect himself. When he began to observe he noticed that they were again in the dark spheres.

'Look, André, we are on the spot where I wanted to be, here lie those beings we have met before. For them it is impossible to return consciously, for they would set the earth on fire.'

'Is this sphere the lowest on this side, Alcar?'

'Yes, my son, here are the people who broke all laws of nature.'

André looked at this misery. There in front of him lay human beings.

He had been here before with his leader.

'I connected myself with one of them on this spot, André. I told you what I noticed, and we have put that down in your second book*). All these beings broke all laws of nature. Oh, if these people were born in a spiritual condition and consciously! If they came into power again which they can certainly accomplish through everything within them, may God have mercy with man on earth if these animals would acquire full consciousness. All these beings are indomitable. They know no bounds; they don't realize what they do. That is why they are in this condition. All these people have sunk very deeply; they are unconscious and just lie here, which may last thousands of years. Yet, one day they will awaken and start a new life.

How much misery haven't I shown you already, André? How much do people suffer? All that, however, is only for the earth, because man on earth must acquire spiritual consciousness. It is not until then that higher life begins and people are open for our life. When I see the deep gaps that these people have to bridge, I think of the misery they have to experience. If there were no end to that, God would be unjust, but they know they have caused this misery themselves.'

'Could they also return to the earth if they wished?'

'Everyone can return, André, as I said, but if all these people would return to the earth in their previous condition, like their last life on earth had been, hell would set in again, for they attack everybody they meet. Once they were on earth, but they forgot themselves in everything. They are the rulers on earth, the wreckers of our human happiness. Yet, God also helps these souls. Inner life arrives on earth; the soul is a living dead being and spends that life on earth in that condition. I told you about that on our previous journey. That life is spent and they are unconscious, their deep inner life is asleep, because this is necessary for further life. However, God comes to the aid of these souls and because they experience life on earth in an apparent dead condition something has changed in them when they enter here. During the last years of that earthly life, however, they must become conscious and when that happens they usually are spiritually insane beings. Do you feel how amazing everything is and how these laws act? That insanity on earth is better than lying here in this darkness. Here, they can't advance, on earth, however, they acquire something, though it is merely

*) See the book: 'A View into the Hereafter', volume II.

511

to belong to the living beings again. Do you understand what I mean, André?'

'If I understand you correctly their own life keeps them imprisoned?'

'Yes, André, that is correct.'

'Aren't they aware of anything, Alcar, not even that they live?'

'No, my son, they are unaware of everything. Thousands of them live on earth in this condition. These souls are deep and all these people can not be fathomed. Yet, we know these people on earth, for when we meet them we think they are insane. These people live on earth but are spiritually asleep. Try to imagine such a condition. Look at these people, they are everywhere, they live in all parts of the world. They are anxious, they do not dare to live, they do not mix with anybody or anything and have no feelings, no desires, for they are living dead. That is the deepest psychic condition we know and we know why those beings are on earth. They are attracted by a higher degree and are usually those who are open to insanity.'

'How remarkable again, Alcar. You haven't told me anything about that yet.'

'No, I haven't, for it was not yet possible. I follow one course, which has been ahead of me for several hundreds of years. I give and explain to you only what you can absorb; I proceed from the lowest condition to the highest. When my work on earth started, I began by appearing before you and establishing a connection. At that time I could not have told you of all those psychological laws and planets, you would also have become insane. I had prepared everything in advance and I initiated you, as you became inwardly awake and conscious. You would not have understood this depth and even now you must adjust yourself properly and clearly in order to be able to feel this depth of the soul.

I said just now that there are many such people on earth and they are the eccentrics. These people stay out of society and they must, for if they would be conscious in that earthly life, my God, what would happen to thousands, no millions of people? However, nothing is known of all these depths of the soul. They cannot be fathomed for they are stupid, are not interested in anything, they can't learn and are simply not capable of normal human thinking. They are adult people, but their inner being is unconscious. Yet, all those people were born like anybody else, and their material bodies may be normal when there is no normal disturbance; it is the soul. The human being received this for he would have been here for thousands of years and God came to his aid again. No spirit, no human being can do anything about that nor change it. No scientist could solve this great spiritual mystery, for these people are beyond any earthly help. They cannot be helped, there is no cure for their illnesses, this is a spiritual problem that only we know. These laws, André, are beyond all others, which, as you will understand, have acquired an existence. Everyone living on earth who may or may not have to perform a task, which is immaterial for that matter, has reached a world of existence. A world of existence means to be something, to possess something, but these people went beyond all bounds. Their inner life keeps them imprisoned. No inner life has sunk so deeply as that of these beings and we know no greater sorrow and misery and ruin. Once these people were conscious, lived on earth, killed thousands of people, were usually the rulers on earth, because they acquired that power.'

'So it is not possible, Alcar, for such a being to be consciously born on earth in this condition?'

'No, they have exceeded that boundary. When they pass away they go to this sphere and are laid down here. All these people have forgotten themselves, destroyed others for a piece of land, for money or gold and for thousands of other things known on earth as property. They were the tyrants of the earth; they brought humanity grief, sorrow and misery. But God knows no rulers, tyrants or wreckers. God gave man everything, His own Divine life. Yet, all these people did not understand this. This deep mystery resides in our life, in front of you are human problems, but we know all those problems. All those rulers, those wreckers must proceed and that is why there is reincarnation on earth; they could not otherwise advance. However, on earth they are the mental defectives, the eccentrics, and one wonders why those people live. They see in them the spiritually poor, which they actually are, but the spiritual meaning is the one I explained to you. It will be clear to you, my son, that we know all these problems of the soul, we know where and how they live, we know whom they will be attracted by, for that is also a great wonder. The law of cause and effect has to do with this; the parents have to make up to this life.

For everything and everything, however deep for people on earth, the explanation can be found on this side, for this is fixed in man, one must feel it and be able to see into one's lives. We can connect ourselves with everything that lives. Now let a psychologist try to analyze it, that is impossible, isn't it? Since we know that a wrong thought must be set right, must be corrected and made up, then most certainly all this misery poured out over thousands of people. There have been rulers who are still held in esteem merely because they were geniuses, but who had thousands of people killed. They will have to make up for that killing. We see them and I know where some of them live on earth in your time. You should see them, my son, those spiritually poor, those children of God, but first look into their past. It is a great mystery, but those are spiritual laws.

There is one being who killed millions of people. Just imagine his struggle, his misery and sorrow in the future. He will have to sleep for thousands of years; it is not until then that he will also be born. He will be a feeble minded, insane, and a living dead being.

Oh, if once that spiritual veil was lifted for people and scientists on earth. How they would tremble and shiver from all these truths.'

'How terrible such a task on earth is, Alcar.'

'Such a task, my son, is a great mercy, but when they forget themselves they will all perish. Such a task is only terrible when they resort to those deeds and kill their fellow human beings. The others who seek the good can do a lot of good and when they are in power it means a mighty bliss for mankind and quiet and peace on earth.

If such a monster were given his full consciousness on earth, he would again try to attain a high social position and you'll understand what would happen then. It is therefore possible in the lowest degrees of this darkness to experience reincarnation. This new birth serves no other purpose and they experience their own problem. It is not possible for these beings to achieve anything in that new life on earth for they experienced that already and forgot themselves completely.

So this is the very last possibility for the planet earth we can receive from God. It is one chance and it has to happen. This is a great and sacred wonder, my son, for which we have to bend our head.

The soul I spoke of descended on earth and was born. That inner life would experience poverty, for it would ruin others if it had wealth. Now wouldn't it be possible, hear what I say, for this inner life to be born to parents with a lot of earthly property? Surely that should be possible, for how many parents haven't acquired that?

Let me tell you, my son, that it is not possible for this law is infallible. This is that great spiritual mystery of which we on this side don't know anything either. No spirit, however high on this side, knows these Divine laws.

That amazing event happens the way it must happen, it was asked and prayed for in advance. That wonder happens and by whom? Only through God, only God can give that and we know nothing about it. So that human being is born and only experiences what he is on earth for.

Do you feel this mighty wonder, my son? It is a mighty and amazing event only God knows, of which no prince of love knows anything.

Those who have reached the All can't know this or the pyramid would have been completed.

That is God, André, and a Divine event for which we can and must pray and bend our head. There is one law that governs and directs everything and that is God, the visible and invisible God we know on this side, Who created the universe, man and animal. God assists His children in everything, but this help is not understood, nor accepted. God allows me and you and billions of others to do something for ourselves and for others, when we seek higher things. Is it clear to you what God is?'

'Where is this leading to, Alcar, can all this be understood on earth?'

'To the depth we all feel, my son, and for which we bend our head, even if we think we feel and know something of creation, even if this is our possession.

Do you understand, André, that all of us are powerless when God says; now it is enough? And do you also understand that we can only ask that God Who rules everything to help us with these words: 'Thy will be done'? This, my son, is the only prayer we may say, only then do we want to be children like God wants us to be.

'Thy will be done, oh, my Father in heaven, I want to be a child, only Your child.'

People think that praying is not necessary because everything is present, the universe, man and animal. What is God and where is God, if there is a God, why then all that misery on earth? Can't God interfere? Can God allow His own children to be ruined? Is God a Father of love? That great mystery, André, is beyond understanding and cannot be felt, neither by spirit nor by man. This calls us to a halt, but the more love we acquire and feel for all the life of God, the clearer becomes the mystery of God and we receive in accordance with the love we have.

God is light, love and life. If God were not love, there would come no end to all this misery here in front of you. This is reincarnation on earth; it is the wonder of God we know on this side. That is what I want to explain to you and what cannot yet be accepted on earth, for one does not know anything about it.

Do you now feel how deep and sacred reincarnation is? That we experience it as human beings and yet do not know anything about it? That this is necessary, because we can't digest what belongs to those previous lives? That God also comes to our aid in this respect? Birth on earth obliterates everything and yet, deep within us lies the past, it is fixed within us, it lives in us, it is ourselves.'

'Is that the reason, Alcar, why controlling spirits when asked about reincarnation cannot tell anything about it?'

'Yes, because those who live here and have not yet attained that level, can't know. The higher spirits know all those laws and know that only God can give us that mercy, but they also keep silent, though they know it is possible.'

'And does this apply to every human being, Alcar?'

'Yes, André. But on this side we can only do what is in our inner being and to that end we must exert all our energies.'

'If I understand you correctly, only those who yearn for this wonder will experience it.'

'Indeed, my son. Those who want that and long for it are busy with themselves and can't think of anything else. Those beings are not aware of anything any more; they feel and think only of this event. While thinking and feeling, many work on some task or other and wait for the moment when they begin to feel this action.'

'Does it occur in them of its own, Alcar?'

'Yes, André, and then man experiences this wonder. What happens I'll explain later. It is therefore possible here in this darkness to return to the earth and that is a mighty grace for those who would otherwise lie here for thousands of years before they would awaken. Look at all those people, how deeply they have sunk. Nevertheless, God comes to their assistance. It will therefore be clear to you that only reincarnation on earth can help them; it is the possibility to get out of here. We have learned to know these laws, reincarnation is possible from all spheres.'

'How natural that is too, Alcar.'

'We human beings cannot be grateful enough, my son, for everything we received. However terrible these lives have been, there is an end to them, all that misery must dissolve; they, too, are children of God.'

'How well you convinced me of a Father of love, Alcar. On earth all those people are doomed. They are banned forever from the spheres of light and there is no end to their misery. The heavens are closed for them forever, that's what the priests say and propagate. How dreadful their preaching is now that I learn to know all this. It would be far better to say nothing, not a word about God, instead of preaching that falsehood throughout their life on earth.'

'Indeed, André, that's right. They do not know their God, a Father Who loves all His children. Everybody has his own God; their eyes won't be opened until on this side. It is not until then that they learn of all these laws and possibilities, here, they bend their head and do not know how to make up for it. I told you of them, I showed you where they live, and they all belong to the living dead.

Come, we'll go on, there is still more I must explain to you.'

André looked at all those beings once more. He felt deep compassion for all these people. He thought of the words his leader Alcar once spoke. Rich on earth and poor in spiritual feeling, that's what they all were. How had all those lives been? He trembled and shuddered because of all this misery. However, one day they would also reach the spheres of light. How great God was, how infallible all these laws were and nothing was known of it on earth. He followed his leader. He now lived in the deepest hells known on this side. During his first departures from the body he had been here with Alcar. How much Alcar had explained to him. He now understood spiritual life, he now felt how true everything was, how natural these laws were.

'Can those who live in the land of hatred go wherever they like, Alcar?'

'Yes, my son, those people are conscious, these here are unconscious. These people have broken the laws of nature, also in the spheres above this one for we also see and know spiritual transitions in these spheres.

Look, André, an other hell, we have also been here before.'

Hands reached out of cracks and those hands were like claws. André shivered, because he saw they were bloodstained.

'How is it possible, Alcar, I see blood!'

'Human beings are living here, André, people like you and me, children of God. Like the angels of the spheres of light, they also have the spark of God, are attuned to God. All of them have forgotten themselves. The blood of others sticks on their hands, they live in a condition like their inner life on earth has been.'

'Can these beings also go back to earth?'

'They can, it is possible, my son. Otherwise they could not free themselves.'

'What happens, Alcar, how do they get away from here?'

'When they are about to receive reincarnation, they will be overcome by a deep sleep and dissolve slowly but surely. They are subsequently attracted by the world of the unconscious and we see them on earth again.'

'How grateful we should be that this is possible, Alcar. So these beings were brought here from the earth?'

'When their end came on earth and they died they were brought to this place. Then they woke up and this life begins and they know they are imprisoned.'

'Would they be aware of that?'

'Certainly, they know they are locked up and try to free themselves, but that is not possible.'

'What did all these people do wrong having to live here?'

'I'm not going to connect you, André, you would not now be able to digest all these horrors. I assure you that God does not allow anything to happen to us, if it is not necessary. Their life on earth was terrible. All these souls, these people, none excluded, André, have killed, tormented, tortured and destroyed thousands of people on earth. All of them are demons; they are geniuses of evil. You surely feel that if nobody helps them they can't get out of here, for they have no spiritual property. They are poor in feeling and don't know that it is possible to proceed. God would not be a Father of love if He left His children alone. However, they cannot stay here. Help is needed. It is not possible to talk to them of a higher life. They cling to you and are again prepared to kill anybody. Their life is disgusting and horrible and yet there will come an end to this. All of them have forgotten themselves. But haven't we all forgotten ourselves? Is there one being in the spheres of light who can say that of himself? No, my son, they all have forgotten themselves, one time, thousands of years ago they were one of those, even though they have already reached the spheres of light.

We have been here before, but I could not explain all these possibilities to you at the time, you would not have understood them. Now, however, we have reached that stage and I can connect you with reincarnation. God, therefore, also comes to their aid and then reincarnation occurs. Everything is deep and mighty, André, and we cannot be grateful enough to God. Is it clear to you that God is love? That we human beings must receive this, or we would not advance any more? There is no end to their life, they have no spiritual property and cannot get out of here. Reincarnation sets them free and they receive a new material organism. Thus, there is no other possibility of advance for them.'

'What will their life on earth be like, Alcar?'

'Life of these people will be hard, André. They may try whatever they want, but they will come to nothing. Millions of these people live on earth and all these souls have to make up. One law keeps them captive, their life on earth is a great mystery and they feel lost. They don't reach a high social position, they spoiled all that. There is something, André, which makes them invariably feel: up to here and no further.

You see, such are those unfathomable laws of God and man curses his Father, because he does not understand his own life and does not know all these laws. That mystery lives on earth, seeks an existence and everything fails all his life. Consequently, every human condition on earth is a deep spiritual mystery, as will now be clear to you. Every human being has his own karma, which is and means the past.

Where would you rather live, André, here in deep darkness, where it is cold and miserable, or on earth in a material organism with the sun and people around? If one can accept all this, life on earth is not so difficult, for one experiences what one has done wrong. However, people revolt, for why do others have everything? As you see, this deep problem can only be solved on this side. There is a power that rules everything, the power through which man and animal, stars and planets were born. That power guards; and drives and says up to here and no further, when people have broken all laws of nature. We are confronted by this wonder, this deep and mighty problem that we have learned on this side and we are grateful for everything. Look around, André, see how much misery there is and these are human beings. I

519

showed you all this before, but now I was allowed to explain the meaning of all these spiritual wonders and problems we know.

They are living in cracks and holes and wherever you look there are God's children. They all have the Divine Spark, but they have to awaken.'

'What do they achieve on earth, Alcar?'

'I told you already, they can't achieve anything. They'll just live here and in this way that earthly life will pass and they'll again enter here, then, however, they can move. Do you feel how wonderful it is, André?'

'Yes, Alcar, they belong to the living ones again?'

'Exactly, that's right and that is God's intention. Once free of this life they crawl about and proceed to reach the land of hatred. I explained this also to you on our other journeys. They have returned to life by that new birth. And this, my son, is a great mercy, for which we cannot be grateful enough to God; there would not otherwise come an end to this darkness. We do not know damnation; God loves all His children, also these children who broke all laws of nature. The higher we come, the more the spheres and also the people change. You know that there are seven spheres of hell. The deep darkness dissolves already and as we ascend you will be able to see better. The people who live here crawl about like animals, but they are free in their doings and can go wherever they like. Yet, their hell keeps them imprisoned and I told you already why. We have put that down in the first three books.*)

Come, André, a little further and higher you will see those who have reached an other condition.'

The deep darkness dissolved a little and now André could observe better. He had been here before, in front of him he saw those beings. They crawled on hands and knees and their horrible physique hardly resembled human beings.

'Is it clear to you, André?'

'Yes, Alcar, everything, I understand you perfectly.'

'Those, here above, the ones that live at a higher level of hell are not yet accessible to reincarnation. All those people lived to the full on earth and I also explained those spiritual conditions to you. When you ask them how they feel, they think their life is not at all bad. We, however, shudder at their conception of life and are disgusted by their passions.

These people remain in those dark spheres until one day they will

*) The three volumes of the book 'A View into the Hereafter'.

awaken and want to begin a higher life. My point is to show you that reincarnation is not yet possible for them, for they are conscious and must try to free themselves from this hell. Though it may take centuries, one day they will begin, but only, as I said, when that sacred activity is conscious within them. They themselves awaken those laws of nature and when this happens they pass on into that activity and have to experience it.'

'And that also applies to the higher being, Alcar?'

'Yes, André, I'll explain that to you in a minute. As I said, this is for everybody, God makes no difference. What applies to these beings also applies to those who have reached the spheres of light.'

'Those who live in the Land of Hatred, Alcar? Can they also return to the earth?'

'Those who live in the Land of Hatred are animal-like beings and conscious in their life. Do you feel what this means? I just said that all those people must awaken first, it is not until then that they will feel remorse and ask their God to be allowed to make up for it. We know, however, that hundreds of years will pass before they reach that stage. They experience life on earth again, though this time as astral beings. They can nevertheless receive this mercy.'

'If I understand you correctly, Alcar, it is rather possible to be born from the deepest hells than from the Land of Hatred?'

'Indeed, my son, quite true. They just lie there in the deepest darkness and can't move. In the Land of Hatred, however, there is activity and they can go wherever they like. It is a matter of course that all these people have to awaken and begin an other life. We see many possibilities in their life, in the deepest darkness there is only one possibility: reincarnation as a result of which their condition changes.

After the Land of Hatred the Land of Twilight follows which borders the Land of Hatred. In those spheres, however, people have cut themselves off from reincarnation, because they belong to the living ones. Do you feel that too, André?'

'Yes, Alcar, it is very clear to me. They don't want anything else, they only think of what they want to have and they find that on earth.'

'Very good, André, this is what I wanted to explain. Those down there have but one desire, but those living in the Land of Hatred and in the Land of Twilight have thousands of desires and this excludes them from reincarnation.

Consequently a person who is absorbed in his own problem cannot think of anything else and it is not until then that these wonders happen. They feel remorse, André, and want to make up. However, hundreds of years may pass before this prayer is heard. I have experienced all that, I have learned to understand all those problems on this side and I am very grateful to God. When I was in the darkness to help others, I met a woman whom I wanted to convince of a higher life. No matter how I tried to reach her, I found it impossible. I hurried back to the higher spheres and asked my master what I should do to help this poor soul. She had a great problem, nobody could help her, only God could give her what would change her life. My master said: 'Brother Alcar, just wait. There is only one power able to help and that power is God, but it is the being itself that must activate those laws and powers.'

'But, I said, the sorrow and remorse she feels are terrible.'

My master looked at me and said: 'Yes, my brother, she lives, she is awake and conscious and she yearns, but her yearning is not intense enough yet to activate that process. Go back and see what she is like, follow her and you will learn to know this wonder and notice how infallible all this is.'

I descended once more, André, and I saw this wonder take place. Slowly but surely she dissolved and disappeared, she had entered another world. I returned again to the spheres of light and told my master. He said to me: 'If this had not happened, thousands of years might pass and she would still remain in her own condition and that torment is beyond description. However, God helps all of us, but only if we earnestly want to. Would God be a Father of love if he denied this to His own life? Now follow her on earth, I'll tell you where she'll be born, watch this life mature. See what happens in that short life on earth and you learn to understand the Divine laws.

I returned to the earth, André, and followed that life. This soul experienced her own problems and God granted her this mercy in order to come to herself. And she came to herself and when she left that life on earth when death called her, she entered here and was delivered from that terrible remorse, so that she was open for a new life.'

'How mighty that is, Alcar.'

'I told you already, André, we cannot be grateful enough to our Father. Time and again God helps His children. Where prayers do not help, the laws of nature do. That life is experienced, the deed dissolves and the soul is happy and begins a new life. Is that clear to you, André? Then you feel that God's love is in everything and that we, human beings, can receive everything if we earnestly want to. This belongs to our life; it is the reincarnation on earth and a mighty grace of God. When we have completed our cycle of life on earth, we learn to know all these Divine laws.

The possibility for these souls to free themselves from their own misery is, as I said before, also available to the higher being who wants to do something for the earth. The higher being also has and knows his own problems.

When we begin to understand this life, André, and feel what we received and were allowed to experience during all those millions of years, an other feeling develops within us, which is gratitude. But how can we show that gratitude? There are thousands of ways and means for that.

First of all we can be of use on this side, in the hell and in the spheres of light, as well as on earth. We can descend into these spheres, where much work is to be done. Nearly everyone descends into this darkness to help others. Many go to the earth and help their friends and their sisters and brothers. Others again want to bring something on earth, to achieve something there to thank God for everything. That is also possible and they are born again.

Now I'll pass on to the time when the earth was to receive art. Meanwhile we'll return to the spheres of light, while on our way, I'll tell you about it. We'll leave the darkness, André, and you won't come back here for the time being. Have you any more questions?'

'No, Alcar, I understood you in everything.'

'Splendid, André. Surely you have understood that, whatever is on earth, came from this side? There is nothing on earth that has not been received from their sisters and brothers on this side. We discussed that on our previous journey, now I'm going to explain it because it is part of reincarnation on earth.

Everything present on earth we brought by inspiration, but also by reincarnation. Thus, beings were born who came to the earth for art, because the earth needed art. The object achieved thereby was that people became interested in higher things. I'm going to connect you with that condition and show you how this happened. Wherever we are, starting from the first sphere, we see spiritual beings preparing themselves to receive this grace.

Is it clear to you, André, why all these beings had to reach the first sphere before reincarnation is possible?'

'Yes, Alcar, it is quite clear, for all those people first have to make themselves free of everything.'

'Exactly, André, they must earn it, attain a spiritual possibility of existence in order to activate those laws. It is possible in the lower three hells but subsequently people are conscious and because they are conscious their inner life is different and that activity is not possible any more. Thus, they continuously proceed and once they have attained that aim, they get to know these laws which have been activated by their remorse.'

'How many wonders there are on this side, Alcar, and how natural everything is. How great is the mercy to be allowed to receive this. Did you experience reincarnation, Alcar?'

'Yes, my son, I also was one of those who were allowed to experience this grace, but I'll tell you about that later.'

'Is this the Land of Twilight where Gerhard lived, Alcar?'

'Yes, André, we'll soon be in the first sphere.'

'So, reincarnation is not possible from this sphere?'

'No, for they have to experience other problems and consequently have plenty on their mind, they are therefore not open to deeper experiences.'

'That is quite clear, Alcar, I now understand perfectly.'

'This must be clear, my boy. All those people have a different spiritual attunement, they experience their own life and cannot think of anything else.'

'When a human being is born again, Alcar, and dies on earth, hasn't anything changed when they enter here?'

'Yes, certainly. If they make progress on earth, they'll notice it instantly on this side.'

'Are they aware of that?'

'No, that is not possible. It is not until in the fourth sphere that we can perceive this. I told you about that too, and I'll show you this, when I'm going to connect you with my own life. There is a change and it is achieved in that life on earth.'

'Can't they sink back, Alcar?'

'No, that is not possible either, those powers are within us. Do you feel what I mean, André?'

'Yes, Alcar, this is also clear to me.'

'Before we are born on earth, we meditate for years and prepare for this mighty event.'

'Did it take you a long time, Alcar?'

'About half a century.'

'I beg your pardon, fifty years?'

'Yes, my son, fifty years by worldly standards I needed to prepare myself for this task.'

'What you explain is a new wonder again.'

'I had to be prepared inwardly in order to be able to receive this great mercy, before birth on earth could follow. When I entered this life again, I had attained a higher sphere, which I only realized later. Consequently, I had earned that higher condition during life on earth.'

'Everything is so amazing, Alcar, I have no words for it.'

'Look, André, there is the first sphere. We now go to the temple of art where I am going to connect you with the past. You'll see what happened on this side at that time, several centuries ago. I try to convince you of reincarnation in various ways. We'll enter over there. You have been there before, André, it is the temple of the art of painting and sculpture. That's where I want to be. I have also shown you this temple in the second sphere. Here, however, this temple has an other meaning.

During the years when art was to come on earth, it emanated from this temple. That's where the artists lived and these beings would be born on earth again. I promised to tell you about it. This art, I mean the art of the old masters, is of very high quality. Why did all these artists live in that golden age? Why did they live in that age and aren't they here any more? I'll answer those questions. People on earth still paint, but they cannot come up to that level. Such masters will not come on earth again, they can't come there any more, or they would bring an art that cannot be understood on earth. What do we achieve? That is taken into account here. I told you that the art of the second and third sphere is not understood any more. If it was born on earth it would be a revelation, but this revelation would not be felt either. It is beyond their feeling and the passions of mankind would be roused, merely by our art. At the time I also told you that my art was stolen and that some people got killed, just because they wanted to possess a painting to cash in on it. That is a disturbance and if that higher art were given it would happen again, and that on a much larger scale.

The art to be given to the earth in those days came from this sphere and some of the masters were already connected with the second sphere, though only a few. It was felt here what would happen and it was here in the first sphere that the masters began to prepare themselves. They meditated before that tremendous event was to happen. Come, André, we'll go inside.'

André followed his leader and he recognized this magnificent building. At once Alcar was welcomed. A spirit of the light approached Alcar and paid him welcome. André heard him speak. This spirit wore a magnificent garment and André understood that he was a master from the third sphere. André recognized his sphere by his garment and his inner light. Alcar beckoned André to come nearer and the spirit went away.

'Look, André, art, spiritual art. They are young artists who lived on earth and are now training on this side. You know that this is possible. I also told and explained that they had better descend into the darkness to do work there instead of paint here. But these temples are open to man and everyone who wants can qualify for art. Strong spirits, however, feel what they could do and they descend and achieve much in a short period of time, as you know from Gerhard. That's not my point, though, for this has been going on here for thousands of years. When they have finished painting they will come to themselves.'

'Why are they not told, Alcar?'

'That is pointless, my boy. They have that feeling and they must experience it, they will not otherwise advance. Do you realize how intense our feelings are and that we can't do or feel anything but what occupies our mind? Do you feel then that those poor beings down here suffocate in and through their own life? That they cannot move an inch and first have to experience that before they can think of other things? This master who recognized me is here, because he does good work and convinces them of their wrong feelings, when necessary. Life on earth is similar and we see this reflected in the spheres, though only in the first sphere, since the first sphere is like the earth.

In the second sphere people need not be stimulated any more, they have that willpower and have advanced that far. Here, they paint, in other conditions in this sphere they walk around and seek their life in nature, they try to fathom how everything grows and lives; though it does not bring them any further.

526

I also painted and thought I could achieve everything through it. But it is not possible for our inner life. We understand and possess art and our sensitivity has developed, but that does not get us any further, for one must serve here, one must serve life.

Look, André, all these people try to achieve something in art, but I'm interested in the past and I'm going to connect you with it.'

André began to observe. He saw many beings in front of him.

'These spiritual beings, André, were gathered here many centuries ago. Many of them were born on earth and I am among them.'

'I beg your pardon?'

'That I am among them, André. Search and you'll find me.'

André followed all of them. He was startled, for there he saw his leader. My God, how is it possible?

'Yes, it is you, I recognize you, Alcar, you are that being. It is a great wonder, Alcar.'

'Look, over there, André, our master, like him who welcomed me a minute ago.'

André looked in that direction. He felt art in that human being. He was a genius. He lived in art and his radiance also reflected art.

'What does this mean, Alcar?'

'It means that this being has reached his highest degree in art for this sphere. His feeling is open for art only; he is nothing but art. You see that feeling in his radiance. There are beings on this side who have qualified for other studies and that can also be seen in their aura. He is only art and a master at that, although that does not mean that he has much love. His love is as in the first sphere and that's where he lives. I'm there too, I must tell you of my arrival on this side and I'll presently refer to my own life.

As I said just now, I arrived at the border of the first sphere and I also wanted to achieve something in art, while attaining a new birth as well.

All these people, André, were born again, just as I was. What you observe now is the moment we prepared ourselves. A higher being would convince us of that mission, and that happened. There was a desire in us to be allowed to bring this on earth. There was art on earth, but art would now reach its peak, if this could be given.

That message came from the higher cosmic masters, who not only governed the spheres, but also followed evolution on earth. They knew what people on earth would do with all that art; it served to raise the human level. First the art of painting and sculpture and subsequently the music. Music, too, was brought on earth from this side. We prepared ourselves on this side and many were masters. We had that feeling and yearned to be allowed to bring it on earth. But where did those feelings come from? From ourselves? Was I conscious and had I already got that far in this sphere that I felt this consciously? I pose those questions, André, to explain to you that I did not have these feelings. The cosmic masters made those feelings awaken in us, they were the ones who influenced us in silence and from afar, and things happened as follows.

Many secluded themselves and meditated. That is only possible in this nature and while doing some work or other. Subsequently, we all went to the earth and observed what man did. Though this took a number of years, our art was ready. However, none of us was aware of that higher influence, although that influence brought us in the required condition. Years went by and the time approached when that art would be brought on earth. One after the other disappeared. However much we tried to find one another, it proved impossible. In reality we all dissolved and passed on into the world of the unconscious.

I know all my fellow artists who were on earth at the time. This master also became my master on earth and I showed him to you on this journey. But how was it possible, André, that we would meet again here? As a matter of course we knew nothing of this mission while on earth, and yet one became the master of the other. As soon as one had accomplished his task, another was born and that happened as in the case of the pyramid, in a number of years. Do you feel this mighty wonder, my son?

We lived in the south and in the west, in various cities on earth. This master, André, is well known on earth and when I presently mention my own name on earth associated with this work, this name is also known. How many names have we had on earth? This one, however, is dear to me and I can always think back to it.

He, my master on earth, once, however, thousands of years ago, my husband. However unbelievable this is for the earth, I was allowed to explain this to you on this side and every human being will be connected with that on this side.

We were allowed to bring this on earth, for this side wanted to present it to the earth. This also happened in respect of the art of sculpture.

One of the greatest geniuses known on earth came from this side. All those masters, my son, were born again, because this had a cosmic meaning. As I told you, what was possible for the pyramid, and all those poor beings here in the dark spheres, the suicides, and those who broke all spiritual laws, is also possible for a being of higher spiritual attunement who has to bring something and must do so for the good. All, non excluded, became artists. Those gifts were in us in our youth. That is obvious, for we were born for the sake of art and this is simple when one knows the spiritual meaning. I would not have been able to do anything else or use my powers for a different purpose, for I had no feelings for anything else. I was essentially inspired by art and this was not only my property, we were also helped from this side.

I was religious and that is why I created religious representations. Those feelings were in me, though none of us understood that. How could we have understood this meaning, now that we know that everything dissolves by birth and that we are only aware of our present life? I'll refer to this later, André, I must first explain other wonders and to that end we go out into nature and presently back to Golgotha to connect you with an other being.'

Alcar went outside and André followed his leader. Again he had learned new wonders. He felt great respect for everything; how natural everything really was. If it wasn't it could not be a revelation. Alcar had been a great artist and now he lived in the spirit and was a master from the fifth sphere. How he admired his leader!

They walked for quite some time and he felt that his leader returned to the quietude. He now walked in the first sphere and the deeper he descended into this life, the more he felt that he had been here more than once, he had been here with his leader, but this was different. He recognized all this beauty and the more Alcar explained to him, the deeper he began to understand this great mystery he felt deeply within himself. Together with these feelings all previous remembrances came back to him. He still could not find words for it and yet it must have a meaning, that was a dead certainty to him because it was too intense, but he felt sure he would get an answer. Presently Alcar would explain his own past and he would wait.

In front of him were spiritual beings. All walked along and were lost in thought. He noticed that some of them were enveloped in a dense haze, while others were more transparent.

'What does it mean, Alcar?'

'This means that they are here with their beloved ones and will presently descend. I also wanted to explain this to you.'

'Are they aware of that?'

'Yes, André, they know they will leave soon, but they are joined together forever and will remain so. I told you about it on our last journey. One of them descends into the world of the unconscious and the other remains on this side and becomes the guiding spirit for this human being on earth.'

'Haven't you told me, Alcar, that this is possible only in the fourth sphere?'

'Yes, André, but I merely touched upon this problem and this has a meaning.'

'Do you feel that this being has to perform a spiritual mission?'

'Yes, I feel and see that.'

'Are they separated during that life on earth?'

'Didn't I tell you many times that we can never be separated? They are one forever and will remain so. She, this soul, brings something on earth and also has to make up for something. I, too, had to make up for something when I was on earth, as well as all those who were born there with me. This human being is the inspiration for her and will raise her on earth to a high level.'

'How difficult that is, Alcar. What age will she reach?'

'Sixty to seventy years.'

'That other being is alone and must endure that she is ridiculed and provoked, for she'll no doubt receive and experience her share of misery and sorrow and many other things?'

'You felt that correctly, André. She will meet someone on earth and make something up to that being. She'll also bring something which is to free herself in that time from what stops her here and prevents her development.'

A new wonder, André thought.

'How terrible that must be, Alcar.'

'Do you think you could not accomplish this, now that you know all this, or that you could not do it?'

'I don't know, it seems so difficult to me. I do feel already that when she'll meet that other being he'll not understand her when she descends into the mother organism. That is terrible, because that life will be so difficult. Oh, what depth and what sacrifice.'

'This wonder is deep, André, though it is no sacrifice. You heard what I said, that she'll also make up? In that case it is no sacrifice, but a mercy, a great mercy, that God gives to all His children when we must make up in that life, and can achieve that in one short life on earth. If the person we have to make up to is on earth and we are already on this side, isn't that better than waiting for years on end before we can proceed on this side? It irrevocably stops us; it impedes our development, for we can't advance while that particular being lives on earth. Do you feel the mighty wonder of this condition, and that it is a great mercy when this happens?

A lot is accomplished in that life, and when the end comes all sorrow is over and they are united forever. Then they are sisters and brothers in the spirit and proceed on this side.'

'I think it is terrible, Alcar. The way the spirit that remains on this side must suffer.'

'Have you properly understood Lantos' life? What did he do when that time came? He connected his own soul with Roni and experienced that she was bound hand and feet. And yet, it is a thousand times better than having to wait here and being unable to advance.'

'If I understand you correctly, you mean the following. When I cause harm to someone on earth and I have returned to the spheres, but that human being goes back to the earth again, I have to wait anyway until I made it up? Can't others do that for me?'

'No, only they have to do with your life, they experienced that sorrow and not those others. You can do much for others, but you'll nevertheless meet those others again, for they are the ones who prevent our development. That is the law of cause of effect.'

'Surely these are not big mistakes, Alcar?'

'You mean because they are living in the first sphere?'

'Yes, that's what I meant.'

'Those who have reached the first sphere may have to make up great sins and mistakes and nevertheless have entered here.'

'You never told me about that, Alcar.'

'That was not possible. Only now can I discuss these spiritual laws, you would not have understood them. I will now discuss these laws, for all these conditions have to do with reincarnation. We can enter the first sphere on this side when we are free from hatred, passion and

531

violence and already possess love, although we still have sins and faults that we can make up for only now. Usually that wonder happens of which I have just told you.'

'What you now explain to me is quite wonderful.'

'Do not forget, André, that the first sphere is like the earth. There are two more spheres to reach the first spiritual sphere of existence.'

'I'm beginning to feel it, Alcar. How remarkable this is too. It did not cross my mind.'

'Everything must and shall dissolve in the first sphere, André. It is not until then that we can proceed.'

'And to that end many of them return to the earth?'

'Yes, André, to make up for the sins and faults and also to serve.'

'How will they find each other, Alcar?'

'That is taken care of by those living on this side.'

'So this spirit will connect her in due course, whereas she is his own life, his own soul?'

'Yes, André, that's the way it happens. I ask you once again, couldn't you do this and also bring something on earth and make up? Is that gratitude not in you? We have all been able to, nobody excluded. Many human beings on earth wonder why God brings people so closely together, but one learns from the other. One being returns for his inner life, an other to bring something to the earth and mankind. There are thousands of possibilities for us to return to the earth, though for a fixed aim and that is achieved. I know many scientists who are on earth, and were born there merely for an invention for the benefit of mankind. Only a short time ago two geniuses arrived here who had returned to bring something to the earth and science, by which thousands of people could be released from their terrible illnesses. Had these beings not been reincarnated on earth and had there not been beings on this side to inspire them, they would not have achieved anything there. But this had been experienced and accomplished in advance and they returned to the earth for that purpose. This is also possible for other disciplines. If the doctors did not return to the earth from this side to leave something for mankind, no progress would ever be made. They were born again and returned after completing their task and they saw that they had not been on earth in vain.

While on earth they were unaware of it, here, however, they passed on into the past and were happy that it had been achieved. This is as old as the earth occupies a place in the universe. I explained that to you. From the moment when hell and the spheres of light commenced, spiritual beings already returned in a material organism and brought their knowledge to the earth.

Here, André, nobody asks what we must experience; we want to experience for we are all serving. We want to make up and feel this as a mercy. Everybody does and all pass on into it and one day they will have advanced that far. Those beings cannot be stopped. Look at them, André, and feel their tremendous inspiration. They work their way through and that way is paved from this side. Beings watch on this side, and these beings are supervisors, the guardian angels of those on earth. They are closely connected and they all have a task to accomplish what they are serving for. Thousands of beings have a task on this side and that task is accomplished; that work cannot be destroyed, it shall and must be done, however much they may be opposed, for they all want to. They have a sacred urge to create. That is spiritual ardour, my son, a sacred ardour that flares up and warms others. How many spiritual beings are there on earth for our work? How many spiritual leaders are there on this side helping those on earth? They now live in all parts of the world, for it is now the century of nourishment for the mind.

People returned from this side for the art of sculpture and painting and brought on earth what they were to bring. As I said, these two beings are very closely connected and will remain so forever.'

'And will she pass into other hands, Alcar?'

'What are hands, my son, what is a material body? A magnificent garment, but we think differently. We only ask after the inner life, that material organism is of no use to us on this side. Inner life, that is our bliss. On earth people commit murder for the sake of that garment, but we, on this side, just go our way and wait until inner life is ready. That is the eternal truth, that is what we love and that goes on forever, André. We see and feel that differently, for deep inner life is not touched, nor set in vibration. Here, it awakens, here it lives, there it is deeply hidden in man's inner life. I could tell you a lot about that as well and you would see it differently, but that is not possible now.

On this side, André, life is feeling, feeling is love and light, warmth and happiness. The material organism is only temporary and dies. On earth the body is loved, here we love inner life. Consequently, the depth of inner life is not touched, cannot be set in vibration, for here lives the being that is able to and has the same attunement. That is the inner connection and it is pure happiness when it is felt. Otherwise it has no meaning and is of no value.

No, André, she'll go and with her thousands of others. She will presently dissolve and the male being begins his task and waits until he can reach her. Feel the depth of this mighty wonder, my son, and be grateful that it is possible.'

'What a sacrifice, what a strength and inspiration, Alcar!'

'They both feel this mercy and will always feel it. Look at this young spirit, she returns. She'll become a mother and she'll experience this on earth. Somebody is waiting on earth and they will meet on that large earth. When she has experienced that, for nothing can prevent it, she'll return to the spheres and proceed on this side. Everything has then been accomplished and experienced and at the same time suffered and made up. She'll consciously experience this mighty event, which is not understood on earth; all this resides in her deep inner being. Aren't those wonders, André? Isn't this mighty and shouldn't we feel grateful to God? Shall we feel this gratitude within us now that we know this?

I think so, André, for it can't be otherwise. We'll feel and think that way, it is in us and we experienced it. I can explain this condition to you in all spheres, even in the highest spheres, but in that case this task is a particular one and is related to a mighty event on earth.

All this is only for the development of mankind, because those higher beings could not bring anything else on earth. That would be a mission of the highest order and that being is then a great personality on earth. They bring wisdom and happiness and this has a cosmic meaning.

Those now returning to the earth bring nourishment for the mind, or science or technique. Both follow one course and will reach the aim envisaged.

This happened during all those millions of years and this would no longer occur now that mankind needs it so badly, now that God's kingdom will be established? You, André, and millions with you live in a particular century, mankind on earth will experience that. We on this side are ready; we only wait to be allowed to begin. Now of all times we bring nourishment for the mind, for that century has approached and people are open for it. Now, our mediums are no longer burnt and we can complete our work. I told you about that too. In former days, several centuries ago, people were sent to the stake, now, they dare not do that any more, because they have advanced and began to think and feel differently. At that time, my son, we ourselves destroyed others and now we are making up for what we destroyed in those days. Yet, we pulled down what others built up. Those others are now the beings who live in the sixth and seventh heaven and look back on what they once accomplished. Is all this so unbelievable, so strange?

For mankind on earth these are problems, on this side they are the truth and a great mercy. They still think we are insane, but later they'll do what we do now and they'll thank their Father in heaven for all this mercy.

We'll now go to the temple of music. These beings were also born on earth. They prepared themselves here and all returned to the earth. We'll enter over there; you have also been here with me before.

All this was achieved in a few centuries, my son, and during those centuries geniuses lived on earth. Music is still composed and paintings are made and there is also sculpture, but the great genius who lived here is not here any more and will not be born on earth again. If this should happen thousands of years will have passed, and that would still be too soon, for the development of mankind proceeds slowly.

Come, André, follow me, you'll hear spiritual music from the past.'

André entered the building, which was full of people. Already from afar he heard spiritual music which he had been allowed to hear before in other spheres. That had been in the fourth and sixth sphere, he had experienced that Divine event. Art was practiced in life after death, all arts known on earth, but how mighty this music was. Thousands of beings were together here, the building was entirely open and he understood what this meant. It was quiet. There were flowers everywhere, birds flew in and out and were the friends of the spiritual beings. And this was only the first sphere!

The performance seemed to have come to an end, for all went away. A pity, he thought. Masters of art were gathered here and interpreted what they felt inwardly. The instruments were like those on earth, though many could not be compared and described.

Alcar said to him: 'Come, André, we'll go on to the interior of the building.'

He followed Alcar. Who would believe him? Nobody, for this was altogether too mighty, too incredible for people on earth. Yet, he experienced all this, he had departed from the body and left his material organism. He saw more beings from the earth over here but they would presently be unaware that they had been here. Yet, in their sleep, as they would say, they had heard beautiful music and, however strange it was, spoken to their father and mother who had passed away a long time ago. This was nevertheless reality and one day they'll see it. When they enter here to stay forever, they'll see that they have been here before more than once. He clearly recognized those who still lived on earth. Great was their happiness. Look how they radiated! Man wasn't aware of that either when he woke up in the morning.

No, life on earth suppressed everything; everything dissolved therein and obscured that picture. It was splendid to see them this way. Fathers and mothers were together; a mother visited her child. This, too, was a mercy, a very great mercy. They could cope with life again and that deep grief had mitigated in the morning.

Alcar walked on but now he halted and waited for him.

'Here, André, I am on the spot where, several centuries ago, human beings prepared to bring their art on earth. Not one, but dozens prepared themselves. All of them returned to this side long ago. One of them passed away at an early age. Look, there, in front of you, André.'

At the same moment André began to observe.

'There, in front of you, that is the spirit I mean, André.'

'I know him, Alcar. His spiritual countenance is like his physical countenance on earth.'

'Yes, André, that's right, that is what I wanted to show you. That, too, is a spiritual phenomenon we only know. In that case inner life dominates the physical body and radiates through that dense garment.'

'I know whom you mean, Alcar, he was a genius. You mean Mozart?'

'Yes, André, that was his name on earth. It was his task to bring this art on earth and that art came from this sphere. Knowing his art and feeling his inner life, you can imagine what art of the second, third, fourth, fifth, sixth and seventh sphere is like. What he brought on earth is mighty enough, not to speak of the art of the higher spheres. Many others came with him and I could point them all out to you, if I connected myself with their past. They lived here, they were born on earth and when they had finished they passed on. That was all they had to do. That art was perfect and everyone created in accordance with his own feelings. There are always artists on earth but these were there only once and can only be born once. They cannot be equalled and they

536

were born on earth for that purpose. They all brought the highest and very latest. Now isn't it remarkable, André, that they are not on earth any more? Why were those people in Egypt and are they no longer there? I told you, they were all born merely for that purpose, and if this had not been possible, there would be no pyramid, no art, no science, nothing on earth. These beings, however, lived on this side, in our hereafter and on all those planets we know.

Now we'll visit one more being who prepared himself on this side for his great task, to bring his art, his love and his religion on earth. He, too, was a genius, one of the greatest we know. He was unique in his art and he was assisted from this side. I could mention all those names of famous people and also show you that they lived on this side. We have known them as spirits; they lived here among us. We also know where they live at this moment. They proceed and will advance here, though some of them are again on earth for they have to make up. Come, André, we'll go back to Jerusalem.

These are wonders, my son, but great is the mercy all of us received from God. This is possible only through reincarnation for we as spirits can receive a new physical garment. All this is mighty and elevated, this is to be grateful to Him Who will never forget us. Everything is love, is inspiration, a holy ardour that is within them and which they have acquired in these thousands of centuries. Pure love inspires. It is passing on into an other being, it is feeling and experiencing, it means adjusting to what we want to bring. God gave us everything and, how many times did I tell you, God gave us His own sacred life. We are inspired by Him and can receive that pure inspiration. But God helps us if we do not understand that inspiration. Many will go to ruin and seek until they have found the inspiration and the being. However, those who really create do so by their own inner possession. It is only pure love that creates wonders.

Look, André, we are already on earth. In a little while we will be in Jerusalem again.'

'Why is it, Alcar, that everything is so clear to me on this journey?'

'I'll tell you later when you understand yourself and you'll know why and what for. Then I can answer all your questions you put on this journey and the previous ones. Have a little more patience and this deep mystery will be solved. We'll pass on to Golgotha, there is nothing to keep us in Jerusalem.'

Below them lay the Holy Land. André was again on the spot where Christ had lived. What was he going to experience this time? He felt that he was connected again, but this connection differed from the one he experienced when they were here last time.

Alcar was completely lost in thought. Slowly he walked up and André followed his leader. He, too, thought again of this terror. He still trembled because of what he had been allowed to experience here. Again he saw beings. There were always people here, but only spirits; they had been living on this side for a long time. Alcar went on. Soon they reached the crest of Golgotha.

Alcar said to him: 'Here I'm going to connect you with a great wonder and with the past of a spiritual being. This was also shown to me and I returned to the spheres after my last life on earth. I'm going to explain, André, what a mission on earth means and what is required to be able to accomplish that mission and to feel it intensely. Those who can't are neither capable of accomplishing their task successfully and that mission will come to nothing. We must know that beforehand, or our life on earth will become a failure. All that work, all that trouble would have been in vain, and that is not possible, for we would break down more than we would build up. Especially in the case of spiritual work we must know this and calculate it, and that is possible because we can fathom and feel the inner life of those suitable for this work. We know then whether they'll experience that life on earth correctly or that they'll forget themselves and somehow live to the full. For a spiritual mission he or she must therefore be up to this task, they cannot otherwise descend. This only applies when we receive this mercy and do work for the masters. If a human being is on earth for himself, and consequently for his own development and he experiences something or other it is up to him to make something of that life. However, in the case of a spiritual task, when an artist or a medium is doing work for our world, we must know whether they can cope or will collapse under their work. They all meditated on this side to acquire their art and to feel everything intensely and when they were ready they descended into the world of the unconscious, shrouded in a veil of light. They will awaken on earth and as they mature physically, inner life awakens and they will only feel that for which they came on earth. For this being it was music. He only came to bring mankind an interpretation in music of the life and suffering of Christ. I myself painted Christ, others interpreted His life in poetry, still others in music, like we experience this holy feast in the spheres.

Now I'm going to connect you. You'll see, André, how a spiritual being on this side got ready to bring this great mission on earth. Look, my son.'

André began to observe again. He saw the illuminated cross that was ever present here. Below this illuminated cross, invisible for human beings on earth, he noticed a spiritual being. This being was lost in prayer. Deep was the silence he now felt and it was a sacred moment for him.

'Stand here near me, André, and give me your hand. You'll hear and see what happened at that time.'

The being was still lost in prayer. André began to see and feel. The being experienced something in the depth of his soul and André clearly felt what this human being was thinking of, and what happened in him. He had to experience this on Golgotha, it could not be experienced anywhere else. André felt what he was thinking. This human being followed the life and suffering of Christ. He followed everything from His birth onward. Now he had arrived at the place where the most terrible thing that was ever to occur had happened. He followed that horrible event and acquired that event. However, André felt and heard still more.

He heard beautiful singing and he looked up, for it came from the side beyond, from the spheres of light. That being heard this singing and he experienced it deeply in his inner life. Subsequently, André suddenly heard beautiful music and this swelled to a mighty entirety. He felt the meaning and he trembled for emotion. This singing and this sublime music interpreted the life and suffering of Christ.

Now he understood the complete meaning and felt what this being was here for and why he was connected. This was a sacred moment. It was the love for Christ; it was gratitude for the perfect Human Being Who had given Himself entirely for mankind. This being intensely felt this awe-inspiring event. It passed through his soul and he experienced this great wonder in the depth of his own life, which wonder came to life within him. This human being became inspired. This was spiritual inspiration, pure and mighty, this was spiritual bliss, a prayer interpreted by music and singing. The angels were singing for him, everything was ready in the spheres and he heard this sublime music and absorbed everything.

When the being had experienced this, he got on his feet and looked up. Above him he saw the illuminated cross and behind it were the angels. At this moment a light shone to the earth and irradiated this human being. He knelt down again, bent his head and was lost in prayer once more. This lasted some length of time. André still heard the spiritual singing. A tremendous happiness now rose in him. Oh, how deeply he felt everything, how mighty this event was for him. This human being was lifted, he was radiated and a dense haze enveloped him completely. André felt he was not aware of it. That spiritual veil condensed and now he was completely closed off, so that he lived as it were, in a spiritual dwelling. He would not be able to free himself from it. This remained, unless the higher beings would free themselves from him and withdraw, but that was not the intention. This spiritual being was now completely closed off. He now lived in what he had just experienced and could not be influenced. He felt that this spirit had concentrated on this event for many years and that he experienced this time and again and that the end had now come.

What would happen now? André saw that he went away. Once more he cast a glance at the luminous cross, then he knelt down again and prayed, prayed ardently and sent his love to those from whom he had received all this. André subsequently saw a luminous shape appearing from space.

This spirit put his hands on the head of the human being and radiated him for a long time. The luminous figure then looked up and a golden glow irradiated him. André understood this too. He was the leader, an angel who had connected himself with him. These beings were one. They had the same feelings and longings and both felt what would happen. They had passed on into this and would presently experience. This was a marvellous and sacred event. Pure, very pure were the thoughts of this spiritual being. They were at the beginning of a mighty work, though André did not know yet what they were going to do. He did feel though that this meant a mission, but was it for the earth? Would this being be born on earth? It must be. He saw that the luminous figure dissolved. André then felt that he must have arrived at a conclusion, for he jumped up and went away.

'We shall follow him, André. A great wonder is going to happen.'

André saw that he was floating over the earth and Alcar followed him. He returned to the spheres. Alcar also returned and kept following him. Now André experienced another wonder. He saw that this being became more transparent, as if he dissolved. He could still see him; presently this would not be possible any more. André felt this mighty and deep wonder. This being was to be born on earth. He was still visible, he could still see his shape, slowly he saw this being disappear before his eyes and dissolve completely.

Alcar looked at him and said: 'This being was born on earth and had to accomplish a spiritual mission. This what you saw was the final moment, though his preparation took half a century. He prepared himself for many years, as did his spiritual leader you also saw. He is ready now and he is already in the world of the unconscious and will be born soon. This being became a composer and, as I said, he had to accomplish a spiritual mission. Have you ever heard on earth of the 'St. Matthew Passion', André?'

'Yes, Alcar, now I understand. What a wonder.'

'What you heard there came from this world. This being prepared himself for it to give it to the earth. It expresses the life, suffering and death of Christ. Those who hear and want to hear that experience what happened on this side, where so many beings and angels assisted. When you experience that, my son, you descend into the life of Christ.

You will experience through singing and music what you witnessed when we were there. Those who experience it properly won't commit any more sins or make mistakes. Those on earth who understand this feel that this must be a spiritual mission, and that he was solely on earth for that purpose. Those who feel this feel God and the life and suffering of His perfect Child, Jesus Christ.

This is a spiritual mission. This happened and it was worked out in advance. This human being was born in this place where he was destined to be born, and was suitable for this task. He became a composer, he could not have become anything else, his soul was connected with that mighty event, he felt as one, entirely one with our Master Jesus Christ.

That is what he brought on earth and for that purpose he served his leaders. He had not only acquired this; he was also influenced and guided by them from his youth.

Isn't this sacred, André? Can people on earth imagine this? Do they feel how mighty it is when they listen and what happens on this side? What was required to accomplish this? Can they completely connect themselves the way he had to, in order to be able to achieve this? He was one of the very greatest who lived at the time, the age of music. He came to the earth for that purpose.

Isn't this a special circumstance and can't it be accepted? He was a master of his art, as we were all master in those days. You have seen that they were all here and returned to the earth. Could those who serve art on earth again be able to reach that high level? No, that is impossible, for this was a mission that came from our side. This human being experienced this awe-inspiring event below the cross, on the spot where Christ was killed. When he was ready he descended and was born on earth. This can only happen once, André, and that is why it is a spiritual mission. This was possible only once and cannot happen a dozen or more times. Mankind on earth possesses this art and it will remain there. It is perfect and sacred and it has a deep and pure meaning, as I showed you.

It is on earth now and for many people this wonder of creative power is too incomprehensible. We know as he does that this was given to mankind many, many years too early and yet that mighty event did not come a second too early or too late. The time was due, for nothing can be given unless it is known here that it is possible.

Mankind is still asleep and it will be years before they understand and intensely feel this sacred and awe-inspiring message, as it was felt and experienced by him and others.

This was a master of art and for this he brought himself. Oh, that people on earth may realize what is already on earth. So much has already been given to the earth, but they don't understand anything yet of all these sacred things, for which beings returned to the earth and experienced reincarnation. He brought himself as others did, like Christ taught us, it is not otherwise possible and a mission would be a failure.

Those who find this dull do not feel what they have received and belong to the living dead and do not understand that this is a pure and sacred prayer. When they listen, others pray for them in music and singing and raise them, so that they are connected. There are many inventions on earth so that they can listen to this mighty music all over the earth. To enable them to listen to it, the scientists came to the earth and were supported from our side, for they were also instruments in the spirit. In this way everything comes from this side, my son, otherwise nothing would have been on earth.

That human being came to rest here, he felt the art and the thoughts arose that became conscious on earth and were expressed.

I could show this to you in a hundred ways, but it will be clear to you now that it is as I said. What more can I say? All those other masters are known on earth and their names will never die, I'm not concerned with their names but with what was brought and that reincarnation on earth is possible.

There were great and very great masters of art on earth. There will be times, however, when they are forgotten and the noise of the jungle dominates everything. Yet, mankind will come to rest again and awaken once more. They will turn to this music and the masters will be honoured again and their creations experienced. This happens time and again. One day the earth and people will have advanced that far and understand what they possess. What has been brought from this side will remain for it is a spiritual mission, like all things given from this side for the benefit of mankind.

When you listen again, André, you'll see the picture I showed you and you'll begin to understand the life of our Lord. The spirits then pray for you and you merely have to follow that. You'll be connected with the spheres and your eyes will be full of tears and you can cry your eyes out. Don't be ashamed of it, we are also deeply moved when we listen to this event. It was ready before it was given to the earth. This applies to every spiritual mission. We are one here and we experience what Christ experienced and felt.'

'It is mighty, Alcar, I'm deeply moved. I did not expect this either. I can't say much, but I am most grateful for having been allowed to experience this and for everything you explained to me on this journey.'

'We'll go back to the spheres, André, to the place where I arrived when my life in the south came to an end. I told you after all that I would return there, that moment has come and I'll now follow my own life. Subsequently we'll go to the earth and after that we'll return to the spheres, for it is necessary and I must explain other wonders. When I have explained all that, André, we'll go to a certain place in the spheres as a final experience and, by having you experience something, I'll answer your hundreds of questions and feelings, which have arisen of late on this journey and on earth.

First of all we'll go to the Land of Twilight, the sphere where Gerhard also entered when he arrived here from the earth. I also entered that sphere, as I told you. We'll soon be there and I'll immediately pass on into that condition. I'll follow my own life there and you'll see that I, too, was born again.'

'How remarkable all this is, Alcar. Oh, if only people on earth could accept this, how different their life would be! How much could they acquire, there is so much to learn. How mighty everything is and how great is God.'

'Didn't I tell you that you would see wonders? Those wonders still happen on earth. People are still born on earth from this side who have to accomplish a task, like those others. Evolution goes on, time and again they need other things, be it science, nourishment for the mind and so on. Souls are preparing here to perform a task, and however insignificant those missions may be, they are all for the benefit of the earth and serve mankind. As I said, this has been going on for millions of years, from the moment the first human beings reached the spheres of light. We receive this from God and it is a mighty grace. This is for all of us, everyone can receive it when feelings of gratitude and love rise in them and they begin to understand what we received from God in all those lives. Then, we all want to do something and give ourselves, and that is possible.

Look, André, we are in the Land of Twilight, I lived here. When I had died on earth I awoke in this place which was my spiritual attunement. Most people arrive here from the earth and they are all not good or bad, though they have no spiritual possession. I, too, was convinced of my life, here I was stirred up and my inner being awakened. I was a little ahead of Gerhard and that is why I decided to let him tell of his spiritual life, so that I would not have to do it later. Gerhard expressed, as it were, my own life, for I also descended into the darkness to acquire something. I remained down there for years. I helped thousands of beings and in that way I accepted my higher condition. I felt the way Gerhard lived and felt, but there was art in me. You'll now understand that I connected myself with Gerhard when I knew that he was to come to this side, to let him tell of his own life and because you had known Gerhard on earth.

I sent one of my own assistants to him and you also know now that this was arranged in advance. Gerhard was convinced. He descended into the hell, experienced thousands of wonders, although they were demonic powers and influences, and in doing so he reached the first

sphere. I also experienced that, André. When you follow and understand his life you'll know what my life was like in those days and you
can feel it. I was, therefore, like Gerhard, I was aware that my possession resided therein and once I understood this I wanted to reach the
first sphere at all cost. I said that there are many people of the earth
who enter here and give themselves, but who have never been able to
do so on earth. That again is a great mystery. Those beings were on
earth to make up for something and have done so, but were to die there
at an early age. Gerhard was one of those beings; he had those powers
through which he was able to reach the first sphere in a short period of
time. For many others this is not so easy as they don't have this depth.

For Gerhard this depth was his great willpower. Others also arrive in
this sphere, though they are not as strong as Gerhard. This proves that
all beings feel differently, that we admittedly possess one love but that
we have different qualities. We are one in love, though not in art and
feelings and what one being is able to do the other isn't, even though he
lives in the same condition, in one sphere. Some feel for art, others for
science and others again have different feelings, not only on earth, but
also on this side. So his life was like mine when I entered here.

Consequently, we now go to the first sphere where I'll continue. When
I entered, my feelings for art awakened. At the beginning I made a
journey and assumed my own sphere and I subsequently turned to art.
I did not stay there though. The others proceeded and indulged in
spiritual art, but at times I descended to the earth and into the dark
spheres for long periods of time to help others. My master supported
me in everything and he understood me perfectly. 'Go on the way you
do', he said, 'there will be a great surprise later.'

I again descended into the hell, helped many unfortunate people
there and subsequently returned to the spheres of light to devote myself completely to art. On earth I had already attained a considerable
level, though not yet the level I could reach as a master. Here my feeling for art awakened. I also learned to know life in the darkness, though
I did not understand that I was followed in everything from the higher
spheres. Even then, André, I was under the leadership of my master
Cesarino. This master was to accomplish a mission to the earth, to
which end many assistants were needed. I became one of his thousands
of assistants. That way the first years went by. Slowly but surely the
fifteenth century approached. I went on feeling the life God created

545

and in this way my art developed. Then, when I thought it would do me good I asked my master permission to make a long journey. 'I'll go with you', he said.

We went to the earth and I studied my art, which I had already left behind in the south. At that time, however, I had not advanced that far. That desire now rose in me to be allowed to give to the earth what I now possessed and I asked my master whether that was possible.

He said to me: 'For our Father in heaven everything is possible.'

'Can't you say for sure?'

'We know a lot, brother, but it is a mercy when this happens.'

'Can't I acquire that mercy? Can't I ask my Father in heaven for that?'

'Are you prepared to accept everything that you might experience on earth?' he replied.

'Is that so terrible?'

'Don't forget that you possess light here, you feel happy, you are free from cold and hardship, from every passion and when you accept a material body, that body belongs to the physical world. If you want it to be born and live there, you must accept everything the earth may give you. Also illness, for you'll have to contend with that, nobody on earth can set himself free of it. I need not tell you that, for you know this life, we have been in the sphere of the earth and you made a study of it. You'll experience that again, although your life will differ from the life of those who are there for some deed or other. You also have to make up and this life could be considered a happy one. Once again, only God can give you that, we can't say anything with certainty, for these are God's sacred laws, which cannot be changed.'

After that I took long walks in the spheres and I arrived at a decision. You have seen my fellow artist and me, so I can leave that out. I prepared myself, André, though I did not understand yet that this had started a long time beforehand.

When I began that journey on earth with my own master it was already part of this event. The years went by and many began to feel this approaching event. All were convinced where they wanted to go to and realized what they accepted.

Here in the spheres we possessed something, we were free from cold and illness, we were happy, and we might experience a lot of misery on earth, but we could not have stayed here. I again descended into the darkness, where the brothers also suffer, but by working there an other sphere is attained and one serves, though this serving is not so simple, for you know the hell. The time came when I began to feel it.

Many years had gone by in complete devotion to art. Then followed the years of meditation and I felt that wonder rise in me. None of us spoke about it; this was too deep and too wonderful for life itself and beyond description. You feel that you become very quiet and you want to be alone all the time. It is as if the entire creation lies within you. I often wandered in nature and at times I descended into the darkness again to help others. Suddenly I felt that awe-inspiring activity rise in me and I returned to the spheres. Then, my son, the wonder happened that you experienced a while ago.

I dissolved; I felt that I was raised into an other world, an other condition. I saw that I faded away. An unbelievable wonder happened within me.

Although I thought I was alone, I heard my master say: 'Farewell, my brother, we'll meet again on earth. There you will seek the deep meaning of this event, though you won't solve this spiritual mystery, for you won't be aware of this life any more.'

I subsequently felt myself sink away deeply and I did not hear anything any more.

After I awakened on earth, and as a youth, I had a feel for art. I got to know my master and however strange it may seem, it was as if I had met him before. I felt great affection for him, but I could not unravel this mystery. There were more artists on earth like we were, who gave themselves completely. These beings lived in Italy, Holland and many other countries. One of them displayed his mastership in your own country; he was also on this side and experienced what I had, just like all those others. I don't need to mention his name, we are all known all over the earth.

We came for one task, André, and served art, the earth and all mankind was to receive this wonder. We all gave our entire personality. This was our mercy, my brothers' and mine, and the art we left is being held in esteem. Visit museums, look at our paintings and feel what it means. Try to connect yourself with our art, it will be as if you feel this wonder, especially since you know all this.

This was a mission as well and we brought ourselves, stimulated by our masters. Many people now admire our art, but I would like to tell them this: 'When you see our art, try to feel what lies behind it and

547

linger a while on our side. What you admire was given you in order to awaken. It happened through inspiration and this inspiration came from the side beyond. We could not have attained that level if we had not been connected.

Think of this and above all that this happened because reincarnation on earth is possible. This cannot be achieved on earth, I mean by those who have not felt the depth of this mighty event, who have not experienced those many years of meditation and not reached that spiritual level in art. This, too, happens only once. No more beings will be born on earth who can achieve this. That has happened, it is past and this is the meaning. If I can reach one of you now, that you know this, and may convince you of your eternal life, this work and my art have not been in vain and all my pains have been rewarded.

On earth I was Antonie van Dijck and I was allowed to bring my art which I acquired on this side. I was able to do this and all the others with me, for reincarnation is possible and a mercy of God. Feel this depth, my sisters and brothers; you too might experience it. One day you'll enter this life and we'll convince you of it.

We now go to the earth, André. Soon we'll be there where I have something to tell you.'

Floating through space Alcar returned to the earth. André thought everything over. How many wonders had he been allowed to experience. How mighty everything was, he could repeat that thousands of times. He kept thinking all the time. How closely one thing was connected with the other! Everything was fixed and that applied to every human being. Everyone experienced his own karma, cause and effect and there was nobody on earth unless he had to make up. All people were on earth for a fixed purpose, for everyone had done good and wrong things. All had been born there and were born again.

Oh, what bliss, how deep and mighty everything he had experienced was. If only they could accept it, how different their life would become. They would learn to understand death and their fear of the unknown would disappear.

Oh, how clear everything was. What more could he say? He understood everything and however deep and amazing everything was, it was so very natural. This life was magnificent, God's laws were deep and sacred when man, the soul, received that mercy once again to correct his wrong things.

548

He could not think properly now, for he felt that he should concentrate on Alcar to be able to experience all those wonders. He should not think anyway, there was too much in him, he was overflowing with spiritual wisdom.

'Look, André, we are where I wanted to be. You were thinking and meditating while I quickly followed my way, now we'll enter my home on earth. Do you remember that we have been here?'

'Yes, Alcar.'

'When we were about to set out on these long journeys, I promised you that we would return here. Now think of everything I explained to you, what you experienced and where we have been in that period. I only followed the past and I could tell all that apart, for I followed a silver thread connecting the events of my life and of others. I only needed to concentrate and everything manifested itself for me and I saw what I had experienced thousands of years ago.

This is not difficult, André, though it is incomprehensible to you. Everything is mighty, for it has to do with our lives and with God and creation and because everything is love. I am grateful and so are many others who followed us wherever we have been, which will become clear to you soon, that we have advanced that far and that this has happened. We'll go on in a minute, for we won't stay here long and return to the spheres, where I must explain other wonders to you. You surely feel that the end of this journey is nearing? Then this mighty event is over and you have experienced creation and many, many wonders. My mightiest and most difficult task will be accomplished, for which I'm grateful to God. I lived here. You have seen my friend and me here and you heard us speak, I connected you with my own past. In Jerusalem I showed you that he was my own child and that I have not seen him since. When I met him there I did not understand why I loved him so much. But, and do listen now, I would not have loved him so much if an other being had not loved through me. So, a being loved through me and the love I felt was laid in me from the invisible world with a fixed purpose.

At the time, however, this was a mystery for me, now, however, I know and understand this mystery. I also know who did this and why it also happened.

Just feel this deep wonder, my son. It was known thousands of years beforehand what I was going to experience and that this would happen. In this life, I was not aware of my reincarnation, but there were beings who had followed me and knew that I would be born. That also happened with an intention, which will become clear to you soon when we have got that far. Here I lived and met him. I also told you that he made a big mistake. That mistake was that he gave himself to an other being, as a result a child was born which he did not accept. That being went to ruin, for grief struck her deeply. She did not put an end to her life, but she sank into despair. She was left behind with her child and he did not accept. Later on he had to accept but then it was too late.

We can't see through this, but when it is all over and we enter on this side, we see cause and effect and experience all these spiritual laws and mysteries.

I told you already on our first journey that he tried to make it all up at an advanced age, but in doing so that law is still in force. It would be made up one day, but in quite a different way. He, however – you know he was once a scientist – also wanted to create his own condition in his last life. He reached that level in France, but he entered the world of the unconscious discontentedly and would be born again. When he was born again he joined the army and passed once more into this life. In his next life I met him.

My feelings for him developed and I loved him like my own child. As I told you, that love was laid in me, I loved him through others, I would not have felt this otherwise. Just imagine this. They wanted me to love him, for one day I would meet him again and we would be connected. One day, but how many years in advance was it felt and known that this would happen?

It was known already in Jerusalem and my path was guided. I had not seen him during all those years. During my last life my love for him ever deepened. You know already that he didn't achieve anything. In that life he could have, as in that other life, attained much, but he wasted his time and was not interested in anything. This also had a profound meaning.

The soul living in the human body must and wants to try to attain a social level on earth. We all get that far, every human being will achieve that and to that end only energy, willpower, perseverance, ambition and some violence are required, that is already sufficient to create our own condition. Once the soul has reached such an sensitive state and condition, things are straightforward. That which we want to achieve

550

will be attained, for the qualities needed for that are within us, they are our character traits I just mentioned.

We have acquired those traits in those many, nay hundreds of lives and if this life is capable, if, for instance, the parents have the necessary means, you surely feel that what we have intended is already within reach. Now he was in an other sensitive state and already freed from worldly ambition and many other terrestrial traits. One day this will happen to every human being, because we then pass on to spiritual life. All worldly honour has no meaning any more; we are not prepared to exert ourselves for that, not even if it was a free gift. Such people live on earth and that is not so strange after all. There are people who would give their life for a worldly title. Others, however, would not even like to have such a title, for nothing, because they don't care. However, that is a law, it has a certain meaning, for, if one lacks that strength, one wants this title, for it is of moment on earth. If one no longer cares about it, one must therefore have that strength.

It also means that once they must have known those titles or whatever, or they would see to it that they possess many of them, for with these the earth and mankind lie at their feet.

This is my point; I want to explain this to you. That is what he experienced, he did not care about anything, not about titles and he was unaware of its meaning. We know now that he was a scholar. I showed and explained his death, so there is no need to go into that any more. In this life, when I was an artist, I met him and we became good friends. Once, however, he had been my child and once I took his life, I subsequently gave my life in return and I met him again later and he was my own child once again. Do you remember, André?'

'Yes, Alcar, I know everything.'

'I'll go on then. My end on earth came and I entered the spiritual world. We'll follow that now. There is nothing else to show you here and I close this past and I'll not return here any more. We now go to the second sphere, André.

We'll leave the earth again and when we return this journey will be over. I awakened in the second sphere, between the second and third sphere. I had therefore been able to acquire that higher level by my life as an artist, for you know that I descended to the earth from the first sphere. We'll go on to that level, you'll see me awaken and also how I changed, which I can show you now.'

'What wonders did you experience, Alcar.'

'We all experience thousands of wonders, André, and all people will experience these wonders when they enter here. They have to experience it, because they will descend into their past when they have completed their cycle of life on earth. You no doubt feel how deep everything is and this is bound to be mighty, for we human beings have been on our way for millions of years. We have discarded and accepted thousands of lives. We passed on from one life to another and all those lives served to acquire spiritual love and to show our gratitude. We receive again all the time and this also serves to make up.

While making up we also experience a lot of worldly pleasures.

I was welcomed everywhere, I moved in English court circles, made many friends and acquaintances there and yet I also made up and experienced what was reserved for me. That is a mighty grace and to show our gratitude.

Look, André, the second sphere, here I awoke. I woke up on a high mountain and had my own spiritual dwelling. Before I went to the earth I gave myself completely, I told you about it. I'll now connect myself with that time and consequently pass on to the second sphere, so that you can see what has changed in and around me.'

André also observed this wonder.

'I am now as I was when I entered here. As I advance and connect myself with other spheres, for I am able to do so, my outer appearance will change, which is reflected on my face. You know my face and my possession, which is the fifth sphere, where I now live. That is also clear to you, isn't it?'

'Yes, Alcar.'

'So I woke up here, André. The being who convinced me of my life on earth was the one who roused my love for my friend. I knew I had died. When I was ready and had assumed my sphere, other wonders were shown to me. When I understood those wonders I again descended into the darkness and stayed there for many years. I subsequently went to the earth to visit him and I helped him there with a few things that were on his mind and he could not cope with. I returned to the darkness again and I wanted to try and attain the spheres, for me the third sphere, within a period of ten to twenty years. I worked on myself and nothing was too much for me. However, I retained my master. I was completely unaware of my former life in the south; neither was it explained to me, that would happen later.

Meanwhile the years went by. I acquired many spiritual laws and learned to know all spiritual degrees of the hell in those times. Then the time came when my friend would die and I showed that scene to you during the first departure from the body. I connected you with his passing away. Do you remember, André?'

'Yes, Alcar, I am quite aware of everything.'

'Well then, when he had entered here I had meanwhile reached the third sphere. Day and night, speaking in worldly terms, I was down there and you know how difficult that work is. Those who want, can make rapid progress and I attained that sphere in a very short period of time, though twenty-five years had gone by. I had a powerful will and I did not relax until I had achieved that. I admittedly say that I did not relax, and had a will, but this was also given to me and inspired in me by my master who had other and mightier plans which I was unaware of and would not have been able to understand. I was then called to my friend and I convinced him of his eternal life. You know that too.

Next we took long walks. We visited the earth and the darkness again and I taught him what I had acquired already. Now we both were on this side. From time to time we were alone, for I was being prepared for other things.

Then my master came to see me.

He told me that an other era would come on earth and that from this side nourishment for the mind would be given to the earth. Many were to do work there for the higher masters and become their assistants. There was also a task for me and I felt happy about it.

He said to me: 'Brother, a mighty task awaits us. You have advanced far enough now to accomplish an other task. You can acquire a lot in two centuries. You have learned to know the earth and the spheres, how God created us and what is the meaning of our life on earth and on this side. Would you like to perform a task on earth?'

'Gladly', I promptly said, 'tell me what I should do.'

The master said: 'On this side you'll learn the physical organism and everything necessary to help mankind on earth. But that is not the main point. You must acquire what you know of our life, you must experience it again and adjust yourself to that task. I'll come back to you later.'

My master went away and I contemplated everything. Again I descended to my friend and we took long walks. We went to the earth once more, studied all material laws there and returned to the darkness. After that my friend awoke, I told you that too, André. I refer to this only now.'

'Do you know', he said, 'what the earth needs and what I felt there already? Do you know, dear friend, why I came to nothing? All this is now clear to me. I'll tell you. Nourishment for the mind, my brother, only love and happiness, that is what the earth and mankind need. But there is something else, my brother, what I wanted to ask you and what keeps my mind occupied. Where is the girl I made unhappy? Do you know that? Could you connect me with her?'

'No', I said, 'that is impossible. I advise you first to do everything to reach the first sphere, not until then can you search for her.'

'He descended and did good work in the darkness. It took him ten years before he could enter the first sphere. When he entered the first sphere I was the first one to welcome him. How happy he was. We subsequently made long journeys and were everywhere. After that he experienced those Divine feelings I had already felt and experienced and which mean reincarnation on earth.

'Is that possible?' he asked.

'For God everything is possible', I said.

'It is a wonder for I feel what I would like to do. Believe me, I want to make up, to make up everything, because it holds me back. Where does she live? Is she still on earth? That is impossible, isn't it? Where would she be?'

I said to him: 'Have a little more patience. I'll investigate and ask my master if I may see her, then I'll come back to you.'

I returned to my own sphere and saw my master. I could always find him, wherever I was, which I did not understand until later. At the time this master lived already in the seventh sphere and was the mentor over all spheres. My friend meanwhile went to the darkness to help the unfortunate ones. In the temple of the soul I was connected with my life and his and also with her whom he was looking for and to whom he had to make up. I now knew what I wanted to know. I was allowed to experience and receive all this for him and for my task, which I likewise did not understand until later.

After a long time I went back to him in the darkness and found him at work. I told him what I knew and advised him just to go on and wait. I would come back when he let me feel this. I returned to my own sphere, for I had already started that study. I did not hear from him for years. He remained down there and I prepared for that other task, which was not given to me until later. I did not yet know its purpose, though I had some idea. I then felt that he called me and I went straight back to him. We took long walks again and he told me that everything was clear to him.

'Do you know what awaits you?' I asked him.

'I am aware of everything', he said. 'I want to serve, if possible. I'll pray and ask God for that. Shall I see her again and do you know whether she will be born? How happy I would be if God would allow that. Who is going to help me?'

'You must wait and see, perhaps it will be given you.'

'We set out on a journey again and visited the earth. During that time he began to feel that wonder and I also told you that. Do you remember, André?'

'Yes, Alcar, you told me.'

André, however, felt himself sink back in his own life. It was as if he began to feel a great mystery, an enormous problem and that this mystery would now be solved. He nevertheless waited to hear what his leader was going to say.

'His sensitivity, my son, became ever deeper and now he experienced what we all experienced and what I explained to you. I told you that I lost sight of him and that I thought I knew where he was. I knew this, André, but I could not tell you yet at the beginning of our first journey. Now the time has come and I can explain this to you.

He felt ready and would return. This feeling had come into him. We were together in nature and waited for things to happen. We discussed all possibilities we felt and understood. Then he dissolved in front of me and I called out to him: 'Till we meet again on earth and on this side.'

He descended into the world of the unconscious and was born on earth. He, too, was enveloped in a dense haze and that veil would be lifted on earth. A mighty task awaited me, for I had a lot to acquire. As I said, my friend was enveloped in a dense haze and in that haze lay my connection with him on earth.

He would meet her again and I had to see to that. I received my directions from my master, which I had to pay attention to. I now had time to prepare myself. I followed my way through the spheres and visited together with my master what you experienced during your departures from the body. I acquired all that. In this way the time went by. He was subsequently born on earth, André. My master sought contact on earth and that connection was found. He was born in a small town to simple people and that was also fixed, for he had to make up to his mother.

He was protected in his youth and finally the time arrived that I could connect him with her, for she was also on earth. It seems impossible to people on earth that human beings who are thousands of miles away from one another can be connected, but on this side that is very easy. He was subsequently introduced to a seance group. My master had obtained this contact and he was to be accepted in that circle in order to awaken. He had that sensitivity, we only had to awaken and open him. We maintained this connection on this side.

And now, my boy, the time has come to answer all your thoughts, your questions of why and what for, where my friend lives, your mediumship and many other things that you asked me during the journeys we have made. Now, André, the moment has arrived.

You surely feel a lot, because I picked up your thoughts. I ask you to control yourself for a while. I'll help you, my boy. I'll show you something that will answer your many questions and thoughts. I told you about that as well. By experiencing this, you'll pass into all those questions and this deep but natural mystery will be solved for you. I'll now show you all your lives, André, to that end we must go back to the first sphere. Come, follow me, André.'

André became very quiet inside. Yes, he felt everything, he now understood himself. My God, he thought, how is it possible. For him it was a great and sacred wonder. He now understood everything; he felt the beginning of creation and also his mediumship. A tremendous tension rose in him. He would for preference have lifted Alcar, or fallen on his knees to thank him for everything. With a supreme effort he forced himself to be quiet. He still had to control himself, but it was ever so difficult.

André floated on and was deeply lost in thought. He dared not look at Alcar. Not a word was spoken. Alcar would reveal everything to him in one condition. He already felt what wonder this would be. He quietly prayed for strength, he asked his Father in heaven to help him. He prepared himself. It was quiet in him, relaxed, yes, he felt completely relaxed. A mighty feeling of happiness rose in him. He felt that he was being helped and he also knew and understood now where that power came from. Oh, my God, what wonders, what might, how tremendous all these laws of nature were. His leader could go there in a flash and yet it took quite some time and he understood this also. He felt and understood everything. An other personality now forced itself upon him. It was the being he had felt on earth and this emanated from his deep inner self. It was his own previous life: it could not be anything else.

I was Alcar's son, I am his friend, and I have been with him during all those lives. He now felt Jerusalem. Oh, my God, how natural everything is. We have known each other for thousands of centuries. My Father, what a problem, and he had been allowed to experience that problem.

He now felt himself on earth and at the same time in the spheres. For him there were no spiritual secrets any more. It was all so incredible, though he had to accept everything Alcar had explained everything from the beginning to the end. Eternity had awakened in him. How did he feel life at the side beyond? This could not be otherwise. He had made all those journeys in former days together with Alcar. He also understood his mediumship now, he needed no more telling and explaining. Everything, all those secrets were in one condition. He kept thinking, however, for there were thousands of thoughts in him and he had to try and digest all that.

He now understood himself and his life on earth, which was also open to him. My God, how grateful I should be to You! His entire youth passed in his mind. Now other thoughts rose in him and he knew where Alcar was going. He felt and knew it because he felt like 'then', before he was to return to earth. What wonder! How glad he was that he had understood his gifts. He now understood that Alcar had kept all those gifts in his own hands, he would not have known what to do with them and would never have been able to cope with them. All those gifts were too much for an earthly being, but Alcar had gradually opened him completely. He now felt conscious and there was nothing left in him that he did not understand.

Finally Alcar said to him: 'Look, André, we'll enter there.' Alcar looked at him and smiled.

'Wonderful, André, and yet, we ourselves are that wonder. Do you know now what you are going to experience?'

'Yes, Alcar, I know. I see Cesarino. He is your master, as you told me on our first journey. I know and I am very grateful, Alcar.'

'Do not thank me, my boy, but God. I'm also grateful. Look, we are already where we should be. Is this also familiar to you? Isn't it wonderful, André?'

'It is all so natural, so mighty and exalted, Alcar. You are my father, my mother, my sister and brother, you are everything to me and now everything is reality. It is you, it has been you all the time, now everything is open to me.'

Alcar entered the building. He was welcomed at the entrance by his master. André followed. The master approached Alcar, took both his hands and said: 'My brothers, God be with you.'

He then said to André: 'My brother André.'

André looked at Alcar's master.

'There is not much to say, André, once we were here and at the entrance I said to you some centuries ago, look to the right and to the left, above and below and learn to know that. You did, it is your possession now and we'll disclose that to mankind, for our work is nearly accomplished and will be passed on to the earth. I am very grateful to you and to your brother Alcar and ask our Father to bless our work. You know everything now, I don't have to explain anything. I just want to add this: When you are back on earth in you physical organism and you meet her, my sister on earth with whom I connected you, tell her, and you know whom I mean, that I thank her for everything. I thank all who have been connected with her and all my sisters and brothers on earth.

Tell her that I'll welcome her on this side and she'll recognize our flowers. I greet her from this side.

My brother André, you'll bring this message from me to her who followed me in everything. I also thank you and bless you for your work, for you did our work and that of a thousand others. Until then, André, we'll meet again in the spheres. Farewell, until we meet on this side. Your Cesarino.'

The master dissolved before his eyes, which André had experienced before. He still heard: 'We'll meet again on this side, André. You are still needed on earth, but when your task is complete we'll come and pick you up. May God bless our work.'

André sank down. When he woke up he found himself with his leader in nature. There were flowers and birds around him and tears were rolling down his cheeks, for it had moved him profoundly. How happy he felt.

He took Alcar's hands in his and said: 'Did I make things very difficult for you on earth, Alcar?'

'You did your best, André.'

'Why did you give me this name, Alcar?'

'Because it was your name once.'

'Was that in France?'

'Yes.'

'How is it possible, Alcar. It is all so true, do help me digest this. I'll try to be strong, but oh, it is so mighty. What will people on earth think of this? Will they be able to accept it?'

'Yes, André, there are people who accept this gratefully. All our sisters and brothers will help us to circulate this work. However, there are also people who find us insane. Let them do as they like, André, one day they'll see and accept all this.'

'How well you have connected me on earth, Alcar, and now I also understand why we were not allowed to keep our baby.'

'Everything is fixed, my son, or is cause and effect.'

'How many books could you write on this subject?'

'Dozens, André, if I wanted to deal with everything we would never finish writing. I only gave flashes of before and after creation, of what awaits all of us and what we have experienced together. You'll receive all this in three volumes within a short time.'

'And what happens after that, Alcar?'

'You will depart from your body again and I'll tell and explain more of your last three lives.'

'Will that also be recorded?'

'No, André, that is important only for yourself. Just wait, my boy. You are entirely conscious now; there is nothing living on this side which is hidden from you. You are now spiritually and cosmically conscious. Do you realize what that means on earth?'

'I know, Alcar. But how am I to cope with everything, how shall I be able to digest this on earth?'

'I'll help you with that. This year is difficult for you, but you'll manage.'

'How well did you figure everything out beforehand, Alcar. There is no flaw in it, everything fits. You were with me from the very beginning, in my youth and when I matured and moved to the city. How is it possible! After that, meeting her. I won't forget anything and I am prepared to do everything to make her happy. How grateful we should be. How great God's love is! But how did you manage to conceal this, when we were together?'

'After all, André, you knew nothing of your lives. Not until you were allowed to experience all this did you become conscious. I gradually gave you nourishment for the mind while descending ever deeper into this world, which was present deep down in you. The closer I approached reincarnation, the clearer it became for you. I ask you, André, why should people not be able to accept this? Is this so strange, so unnatural? They will experience it, here on this side, for one day they will also come to this side. They will all be welcomed and convinced here. God knows that I speak the truth, this will happen.

Now this is mediumship, my son, which we spirits hold in our own hands. Those who can submit, who can listen on earth, who want to follow us implicitly, can receive nourishment for the mind and do something for mankind.

André, I am grateful, most grateful to you, you have understood me in everything and followed me.

I would like to add this to mankind on earth: 'My sisters and brothers. This is mediumship. Those who can submit will receive spiritual wisdom. Follow everything I said in these ten years and have a look at this end. If I had not known and had not been able to oversee this end, which was my task and work, I would have lost myself in all these spiritual and natural laws. No man on earth could do this. But I was prepared and so was André. I only needed to connect myself with him and our work could start.

I drew from his subconscious and yet I had everything, all those gifts, in my own hands. We know this subconscious, for we once lived in that reality, it is the sum total of the lives we have experienced. What is subconscious? Do I still have to explain this? Feel your own depth, your inner life, the feelings that are within you.

There are thousands of beings on earth now who work for the side beyond. The earth needs nourishment for the mind and that is why these things happen.

For God is love! Do I have to show again that God is love? Do feel my sisters and brothers, all this is present in your own life, but you should be able to feel it, learning cannot help you.

Once I lived on your earth and I mentioned my last name, though I won't pursue this in greater depth, for worldly names have no meaning on this side. I wrote in one of André's books: He who calls himself master on earth is a pupil on this side. Is it clear now why I could say that? Am I not a pupil? I am grateful, most grateful and happy as a child that I was allowed to do something for you and for the earth out of which I was born. I now do and achieve far more than when I was a master of art in that life. Seize all this with both hands and don't give up. One day you'll come to this side and you'll see the truth of it all.

I ask you: Would André have been able to do all this? Could he have invented all this? No, for why was he born in that little town? Because he should not acquire anything of the earth, or he could not have accepted me completely. Now his mind was completely empty and he was thankful, very thankful that I came to him.

Who is prepared to accept us who possesses everything on earth? Then you do not need us, for what you possess, all those riches, will stop you.

André was destined to be born there and to possess nothing, not until then could I reach him. And this happened. Do you feel this wonder? Haven't I shown this in everything? This wonder of God happened and we waited here until we could begin. Although there will be people who say that it is too good to be true, it is the holy truth. We proceed, ever further and there will be no more sorrow for you when you possess love for others. Later, the world will crave and yearn for it. At present, however, we are not understood, neither was he who interpreted Christ and came to the earth for that task. One day, your time has come and then we'll meet again on this side.

I am so grateful to my Father in heaven that I sit here beside my brother André and may think of you and that I'll soon be allowed to tell this. God knows that I spoke the holy truth.

If spirits come to you and tell you that this is not possible, know then, brothers and sisters, that they pass off as higher beings but that they do not know the light. They come with fine words to express their love and yet, be on your guard.

I'll leave now and I thank all who have helped and supported me from the bottom of my heart. These books will be read, they belong to your own century. It is God's will, for the time has come that mankind can receive everything from our side. I greet you, my sisters and brothers, we'll meet again on this side.

Have you any more questions, André?'

'Is that what the masters assigned to you, Alcar?'

'Yes, André, and with this I have accomplished my actual task. I thank God for this mercy.'

'I have no more questions, Alcar.'

'This is the place where we were before you returned to the earth. Here we have experienced everything beforehand, then the mightiest wonder we know, which is reincarnation on earth, happened. You were allowed to experience wonders of the spirit and this is meant for every human being living on earth.

I dedicate the three parts of this book to your wife, André, and to mankind. Remember me to her. And now quickly back to your physical body.'

In the spheres André received Alcar's blessing. They subsequently returned to the earth and André entered his home. He could not say a word, but he knelt down before his leader and thanked him inwardly for everything.

Alcar said to him: 'Will you continue to feel my presence as before, now that you know everything about me and yourself, André?'

'Yes, Alcar, I could not do otherwise.'

'Farewell, my boy, you'll soon be with me and do not forget that I'll always guard and help you with everything.'

André descended into his physical organism and this journey was over. He had again been allowed to experience many wonders and problems, for which he was very grateful.

May God's blessing rest on this work.


THE END

# PUBLISHER'S NOTE

## Jozef Rulof (1898-1952)

Jozef Rulof was born at 's Heerenberg, a small village in the east of the Netherlands, in 1898. From early childhood he was guided by a light-radiating personality only visible to him, who, later on, revealed himself as a master from the hereafter. It is this personality that the author will get to know as his master Alcar.

When Jozef Rulof had moved to a large city in the west of Holland, his master took his life in his hands and began the spiritual development of his instrument, which finally resulted in his unparalleled level of mediumship, a mediumship unique in this world.

His mediumship as a writer begins during the early thirties when he receives the first volume of his first book 'A View into the Hereafter' from the Side Beyond. In this book his master does not call him Jozef Rulof but André Hendriks. The reason for this metonymy is explained comprehensively in the trilogy entitled: 'Jeus of Mother Crisje' which deals with his life and which was published much later. It will be evident to the reader of the above trilogy that master Alcar could not develop the contact with his instrument in an other way.

During the years that 'A View into the Hereafter' was produced there was but little interest in messages which could reach us from life after death, the Side Beyond. Master Alcar was first of all concerned with reaching those persons who base their faith on the message of the church and bible.

The tenor of 'A View into the Hereafter' should be seen in this light. The first volume was published in 1933 and the third volume appeared in 1936. In spite of its apparent 'age' this book is still very relevant to our times, as appears from the interest shown in it. One reason for this is that a lot of people are nowadays seeking the reality of life, which is endorsed by the many films which have appeared on this subject and will yet be produced.

The first object of this book from the Side Beyond was to free man from fear of death.

Vital questions had to be answered, such as: Is there life after death? Is there a heaven and hell? Is there a last judgement? Is it true that

God dooms His life? Is God unjust? Why do some mothers lose their children at such an early age? What may the consequences of cremation be? Has man got his life in his own hands or is his life exclusively controlled by God?

Those who had obtained light on the side beyond were determined to share their conviction of the reality of life, their acquired wisdom and bliss, with man on earth. This was done by using earthly language, consistent with our consciousness.

It will be obvious that not all vital questions could be discussed in 'A View into the Hereafter'. To this end more books were required. Many questions remained, such as: How did God's Creation come about? Where have we come from and where do we finally go to? What is the ultimate object of life? Are there more inhabited planets? Does reincarnation exist? What is the meaning of the various races on earth? Can man really finish life by committing suicide? What is the meaning and cause of obsession? Of addiction? What are twin-souls? What is the fundamental significance of father- and motherhood for all life?

All these questions and a great many more are amply dealt with in the series of books Jozef Rulof and the masters left behind. The books are there for your information!

The titles of these books you will find in the folder enclosed in this book.

The Publisher
April, 2000

Do you want more information?

Visit our website www.wayti.com or send your letter to:
Wayti Publishing House Foundation
P.O. box 348
7300 AH Apeldoorn – the Netherlands